Israel
Biblical Sites Travel Guide

ISRAEL

Biblical Sites Travel Guide

Todd M. Fink

ISRAEL
Biblical Sites Travel Guide

by
Todd M. Fink

Published by Selah Book Press

Cover Illustration Copyright © 2021 by Selah Book Press
Cover design by Selah Book Press

Copyright © 2021 by Todd M. Fink

ISBN-13: 978-1-944601-27-0
ISBN-10: 1-944601-27-9

Second Edition

All rights reserved. No part of this publication may be reproduced or transmitted in any form or by any means, electronic or mechanical, including photocopy, recording, or any information storage retrieval system, without permission in writing from the copyright owner.

ISRAEL

Biblical Sites Travel Guide

Todd M. Fink

ISRAEL
Biblical Sites Travel Guide
by
Todd M. Fink

Published by Selah Book Press

Cover Illustration Copyright © 2021 by Selah Book Press
Cover design by Selah Book Press

Copyright © 2021 by Todd M. Fink

ISBN-13: 978-1-944601-27-0
ISBN-10: 1-944601-27-9

Second Edition

All rights reserved. No part of this publication may be reproduced or transmitted in any form or by any means, electronic or mechanical, including photocopy, recording, or any information storage retrieval system, without permission in writing from the copyright owner.

Scripture References are taken from the following Bible versions:

New American Standard Bible®,
Copyright © 1960, 1962, 1963, 1968, 1971, 1972, 1973,
1975, 1977, 1995 by The Lockman Foundation
Used by permission. (www.Lockman.org)

The Holy Bible, English Standard Version® (ESV®)
Copyright © 2001 by Crossway,
a publishing ministry of Good News Publishers.
All rights reserved.
ESV Text Edition: 2007

The Holy Bible, New International Version®, NIV® Copyright © 1973, 1978, 1984, 2011 by Biblica, Inc.® Used by permission. All rights reserved worldwide.

The Holy Bible, New King James Version®. Copyright © 1982 by Thomas Nelson, Inc. All rights reserved.

The NET Bible®, New English Translation (NET) Scripture quoted by permission. Quotations designated (NET) are from the NET Bible® copyright ©1996-2006 by Biblical Studies Press, L.L.C.

Scripture in bold is emphasis added by the author.

Table of Contents

Table of Contents vi
Acknowledgments 1
Israel: Land of the Bible 2

Jerusalem Sites **4**

    Jerusalem Overview 5
    Jerusalem Sites Overview 11
    Antonia Fortress 16
    Chapel of the Ascension: Ascension and Return of Christ 22
    Church of the Holy Sepulchre 28
    City of David Overview 43
    Dominus Flevit: Triumphal Entry 49
    Eastern Gate 55
    Garden of Gethsemane & Church of All Nations 64
    Garden Tomb: Death, Burial, and Resurrection of Christ 69
    Gethsemane to Golgotha: Christ's Path to the Cross 76
    Hezekiah's Broad Wall 85
    Hinnom Valley 93
    House of Caiaphas 98
    Kidron Valley 103
    Mary's Tomb 108
    Mount of Olives Overview 113
    Pater Noster Church 119
    Pilate's Palace & Praetorium 131
    Pool of Bethesda & St. Anne Church 132

Pool of Siloam 138
Temple Mount Overview 143
Temple Mount Southern Stairs 150
Tomb of the Prophets 155
The Upper Room 158
The Via Dolorosa 165
Walls of Jerusalem History 173
Western Wall and Tunnel 180
Other Sites in Jerusalem 187

Sea of Galilee Sites 197

Sea of Galilee Overview 198
Bethsaida 205
Calling of the Disciples 210
Capernaum 215
Chorazin 223
Feeding the 5,000 228
Jesus Walks on the Water, Calms the Storm and Sea 233
Kursi 239
Magdala: Mary Magdalene 244
Mount Arbel 249
Mount of Beatitudes 255
Sower's Cove: Parables of the Kingdom 260
Tabgha 265
Yardenit Baptismal Site 271
Other Sites Around the Sea of Galilee 273

Northern Israel Sites 278

    Beth-Shean 279

    Beth-Shean Amphitheater/Hippodrome 287

    Caesarea Philippi 295

    Caesarea Maritime 303

    Cana 308

    Dan 312

    Gideon's Spring 318

    Hazor 325

    Jordan River Overview 331

    Megiddo: Valley of Armageddon 337

    Mount Carmel 344

    Mount Tabor 352

    Nazareth Overview 358

    Nazareth: Church (Basilica) of the Annunciation 364

    Sepphoris (Tsipori, Zippori) 368

    Other Sites in Northern Israel 374

Central Israel Sites 378

    Tel Ai 379

    Bethel 387

    Bethlehem Overview 394

    Bethlehem: Church of the Nativity 400

    Bethlehem: Herodian Fortress 407

    Bethlehem: Shepherds' Field 414

    Beth-Shemesh 420

Emmaus Nicopolis 427

  Gezer 432

  Gibeon 436

  Gilgal 445

  Inn of the Good Samaritan 452

  Jericho 458

  Joppa (Jaffa, Yafo) 468

  Jordan River: Baptismal Site of Jesus 472

  Jordan River: Crossing into the Promised Land 479

  Judean Wilderness 486

  Qumran and the Dead Sea Scrolls 492

  Samaria 499

  Shechem 508

  Shiloh 520

  St. George's Monastery 527

  Valley of Elah 533

  Other Sites in Central Israel 540

Southern Israel Sites 545

  Tel Arad 546

  Tel Beersheba 554

  En Gedi 560

  Exodus, Red Sea, and Mount Sinai 564

  Hebron 576

  Kadesh Barnea 582

  Lachish 590

  Masada 598

    Sodom and Gomorrah 605

    Timna Park: Tabernacle Replica 614

    Other Sites in Southern Israel 622

Timeline of Israel 627

Maps of Israel 633

    Twelve Tribes of Israel 634

    Divided Kingdom 635

    Regions of Israel 636

    Israel Today 637

Travel Orientation 638

    Understanding the Holy Sites in Israel 639

    How to Get the Most Out of Your Holy Land Trip 642

    Understanding Group Travel Dynamics 644

    Travel Tips for Israel 646

    Packing List 647

About the Author 650

    Books by Todd M. Fink 651

    Connect with Todd 652

Acknowledgments

First and foremost, God deserves all the credit and glory for this book. He gave the desire, resources, time, strength, perseverance, and the ability to write it.

Secondly, for some unexplainable reason, God has filled the hearts of my wife and I with a deep desire to help people see the context of where the Bible took place. Of course, we know this desire is none other than God's sovereign work and grace. It's been a rich joy to have a small part in working with God's grace to provide this book.

What you as a reader find useful in this book, please give the glory and credit to God. What you find that is not useful or to your liking, please place the blame on the author.

Thirdly, I would like to thank my lovely wife, Letsy, for doing much of the research on the secondary "Other Sites of Interest" at the end of each section of the book. Significant time and effort were spent investigating these places.

Lastly, I'd like to thank my son, Joel, for helping with formatting, layout, and proofreading. He was a real trooper, and his contribution was invaluable.

My prayer is that God might use this book in your life to deepen your faith, your understanding of who God is, and how He has used the land of Israel and its people to communicate His eternal message to the world.

Israel: Land of the Bible

The Bible is not a fairy tale written in an unknown time, in an unreal place, and with unreal people. On the contrary, the Bible was written in real-time, in a real place, and with real people. The better we understand the context of the time, place, and people of the Bible, the better we will understand the Bible itself. In other words, by understanding the **world of the Bible** better, we can understand the **words of the Bible** better.

For a person of faith whose beliefs are engrained in the Bible, there is no place on earth like the Holy Land. In this narrow strip of land that connects the three major continents of Africa, Asia, and Europe, God sovereignly placed the land of Israel. It lies on the crossroads of the world and has affected virtually every civilization on earth.

From its barren hills and fertile plains, a message went out from a tethered and worn prophet that still applies today: *"... and many peoples shall come, and say, 'Come, let us go up to the Mountain of the Lord, to the House of the God of Jacob; that He may teach us His ways and that we may walk in His paths. For out of Zion will go forth the law, and the word of the Lord from Jerusalem'"* (Isaiah 2:3–4).

Located on a tiny land bridge between Africa and Asia, there were few travel options between the two continents except through Israel. Therefore, whoever wanted to trade between the two continents, or control the known world, had to conquer and control Israel. For this reason, there have been more wars and conflicts in Israel than in any other country on earth. God positioned Israel in this unique location so He could influence the world and be on "Center Stage." In so doing, God's message of who He is, and His message of salvation and hope, is reaching the entire world.

For nearly 2,000 years, pilgrims of faith have come from all over the world to visit and experience the Holy Land, the land of their spiritual heritage. With Bibles in hand, these pilgrims have walked where Jesus walked and prayed in the places He preached and prayed. For Christians, there is just simply no place like Israel. As we traverse and experience the Holy Land, the better we understand Israel's land, places, and people. This great privilege allows us to better understand God's message written to us on the holy pages of Scripture, and as a result, live lives that glorify and fulfill God's purpose for our existence.

This book is divided into five main sections:

1. Jerusalem Sites
2. Sea of Galilee Sites
3. Northern Israel Sites
4. Central Israel Sites
5. Southern Israel Sites

Each section is arranged in alphabetical order for your convenience.

Jerusalem Sites

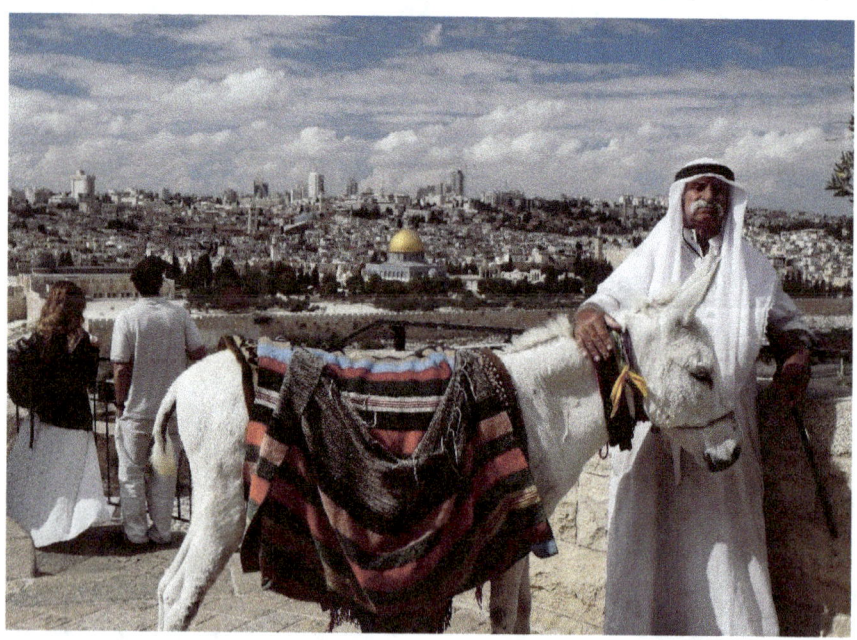

Jerusalem Overview

Location

1. Jerusalem is in the central part of Israel, about 33 miles (53 km.) east of Tel Aviv and the Mediterranean Sea.
2. It's situated at an altitude of 2,600 ft. (800 m.) above sea level and is one of the highest cities in Israel.
3. It's located on a mountain that is well protected. For this reason, it was hard to capture by enemy forces.
4. Jerusalem rests primarily upon bedrock, so everything was well preserved.
5. Jerusalem is the Old Testament, Mount Moriah.

Historical Background

1. Jerusalem means "City of Peace."
2. It's mentioned over 500 times in the Bible.
3. It's first mentioned as the city in which King Melchizedek, King of Salem (Jerusalem), lived (Gen. 14:17). Melchizedek was a figure of Christ as he had neither beginning of days or end of life.

   Hebrews 7:1: *For this Melchizedek, king of **Salem**, priest of the Most High God, who met Abraham as he was returning from the slaughter of the kings and blessed him, 2 to whom also Abraham apportioned a tenth part of all the spoils, was first of all, by the translation of his name, king of righteousness, and then also king of **Salem**, which is **king of peace**.*
4. Jerusalem is the special dwelling place of God on this earth.

   Psalms 76:2: *His tent is in **Salem**, his dwelling place in Zion.*

   Psalm 135:21: *Praise be to the LORD from Zion, to him who dwells in **Jerusalem**. Praise the LORD.*

5. In Jerusalem, on Mount Moriah, Abraham was to offer Isaac, his firstborn son, to God, on the very place the temple would later be built.

   Genesis 22:2: *Then God said, "Take your son, your only son, Isaac, whom you love, and go to the region of **Moriah**. Sacrifice him there as a burnt offering on one of the **mountains** I will tell you about."*

6. Jerusalem was partially conquered by the Israelites when they entered the Promised Land.

7. Jerusalem was then later fully conquered by King David.

8. King David purchased the original Temple Mount in Jerusalem from Araunah when it was just a threshing floor. He purchased it to build an altar to the Lord.

9. Afterward, King David set up his throne in Jerusalem, and it became the ruling center of Israel from then on.

10. King Solomon then built the Temple in 960 AD on the exact location where Abraham was going to sacrifice Isaac. This exact location was also the very threshing floor that King David had purchased.

    2 Chronicles 3:1: *Then Solomon began to build the temple of the LORD in **Jerusalem** on Mount Moriah, where the LORD had appeared to his father, David. It was on the threshing floor of Araunah the Jebusite, the place provided by David.*

11. At the dedication of the temple Solomon built, the temple was so filled with the glory of God that the priest had to withdraw and suspend their dedication service.

    1 Kings 8:10–11: *When the priests withdrew from the Holy Place, the cloud filled the temple of the LORD. 11 And the priests could not perform their service because of the cloud, for the glory of the LORD filled his temple.*

12. Jerusalem became the center of worship in Israel.

13. The kings of Israel reigned from Jerusalem.

Jerusalem Sites

14. The prophets of Israel spoke and ministered in Jerusalem.
15. Unfortunately, the first temple built by Solomon was destroyed in 586 BC by Babylon because of God's judgment on Israel for their disobedience to Him.
16. The altar and foundation of the second temple were built by Zerubbabel in 535 BC.
17. The construction of the second temple was completed in 515 BC.

    Ezra 6:3: *In the first year of King Cyrus, the king issued a decree concerning the temple of God in **Jerusalem**: Let the temple be rebuilt as a place to present sacrifices, and let its foundations be laid.*

18. Nehemiah then arrived to rebuild the city and walls of Jerusalem in 445 BC.

    Nehemiah 2:17: *Then I said to them, "You see the trouble we are in: **Jerusalem** lies in ruins, and its gates have been burned with fire. Come, let us rebuild the wall of Jerusalem, and we will no longer be in disgrace."*

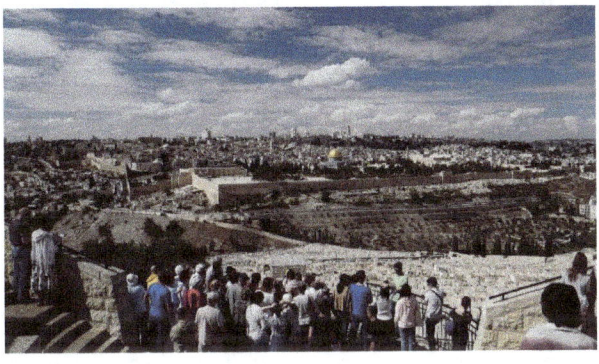

19. The Temple Mount Platform was then later enlarged tremendously by King Herod in 19 BC.
20. On top of the Temple Mount Platform (and over the existing second temple, which was later removed), King Herod built a new massive temple in 19 BC and was made more beautiful than any before it.
21. It was at this temple built by Herod that Christ and the disciples would minister.
22. Jesus was circumcised at the temple in Jerusalem after being born in Bethlehem.
23. Magi from the east came to visit Jerusalem to witness the birth of Jesus, the Messiah King.

    Matthew 2:1: *After Jesus was born in Bethlehem in Judea, during the time of King Herod, Magi from the east came to **Jerusalem**.*

24. Scripture records that Jesus appeared in Jerusalem at the age of 12, and His parents visited there regularly.
25. At the temple in Jerusalem is the place where Christ was tempted by the Devil to throw himself down headlong.
26. Christ visited and ministered in Jerusalem at least 10 times during His ministry years.
27. Christ died on the Cross in Jerusalem.

   Matthew 16:21: *From that time on Jesus began to explain to his disciples that he must go to **Jerusalem** and suffer many things at the hands of the elders, chief priests and teachers of the law, and that he must be killed and on the third day be raised to life.*
28. Christ ascended to heaven in Jerusalem from the Mount of Olives.
29. Pentecost and the coming of the Holy Spirit happened in Jerusalem.

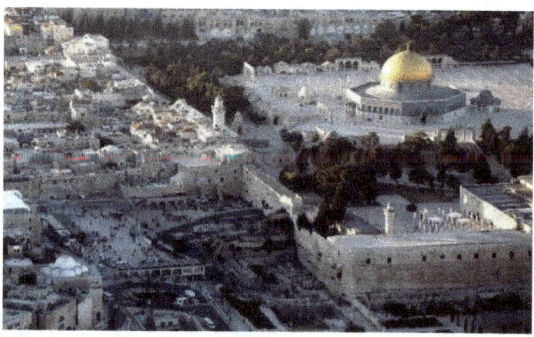

30. The Early Church was born in Jerusalem.

   Acts 2:1, 5–6, 41: *When the day of Pentecost came, they were all together in one place. 5 Now there were staying in **Jerusalem** God-fearing Jews from every nation under heaven. 6 When they heard this sound, a crowd came together in bewilderment, because each one heard them speaking in his own language. 41 Those who accepted his message were baptized, and about three thousand were added to their number that day.*
31. The Apostle Paul grew up in Jerusalem under Gamaliel (Acts 22:3). He probably sat at the Southern Stairs (Rabbi's Stairs), learning from Gamaliel.
32. Stephen was martyred in Jerusalem, as recounted in Acts 7.
33. Unfortunately, Jerusalem was destroyed in 70 AD by the Romans due to Christ's judgment on it for the Jew's rejection of Him as their Messiah.
34. It was destroyed again in 132 AD in the Bar Kokhba Revolt. Later, Hadrian rebuilt and renamed it Aelia Capitolina.
35. It was later conquered by Muslims in 636 AD.

Jerusalem Sites

36. In 691 AD, the Dome of the Rock was built where the temple once stood.
37. It was captured by the Crusaders in 1099 AD.
38. It was re-captured by the Muslims in 1187 AD.
39. It was ruled by the Mamluks in 1291 AD.
40. It was ruled by the Ottomans in 1516 AD.
41. Most of the walls and gates of Jerusalem that exist today were built around 1537 AD.
42. The nation of Israel was supernaturally re-gathered after almost 2,000 years of being scattered and became a nation again in 1948.

43. Christ will return to Jerusalem in power and great glory on the Mount of Olives at the end of the Great Tribulation Period.
44. The final judgment at the end of the Great Tribulation takes place in Jerusalem in the Kidron Valley.
45. Christ will reign for 1,000 years from Jerusalem after the Great Tribulation Period.
46. There will be a New Jerusalem that will be the center of the new heavens and new earth for eternity.

Places of Interest

1. Temple Mount
2. Western Wall
3. Southern Stairs
4. Church of the Holy Sepulchre
5. Kidron Valley
6. Garden of Gethsemane
7. Triumphal Entry
8. Mount of Olives
9. City of David

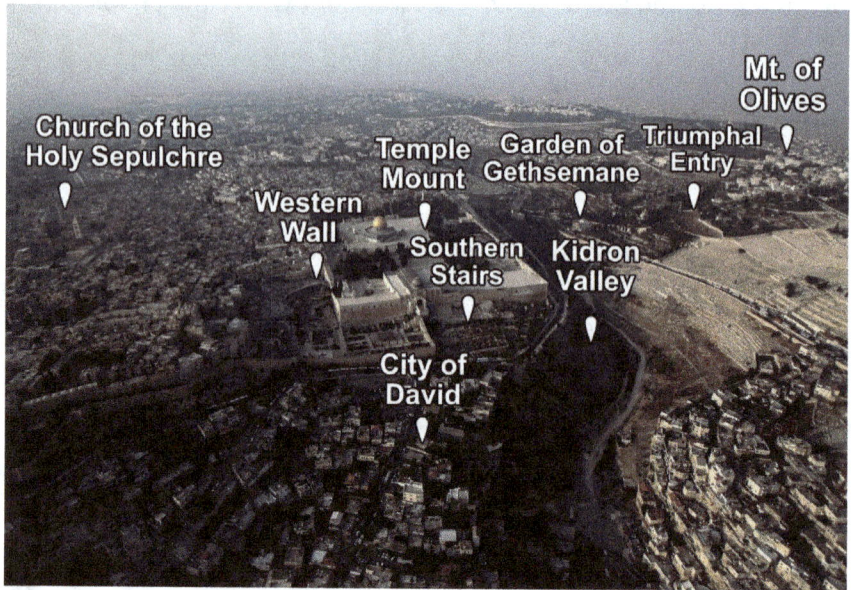

Faith Lesson from Jerusalem

1. Jerusalem has played a key role as the center of God's dwelling place and ministry on this earth.
2. It will be the place Christ returns to in power and great glory at the end of the Great Tribulation Period. Believers will return with Him at this event. Will you be coming with him in glory or be judged by Him when He comes?
3. Christ will reign in Jerusalem over all the earth during the Millennial Reign. Will you be among those who reign with Him?
4. There will be a New Jerusalem created by God which will be His new eternal dwelling place on the new earth. Those who are followers of Christ will have the privilege of living in or visiting this new city forever. Are you saved, and will you be in heaven where the New Jerusalem will be?

Journal/Notes:

Jerusalem Sites Overview

Summary of all the Biblical Sites and Their Locations

1. Mount of Olives
2. Bethphage
   - Beginning of the Triumphal Entry.
3. Chapel of Ascension
   - Place from which Christ ascended to heaven and will return to in power and great glory at the end of the Great Tribulation.
4. Pater Noster Church
   - Place Christ taught the Lord's Prayer.
5. Tombs of the Prophets
   - Haggai, Zechariah, and Malachi.
6. Triumphal Entry Pathway
   - The road Christ descended on Palm Sunday, the Sunday before His crucifixion on Friday.
7. Church of Dominus Flevit
   - Place Christ wept over Jerusalem on the Triumphal Entry and prophesied her future destruction.
8. Church of Mary Magdalene
   - Christ cast out seven demons from Mary, and she became a passionate follower of Christ.
9. Garden of Gethsemane – Church of All Nations
10. Tomb of Mary (mother of Jesus)
11. Kidron Valley (Valley of Jehoshaphat)
    - Place Christ will gather the nations in judgment at the end of the Tribulation Period, and their blood will flow to the depth of a horse's bridle down toward the Dead Sea and beyond.
12. Temple Mount
    - It was enlarged by Herod the Great. It's the size of 35 football fields (35 acres, 14 hectares).
    - The original temple was located exactly where the Dome of the Rock is today.
    - Place the prophets ministered.

Israel Biblical Sites Travel Guide

- The glory of the Lord filled the temple here.
- Place Christ ministered.
- Place the apostles ministered.
- Place the early church met.
- The Antonia Fortress was located just north of the Temple Mount.

13. Dome of the Rock (not a mosque but a shrine)
14. Western Wall
    - It was part of the original wall of the Temple Mount Herod built.
    - It existed during the time of Christ.
    - It is the closest place (for a large gathering) to the original temple where the Jews pray.
15. Pool of Bethesda - St. Anne Church
    - A lame man was healed here after waiting 38 years.
16. Via Dolorosa (painful path)
    - It's the believed path Christ took on the way to the Cross.
    - It has 14 stations.
17. Gordon's Garden Tomb – Golgotha
18. Church of the Holy Sepulchre
19. Absalom's Tomb
20. Southern Stairs
    - Place Christ taught His disciples.
    - Likely location of Pentecost.
21. City of David
22. David's Palace
23. Gihon Spring
24. Wall repaired by Nehemiah
25. Pool of Siloam
26. Hinnom Valley
    - Gehenna – Idea of hell and eternal burning.
27. House of Caiaphas
    - Place Peter denied Christ.
    - Place Christ was condemned before Ananias and Caiaphas the high priest.

Jerusalem Sites

28. Tomb of David
29. The Upper Room
30. Herod's Palace – Later, it would become Pilate's Palace
31. Citadel of David

Gates of Jerusalem

1. Eastern Gate (Golden Gate, Shushan Gate)
   - Gate Christ regularly entered on His way to the temple from the Mount of Olives.
   - Peter and James healed a lame man after entering this gate.
   - Closed by Ottoman Turkish Muslims in 1541 AD.
2. Lions Gate (Stephen's Gate)
3. Herod's Gate

Israel Biblical Sites Travel Guide

4. Damascus Gate
5. New Gate
6. Jaffa Gate
7. Zion Gate
8. Dung Gate

Jerusalem Sites

Journal/Notes:

Israel Biblical Sites Travel Guide

Antonia Fortress

Location

1. The Antonia Fortress was located just outside the Temple Mount area on its northwestern side.
2. Today, Umariya Elementary School and a convent of the Sisters of Zion lie atop its ruins.
3. Some of the ruins can be accessed through the Convent of the Sisters of Zion.
4. Tradition places the Antonia Fortress as the beginning point of the Via Dolorosa (painful path).

Historical Background

1. The Antonia Fortress was a military headquarters and barracks built by Herod the Great in 19 BC to protect the Temple Mount area and the city of Jerusalem. It was named after Herod's patron, Mark Antony.
2. Some believe Jesus appeared before Pilate here and was condemned to death by crucifixion.
3. Others believe that Pilate's Headquarters, also called Pilate's Palace or Praetorium, was the place Christ appeared before Pilate. It's located on the northern side of Jerusalem, just south of the Jaffa Gate. The evidence points strongly in favor of this location as the place of Christ's trial and condemnation.
4. Some believe that the Antonia Fortress encompassed all the current Temple Mount and that the original temple and Temple Mount were in the City of David. However, Scripture clearly states that at the dedication of the temple that Solomon built that the Ark of the covenant was brought "**out of the City of David**" to the temple. *"Then Solomon assembled to Jerusalem the elders of Israel and all the heads of the tribes, the leaders of the fathers' households*

*of the sons of Israel, to bring up the ark of the covenant of the Lord **out of the City of David**, which is Zion"* (2 Chron. 5:2).

If the Ark was brought out of the City of David to the temple, then the temple couldn't have been in the City of David. There is also overwhelming historical and archaeological evidence, and the writings of the famous Jewish historian Flavius Josephus, that contradict the belief that the Antonia Fortress encompassed all the Temple Mount.

Evidence that the Temple Mount was not the Antonia Fortress.

1. Contrary to what some say, the current Temple Mount existed long before the Romans arrived. The Temple Mount foundation, or platform, was first built by Solomon. Then Hezekiah enlarged it. Later, its foundations were repaired during the time of Zerubbabel when the second temple was built. We see evidence of this in the ancient stones around the Eastern Gate. They date back to the time of Solomon, Hezekiah, Zerubbabel, and Nehemiah.

2. Later, in around 141 BC, the Hasmoneans built an extension to the southern end of the Temple Mount. This can be seen in the Eastern Wall, where the bend in the wall exists. Thus, there is a change in stone styles from earlier periods to the Hasmonean period.

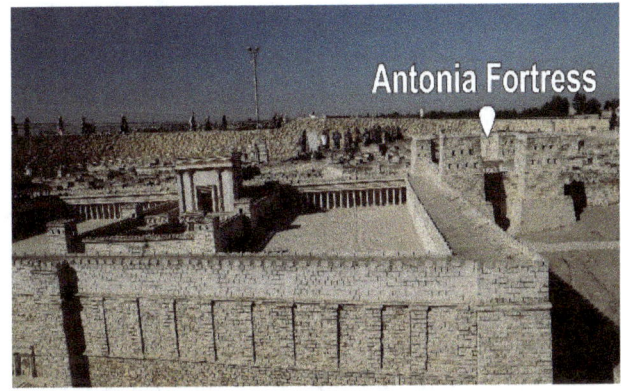

Model of what the Antonia Fortress may have looked like

3. Then, in around 19 BC, Herod the Great began to enlarge the Temple Mount Platform. He would double the size of what it was during the Hasmonean period. This can be seen in the Eastern Wall as well, where there is a seam in the wall. The stone styles change from Hasmonean to Herodian. Josephus confirms this: *"Accordingly, in the fifteenth year of his reign [23-22 BC], Herod rebuilt the temple, and encompassed a piece of land about it with a*

wall, which land was twice as large as that before enclosed. The expenses he laid out upon it were vastly large also, and the riches about it were unspeakable" (Wars of the Jews, Bk 1, Ch. 21, Sect. 401).

Therefore, the current Temple Mount existed long before the Romans arrived and was not expanded to be a Roman Fort.

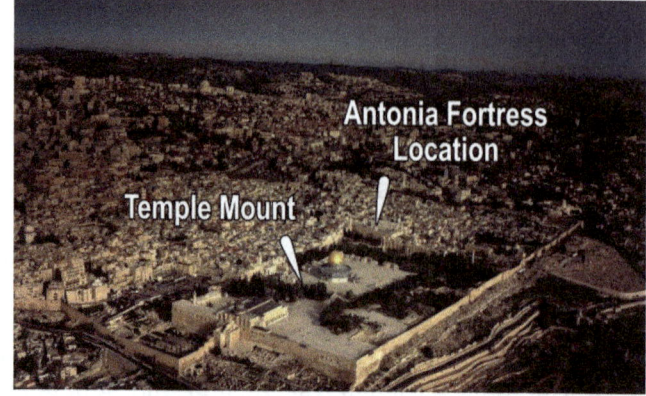

4. There are also no historical records that a Roman Legion was stationed in Jerusalem before 66–67 AD. At this time, the Jews had revolted and recaptured Jerusalem from Roman control. The 10th Roman Legion was then moved to Jerusalem to conquer it. This was a fulfillment of Christ's prophecy. The city was destroyed and conquered in 70 AD.

5. Facts about the 10th Roman Legion.
   - It was founded in around 41 or 40 BC. It was also called the X Fretensis or Legio X.
   - It was never stationed in Jerusalem until it arrived to overthrow the Jewish rebellion that had taken place wherein the Jews overtook the Roman Soldiers who were in Jerusalem and regained control. It was the 10th Roman Legion, led by Vespasian, that would win the battle to recapture Jerusalem from the Jews in 70 AD.
   - From 67 onward, X Fretensis fought in the war against the Jews. It was commanded by Marcus Ulpius Trajanus, the father of the future emperor. The supreme commander of the Roman forces in Judaea was general Vespasian, who was to become emperor during the civil war that broke out after the suicide of Nero in 68 AD.
   - After the conclusion of the Jewish revolt in around 73 AD, Legio X was garrisoned at Jerusalem. Their main camp was positioned on the Western Hill, located in the southern half of

the old city, now leveled of all former buildings. The camp of the Tenth was built using the surviving portions of the walls of Herod the Great's palace, demolished by order of Titus. The camp was at the end of the cardo maximus of Aelia Capitolina (Pace, H. Geva, "*The Camp of the Tenth Legion in Jerusalem: An Archaeological Reconsideration,*" IEJ 34, 1984, pp. 247-249).

6. Josephus clearly describes and clarifies that the Antonia Fortress was destroyed by the Romans when they conquered and tore down the temple in 70 AD: *"Titus now ordered the troops that were with him to raze the foundations of Antonia and to prepare an easy ascent [into the Temple Mount] for the whole army"* (Wars Ch. 6, Sect 93). *"Meanwhile, the rest of the Roman army, having in seven days overthrown the foundations of Antonia, had prepared a broad ascent to the Temple"* (Wars Ch. 6, Sect. 149).

It is vital to understand that when Josephus wrote this, it was in 70 AD, more than 70 years after Herod enlarged the Temple Mount Platform. Also, the Tenth Roman Legion never was stationed in Jerusalem until after it was conquered in 70 AD. So, the idea that the current Temple Mount Platform was built for the Tenth Roman Legion is entirely false.

7. If the Antonia was destroyed in seven days, it reveals that it wasn't that big. Also, it was destroyed, so there is no way the current Temple Mount could be the Antonia Fortress.

Places of Interest
1. Ecce Homo Arch (behold the man)

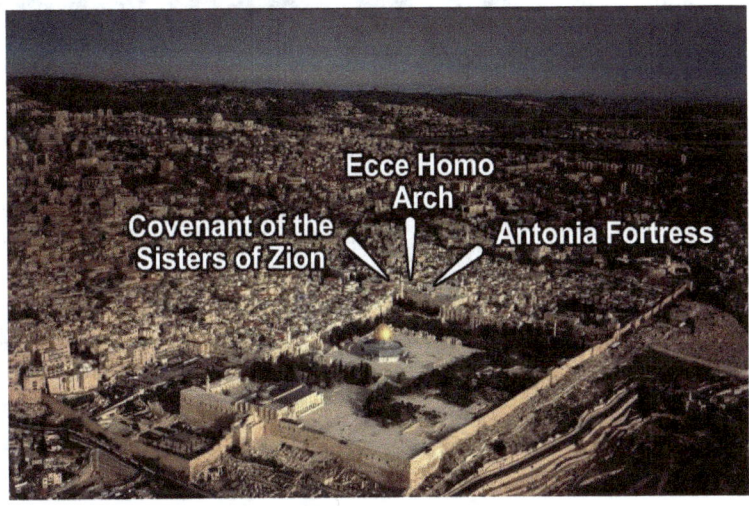

2. Convent of the Sisters of Zion
3. Pavement stones with Roman carved games on them.
4. Pavement stones with carved grooves.
5. Temple Mount

The Antonia Fortress in the Bible

1. **The Antonia Fortress is the believed place where the Via Dolorosa begins.**

   Tradition places the Antonia Fortress as the beginning place of the Via Dolorosa. However, the site with the best evidence for being the beginning place of the Via Dolorosa is Pilate's Palace, located just south of the Jaffa Gate.

2. **Paul addressed an angry mob from the Antonia Fortress.**

   Acts 21:27–40: *When the seven days were almost over, the Jews from Asia, upon seeing him [Paul] in the temple, began to stir up all the crowd and laid hands on him, 28 crying out, "Men of Israel, come to our aid! This is the man who preaches to all men everywhere against our people and the Law and this place; and besides he has even brought Greeks into the temple and has defiled this holy place." 29 For they had previously seen Trophimus the Ephesian in the city with him, and they supposed that Paul had brought him into the temple. 30 Then all the city was provoked, and the people rushed together, and taking hold of Paul they dragged him out of the temple, and immediately the doors were shut. 31 While they were seeking to kill him, a report came up to the commander of the Roman cohort that all Jerusalem was in confusion. 32 At once he took along some soldiers and centurions and ran down to them; and when they saw the commander and the soldiers, they stopped beating Paul. 33 Then the commander came up and took hold of him, and ordered him to be bound with two chains; and he began asking who he was and what he had done. 34*

   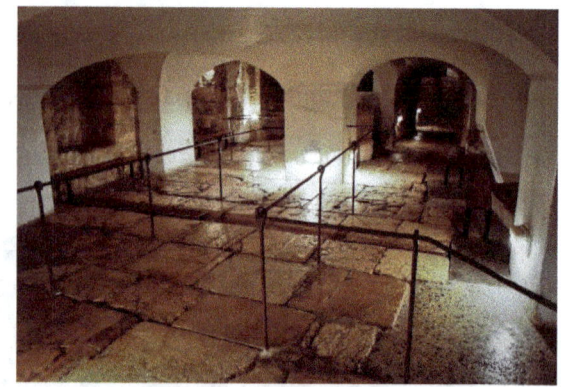
   Original stone floor of the Antonia Fortress

Jerusalem Sites

*But among the crowd some were shouting one thing and some another, and when he could not find out the facts because of the uproar, he ordered him to be **brought into the barracks**. 35 **When he got to the stairs**, he was carried by the soldiers because of the violence of the mob; 36 for the multitude of the people kept following them, shouting, "Away with him!" 37 As Paul was about to be **brought into the barracks**, he said to the commander, "May I say something to you?" And he said, "Do you know Greek? 38 Then you are not the Egyptian who some time ago stirred up a revolt and led the four thousand men of the Assassins out into the wilderness?" 39 But Paul said, "I am a Jew of Tarsus in Cilicia, a citizen of no insignificant city; and I beg you, allow me to speak to the people." 40 When he had given him permission, Paul, standing on the stairs, motioned to the people with his hand; and when there was a great hush, he spoke to them in the Hebrew dialect.*

Faith Lesson from the Antonia Fortress

1. Paul suffered at the Antonia Fortress for his faith. Are we willing to boldly proclaim our faith and suffer as a result if necessary?
2. Paul shared his testimony often. Do we have our testimony memorized, and do we share it when talking to others about God?

Journal/Notes:

Chapel of the Ascension: Ascension and Return of Christ

Location

1. The Chapel of the Ascension sits at the highest place on the Mount of Olives.
2. Near the Ascension Chapel is the Russian Orthodox Church of the Ascension, built in 1870, which is another traditional site of the ascension. It is located near a tall tower in the village of A-Tur.

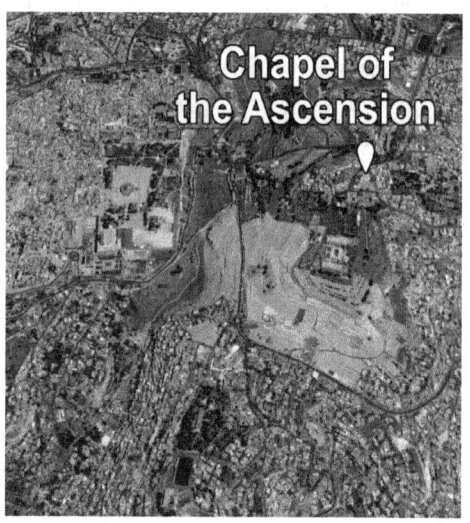

Historical Background

1. Early Christians soon memorialized this place after Christ's resurrection.
2. In 384 AD, a pilgrim named Egeria found two footprints embedded in a rock that she claimed were those of Christ when He ascended to heaven.
3. Constantine's mother, Helena, had a church built here as a memorial chapel at the end of the 4th century.
4. This chapel was rebuilt in the 7th century.
5. It was again rebuilt by the Crusaders around 1100 AD.
6. In 1198 AD, the chapel was destroyed by Saladin under Ottoman Muslim conquest, and a mosque was built on its site. However, part of the original chapel was left intact. The bases of the columns can be seen today.
7. At this time, since the chapel was primarily used by Christians, a mosque was built during the Ottoman period on the south side of the compound, and the chapel was converted into a Muslim shrine.
8. Today, both Christians and Muslims visit this place, and it's open to all.
9. Because it's the highest place on the Mount of Olives, it's the

Jerusalem Sites

believed place from where Christ ascended back to heaven.

10. It's also the believed place where Christ will return to earth at His second coming.

Places of Interest

1. Chapel of the Ascension
2. Russian Orthodox Church of the Ascension
3. Mount of Olives
4. Old City Jerusalem

Location of the Chapel of Ascension in the Bible

1. Christ ascended back to heaven from the top of the Mount of Olives.

Acts 1:6–12: *So when they had come together, they asked him, "Lord, will you at this time restore the kingdom to Israel?" 7 He said to them, "It is not for you to know times or seasons that the Father has fixed by his own authority. 8 But you will receive power when the Holy Spirit has come upon you, and you will be my witnesses in Jerusalem and in all Judea and Samaria, and to the end of the earth." 9 And when he had said these things, as they were looking on, **he was lifted up, and a cloud took him out of their sight**. 10 And while they were gazing into **heaven as he went**, behold, two men stood by them in white robes, 11 and said, "Men of Galilee, why do* you stand looking into heaven? This Jesus, who was taken up from you into heaven, **will come in the same way as you saw him go into heaven**." 12 Then they returned to Jerusalem from the **mount called Olivet**, which is near Jerusalem, a Sabbath day's journey away.

2. **The return of Christ to earth will be one of the greatest culminating events in Scripture.**

   Zechariah 14:4: *On that day his feet shall stand on the* **Mount of Olives** *that lies before Jerusalem on the east, and the Mount of Olives shall be split in two from east to west by a very wide valley, so that one half of the Mount shall move northward, and the other half southward.*

3. **Every being that has ever been created will see Christ's return.**

   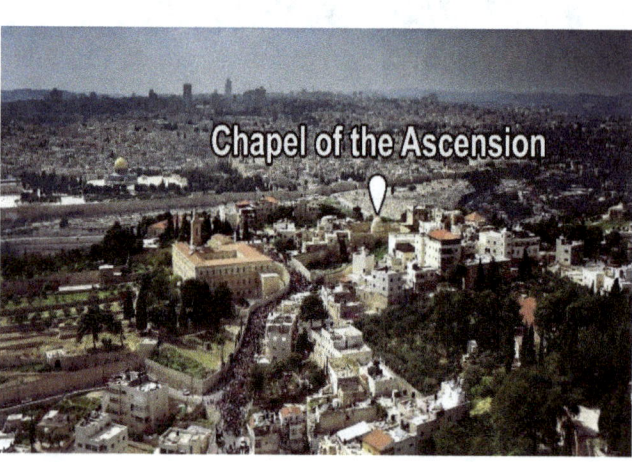

   Revelation 1:7: *Behold, he is coming with the clouds, and every eye will see him, even those who pierced him, and all tribes of the earth will wail on account of him. Even so. Amen.*

4. **Christ's return conquers and flips all evil powers into submission to Him.**

   Revelation 19:15: *From his mouth comes a sharp sword with which to strike down the nations, and he will rule them with a rod of iron. He will tread the winepress of the fury of the wrath of God the Almighty.*

5. **Christ coming will be in extreme power and great glory.**

   Matthew 24:29–31: *Immediately after the tribulation of those days the sun will be darkened, and the moon will not give its light, and the stars will fall from heaven, and the powers of the heavens will be shaken. 30 Then will appear in heaven the sign of the Son of Man, and then all the tribes of the earth will mourn, and they will*

Jerusalem Sites

see the Son of Man coming on the clouds of heaven with power and great glory. 31 And he will send out his angels with a loud trumpet call, and they will gather his elect from the four winds, from one end of heaven to the other.

Revelation 6:12–17: *When he opened the sixth seal, I looked, and behold, there was a great earthquake, and the sun became black as sackcloth, the full moon became like blood, 13 and the stars of the sky fell to the earth as the fig tree sheds its winter fruit when shaken by a gale. 14 The sky vanished like a scroll that is being rolled up, and every mountain and island*

was removed from its place. 15 Then the kings of the earth and the great ones and the generals and the rich and the powerful, and everyone, slave and free, hid themselves in the caves and among the rocks of the mountains, 16 calling to the mountains and rocks, "Fall on us and hide us from the face of him who is seated on the throne, and from the wrath of the Lamb, 17 for the great day of their wrath has come, and who can stand?"

6. **Believers and angels will return with Christ in power and great glory as well.**

    Revelation 19:11–15: *Then I saw heaven opened, and behold, a white horse! The one sitting on it is called Faithful and True, and in righteousness he judges and makes war. 12 His eyes are like a flame of fire, and on his head are many diadems, and he has a name written that no one knows but himself. 13 He is clothed in a robe dipped in blood, and the name by which he is called is The Word of God. 14 And the **armies of heaven, arrayed in fine linen**, white and pure, were following him on white horses. 15 From his mouth comes a sharp sword with which to strike down the nations, and he will rule them with a rod of iron. He will tread the winepress of the fury of the wrath of God the Almighty.*

7. **Christ will judge the nations and separate the sheep (believers) from the goats (unbelievers).**

   Revelation 14:17–20: *Then another angel came out of the temple in heaven, and he too had a sharp sickle. 18 And another angel came out from the altar, the angel who has authority over the fire, and he called with*

   Mount of Olives

   a loud voice to the one who had the sharp sickle, "Put in your sickle and gather the clusters from the vine of the earth, for its grapes are ripe." 19 So the angel swung his sickle across the earth and gathered the grape harvest of the earth and threw it into the great winepress of the wrath of God. 20 And the winepress was trodden outside the city, and blood flowed from the winepress, as high as a horse's bridle, for 1,600 stadia [200 miles or 300 km].

8. **The judgment of unbelievers will be severe.**

   Zechariah 14:12: *And this shall be the plague with which the LORD will strike all the peoples that wage war against Jerusalem: their flesh will rot while they are still standing on their feet, their eyes will rot in their sockets, and their tongues will rot in their mouths.*

Faith Lesson from the Location of the Chapel of the Ascension

1. Christ proved to be God in ascending in a glorified body back to heaven. Do we believe Jesus is God?
2. Every being that has ever been created will see Christ's return in power and great glory.
3. Christ's return conquers and flips all evil powers into submission to Him.
4. Christ coming will be in extreme power and great glory.

Jerusalem Sites

5. Christ will physically return to the Mount of Olives.
6. Believers and angels will return with Christ in power and great glory as well.
7. Christ will judge the nations and separate the sheep from the goats.
8. Are we living a devoted life to Christ and serving Him?
9. Are we living a life that is watchful and ready?
10. Will we be among those who come with Christ at His return or those whom Christ judges?

Chapel of the Ascension – Jerusalem in the background

Journal/Notes:

Israel Biblical Sites Travel Guide

Church of the Holy Sepulchre

Location

1. The Church of the Holy Sepulchre is located about 450 yards (415 m.) west of the Temple Mount.
2. It was located outside the city walls during the time of Christ.
3. It's the believed place where Christ was crucified, buried, and rose from the dead.
4. It's the ending place to the Via Dolorosa path, and the last 5 stations are located at it.
5. It's visited by over a million people every year.

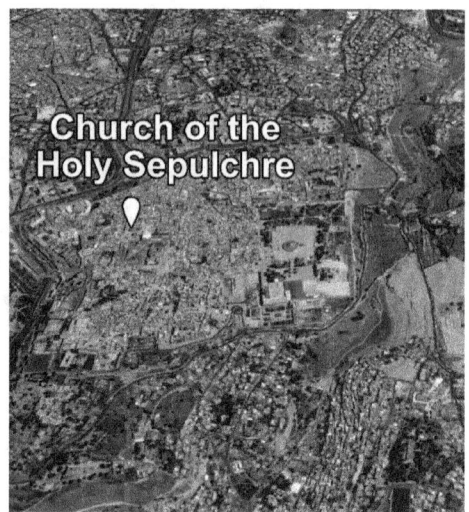

Historical Background

1. The Church of the Holy Sepulchre is the most important holy site in Christianity and is visited by over one million pilgrims every year.
2. The place of Calvary was once a stone quarry that supplied stone for the building of the temple and so forth. During the time of Christ, there was a gate to Jerusalem called the Gennath Gate, which means garden gate. This gate has been discovered in recent times. It is in a little different location than the Jerusalem model, as the model was built before the gate was discovered. Josephus makes mention of this gate in his historical writings as well. There was a road that passed by the stone quarry for travelers entering and leaving Jerusalem. Because the quarry had fallen out of use many years before Christ, it slowly developed into a garden with a cistern and pool of water nearby. Some of the rock was left, and upon it, the Romans crucified people. This rock can be seen in the Church of the Holy Sepulchre today. It was an ideal place because it was just outside the city and located on a well-traveled road. The

Jerusalem Sites

Romans crucified people in the most visible places possible, so all would learn what would happen to them if they disobeyed Roman laws. There were also tombs in the rock faces that were used for burials.

Scripture states in John 19:20 that the place of crucifixion was near the city of Jerusalem, so this place fits the biblical narrative well: *"Therefore, many of the Jews read this inscription, for the place where Jesus was crucified was near the city; and it was written in Hebrew, Latin and in Greek."*

Substantial remains of the First Wall have been found in the Jewish Quarter of the Old City of Jerusalem. In these latter excavations, the remains of the Gennath (Garden) Gate and the beginning of what is believed to be the Second Wall have been found, just where Josephus described them as being (cf. War 5.146).

Entrance to the church

The name "Garden Gate" indicates that a garden must have been located nearby. Excavations below the Church of the Holy Sepulchre and the Lutheran Church of the Redeemer show that this area used to be an ancient quarry, which was later abandoned. The excavators believe that the area was then filled with good soil, presumably to turn the ugly quarry remains into a beautiful garden.

An additional area by the rock quarry became a cistern as the city developed.

From the Gospels, we know that Jesus was crucified in a place called "Calvary" and buried in a garden that was in the same place as Joseph of Arimathea's tomb. The front wall of the tomb faced east so the early morning sun could illuminate it. According to Hebrews 13:12, Jesus was crucified outside the city.

Some people have a problem that the place of crucifixion and the tomb of Jesus are so close together in the Church of the Holy Sepulchre. However, John 19:41 states: *"Now in the place where He was crucified there was a garden, and in the garden a new tomb in which no one had yet been laid."* So, Scripture clearly indicates that the crucifixion and tomb were nearby to each other.

3. According to tradition, the early Christian community of Jerusalem worshiped at this site of the crucifixion from the time of the resurrection until 135 AD, when Emperor Hadrian destroyed and rebuilt Jerusalem. Visiting the burial sites of rabbis was a common practice that is even done to this day by the Jews. So, there is no doubt the early Christians would have visited the place where Christ died and rose again as well. There was no one like Jesus, so His followers knew exactly where Golgotha was and venerated it. There is no way this spot would have been lost or forgotten by them.

   For example, shortly after the resurrection of Christ, the Upper Room was converted into a church, and the apse (which is a half-round circle with a dome shape) pointed toward the crucifixion, burial, and resurrection place of Christ. This gives significant evidence that this place was venerated and visited early on after Christ's resurrection. Because this place was so important, the apse of the Upper Room Church pointed toward it and not the temple.

   Another interesting fact is that there are also burial tombs in the Church of the Holy Sepulchre that date to the time of Christ. They are of the type that were used from about 37 BC to around 70 AD. These tombs clearly indicate that this area had tombs and was outside the City of Jerusalem during the time of Christ, as regular people were not buried within the city.

4. About 10 years after the crucifixion of Christ, a wall was built by King Agrippa I that enclosed the area of Christ's execution and burial within the city. This accounts for why the Holy Sepulchre is located inside the Old City walls of Jerusalem today.

5. The next major event that affected the site of the crucifixion and tomb of Christ was a major Jewish rebellion against the Romans called the Bar Kokhba revolt in around 132 AD. Because of the revolt, the Roman Emperor Hadrian destroyed much of Jerusalem and changed its orientation. He renamed the city Aelia Capitolina, and the country of Israel to Palestine, which was a Philistine name. His desire was to erase the Jewish connection to the land because of the Jew's continual rebellions and uprisings. He constructed a main street that ran north and south called the Cardo Maximus

(which means heart, or center of). He also desecrated the place of the crucifixion and resurrection that the early Christians had venerated, and in its place, he built a large platform that filled in the quarry and had upon it a large temple dedicated to Jupiter and Aphrodite, an ancient Greek goddess of sexual love and beauty, identified with Venus by the Romans. Hadrian was so intent on destroying any connection to the land by the Jews and the Christians that he buried all the evidence of the crucifixion and tomb of Christ under a platform that housed his large temple to Jupiter and Venus. Hadrian laid out the new City of Jerusalem so that the major streets led to his temple to Jupiter and Venus, which again were over the remains of the crucifixion and tomb of Christ.

Hadrian's Temple to Jupiter & Venus

Eusebius, the bishop of Caesarea, Israel, who lived from 260 to 339 AD, gave a chronological account of the development of Early Christianity from the 1st century to the 4th. He was an eyewitness to some of the events Hadrian did and wrote down what he saw. Regarding the desecration of the crucifixion and tomb of Christ, Eusebius says: *"The Romans brought a quantity of earth from a distance with much labor and covered the entire spot and buried it. Then having raised this to a moderate height, they paved it with stone."* What he described was the raised platform Hadrian built, upon which he erected his temple to Jupiter and Venus. This platform had retaining walls around it, of which some can still be seen inside the Church today. Also, some of the stairs leading up to the temple of Hadrian can be seen today in the lower part of the church to the east.

Eusebius goes on to say that: *"The monument of his most holy passions so long ago buried beneath the ground."* Here he is describing the place of the crucifixion and tomb of Christ that were buried. Hadrian also minted a coin depicting the temple he built upon Golgotha. The temple of Hadrian would remain in place for another 200 years or so until the time of the Roman Emperor, Constantine.

6. In 313 AD, a major change happened in the Roman Empire when Constantine legalized Christianity. Later, because his mother was so passionate about Christ, she made a trip to the Holy Land to build churches over the main events of Christ's life. She built the Church of the Nativity in Bethlehem, the Church of the Ascension on the Mount of Olives (currently known as the Pater Noster Church), the Church of the Annunciation in Nazareth, and the Church of the Holy Sepulchre.

   The Roman Emperor Constantine had the temple Hadrian had erected to Jupiter and Venus demolished to make way for the Church of the Holy Sepulchre. In the process of the demolition, the tomb and crucifixion site of Jesus were uncovered once again, and the Church of the Holy Sepulchre was erected. Additionally, Constantine's mother, Helena, is claimed to have discovered the relic of the Cross of Jesus at this time as well. The church was dedicated in 335 AD.

7. Now let's see what Jerome says about the fact that Hadrian's temple was located on the top of the crucifixion and tomb site of Christ. Jerome lived from 347 to 420 AD. In about 389 AD, he established a monastery at Bethlehem and translated the Hebrew Bible into Latin. Bethlehem is very close to Jerusalem, so Jerome was an eyewitness to what he wrote.

   Here's what Jerome tells us: *"From the time of Hadrian to the reign of Constantine, the spot which had witnessed the resurrection was occupied by a figure of Jupiter while on the rock where the cross had stood a marble statue of Venus was set up by the heathen and became an object of worship. The original persecutors indeed suppose that by polluting our holy places, they would deprive us of our faith in the passion and in the resurrection."* So Jerome confirms that from the time of Hadrian to Constantine, the temple Hadrian built was located on top of Golgotha.

   So, in the place where Christ died for the sins of humanity, Hadrian set up a temple to false gods who promoted deep immoral sins. What a contrast.

8. Eusebius, whom we referred to earlier, describes the destruction of Hadrian's temple by Constantine: *"As soon as his [Constantine's]*

Jerusalem Sites

commands were given, these engines of deceit were cast down from their proud eminence to the very ground and the dwelling places of error with the statues and the evil spirits which they represented were overthrown and utterly destroyed. Nor did the emperor's zeal stop here, but he gave further orders that the materials of what was thus destroyed, both stone and timber, should be removed and thrown as far from the spot as possible, and this command also was speedily executed."

Eusebius continues: *"The emperor, however, was not satisfied with having proceeded thus far, once more fired with holy adjure he directed that the ground itself should be dug up to come to a considerable depth and the soil which had been polluted by the foul impurities of demon worship transported to a far distant place. This also was accomplished without delay, and as soon as the original surface of the ground beneath the covering of the earth appeared, immediately the venerable and Holy Monument of our Savior's resurrection was discovered. Then indeed did the most holy cave [referring to the tomb] present a faithful similitude of his return to life and that after lying buried in darkness, it again emerged to light and afforded to all who came to witness a sight a clear and visible proof of the wonders of which that spot had once been seen, a testimony to the resurrection of the Savior clearer than any voice could give."*

Eusebius then speaks about the Church of the Holy Sepulchre that Constantine built: *"Accordingly, on the very spot which witnessed the Savior's suffering, a new Jerusalem was constructed where at the side opposite to the Sepulchre [Jesus's tomb] which was the eastern side, the church itself was erected, a noble work rising to a vast height and a great extent in length and breadth."*

Eusebius now describes the construction of the Church of the Holy Sepulchre by Constantine: *"Thereupon the Emperor issued sacred* edicts, and when he had provided an abundant supply of all the things required for the project, he gave orders that a House of Prayer worthy of God should be erected round about the cave of salvation [he is speaking about the tomb], and on a scale of rich and imperial costliness to be greater than anything else that had been built on earth." So Constantine built a large mausoleum over the place of the tomb. A mausoleum is a structure designed for burial or entombment above the ground.

9. Another eyewitness account that the Church of the Holy Sepulchre was located on the site of the crucifixion and tomb of Christ comes from the Pilgrim of Bardot from 333AD: *"On your left is a little hill of Golgotha where the Lord was crucified, about a stone's throw from it is the Crypt where they laid his body and from where he rose again on the third day. These are present by order of Constantine. There has been built a basilica that is a church of wondrous beauty."*

10. A quote from another pilgrim's account of a worship service in the Church of the Holy Sepulchre comes from 380 AD: *"I know you were eager to know about the services they have daily in the holy places, I shall tell you about them. When the first cock has crowed, the bishop straightaway enters and goes into the tomb and the anastasis [anastasis means resurrection and is the round rotunda dome place in the church over the tomb of Christ] and the whole crowd streams into the Anastasis which is already ablaze with many lamps. Then the bishop standing inside the screen takes the gospel and advances to the door of the tomb, where he himself reads the account of the Lord's resurrection. When the gospel is finished, the bishop comes out and is taken with hymns to the cross, and they all go with him to the great church, the martyrium. The people assemble in the great church built by Constantine upon Golgotha."*

Tomb of Christ

11. Another amazing piece of evidence is found at the Basilica of Santa

Jerusalem Sites

Pudenziana, which is recognized as the oldest place of Christian worship in Rome. In the apse of the building is a mosaic of Christ and the Church of the Holy Sepulchre in the background. So, we actually have a photo of what Constantine's Church of the Holy Sepulchre looked like. This is strong evidence for the authenticity of this place.

12. In addition, more substantial evidence supporting the Church of the Holy Sepulchre as the true site of Golgotha is found in Madaba, Jordan. The Madaba Mosaic Map is part of a floor mosaic in the early Byzantine church of St. George in Madaba, Jordan. The map is of the Middle East, and part of it shows the oldest surviving original depiction of the Holy Land and Jerusalem. In the map of Jerusalem, the Church of the Holy Sepulchre can be found in the center of the city. This reveals that the church existed and was venerated as the site of Jesus' death and resurrection. The map dates to around 550 AD.

13. The next big change to the church took place during the Persian conquest in 614 AD when the church was pillaged and suffered significant damage. However, it was restored by the monk, Modestus. According to tradition, it was during this time that the relic of the True Cross was also taken and then recovered in 630 AD.

14. In 648 AD, Jerusalem came under Muslim rule, but Christians could still make pilgrimages to the church.

15. In 1009 AD, the Muslim Caliph al-Hakim gave orders for all churches to be destroyed. This proved fatal for the Church of the Holy Sepulchre, which was singled out in particular and destroyed beyond recognition. During the destruction of the church, the tomb of Christ was largely destroyed. However, some of the rock of the tomb and its location were still preserved.

16. The church was again restored at a large expense by Emperor Constantine IX Monomachos and Patriarch Nicephorus of Constantinople in 1048 AD.

17. The Crusaders renovated the church in 1112 AD and reconsecrated it in 1149 AD. Much of what is seen today of the church is from the Crusader renovations in around 1112 AD, although portions are part of the original church of Constantine.

    As 12th-century maps reveal, the Holy Sepulchre in Jerusalem was the spiritual focus of Christendom and its most important pilgrimage center. The church was laid out to enable pilgrims to move from chapel to chapel, their visit culminating in the Holy Sepulchre itself.

The church that the Crusaders built included the courtyard where Golgotha was believed to have been and enclosed everything under one roof within a magnificent cathedral.

The entrance to the church was changed from the east end and placed on the south side. The Basilica of Helena, accessed from stairs leading downward, was built. This is the believed place where Helena found the true Cross of Christ. It was originally in a hole under the quarry. The entrance to Calvary was from the outside of the church, with stairs leading upwards to a platform where all the events of the crucifixion are located.

The Basilica of the Martyrium was changed, and everything was housed under the roof of the cathedral. The apse of the church Constantine built for the crucifixion site faced west.

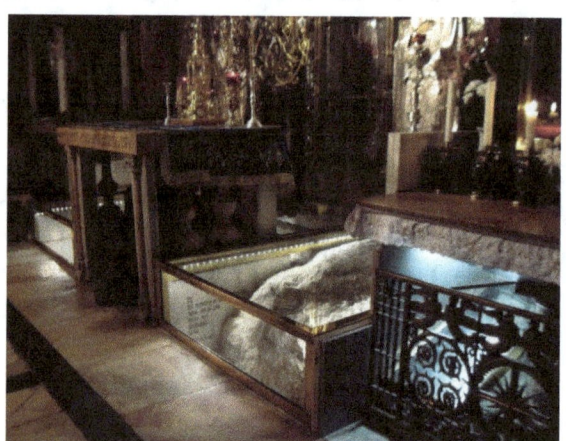

Part of the rock of Golgotha today

Today it faces east. The sites of the crucifixion and tomb have remained in the same places since the time of Christ. Only the buildings around them have changed.

An Edicule was built over the tomb of Christ, and within it is the Chapel of the Angels and what's left of Christ's tomb.

18. The right-hand door was blocked up after the Muslim reconquest of the city in 1187 AD. Now the entrance consists of just one large single door.

19. The three primary custodians of the church were appointed when the Crusaders ruled Jerusalem. They are the Greek Orthodox, the Armenian Apostolic, and Roman Catholic churches. In the 19th century, the Coptic Orthodox, the Ethiopian Orthodox, and the Syrian Orthodox also acquired responsibilities, but in a smaller way. Each church denomination agrees to times and places of

worship.
20. A Muslim family has been given the key for opening and closing the church doors since 1187 AD, when Muslims seized control of Jerusalem.
21. After a fire, the last major changes to the church took place in around 1808. The Edicule over the tomb was renovated. The central Catholicon was closed, which was at one time where part of the courtyard of Constantine's church was located. New stairs leading up to Calvary were changed from outside the church to inside. Today you enter from just inside the church, turn right, and take steep stairs up to the platform of Calvary.

    The Edicule, or tomb of Christ, has been renovated several times since the Crusaders. It suffered an earthquake in 1927 and was shored up, and then recently, in 2016, underwent another renovation. As mentioned earlier, there is nothing but the floor and back edge of the tomb that is from the time of Christ.
22. Because of all the adornments and construction over the centuries, it is hard to imagine how the site would have looked like in the time of Christ. However, these 2,000 years of activity and tradition give greater weight to its authenticity. Some people have an adverse reaction to the atmosphere inside the church. However, this is what we should expect from a place that has been venerated for two millenniums.

    Now in archaeology, one of the most important factors in locating an authentic site is having one thing built upon another. The Church of the Holy Sepulchre has around 2,000 years of such history. For me personally, there is no doubt this is the genuine place where Christ was crucified, buried, and rose from the dead to pay for our sins. All of the evidence and historical writings from eyewitnesses provide overwhelming evidence that points to the authenticity of this site.

Places of Interest
1. The Chapel of the Franks (Station 10 of the Via Dolorosa) is located at the right of the entrance to the church.
2. A stairway on the right, just inside the entrance, leads to Calvary (or Golgotha), the place where Jesus was crucified.
3. Chapel of the Nailing of the Cross (Station 11). It features a 12th century mosaic of Jesus being nailed to the Cross.

4. The Greek Orthodox Calvary contains the believed Rock of Calvary around which the church was built. The rock can be seen under a glass cover on either side of the main altar. Beneath the altar is a hole that permits people to touch the rock.

5. The Crucifixion Altar marks the place where Christ was crucified (Station 12). A silver disk with a central hole underneath the altar marks where the Cross stood.
6. The Stone of Unction (Station 13), located just after entering the church, commemorates the preparation of Jesus' body for burial. Behind the Stone of Unction is a mosaic depicting Christ's anointing for burial.
7. Underneath the large dome of the church (rotunda) is the Tomb of Christ itself (Station 14). It is housed in a large shrine and is referred to as the Edicule. It is supported by scaffolding on the outside to protect it from possible earthquakes.
8. The Chapel of Adam enshrines a cracked slab of rock behind glass which is believed to have been caused by the earthquake after Christ died on the Cross.
9. The Catholicon (Greek Orthodox cathedral) area was the main part of the Crusader church.
10. Armenian Shrine and Chapel of the 3 Marys (Mourning Place). It marks the place where they watched the crucifixion of Christ.

Jerusalem Sites

11. In 2016 an archaeological team was given permission to lift the marble slate covering the tomb and found under it an older marble slab with a carved cross on it, and underneath it the original limestone burial bed of Christ.
12. The Coptic Chapel is located behind the tomb of Jesus.
13. The Jacobite (Syrian) Chapel is located in the original 4th-century Constantine church walls. Within this chapel are burial tombs, one of which is believed to be that of Joseph of Arimathea.
14. Chapel of Mary Magdalene. Dedicated to the encounter Christ had with Mary after His resurrection.
15. Franciscan Church of the Aspiration of Mary. Dedicated to the meeting between Christ and His mother, Mary, at Christ's crucifixion.
16. Arches of the Virgin Mary
17. Greek Orthodox Chapel of the Prison of Jesus
18. St. Longinus Chapel. Longinus was the believed Roman Centurion who commanded the soldiers that stood watch at Golgotha. He was an eyewitness of the final moments of Jesus and proclaimed that Jesus was truly the Son of God.

Church of the Holy Sepulchre today

19. Chapel of St. James
20. Chapel of John the Baptist
21. Division of the Holy Robes. The place commemorating the dividing of Christ's clothing.
22. Derision Chapel. This place commemorates how the mob derided Jesus by mocking and laughing at him while He hung on the Cross.
23. Armenian Chapel of St. Helena. Within this area is the Chapel of the Invention (discovery) of the Cross of Jesus.
24. Rock of Golgotha enclosed in glass.

Jerusalem Sites

Church of the Holy Sepulchre in the Bible

1. **Jesus arrives at Golgotha and is stripped of His garments (Station 10 of the Via Dolorosa. For all stations, see Via Dolorosa.).**

   John 19:23-24: *When the soldiers had crucified Jesus, they took his garments and divided them into four parts, one part for each soldier; also his tunic. But the tunic was seamless, woven in one piece from top to bottom, 24 so they said to one another, "Let us not tear it, but cast lots for it to see whose it shall be." This was to fulfill the Scripture which says, "They divided my garments among them, and for my clothing they cast lots."*

2. **Jesus is nailed to the Cross (Station 11).**

   John 19:17-18: *And he went out, bearing his own cross, to the place called The Place of a Skull, which in Aramaic is called Golgotha. 18 There they crucified him, and with him two others, one on either side, and Jesus between them.*

3. **Jesus dies on the Cross (Station 12).**

   Luke 23:44-45: *It was now about the sixth hour [12:00 pm], and there was darkness over the whole land until the ninth hour [3:00 pm], 45 while the sun's light failed. And the curtain of the temple was torn in two. Then Jesus, calling out with a loud voice, said, "Father, into your hands I commit my spirit!" And having said this he breathed his last.*

   Altar of the Nailing of Christ to the Cross

4. **Jesus' body is removed from the Cross (Station 13).**

   John 19:38-40: *After these things Joseph of Arimathea, who was a disciple of Jesus, but secretly for fear of the Jews, asked Pilate that he might take away the body of Jesus, and Pilate gave him permission. So he came and took away his body. 39 Nicodemus also, who earlier had come to Jesus by night, came bringing a mixture of myrrh and aloes, about seventy-five pounds in weight. 40 So they took the body of Jesus and bound it in linen cloths with the spices, as is the burial custom of the Jews.*

5. **Jesus is placed in the tomb (Station 14).**

   John 19:41–42: *Now in the place where he was crucified there was a garden, and in the garden a new tomb in which no one had yet been laid. 42 So because of the Jewish day of Preparation, since the tomb was close at hand, they laid Jesus there.*

6. **Jesus raises from the dead.**

   Matthew 28:5–6: *The angel said to the women, "Do not be afraid; for I know that you are looking for Jesus who has been crucified. 6 He is not here, for He has risen, just as He said. Come, see the place where He was lying."*

Faith Lesson from the Church of the Holy Sepulchre

1. While we might not agree with the decorations and atmosphere of the Church of the Holy Sepulchre, do we appreciate all the devotion and sacrifice that has been made to remember and commemorate all Jesus did for us on the Cross?

2. The fact that this place, along with many others, has been preserved and set aside to honor Christ and the events of the Bible provide powerful evidence regarding the historicity of Christ and the truthfulness of the Bible. Do we truly believe the Bible and everything written in it?

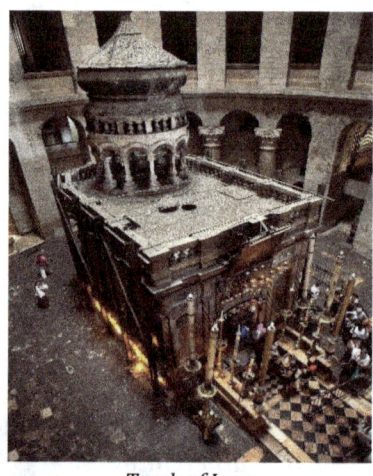
Tomb of Jesus

3. There is another place that is considered an option as to where Christ died and rose again, and it's called the Garden Tomb. It's just a stone's throw away. However, because we worship a person and not a place, the exact location isn't the main thing. We can worship Christ and all He did for us anywhere.

Journal/Notes:

City of David Overview

Location

1. The City of David is located just south of the Temple Mount on a plateau ridge.
2. It's where all the history of Jerusalem began.
3. It is strategically located with the Kidron Valley to the east, the Tyropoeon Valley to the West, and the Hinnom Valley to the south. These valleys provide it with natural protection.

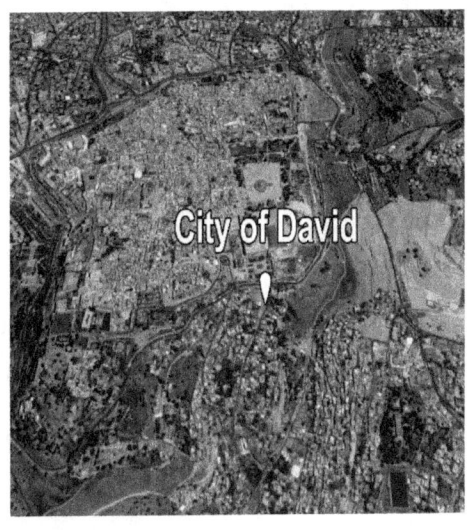

Psalm 125:2: *As the mountains surround Jerusalem, so the Lord surrounds His people from this time forth and forever.*

4. It has been the most excavated site in Israel over the past 150 years.

Historical Background

1. It was 3,000 years ago that King David made the City of David, also known as Jerusalem, the capital of Israel.
2. Before David, it was Abraham who would traverse here when he met with Melchizedek, the King of Salem (Salem was later called Jerusalem).
3. Later, Abraham would be willing to offer his son, Isaac, to the Lord on Mount Moriah, which is just above the City of David.
4. The City of David had an amazing source of freshwater known as the Gihon Spring.
5. The City of David is also referred to as Zion in Scripture.

   2 Samuel 5:7: *Nevertheless, David captured the stronghold of Zion, that is the city of David.*

Israel Biblical Sites Travel Guide

Places of Interest

1. A theater with an excellent movie showing the history of the City of David.
2. Bet Hatsofeh Lookout – Great place to see a panoramic view of the City of David and the sites around it.
3. Palace of King David
4. Stepped Stone Retaining Wall
5. Ancient 3,000-year-old walls.
6. Walls Nehemiah repaired.
7. House of Ahiel (four-room house).
8. Burnt Room – Evidence of a room that was burnt during the Babylonian destruction in 586 BC.

Jeremiah 52:12–13: *In the fifth month, on the tenth day of the month—that was the nineteenth year of King Nebuchadnezzar, king of Babylon— Nebuzaradan the captain of the bodyguard, who served the king of Babylon, entered Jerusalem. 13 And he **burned** the house of the Lord, and the king's house and all the houses of Jerusalem; every great house he **burned** down.*

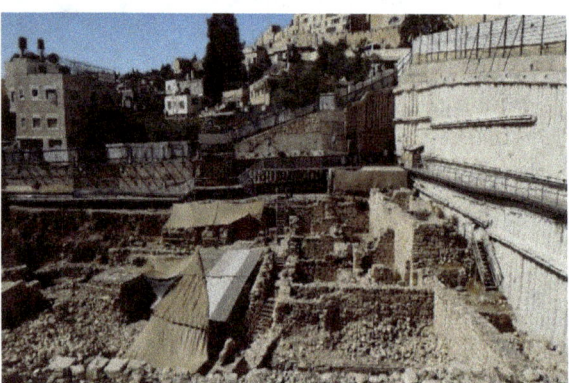
Givati excavations by the City of David

9. Recent discoveries unearthed two bullae (clay seals) dating to the beginning of the 6th century BC, bearing the names "Gedaliah Ben Pashur" and "Yehuchal Ben Shelemayahu." Both officials are named in Jeremiah 38:1: *Then . . . Gedaliah the son of **Pashur**, and **Jucal** the son of Shelemiah . . . heard the words that Jeremiah had spoken unto all the people.* This is the first time two bullas from a single Bible verse have been discovered in one place.
10. Jeremiah's Dungeon. Jeremiah 38:6: *"So they took Jeremiah and cast him into the cistern of Malchiah, the king's son, which was in the court of the guard, letting Jeremiah down by ropes. And there was no water in the cistern, but only mud, and Jeremiah sank in the*

Jerusalem Sites

mud."

11. Gihon Spring
    - Jerusalem's main water source.
    - King Solomon was anointed here along with many other kings.
    - King Hezekiah diverted the water down to the Pool of Siloam.
12. Hezekiah's Water Tunnel
13. Canaanite Tunnel
14. Warren Shaft System
15. Melchizedek's Temple
16. Ancient 3,000-year-old walls.
17. Tomb of King David
18. Pool of Siloam – Siloam means "safe."
    - Herod the Great enlarged the Pool of Siloam to make it a massive mitzvah.
    - A blind man was healed here by Christ.
19. Pilgrim's Road leading up to the temple from the Pool of Siloam called the Herodian Street. Countless Jews used it to ascend to the temple. There is no doubt Jesus walked this road as well.
20. There was a canal under the Herodian Street that was used for waste purposes. In this tunnel, thousands of Jews were

slaughtered by the Romans in 70 AD as they tried to escape the city.

21. In this same tunnel, a rare gold bell that was sewn onto priests' garments, an ancient silver shekel which was used to pay the half-shekel temple tax, and a Roman sword with its leather sheath still partly intact have been recently discovered.
22. Excavations in Givati parking lot in the City of David.

City of David in the Bible

1. **Before King David conquered this site, it was known as the City of Jebus.**

   1 Chronicles 11:3–5: *So all the elders of Israel came to the king at Hebron, and David made a covenant with them in Hebron before the Lord; and they anointed David king over Israel, according to the word of the Lord through Samuel. 4 Then David and all Israel went to Jerusalem (that is, **Jebus**); and the Jebusites, 5 the inhabitants of the land, were there. The inhabitants of **Jebus** said to David, "You shall not enter here." Nevertheless, David captured the stronghold of Zion (that is, the city of David).*

   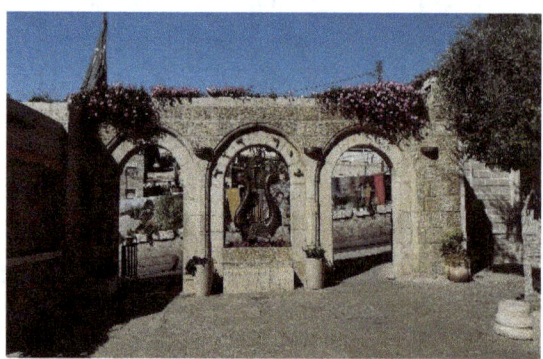
   Entrance to the City of David

   2 Samuel 5:9: *So David lived in the stronghold and called it the city of David. And David built all around from the Millo and inward.*

2. **David built houses for himself and prepared a place for the Ark of the Covenant in the City of David.**

   1 Chronicles 15:1: *Now David built houses for himself in the city of David; and he prepared a place for the ark of God and pitched a tent for it.*

3. **David brought the Ark of the Covenant to the City of David.**

   2 Samuel 6:12: *Now it was told King David, saying, "The Lord has blessed the house of Obed-edom and all that belongs to him, on account of the ark of God." David went and brought up the ark of*

Jerusalem Sites

God from the house of Obed-edom into the city of David with gladness.

4. **David strongly desired to build a house for the Lord, but God said no because he was a man of war. However, he made all the plans and prepared much of the materials his son, Solomon would use to build the House of the Lord.**

   1 Chronicles 22:5: *Now David said, "Solomon my son is young and inexperienced, and the house to be built for the Lord must be exceedingly magnificent, famous and glorious throughout all countries. I will now make preparation for it." So David made abundant preparations before his death.*

   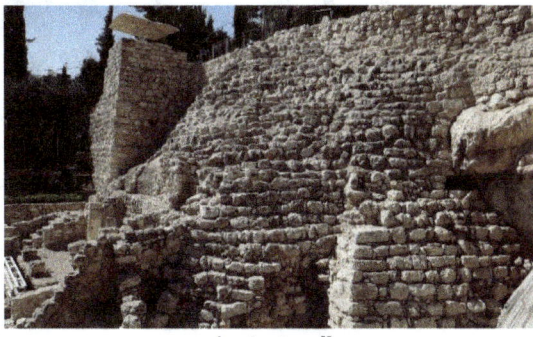
   Ancient walls

5. **From David's palace rooftop, he saw Bathsheba bathing and committed a serious sin.**

   2 Samuel 11:2: *It happened, late one afternoon, when David arose from his couch and was walking on the roof of the king's house, that he saw from the roof a woman bathing; and the woman was very beautiful.*

6. **David died and was buried in the City of David.**

   1 Kings 2:10: *Then David slept with his fathers and was buried in the city of David.* David's tomb is located close to the City of David.

7. **King Solomon was anointed as king at the Gihon Spring.**

   1 Kings 1:45: *Zadok the priest and Nathan the prophet have anointed him king in Gihon, and they have come up from there rejoicing, so that the city is in an uproar. This is the noise which you have heard.*

8. **After David built his palace and much of the city of David, his son, Solomon, built the temple just north of the City of David.**

   1 Kings 6:1: *In the four hundred and eightieth year after the people of Israel came out of the land of Egypt, in the fourth year of Solomon's reign over Israel, in the month of Ziv, which is the second month, he began to build the house of the Lord.*

9. **The people would go up from the City of David to the temple to worship God.**

   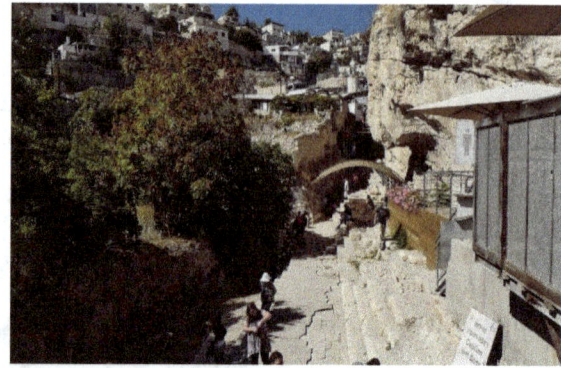
   Pool of Siloam

   Isaiah 2:3: *And many peoples shall come, and say: "Come, let us go up to the mountain of the Lord, to the house of the God of Jacob, that he may teach us his ways and that we may walk in his paths."*

10. **Later, King Hezekiah built a tunnel to divert the water from the Gihon Spring (the city's water source) down to the Pool of Siloam to keep the water inside the city walls so warring armies (the Assyrians) couldn't cut off the water to the city.**

    2 Chronicles 32:30: *This same Hezekiah closed the upper outlet of the waters of Gihon and directed them down to the west side of the city of David.*

Faith Lesson from the City of David

1. The City of David has provided overwhelming archaeological evidence supporting the truthfulness of Scripture. Do we embrace this evidence that is yielding more and more proof that the Bible is true and historically accurate?
2. The City of David, along with Jerusalem, was destroyed by the Babylonians because of Israel's disobedience to God. Do we understand that obedience brings life and peace, but disobedience brings death and destruction?
3. In what areas of my life am I experiencing pain and problems because of disobedience to God's Word?

Journal/Notes:

Dominus Flevit: Triumphal Entry

Location

1. The Triumphal Entry begins at the upper part of the Mount of Olives and winds its way down to the bottom of the mountain to the Garden of Gethsemane.
2. A church called Dominus Flevit is located halfway down the western slope of the Mount of Olives and marks the place where Jesus wept over the future fate of Jerusalem.

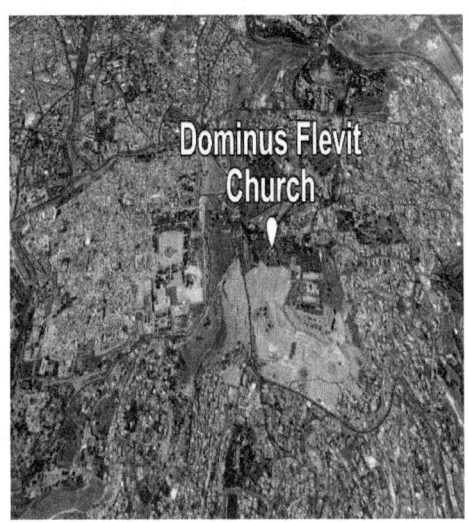

Historical Background

1. The Triumphal Entry was a major event in the life of Jesus wherein He entered Jerusalem on the Sunday before He would be crucified (Friday the Passover) and rise from the dead the following Sunday.
2. This event was designed by Christ to broadcast to the Nation of Israel that He was their Passover Lamb.
3. It is also referred to as Palm Sunday because palm branches were laid on the road as Jesus rode into Jerusalem on a donkey.
4. It would mark Christ's last days of intensive teaching and His condemnation of the Jews for rejecting Him and His message.
5. It would be the beginning of Christ's last week on earth.
6. The Dominus Flevit Church was built in 1953 to commemorate this important event.
7. The current church stands on the ruins of a 6th-century Byzantine church, and some mosaics of the church still remain.
8. Dominus Flevit is Latin and means "the Lord wept."

Places of Interest

1. Bethphage (beginning point of the Triumphal Entry)
2. Mount of Olives

3. Triumphal Entry Path
4. Dominus Flevit Church
5. Garden of Gethsemane
6. Temple Mount
7. The western window of the Dominus Flevit Church provides a beautiful view of the Temple Mount.
8. A mosaic on the altar of the Dominus Flevit Church has an illustration of a hen gathering her chickens, which is based on Luke 13:34: *O Jerusalem, Jerusalem, the city that kills the prophets and stones those sent to her! How often I wanted to gather your children together, just as a hen gathers her brood under her wings, and you would not have it!*
9. Ancient burial caves located by the Dominus Flevit Church.

Triumphal Entry in the Bible

1. The Triumphal Entry was prophesied in the Old Testament.

Some 450–500 years before Christ, the Prophet Zechariah prophesied: *"Rejoice greatly, O daughter of Zion! Shout, O daughter of Jerusalem! Behold, your King is coming to you; He is just and having salvation, lowly and riding on a donkey, a colt, the foal of a donkey"* (Zech. 9:9).

2. **The Triumphal Entry was fulfilled in the New Testament.**

   Matthew 21:7–9: *They brought the donkey and the colt, laid their clothes on them, and set Him on them. 8 And a very great multitude spread their clothes on the road; others cut down branches from the trees and spread them on the road. 9 Then the multitudes who went before and those who followed cried out, saying: "Hosanna to the Son of David! Blessed is He who comes in the name of the LORD!' Hosanna in the highest!"*

3. **Palm Sunday was also the fulfillment of the Prophet Daniel's "seventy sevens" prophecy.**

   Daniel 9:25: *Know therefore and understand, that from the going forth of the command to restore and build Jerusalem until **Messiah the Prince**, there shall be seven weeks and sixty-two weeks; the street shall be built again, and the wall, even in troublesome times.*

4. **The Triumphal Entry, which occurred the Sunday before the Passover, was also lamb selection day for the Passover.**

   According to Exodus 12, this was the day set aside for each Israelite family to choose the lamb they would kill for their Passover meal. The blood from their lamb was to be put on the doorposts of their homes so the angel of death would not kill their

   Dominus Flevit Church

   firstborn children. The Passover was celebrated each year to mark their deliverance from Egypt and how God had miraculously saved them. The fact that Christ entered Jerusalem on this very day was no accident. He was proclaiming Himself as the Passover Lamb, not only for the Israelites but for all humanity.

5. **Christ entered Jerusalem, riding on a donkey.**

   Luke 19:28–35: *And when he had said these things, he went on ahead, going up to Jerusalem. 29 When he drew near to Bethphage* and Bethany, at the mount that is called Olivet, he sent two of the disciples, 30 saying, "Go into the village in front of you, where on entering you will find a colt tied, on which no one has ever yet sat. Untie it and bring it here. 31 If anyone asks you, 'Why are you untying it?'

View of Jerusalem from the Triumphal Entry Path

you shall say this: 'The Lord has need of it.' 32 So those who were sent went away and found it just as he had told them. 33 And as they were untying the colt, its owners said to them, "Why are you untying the colt?" 34 And they said, "The Lord has need of it." 35 And they brought it to Jesus, and throwing their cloaks on the colt, they set Jesus on it.

- **The meaning of a donkey:**

  A donkey was a symbol of peace; a horse was a symbol of war. Christ came to make peace with mankind during His first coming by dying for our sins. However, at His second coming, He will come riding a horse to wage war with mankind and judge them for their sinful rejection of Him.

6. **The crowd took branches of palm trees and cried out, "Hosanna! Blessed is he who comes in the name of the Lord."**

   John 12:13: *So, they took branches of palm trees and went out to meet him, crying out, "Hosanna! Blessed is he who comes in the name of the Lord, even the King of Israel!"*

   - **The meaning of the palm branches:**

     It was a cry for deliverance from Roman occupation. The last time the Israelites had their freedom during the Maccabean rule from 167–63 BC, their money had the symbol of a palm branch as a sign of freedom. It was like the national flag of a country. It was the Jew's way of saying that they wanted Christ to be their King and deliver them from the Romans.

Jerusalem Sites

7. **At the place marked by the church, Dominus Flevit, Christ paused and wept over Jerusalem.**

   Luke 19:41–44: *And when he drew near and saw the city, **he wept over it**, 42 saying, "Would that you, even you, had known on this day the things that make for peace! But now they are hidden from your eyes. 43 For the days will come upon you, when your enemies will set up a barricade around you and surround you and hem you in on every side 44 and tear you down to the ground, you and your children within you. And they will not leave one stone upon another in you, because you did not know the time of your visitation."*

   - There are only two times in the Bible where it is noted that Christ wept. The first time was at the death of Lazarus, and the second during His triumphal entry into Jerusalem. Both places are located on the Mount of Olives.

   Dominus Flevit Church

   - In this account of Christ weeping, He wept for those who aren't saved and the judgment that awaits them.
   - Within 40 years, in 70 AD, Jesus' prophecy was fulfilled. Roman legions **besieged** Jerusalem and, after six months of fighting, burnt the temple and leveled the city.

8. **The first time Christ wept took place at the death of Lazarus just a week or so earlier on the backside of the Mount of Olives.**

   John 11:33–36: *When Jesus saw her weeping, and the Jews who had come with her also weeping, he was deeply moved in his spirit and greatly troubled. 34 And he said, "Where have you laid him?" They said to him, "Lord, come and see." 35 Jesus wept. 36 So the Jews said, "See how he loved him!"*

   - In this account, Christ weeps for those who suffer.

Faith Lesson from the Triumphal Entry

1. The Triumphal Entry was a prophesied event from the Old Testament and reveals the validity of Scripture and God's sovereignty.
2. Christ wept over Jerusalem because they rejected Him and the judgment that would await them as a result. Does Christ weep for you because you don't know Him and will be separated from Him in hell for all eternity?

Triumphal Entry Path

3. Christ wept with those at the death of Lazarus. Does Christ weep with you as He understands your pain and suffering?

Journal/Notes:

Jerusalem Sites

Eastern Gate

Location

1. The Eastern Gate is located on the eastern side of the Temple Mount and faces the Mount of Olives.
2. It is an important gate because it plays a central role in Scripture and prophecy.
3. The current Old City of Jerusalem is surrounded by a wall containing eight gates.
   1. Lions Gate (Stephen's Gate)
   2. Eastern Gate (Golden Gate, Shushan Gate)
   3. Dung Gate
   4. Zion Gate
   5. Jaffa Gate
   6. New Gate
   7. Damascus Gate
   8. Herod's Gate
4. The Eastern Gate is unique in that it is sealed shut.
5. It is the oldest gate in Old City Jerusalem.

Historical Background

1. The original Eastern Gate was built by Solomon (960 BC) or, at a later date, by Hezekiah (715 BC). The ancient posts located inside the gate today, along with the stones beside the gate of the Eastern Wall, date back to these time periods and would affirm its early existence and location at its present-day site.
2. It's very likely that Nehemiah rebuilt the Eastern Gate when he rebuilt the walls of Jerusalem in around 444 BC. Some believe the original gate was then named the Eastern Gate by Nehemiah at

this time.

3. Herod the Great then rebuilt the Eastern Gate in around 19 BC and added a stairway, or rebuilt an existing one that led up to the gate. This stairway ran alongside the Eastern Wall. In the 1860s, Charles Warren discovered an outer wall that enclosed the stairway leading up to the Eastern Gate that Herod had built.

4. The best evidence suggests that the gate was then rebuilt during the Umayyad period (661–750 AD), on the foundations of the earlier gate dating to the time of Solomon or Hezekiah. Part of the gate from this time period has been preserved.

   As mentioned, the remains of two massive ancient gateposts are

   Eastern Gate

   preserved inside this gate. These gateposts are situated in the same line as the Eastern Wall of the Temple Mount. They also line up with the lower massive stone masonry on both sides of the Golden Gate. The gateposts, along with the masonry sections of the Eastern Wall, suggest they are all part of the same construction. The upper part of the southern gatepost is level with the top of the ancient stone masonry that can be seen south of the Golden Gate. The gatepost in the northern part of the gate is one stone course higher and is located just one stone course lower than the surface of the Temple Mount. These two ancient gateposts belong to the gate dating back to the First Temple period, most likely the Shushan Gate mentioned in Mishnah Middot 1.3. This gate was the only gate in the Eastern Wall at that time.

5. The current gate that is seen today was rebuilt by Suleiman in around 1541 AD and was built on the foundations of the earlier gates. The Eastern Gate's outer facade today consists of two blocked-up gateways decorated with detailed carved relief arches.

6. The original gate was thought to have been discovered in 1969 by Dr. James Fleming and was believed to be east of the current Eastern Gate a bit and about 8 feet (2.5 m) lower. However, after significant research and archaeological work was done and

Jerusalem Sites

analyzed, it appears what Dr. Fleming found were arches of a stairway that led up to the Eastern Gate that Herod the Great built. Again, inside the gate are ancient posts that date back to the First Temple period. These reveal that the level of the current Eastern Gate is relatively the same as it has always been.

The bedrock beneath the Eastern Gate rises sharply upwards from the Kidron Valley to the Temple Mount, so this would make it very unlikely that the original gate was beneath the current one as the bedrock would be in the way and prevent this.

Copyright: Leen Ritmeyer

Moreover, the stones of the arch that Dr. Fleming discovered are Herodian, which are much later than the original Eastern Gate, making it unlikely the arch that was discovered was part of the top of the Eastern Gate. Again, reputable archaeologists now believe that what Dr. Fleming discovered was one of the arches of the stairway leading up to the Eastern Gate. Herod built this stairway, so the stone type that was found would match this time era.

However, it should be noted that what Dr. Fleming discovered does provide more evidence that the Eastern Gate's current location is accurate.

7. The Eastern Gate gives the most direct access to the Temple Mount from the Mount of Olives.

8. The Eastern Gate is unique in that it is completely sealed shut. Some commentators see the Eastern Gate's obstruction as a fulfillment of biblical prophecy.

It was closed by the Muslims in 810 AD, reopened in 1102 AD by the Crusaders, and then walled up by Saladin after regaining Jerusalem in 1187 AD. Ottoman Sultan Suleiman rebuilt it together with the city walls and again walled it up in 1541 AD, and it has stayed that way until today.

It's believed that the closing of the Eastern Gate was to prevent the Jewish Messiah from gaining entrance to the temple on the Temple Mount.

Muslims also put a cemetery directly in front of the gate as an extra layer of precaution, believing that the Messiah, being a good Jew, would not walk through it and become unclean in doing so. However, whatever Christ touches becomes clean, so that presents no problem.

9. Jewish tradition states that the Messiah will pass through the Eastern Gate when He comes to rule. For Christians, Christ already

did this at His first coming and will do it again at His second coming.

Ezekiel 44:1–3: *Then he brought me back to the outer gate of the sanctuary, which faces east. And it was shut. 2 And the Lord said to me, "This gate shall remain shut; it shall not be opened, and no one shall enter by it, for the Lord, the God of Israel, has entered by it. Therefore, it shall remain shut. 3 Only the prince may sit in it to eat bread before the Lord. He shall enter by way of the vestibule of the gate, and shall go out by the same way."*

10. Though it is formally called the Eastern Gate, it is also known as the Golden Gate, the Gate of Eternal Life, the Mercy Gate, the Shushan Gate, and sometimes as the Beautiful Gate. Scripture says in Acts 3:1–10 that the Beautiful Gate was one of the temple gates. This would make the Nicanor Gate the best candidate for being the Beautiful Gate.

11. Some believe the Eastern Gate was in direct alignment with the gate into the temple's outer court, inner court, and main entrance doors.

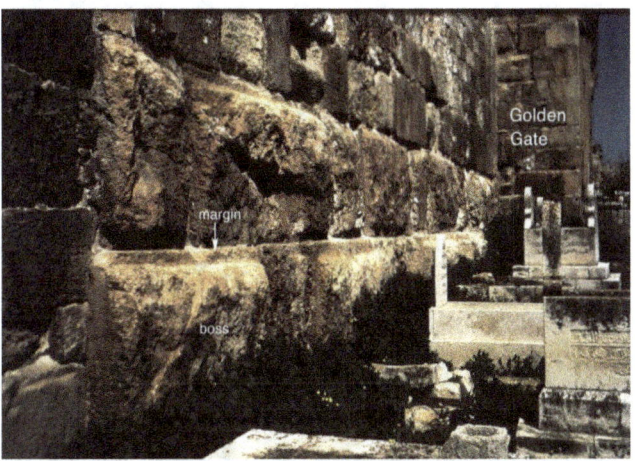

Ancient Stones by the Eastern Gate – Copyright Leen Ritmeyer

This belief comes from a misunderstanding of a writing in Middot 2.4 (which is part of the Jewish Mishnah) that says: *"All the walls there were high, save only the eastern wall because the [High] priest that burns the [Red] heifer and stands on top of the Mount of Olives should be able to look directly into the entrance of the sanctuary when the blood is sprinkled."*

However, the view from the top of the Mount of Olives through the Eastern Gate would only allow one to see into the ground because the gate was lower than the temple. So, this presents an impossibility as you cannot look from a higher elevation through a lower gate and then see something that is higher than that gate.

Therefore, a line of vision from the top of the Mount of Olives through the Eastern Gate makes it impossible to see anything on the Temple Mount, let alone the temple. Therefore, it appears that what was meant in the writing of Middot 2.4 referred to the Nicanor Gate. This was an outer gate of the temple complex. From the top of the Mt. of Olives, one could easily look directly through the Nicanor Gate and see the sanctuary.

Therefore, the Eastern Gate was not in alignment with the temple as some suggest. The original temple has very strong evidence that it was on the exact location where the Dome of the Rock stands today.

12. Some also believe that during the time of Christ, according to the Mishnah (collection of Jewish oral laws), a bridge (causeway) led out of the Temple Mount eastward over the Kidron Valley, extending as far as the Mount of Olives. The Hebrew word for causeway is *Kevesh*, usually translated as "ramp," not as "bridge." It is very unlikely there was a major causeway spanning the Kidron Valley as it would have been massive in size, extremely difficult to build, and expensive. This causeway mentioned most likely refers to the stairway leading up to the Eastern Gate that ran along the eastern wall. However, if there would have been a causeway or bridge that did exist, it would have been on a small scale.

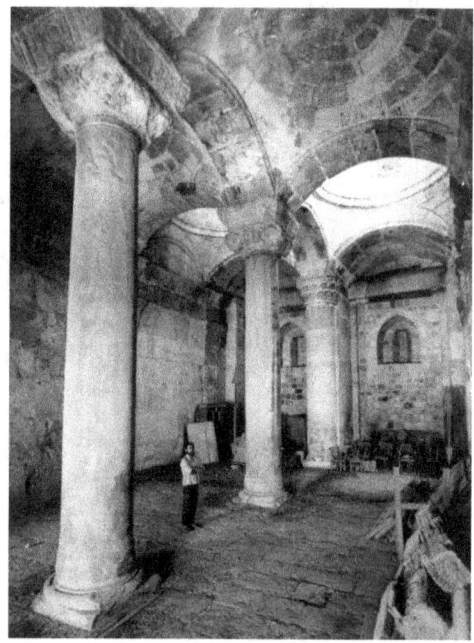
Ancient gateposts inside the Eastern Gate
Copyright Leen Ritmeyer

13. It should also be mentioned that the archaeological evidence supporting the Eastern Gate as being authentic provides strong evidence that the original temple was located on the current Temple Mount. Additionally, the ancient stones of the Eastern Wall dating back to the first temple period validate the temple's

Jerusalem Sites

location as well.

Places of Interest

1. Eastern Gate
2. Ancient Gate Posts
3. Ancient Stone Masonry
4. Eastern Wall
5. Stairway Leading Up to the Eastern Gate
6. Outer Wall Encompassing the Stairway
7. Temple Mount
8. Nicanor Gate
9. Original Location of the Temple
10. Inner and Outer Courts of the Temple
11. Mount of Olives
12. Other Gates of Old City Jerusalem

The Eastern Gate in the Bible

1. **It is the likely gate the ashes of the Red Heifer sacrifice were carried through and then deposited in a clean place outside the city (Num. 19:1–10).**

2. **The glory of the Lord left the temple because of Israel's disobedience.**

   Ezekiel 10:18–19: *Then the glory of the Lord went out from the threshold of the house, and stood over the cherubim. 19 And the cherubim lifted up their wings and mounted up from the earth before my eyes as they went out, with the wheels beside them. And they stood at the entrance of the **east gate of the house of the Lord**, and the glory of the God of Israel was over them.*

   Ezekiel 11:23: *And the glory of the Lord went up from the midst of the city and stood on the mountain that is on the **east side of the city [Mount of Olives]**.*

3. **The glory of the Lord will return to the temple at Christ's second coming.**

   Ezekiel 43:1–5: *Then he led me to the gate, **the gate facing east**. 2 And behold, the glory of the God of Israel was coming from the east. And the sound of his coming was like the sound of many waters, and the earth shone with his glory. 3 And the vision I saw was just like the vision that I had seen when he came to destroy the city, and just like the vision that I had seen by the Chebar canal. And I fell on my face. 4 As the glory of the Lord entered the temple by the gate facing east, 5 the Spirit lifted me up and brought me into the inner court; and behold, the glory of the Lord filled the temple.*

   Zechariah 14:4: *On that day his feet shall stand on the **Mount of Olives that lies before Jerusalem on the east**, and the Mount of Olives shall be split in two from east to west by a very wide valley, so that one half of the Mount shall move northward, and the other half southward.*

4. **When Jesus entered Jerusalem from the Mount of Olives on Palm Sunday (Triumphal Entry), He most likely used the Eastern Gate.**

   Luke 19:37–38: *As he was drawing near—already on the **way down the Mount of Olives**—the whole multitude of his disciples began to rejoice and praise God with a loud voice for all the mighty works that they had seen, 38 saying, "Blessed is the King who comes in the name of the Lord! Peace in heaven and glory in the highest!"*

   Luke 19:45–46: *And he **entered the temple** and began to drive out those who sold, 46 saying to them, "It is written, 'My house shall be a house of prayer,' but you have made it a den of robbers."*

5. **It is the gate that Jesus would have entered and exited**

through repeatedly as He taught in the temple and then retreated to the Mount of Olives to rest and sleep.

Luke 21:37–38: *And every day he was teaching in the temple, but at night he went out and lodged on the **mount called Olivet**. 38 And early in the morning all the people came to him in the temple to hear him.*

6. **Just inside the Eastern Gate was where Peter and John healed a lame man.**

Acts 3:1–10: *Now Peter and John went up together to the Temple at the hour of prayer, the ninth hour, 2 and a certain man lame from his mother's womb was carried whom they laid daily at the **gate of the temple which is called Beautiful** to ask alms from those who entered the temple. 3 Seeing Peter and John about to go into the temple, he asked to receive alms. 4 And Peter directed his gaze at him, as did John, and said, "Look at us." 5 And he fixed his attention on them, expecting to receive something from them. 6 But Peter said, "I have no silver and gold, but what I do have I give to you. In the name of Jesus Christ of Nazareth, rise up and walk!" 7 And he took him by the right hand and raised him up, and immediately his feet and ankles were made strong. 8 And leaping up, he stood and began to walk, and entered the temple with them, walking and leaping and praising God. 9 And all the people saw him walking and praising God, 10 and recognized him as the one who sat at the **Beautiful Gate** of the temple, asking for alms. And they were filled with wonder and amazement at what had happened to him.*

Faith Lesson from the Eastern Gate

1. The Eastern Gate has seen many prophecies fulfilled.
2. There are still more prophecies it will witness.
3. Prophecy proves the Bible is accurate and that we can place our full confidence in it.
4. If all past prophecies have been fulfilled, we can rest assured that what is still prophesied will also come to pass.
5. Do we fully believe the prophecies in the Bible, and are we living in such a way that proves it?

Journal/Notes:

Garden of Gethsemane & Church of All Nations

Location

1. The Garden of Gethsemane and the Church of All Nations are located at the base of the Mount of Olives.
2. The Church of All Nations is built over the rock on which Jesus is believed to have prayed in agony the night He was arrested and then condemned to crucifixion.

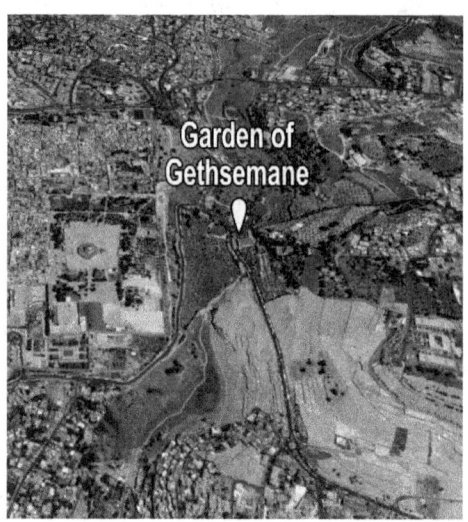

Historical Background

1. The current church rests on the foundations of two earlier churches, a 4th-century Byzantine Basilica, destroyed by an earthquake in 746 AD, and a small 12th-century Crusader chapel abandoned in 1345 AD.
2. The current church, called the *Church of All Nations*, or also called the *Basilica of the Agony*, was consecrated in 1924.
3. It is a Catholic Franciscan church and was built using donations from 12 nations. Therefore, it is called the Church of All Nations.
4. Gethsemane means "Oil Press" in Hebrew. The main source of oil in Israel was from olives, so it is also known as an olive press.
5. It was an olive orchard with an olive press in it. As a result, it became known as the Garden of Gethsemane.
6. How fitting it would be called Gethsemane, as Christ would be pressed here beyond measure. Even to the point of His sweat becoming like drops of blood.

Places of Interest

1. Church of All Nations
2. Garden of Gethsemane

Jerusalem Sites

3. Mount of Olives
4. Temple Mount
5. Old City Jerusalem
6. Rock inside the church upon which Jesus prayed in agony.
7. Mosaic on the wall above the Stone of Agony depicting Christ praying and an angel consoling Him.
8. Old olive trees dating to the time of Christ.
9. The roof of the church has 12 domes, one for each country that donated to the church's construction costs.
10. The dim lighting in the church gives the sense of the night in which Christ prayed in agony.
11. Glass plates on the floor of the church where mosaics of the Byzantine church from the 4th century are located.
12. The front of the church on the outside has 4 pillar columns, each representing an author of the 4 Gospels.

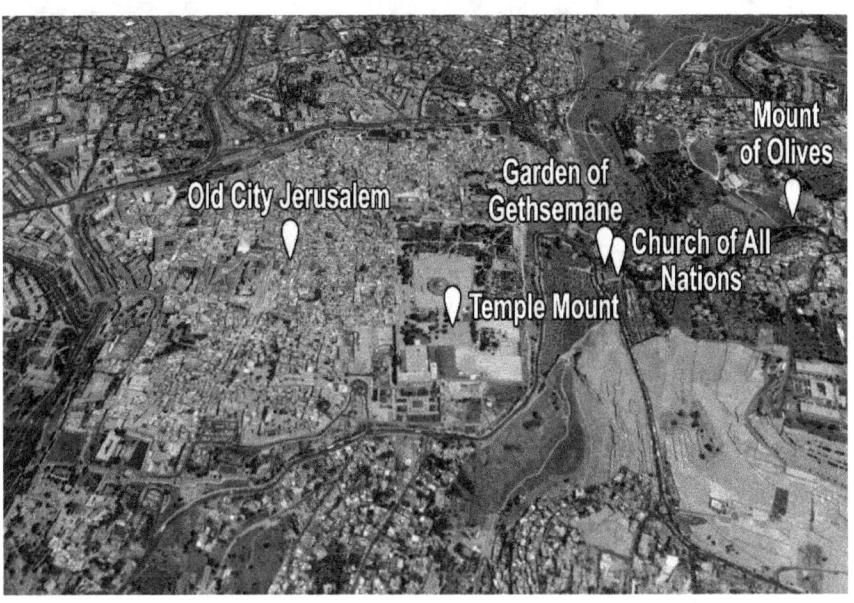

Garden of Gethsemane in the Bible

1. Jesus spent His last evening on earth praying in great agony before His crucifixion the following day.

Luke 12:50: *I have a baptism to be baptized with, and how great is my distress until it is accomplished!*

2. **Christ became sorrowful, even to the point of death.**

   Matthew 26:36–39: *Then Jesus went with them to a place called Gethsemane, and he said to his disciples, "Sit here, while I go over there and pray." 37 And taking with him Peter and the two sons of Zebedee, he began to be sorrowful and troubled. 38 Then he said to them,* **"My soul is very sorrowful, even to death***; remain here, and watch with me." 39 And going a little farther he fell on his face and prayed, saying, "My Father, if it be possible, let this cup pass from me; nevertheless, not as I will, but as you will."*

3. **Christ taught us how to overcome temptation.**

   Matthew 26:40–41: *And he came to the disciples and found them sleeping. And he said to Peter, "So, could you not watch with me one hour? 41* **Watch and pray that you may not enter into temptation***. The spirit indeed is willing, but the flesh is weak."*

4. **Christ departed and prayed a second time.**

   Matthew 26:42–43: *Again, for the second time, he went away and prayed, "My Father, if this cannot pass unless I drink it, your will be done." 43 And again he came and found them sleeping, for their eyes were heavy.*

   Believed rock upon which Jesus prayed

5. **Christ prayed a third time.**

   Matthew 26:44: *So, leaving them again, he went away and prayed for the third time, saying the same words again.*

6. **Christ's sweat became like great drops of blood.**

   Luke 22:43–44: *And there appeared to him an angel from heaven, strengthening him. 44 And being in an agony he prayed more earnestly; and* **his sweat became like great drops of blood falling down to the ground.**

7. Christ was arrested and taken captive by the Jews.

Matthew 26:45–50: *Then he came to the disciples and said to them, "Sleep and take your rest later on. See, the hour is at hand, and the Son of Man is betrayed into the hands of sinners. 46 Rise, let us be going; see, my betrayer is at hand." 47 While he was still speaking, Judas came, one of the twelve, and with him a great crowd with swords and clubs, from the chief priests and the elders of the people. 48 Now the betrayer had given them a sign, saying, "The one I will kiss is the man; seize him." 49 And he came up to Jesus at once and said, "Greetings, Rabbi!" And he kissed him. 50 Jesus said to him, "Friend, do what you came to do." Then they came up and laid hands on Jesus and seized him.*

8. Jesus voluntarily surrendered to the Jews.

Matthew 26:51–56: *And behold, one of those who were with Jesus stretched out his hand and drew his sword and struck the servant of the high priest and cut off his ear. 52 Then Jesus said to him, "Put your sword back into its place. For all who take the sword will perish by the sword. 53 Do you think that I cannot appeal to my Father, and he will at once send me more than twelve legions of angels [60,000 angels]? 54 But how then should the Scriptures be fulfilled, that it must be so?" 55 At that hour Jesus said to the crowds, "Have you come out as against a robber, with swords and clubs to capture me? Day after day I sat in the temple teaching, and you did not seize me. 56 But all this has taken place that the Scriptures of the prophets might be fulfilled." Then all the disciples left him and fled.*

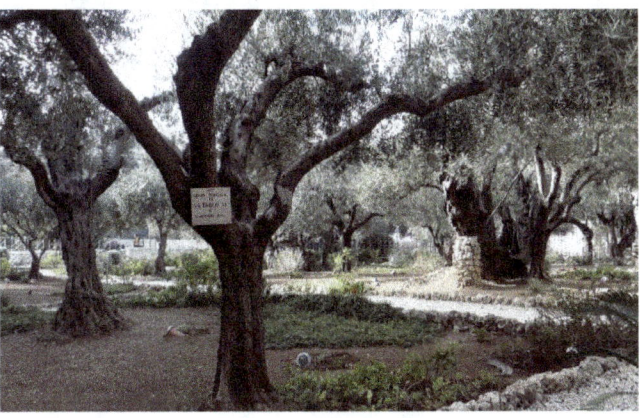
Garden of Gethsemane

In the Old Testament, one angel killed 185,000 Assyrian soldiers. This means 12 legions of angels (60,000) could have killed 11 billion people. This is more than the entire earth's current population. The earth's population during the time of Christ was only around 300 million.

Faith Lesson from the Garden of Gethsemane

1. The spiritual weight of paying for the sins of the world was far greater for Christ to bear than His physical sufferings. Have we really contemplated the price Christ paid for our salvation?
2. Christ taught us to overcome temptation through prayer. Do we follow His example?
3. If there is no hell, then the suffering of Christ has little purpose. Do we believe in hell and speak about it, or do we avoid it?
4. Christ provided us the perfect example of how we should choose God's will over our own. In the same way Christ submitted to the will of the Father, do we submit to God as well?

Church of All Nations at the Garden of Gethsemane

Journal/Notes:

Garden Tomb: Death, Burial, and Resurrection of Christ

Location

1. Gordan's Garden Tomb is located just 250 yards (220 m.) to the north of the Damascus Gate of Old City Jerusalem.
2. It provides a serene setting in a garden-like place to meditate and reflect upon the death, burial, and resurrection of Christ.
3. It is considered by many as the location of Golgotha.
4. The traditional location of Golgotha is at the Church of the Holy Sepulchre.
5. Both places have evidence of being the location of Golgotha. However, the Church of the Holy Sepulchre has more tradition, evidence, and history supporting it as the most authentic site.
6. Both places are within a stone's throw of each other, so regardless of the location, we are still in close vicinity of Golgotha.
7. Because we worship a person and not a place, the exact location is not necessary for understanding and reflecting on what Christ did for us at Golgotha.

Historical Background

1. The property of the Garden Tomb was purchased in 1894 by the Garden Tomb Association.
2. It is a Charitable Trust based in the United Kingdom and is made up of people from many different denominations and national backgrounds.
3. Their passion is to help people understand all Christ did for them on the Cross.
4. The site is maintained by volunteers that come from around the

globe and join a team of local Palestinians and Israelis.

Places of Interest

1. Garden Tomb – A cave-like tomb that can be entered. It has a channel at the entrance where a stone could be rolled to cover and uncover the tomb.
2. A rock face cliff shaped like a skull, which is believed to be Golgotha.
3. Damascus Gate
4. Old City Jerusalem
5. Church of the Holy Sepulchre

Death, Burial, and Resurrection of Christ in the Bible

1. **At 3:00 pm, Friday afternoon, Jesus died. This happened at the exact time the sacrificial lamb for the Passover was to be killed.**

   Matthew 27:45–53: *Now from the sixth hour [12:00 pm] there was darkness over all the land until the ninth hour [3:00 pm]. 46 And about the ninth hour Jesus cried out with a loud voice, saying, "Eli, Eli, lema sabachthani?" that is, "My God, my God, why have you forsaken me?" 47 And some of the bystanders, hearing it, said, "This man is calling Elijah." 48 And one of them at once ran and took a sponge, filled it with sour wine, and put it on a reed and gave it to*

Jerusalem Sites

him to drink. 49 But the others said, "Wait, let us see whether Elijah will come to save him." 50 And Jesus cried out again with a loud voice and yielded up his spirit. 51 And behold, the curtain of the temple was torn in two, from top to bottom. And the earth shook, and the rocks were split. 52 The tombs also were opened. And many bodies of the saints who had fallen asleep were raised, 53 and coming out of the tombs after his resurrection they went into the holy city and appeared to many.*

2. **Jesus' body was taken down from the Cross and placed in a tomb.**

   John 19:41–42: *Now in the place where he was crucified **there was a garden**, and **in the garden a new tomb** in which no one had yet been laid. 42 So because of the Jewish day of Preparation, since the tomb was close at hand, they laid Jesus there.*

3. **Jesus' body was given to Joseph of Arimathea, prepared for burial, and placed in Joseph's own tomb.**

   Matthew 27:57–61: *As evening approached, there came a rich man from Arimathea, named Joseph, who had himself become a disciple of Jesus. 58 Going to Pilate, he asked for Jesus' body, and Pilate ordered that it be given to him. 59 Joseph took the body, wrapped it in a clean linen cloth, 60 and placed it in his own new tomb that he had cut out of the rock. He rolled a big stone in front of the entrance to the tomb and went away. 61 Mary Magdalene and the other Mary were sitting there opposite the tomb.*

   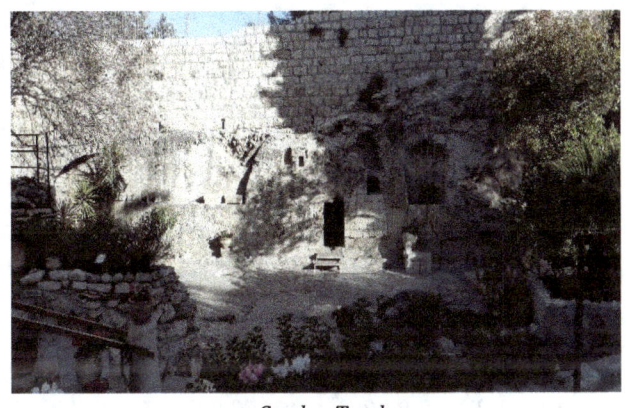
   Garden Tomb

4. **The Tomb of Jesus was sealed and secured by the Romans.**

   Matthew 27:62–66: *The next day, the one after Preparation Day, the chief priests and the Pharisees went to Pilate. 63 "Sir," they said, "we remember that while he was still alive that deceiver said, 'After three days I will rise again.' 64 So give the order for the tomb to be* made secure until the third day. Otherwise, his disciples may come and steal the body and tell the people that he has been raised from the dead. This last deception will be worse than the first." Pilate said to them, "You have a guard of soldiers. Go, make it as secure as you can." 66 So they went and made the tomb secure by sealing the stone and setting a guard.

5. **On Sunday morning, very early, Jesus rose from the dead.**

   Matthew 28:1–10: *After the Sabbath, at dawn on the first day of the week, Mary Magdalene and the other Mary went to look at the tomb. 2 There was a violent earthquake, for an angel of the Lord came down from heaven and, going to the tomb, rolled back the stone and sat on it. 3 His appearance was like lightning, and his clothes were white as snow. 4 The guards were so afraid of him that they shook and became*

   Garden Tomb

   like dead men. 5 The angel said to the women, "Do not be afraid, for I know that you are looking for Jesus, who was crucified. 6 He is not here; he has risen, just as he said. Come and see the place where he lay. 7 Then go quickly and tell his disciples: 'He has risen from the dead and is going ahead of you into Galilee. There you will see him.' Now I have told you." 8 So the women hurried away from the tomb, afraid yet filled with joy, and ran to tell his disciples. 9 Suddenly Jesus met them. "Greetings," he said. They came to him, clasped his feet and worshiped him. 10 Then Jesus said to them, "Do not be afraid. Go and tell my brothers to go to Galilee; there they will see me."

6. **Mary Magdalene is our example of what it means to love the Lord your God with all your heart, soul, mind, and strength.**

   John 20:11–18: *But Mary stood weeping outside the tomb, and as she wept, she stooped to look into the tomb. 12 And she saw two*

Jerusalem Sites

angels in white, sitting where the body of Jesus had lain, one at the head and one at the feet. 13 They said to her, "Woman, why are you weeping?" She said to them, "They have taken away my Lord, and I do not know where they have laid him." 14 Having said this, she turned around and saw Jesus standing, but she did not know that it was Jesus. 15 Jesus said to her, "Woman, why are you weeping? Whom are you seeking?" Supposing him to be the gardener, she said to him, "Sir, if you have carried him away, tell me where you have laid him, and I will take him away." 16 Jesus said to her, "Mary." She turned and said to him in Aramaic, "Rabboni!" (which means Teacher). 17 Jesus said to her, "Do not cling to me, for I have not yet ascended to the Father; but go to my brothers and say to them, 'I am ascending to my Father and your Father, to my God and your God.'" 18 Mary Magdalene went and announced to the disciples, "I have seen the Lord"—and that he had said these things to her.

7. The Roman soldiers reported to the chief priests.

Matthew 28:11–15: *While the women were on their way, some of the guards went into the city and reported to the chief priests everything that had happened. 12 When the chief priests had met with the elders and devised a plan, they gave the soldiers a large sum of money, 13 telling them,*

Inside the Garden Tomb

"You are to say, 'His disciples came during the night and stole him away while we were asleep. 14 If this report gets to the governor, we will satisfy him and keep you out of trouble.'" 15 So the soldiers took the money and did as they were instructed. And this story has been widely circulated among the Jews to this very day.

8. The disciples responded in unbelief to the report from the women that Christ had risen from the dead.

Luke 24:9–11: *When they came back from the tomb, they told all these things to the Eleven and to all the others. 10 It was Mary*

Magdalene, Joanna, Mary the mother of James, and the others with them who told this to the apostles. 11 But they did not believe the women, because their words seemed to them like nonsense.

9. **Jesus appeared to the disciples.**

   Luke 24:36–47: *While they were still talking about this, Jesus himself stood among them and said to them, "Peace be with you." 37 They were startled and frightened, thinking they saw a ghost. 38 He said to them, "Why are you troubled, and why do doubts rise in your minds? 39 Look at my hands and my feet. It is I myself! Touch me and see; a ghost does not have flesh and bones, as you see I have." 40 When he had said this, he showed them his hands and feet. 41 And while they still did not believe it because of joy and amazement, he asked them, "Do you have anything here to eat?" 42 They gave him a piece of broiled fish, 43 and he took it and ate it in their presence. 44 He said to*

   Rock face cliff believed to be Golgotha

   them, "This is what I told you while I was still with you: Everything must be fulfilled that is written about me in the Law of Moses, the Prophets and the Psalms." 45 Then he opened their minds so they could understand the Scriptures. 46 He told them, "This is what is written: The Christ will suffer and rise from the dead on the third day, 47 and repentance and forgiveness of sins will be preached in his name to all nations, beginning at Jerusalem."

10. **Christ appeared to many others after His resurrection.**

    1 Corinthians 15:3–8: *For I delivered to you as of first importance what I also received: that Christ died for our sins in accordance with the Scriptures, 4 that he was buried, that he was raised on the third day in accordance with the Scriptures, 5 and that he appeared to Cephas, then to the twelve. 6 Then he appeared to more than five hundred brothers at one time, most of whom are still alive, though some have fallen asleep. 7 Then he appeared to James, then to all the*

apostles. 8 Last of all, as to one untimely born, he appeared also to me [Apostle Paul].

Faith Lesson from the Garden Tomb

1. The death, burial, and resurrection of Christ are true historical events that form the foundation of the Christian Faith.
2. Without Christ's death on the Cross, our sins are not forgiven.
3. Without Christ's resurrection, our faith is in vain (1 Cor. 15:14).
4. No other self-acclaimed prophet has risen from the dead. The fact that Christ did separates Him from all others, proving that He was God in the flesh.
5. The resurrection proves that all believers will receive resurrected bodies after death.
6. Mary Magdalene was the first woman Christ appeared to and encapsulates what it means to love the Lord your God with all your heart, soul, mind, and strength. Do we love the Lord as Mary did?

Sign inside the tomb door

Journal/Notes:

Gethsemane to Golgotha: Christ's Path to the Cross

Location

1. Gethsemane is located at the base of the Mount of Olives and just east of the Temple Mount.
2. Golgotha has two general options for its location.

    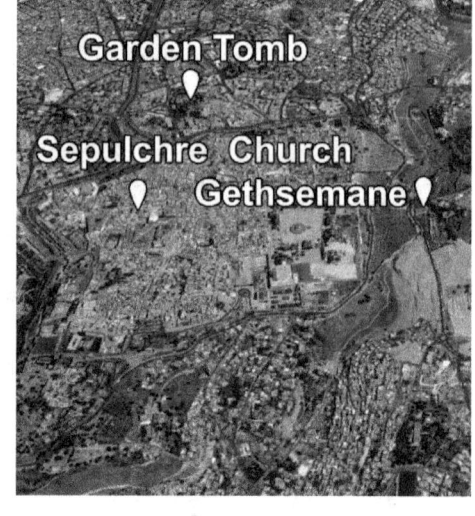

    - The traditional site of the Church of the Holy Sepulchre provides the most evidence as being the true site.
    - Another option is the Garden Tomb. There is a rock face cliff that looks like the face of a skull. Over the years, it has deteriorated but still resembles a face.
3. Because we worship a person and not a place, the location isn't as important as what happened. Both sites are close to each other, so we know they're both in the vicinity of the historical Golgotha.

Historical Background

1. The death, burial, and resurrection of Christ were actual events that happened in history.
2. They were prophesied in the Old Testament and fulfilled in the New Testament.
3. There were hundreds, if not thousands, of eyewitnesses to Christ's resurrection (1 Cor. 15:6).
4. Within decades of Christ's resurrection, Roman and Jewish historians wrote about Jesus and the events surrounding Him.
5. There is more evidence regarding Christ's existence than Julius Caesar.
6. No other person has changed history as Christ did.

Jerusalem Sites

7. Christ's disciples were willing to die for their faith in Him.
8. Throughout history, and today, billions of people confess Christ as their Savior, and that He lives within them and has changed their lives.

Places of Interest

1. Gethsemane
2. House of Caiaphas
3. Antonia Fortress
4. Herod's Palace – Pilate's Judgment Hall
5. Church of the Holy Sepulchre
6. Garden Tomb
7. Via Dolorosa

Gethsemane to Golgotha in the Bible

1. **Jesus began the journey praying in the Garden of Gethsemane.**

   Matthew 26:36–38: *Then Jesus went with them to a place called Gethsemane, and he said to his disciples, "Sit here, while I go over there and pray." 37 And taking with him Peter and the two sons of Zebedee, he began to be sorrowful and troubled. 38 Then he said to them, "My soul is very sorrowful, even to death; remain here, and watch with me."*

2. **Jesus was arrested in the Garden of Gethsemane very late at night.**

   Matthew 26:47: *While he was still speaking, Judas came, one of the twelve, and with him a great crowd with swords and clubs, from the chief priests and the elders of the people.*

   Church of all Nations at Garden of Gethsemane

3. **Jesus was brought before Annas, the father-in-law of Caiaphas, the High Priest.**

   John 18:12–13: *So the band of soldiers and their captain and the officers of the Jews arrested Jesus and bound him. 13 First they led him to Annas, for he was the father-in-law of Caiaphas, who was high priest that year.*

4. **Christ was brought before Caiaphas, the High Priest.**

   Matthew 26:57: *Then those who had seized Jesus led him to Caiaphas the high priest, where the scribes and the elders had gathered.*

5. **While at the house of Caiaphas, Peter denied Christ 3 times.**

   Luke 22:61–62: *And the Lord turned and looked at Peter. And Peter remembered the saying of the Lord, how he had said to him, "Before the rooster crows today, you will deny me three times." 62 And he went out and wept bitterly.*

6. **The religious leaders condemned and beat Jesus at the house of Caiaphas.**

   Matthew 26:65–68: *Then the high priest tore his robes and said, "He has uttered blasphemy. What further witnesses do we need? You have now heard his blasphemy. 66 What is your judgment?" They answered, "He deserves death." 67 Then they spit in his face and struck him. And some slapped him, 68 saying, "Prophesy to us, you Christ! Who is it that struck you?"*

7. **Christ most likely spent the rest of the night in a dungeon at**

the house of Caiaphas, the High Priest.

8. **Early the next morning, Christ was brought before Pilate to be judged.**

    John 18:28: *Then they led Jesus from the house of Caiaphas to the governor's headquarters. It was early morning. They themselves did not enter the governor's headquarters, so that they would not be defiled, but could eat the Passover.*

9. **Judas, the disciple who betrayed Christ, hanged himself.**

    Matthew 27:3–5: *Then when Judas, his betrayer, saw that Jesus was condemned, he changed his mind and brought back the thirty pieces of silver to the chief priests and the elders, 4 saying, "I have sinned by betraying innocent blood." They said, "What is that to us? See to it yourself." 5 And throwing down the pieces of silver into the temple, he departed, and he went and hanged himself.*

    Field of Blood in the Hinnom Valley

10. **Jesus appeared before King Herod.**

    Luke 23:5–7: *But they were urgent, saying, "He stirs up the people, teaching throughout all Judea, from Galilee even to this place." 6 When Pilate heard this, he asked whether the man was a Galilean. 7 And when he learned that he belonged to Herod's jurisdiction, he sent him over to Herod, who was himself in Jerusalem at that time.*

    Luke 23:11: *And Herod with his soldiers treated him with contempt and mocked him. Then, arraying him in splendid clothing, he sent him back to Pilate.*

11. **Jesus appeared again before Pilate; Pilates's wife warned him about condemning Jesus, Barabbas was released.**

    Matthew 27:19–23: *While he was sitting on the judgment seat, his wife sent him a message, saying, "Have nothing to do with that righteous Man; for last night I suffered greatly in a dream because of Him." 20 But the chief priests and the elders persuaded the crowds* to ask for Barabbas and to put Jesus to death. 21 But the governor said to them, "Which of the two do you want me to release for you?" And they said, "Barabbas." 22 Pilate said to them, "Then what shall I do with Jesus who is called Christ?" They all said, "Crucify Him!" 23 And he said, "Why, what evil has He done?" But they kept shouting all the more, saying, "Crucify Him!"

12. Pilate had Jesus beaten in an attempt to appease the Jews.

John 19:1-6: *Then Pilate took Jesus and flogged him. 2 And the soldiers twisted together a crown of thorns and put it on his head and arrayed him in a purple robe. 3 They came up to him, saying, "Hail, King of the Jews!" and struck him with their hands. 4 Pilate went out again and said to them, "See, I am bringing him out to you that you may know that I find no guilt in him." 5 So Jesus came out, wearing the crown of thorns and the purple robe. Pilate said to them, "Behold the man!" 6 When the chief priests and the officers saw him, they cried out, "Crucify him, crucify him!" Pilate said to them, "Take him yourselves and crucify him, for I find no guilt in him."*

Pilates Palace – Judgment Hall

13. Pilate condemned Jesus to death by crucifixion.

Matthew 27:24–26: *So when Pilate saw that he was gaining nothing, but rather that a riot was beginning, he took water and washed his hands before the crowd, saying, "I am innocent of this man's blood; see to it yourselves." 25 And all the people answered, "His blood be on us and on our children!" 26 Then he released for them Barabbas, and having scourged Jesus, delivered him to be crucified.*

14. Jesus was led out to be crucified at Golgotha.

John 19:16–17: *So he delivered him over to them to be crucified. So they took Jesus, 17 and he went out, bearing his own cross, to the place called The Place of a Skull, which in Aramaic is called Golgotha.*

15. **Because Christ's body was so physically damaged, Simon of Cyrene was forced to carry Christ's cross the rest of the way.**

    Matthew 27:32–33: *As they went out, they found a man of Cyrene, Simon by name. They compelled this man to carry his cross. 33 And when they came to a place called Golgotha (which means Place of a Skull)."*

16. **Jesus was crucified at 9:00 Friday morning on Passover day.**

    Mark 15:25: *And it was the third hour [9:00 am] when they crucified him.*

17. **Christ on the Cross.**

    Matthew 27:34–37: *They offered him wine to drink, mixed with gall, but when he tasted it, he would not drink it. 35 And when they had crucified him, they divided his garments among them by casting lots. 36 Then they sat down and kept watch over him there. 37 And over his head they put the charge against him, which read, "This is Jesus, the King of the Jews."*

18. **Jesus was mocked by those who passed by, the chief priest, scribes, and elders.**

    Matthew 27:38–43: *Then two robbers were crucified with him, one on the right and one on the left. 39 And those who passed by derided him, wagging their heads 40 and saying, "You who would destroy the temple and rebuild it in three days, save yourself! If you are the Son of God, come down from the cross." 41 So also the chief priests, with the scribes and elders, mocked him, saying, 42 "He saved others; he cannot save himself. He is the King of Israel; let him come down now from the cross, and we will believe in him. 43 He trusts in God; let God deliver him now, if he desires him. For he said, 'I am the Son of God.'"*

19. **One of the robbers who was crucified with Christ believed in Christ and received Him as Savior.**

    Luke 23:39–43: *One of the criminals who were hanged railed at* him, saying, "Are you not the Christ? Save yourself and us!" 40 But the other rebuked him, saying, "Do you not fear God, since you are under the same sentence of condemnation? 41 And we indeed justly, for we are receiving the due reward of our deeds; but this man has done nothing wrong." 42 And he said, "Jesus, remember me when you come into your kingdom." 43 And he said to him, "Truly, I say to you, today you will be with me in paradise."

20. Jesus dies on the Cross.

Luke 23:46–49: *Then Jesus, calling out with a loud voice, said, "Father, into your hands I commit my spirit!" And having said this he breathed his last. 47 Now when the centurion saw what had taken place, he praised God, saying, "Certainly this man was innocent!" 48 And all the crowds that had assembled for this spectacle, when they saw what had taken place, returned home beating their breasts. 49 And all his acquaintances and the women who had followed him from Galilee stood at a distance watching these things.*

21. From noon until 3:00 pm, darkness fell on the earth.

Matthew 27:45–50: *Now from the sixth hour [12:00 pm], there was darkness over all the land until the ninth hour [3:00 pm]. 46 And about the ninth hour Jesus cried out with a loud voice, saying, "Eli, Eli, lema sabachthani?" that is, "My God, my God, why have you forsaken me?" 47 And some of the bystanders, hearing it, said, "This man is calling Elijah." 48 And one of them at once ran and took a sponge, filled it with sour wine, and put it on a reed and gave it to him to drink. 49 But the others said, "Wait, let us see whether Elijah will come to save him." 50 And Jesus cried out again with a loud voice and yielded up his spirit.*

Route to Calvary from Pilate's Palace

22. The temple curtain was torn in two, and many people rose from the dead and appeared to others.

Matthew 27:51–53: *And behold, the curtain of the temple was torn*

Jerusalem Sites

in two, from top to bottom. And the earth shook, and the rocks were split. 52 The tombs also were opened. And many bodies of the saints who had fallen asleep were raised, 53 and coming out of the tombs after his resurrection they went into the holy city and appeared to many.

23. Jesus' body is taken down from the Cross and placed in a tomb.

John 19:38–42: *After these things, Joseph of Arimathea, who was a disciple of Jesus, but secretly for fear of the Jews, asked Pilate that he might take away the body of Jesus, and Pilate gave him permission. So he came and took away his body. 39 Nicodemus also, who earlier had come to Jesus by night, came bringing a mixture of myrrh and aloes, about seventy-five pounds in weight. 40 So they took the body of Jesus and bound it in linen cloths with the spices, as is the burial custom of the Jews. 41 Now in the place where he was crucified there was a garden, and in the garden a new tomb in which no one had yet been laid. 42 So because of the Jewish day of Preparation, since the tomb was close at hand, they laid Jesus there.*

Church of the Holy Sepulchre – Believed place of Calvary

24. The tomb of Jesus was secured by the Romans.

Matthew 27:65–66: *Pilate said to them, "You have a guard of soldiers. Go, make it as secure as you can." 66 So they went and made the tomb secure by sealing the stone and setting a guard.*

25. Three days later, Christ rose from the dead and proved victorious over sin and death.

1 Corinthians 15:3–8: *For I delivered to you as of first importance what I also received: that Christ died for our sins in accordance with the Scriptures, 4 that he was buried, that he was raised on the third day in accordance with the Scriptures, 5 and that he appeared to Cephas, then to the twelve. 6 Then he appeared to more than five hundred brothers at one time, most of whom are still alive, though*

some have fallen asleep. 7 Then he appeared to James, then to all the apostles. 8 Last of all, as to one untimely born, he appeared also to me [Apostle Paul].

Faith Lesson from Gethsemane to Golgotha

1. Christ was beaten on at least 3 occasions, and His body was so damaged He couldn't even carry His cross.
2. Christ suffered both physically and spiritually for us.
3. What He suffered spiritually was far more than His physical suffering.
4. He suffered the penalty of eternity in hell for each person who trusts in Him as their Savior.

    Isaiah 53:5: *But he was wounded for our transgressions; he was crushed for our iniquities; upon him was the chastisement that brought us peace, and with his stripes we are healed.*
5. Jesus died on the Cross at the exact time the sacrificial lamb of the Passover was to be sacrificed. This was no accident but was sovereignly arranged by God to show that Christ was the Passover Lamb once and for all.
6. Words fail to express what Christ went through for us so He could restore us to Himself and have an eternal relationship with us.
7. Do we comprehend and appreciate this reality?
8. Because of His great sacrifice, we can have our sins forgiven and receive the gift of eternal life. Have you received Christ as your Lord and Savior?

Journal/Notes:

Jerusalem Sites

Hezekiah's Broad Wall

Location

1. Hezekiah's Broad Wall connected the lower part of the City of David with the west side of the Temple Mount.
2. The part that is visible today is located just north of the Hurva Synagogue and to the left of Bonei ha-Khoma St.

Historical Background

1. After the dividing of the nation of Israel into two kingdoms (Israel and Judah) after King Solomon, God sent prophet after prophet to warn them to turn from their sinful ways and follow Him. However, all these warnings fell on deaf ears.
2. All the 19 kings who reigned in the Northern Kingdom of Israel did not follow the Lord but acted wickedly.
3. As a result, the northern kingdom of Israel was conquered and taken into captivity in 722 BC by the Assyrians.

   2 Kings 18:11–12: *Then the king of Assyria carried Israel away into exile to Assyria, and put them in Halah and on the Habor, the river of Gozan, and in the cities of the Medes,* **12 because they did not obey the voice of the Lord their God,** *but transgressed His covenant, even all that Moses the servant of the Lord commanded; they would neither listen nor do it.*
4. The Assyrian army was brutal and known for its torturous tactics. They intentionally instilled fear in the hearts of those they conquered to cause other countries to surrender instead of fighting.
5. By 701 BC, the Assyrians, headed by Sennacherib, invaded Judah, the Southern Kingdom of Israel, because of their disobedience to God.
6. According to an Assyrian stele found in the ruins of the royal

palace of Nineveh, Sennacherib conquered 46 cities in Judea prior to attempting to conquer Jerusalem.
7. God allowed most of Judah to be conquered but protected Jerusalem because of Hezekiah's obedience to Him.
8. As Hezekiah began to prepare for what he knew would be a terrible siege by a merciless Assyrian war machine, he had to figure out how to protect his people. This meant building new defenses.
9. During the time of Hezekiah, Jerusalem's urban population had grown far outside the city's old walls and was unprotected.
10. King Hezekiah fortified the existing walls of the city and rapidly built a new wall to protect those living outside the city walls.

    2 Chronicles 32:5: *He set to work resolutely and **built up all the wall that was broken down** and raised towers upon it, and outside it **he built another wall**, and he strengthened the Millo in the city of David. He also made weapons and shields in abundance.*

    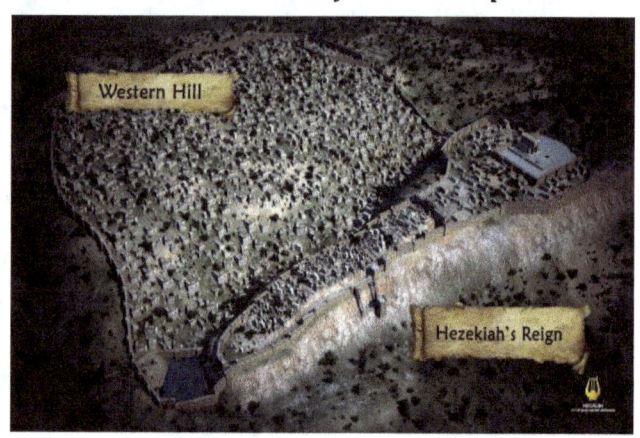
    Hezekiah's Broad Wall – Western Hill expansion

11. Hezekiah's new wall measured about 22 ft. wide (7 m.) by 25 ft. high (8 m.).
12. It was a massive undertaking and measured around 2.5 miles (4 km.) in length.
13. A portion of the wall was discovered in the 1970s by Israeli archaeologist Nahman Avigad and dated to the reign of King Hezekiah (716-687 BC).
14. It was called "Hezekiah's Broad Wall" by archaeologists because of its width.
15. King Hezekiah also built a water tunnel to keep the water from the Gihon Spring inside the city walls so the Assyrians couldn't cut off

Jerusalem Sites

the water supply (2 Chron. 32:3–4). The curving tunnel is 583 yards (533 m.) long and has an altitude difference of 12 inches (30 cm.) between its two ends. It was chiseled from both ends to the middle at the same time. It took the water from the Gihon Spring under the mountain to the Pool of Siloam below the City of David.

Places of Interest
1. Hezekiah's Broad Wall – Only a small section can be seen today.
2. Gihon Spring
3. Pool of Siloam
4. Hezekiah's Tunnel
5. City of David
6. Temple Mount

Hezekiah in the Bible

1. **King Hezekiah's father, Ahaz, was a wicked king. He closed the doors of the temple and burned his children in sacrificial worship to false gods.**

2. **King Hezekiah was a godly king who reopened the temple and restored worship to God.**

    2 Kings 18:3-6: *And he did what was right in the eyes of the Lord, according to all that David his father had done. 4 He removed the high places and broke the pillars and cut down the Asherah. And he broke in pieces the bronze serpent that Moses had made, for until those days the people of Israel had made offerings to it (it was called Nehushtan). 5 He trusted in the Lord, the God of Israel, so that there was none like him among all the kings of Judah after him, nor among those who were before him. 6 For he held fast to the Lord. He did not depart from following him, but kept the commandments that the Lord commanded Moses.*

    Hezekiah's Water Tunnel

3. **King Hezekiah chose not to serve the King of Assyria.**

    2 Kings 18:7: *And the Lord was with him; wherever he went he prospered. And he rebelled against the king of Assyria and did not serve him.*

4. **Sennacherib, the King of Assyria, conquered the southern part of Judah, including the mighty city of Lachish. King Hezekiah tried to keep him at bay by paying him money.**

    2 Kings 18:13-16: *Now in the fourteenth year of King Hezekiah, Sennacherib king of Assyria came up against* **all the fortified cities of Judah** *and seized them. 14 Then Hezekiah king of Judah sent to the king of Assyria at* **Lachish**, *saying, "I have done wrong. Withdraw from me; whatever you impose on me I will bear." So the king of Assyria required of Hezekiah king of Judah three hundred*

Jerusalem Sites

talents of silver and thirty talents of gold. 15 Hezekiah gave him all the silver which was found in the house of the Lord, and in the treasuries of the king's house. 16 At that time Hezekiah cut off the gold from the doors of the temple of the Lord, and from the doorposts which Hezekiah king of Judah had overlaid, and gave it to the king of Assyria.

5. **King Sennacherib made plans to conquer Jerusalem.**

   2 Kings 18:17: *Then the king of Assyria sent Tartan and Rab-saris and Rabshakeh from Lachish to King Hezekiah with a large army to Jerusalem. So they went up and came to Jerusalem.*

6. **King Sennacherib mocked King Hezekiah and the God of Israel.**

   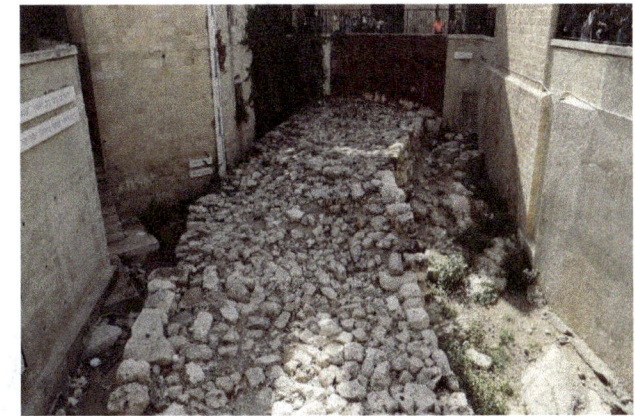

   Hezekiah's Broad Wall exposed today

   2 Kings 18:32–35: *And do not listen to Hezekiah when he misleads you by saying,* **"The Lord will deliver us."** *33 Has any of the gods of the nations ever delivered his land out of the hand of the king of Assyria? 34 Where are the gods of Hamath and Arpad? Where are the gods of Sepharvaim, Hena, and Ivvah? Have they delivered Samaria out of my hand? 35 Who among all the gods of the lands have delivered their lands out of my hand, that the* **Lord should deliver Jerusalem out of my hand***?'"*

7. **King Hezekiah humbled himself before God and sent for the Prophet Isaiah.**

   2 Kings 19:1–7: *And when King Hezekiah heard it, he tore his clothes, covered himself with sackcloth and entered the house of the Lord. 2 Then he sent Eliakim who was over the household with Shebna the scribe and the elders of the priests, covered with sackcloth, to Isaiah the prophet the son of Amoz. 3 They said to him, "Thus says Hezekiah, 'This day is a day of distress, rebuke, and rejection; for children have come to birth and there is no strength to*

deliver. 4 Perhaps the Lord your God will hear all the words of Rabshakeh, whom his master the king of Assyria has sent to reproach the living God, and will rebuke the words which the Lord your God has heard. Therefore, offer a prayer for the remnant that is left.'" 5 So the servants of King Hezekiah came to Isaiah. 6 Isaiah said to them, "Thus you shall say to your master, 'Thus says the Lord, "Do not be afraid because of the words that you have heard, with which the servants of the king of Assyria have blasphemed Me. 7 Behold, I will put a spirit in him so that he will hear a rumor and return to his own land. And I will make him fall by the sword in his own land."

8. **King Sennacherib once again threatened King Hezekiah and spoke against the God of Israel.**

   2 Kings 19:9–12: *So he sent messengers again to Hezekiah, saying, 10 "Thus shall you speak to Hezekiah king of Judah: 'Do not let your God in whom you trust deceive you by promising that Jerusalem will not be given into the hand of the king of Assyria. 11 Behold, you have heard what the kings of Assyria have done to all lands, devoting them to destruction. And shall you be delivered? 12 Have the gods of the nations delivered them, the nations that my fathers destroyed.'"*

9. **Hezekiah sought the Lord's help.**

   2 Kings 19:14–19: *Then Hezekiah took the letter from the hand of the messengers and read it, and he went up to the house of the Lord*

and spread it out before the Lord. 15 Hezekiah prayed before the Lord and said, "O Lord, the God of Israel, who are enthroned above the cherubim, You are the God, You alone, of all the kingdoms of the earth. You have made heaven and earth. 16 Incline Your ear, O Lord, and hear; open Your eyes, O Lord, and see; and listen to the words of Sennacherib, which he has sent to reproach the living God. 17 Truly, O Lord, the kings of Assyria have devastated the nations and their lands 18 and have cast their gods into the fire, for they were not gods but the work of men's hands, wood and stone. So they have destroyed them. 19 Now, O Lord our God, I pray, deliver us from his hand that all the kingdoms of the earth may know that You alone, O Lord, are God."

10. God answered Hezekiah's prayer.

2 Kings 19:20–22: *Then Isaiah the son of Amoz sent to Hezekiah saying, "Thus says the Lord, the God of Israel, 'Because you have prayed to Me about Sennacherib king of Assyria, I have heard you.' 21 This is the word that the Lord has spoken against him: 'She has despised you*

and mocked you, the virgin daughter of Zion; She has shaken her head behind you, The daughter of Jerusalem! 22 'Whom have you reproached and blasphemed? And against whom have you raised your voice, and haughtily lifted up your eyes? Against the Holy One of Israel!'"

2 Kings 19:32–34: *Therefore, thus says the Lord concerning the king of Assyria, "He will not come to this city or shoot an arrow there; and he will not come before it with a shield or throw up a siege ramp against it. 33 By the way that he came, by the same he will return, and he shall not come to this city, declares the Lord. 34 For I will defend this city to save it for My own sake and for My servant David's sake."*

11. God miraculously destroyed King Sennacherib and his army.

2 Kings 19:35-37: Then it happened that night that the angel of the Lord went out and struck 185,000 in the camp of the Assyrians; and when men rose early in the morning, behold, all of them were dead. 36 So Sennacherib king of Assyria departed and returned home, and lived at Nineveh. 37 It came about as he was worshiping in the house of Nisroch his god, that Adrammelech and Sharezer killed him with the sword; and they escaped into the land of Ararat. And Esarhaddon his son became king in his place.

Faith Lesson from the Life of King Hezekiah

1. Even though Hezekiah had a wicked father, he chose to serve the Lord.
2. No matter what our background might be, and the parents we have, God can still use us greatly if we yield ourselves entirely to Him.
3. He was extremely dedicated to God.

    2 Kings 18:5-6: He trusted in the Lord, the God of Israel; so that after him there was none like him among all the kings of Judah, nor among those who were before him. 6 For he clung to the Lord; he did not depart from following Him, but kept His commandments, which the Lord had commanded Moses.

4. He trusted in God during times of great trials.
5. God blessed him and protected him because of his faith and dedication to Him.
6. He worked hard to fortify the old walls, built a huge new wall, and protected the water source of the city. All this was good but not needed as God supernaturally protected Jerusalem because Hezekiah trusted in the Lord.
7. King Hezekiah lived the kind of life God blesses. Are we following his example?

Journal/Notes:

Jerusalem Sites

Hinnom Valley

Location

1. The Hinnom Valley is located just to the southeast of Old City Jerusalem.
2. It joins the Kidron Valley just to the southeast of Old City Jerusalem.
3. Today it looks nothing like it did during the Old and New Testament periods.
4. It was an ugly place where ugly things happened.

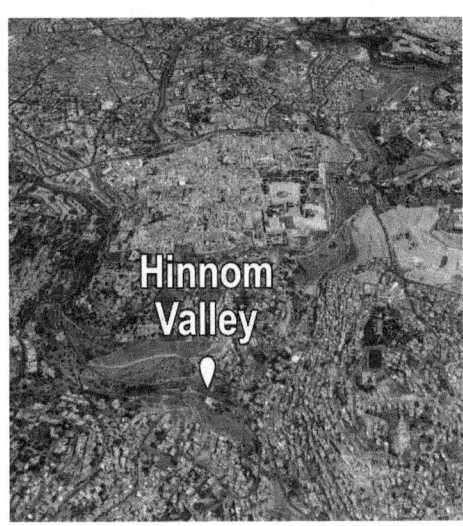

Historical Background

1. In the Hinnom Valley, the city dumped its waste and burned its trash.
   - Because the Hinnom Valley is located on the southeast side of Jerusalem, the prevailing winds carry the winds away from the city. For this reason, it became the city dump.
   - Dead animals from the temple sacrifices were thrown there to rot and be eaten by worms and maggots.
   - Trash was burnt here.
   - The city sewage was emptied here.
   - It was smelly, ugly, burning, crawling with worms, full of rot, and full of disease.
2. During the Old Testament period, many of the Israelites sacrificed their children to the false gods of Molech and Baal in the Hinnom Valley.

   Leviticus 20:2: *You shall also say to the sons of Israel: "Any man from the sons of Israel or from the aliens sojourning in Israel who gives any of his offspring to Molech, shall surely be put to death; the people of the land shall stone him with stones."*

3. What did worship to Molech entail?
   - It is believed that the idols of Moloch were giant metal statues of a man with a bull's head. Each image had a hole in the abdomen and outstretched forearms that made a kind of ramp to the hole. A fire was lit in or around the statue, and babies were placed in the statue's arms or in the hole. When a couple sacrificed their firstborn, they believed that Moloch would ensure financial prosperity for the family and future children.
   - It was a custom to beat drums and play music loudly. Some believe this was done to drown out the babies' screams from reaching their parents' ears.
4. What did worship to Baal entail?
   - Baal worship was rooted in sensuality and involved ritualistic prostitution in the temples. At times, appeasing Baal required human sacrifice, usually the firstborn of the one making the sacrifice.

Hinnom Valley

5. With its pagan history and burning sewer stench, Jerusalem's Hinnom Valley serves as a vivid metaphor for both the Christian and Jewish concept of hell.
6. By Jesus' time in the New Testament, the Greek translation of Hinnom Valley, "Gehenna," became a synonym for hell. For this reason, the English New Testament versions of the Bible translate Gehenna as hell.

Places of Interest

1. Hinnom Valley
2. Kidron Valley
3. Temple Mount
4. City of David
5. Field of Blood – Land purchased from the 30 pieces of silver paid to Judas for betraying Christ.

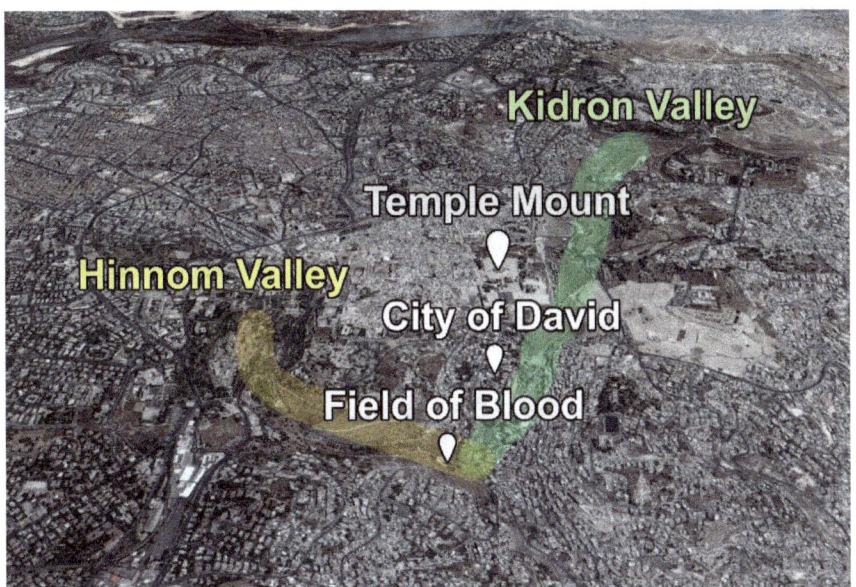

Hinnom Valley in the Bible

1. **The Prophet Jeremiah strongly condemned the worship of Molech.**

   Jeremiah 32:31–35: *This city has aroused my anger and wrath, from the day it was built to this day, so that I will remove it from my sight 32 because of all the evil of the children of Israel and the children of Judah that they did to provoke me to anger—their kings and their officials, their priests and their prophets, the men of Judah and the inhabitants of Jerusalem. 33 They have turned to me their back and not their face. And though I have taught them persistently, they have not listened to receive instruction. 34 They set up their abominations in the house that is called by my name, to defile it. 35 They built the high places of **Baal** in the **Valley of the Son of Hinnom**, to offer up their sons and daughters to **Molech**, though I did not command them, nor did it enter into my mind, that they should do this abomination, to cause Judah to sin.*

2. **Several of the Kings of Israel worshiped Molech and Baal.**

   2 Chronicles 28:1–4: *Ahaz was twenty years old when he became king, and he reigned sixteen years in Jerusalem; and he did not do right in the sight of the Lord as David his father had done. 2 But he walked in the ways of the kings of Israel; he also made molten images for the Baals. 3 Moreover, he burned incense in the valley of*

Ben-hinnom and burned his sons in fire, *according to the abominations of the nations whom the Lord had driven out before the sons of Israel. 4 He sacrificed and burned incense on the high places, on the hills and under every green tree.*

2 Chronicles 33:5–6: *For he [King Manasseh] built altars for all the host of heaven in the two courts of the house of the Lord. 6 He made his sons pass through the fire in the* **valley of Ben-hinnom**; *and he practiced witchcraft, used divination, practiced sorcery and dealt with mediums and spiritists. He did much evil in the sight of the Lord, provoking Him to anger.*

3. **God destroyed the nations that previously lived in Israel because of their evil worship of false gods.**

   Deuteronomy 20:16–18: *But in the cities of these peoples that the Lord your God is giving you for an inheritance, you shall save alive nothing that breathes, 17 but you shall devote them to complete destruction, the Hittites and the*

   Hinnom Valley

   Amorites, the Canaanites and the Perizzites, the Hivites and the Jebusites, as the Lord your God has commanded, 18 that they may not teach you to do according to all their abominable practices that they have done for their gods, and so you sin against the Lord your God.

4. **When Christ wanted to communicate the concept of coming judgment and hell, He used Gehenna (Hinnom) as an example.**

   Mark 9:42–49: *Whoever causes one of these little ones who believe to stumble, it would be better for him if, with a heavy millstone hung around his neck, he had been cast into the sea. 43 If your hand causes you to stumble, cut it off; it is better for you to enter life crippled, than, having your two hands, to go into hell, into the unquenchable fire, 44 where their worm does not die, and the fire is not quenched. 45 If your foot causes you to stumble, cut it off; it is better for you to enter life lame, than, having your two feet, to be cast into hell, 46 where their worm does not die, and the fire is not quenched. 47 If your eye causes you to stumble, throw it out; it is better for you to enter the kingdom of God with one eye, than, having two eyes, to be cast into hell, 48 where their worm does not die, and the fire is not quenched. 49 For everyone will be salted with fire.*

Luke 12:5: *But I will warn you whom to fear: fear the One who, after He has killed, has authority to cast into **hell**; yes, I tell you, fear Him!*

5. **Interestingly, the Field of Blood which was purchased from the 30 pieces of silver Judas received to betray Christ, is in the Hinnom Valley. Today, there's a monastery marking this spot called, Akeldama.**

Faith Lesson from the Hinnom Valley

1. Worship of false gods is ugly and destructive. Today, in a metaphorical sense, we can also sacrifice our children on the altar to false idols if we neglect God and don't raise our children to fear Him.
2. Hell is a true reality, even though it might seem unjust or uncomfortable.
3. Coming judgment is certain and will take place.
4. Are we genuinely saved and walking with God so we will escape the judgment to come?

Akeldama Monastery – Field of Blood

Journal/Notes:

Israel Biblical Sites Travel Guide

House of Caiaphas

Location

1. The House of Caiaphas, also known as the Church of Saint Peter in Gallicantu (cock's crow in Latin), is located on the eastern slope of Mount Zion, just outside the Old City of Jerusalem.
2. It can be accessed by Malki Tsedek Street.
3. It is administered by the Roman Catholic Church.

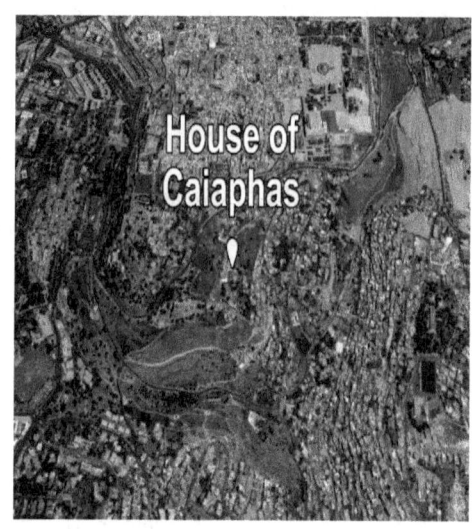

Historical Background

1. The church consists of four levels: (1) the upper church, (2) the middle church, (3) the guardroom, and (4) the cistern (dungeon).
2. According to tradition, the church is the believed site of the House of Caiaphas.
3. A Byzantine church was built on this site in 457 AD.
4. It was later destroyed by Muslims in 1010.
5. It was rebuilt by the Crusaders in 1102 and given its present name.
6. It was destroyed in 1219 by the Turks.
7. Later, a chapel was built in 1300.
8. The church fell in ruins again by 1320.
9. The church that exists today was rebuilt in 1931.

Places of Interest

1. In the Courtyard of the church is a statue that recalls the events of Peter's denial of Jesus. It shows Peter, the rooster that crowed, a maid, a servant, and a Roman soldier.
2. On the roof of the church is a rooster on a black cross, a symbol of Peter's denial of Christ before the cock crowed.

Jerusalem Sites

3. The main sanctuary, located on the first floor, contains large multi-colored mosaics portraying figures from the New Testament.
4. On the second floor is a chapel that utilizes stone from ancient grottos as its walls. It also has mosaics from a 5th-century Byzantine church that previously existed at this site.
5. Above the cistern is the Guard Room. It overlooks the cistern (dungeon).
6. On the lower floor is a cistern (dungeon) where it's believed Christ was placed the night He was tried and condemned by Caiaphas.
7. Ruins and excavations outside the church at ground level.
8. A walkway with steps that run beside the church that was used for ascending and descending from Mount Zion to the Kidron Valley.
   - They were most likely used by Jesus and His disciples as they went from the Upper Room, where they celebrated the Passover meal on Mount Zion, to the Garden of Gethsemane.
   - Later, Christ would use these same steps as He was brought from Gethsemane, which led through the Kidron Valley, to the House of Caiaphas.
9. Upper viewing area where many sites can be seen. One of them is the Akeldama Monastery, which marks the place called the Field of Blood. The religious leaders purchased this property with the

money Judas threw at their feet just before he went and hanged himself.
10. Upper Room
11. Mount Zion
12. Kidron Valley
13. Garden of Gethsemane

House of Caiaphas in the Bible

1. **Christ foretold that Peter would deny Him 3 times.**

   Mark 14:27-31: *And Jesus said to them, "You will all fall away, for it is written, 'I will strike the shepherd, and the sheep will be scattered.' 28 But after I am raised up, I will go before you to Galilee." 29 Peter said to him, "Even though they all fall away, I will not." 30 And Jesus said to him, "Truly, I tell you, this very night, before the rooster crows twice, **you will deny me three times**." 31 But he said emphatically, "If I must die with you, I will not deny you." And they all said the same.*

   House of Caiaphas

2. **Jesus appeared before Caiaphas, the High Priest, just after being arrested in the Garden of Gethsemane.**

   Matthew 26:57-68: *Then those who had seized Jesus led him to Caiaphas the high priest, where the scribes and the elders had gathered. 58 And Peter was following him at a distance, as far as the courtyard of the high priest, and going inside he sat with the guards to see the end. 59 Now the chief priests and the whole Council were seeking false testimony against Jesus that they might put him to death, 60 but they found none, though many false witnesses came forward. At last two came forward 61 and said, "This man said, 'I am able to destroy the temple of God, and to rebuild it in three days.' 62 And the high priest stood up and said, "Have you no answer to* make? What is it that these men testify against you?" 63 But Jesus remained silent. And the high priest said to him, "I adjure you by the living God, tell us if you are the Christ, the Son of God." 64 Jesus said to him, "You have said so. But I tell you, from now on you will see the Son of Man seated at the right hand of Power and coming on the clouds of heaven." 65 Then the high priest tore his robes and said, "He has uttered blasphemy. What further witnesses do we need? You have now heard his blasphemy. 66 What is your judgment?" They answered, "He deserves death." 67 Then they spit in his face and struck him. And some slapped him, 68 saying, "Prophesy to us, you Christ! Who is it that struck you?"

Statue marking Peter's denial of Christ

Luke 22:63–65: *Now the men who were holding Jesus in custody were mocking him as they beat him. 64 They also blindfolded him and kept asking him, "Prophesy! Who is it that struck you?" 65 And they said many other things against him, blaspheming him.*

3. **Peter denied Christ.**

Matthew 26:69–75: *Now Peter was sitting outside in the courtyard. And a servant girl came up to him and said, "You also were with Jesus the Galilean." 70 But he denied it before them all, saying, "I do not know what you mean." 71 And when he went out to the entrance, another servant girl saw him, and she said to the bystanders, "This man was with Jesus of Nazareth." 72 And again he denied it with an oath: "I do not know the man." 73 After a little while the bystanders came up and said to Peter, "Certainly you too are one of them, for your accent betrays you." 74 Then he began to invoke a curse on himself and to swear, "I do not know the man."* **And immediately the rooster crowed.** *75 And Peter remembered the saying of Jesus, "Before the rooster crows, you will deny me three times." And he went out and wept bitterly.*

4. **It's believed Jesus spent the night in a cistern (dungeon) at the House of Caiaphas before being taken to Pilate the next morning.**

   Matthew 27:1-2: *When morning came, all the chief priests and the elders of the people took counsel against Jesus to put him to death. 2 And they bound him and led him away and delivered him over to Pilate the governor.*

Faith Lesson from the House of Caiaphas

1. Peter had walked with Christ for 3 ½ years. He had heard numerous times that Christ would die and rise again.
2. Just hours before Peter's denial of Christ, he said he would suffer and die with Christ if need be. But when reality set in, he abandoned Christ and denied Him 3 times.
3. He later wept bitterly and thought his relationship with Christ and ministry was finished. However, Christ restored Peter to fellowship and ministry at the Sea of Galilee.
4. How can we deny Christ in our own lives?
   - Do we deny His word, the truths in His word, or the clarity of the gospel in any way?
   - Do we deny we know Him by remaining silent when Christ or the Bible are attacked, slandered, or diminished?
   - Do we deny Him by not sharing the gospel with others?
   - Do we deny Christ by not spending time with Him in prayer, daily devotions, and Bible reading?
   - Do we deny Christ when it costs us to be identified with Him or persecuted for our faith in Him?

Journal/Notes:

Jerusalem Sites

Kidron Valley

Location

The Kidron Valley, also called the Valley of Jehoshaphat, lies between the Old City of Jerusalem and the Mount of Olives.

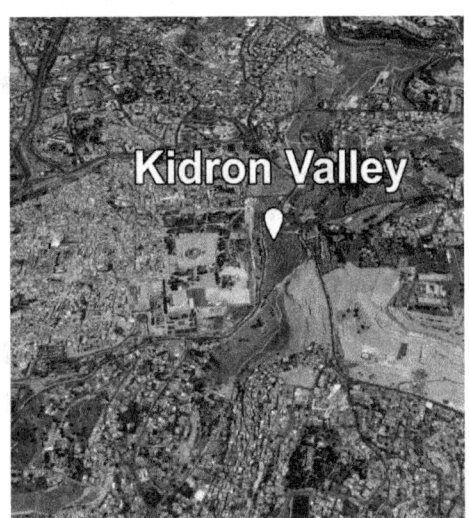

Historical Background

1. The Kidron Valley was much deeper in biblical times.
2. It is referred to repeatedly in Scripture as a place of judgment.
3. It is also called the *Winepress* of God's wrath.

Places of Interest

1. Kidron Valley
2. Absalom's Tomb
3. Zechariah's Tomb
4. Mount of Olives
5. Temple Mount
6. City of David

Kidron Valley and the Judgments of God in the Bible

1. **God will gather the nations to the Kidron Valley at the end of the Great Tribulation Period and judge them.**

   Joel 3:1–3: *For behold, in those days and at that time, when I restore the fortunes of Judah and Jerusalem, 2 I will gather all the nations and bring them down to the **Valley of Jehoshaphat**. And I will enter into judgment with them there, on behalf of my people and my heritage Israel, because they have scattered them among the nations and have divided up my land, 3 and have cast lots for my people, and have traded a boy for a prostitute, and have sold a girl for wine and* *have drunk it.*

2. It is the Winepress of God's wrath.

Revelation 14:14–20: *Then I looked, and behold, a white cloud, and seated on the cloud one like a son of man, with a golden crown on*

his head, and a sharp sickle in his hand. 15 And another angel came out of the temple, calling with a loud voice to him who sat on the cloud, "Put in your sickle, and reap, for the hour to reap has come, for the harvest of the earth is fully ripe." 16 So he who sat on the cloud swung his sickle across the earth, and the earth was reaped. 17 Then another angel came out of the temple in heaven, and he too had a sharp sickle. 18 And another angel came out from the altar, the angel who has authority over the fire, and he called with a loud voice to the one who had the sharp sickle, "Put in your sickle and gather the clusters from the vine of the earth, for its grapes are ripe." 19 So the angel swung his sickle across the earth and gathered the grape harvest of the earth and threw it into the **great winepress of the wrath of God.** *20 And the winepress was trodden outside the city, and blood flowed from the winepress, as high as a horse's bridle [5 ft. or 1.75 m.], for 1,600 stadia [200 miles, or 300 km.].*

The flow of the river of blood from the Kidron Valley will run east

Jerusalem Sites

toward the Dead Sea, then go south toward the Red Sea.

3. **The judgments of God throughout history.**
   1. God judged Satan and the angels who rebelled against Him. They are now called demons.
   2. God judged Adam and Eve for their disobedience.
   3. God judged the ancient world by sending a great flood upon the whole earth.
   4. God judged Sodom and Gomorrah.
   5. God judged the Canaanite nations and commanded Israel to destroy them because of their great wickedness.

Kidron Valley looking north

   6. God gave clear warnings of blessings and curses to the Israelites in Deuteronomy chapters 27 and 28.
   7. The nation of Israel disobeyed God repeatedly and was eventually deported from their land. This was a fulfillment of Deuteronomy chapters 27 and 28.
   8. Contrary to what many people believe, Christ talked more about hell than heaven.
   9. Today, there is very little mention of the judgments of God.

4. **The ultimate judgment awaits those who reject Christ's offer of salvation.**

   Christ was the leading figure who talked about hell in the Bible. He described hell as:
   1. A fiery lake of burning sulfur that is unquenchable and never goes out (Matt. 25:46; Mark 9:43–44; Rev. 21:8).
   2. Everlasting destruction away from the presence of the Lord (2 Thess. 1:9).
   3. Where people gnash their teeth in pain (Matt. 13:50).
   4. Where the devil and the demons suffer (Matt. 25:41).
   5. A gloomy dungeon (2 Pet. 2:4).

6. Where the worm never dies (Mark 9:48).
7. A fiery furnace (Matt. 13:42).
8. Where people will be salted with fire (Mark 9:49).
9. A place of weeping (Matt. 13:50).
10. A place of utter darkness (Jude 1:13).
11. A place of fiery flames (Luke 16:24).
12. A place of torment (Luke 16:28).

According to Christ, hell is a real place, and many will choose to go there because of their rejection of Him. They choose materialism, pleasure, and the pride of life over the salvation of their souls and the eternal riches of Christ.

5. **The final judgment of God at the Great White Throne.**

    Revelation 20:11–15: *Then I saw a great white throne and him who was seated on it. From his presence, earth and sky fled away, and no place was found for them. 12 And I saw the dead, great and small, standing before the throne, and books were opened. Then another book was opened, which is the book of life. And the dead were judged by what was written in the books, according to what they had done. 13 And the sea gave up the dead who were in it, Death and Hades gave up the dead who were in them, and they were judged, each one of them, according to what they had done. 14 Then Death and Hades were thrown into the lake of fire. This is the second death, the lake of fire. 15 And if anyone's name was not found written in the book of life, he was thrown into the lake of fire.*

    Absalom's Monument in the Kidron Valley

6. **Why does God give more time and attention to judgment than blessings?**
    1. In the two foundational passages given to the Israelites regarding blessings for obedience and curses for disobedience

to God (Leviticus 26 and Deuteronomy 27 and 28), about 17% of the verses deal with blessings and 83% deal with curses.
2. Additionally, Christ followed this same pattern and talked more about hell than heaven.
3. This pattern reveals that God has designed the human heart in such a way that it responds better to warnings than blessings.
4. This is so because blessings are optional, but judgment is not. We can choose the blessings if we want, but we can't choose to escape judgment for disobedience.

Kidron Valley looking south

Faith Lesson from the Kidron Valley

1. Do we realize God is a God of love, but He is also a God of justice?
2. Do we realize the reality of the judgments of God?
3. Do we believe in a literal hell, and do we talk about it like Christ did?
4. Do we understand that God has done everything possible to save us, but if we reject Him, then we are choosing separation from Him in hell instead?
5. Have I received Christ as my Savior, and am I living for Him?
6. Am I telling others about Christ's offer of eternal life?

Journal/Notes:

Mary's Tomb

Location

The Tomb of Mary (mother of Jesus), also known as the Church of the Sepulchre of St. Mary, is located just a little north of the Garden of Gethsemane in the Kidron Valley.

Historical Background

1. The New Testament is silent regarding the death and burial of Mary, but strong Christian tradition places her tomb at this site.
2. The church is in an underground rock-cut cave in the shape of a cross. It has a wide staircase leading down to the church. It is dimly lit and has blackish ceilings due to centuries of candle burning.
3. The church began as burial caves that were cut into the rock in the 1st century.
4. These caves were later expanded in 455 AD into a cross-shaped church with the tomb of Mary in its center.
5. The large crypt containing the empty tomb in the church is all that remains of an early 5th-century church.
6. In the 6th century, an octagon-shaped church was built on the upper level, covering the tomb. However, it was destroyed in the Persian invasion in 614 AD.
7. During the Crusader period (1130), the church was rebuilt and included a Benedictine monastery called the Abbey Church of St. Mary of Jehoshaphat. Unfortunately, Saladin destroyed virtually everything in 1187 except for the south entrance and staircase.
8. After the Crusaders left, the site was taken over by Franciscans. Since that time, it has been shared by Greeks, Armenians, Syrians, Copts, Abyssinians, and Muslims.

Jerusalem Sites

9. Muslims also worship here, and in the wall to the right of the Tomb of Mary is a mihrab niche giving the direction of Mecca. It was installed after Saladin's conquest in the 12th century.
10. According to Catholic tradition, Mary ascended into heaven. Her tomb at this church is empty and is a shrine honoring this event. However, there is no proof of Mary ascending to heaven, and Protestants believe Mary died a natural death.

Places of Interest

1. The modern upper level of the church.
2. Forty-seven steps leading down to the dimly lit church.
3. On the way down the steps, there are 2 chapels. On the left side is the chapel of Joseph, Mary's husband, and on the right side is the chapel of Mary's parents, Hanna (Anna) and Joachim.
4. Mary's Chapel
5. Mary's Tomb
6. Copt Altar
7. Garden of Gethsemane

8. Kidron Valley (Valley of Jehoshaphat)
9. Temple Mount

The Life of Mary in the Bible

1. **Mary was a godly woman who had the privilege of being the mother of Jesus.**

    Luke 1:26–31: *Now in the sixth month the angel Gabriel was sent from God to a city in Galilee called Nazareth, 27 to a virgin engaged to a man whose name was Joseph, of the descendants of David; and the virgin's name was Mary. 28 And coming in, he said to her,* **"Greetings, favored one!** *The Lord is with you." 29 But she was very perplexed at this statement and kept pondering what kind of salutation this was. 30 The angel said to her, "Do not be afraid, Mary; for you have* **found favor with God**. *31 And behold, you will conceive in your womb and bear a son, and you shall name Him Jesus."*

    Entrance to Mary's Tomb

2. **Mary treasured the privilege of being Christ's earthly mother.**

    Luke 2:19: *But Mary treasured all these things, pondering them in her heart.*

3. **Being the mother of Jesus would come at a high price.**

    Luke 2:34–35: *And Simeon blessed them and said to Mary, His mother, "Behold, this Child is appointed for the fall and rise of many in Israel, and for a sign to be opposed— 35 and a* **sword will pierce even your own soul**—*to the end that thoughts from many hearts may be revealed."*

4. **Mary was an obedient woman, submitting to God and her husband in all things.**

    Matthew 2:13: *Now when they had gone, behold, an angel of the*

Lord appeared to Joseph in a dream and said, "Get up! Take the Child and His mother and flee to Egypt, and remain there until I tell you; for Herod is going to search for the Child to destroy Him."

5. **Because Christ's earthly father, Joseph, is not mentioned after Christ was 12 years old, and because Christ entrusted the Apostle John with her care at His death, it appears she became a widow at an early age.**

   John 19:25–27: *But standing by the cross of Jesus were His mother, and His mother's sister, Mary the wife of Clopas, and Mary Magdalene. 26 When Jesus then saw His mother, and the disciple whom He loved standing nearby, He said to His mother, "Woman, behold, your son!" 27 Then He said to the disciple, "Behold, your mother!" From that hour the disciple took her into his own household.*

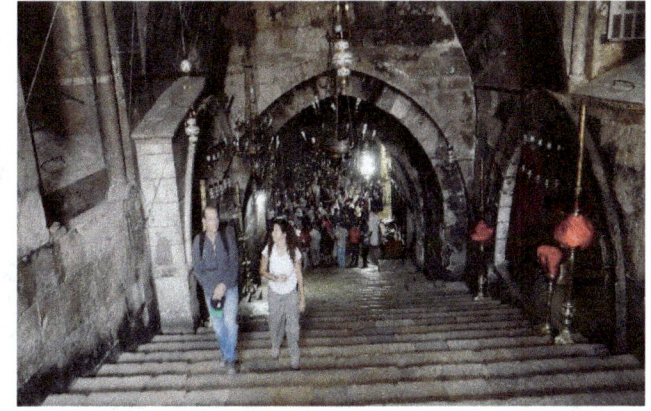

Stairs leading down to the church

6. **Mary did not remain a virgin as she had 4 other sons and several daughters after Jesus was born.**

   Matthew 15:55–56: *Is not this the carpenter's son? Is not His mother called Mary, and His brothers,* **James** *and* **Joseph** *and* **Simon** *and* **Judas***? 56 And* **His sisters, are they not all with us***?*

7. **Mary witnessed the crucifixion of her Son on the Cross.**

   John 19:25: *Therefore, the soldiers did these things. But standing by the cross of Jesus were His mother, and His mother's sister, Mary the wife of Clopas, and Mary Magdalene.*

8. **Mary continued to support the apostles and was part of serving the cause of Jesus after His resurrection.**

   Acts 1:14: *All these with one accord were devoting themselves to prayer, together with the women and* **Mary the mother of Jesus***, and his brothers.*

Faith Lesson from the Life of Mary

1. Mary was a deeply devoted woman to be honored, but nowhere in Scripture is she worshiped, or are we commanded to worship or pray to her.
2. We could learn a lot from the life of Mary and should emulate her faith and devotion to God.
3. Mary was highly favored by the Lord because of her obedience to Him. When we obey and seek the Lord, we are favored by Him as well.
4. Our obedience doesn't earn God's love, but it does bring blessing and favor.
5. Contrary to what many believe, Mary did not stay a virgin. The Bible says she had 4 sons and other daughters. We should believe the Bible over what any church or religion teaches.
6. What is your highest authority in life, God and His Word, or what people say?

Mary's Chapel

Journal/Notes:

Jerusalem Sites

Mount of Olives Overview

Location

The Mount of Olives is located just opposite the Temple Mount on the east side of Old City Jerusalem.

Historical Background

1. The Mount of Olives has played a significant role in the Bible.
2. From the top of the Mount of Olives, Christ ascended back to heaven.
3. It is where Christ, along with all believers, will return to at Christ's second coming.

Places of Interest

1. Kidron Valley (Valley of Jehoshaphat)
2. Garden of Gethsemane
3. Mary's Tomb (mother of Jesus)
4. Church of Mary Magdalene
5. Church of Dominus Flevit (where Christ wept over Jerusalem)
6. Triumphal Entry Path
7. Bethphage (beginning place of the Triumphal Entry on the backside of the Mount of Olives)
8. Tomb of Lazarus (backside of the Mount of Olives)
9. 3,000-Year-Old Cemetery with 150,000 Gravesites
10. Chapel of the Ascension (where Christ ascended to heaven and will return to at His second coming)
11. Pater Noster Church (where Christ taught the Lord's Prayer)
12. Absalom's Monument
13. Tomb of the Prophets (Haggai, Zechariah, and Malachi)

Mount of Olives in the Bible

1. **When King David's son, Absalom, tried to take over the kingship, David ascended the Mount of Olives as he fled Jerusalem.**

   2 Samuel 15:30: *But David went up the **ascent of the Mount of Olives**, weeping as he went, barefoot and with his head covered. And all the people who were with him covered their heads, and they went up, weeping as they went.*

2. **It's where Jesus regularly stayed when He ministered in Jerusalem.**

   Luke 21:37: *And every day he was teaching in the temple, but at night he went out and lodged on the mount called Olivet.*

3. **It's the believed place where Christ taught His disciples to pray after visiting Mary and Martha's home in Bethany (Pater Noster Church).**

   Luke 11:1: *One day Jesus was praying in a certain place. When he finished, one of his disciples said to him, "Lord, teach us to pray, just as John taught his disciples."*

4. **On the backside of the Mount of Olives (at Bethany), Christ raised Lazarus from the dead.**

   John 11:32–36: *Now when Mary came to where Jesus was and saw him, she fell at his feet, saying to him, "Lord, if you had been here, my brother would not have died." 33 When Jesus saw her weeping, and the Jews who had come with her also weeping, he was deeply moved in his spirit and greatly troubled. 34 And he said, "Where have you laid him?" They said to him, "Lord, come and see." 35 Jesus wept. 36 So the Jews said, "See how he loved him!"*

5. **Jesus descended the Mount of Olives during His Triumphal Entry (Triumphal Entry Path).**

   Luke 19:35–38: *And they brought it [colt of a donkey] to Jesus, and throwing their cloaks on the colt, they set Jesus on it. 36 And as he rode along, they spread their cloaks on the road. 37 As he was drawing near—already on the way* **down the Mount of Olives**—*the whole multitude of his disciples began to rejoice and praise God with a loud voice for all the mighty works that they had seen, 38 saying, "Blessed is the King who comes in the name of the Lord! Peace in heaven and glory in the highest!"*

   Mount of Olives

6. **Christ wept over Jerusalem from the Mount of Olives (Church of Dominus Flevit).**

   Luke 19:41–44: *And when he drew near and saw the city, he wept over it, 42 saying, "Would that you, even you, had known on this day the things that make for peace! But now they are hidden from your eyes. 43 For the days will come upon you, when your enemies will set up a barricade around you and surround you and hem you in on every side 44 and tear you down to the ground, you and your children within you. And they will not leave one stone upon another in you, because you did not know the time of your visitation."*

7. **The Garden of Gethsemane, located at the base of the Mount of Olives, is where the suffering of Christ began.**
   - Christ's sweat became like drops of blood.

     Luke 22:39-44: *And he came out and went, as was his custom, to the Mount of Olives, and the disciples followed him. 40 And when he came to the place, he said to them, "Pray that you may not enter into temptation." 41 And he withdrew from them about a stone's throw, and knelt down and prayed, 42 saying, "Father, if you are willing, remove this cup from me. Nevertheless, not my will, but yours, be done." 43 And there appeared to him an angel from heaven, strengthening him. 44 And being in an agony, he prayed more earnestly; and his sweat became like great **drops of blood falling** down to the ground.*

   Gethsemane at the base of the Mount of Olives

   - Peter cut off the ear of the High Priest's guard.
   - Christ was arrested, and the disciples fled.

8. **Christ's return and the destruction of Jerusalem were foretold from the Mount of Olives.**

   Matthew 24:3: *As he sat on the **Mount of Olives**, the disciples came to him privately, saying, "Tell us, when will these things be, and what will be the sign of your coming and of the close of the age?"*

9. **On the top of the Mount of Olives is where Christ ascended back to heaven (Chapel of the Ascension).**

   Acts 1:9-11: *And when he had said these things, as they were looking on, he was lifted up, and a cloud took him out of their sight. 10 And while they were gazing into heaven as he went, behold, two men stood by them in white robes, 11 and said, "Men of Galilee, why do you stand looking into heaven? This Jesus, who was taken up from you into heaven, will come in the same way as you saw him go into heaven."*

10. On top of the Mount of Olives is where Christ will return at the end of the Tribulation Period.

Matthew 24:29–31: *Immediately after the tribulation of those days the sun will be darkened, and the moon will not give its light, and the stars will fall from heaven, and the powers of the heavens will be shaken. 30 Then will appear in heaven the sign of the Son of Man, and then all the tribes of the earth will mourn, and they will see the Son of Man coming on the clouds of heaven with power and great glory. 31 And he will send out his angels with a loud trumpet call, and they will gather his elect from the four winds, from one end of heaven to the other.*

Triumphal Entry Path

Zechariah 14:4: *On that day his feet shall stand on the **Mount of Olives** that lies before Jerusalem on the east, and the **Mount of Olives** shall be split in two from east to west by a very wide valley, so that one half of the Mount shall move northward, and the other half southward.*

11. At the base of the Mount of Olives lies the Kidron Valley (Valley of Jehoshaphat), where Christ will judge unbelievers at the end of the Tribulation Period.

Joel 3:2: *I will gather all the nations and bring them down to the **Valley of Jehoshaphat**. And I will enter into judgment with them there, on behalf of my people and my heritage Israel, because they have scattered them among the nations and have divided up my land.*

Revelation 14:19–20: *So the angel swung his sickle across the earth and gathered the grape harvest of the earth and threw it into the great winepress of the wrath of God. 20 And the winepress was trodden **outside the city**, and blood flowed from the winepress, as high as a horse's bridle, for 1,600 stadia [200 miles, 300 km.].*

Faith Lesson from the Mount of Olives

1. Christ's return on the Mount of Olives is where everything culminates and flips. Righteousness becomes dominant, and evil bows its knees.
2. We will return with Christ in power and great glory. What a hope we believers have in Christ.
3. We will reign with Christ for 1,000 years from Jerusalem during Christ's Millennial Reign.

Graves on the Mount of Olives

4. Because of our hope as believers, are we motivated to serve Christ and live for Him?

Journal/Notes:

Pater Noster Church

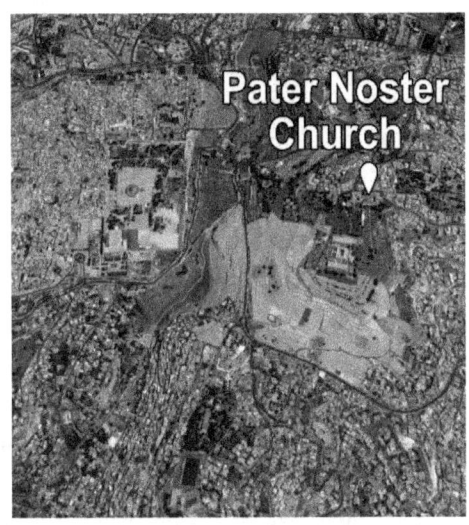

Location

1. The Church of Pater Noster is located on the top of the Mount of Olives, just below the Chapel of the Ascension.
2. It is part of a Carmelite monastery, also known as the Sanctuary of the *Eleona* (Greek for olive grove).

Historical Background

1. Pater Noster means "Our Father" in Latin.
2. The church is overseen by the Carmelite Cloistered Sisters.
3. It is located on the site of the ruins of the Eleona Basilica, built in the 4th century by Constantine.
4. The Byzantine church was built over a cave, where according to tradition, was the place Jesus taught his disciples how to pray.
5. The church was destroyed by the Persians in 614 AD, but the memory of Jesus' teaching continued to be associated with it. Some of the Byzantine church remains can be seen in the backyard outside of the present courtyard.
6. When the Crusaders arrived, the site was explicitly associated with the Lord's Prayer, so the Crusaders rebuilt part of the church in 1099.
7. In 1872, a Carmelite convent was built that preserved and restored the foundations of the 4th-century Byzantine church.
8. In 1874, the present church was built on the north side of the ruined church. A large monastery was also built next to the church and grotto.
9. A new church was partially built in 1915 but is still unfinished. The half-restored church has the same dimensions as the original, and the garden outside the three doors outlines the open-aired

area. Work on the church was abandoned in 1927 when funds ran out, leaving the base and walls uncovered.
10. It is very likely that Jesus prayed in this vicinity because He had just visited Mary and Martha's house in Bethany, a short distance away.
11. Jesus also regularly prayed on mountain tops, so the top of the Mount of Olives would be a natural fit.

Places of Interest

1. The church has 140 large ceramic plaques containing the Lord's Prayer in many languages.
2. The cave where it is believed Jesus taught about prayer is in an enclosed courtyard in front of the church and down a few stairs. The cave was partially collapsed when discovered in 1910.
3. To the left of the church's south door is an area paved with mosaics and identified as a baptistery.
4. The backyard of the church is where the original Byzantine church was located.
5. Bethany – The town of Mary, Martha, and Lazarus.
6. Top of the Mount of Olives
7. Chapel of the Ascension
8. Old City Jerusalem

The Lord's Prayer in the Bible

In the New Testament, the Lord's Prayer is mentioned two times. The first and longer form is found in Matthew 6 and is part of the Sermon on the Mount. The shorter form is in Luke 11 and is a response given by Jesus to a request by one of his disciples to teach them to pray as John taught his disciples.

1. **Jesus was asked to teach His disciples how to pray.**

   Luke 11:1–4: *It happened that while Jesus was praying in a certain place, after He had finished, one of His disciples said to Him, "Lord, teach us to pray just as John also taught his disciples." 2 And He said to them, "When you pray, say: **Father, hallowed be Your name. Your kingdom come. 3 Give us each day our daily bread. 4 And forgive us our sins, for we ourselves also forgive everyone who is indebted to us. And lead us not into temptation.**"*

2. **Christ gave examples of how we should pray.**

   Luke 11:5–13: *Then He said to them, "Suppose one of you has a friend, and goes to him at midnight and says to him, 'Friend, lend me three loaves; 6 for a friend of mine has come to me from a journey, and I have nothing to set before him'; 7 and from inside he answers and says, 'Do not bother me; the door has already been shut and my children and I are in bed; I cannot get up and give you anything.' 8 I tell you, even though he will not get up and give him anything because he is his friend, yet because of his **persistence** he will get up and give him as much as he needs. 9 So I say to you, ask, and it will be given to you; seek, and you will find; knock, and it will be opened to you. 10 For everyone who asks, receives; and he who seeks, finds; and to him who knocks, it will be opened. 11 Now suppose one of you fathers is asked by his son for a fish; he will not give him a snake*

Pater Noster Church

instead of a fish, will he? 12 Or if he is asked for an egg, he will not give him a scorpion, will he? 13 If you then, being evil, know how to give good gifts to your children, how much more will your heavenly Father give the Holy Spirit to those who ask Him?"

3. **Jesus also taught about how to pray in the Sermon on the Mount.**

   Matthew 6:5–15: *And when you pray, you must not be like the hypocrites. For they love to stand and pray in the synagogues and at the street corners, that they may be seen by others. Truly, I say to you, they have received their reward. 6 But when you pray, go into your room and shut the door and pray to your Father who is in secret. And your Father who sees in secret will reward you. And when you pray, do not heap up empty phrases as the Gentiles do, for they think that they will be heard for their many words. 8*

   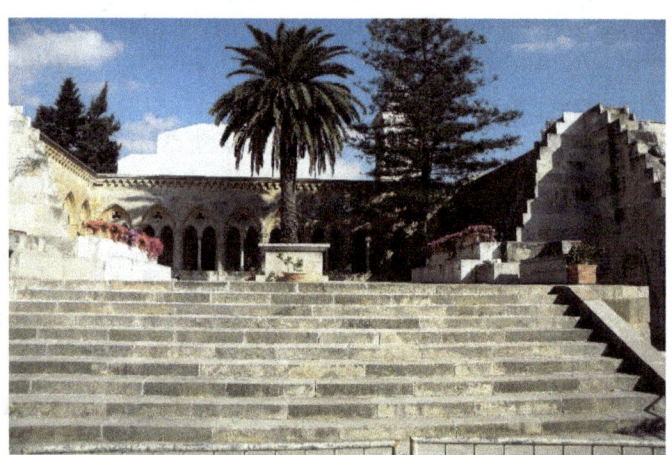

   Pater Noster Church

   Do not be like them, for your Father knows what you need before you ask him. 9 Pray then like this: **Our Father in heaven, hallowed be your name. 10 Your kingdom come, your will be done, on earth as it is in heaven. 11 Give us this day our daily bread, 12 and forgive us our debts, as we also have forgiven our debtors. 13 And lead us not into temptation, but deliver us from evil.** *14 For if you forgive others their trespasses, your heavenly Father will also forgive you, 15 but if you do not forgive others their trespasses, neither will your Father forgive your trespasses.*

Faith Lesson from the Lord's Prayer

1. Jesus prayed regularly and was in constant communion with the Father. Do we do the same?
2. We should not pray repetitious phrases but should pray in a sincere and heartfelt manner.
3. The Lord's Prayer is not an exact phrase we must pray but gives us principles of how to pray.
4. Jesus taught that we should be persistent in prayer.
5. Jesus taught that He is a good loving Father who delights in answering prayer when it's best for us and His sovereign will.

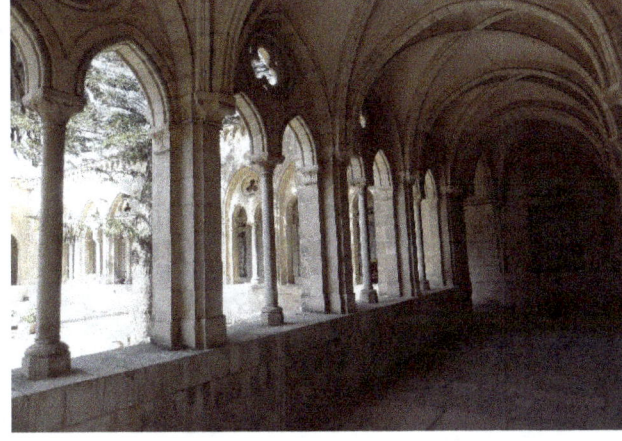
Hallway with ceramic plaques

6. Jesus taught that if we expect God to forgive us, we should forgive others as well. Do we have people in our lives we need to forgive?

Journal/Notes:

Pilate's Palace & Praetorium

Location

1. John 18:28-29: *Then they brought Jesus from Caiaphas into the Praetorium [governor's headquarters, ESV; palace of the Roman governor, NIV], and it was early; and they themselves did not enter the Praetorium so that they would not be defiled, but might eat the Passover. 29 Therefore, Pilate came out to them and said, "What accusation are you bringing against this Man?"*

2. Where was Pilate's Palace, also known as Pilate's Praetorium or headquarters, located? Some believe it was located at the Antonia Fortress. I once thought this as well. However, after much research and considering the archaeological evidence, I now believe the best option is Pilate's Palace, which is located just south of the Jaffa Gate. Pilate's Palace was first built and used by King Herod and later used by Pilate and other Roman governors.

3. Herod's Palace Fortress in Jerusalem is located adjacent to the western city wall of Old Jerusalem, in the area now encompassing the Armenian Quarter. It begins at the Kishle building and ends at the present line of the modern (Ottoman period) wall west of Zion Gate. It consisted mainly of two palace wings running north and south and had in the middle of the two ends a large garden. In the area of the Citadel of David and Jaffa Gate, just north of Pilate's Palace, Herod erected three large towers for additional protection in case of pending danger.

4. If the location of the trial of Jesus took place at Pilate's Palace, then the location of the Via Dolorosa would be different than it is today. You can see in the Google map here where the likely route could have been.
This route would have led Jesus outside the city walls to Calvary

Jerusalem Sites

(modern-day Church of the Holy Sepulchre). This route is very likely as the Romans afflicted their criminals with maximum humiliation in order to teach others not to do the same. Of course, in the case of Christ, He was entirely innocent, and the Jews and the Romans were the actual criminals.

Historical Background

1. Herod's Palace at Jerusalem was built in the last quarter of the 1st century BC by Herod the Great, King of Judea, from 37 to 4 BC. It was the second most important building in Jerusalem, after the temple itself.
2. Pilate was the Roman governor of Judea, appointed by the emperor of Rome. He lived in Caesarea, the capital of the Roman province of Judea, but when he was in Jerusalem, he resided at Herod's Palace, which served as the praetorium, or governor's palace.
3. As mentioned, some believe Pilate's Palace was in the Antonia Fortress. This belief seems to be based on the idea that the Roman governor would have had his residence inside the barracks of the Antonia Fortress. However, this is an incorrect understanding of the geography and topography of the crucifixion account. Underneath the Antonia Fortress is a Roman period stone pavement found in the structure and associated with the "stone pavement" at the Praetorium mentioned in the Trial of Jesus story in John 19:13. However, the pavement in the Antonia Fortress is from the 2nd century AD when the Roman emperor, Hadrian, rebuilt much of Jerusalem. Ancient sources and accounts such as Josephus and Philo relate that the Praetorium of Jerusalem was the former palace of Herod the Great. At the Praetorium, Jesus was standing on the "Pavement" while Pilate took his place at the bema or "judgment seat" (John 19:8-13).

Trial Location

4. As mentioned, according to reliable sources, the governor's residence in Jerusalem was the complex of the former palace of Herod the Great, which was located on the western side of the current Old City of Jerusalem. Josephus related that the Roman governor, Florus, took up residence in Jerusalem at the former palace of Herod the Great, where the bema was located. Philo also indicated that the Praetorium was in the palace of Herod since that is where Pilate initially installed the golden shields for Tiberius. The Gospel of Mark records that at the trial of Jesus, the Roman soldiers took Jesus into the palace, which is the Praetorium (Mark 15:16).

Judgement platform where Christ was tried and condemned

5. Because of archaeological excavations, the Praetorium and its pavement, the bema, or judgment seat, and one of the gates can be seen today. These provide a historical background context to the trial of Jesus account and demonstrate the accuracy of the Gospel stories of this event.

6. Excavations dating from 1999–2000, underneath an abandoned Ottoman-period prison known as the Kishle, which is part of the Tower of David complex, Israel Antiquities Authority archaeologist Amit Re'em uncovered the foundation walls and sewage system of Herod's Palace in Jerusalem. Tours can be taken via the Tower of David Museum that will showcase these findings.

7. The Jewish historian Josephus tells us that Herod's Palace Complex in Jerusalem was built in the last quarter of the first century BC and was comprised of a palace that had two wings and was divided by pools and gardens. It was protected by three large towers on the northwestern corner of the complex. Excavations carried out by different archaeological teams since the 1960s have uncovered various remains of the palace foundations. However, very little has been found of the actual walls and building itself. This presents no problem and can easily be accounted for due to

the many destructions of Jerusalem over the centuries.

8. Using a similar construction style as Herod's Temple, Herod's Palace was constructed on an elevated platform of retaining walls rising 13 to 16 feet (4.5 m) above ground level. Its measurements consisted of about 1,000 feet long (304 m), running north and south by 180 feet wide (56 m) running east to west. As mentioned, it consisted of two main buildings, each with its own banquet halls, baths, and accommodations for hundreds of guests. The two wings were named after Agrippa and Caesar. In the center of the palace were gardens with porticoes, statues, idols, and so forth. The grounds included groves, canals, and ponds fitted with bronze fountains. The praetorium at the Palace was, after Herod's death, the official residence of the Roman governors when they came to

Jerusalem during major Jewish festivals. For this reason, this site was most likely where Pontius Pilate resided and the place where the trial of Jesus of Nazareth took place.

9. In addition to a Roman cohort (about 400–500) of soldiers that were stationed at the Antonia Fortress, there was a substantial number of Roman soldiers stationed at Pilate's Palace Complex. There were also Roman soldier encampments around the city when needed as well.

10. There was a gate leading out of the Palace Complex on the western side of the palace for security purposes. This gate also served as an escape route that Herod and others would have used if the palace was attacked from within Jerusalem. It was in this area that Simon of Cyrene was arriving from the open country and was obligated to carry the cross of Christ. There was no open country access around the Antonia Fortress, so this is another big piece of evidence that Pilate's Palace is the authentic site of the trial of Jesus.

Places of Interest
1. Pilate's Palace
2. Gate Entrance Between Pilate's Palace and Stone Pavement
3. Preserved Stone Pavement

Jerusalem Sites

4. Bema Seat – Judgment Seat
5. Outside Pilate's Palace – Open Country
6. Jaffa Gate
7. Citadel of David
8. Three Towers Herod Erected
9. Likely Route of the True Via Dolorosa

Pilate's Palace in the Bible

1. **Jesus was brought before Pilate outside Pilate's Palace by the Jewish leaders.**

   John 18:28–29: *Then they brought Jesus from Caiaphas into the Praetorium [governor's headquarters, ESV; palace of the Roman governor, NIV], and it was early; and they themselves did not enter the Praetorium, so that they would not be defiled, but might eat the Passover. 29 Therefore, Pilate came out to them and said, "What accusation are you bringing against this Man?"*

2. **The Jewish leaders seek the death penalty for Jesus by crucifixion.**

   Trial Location

   John 18:30–31: *They answered and said to him, "If this Man were not a criminal, we would not have handed Him over to you." 31 So Pilate said to them, "Take Him yourselves, and judge Him according to your law." The Jews said to him, "We are not permitted to put anyone to death." 32 This happened so that the word of Jesus which He said, indicating what kind of death He was going to die, would be fulfilled.*

3. **Pilate talks with Jesus inside his palace.**

   John 18:33: *Therefore, Pilate entered the Praetorium again, and summoned Jesus and said to Him, "You are the King of the Jews?" 34 Jesus answered, "Are you saying this on your own, or did others tell you about Me?"*

4. **Pilate comes outside his palace and speaks again with the Jewish leaders.**

   John 18:38: *And after saying this, he came out again to the Jews and said to them, "I find no grounds at all for charges in His case.*

5. **Pilate has Jesus flogged inside his palace.**

   John 19:1–3: *So Pilate then took Jesus and had Him flogged. 2 And the soldiers twisted together a crown of thorns and placed it on His head, and put a purple cloak on Him; 3 and they repeatedly came up to Him and said, "Hail, King of the Jews!" and slapped Him in the face again and again.*

6. **Pilate comes out again with Jesus to the Jewish leaders after flogging Jesus.**

   Stone Pavement

   John 19:4–7: *And then Pilate came out again and said to them, "See, I am bringing Him out to you so that you will know that I find no grounds at all for charges in His case." 5 Jesus then came out, wearing the crown of thorns and the purple robe. And Pilate said to them, "Behold, the Man!" 6 So when the chief priests and the officers saw Him, they shouted, saying, "Crucify, crucify!" Pilate said to them, "Take Him yourselves and crucify Him; for I find no grounds for charges in His case!" 7 The Jews answered him, "We have a law, and by that law He ought to die, because He made Himself out to be the Son of God!"*

7. **Pilate goes back inside his palace and speaks with Jesus again.**

   John 19:8–12: *Therefore, when Pilate heard this statement, he was even more afraid; 9 and he entered the Praetorium again and said to Jesus, "Where are You from?" But Jesus gave him no answer. 10 So Pilate said to Him, "Are you not speaking to me? Do You not know that I have authority to release You, and I have authority to crucify You?" 11 Jesus answered him, "You would have no authority over Me at all, if it had not been given to you from above; for this reason, the one who handed Me over to you has the greater sin." 12 As a result of this, Pilate made efforts to release Him; but the Jews shouted, saying, "If you release this Man, you are not a friend of Caesar; everyone who makes himself out to be a king opposes Caesar!"*

8. **Pilate comes out again with Jesus and speaks to the Jewish leaders.**

    John 19:13: *Therefore, when Pilate heard these words, he brought Jesus out, and sat down on the judgment seat at a place called The Pavement—but in Hebrew, Gabbatha.*

9. **Simon of Cyrene is obligated to carry Christ's cross. He is coming from outside the city when this takes place.**

    Luke 23:26: *And when they led Him away, they seized a man, Simon of Cyrene, as he was coming in from the country, and placed on him the cross to carry behind Jesus.*

Faith Lesson from Pilate's Palace

1. The Jewish leaders were responsible for crucifying Christ because they were jealous of him. They were filled with selfish ambition and cared more about themselves than God. Are we guided and motivated out of jealousy and envy? Are we more concerned about our own kingdom than the Kingdom of God?

2. Pilate had supernatural warnings from God and knew that what he was doing was wrong. However, he chose to obey the pressure of people rather than choosing the fear of the Lord. What about us? Do we often do the same and yield to the pressure of others rather than doing what is right?

3. Christ willingly went to the Cross, knowing that He had come into the world for this purpose. Have we received His gift of salvation by grace through faith?

Journal/Notes:

Pool of Bethesda & St. Anne Church

Location

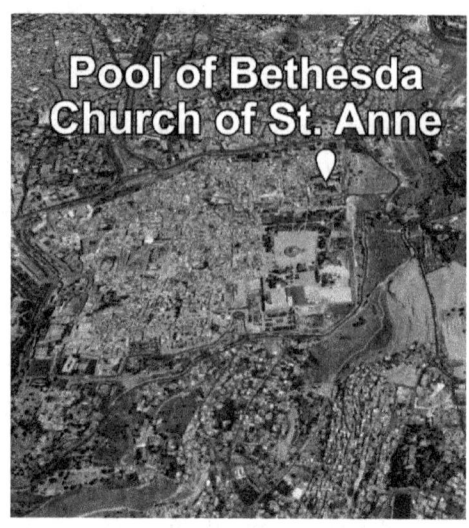

1. The Pool of Bethesda is located on the property of the Church of St. Anne.
2. It's located just inside the Lions' Gate at the eastern entrance of the Old City.
3. The Church of St. Anne is known for its extraordinary acoustics, and visitors singing hymns of praise to God can often be heard there.
4. The ruins of the Jewish, Roman, Byzantine, and Crusader eras are still well preserved at the Pool of Bethesda.

Historical Background

1. The Pool of Bethesda marks the place where a sick man was healed.
2. Bethesda means "House of Mercy" and has been associated with a place of healing for many years. According to the Gospel of John, Bethesda was a bathing pool with five porticoes or porches. Remains of part of these porticoes can still be seen today.
3. It should be noted that the pool that can be seen today is the corner of the southern pool. You will also note that it is significantly below the level of the city today. That is because Jerusalem is really a large tel. A tel is something that develops and grows in height as one civilization builds upon another. Therefore, since the time of Christ, the city has been destroyed and rebuilt many times. That is why the pool is below the surface of the city today.
4. In around 700 BC, during the time of King Hezekiah, there was a large cistern built here to capture water from the area for the use of purification and animal preparations of the temple.
5. Later, in around 200 BC, another pool was built beside the first

one. The first pool would become known as the Southern Pool and the second one as the Northern Pool.

6. These pools, also known as cisterns, were close to the Temple Mount, and there was a gate nearby known as the sheep gate that led up to the Temple Mount.

7. In the first century BC, before the birth of Christ, there were healing baths built here dedicated to the Greek false god, Asclepius.

8. When the Roman Emperor, Hadrian, rebuilt Jerusalem as Aelia Capitolina in 135 AD, he built a large temple to Asclepius and Serapis, the Greek false gods of healing and believed deity.

9. After Christianity became the state religion of the Roman Empire, the temple Hadrian had erected was torn down, and a large Byzantine Basilica was built over its ruins in around 450 AD.

Pool of Bethesda – St. Anne Church

10. Close to the Byzantine Basilica was a grotto dedicated to the believed place where Mary's parents, Anne and Joachim, lived and where Mary, the mother of Jesus, was born.

11. In 614 AD, the Byzantine Basilica was destroyed by the Persians. Later, in 1138 AD, the Basilica of St. Anne was erected over the site of the grotto believed by the Crusaders to be the birthplace of Mary, mother of Jesus. The church is dedicated to Anna and Joachim, who, according to tradition, lived here, and the site where their daughter, Mary, was born in a cave which is located under the basilica. It is one of the most preserved Crusader churches in Israel. In 1192, after the fall of the Crusader Kingdom, Saladin turned the church into a theological school for the study of the Quran, which is commemorated in an inscription above the entrance to the church.

12. The New Testament says nothing about the birthplace of Mary. However, an ancient tradition found recorded in the apocryphal

Gospel of James, which dates from around AD 150, places the house of Anne and Joachim close to the temple area.

13. Three episodes from the life of the Mary are depicted at the front of the high altar in the Church of St Anne: (1) the Annunciation on the right (2) the Descent of Jesus from the Cross in the center, and (3) the Nativity of Jesus on the left. On the left-hand side of the altar is an illustration of the education of Mary by St Anne. On the right-hand side is a portrayal of the Presentation of Mary at the temple. A flight of stone steps descends from the south aisle to the crypt. This cave is the supposed remains of the house of Anne and Joachim, and the birthplace of Mary. Here, in a tiny chapel with a domed ceiling, an altar is dedicated to the birth of Mary.

14. In 1192, after the fall of the Crusader Kingdom, Saladin turned the church into a theological school for the study of the Quran, which is commemorated in an inscription above the entrance to the church.

15. In the 19th century, the compound was given to the French Catholic Order of the White Fathers. France did extensive restoration work on the church, returning it as closely as possible to the original basilica. A second restoration was necessary after the church was damaged during the Six-Day War in 1967.

Jerusalem Sites

Places of Interest

1. Pool of Bethesda (also used as a cistern and mikvah)
   - South Pool
   - North Pool
   - Pool of Bethesda and its 5 porticoes.
   - Ruins of the Roman Temple of Asclepius (god of healing).
   - Pagan Medicinal Baths.
   - Ruins of a Byzantine Basilica.
   - Ruins of a Crusader Chapel.
2. Sheep Gate (located where the Lions' Gate is today)
3. Antonia Fortress
4. Temple Mount

5. Church of St. Anne
   - Altar at the front of the church depicting three events: (1) the Annunciation on the right (2) the descent of Jesus from the Cross in the center, and (3) the birth of Jesus on the left.
   - Crypt dedicated to Mary's birth.
   - On the right-hand side is a portrayal of the Presentation of Mary at the temple.

- Crypt dedicated to Mary's birth

Pool of Bethesda in the Bible

1. **It was a place where many came to be healed during the time of Jesus.**

   John 5:1-4: *After these things, there was a feast of the Jews, and Jesus went up to Jerusalem. 2 Now there is in Jerusalem by the sheep gate a **pool, which is called in Hebrew Bethesda**, having five porticoes. 3 In these lay a multitude of those who were sick, blind, lame, and withered, waiting for the moving of the waters; 4 for an angel of the Lord went down at certain seasons into the pool and stirred up the water; whoever then first, after the stirring up of the water, stepped in was made well from whatever disease with which he was afflicted.*

2. **A sick man had been going to this pool for healing for 38 long years.**

   John 5:5: *A man was there who had been ill for thirty-eight years.*

3. **Jesus healed the sick man.**

   John 5:6-9: *When Jesus saw him lying there, and knew that he had already been a long time in that condition, He said to him, "Do you wish to get well?" 7 The sick man answered Him, "Sir, I have no man to put me into the pool when the water is stirred up, but while I am coming, another steps down before me." 8 Jesus said to him, "Get up, pick up your pallet and walk." 9 Immediately the man became well, and picked up his pallet and began to walk.*

4. **Christ revealed to the man why he had been sick for so long.**

   John 5:9-14: *Now it was the Sabbath on that day. 10 So the Jews were saying to the man who was cured, "It is the Sabbath, and it is not permissible for you to carry your pallet." 11 But he answered them, "He who made me well was the one who said to me, 'Pick up your pallet and walk.'" 12 They asked him, "Who is the man who said to you, 'Pick up your pallet and walk?'" 13 But the man who was healed did not know who it was, for Jesus had slipped away while there was a crowd in that place. 14 Afterward, Jesus found him in the temple and said to him, "Behold, you have become well; **do not sin anymore, so that nothing worse happens to you.**"*

5. **Jesus made Himself equal with God.**

   John 5:15-18: *The man went away and told the Jews that it was Jesus who had made him well. 16 For this reason, the Jews were persecuting Jesus, because He was doing these things on the Sabbath. 17 But He answered them, "My Father is working until now, and I Myself am working." 18 For this reason, therefore, the Jews were seeking all the more to kill Him, because He not only was breaking the Sabbath, but also was calling God His own Father,* **making Himself equal with God.**

Faith Lesson from the Pool of Bethesda

1. The sick man had faith in God as he was in a place where miracles happened. Do we have faith that God can help us with our problems?

2. The sick man was patient and went to the Pool of Bethesda regularly for 38 long years. Are we patient and remain faithful even if we don't understand sickness or problems we might have?

Pool of Bethesda in Jesus' day

3. The sick man was alone as no one would help him get into the pool to be healed. Do we need others to help us with our problems because we are alone?

4. It appears some sinful activity caused his disability because Jesus told him to stop sinning, or something worse might happen. Is it possible our sicknesses could be caused by disobedience and sin in our lives?

Journal/Notes:

Pool of Siloam

Location

1. The Pool of Siloam was uncovered in 2004 during a water pipe break.
2. It is in the lower part of the City of David.
3. It is located on a main road that headed up to the Southern Gate entrance to the temple.

Historical Background

1. The Pool of Siloam was a large purification mitzvah for the Jewish holy festivals like the Passover, Feast of Tabernacles, Pentecost, etc.
2. The historian, Josephus, who lived during the time of Christ, records that up to a million Jews would make pilgrimages to Jerusalem on these holy festivals. These Jews had to be purified before entering the Temple Mount, so the Pool of Siloam was a popular place for purification.
3. It was the size of two Olympic-sized swimming pools.
4. It has the same kind of stones and style as the Southern Stairs.
5. Its water source comes from the Gihon Spring in the City of David.
6. The water runs through Hezekiah's Tunnel, which was built in 700 BC to prevent Jerusalem's water source from being cut off by the warring army of the Assyrians.

Places of Interest

1. Pool of Siloam
2. Road from the Pool of Siloam leading up to the southern entrance to the temple.
3. Southern Temple Entrance
4. Gihon Spring
5. City of David

6. Temple Mount

Pool of Siloam in the Bible

1. **Jesus performed an amazing miracle here by healing a blind man.**

   John 9:1–7: *As he passed by, he saw a man blind from birth. 2 And his disciples asked him, "Rabbi, who sinned, this man or his parents, that he was born blind?" 3 Jesus answered, "It was not that this man sinned, or his parents, but that the works of God might be displayed in him. 4 We must work the works of him who sent me while it is day; night is coming, when no one can work. 5 As long as I am in the world, I am the light of the world." 6 Having said these things, he spit on the ground and made mud with the saliva. Then he anointed the man's eyes with the mud 7 and said to him, "**Go, wash in the pool of Siloam**" (which means Sent). So he went and washed and came back seeing.*

2. **Why did Jesus make clay out of dirt and His saliva?**
   - To possibly show that He was the Creator and formed Adam and Eve out of the dust of the ground.

3. **Why was the blind man healed at the Pool of Siloam?**
   - It was a key purification place, and multitudes of people were likely present to witness the miracle.

- It was an example of living water: John 7:37–38: *Now on the last day, the great day of the feast, Jesus stood and cried out, saying, "If anyone is thirsty, let him come to Me and drink. 38 He who believes in Me, as the Scripture said, 'From his innermost being will flow **rivers of living water**.'"*

4. **Confrontation between the blind man and the religious leaders.**

    John 9:28–34: *And they reviled him, saying, "You are his disciple, but we are disciples of Moses. 29 We know that God has spoken to Moses, but as for this man, we do not know where he comes from." 30 The man answered, "Why, this is an amazing thing! You do not know where he comes from, and yet he opened my eyes. 31 We know that God does not listen to sinners, but if anyone is a worshiper of God and does his will, God listens to him. 32 Never since the world began has it been heard that anyone opened the eyes of a man born blind. 33 If this man were not from God, he could do nothing." 34 They answered him, "You were born in utter sin, and would you teach us?" **And they cast him out** [of the synagogue and fellowship].*

    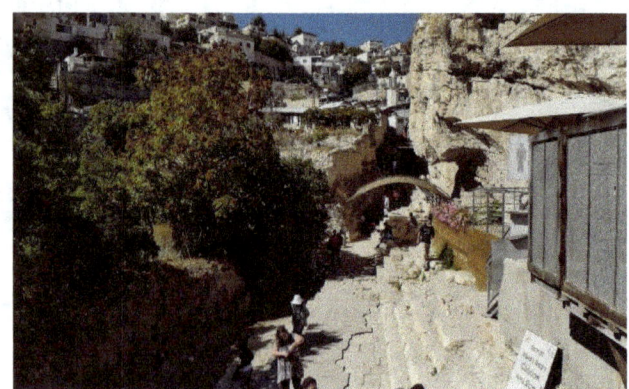
    Pool of Siloam

5. **Later, this man also received spiritual sight and became a follower of Christ.**

    John 9:35–38: *Jesus heard that they had **cast him out**, and having found him he said, "Do you believe in the Son of Man?" 36 He answered, "And who is he, sir, that I may believe in him?" 37 Jesus said to him, "You have seen him, and it is he who is speaking to you." 38 He said, "Lord, I believe," and he worshiped him.*

6. **Jesus pronounced judgment on those who refuse the light God gives them.**

    John 9:39–41: *Jesus said, "For judgment I came into this world, that those who do not see may see, **and those who see may become***

Jerusalem Sites

***blind**." 40 Some of the Pharisees near him heard these things, and said to him, "Are we also blind?" 41 Jesus said to them, "If you were blind, you would have no guilt; but now that you say, 'We see,' your guilt remains."*

Faith Lesson from the Pool of Siloam

1. The blind man received physical sight because of Jesus.
2. Later, he would receive spiritual sight as well and believe in the Lord Jesus Christ as his Lord and Savior. Have we received spiritual sight by being born-again?
3. The blind man was cast out of the synagogue, which was an enormous price to pay for a Jew. Are we willing to pay any price to follow Christ?
4. If we refuse the light God gives us, we can become spiritually blind like the Pharisees and religious leaders of Jesus' day.

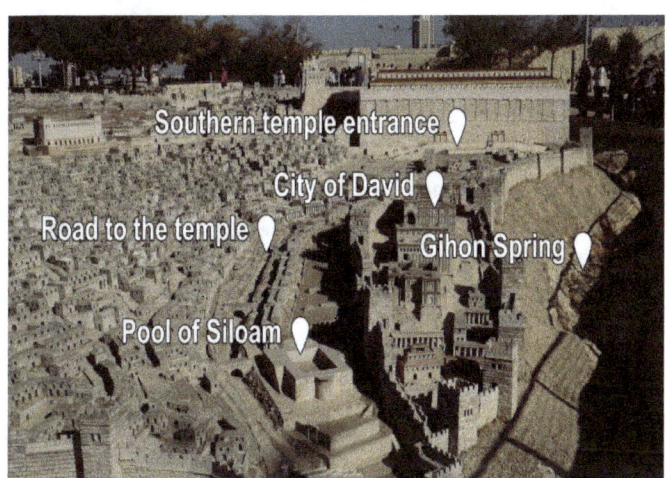

Pool of Siloam in the time of Christ

5. Contrary to what many believe, God does not always heal everyone and has more than one purpose for sickness.

Seven Biblical Purposes for Sickness and Ailments

1. Sickness for the glory of God.

    Example of the blind man Jesus healed at the Pool of Siloam: John 9:3: *Jesus answered, "It was not that this man sinned, or his parents, but that the works of God might be displayed in him."*

2. Sickness for disciplining believers living in sin.

    Example of believers who partook of the Lord's Supper with sin in their lives: 1 Corinthians 11:30: *For this reason, many among you are weak and sick, and a number sleep.*

3. Sickness to keep us humble and dependent on God.

   Example of the Apostle Paul: 2 Corinthians 12:7: *So to keep me from becoming conceited because of the surpassing greatness of the revelations, a thorn was given me in the flesh, a messenger of Satan to harass me, to keep me from becoming conceited.*

4. Sickness that allows us to glorify God in the midst of our suffering as we show our love and devotion to God despite our problems.

   Example of the life of Job: Job 13:15: *Though He slay me, yet will I trust Him.*

5. Sickness for transforming us into the image of Christ.

   Romans 8:28–29: *And we know that for those who love God all things work together for good, for those who are called according to his purpose. 29 For those whom he foreknew he also predestined to be conformed to the image of his Son.*

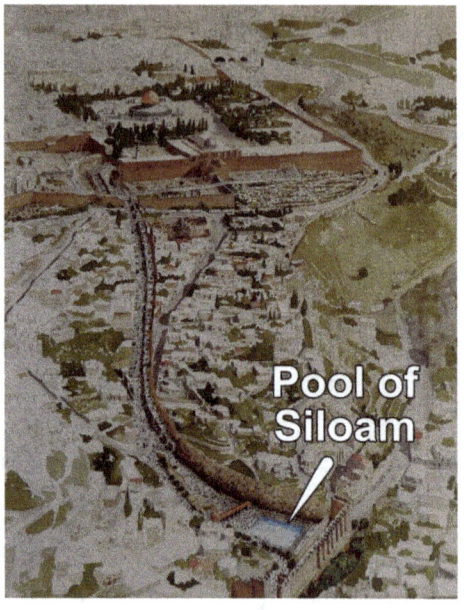

6. Sickness that will develop within us a greater appreciation for heaven and all its pleasures.

   2 Corinthians 4:17: *For our light affliction, which is but for a moment, is working for us a far more exceeding and eternal weight of glory.*

7. Sickness unto death.

   Eventually, we're all going to die regardless of what happens: example of the Prophet Elisha.

Journal/Notes:

Jerusalem Sites

Temple Mount Overview

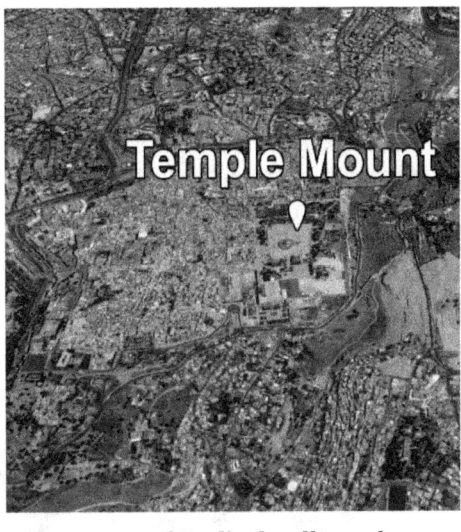

Location

1. The Temple Mount is located on the eastern side of Old City Jerusalem.
2. It occupies 1/6 of the current city.
3. It's 35 acres (14 hectares) in size, the equivalent of 35 football fields.

Historical Background

1. The Temple Mount has played a "center stage" role for much of Israel's history and has functioned as the center of God's dwelling place and ministry on this earth.
2. It will play a key part during the Millennial Reign of Christ on the earth as well.
3. God has chosen to focus His presence and attention here like a laser beam from heaven like no other place.
4. First Temple: the temple Solomon built.
5. Second Temple: the temple Zerubbabel oversaw after the deportation and return of the Jews.
6. King Herod's Temple: it would seem like this would be called the Third Temple, but because the Second Temple wasn't destroyed by enemies, but that Herod built over it a new temple and then removed the old one inside, it's still referred to as the Second Temple.
7. Some believe that the Antonia Fortress encompassed all the current Temple Mount and that the original Temple Mount was in the City of David. However, Scripture clearly states that at the dedication of the temple that Solomon built that the Ark of the covenant was brought "**out of the City of David**" to the temple. *"Then Solomon assembled to Jerusalem the elders of Israel and all the heads of the tribes, the leaders of the fathers' households of the sons of Israel, to **bring up the ark of the covenant of the Lord out***

of the City of David, which is Zion" (2 Chronicles 5:2). If the Ark was brought out of the City of David to the temple, then the temple couldn't have been in the City of David.

Places of Interest

1. Temple Mount
2. Archaeological, historical, and eyewitness accounts place the location of the first and second temples directly on top of the Dome of the Rock.
3. Western Wall
4. Eastern Gate
5. Southern Stairs
6. Antonia Fortress
7. Royal Stoa – Location close to where Pentecost likely took place.

The Temple Mount in the Bible

1. The Temple Mount is also called Mount Moriah and was the place where Abraham was to sacrifice his son, Isaac, to God.

Genesis 22:1–2: *After these things God tested Abraham and said to him, "Abraham!" And he said, "Here am I." 2 He said, "Take your son, your only son Isaac, whom you love, and go to the land of **Moriah**,*

Jerusalem Sites

and offer him there as a burnt offering on one of the mountains of which I shall tell you."

2. **King David purchased the original Temple Mount when it was a threshing floor in order to build an altar to the Lord.**

    1 Chronicles 21:18: *Now the angel of the LORD had commanded Gad to say to David that David should go up and raise an altar to the LORD on the threshing floor of Ornan [also called Araunah] the Jebusite.*

3. **King Solomon then built the temple in this exact location.**

    2 Chronicles 3:1: *Then Solomon began to build the house of the LORD in Jerusalem on Mount Moriah, where the LORD had appeared to David his father, at the place that David had appointed, on the threshing floor of Ornan the Jebusite.*

4. **During the dedication of Solomon's temple, the glory of the Lord filled it in such a way that the priests had to suspend their activities until God's glory subsided.**

    1 Kings 8:10–11: *And when the priests came out of the Holy Place, a cloud filled the house of the LORD, 11 so that the priests could not stand to minister because of the cloud, for the glory of the LORD filled the house of the LORD.*

    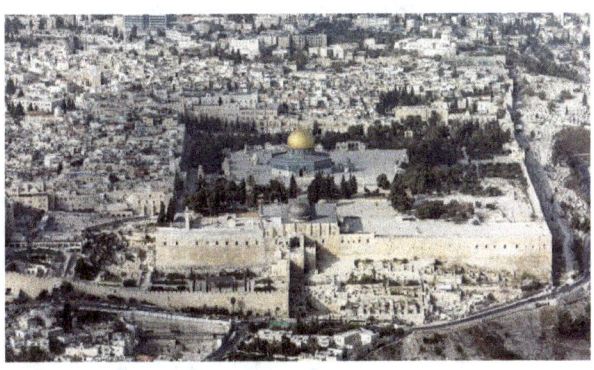
    Temple Mount

5. **The prophets spoke to the nation of Israel from the Temple Mount.**

6. **The first temple was destroyed in 586 BC by Babylon because of Israel's continued disobedience to God.**

    2 Kings 24:10: *At that time the servants of Nebuchadnezzar king of Babylon came up to Jerusalem, and the city was besieged.*

7. **The temple was rebuilt again from 535-515 BC under Zerubbabel.**

    Ezra 6:3: *In the first year of Cyrus the king, Cyrus the king issued a decree: Concerning the house of God at Jerusalem, let the house be rebuilt, the place where sacrifices were offered, and let its foundations be retained. Its height shall be sixty cubits and its breadth sixty cubits.*

8. **Nehemiah rebuilt the wall of Jerusalem in 444 BC.**

    Nehemiah 2:17: *Then I said to them, "You see the trouble we are in, how Jerusalem lies in ruins with its gates burned. Come, let us build the wall of Jerusalem, that we may no longer suffer derision."*

9. **The Temple Mount was enlarged enormously by King Herod in 19 BC to the size it is today.**

    God, in His sovereignty, made the Temple Mount large enough to handle the crowds Jesus would teach, the 3,000 saved at Pentecost, the 5,000 saved in Acts 4, and a place the Early Church could meet and grow in.

10. **Herod also made the temple more beautiful than any before it, and it was three times bigger than the current Dome of the Rock.**

11. **Zachariah received the vision of having a son (John the Baptist) while serving at the temple.**

    Luke 1:13: *But the angel said to him, "Do not be afraid, Zechariah, for your prayer has been heard, and your wife Elizabeth will bear you a son, and you shall call his name John."*

12. **Jesus was dedicated to the Lord at the temple.**

    Luke 2:22: *And when the time came for their purification according to the Law of Moses, they brought him up to Jerusalem to present him to the Lord.*

    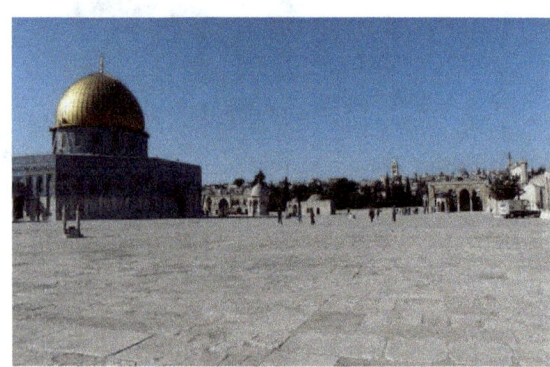

    Temple Mount

13. **At the age of 12, Jesus appeared and dialogued with the religious leaders at the temple.**

    Luke 2:46–47: *After three days they found him in the temple, sitting among the teachers, listening to them and asking them questions. 47 And all who heard him were amazed at his understanding and his answers.*

Jerusalem Sites

14. **The temple was where Christ was tempted by the Devil to throw himself down headlong.**

    Luke 4:9–12: *And he took him to Jerusalem and set him on the pinnacle of the temple and said to him, "If you are the Son of God, throw yourself down from here, 10 for it is written, "He will command his angels concerning you, to guard you,' 11 and "On their hands they will bear you up, lest you strike your foot against a stone.'" 12 And Jesus answered him, "It is said, 'You shall not put the Lord your God to the test.'"*

15. **Christ taught at the temple on a frequent basis.**

    Luke 19:47: *And he was teaching daily in the temple.*

16. **Christ drove out the moneychangers on the Temple Mount.**

    Mark 11:15–17: *And they came to Jerusalem. And he entered the temple and began to drive out those who sold and those who bought in the temple, and he overturned the tables of the money-changers and the seats of those who sold pigeons. 16 And he would not allow anyone to carry anything through the temple. 17 And he was teaching them and saying to them, "Is it not*

    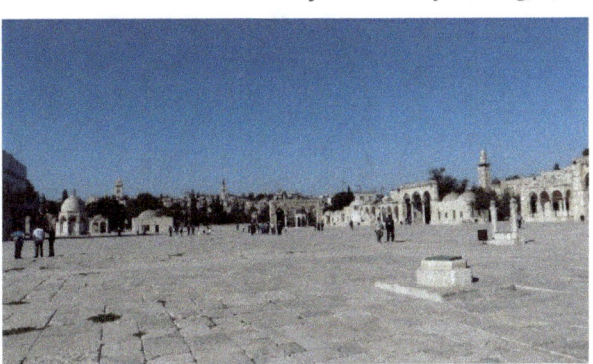
    Temple Mount

    written, 'My house shall be called a house of prayer for all the nations'? But you have made it a den of robbers."

17. **Christ was tried before Pilate next to the Temple Mount at the Antonia Fortress.**

18. **Next to the Temple Mount, at the Southern Stairs, is the likely place where Pentecost took place, 3,000 were saved, and the Early Church was born.**

    Acts 2:41: *Then those who gladly received his word were baptized; and that day about three thousand souls were added to them.*

19. **A lame man was healed on the Temple Mount by Peter and John, causing 5,000 men to be saved.**

    Acts 3:1–8: *Now Peter and John were going up to the temple at the* hour of prayer, the ninth hour. 2 And a man lame from birth was being carried, whom they laid daily at the gate of the temple that is called the Beautiful Gate to ask alms of those entering the temple. 3 Seeing Peter and John about to go into the temple, he asked to receive alms. 4 And Peter directed his gaze at him, as did John, and said, "Look at us." 5 And he fixed his attention on them, expecting to receive something from them. 6 But Peter said, "I have no silver and gold, but what I do have I give to you. In the name of Jesus Christ of Nazareth, rise up and walk!" 7 And he took him by the right hand and raised him up, and immediately his feet and ankles were made strong. 8 And leaping up he stood and began to walk, and entered the temple with them, walking and leaping and praising God.

Acts 4:4: *But many of those who had heard the word believed, and the number of the men came to about five thousand.*

20. **The Temple Mount became the meeting place of the Early Church.**

Temple Mount

Acts 2:46–47: *And day by day, attending the temple together and breaking bread in their homes, they received their food with glad and generous hearts, 47 praising God and having favor with all the people. And the Lord added to their number day by day those who were being saved.*

21. **Close to the Temple Mount, Stephen was martyred (Acts 7).**
22. **Because Israel rejected Christ, their Messiah, Jerusalem, and the Temple Mount were destroyed in 70 AD by the Romans.**

Luke 19:41–44: *And when he drew near and saw the city, he wept over it, 42 saying, "Would that you, even you, had known on this day the things that make for peace! But now they are hidden from your eyes. 43 For the days will come upon you, when your enemies will set up a barricade around you and surround you and hem you in on every side 44 and tear you down to the ground, you and your*

Jerusalem Sites

children within you. And they will not leave one stone upon another in you, because you did not know the time of your visitation.

23. **The Anti-Christ will commit the abomination of desolation on the Temple Mount during the middle of the Tribulation Period.**

    2 Thessalonians 2:3–4: *Let no one in any way deceive you, for it will not come unless the apostasy comes first, and the man of lawlessness is revealed, the son of destruction, 4 who opposes and exalts himself above every so-called god or object of worship,* **so that he takes his seat in the temple of God,** *displaying himself as being God.*

24. **Christ will reign from the Temple Mount (along with believers) for 1,000 years after the Tribulation Period.**

    Revelation 20:6: *Blessed and holy is the one who shares in the first resurrection! Over such the second death has no power, but they will be priests of God and of Christ, and they will* **reign with him for a thousand years.**

Temple Mount

Faith Lesson from the Temple Mount

1. In the Old Testament, the temple was a focal place where God dwelt. In the New Testament, believers are now the temple in which God dwells.

    1 Corinthians 3:16–17: *Do you not know that you are God's temple and that God's Spirit dwells in you? 17 If anyone destroys God's temple, God will destroy him. For God's temple is holy, and you are that temple.*

2. What kind of temple are we?

Journal/Notes:

Temple Mount Southern Stairs

Location

The Southern Stairs are located at the southern part of the Temple Mount at the Davidson Center.

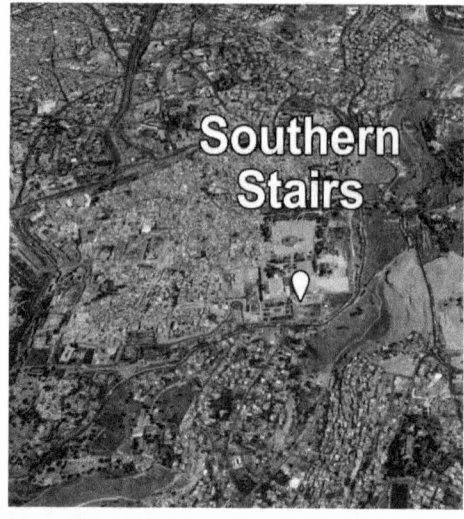

Historical Background

1. The Southern Stairs were the main entrance to the Temple Mount during the time of Christ.
2. King Herod had them redone and made them staggered so no one could enter the presence of God without being thoughtful in the process.
3. The width of the stairs was hundreds of feet wide, so they provided plenty of space for congregating and teaching.
4. They were the main access to the temple from the City of David and the city's western area, where most of the population lived.
5. Multitudes arrived at the Southern Stairs by using a main road (Herodian St.) that connected the Pool of Siloam to the Temple Mount.
6. The Pool of Siloam was a massive mikvah at the lower part of the City of David that the Jews used for purification purposes before entering the Temple Mount.
7. There were also many purification mikvahs at the base of the Southern Stairs as well (around 48 total).
8. The Southern Stairs were also called "The Rabbis' Stairs" or the "Teaching Stairs" as rabbis taught their disciples on them.
9. There is no doubt Jesus would have walked on these stairs and taught His disciples here. It's also likely that the young Apostle Paul sat here under the teaching of Gamaliel (Acts 22:3).
10. The stairs were cut out of the bedrock of the mountain, and part of them can still be seen today.

Jerusalem Sites

11. It's also likely that Pentecost took place or ended up here.

Places of Interest

1. Southern Stairs
2. Royal Stoa – Large public meeting building on the south side of the Temple Mount just above the Southern Stairs.
3. Southern Stair entrance doors to the Temple Mount.
4. Crusader Tower
5. Original Stairs
6. Temple Mount
7. Upper Room

8. Pool of Siloam
9. Road (Herodian St.) from the Pool of Siloam to the Southern Stairs.
10. Mikvahs by the Southern Stairs.
11. City of David
12. Jerusalem in the time of Christ.

The Southern Stairs and Pentecost in the Bible

1. Pentecost means 50.
2. Fifty days after Passover, the Feast of Weeks, also known as the beginning of the harvest, was celebrated. At this feast, the Jews

were to give God the first part of their harvest.

3. Pentecost also marks 50 days from the time the Israelites left Egypt and arrived at Mount Sinai, where God gave them the 10 Commandments and the Law.

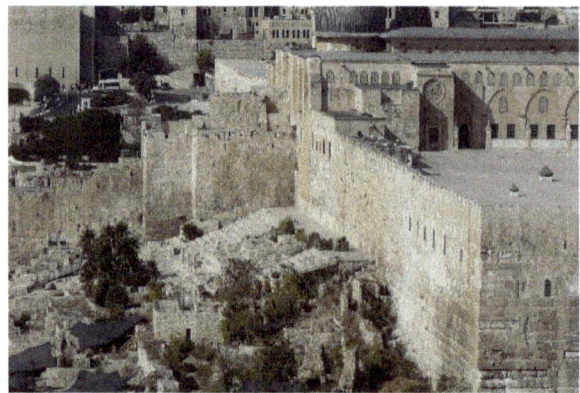
Southern Stairs

4. Pentecost happened 50 days after Passover. There were 40 days from the resurrection of Christ to His ascension, and then 10 days from Christ's ascension to Pentecost, for a total of 50 days.

5. Interestingly, the Jewish nation was born at Mount Sinai 50 days after leaving Egypt, and the Church was born at Pentecost 50 days after Christ's resurrection.

Reasons why Pentecost could have happened at the Southern Stairs.

1. **It is unlikely that all of Pentecost took place in the Upper Room as a large multitude gathered and witnessed this astounding event. The Upper Room couldn't have handled such a large crowd of 15,000–30,000.**

   Acts 2:1–6: *When the day of Pentecost arrived, they were all together in one place. 2 And suddenly there came from heaven a sound like a mighty rushing wind,* **and it filled the entire house** *where they were sitting. 3 And divided tongues as of fire appeared to them and rested on each one of them. 4 And they were all filled with the Holy Spirit and began to speak in other tongues as the Spirit gave them utterance. 5 Now there were dwelling in Jerusalem Jews, devout men from every nation under heaven. 6* **And at this sound the multitude came together**, *and they were bewildered, because each one was hearing them speak in his own language.*

   Acts 2:14: *But Peter, standing with the eleven, lifted up his voice and addressed them:* **"Men of Judea and all who dwell in Jerusalem**, *let this be known to you, and give ear to my words."*

Jerusalem Sites

2. **Scripture says the coming of the Holy Spirit filled a house; it doesn't mention the Upper Room.**
3. **The temple is referred to as the House of the Lord, or just house, in many places in the Bible.**

   John 2:17: *The Zeal for your **house** will consume me.*

   House can also refer to just a covered area as well.

   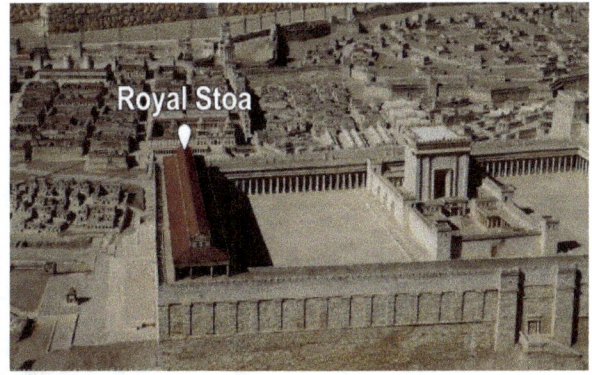

   At the southern side of the Temple Mount, just above the Southern Stairs, was the **Royal Stoa**. It was a public meeting place with a large roof. This could have been a likely place where Pentecost began.

4. **The coming of the Holy Spirit happened at nine in the morning, which was the time of morning prayers at the temple. The disciples regularly went to the temple at the times of prayer.**

   Acts 2:15: *For these people are not drunk, as you suppose, since it is only the third hour [9:00 am] of the day.*

   Acts 3:1: *Now Peter and John were going up to the temple at the **hour of prayer**, the ninth hour.*

5. **Many scholars say that Jerusalem swelled to around 150,000 people or more during the Passover in Christ's time.**
6. **The Temple Mount and Southern Stair area could easily have handled the large crowd of 15,000–30,000 who gathered at Pentecost.**
7. **Acts 2:41 says 3,000 were saved and baptized. At the Southern stairs are mikvah cleansing pools that could have been used to baptize those saved.**
8. **The Southern part of the Temple Mount would have been a natural place for Pentecost to happen as it was a center of public activities.**
9. **In summary, if Pentecost did start at the Upper Room, it quickly moved to an outside area close to the Temple Mount**

as the Upper Room couldn't have handled 15,000–30,000 people. The Southern Stair area had all the mikvahs necessary for baptizing and space to handle such a large crowd.

Faith Lesson from the Southern Stairs and Pentecost

1. Pentecost is a fulfillment of many Old Testament prophecies.
2. It's amazing to see the many pictures in the Old Testament that are fulfilled in the New Testament.

   - The Old Testament Passover lamb is fulfilled by Christ, the New Testament Passover Lamb.
   - The Jewish nation was formally born at Mount Sinai on Pentecost, and the Christian Church was also born on Pentecost.

   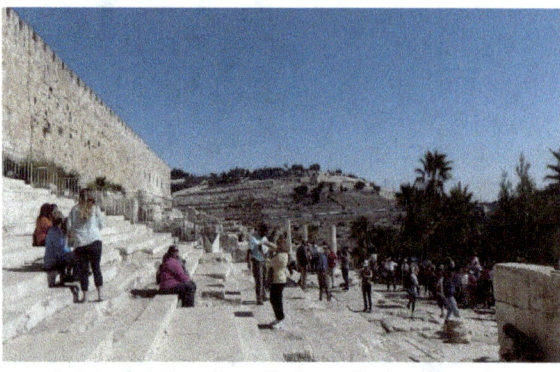
   Original stairs where Christ walked and taught

   - The Passover lamb was sacrificed on Passover afternoon at 3:00 pm, and Christ died on the Cross as our sacrifice at 3:00 pm on Passover also.
3. Do we understand how prophecy fits into validating God's Word?
4. Do we understand the meta-narrative (God's large master plan) of God's story?
5. Do I see how God gave examples and pieces to His meta-narrative in the Old Testament and then fulfilled and amplified these examples in the New Testament?
6. Have I received the Holy Spirit as a result of trusting Christ as my Lord and Savior?
7. Have I been baptized?

Journal/Notes:

Jerusalem Sites

Tomb of the Prophets

Location

1. The Tomb of the Prophets is located on top of the Mount of Olives at the beginning of the Triumphal Entry descent.
2. Just above it is a popular viewing terrace of Old City Jerusalem.

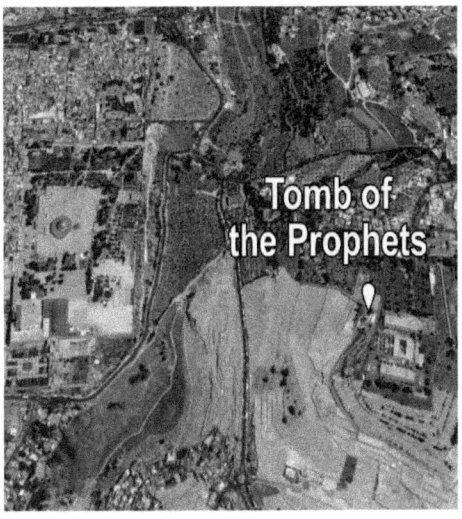

Historical Background

1. The site has 26 burial niches and two adjoining burial caves.
2. According to medieval Jewish tradition, the tombs are those of the prophets Haggai, Zechariah, and Malachi, who lived in the 6th and 5th centuries BC.
3. Haggai, Zechariah, and Malachi are the last books of the Old Testament.
4. Both Jews and Christians venerate the site as the tombs of these prophets. However, some dispute the authenticity of the tombs as being those of the prophets.
5. Inscriptions indicate that the site was also used for the burial of Christians in the Byzantine period.
6. The property is owned by the Russian Orthodox Church but is overseen by a local Arab who lives on top of the tomb.

Places of Interest

1. Tomb of the Prophets
2. Mount of Olives
3. Viewing Terrace above the tombs.
4. Triumphal Entry Path
5. Old City Jerusalem

The Role of the Prophets in the Bible

1. **A prophet was someone called by God to communicate a needed message to God's people or surrounding nations.**
2. **Prophets were also called** *seers* **because God gave them a special ability to discern and know the future.**

   1 Samuel 9:9: *Formerly in Israel, when a man went to inquire of God, he used to say, "Come, and let us go to the seer"; for he who is called a prophet now was formerly called a seer.*

3. **The prophet had two roles: (1) to speak forth God's truth and (2) to predict the future.**
4. **The prophets were to deliver God's message accurately and responsibly, and if they didn't, they were held accountable.**

   Ezekiel 33:7–9: *Now as for you, son of man, I have appointed you a watchman for the house of Israel; so you will hear a message from My mouth and give them warning from Me. 8 When I say to the wicked, 'O wicked man, you will surely die,' and* **you do not speak to warn the wicked from his way**, *that wicked man shall die in his iniquity, but* **his blood I will require from your hand**. *9 But if you on* **your part warn a wicked man to turn from his way** *and he does not turn from his way, he will die in his iniquity, but* **you have delivered your life.**

5. **A prophet sometimes had a unique appearance, i.e., Elijah, John the Baptist, etc.**
6. **A prophet often led a hard life and was generally rejected by those to whom he spoke.**

   Isaiah 6:8–10: *Then I heard the voice of the Lord, saying, "Whom shall I send, and who will go for Us?" Then I said, "Here am I. Send me!" 9 He said, "Go, and tell this people: 'Keep on listening, but do not perceive; keep on looking, but do not understand.' 10 "Render the hearts of this people insensitive, their ears dull, and their eyes dim, otherwise they might see with their eyes, hear with their ears, understand with their hearts, and return and be healed."*

   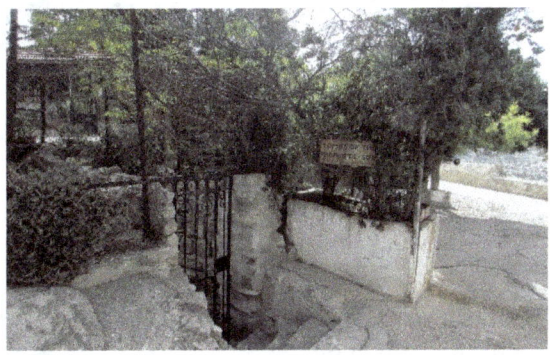
   Tomb of the Prophets entrance

7. **The prophets came from all kinds of backgrounds, used various methods, and spoke to many different audiences.**

Faith Lesson from the Role of the Prophets

1. Today, we are called to be small "p" prophets who speak God's Word to those around us like the prophets of old did.
2. Like the Old Testament prophets, those to whom we are called to speak often reject and persecute us.
3. And like the Old Testament prophets, our lives can be difficult, lonely, and challenging as a result of standing up for the truth.
4. We must know God's Word well in order to share it accurately (2 Tim. 2:15).
5. We are called to speak the truth in love, but nonetheless, we must speak the truth regardless of how others might receive it.

Journal/Notes:

The Upper Room

Location

1. The Upper Room is in a second-story building in Jerusalem that commemorates where Jesus shared the Passover (Last Supper) with His disciples.
2. It is located directly above the Tomb of David and near the Dormition Abbey on Mount Zion.
3. It is also called the Cenacle Room, which means "dining room" in Latin.
4. On the first floor of the building is King David's Tomb. It functions as a synagogue, so a head covering for men must be worn. It is divided into three sections: (1) a small synagogue room, (2) a men's viewing area of David's tomb, and (3) a women's viewing area of the tomb.
5. The location of David's Tomb is just a memorial place as Scripture says he was buried in the City of David (1 Kings 2:10).

Historical Background

1. The Upper Room is believed to be the location of the first Christian church, and evidence of this can be found in the massive stones in the apse of the church on the first floor.
2. Archaeological research reveals the Upper Room is built on top of a church-synagogue built by the first-century Jewish-Christian community of Jerusalem.
3. The location of the Upper Room has been the traditional site of the Last Supper since the 4th century AD.
4. In the 5th century, the church was referred to as "Zion, Mother of all Churches."
5. The Upper Room that pilgrims visit today was built by the Crusaders in the 12th century as part of the Church of St. Mary of

Zion. The Gothic-era columns seen today were from this time era.

6. The buildings around the Upper Room are remains of a Franciscan medieval friary from around 1335.
7. The Upper Room was transformed into a mosque by the Ottomans in 1524, and a prayer niche is embedded in the south wall, directed towards the Islam cities of Mecca and Medina.
8. The Upper Room building is currently managed by the State of Israel Ministry of the Interior.

The Upper Room

9. It's very likely that the Upper Room was used for more than the Passover meal. It could also have been where Christ appeared to His disciples after His resurrection, where Matthias was appointed the apostle to replace Judas, and where the disciples stayed while waiting for Pentecost. Some believe it's also where Pentecost happened or began.
10. It seems logical that all these events shared the same Upper Room as the man who allowed Christ to use his large room for the Passover meal was probably a follower of Christ who continued to allow the disciples to use it.

Places of Interest

1. The Upper Room
    - Crusader Remains
    - Capital on a pillar above the Crusader remains depicting events from the Last Supper.
    - Model of an olive tree symbolizing the Garden of Gethsemane, grapes symbolizing the cup of wine, and wheat symbolizing the bread.
    - Muslim prayer niche from the Ottoman period.
2. King David's Tomb under the Upper Room.
3. Temple Mount Southern Stairs

4. Royal Stoa
5. Mount Zion
6. Temple Mount
7. Zion Gate
8. City of David

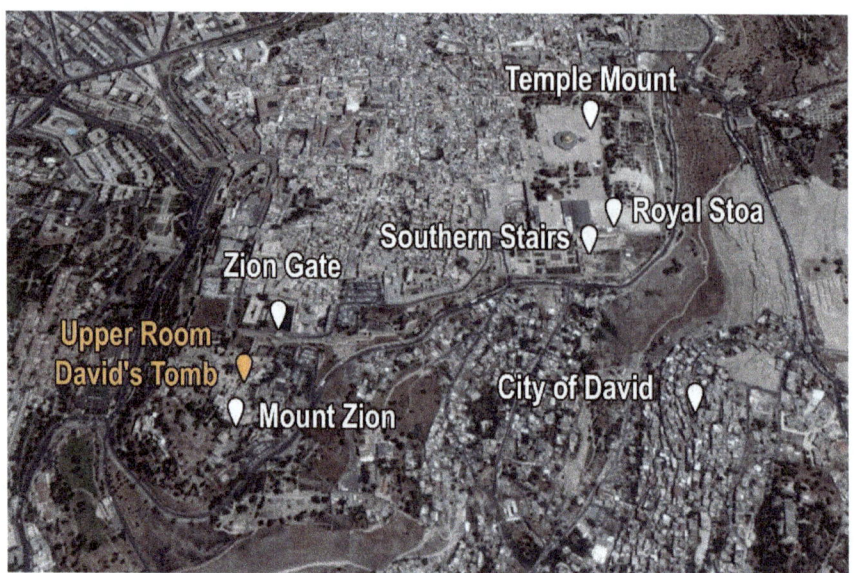

The Upper Room in the Bible

1. **Jesus ate the Passover with His disciples in the Upper Room.**

    Luke 22:11–13: *And tell the master of the house, "The Teacher says to you, 'Where is the guest room, where I may eat the Passover with my disciples?' 12 And he will show you a large upper room furnished; prepare it there." 13 And they went and found it just as he had told them, and they prepared the Passover.*

2. **The Upper Room is the likely place Christ appeared to His disciples after His resurrection.**

    John 20:19: *On the evening of that day, the first day of the week, the doors being locked where the disciples were for fear of the Jews, Jesus came and stood among them and said to them, "Peace be with you."*

3. **After Christ ascended back to heaven, the disciples went to the Upper Room, which was most likely their living quarters while they stayed in Jerusalem.**

Acts 1:13–14: *And when they had entered, they went up to the **upper room**, where they were staying, Peter and John and James and Andrew, Philip and Thomas, Bartholomew and Matthew, James the son of Alphaeus and Simon the Zealot and Judas the son of James. 14 All these with one accord were devoting themselves to prayer, together with the women and Mary the mother of Jesus, and his brothers.*

4. **It's possible that the Upper Room is where Matthias was chosen to replace Judas.**

   Acts 1:15–16: *In those days Peter stood up among the brothers (the company of persons was in all about 120) and said, 16 "Brothers, the Scripture had to be fulfilled, which the Holy Spirit spoke beforehand by the mouth of David concerning Judas, who became a guide to those who arrested Jesus."*

   Inside the Upper Room

   Acts 1:26: *And they cast lots for them, and the lot fell on Matthias, and he was numbered with the eleven apostles.*

5. **Some believe the Upper Room is where Pentecost happened or began.**

   Acts 2:1–4: *When the day of Pentecost arrived, they were all together in one place. 2 And suddenly there came from heaven a sound like a mighty rushing wind, and it filled the entire house where they were sitting. 3 And divided tongues as of fire appeared to them and rested on each one of them. 4 And they were all filled with the Holy Spirit and began to speak in other tongues as the Spirit gave them utterance.*

6. **If Pentecost did begin in the Upper Room, it quickly moved outside somewhere by the Temple Mount Southern Stairs area as a multitude gathered, and 3,000 were saved. The Upper Room couldn't have accommodated the 15,000–30,000 people who would have gathered at this event.**

Acts 2:5–6: Now there were dwelling in Jerusalem Jews, devout men from every nation under heaven. 6 And at this sound the multitude came together, and they were bewildered, because each one was hearing them speak in his own language.

Acts 2:41: So those who received his word were baptized, and there were added that day about three thousand souls.

7. **On the southern side of the Temple Mount, just above the Southern Stairs, was the Royal Stoa. It was a large covered public meeting place. This would be the most likely place where Pentecost began. Also, throughout Scripture, the temple was referred to as a house.**

   (For a more detailed look at where Pentecost happened, please see Temple Mount Southern Stairs.)

The Upper Room and Passover in the Bible

1. **The meaning of the Passover.**

   The Passover was a celebration the Israelites observed each year in remembrance of their deliverance from Egypt as slaves. The last miracle performed by God was the killing of the firstborn of all people and animals. He gave a command to the Israelites, and to the Egyptians as well, to kill a

   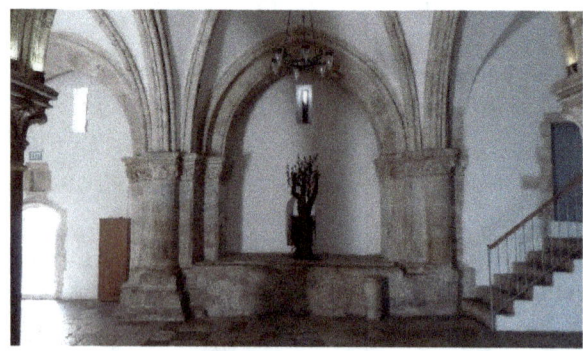
   Inside the Upper Room

   lamb and put its blood on the door mantles and doorpost of their houses. In so doing, God would pass over that home and save those inside. Christ's crucifixion during the Passover was a fulfillment of this covenant act. In the New Covenant, Christ is our Passover Lamb whose blood saves us from death and sin.

2. **The Passover meal began with Jesus washing the disciples' feet.**

   John 13:1–5: Now before the Feast of the Passover, when Jesus knew that his hour had come to depart out of this world to the Father, having loved his own who were in the world, he loved them to the

Jerusalem Sites

end. 2 During supper, when the devil had already put it into the heart of Judas Iscariot, Simon's son, to betray him, 3 Jesus, knowing that the Father had given all things into his hands, and that he had come from God and was going back to God, 4 rose from supper. He laid aside his outer garments, and taking a towel, tied it around his waist. 5 Then he poured water into a basin and began to wash the disciples' feet and to wipe them with the towel that was wrapped around him.

3. **Christ taught about true love and servanthood.**

   John 13:12–16: *When he had washed their feet and put on his outer garments and resumed his place, he said to them, "Do you understand what I have done to you? 13 You call me Teacher and Lord, and you are right, for so I am. 14 If I then, your Lord and Teacher, have washed your feet, you also ought to wash one another's feet. 15 For I have given you an example that you also should do just as I have done to you. 16 Truly, truly, I say to you, a servant is not greater than his master, nor is a messenger greater than the one who sent him."*

   The Upper Room

4. **Christ instituted the New Covenant at the Passover meal.**

   Matthew 26:26–29: *Now as they were eating, Jesus took bread, and after blessing it broke it and gave it to the disciples, and said, "Take, eat; this is my body." 27 And he took a cup, and when he had given thanks, he gave it to them, saying, "Drink of it, all of you, 28* **for this is my blood of the covenant, which is poured out for many for the forgiveness of sins.** *29 I tell you I will not drink again of this fruit of the vine until that day when I drink it new with you in my Father's kingdom."*

5. **The meaning of the bread.**
   - The bread represents Christ's body, which was broken and crucified for our sin.
   - It speaks of the bread that was made without leaven for the rapid departure of the Israelites from Egypt.

- It also represents the Israelite's utter dependence on God for their sustenance during their time in the desert and beyond.
- Christ referred to Himself as the Bread of Life and the True Manna from heaven.
- Christ now becomes our unleavened bread and sustenance.

6. **The meaning of the cup.**
   - The cup represents the blood of Christ that was shed on the Cross for the payment and forgiveness of our sins. The blood being poured out is synonymous with Christ being crucified and shedding His blood.
   - There is also wedding imagery that is used in the taking of the cup. Receiving the cup was used for confirming an Israelite marriage much in the same way our modern-day ring vows do.
   - When we receive the cup, we are confirming our marriage to Christ.

First Church Layout

Faith Lesson from the Upper Room

1. Christ gave a humbling example of true servanthood by washing the disciples' feet. What kind of a servant am I?
2. Christ introduced the New Covenant at the Passover meal. Do I understand the meaning of the bread and the cup?
3. Is Christ my sacrificial Passover Lamb, or am I separated from God and in danger of His judgment?

Journal/Notes:

Jerusalem Sites

The Via Dolorosa

Location

1. The Via Dolorosa starts (Station 1) at the original place of the Antonia Fortress, which is currently a Muslim Elementary School.
2. Station 1 is located on Lions' Gate St., several hundred yards (m.) inside the Old City west of the Lions' Gate.
3. The Via Dolorosa ends at the Church of the Holy Sepulchre.

Historical Background

1. Via Dolorosa means "The Painful Path."
2. It's the route Jesus walked as he went from His trial before Pilate at Antonia's Fortress to His crucifixion at Golgotha.
3. The Via Dolorosa has 14 stations honoring the events that took place as Christ made His way to Golgotha to be crucified.
4. In the 4th century, Byzantine pilgrims followed a similar path to the one taken today but did not stop along the way.
5. During the 8th century, the route changed; it began at the Garden of Gethsemane, headed south to Mount Zion, then returned around the Temple Mount to the Holy Sepulchre.
6. The Franciscans marked out the present route in 1342 after the Ottoman Sultan granted them authority over the Christian holy sites in Jerusalem.
7. Nine of the stations are biblical, and five are taken from traditional beliefs handed down over the centuries.

Places of Interest

1. Lions' Gate

2. Temple Mount
3. Antonia Fortress
4. Church of the Holy Sepulchre
5. Ecce Homo Arch
6. Original Stone Pavement
7. Old City wall in the time of Christ.

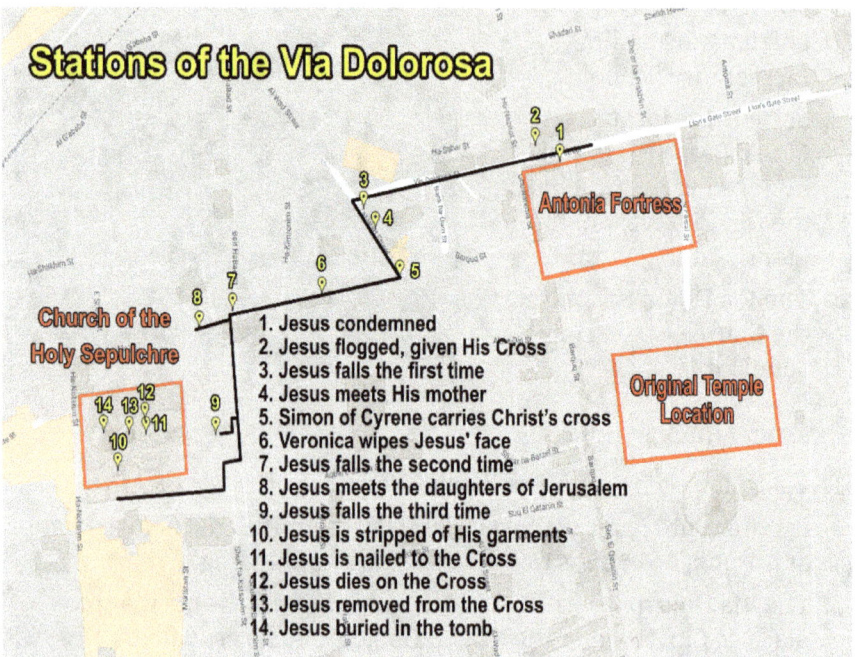

The 14 Stations of the Via Dolorosa

The stations that are biblical will have Bible verses after them clarifying the events (stations 1, 2, 5, 8, 10, 11, 12, 13, 14).

The stations that have been handed down from tradition will just list the event that is believed to have happened there (stations 3, 4, 6, 7, 9).

Stations 1–9 each have a large, rounded metal plaque with Roman numerals marking their locations. Stations 10–14 are located at the Church of the Holy Sepulchre.

1. **Station 1: Jesus is condemned to death.** Location: Umariya Muslim Elementary School, which is where the Antonia Fortress was located. Permission is needed to enter the school courtyard.

Jerusalem Sites

However, if permission is not granted, this event can be commemorated outside the school.

Matthew 27:27: *Then the **soldiers of the governor** took Jesus into the **governor's headquarters, and they gathered the whole battalion** before him.*

Luke 23: 13-25: *Pilate then called together the chief priests and the rulers and the people, 14 and said to them, "You brought me this man as one who was misleading the people. And after examining him before you, behold, I did not find this man guilty of any of your charges against him. 15 Neither did Herod, for he sent him back to us. Look, nothing deserving death has been done by him. 16 I will, therefore, punish and release him." 18 But they all cried out together, "Away with this man, and release to us Barabbas"— 19 a man who had been thrown into prison for an insurrection started in the city and for murder. 20 Pilate addressed them once more, desiring to release Jesus, 21 but they kept shouting, "Crucify, crucify him!" 22 A third time he said to them, "Why, what evil has he done? I have found in him no guilt deserving death. I will, therefore, punish and release him." 23 But they were urgent, demanding with loud cries that he should be crucified. And their voices prevailed. 24 So Pilate decided that their demand should be granted. 25 He released the man who had been thrown into prison for insurrection and murder, for whom they asked, but he delivered Jesus over to their will.*

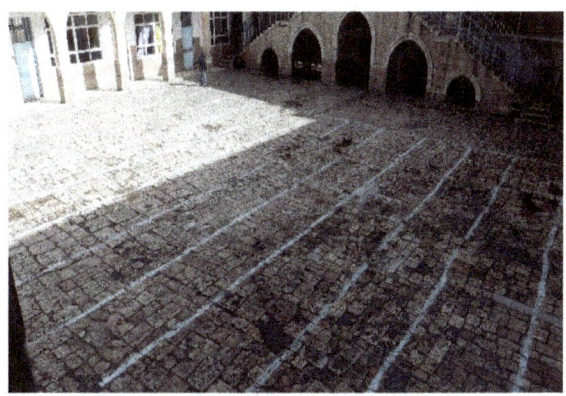
Station 1: Antonia Fortress location

2. **Station 2: Jesus is given His Cross.** Location: Church of Condemnation/Flagellation across from Station 1.

   John 19:16-17: *So he delivered him over to them to be crucified. So they took Jesus, 17 and he went out, bearing his own cross, to the place called The Place of a Skull, which in Aramaic is called Golgotha.*

   ✢ Between Stations 2 and 3 is Ecce Homo Arch (behold the man).

3. **Station 3: Jesus falls the first time.** Location: Take a left (south) at the corner of Via Dolorosa St. and Al Wad St., and Station 3 is immediately on the left.

   ⁜ In front of Station 3 are old stones on the street from the time of Christ that were discovered underneath this area and placed here for all to see.

4. **Station 4: Jesus meets His mother.** Located a short distance southward from Station 3 on El-Wad St.

5. **Station 5: Simon of Cyrene carries Christ's Cross.** Located at the corner of Via Dolorosa St. and El-Wad St. From this corner, the street takes a sharp turn to the right and then starts ascending uphill with a series of stairs along the way.

   Matthew 27:31–32: *And when they had mocked him, they stripped him of the robe and put his own clothes on him and led him away to crucify him. 32 As they went out, they* **found a man of Cyrene, Simon** *by name. They compelled this man to carry his cross.*

   Station 5: Simon of Cyrene carries Christ's cross

6. **Station 6: Veronica wipes the face of Jesus.** Location: Via Dolorosa St. up from station 5.

   According to tradition, Veronica felt compassion when she saw Jesus carrying his cross to Golgotha and gave him her veil so that he could wipe his forehead. Jesus supposedly wiped His face and then handed it back to her with the image of His face miraculously impressed upon her veil. Veronica means true image in Latin.

   ⁜ A short distance before Station 7, part of the original wall of the city can be seen. Golgotha was outside the city during the time of Christ, and this wall marks the exit out of the city.

7. **Station 7: Jesus falls the second time.** Location: On the corner of Via Dolorosa St. and Khan es-Zeit St.

8. **Station 8: Jesus meets the daughters of Jerusalem.** Location: From Station 7, take a step to the right and walk up Ma'alot E-Khanka St. a short distance.

   Luke 23:27–31: *And there followed him a great multitude of the people and of women who were mourning and lamenting for him. 28 But turning to them Jesus said, "Daughters of Jerusalem, do not weep for me, but weep for yourselves and for your children. 29 For behold, the days are coming when they will say, 'Blessed are the barren and the wombs that never bore and the breasts that never nursed!' 30 Then they will begin to say to the mountains, 'Fall on us,' and to the hills, 'Cover us.' 31 For if they do these things when the wood is green, what will happen when it is dry?"*

9. **Station 9: Jesus falls the third time.** Location: Walk back down to Station 7, take a right (south) on Beit HaBad St. Continue on Beit HaBad St. for about 75 yards (70 m.), and you will notice on the right a stairway leading to Station 9. Station 9 is the hardest to find. It's located by the Coptic Patriarchate Building, through a narrow alley.

✝ **Stations 10–14 are at the Church of the Holy Sepulchre.** Location: From Station 9, the Church of the Holy Sepulchre can be accessed two ways: (1) by a green door that leads to the courtyard of the Holy Sepulchre, (2) by returning to Beit HaBad St. and continuing south, then take a right on Shuk ha-Tsaba'im St. and follow it to the Church of the Holy Sepulchre.

Station 10–14: Church of the Holy Sepulchre

10. **Station 10: Jesus is stripped of His garments.** Location: In a room outside the church called *The Chapel of the Franks*, on the right side of the church entrance.

    John 19:23–24: *When the soldiers had crucified Jesus, they took his garments and divided them into four parts, one part for each soldier; also his tunic. But the tunic was seamless, woven in one piece from* top to bottom, 24 so they said to one another, "Let us not tear it, but cast lots for it to see whose it shall be." This was to fulfill the Scripture which says, "They divided my garments among them, and for my clothing they cast lots." So the soldiers did these things.

11. **Station 11: Jesus arrives at Golgotha and is nailed to the Cross.** Location: Just after entering the church, take a right and go up the stairs to the second level. A Franciscan altar marks Station 11.

    John 19:17–18: *And he went out, bearing his own cross, to the place called The Place of a Skull, which in Aramaic is called Golgotha. 18 There they crucified him, and with him two others, one on either side, and Jesus between them.*

12. **Station 12: Jesus dies on the Cross.** Location: Beside Station 11, a Greek Orthodox crucifixion altar marks Station 12.

    Matthew 27:45–54: *Now from the sixth hour [12:00 pm] there was darkness over all the land until the ninth hour [3:00 pm]. 46 And about the ninth hour Jesus cried out with a loud voice, saying, "Eli, Eli, lema sabachthani?" that is, "My God, my God, why have you forsaken me?" 47 And some of the bystanders, hearing it, said, "This man is calling Elijah." 48 And one of them at once ran and took a*

Mural above Station 12

sponge, filled it with sour wine, and put it on a reed and gave it to him to drink. 49 But the others said, "Wait, let us see whether Elijah will come to save him." 50 And Jesus cried out again with a loud voice and yielded up his spirit. 51 And behold, the curtain of the temple was torn in two, from top to bottom. And the earth shook, and the rocks were split. 52 The tombs also were opened. And many bodies of the saints who had fallen asleep were raised, 53 and coming out of the tombs after his resurrection they went into the holy city and appeared to many. 54 When the centurion and those who were with him, keeping watch over Jesus, saw the earthquake and what took place, they were filled with awe and said, "Truly this was the Son of God!"

Jerusalem Sites

- Beside Station 12 is a large, cracked rock believed to have been caused by the earthquake at Christ's death. On the lower level of the church, this rock can be seen as well.

13. **Station 13: Jesus' body is removed from the Cross.** Location: On the ground level of the church across from its entrance. This station is marked by a large marble slab with adornments hanging above it.

    John 19:38–40: *After these things, Joseph of Arimathea, who was a disciple of Jesus, but secretly for fear of the Jews, asked Pilate that he might take away the body of Jesus, and Pilate gave him permission. So he came and took away his body. 39 Nicodemus also, who earlier had come to Jesus by night, came bringing a mixture of myrrh and aloes, about seventy-five pounds in weight. 40 So they took the body of Jesus and bound it in linen cloths with the spices, as is the burial custom of the Jews.*

14. **Station 14: Jesus is laid in the tomb and covered in incense.** Location: In the large rotunda of the church, a large, enclosed tomb marks Station 14.

    John 19:41–42: *Now in the place where he was crucified there was a garden, and in the garden a new tomb in which no one had yet been laid. 42 So because of the Jewish day of Preparation, since the tomb was close at hand, they laid Jesus there.*

    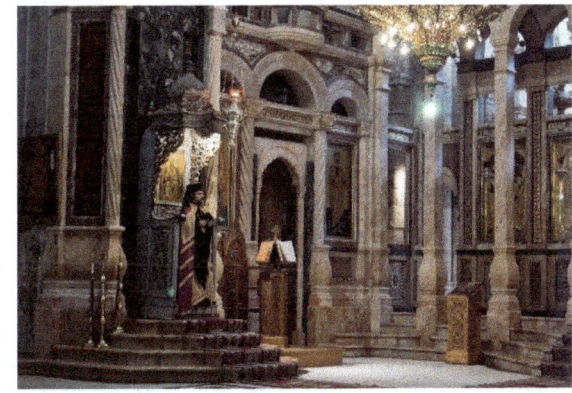
    Tomb of Jesus

    (For a more detailed look at the Church of the Holy Sepulchre, please see Church of the Holy Sepulchre.)

Faith Lesson from the Via Dolorosa

1. Roman crucifixion always took place in the most public areas as possible.
2. Jesus was led through the busy streets for maximum humiliation.
3. Christ's crucifixion happened on the day of Passover, so Jerusalem

was at its busiest time of year, and there could have easily been around 150,000 people present in the city at this time.
4. The blood lost during the floggings, the crown of thorns, and the beatings were unbearable and life-threatening.
5. Christ was so weak that Simon of Cyrene had to carry His cross most of the way to Golgotha.
6. The total time elapsed from Christ's suffering that began in the Garden of Gethsemane to His death on the cross was about 18 hours of sleepless, intense torment and pain.

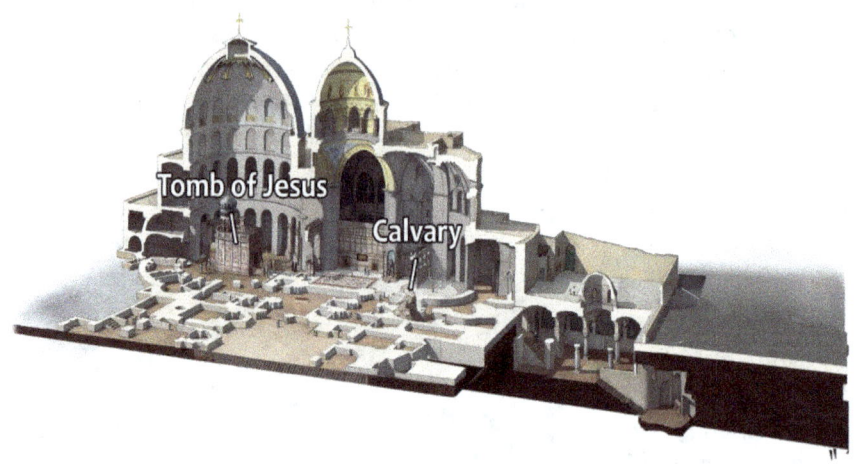

7. The physical suffering was only a drop in the bucket compared to the spiritual suffering Christ endured in order to pay for our sins.
8. Do we really understand the price that was paid for the forgiveness of our sins, the privilege we have of being right with God, and the gift of eternal life in heaven?
9. Do we warn others of the reality of the judgments of God and the price of rejecting Christ's gift of forgiveness and eternal life?
10. If we refuse to believe in the existence of a literal hell, then all Christ suffered has little meaning or purpose. This would be a horrendous slap in the face of Christ for all He did on the Cross.

Journal/Notes:

Walls of Jerusalem History

The First Walls Were Built by the Canaanites

Long before the Israelites entered the Promised Land, the Jebusites lived securely within the walls of Jerusalem. The city was blessed with natural valleys around it that made it easy to defend. The city walls and its fortress provided additional protection.

David Conquered the Jebusite City and Enlarged the City Walls

God was with David and allowed him to capture Jerusalem from the Jebusites. Later, he built stronger and additional walls to fortify the city, and it would become known as the City of David.

2 Samuel 5:6–10: *And the king and his men went to Jerusalem against the Jebusites, the inhabitants of the land, who said to David, "You will not come in here, but the blind and the lame will ward you off"— thinking, "David cannot come in here." 7 Nevertheless, David took the stronghold of Zion, that is, the city of David. 8 And David said on that day, "Whoever would strike the Jebusites, let him get up the water shaft to attack 'the lame and the blind,' who are hated by David's soul." Therefore, it is said, "The blind and the lame shall not come into the house." 9 And David lived in the stronghold and called it the city of David. And David built the city all around from the Millo inward. 10 And David became greater and greater, for the Lord, the God of hosts, was*

with him.

Solomon Added to the Walls of the City

After David died, Solomon built the Temple Mount Platform on Mt. Moriah upon the threshing floor of Araunah. Then he erected the temple upon it and added walls from the City of David to encompass the Temple Mount and temple.

Hezekiah's Broad Wall Expansion of the Western Hill

In 701 BC, the Assyrians, headed by Sennacherib, invaded Judah, the Southern Kingdom of Israel, because of their disobedience to God. According to an Assyrian stele found in the ruins of the royal palace of Nineveh, Sennacherib conquered 46 cities in Judea prior to attempting to conquer Jerusalem.

God allowed most of Judah to be conquered but protected Jerusalem because of Hezekiah's obedience to Him. As Hezekiah began to prepare for what he knew would be a terrible siege by a merciless Assyrian war machine, he had to figure out how to protect his people. This meant building new defenses.

During the time of Hezekiah, Jerusalem's urban population had grown far outside the old walls of the city and were unprotected. King Hezekiah fortified the existing walls of the city and built a new wall in a rapid manner to protect those living outside the city walls.

2 Chronicles 32:5: *He set to work resolutely and built up all the wall that was broken down and raised towers upon it,* **and outside it he built another wall**, *and he strengthened the Millo in the city of David. He also made weapons and shields in abundance.*

Hezekiah's new wall measured 22 ft. wide (7 m.) by 25 ft. high (8 m.). It was a massive undertaking and measured around 2.5 miles (4 km.) in length.

A portion of the wall was discovered in the 1970s by Israeli archaeologist Nahman Avigad and dated to the reign of King Hezekiah (716-687 BC). It was called "Hezekiah's Broad Wall" by archaeologists because of its width.

Hezekiah also built a water tunnel in order to keep the water from the Gihon Spring inside the city walls so the Assyrians couldn't cut off the water supply (2 Chron. 32:3-4). The curving tunnel is 583 yards (533 m.) long and has a fall of 12 inches (30 cm.) between its two ends. It was chiseled from both ends to the middle at the same time. It took the water from the Gihon Spring under the mountain to the Pool of Siloam below the city. Today, this water tunnel is known as Hezekiah's Tunnel.

Nehemiah Rebuilt the City Walls

When the Babylonians conquered and destroyed Jerusalem in 586 BC, they also destroyed the walls and burned the gates with fire. However, God sovereignly moved in the heart of Artaxerxes, king of Persia, to allow Nehemiah to rebuild the walls. Under his leadership and with a small Jewish population, the walls of Jerusalem were rebuilt to dimensions similar to Solomon's day.

Nehemiah 1:1–3: *Now it happened in the month of Chislev, in the twentieth year, as I was in Susa the citadel, 2 that Hanani, one of my brothers, came with certain men from Judah. And I asked them concerning the Jews who escaped, who had survived the exile, and concerning Jerusalem. 3 And they said to me, "The remnant there in the province who had survived the exile is in great trouble and shame. The wall of Jerusalem is broken down, and its gates are destroyed by fire."*

The rebuilding and repair of the wall was a miracle.

Nehemiah 6:15–16: *So the wall was finished on the twenty-fifth day of the month Elul, in fifty-two days. 16 And when all our enemies heard of it, all the nations around us were afraid and fell greatly in their own esteem, for they perceived that this work had been accomplished with the help of our God.*

Jerusalem Sites

Hasmonean Wall Addition

The Jews gained their independence from the Seleucid Empire in 164 BC, led by the Maccabees and Hasmoneans. During this time, known as the Hasmonean period (164–63 BC), Jerusalem was rebuilt along with its walls. It was built to dimensions similar to King Hezekiah's time.

King Herod Addition ~ Jerusalem of Jesus' Day

In 19 BC, the master-builder, King Herod the Great, began his life's most ambitious building project. He undertook the rebuilding of the temple and the Temple Mount on a massive scale. He took the expansion of the Hasmonean Temple Mount and extended it on three sides, to the north, west, and south. This expansion also included some additional wall construction on the north side of the city walls. The archaeology of the Temple Mount today confirms this enlargement. It would be this city layout that would exist during the time of Christ.

Agrippa I Wall Addition

Agrippa I began the construction of an additional wall of the city which was completed at the beginning of the first Jewish-Roman War in 66 AD. This would be the largest area the city walls would encompass.

The City Walls Today

In the 16th century, Suleiman decided to rebuild the city walls on much of the remains of the ancient walls that already existed. However, much of the southern part of the city walls were omitted in the new construction. They were completed in 1538 and are the walls that exist today.

Western Wall and Tunnel

Location

1. The Western Wall, also known as the Wailing Wall (because the Jews weep here during their prayers), is located on the western side of the Temple Mount.
2. The Western Wall Tunnel is accessed on the northern side of the Western Wall Plaza and runs north to the end of the Temple Mount Platform.

Historical Background

1. When the Romans destroyed the temple in 70 AD, part of the western side of the Temple Mount Platform survived. For hundreds of years prior to 1967, people prayed in the small area of the wall that could be seen at that time. However, in 1967, following the Six-Day War, Israelis excavated below the ground level of the wall and found two more stone rows. They then cleared the area around the wall to create the Western Wall Plaza that visitors see today.
2. The Western Wall is part of the retaining wall, or support wall, that Herod the Great built in 19 BC when he enlarged the Temple Mount complex in order to accommodate a larger temple and Temple Mount area. It was a massive undertaking that required exceptional and sophisticated engineering.
3. Unlike many think, the Western Wall was not part of the wall of the temple King Herod Built.

Places of Interest

1. In the Western Wall Plaza area, a walkway bridge can be seen that tourists use to access the Temple Mount.
2. The Western Wall Plaza is divided into two sections: a men's and a

Jerusalem Sites

women's section.

3. The area close to the wall is considered a synagogue, so men must wear a head covering when entering the men's section.
4. Most Jews do not enter on the Temple Mount for fear of unknowingly walking in the place where the Holy of Holies might have been. Plus, Muslims do not want them entering there as well.
5. The Western Wall Plaza is the closest large public area to the temple and Holy of Holies for the Jews. Therefore, it is their most holy site.
6. On the northern side of the Western Wall is Wilson's Arch, which is the modern name for a stone arch whose top is still visible today. It once supported a bridge that provided access to a gate that was level with the surface of the Temple Mount during the time of Jesus. Under this arch is a synagogue where Jews pray and read the Scriptures.
7. The Western Wall Plaza is only 10% of the entire western wall of the Temple Mount Platform. The majority of the wall is accessed by entering what is called "The Western Wall Tunnels." We will see that part shortly.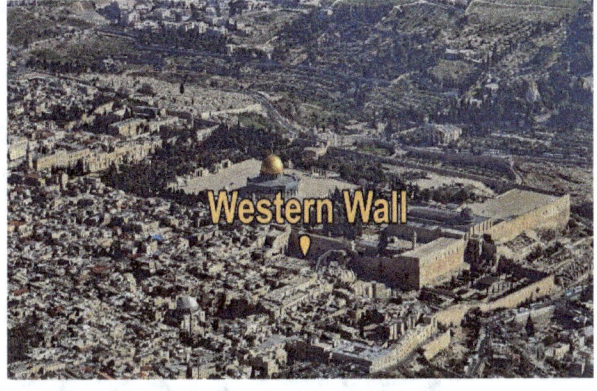
8. The entire length of the Western Wall is 1,575 ft. long (480 m.), almost a third of a mile (.53 km.).
9. On the southernmost end of the Western Wall are stones that the Romans cast down when they destroyed the city in 70 AD, under the leadership of the Roman General, Titus.
10. The broken pavement of the street that the massive stones crushed when they fell is sobering to see.
11. Burn marks remain on some of the stones as a result of fire from the Roman conquest of the city in 70 AD.
12. There are remains of shops that were part of a large shopping plaza at the southern part of the Western Wall.

13. This is the same wall that Jesus and His disciples would have seen.
14. On the Southern Stair entrance to the temple is where Jesus would have taught His disciples and entered the Temple Mount area.
15. At the southernmost end of the Western Wall is a significant stone that stood upon the uttermost southwestern corner of the Temple Mount.
    - It has words written in Hebrew that mean "The Trumpeter's House."
    - A priest would stand at this corner announcing the beginning of the Sabbath and other festival days the Jews celebrated with a loud trumpet blast.

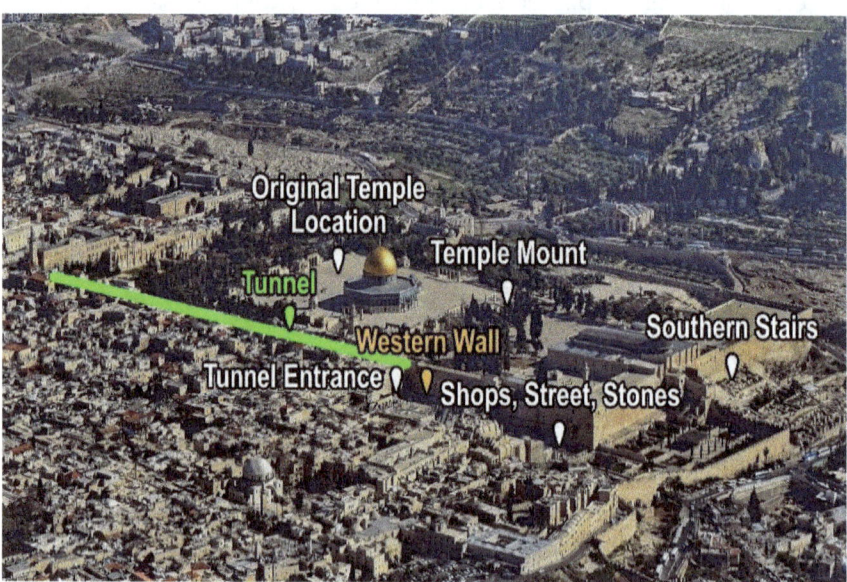

Western Wall Tunnel

1. In order to build the temple on the mountain top of Mount Moriah, there had to be erected supporting walls that could be filled in, so there was a large flat place (platform) upon which to build. King Solomon first did this when he constructed the First Temple in around 950 BC. When the temple was rebuilt under Zerubbabel (535–515 BC), this same platform was used. Later, in 19 BC, King Herod began rebuilding a new massive temple. In order to do so, he had to enlarge the Temple Mount Platform immensely. When he was done, it measured 985 ft. by 1,575 ft. (300 x 480 m.), or the equivalent of 35 football fields in size (35 acres, 14 hectares).

Jerusalem Sites

2. King Herod put 10,000 men to work and trained 1,000 priests as masons so they could work on the most sacred parts of the temple. Construction was begun in 19 BC and finished in 10 years, but the work of decoration was not completed until 64 AD.

3. The temple King Herod built on this massive Temple Mount Platform was enormous in size. Nothing in the known world at that time compared to it in size and beauty. For comparison's sake, the temple Herod built was three times the size of the Dome of the Rock (which measures 65 ft. wide by 115 ft. high, 20 x 35 m.), that can be seen today.

4. In 70 AD, six years after the temple was fully completed, the Romans burned down and destroyed the temple at Jerusalem, and it has never been rebuilt since.

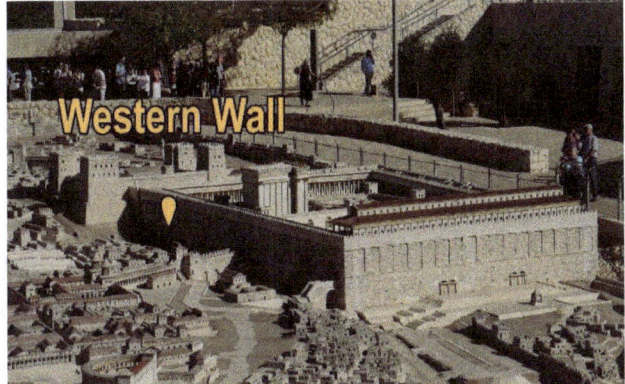
Model of the Temple Mount in Jesus' day

5. Located beside the Western Wall Tour Entrance on the left side, or northern side of the Western Wall, is a synagogue. Here Jews gather to study, read, and pray. This is one of the Jew's most holy synagogues because of its proximity to the original temple wherein the Holy of Holies resided.

6. At the beginning of the Western Wall Tunnel Tour Entrance is a room where the tour begins. Here, tour guides give an overview of the temple Solomon built, the temple Zerubbabel oversaw, and then the temple King Herod built. The history of the Western Wall is meshed in with the history of the temples that once resided next to the Western Wall.

7. Walking along the Western Wall Tunnel, what is known as the master course of stones can be seen. These are some of the first rows of cut stones that support the Temple Mount Western Wall. The largest stone found in the Western Wall measures 44 ft. (13.4 m.) in length (longer than a Greyhound bus). It's almost 12 ft. (3.66 m.) high (taller than a semi-truck trailer). Its width is 14 ft. (4.26

m.) (almost as wide as some highways). It weighs over 600 tons (equivalent to 200 elephants, or ten tanks, or two 747 jumbo jets, including the people and their luggage). There is no machine big enough today to lift it. It was carved outside the city and then placed here. The stones were carved and placed with such precision that not even a credit card will fit between the joints. By comparison, the largest stones in the Egyptian Pyramids are 15 tons.

8. We next come to what is called Warren's Gate. This is the closest place along the Western Wall to where the temple used to be. It is, therefore, according to the Jews, the holiest place in the Western Wall. Just 200 ft. (61 m.) towards the east is where the temple was originally located.

9. The bedrock of the Western Wall of the Temple

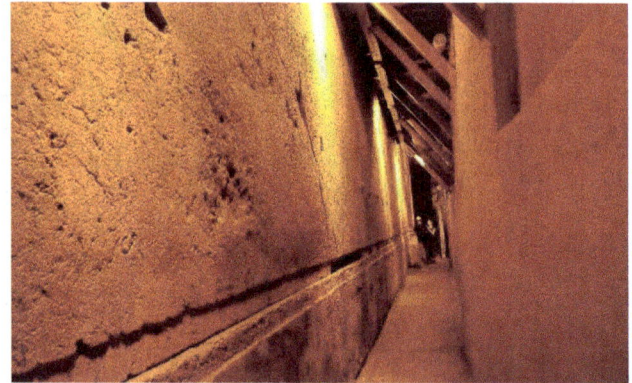

Largest cut stone in the Western Wall Tunnel

Mount can be seen as well. The masons who laid the great stones to build the Western Wall chiseled the bedrock of the mountain to make them look like they were stones, but in reality, they are the bedrock of the mountain upon which the Western Wall rests.

10. Next, the tiles of the original floor where Jesus likely walked are visible in the tunnel.
11. Continuing along the Western Wall Tunnel is a Hasmonean aqueduct built over 2,200 years ago, 200 years before Christ.
12. At the northern end of the Western Wall Tunnel is the Struthion Pool, where water was stored for use in the city of Jerusalem.

Faith Lesson from the Western Wall

1. It's sad that the closest large meeting area the Jews can get to the place where the original temple used to be located is the Western Wall, which in reality, is just part of the supporting wall of the Temple Mount.

Jerusalem Sites

2. It's sad that because of the Jew's repeated refusal to heed God's warnings to obey and follow Him that He sent judgments upon Israel and Jerusalem.
3. It's sad that because the Jews rejected Jesus as their Messiah, Jesus prophesied Jerusalem would be destroyed. This was fulfilled in 70 AD. The reality of this destruction is the overarching fact that can be seen all along the Western Wall.
4. Because of the Jew's continual disobedience to God, He prophesied that the Jews would be scattered to the four corners of the earth. This was fulfilled in 70 AD.

Western Wall & Plaza

5. God also prophesied that He would bring the Jews back to their homeland in the last days. This was fulfilled in 1948.
6. According to many passages in the Bible, God still has a plan for the Jews. He said He would bring them back to their homeland after being scattered for thousands of years. He also says that during the Great Tribulation Period that many Jews, if not most of them, will recognize that Jesus is indeed their Messiah and turn to Him in repentance.
7. Amazingly, we see the first prophecy fulfilled in that the Jews returned to their homeland and have their own country back. Many civilizations have occupied the Holy Land, but God has fulfilled prophecy in bringing the Jews back to their homeland today.
8. The stones here cry out that God's Word is true and is verifiable through the fulfillment of these prophecies.
9. At the Southern Stair entrance area of the Temple Mount is a sad but very true saying, *"The Jerusalem stone, so resilient and supple, bows to the transient follies of humankind, bearing a testimony like*

a hundred witnesses, and yet, remains silent."

10. We find in all that has happened to the Jews a powerful and sobering message for us today. Obedience brings God's blessings, but disobedience brings His discipline.

Fallen stones from the destruction of Jerusalem

1 Corinthians 10:11-12: *Now these things happened to them as an example, but they were written down for our instruction, on whom the end of the ages has come. 12 Therefore let anyone who thinks that he stands take heed lest he fall.*

Journal/Notes:

Other Sites in Jerusalem

Aish HaTorah Observation Point

Aish HaTorah's Observation Deck overlooking the Western Wall is located on top of the Aish HaTorah World Center in the Jewish Quarter and was awarded "One of the Top Ten Panoramic Views in the World." It has a 360-degree view of the most important sites in Jerusalem. From here you can see the Western Wall Plaza, the Temple Mount, Mount of Olives, City of David, Jordanian Hills, and the Judean Desert. There is also a detailed model of the original temple built by King Solomon to help visualize the magnificence of Mount Moriah in the 10th century BC.

Bethany

Bethany is known today by the name of Al-Eizariya or al-Azariya. It's located about 1.5 miles (2.4 km.) east of the Mount of Olives.

In the New Testament, Bethany was the home of Mary, Martha, Lazarus, and Simon the Leper.

Tomb of Lazarus at Bethany

Jesus regularly lodged at Bethany on His travels to Jerusalem, and it's likely He stayed with Mary, Martha, and Lazarus when doing so. He seemed to prefer staying in Bethany rather than Jerusalem (Matt. 21:17; Mark 11:11).

At Bethany, Christ performed the powerful miracle of raising Lazarus from the dead (John 11).

A feast was also celebrated in the house of Simon the leper in Bethany (Matt. 26:1–13; Mark 14:3–9).

Bible Lands Museum

The Bible Lands Museum places into historical context an exciting journey of the people of the Bible and their cultures, bringing greater appreciation and understanding of the biblical stories in the context of human history from a biblical perspective. On display are the great civilizations that rose and flourished in this region: Sumer, Egypt, Babylon, Assyria, Canaan, Persia, Greece, and Rome, who were responsible for the advancements of Western civilization. Established in 1992, the Bible Lands Museum is situated in the city's cultural heart and holds a unique collection dating back to the beginning of written history. There is an audio guide in English and Hebrew.

The Burnt House Museum

This museum is an excavated house from the Second Temple period located six meters below the current street level of the Jewish Quarter in the Old City of Jerusalem. It was inhabited by a wealthy priestly family at the end of the Second Temple period and is believed to have been set on fire during the Roman destruction of Jerusalem in 70 AD. In the early Roman period, this area was the "Upper City," located on the higher hill west of the temple. While in the museum, a visitor can view a short film about the Roman invasion and life in the Second Temple period. The Burnt House is included in the "Jewish Quarter Combined Ticket" purchase, which includes access to the tower at Hurva Synagogue and the Herodian Quarter Museum. The site is located at Tiferet-Yisrael Street, in the Jewish Quarter of the Old City.

The Cardo

A cardo was the Latin name given to the main street in Ancient Roman cities. Evidence for the existence of this ancient Cardo was first found on a mosaic map of Jerusalem. The map was discovered in a Byzantine church in Medeba town in the Moav Mountains of Jordan. This Medeba map was used as a tool to teach the locals about

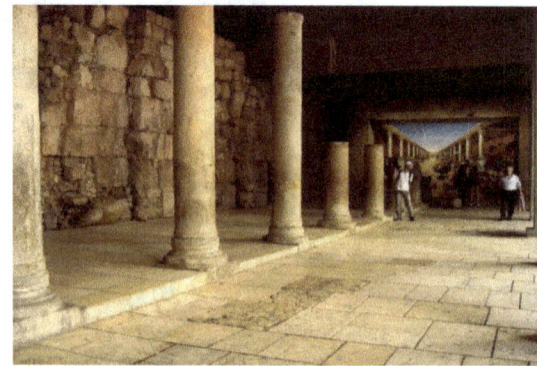

Jerusalem. The Cardo begins at Damascus Gate in the north, running southwards through the Old City, ending at Zion Gate. The north side of the Cardo, from Damascus Gate to David Street, was built during the Roman period in Jerusalem. However, the south side was built in the 6th century, during the times of the Byzantine Empire in Jerusalem, and it extends along the western side of the Jewish Quarter.

Christ Church Jerusalem

Christ Church Jerusalem is an Anglican church located inside the Old City of Jerusalem. It was consecrated by Bishop Samuel Gobat in 1849 and is the oldest Protestant church building in the Middle East. The Church's Ministry Among Jewish People or (CMJ) helped finance the church's construction and have been active in the Land of Israel since the 1820s. Their mission statement reads: *"Driven by a commitment to the God of Israel and the people of Israel, our purpose at CMJ Israel is to represent the Love of Yeshua (Jesus) in word and deed with the Jewish people and Gentiles living in the Land and visiting from abroad."* The church is part of a small compound just inside the Jaffa Gate opposite King David's citadel, and the compound includes the Heritage Centre Museum, Beiṭ Bracha guest house (House of Blessing), which is a bed and breakfast and prayer garden.

The Church of the Nativity of St. John the Baptist

This Catholic church is in the picturesque village of Ein Karem, 4.5 miles (7.5 km.) southwest of Jerusalem. The church and monastery were built over the ruins of ancient layers of the Herodian, Roman, Byzantine, and Crusader periods. Inside the church is a cave, where according to tradition, was the birthplace of John the Baptist. The Franciscan Order of monks purchased the property in 1674 and

restored the church with the aid of the Spanish royal family. In 1941–42 the area west of the church was excavated, discovering graves, rock-cut chambers, wine presses, and small chapels with mosaic tiling. The southern rock-cut chamber contained ceramics dating back to the first century BC, of which is the presumed lifetime of Zechariah, Elizabeth, and John.

Church of St. James

Located within a walled compound in the Armenian Quarter of Jerusalem's Old City is the Church of St. James, honoring two martyred believers of that name — James the Great, one of the first apostles to follow Jesus, and James the Less, believed to be a close relative of Jesus and a key leader of the church in Jerusalem. James the Great was beheaded by Herod Agrippa I, around 44 AD (Acts 12:1-2). James the Less was martyred by temple authorities about 20 years later by being thrown from the temple platform, then stoned to death. Within the church are buried the head of James the Great and the body of James the Less, according to Armenian tradition.

Church of St. John the Baptist

The Greek Church of St. John the Baptist, located in the Christian Quarter of the Old City, can be easily spotted with its distinctive, silvery dome. This is the oldest church in Jerusalem, built in the mid-5th century and restored after the Persians destroyed it in 614 AD. The current building was built between the 8th and 11th centuries by Italian merchants, and in the 12th century, it was renovated by the Crusaders. The ancient church, more than seven meters below street level, is still accessible via a staircase. According to Greek Orthodox tradition, the head of John the Baptist was held in this church. The entrance is located on the Christian Quarter Rd., where it intersects with David St.

Christian Information Center

The Christian Information Center (C.I.C.) has been sponsored by the Franciscan Custody of the Holy Land since 1973. The Center is located opposite the Tower of David, just inside the Jaffa Gate of Jerusalem's Old City. The purpose of the C.I.C. is to provide information about Christianity and the Holy Land – such as holy places and shrines, churches in the region, and aspects of religious and cultural life.

Dormition Abbey

Near the top of Mount Zion, the Church of the Dormition, a 12th-century church, was built on the ruins of the earlier demolished Byzantine church that overlooks the Old City. The location is identified in Christian tradition as the place where the Virgin Mary died or "fell asleep," as the name suggests. Inside, the circular basilica is a mosaic of Mary and of the child Jesus, with the figures of twelve prophets below them. Around the church are six chapels decorated by beautiful mosaics depicting scenes such as Mary and the infant Jesus receiving pilgrims, Jesus' family tree, John the Baptist on the shore of the Jordan River, and other saints. Two spiral staircases lead down to the crypt, where a round pillared room with a sculpture of Mary "asleep" in the center resides. On the ceiling above her is the figure of Jesus, as if watching over her, surrounded by the great women of the Bible.

Herodian Quarter/Wohl Museum of Archeology

The Herodian Quarter was discovered by archeologists when the Jewish Quarter was rebuilt following the Six-Day War. Located underground, it preserves the remains of 6 houses from the Herodian period (the reign of King Herod) that were excavated in 1967 and is considered one of the largest underground archeological sites in the world. In the Herodian period, this part of the city was home to wealthy priestly families. Homes were built on the western hill (today's Mount Zion) overlooking the Temple Mount, with the roof of each home at the basement level of the house above it so that every house enjoyed a clear view of the temple. There are three distinct levels, with the lowest considered to be a mansion with a possible 6,000 square ft. (557 m.) of original floor area. None of the upper stories survived the Roman torching of the city in 70 AD.

Hurva Square Plaza

In the center of the Jewish Quarter, surrounded by a maze of narrow and winding streets, is the Hurva Square Plaza, an open area of outdoor seating with cafes, souvenir shops, and snack bars. On the west side of the square stands the Hurva Synagogue. During the War of Independence in 1948, the 19th-century synagogue was destroyed, then in 2010, it was reconstructed in its original Ottoman style. From the upper balcony, you can enjoy a 360-degree panoramic view of the city. You can purchase the Jewish Quarter special ticket, which includes entry to the Hurva Synagogue, the Wohl Museum of Archeology (Herodian Quarter), the nearby Burnt House, and the Jerusalem Archaeological Park-Davidson Center. This combined ticket requires a reservation made through the Company for the Restoration and Development of the Jewish Quarter and can save you a bit of money if you intend to visit these 4 attractions.

Israel Museum – Shrine of the Book – Model City of Jerusalem

Founded in 1965, the Israel Museum was extensively enlarged, refurbished, and reopened in 2010. Within this sprawling 20-acre (8 hectares) compound, you will find the Archaeology Wing, the Shrine of the Book, the Model of Jerusalem in the Second Temple Period, the Wing for Jewish Art and Life, the Fine Arts Wing, the Youth Wing, and the Art Garden.

The Archaeology Wing tells the story, chronologically, of the ancient Land of Israel, which was home to peoples of different cultures and faiths, from prehistory through the Ottoman Empire.

The Shrine of the Book is a white tiled dome building that houses the Dead Sea Scrolls, which are the oldest biblical manuscripts in the world. These scrolls, along with rare early medieval biblical manuscripts, were found in Qumran in 1947.

The Model of Jerusalem is a reconstruction of 1st-century Jerusalem in the Second Temple period, showing the topography and architecture of the city before its destruction by the Romans in 66 AD. The model is on a scale of 50:1 and is spread over nearly an acre (.4 hectare).

The Jewish Art and Life Wing exhibits four complete synagogues brought from various locations around the world and reconstructed.

Jeremiah's Grotto

Jeremiah's Grotto is a cave located just outside the north wall of Jerusalem, where tradition says Jeremiah wept bitter tears and composed the book of Lamentations. The grotto is under what is called Scull Hill near the Garden Tomb.

Jerusalem Sites

Little Western Wall

The Little Western Wall (also known as Small Kotel) is a small portion of the Western Wall of the Temple Mount located in the Muslim Quarter of the Old City of Jerusalem near the Iron Gate. The Kotel is close to the middle point of the Western Wall of the Temple Mount, and it is the second closest place to the Holy of Holies (outside of the Temple Mount) where Jews can pray. The passage alongside the wall is a courtyard of Ribat Kurd, a hospice for Muslim pilgrims founded in 1293.

Lutheran Church of the Redeemer

The Church of the Redeemer was built on the ruins of the medieval St. Mary la Latine Church. The site is said to have been a hostel and hospital for western pilgrims and served as the Knights of St. John headquarters, where members of the order nursed patients in the complex's hospital. In the late 1800s, the 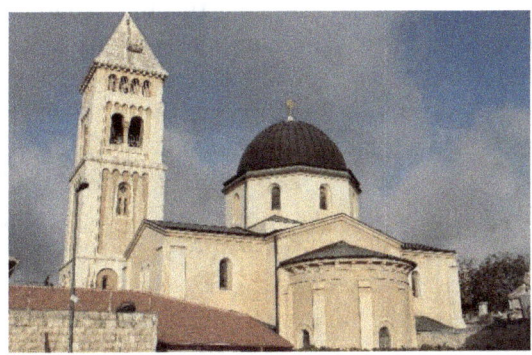 church was reconstructed and personally dedicated by Kaiser Wilhelm. The church is located in the Christian Quarter of the Old City near the famous Church of the Holy Sepulchre. The square bell tower of this Protestant church has graced the Old City's skyline since 1898. It's worth buying a ticket to access the tower for a 360-degree view over the Old City, but be prepared; it's a winding staircase of 170 steps to the top.

Mahane Yehuda Market

The Mahane Yehuda Market, or shuk, is a true old-style market located in the middle of Jerusalem with over 250 vendors. At the market, you can find street singers, musicians, fresh spices by weight, baked goods, meat, cheeses, nuts, housewares, fresh fruits, and vegetables. In and around the market are restaurants, cafes, juice bars, and many small stands selling a variety of local foods and drinks. The market is closed for Shabbat (Sabbath) from Friday evening through Saturday evening. This market is one of the largest and busiest in Jerusalem.

Old City Rooftop Walk

The easiest entry point to the Chabad Street rooftops is from the narrow metal steps on the right as you walk down Rehov Chabad just as it meets St. Mark's Street. You may have to ask for directions as it's not easy to find, but it's worth the effort. You can then explore large amounts of the Old City and enjoy some truly unique views. One of the most fascinating of these is standing over the Old City's central point where the main north-south and east-west roads intersect. At this point, the division of the Old City of Jerusalem into its four quarters – Jewish, Christian, Muslim, and Armenian can be seen.

Ramparts Walk

Walk the walls of the Old City, built around 485 years ago by Suleiman the Magnificent. The Ramparts walk is a great way to get an overview of Jerusalem and the outlying areas. For a small entrance fee, you can climb the ramparts of the Old City and circle the city from above. The walk is divided into two parts: The Northern Ramparts Walk begins at Jaffa Gate and can be exited from New Gate, Herod's Gate, or Lions' Gate. The Southern Ramparts Walk also begins at Jaffa Gate and can be exited from Zion Gate or Dung Gate. The walk requires a lot of stair climbing and descending. Make sure you have enough water with you as once you're on the ramparts, there's no getting off until you reach an exit.

Temple Institute

The Temple Institute is an organization in Israel focused on establishing the Third Temple to be rebuilt on Mount Moriah (Temple Mount Platform) in Jerusalem. The Institute's work touches upon the history of the temple's past, an understanding of the present day, and the divine promise of Israel's future. As part of its ongoing effort to prepare for a future rebuilt temple, the Temple Institute has been preparing more than ninety ritual items suitable for temple use. The Institute's activities include education, research, and development. You can visit and tour their facilities which are located up the stairs to the southeast of the Western Wall Plaza.

Tower of David – Citadel Museum

The Tower of David – Museum of the History of Jerusalem, is located in the medieval citadel known as the Tower of David, near the Jaffa Gate of the Old City. The Museum presents Jerusalem's story, detailing the major events in its history, beginning with the birth of the city in the second millennium BC, until it became the capital of the State of Israel. From the towers of the Citadel, one has a breathtaking 360-view of Jerusalem, the Four Quarters of the Old City, the New City, Mount of Olives, Mount Scopus, the Judean Desert, and the Dead Sea in the distance.

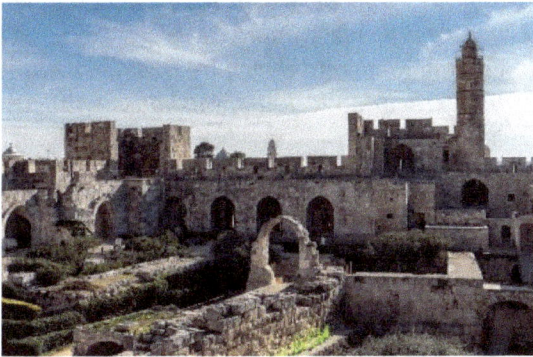

Access to the ruins of King Herod's Palace (Pilate's Palace) is via the museum as well.

Yad Vashem Holocaust Museum

Yad Vashem (meaning: "a monument and a name") Holocaust History Museum is Israel's official memorial to the victims of the Holocaust. Yad Vashem is located on the western slope of Mount Herzl, also known as the Mount of Remembrance, and was established in 1953. It is dedicated to the memory of the Jews who died under Nazi oppression and Gentiles who selflessly aided the Jews.

Zedekiah's Cave (Solomon's Quarries)

Zedekiah's Cave is a 5-acre (2 hectares) underground limestone quarry that stretches under five city blocks of the Muslim Quarter of Old City Jerusalem. It was carved over a period of several thousand years and is a remnant of the largest quarry in Jerusalem. Zedekiah's Cave entrance is just beneath Solomon's Quarries, the Old City wall, between the Damascus and Herod Gates. Just past the narrow entrance, the cave slopes down into a huge 300 ft. (91 m.) long auditorium-like chamber. The drops of water dripping through the ceiling are known as "Zedekiah's tears." Beyond the "auditorium" are a series of man-made galleries hewn by ancient stonecutters into interesting patterns and formations. Access paths cover the entire quarry system and take at least 30 minutes to explore. Chisel marks are visible in many sections, and in some areas huge, nearly finished building blocks are locked into the rock where the stonecutters left them.

Now Solomon had 70,000 transporters, and 80,000 hewers of stone in the mountains, 16 besides Solomon's 3,300 chief deputies who were over the project and who ruled over the people who were doing the work. 17 Then the king commanded, and they quarried great stones, costly stones, to lay the foundation of the house with cut stones (I Kings 5:15–17).

These verses have intrigued scholars who have suggested that the proximity of the Temple Mount (Mount Moriah) to the site of "Zedekiah's Cave" is what prompted King Solomon to utilize the quarry to produce the stones necessary for his building projects. Herod the Great used the main quarry at Zedekiah's Cave for building blocks in the renovation of the temple and its retaining walls, today known as the Western or Wailing Wall. Stones from the quarry may also have been used for the building projects of Herod Agrippa I.

Sea of Galilee Sites

Sea of Galilee Overview

Location

1. The Sea of Galilee is located in the northern part of Israel, known as the Galilee region. Therefore, it's called the Sea of Galilee.
2. It's also referred to in Scripture by other names like Ginnosar, Lake of Gennesar, Gennesaret, Sea of Chinneroth, Kinneret, and Sea of Tiberias.
3. It's about 70 miles (115 km.) north of Jerusalem and about 27 miles (45 km.) east of the Mediterranean Sea.
4. It's a freshwater lake about 8 miles (13 km.) wide by about 12 miles (19 km.) long and 150 ft. (46 m.) deep.
5. It's located about 700 ft. (213 m.) below sea level.
6. It's a key freshwater source for much of Israel.
7. Because of its location, storms can arise quickly and drop down onto its surface without much warning.
8. The Sea of Galilee was located on a main crossroad of the known world during Christ's ministry on earth. This international highway was called the "Via Maris" (Way of the Sea) and linked travel between the 3 continents of Africa, Asia, and Europe.
9. Travelers from these 3 continents were forced to use this route as there were few other options for traveling to and from each continent. This was so because there was a desert to the east that was impassible due to lack of water, and the Mediterranean Sea was located to the west, which was not a realistic option for travel as it was expensive and ships were scarce.
10. The Via Maris passed right along the northern shore of the Sea of Galilee, and there are old ruins and markers showing its existence.
11. The north shore of the Sea of Galilee was even more traveled than the roads and routes leading through Jerusalem.

12. Oftentimes, we might think Christ was hiding out somewhere in a remote location. However, just the opposite was true. He chose the northern shore of the Sea of Galilee (and Capernaum was located at a key place along this route) as a center stage so His message would reach as many people as possible in the world.

13. By spending most of His ministry time in the northern Galilee area, Christ's miracles would travel by word of mouth to the ends of the earth. This laid the groundwork and sowed the seeds of the gospel to the rest of the known world so the evangelization work done later by the apostles would be easier and more acceptable to those who heard the message about Christ.

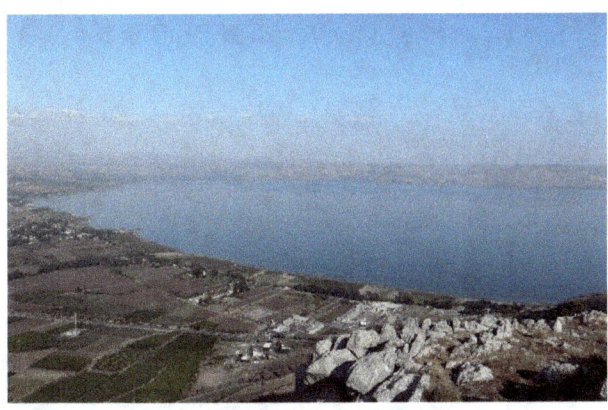
Sea of Galilee from Mt. Arbel

Historical Background

1. Abraham entered the Promised Land through the gateway of the Sea of Galilee when he first journeyed from Ur of the Chaldeans.
2. In Matthew 4, we find that Jesus established his home ministry base in the town of Capernaum, which is located on the northern shore of the Sea of Galilee.
3. At least 6 of the 12 disciples were from right around the Sea of Galilee. These were Peter, Andrew, James, John, Matthew, and Philip.
4. According to Acts 1:11, the rest of the disciples were from the Galilee area as well.

Places of Interest

Listed clockwise, starting at Tiberias

1. Tiberias
2. Mount Arbel – Likely place the Great Commission was given.

3. Magdala – Hometown of Mary Magdalene, from whom Christ cast out 7 demons.
4. Yigal Allon Center – Jesus Boat Museum
5. Calling of the disciples.
6. Tel Chinnereth (Kinneret) – Identified as the biblical city listed by Joshua as one of the fortified cities in the Naftali tribe region (Josh. 19).

7. Tabgha – Restoration of Peter: Church of the Primacy of Saint Peter
8. Tabgha: Church of the Loaves and Fish – The traditional site of the feeding of the 5,000.
9. Mount of Beatitudes – Place from where Christ preached the Sermon on the Mount.
10. Chorazin – One of the 3 towns Jesus cursed because of their unbelief.
11. Sower's Cove – Likely place Christ preached the Parables of the Kingdom sermon.

Synagogue at Capernaum

12. Capernaum – Homebase of Jesus, Franciscan Site
13. Capernaum – Homebase of Jesus, Greek Orthodox Site
14. Capernaum National Park and Peer – Great place to get out into the Sea of Galilee a bit.
15. St. Peter's Fish Restaurant Mifratz-Amnun – Nice restaurant and beach location.
16. Bethsaida traditional location.
17. Bethsaida newly discovered location – New archaeological evidence points to this place as the real Bethsaida.
18. Gamla – Place many Jews jumped to their deaths fleeing the Romans in 67 AD.
19. Sea of Galilee lookout place.
20. Kursi – Demon possessed man healed. Pigs run down a steep slope into the sea just south of Kursi.
21. Feeding of the 5,000 – The most accurate location according to Scripture.
22. Horvat Susita – Old Roman City atop of a hill on the east side of the Sea of Galilee.
23. Yardenit – Nice baptismal site and souvenir store.

24. Hamat Tiberias National Park – Old Ruins of ancient Tiberias.

The Sea of Galilee in the Bible

1. Jesus calmed the sea here two times.
2. Christ fed 5,000 and 4,000 on its eastern shores.
3. Christ walked on water in the northern part of the sea.
4. Christ preached the Sermon on the Mount here, which is His most famous and longest sermon.
5. Jesus cast demons out of a herd of 2,000 pigs here.
6. Christ did the majority of his miracles here in this region.
7. The miraculous "Catch of Fish" was performed here by Jesus.

Boat dock at Capernaum National Park

8. Jesus performed every class of miracle to show He was Lord of every aspect of creation. Here are the kinds of miracles Christ performed:
    - He healed all kinds of sickness.
    - He had power over the demons and the demonic world.
    - He had power over the weather and calmed the sea.
    - He had power over nature and cursed a fig tree, and it died.
    - He had power over animals – He cast demons into a herd of swine, performed miraculous catches of fish, and rode into Jerusalem on an untamed donkey.
    - He had power over food – He fed 5,000 and 4,000 people.
    - He had power over death – He raised a number of people from the dead and rose from the dead Himself.
    - Jesus had power to forgive sins (Mark 2:10).
9. Christ preached the Parables of the Kingdom from its shore.

Sea of Galilee Sites

10. Jesus spent around 50–70% of His ministry time on earth around the Sea of Galilee.
11. The cursing of the unrepentant cities of Chorazin, Bethsaida, and Capernaum was pronounced here by Jesus.
12. The Great Commission was likely given on Mount Arbel, which is the tallest mountain around the Sea of Galilee and has the best view.
13. Jesus appeared here to the disciples after His resurrection.
14. Jesus restored Peter to ministry here.
15. Thirty-four times in the Gospels it's mentioned that multitudes of people followed Jesus. These great crowds could have easily reached 15,000 or more in size.

Matthew 4:23–25: *And he went throughout all Galilee, teaching in their synagogues and proclaiming the gospel of the kingdom and healing every disease and every affliction among the people. 24 So his fame spread throughout all Syria, and they brought him all the sick, those afflicted with various diseases and pains, those oppressed by demons, those having seizures, and paralytics, and he healed them. 25 And **great crowds** followed him from Galilee and the Decapolis, and from Jerusalem and Judea, and from beyond the Jordan.*

Kursi: Demon possessed man healed here

Mark 6:30–34: *The apostles gathered together with Jesus; and they reported to Him all that they had done and taught. 31 And He said to them, "Come away by yourselves to a secluded place and rest a while." (For there were many people coming and going, and they did not even have time to eat.) 32 They went away in the boat to a secluded place by themselves. 33 The people saw them going, and many recognized them and ran there together on foot from all the cities and got there ahead of them. 34 When Jesus went ashore, He saw **a large crowd**, and He felt compassion for them because they were like sheep without a shepherd; and He began to teach them* *many things.*

Faith Lesson from the Sea of Galilee

1. Christ chose to locate His ministry base in Capernaum which was on the Via Maris so He would have maximum impact on a worldwide scale. Do we position ourselves to have maximum impact regarding the ministries we are involved in?
2. Jesus performed every class of miracle to show He was Lord of every aspect of creation. Do we believe Jesus was fully God and fully man at the same time?
3. Christ cursed the 3 towns of Capernaum, Chorazin, and Bethsaida because they heard so much teaching and witnessed many miracles but grew apathetic and hardhearted. Are we becoming apathetic toward Christ and His Word in our own personal lives?
4. Christ gave the Great Commission overlooking the Sea of Galilee. Are we seriously fulfilling the Great Commission, or have we become lazy and apathetic to this key command?

Sea of Galilee at sunset

Journal/Notes

Sea of Galilee Sites

Bethsaida

Location

1. Currently, there are two leading candidates for the true Bethsaida location. The first is the traditional site that has been excavated from 1987 to the present. It sits upon a hill and is located about 1.5 miles or 2.25 km. from the highwater mark of the Sea of Galilee. Because there were no other sites excavated besides this first site, it became the default site. The traditional site is known as Et Tell.

    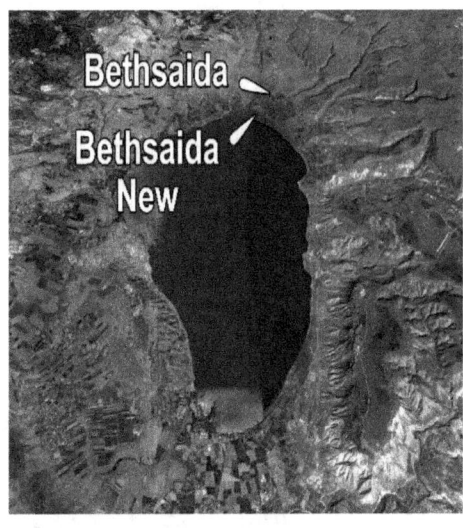

    A new site called El Araj has been recently excavated since 2014, and all the evidence points to it as the best candidate for the true Bethsaida location. It is located at the high-water mark on the northeast side of the Sea of Galilee at the inlet of the Jordan River and fits the biblical and historical records much better than the traditional site.

2. We know from the Bible that Bethsaida was in a desolate, remote place with little population.

    Luke 9:10: *The apostles, when they had returned, told him what things they had done. He took them, and withdrew apart to a **deserted place** of a city called Bethsaida.*

3. The northwestern side of the Sea of Galilee was densely populated in Jesus' time, but the northeastern side where Bethsaida was located was desolate.

4. Bethsaida was a fishing village right on the seashore of the Sea of Galilee. In fact, its name means "House of Fishing."

5. In John 1:44, we find that at least 3 disciples were from here: *Now **Philip** was from **Bethsaida**, the city of **Andrew** and **Peter**.*

    We also know that at least Peter and Andrew were fishermen, so they lived in Bethsaida to be close to the sea.

6. As mentioned, the traditional site of Bethsaida is located 1.5 miles (2.25 km.) from the Sea of Galilee.
   - This presents a challenge as Bethsaida was a fishing village right on the Sea of Galilee.
   - Some have suggested the water level was higher back in Jesus' day, but this cannot be true as Capernaum, Magdala, and other towns are right on the sea. If the water level had been higher, these other towns could not have existed.
   - Pliny the Elder, a first-century Roman writer, called Bethsaida *"One of four lovely cities on the Sea of Galilee."*

Historical Background

1. Bethsaida was a fishing village with several hundred inhabitants during the time of Christ.
2. At least 3 of the 12 disciples were from Bethsaida.

   John 1:44: *Now **Philip** was from Bethsaida, of the city of **Andrew** and **Peter**.*

3. Later on, however, these disciples moved to Capernaum to be closer to where Jesus lived.

Traditional site of Bethsaida

   Mark 1:21: *And they went into **Capernaum**, and immediately on the Sabbath, he entered the synagogue and was teaching.*

   Mark 1:28: *And immediately he left the synagogue and entered the house of Simon and Andrew, with James and John. And at once his fame spread everywhere throughout all the surrounding region of Galilee.*

Places of Interest

1. Et-Tell site of Bethsaida – Traditional Location
2. El Araj site of Bethsaida – New Location
3. Feeding of the 5,000

4. Approximate place Jesus walked on water.
5. Capernaum

Bethsaida in the Bible

1. **Philip, Andrew, and Peter were from Bethsaida (John 1:44).**
2. **Jesus healed a blind man at Bethsaida.**

   Mark 8:22–25: *And they came to **Bethsaida**. And some people brought to him a blind man and begged him to touch him. 23 And he took the blind man by the hand and led him out of the village, and when he had spit on his eyes and laid his hands on him, he asked him, "Do you see anything?" 24 And he looked up and said, "I see people, but they look like trees, walking." 25 Then Jesus laid his hands on his eyes again; and he opened his eyes, his sight was restored, and he saw everything clearly.*

3. **Bethsaida was one of the 3 towns Jesus cursed because of their unbelief in Him after witnessing all His miracles.**

   Matthew 11:21: *Woe to you, Chorazin! Woe to you, **Bethsaida**! For if the mighty works had been done in Tyre and Sidon which were done in you, they would have repented long ago in sackcloth and* *ashes.*

4. **It was close to Bethsaida, where Christ fed the 5,000.**

   Luke 9:10–17: *When the apostles returned, they gave an account to Him of all that they had done. Taking them with Him, He withdrew by Himself to a city called **Bethsaida**. 11 But the crowds were aware of this and followed Him; and welcoming them, He began speaking to them about the kingdom of God and curing those who had need of healing. 12 Now the day was ending, and the twelve came and said to Him, "Send the crowd away, that they may go into the surrounding villages and countryside and find lodging and get something to eat; for here we are in a desolate place." But he said to them, "You give them something to eat." They said, "We have no more than five loaves and two fish—unless we are to go and buy food for all these people." 14 For there were about five thousand men. And he said to his disciples, "Have them sit down in groups of about fifty each." 15 And they did so, and had them all sit down. 16 And taking the five loaves and the two fish, he looked up to heaven and said a blessing over them. Then he broke the loaves and gave them to the disciples to set before the crowd. 17 And they all ate and were satisfied. And what was left over was picked up, twelve baskets of broken pieces.*

   New location of Bethsaida

5. **Not far from Bethsaida, Jesus walked on water and calmed the sea.**

   Mark 6:45–51: *Immediately he made his disciples get into the boat and go before him to the other side, to **Bethsaida**, while he dismissed the crowd. 46 And after he had taken leave of them, he went up on the mountain to pray. 47 And when evening came, the boat was out on the sea, and he was alone on the land. 48 And he saw that they were making headway painfully, for the wind was against them. And about the fourth watch of the night [the last watch before dawn], he came to them, walking on the sea. He meant to pass by them, 49 but when they saw him walking on the sea, they* *thought it was a ghost, and cried out, 50 for they all saw him and were terrified. But immediately he spoke to them and said, "Take heart; it is I. Do not be afraid." 51 And he got into the boat with them, and the wind ceased. And they were utterly astounded.*

Faith Lesson from Bethsaida

1. Like the healing of the blind man, Jesus often heals in different and strange ways. Do we have faith and trust in God regardless of how or if He chooses to heal?
2. Christ cursed the town of Bethsaida because its inhabitants were apathetic, showed unbelief in Christ, and chose not to follow and obey Him. Are we often slow to trust and obey Christ as well?
3. Christ fed the 5,000 in the area of Bethsaida to reveal He was the true bread of life from heaven and that His Word is our spiritual food. In the same way there were 12 baskets of food left over, Christ, as our Bread from Heaven, is also abundant and overflowing in feeding us spiritual food through His Word. Are we eating daily and finding our life from the true Bread of Life?

Ruins at new Bethsaida location

4. Not far from Bethsaida Jesus walked on water and calmed the sea. Am I finding rest and peace in Jesus in the midst of my personal storms of life?

Isaiah 26:3–4: *You keep him in perfect peace whose mind is stayed on you, because he trusts in you. 4 Trust in the Lord forever, for the Lord God is an everlasting rock.*

Journal/Notes:

Calling of the Disciples

Location

It's very likely that the biblical account of the calling of at least 6 of the 12 disciples occurred on the northern shore of the Sea of Galilee. This was the area where most of the fishing was done, and the fishing towns were located.

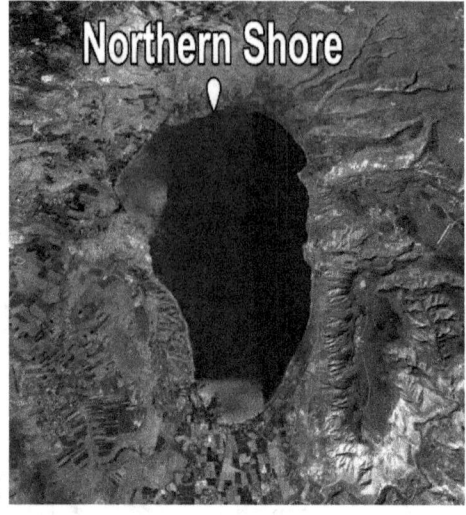

Historical Background

1. While the Bible clearly mentions that 6 of the 12 disciples were from the Sea of Galilee, it's possible more were from this area as well.
2. At the ascension of Christ into heaven, the angels said to the disciples who were standing there: *"Men of **Galilee**, why do you stand looking into heaven?"* (**Acts 1:11**). Now while the text doesn't specify the exact location, it does tell us that all the disciples were from the Galilee area.

Places of Interest

1. Northern Shore of the Sea of Galilee
2. Most likely place several of the disciples were called.
3. Gennesaret
4. Magdala
5. Tabgha
6. Capernaum
7. Bethsaida
8. Sea of Galilee

Sea of Galilee Sites

Calling of the Disciples in the Bible

1. **It appears by looking at the biblical narrative that Jesus had several contacts with some of the disciples before His final call for them to leave everything and follow Him.**

   John 1:35–44: *The next day again John was standing with two of his disciples, 36 and he looked at Jesus as he walked by and said, "Behold, the Lamb of God!" 37 The two disciples heard him say this, and they followed Jesus. 38 Jesus turned and saw them following and said to them, "What are you seeking?" And they said to him, "Rabbi" (which means Teacher), "where are you staying?" 39 He said to them, "Come and you will see." So they came and saw where he was staying, and they stayed with him that day, for it was about the tenth hour. 40 One of the two who heard John speak and followed Jesus was **Andrew**, Simon Peter's brother. 41 He first found his own brother **Simon** and said to him, "We have found the Messiah" (which means Christ). 42 He brought him to Jesus. Jesus looked at him and* said, "So you are Simon the son of John? You shall be called Cephas" (which means Peter). 43 The next day Jesus decided to go to Galilee. He found **Philip** and said to him, "Follow me." 44 Now Philip was from Bethsaida, the city of Andrew and Peter.*

2. **In the following passage, we see what appears to be a final contact with some of the disciples before Jesus' last call for them to follow Him in full-time ministry.**

   Luke 5:1–11: *On one occasion, while the crowd was pressing in on him to hear the word of God, he was standing by the lake of Gennesaret, 2 and he saw two boats by the lake, but the fishermen had gone out of them and were washing their nets. 3 Getting into one of the boats, which was **Simon's**, he asked him to put out a little from the land. And he sat down and taught the people from the boat. 4 And when he had finished speaking, he said to Simon, "Put out into the deep and let down your*

   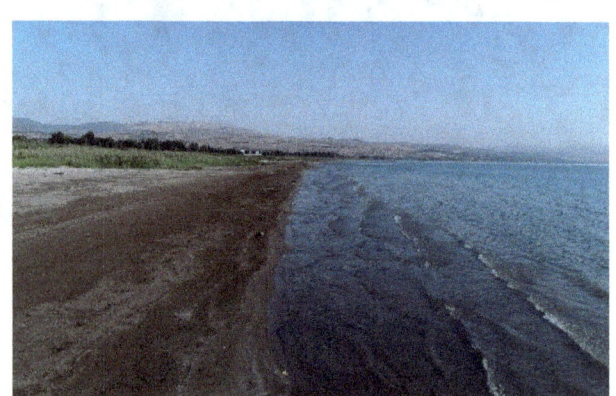

   Northwestern shore of the Sea of Galilee

   *nets for a catch." 5 And Simon answered, "Master, we toiled all night and took nothing! But at your word I will let down the nets." 6 And when they had done this, they enclosed a large number of fish, and their nets were breaking. 7 They signaled to their partners in the other boat to come and help them. And they came and filled both the boats, so that they began to sink. 8 But when Simon Peter saw it, he fell down at Jesus' knees, saying, "Depart from me, for I am a sinful man, O Lord." 9 For he and all who were with him were astonished at the catch of fish that they had taken, 10 and so also were **James** and **John**, sons of Zebedee, who were partners with **Simon**. And Jesus said to Simon, "Do not be afraid; from now on you will be catching men." 11 And when they had brought their boats to land, they left everything and followed him.*

3. **The calling of Matthew, the tax collector.**

   Matthew 9:9: *As Jesus passed on from there, he saw a man*

called **Matthew** sitting at the tax booth, and he said to him, "Follow me." And he rose and followed him.

From Matthew 9:1, we see that the calling of Matthew was close to Capernaum, which is on the northern shore of the Sea of Galilee.

Faith Lesson from the Calling of the Disciples

1. When God calls us to salvation or a certain calling or task, this might sometimes involve a process and have several confirmations. Are you genuinely saved? Is there some special calling or mission you are sensing from the Lord?
2. God wants our complete devotion and obedience. He doesn't want us to add Him onto our lives and make Him an accessory that we go to just when we need help. God refuses to be an ATM. Do I follow Jesus for His blessings only, or am I willing to deny myself and suffer for Him as well?
3. God calls us to be His disciples and devote our entire life to Him. Luke 14:25–27, 33: *Now great crowds accompanied him, and he turned and said to them, 26 "If anyone comes to me and does not hate his own father and mother and wife and children and brothers and sisters, yes, and even his own life, he cannot be my disciple. 27 Whoever does not bear his own cross and come after me cannot be my disciple. 33 So therefore, any one of you who does not renounce all that he has cannot be my disciple."*

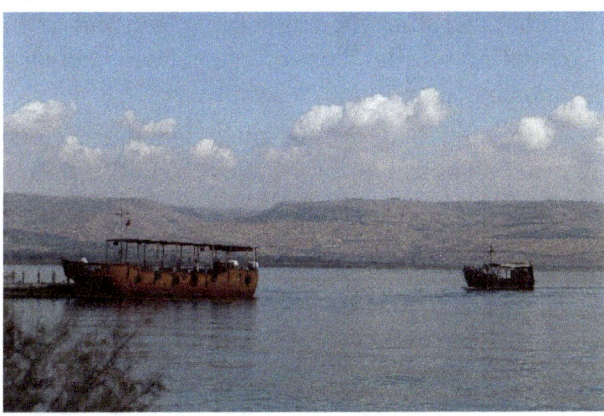

Northern shore of the Sea of Galilee

4. Am I willing to love Christ and follow Him regardless of the cost?
5. In comparison to my love for Christ, all other relationships should fade. The contrast here is that compared to my love for Christ, all other relationships would seem like hate in comparison. Do all my relationships appear as hate in comparison to my love for Christ?

6. Christ said that there would be a great falling away from the faith in the last days, and there would be many false teachers. Unfortunately, in many churches today, a soft version of the gospel is proclaimed. They neglect to emphasize repentance, the judgments of God, the true cost of discipleship, service, and sacrifice. Instead, there is an overemphasis on the blessings of God and how He exists to serve our needs and make us happy rather than us serving Him and finding true joy in our devotion to Him. This soft gospel will likely lead to the great apostasy mentioned in Scripture.

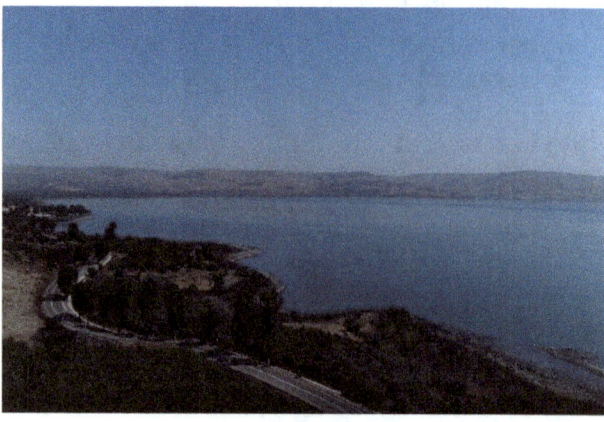

Northern shore of the Sea of Galilee

7. Am I growing deeper in my knowledge of God's Word so I don't fall into the many traps that will lead to the great apostasy of the last days?

Journal/Notes:

Capernaum

Location

1. Capernaum is located on the north shore of the Sea of Galilee.

2. It was located on the Via Maris, which was the main international highway of the known world during the time of Christ.

    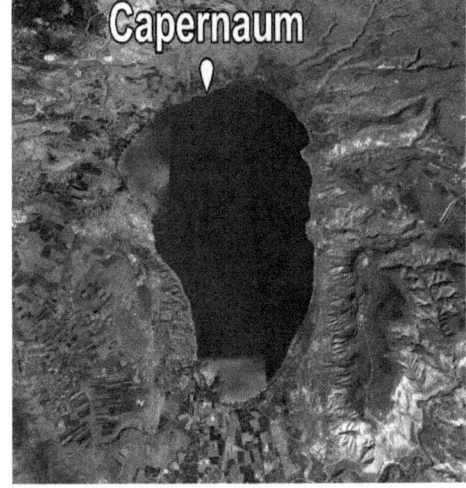

    - The Via Maris linked the three continents of Africa, Asia, and Europe.
    - Travelers were forced to use this route as there were few other options for traveling to and from each continent.
    - The north shore of the Sea of Galilee was even more traveled than the roads and routes leading through Jerusalem.
    - It might appear that Christ set up His ministry base in a remote place. However, just the opposite is true. He chose the northern shore of the Sea of Galilee (and Capernaum was located at a key place along the Via Maris) as a center stage so His message would reach as many people as possible throughout the world.
    - By spending most of His ministry time in the northern Galilee area, Christ's miracles traveled by word of mouth to the ends of the earth. This laid the groundwork and sowed the seeds of the gospel to the rest of the known world. As a result, evangelism done later on by the apostles would be easier and more acceptable.

3. Today, Capernaum is shared between two sites. The Franciscan site receives around 90% of visitors as it possesses the synagogue, Peter's home, village ruins, ancient artifacts, and nice access to the beach. The Greek Orthodox site has chosen to remain basically unexcavated and serene.

Historical Background

1. The name Capernaum is derived from two words, *Caper*, which means village, and *Naum,* which is from the title, Nahum. Therefore, some believe that the town was named after the Prophet Nahum.
2. Capernaum was a fishing village with a population of around 1,000 during the time of Christ.
3. Capernaum became the hometown of Jesus after moving from his boyhood home of Nazareth. It also became the ministry headquarters of Christ during His ministry on earth.

   Matthew 4:13-17: *And leaving Nazareth he went and lived in* **Capernaum** *by the sea, in the territory of Zebulun and Naphtali, 14 so that what was spoken by the prophet Isaiah might be fulfilled: 15 "The land of Zebulun and the land of Naphtali, the way of the sea, beyond the Jordan, Galilee of the Gentiles— 16 the people*

   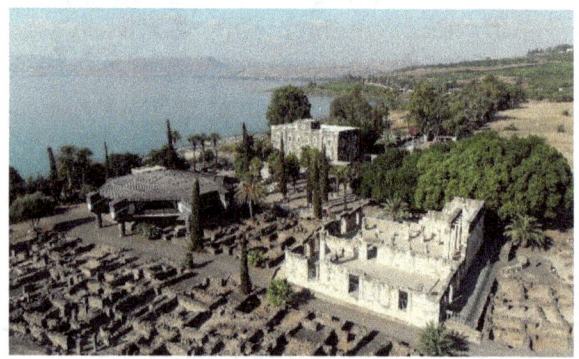

   Capernaum: Franciscan site

   dwelling in darkness have seen a great light, and for those dwelling in the region and shadow of death, on them a light has dawned." 17 From that time Jesus began to preach, saying, "Repent, for the kingdom of heaven is at hand."
4. Capernaum is mentioned more than any other town around the Sea of Galilee.
5. Capernaum was also the home of Peter, James, Andrew, John, and Matthew.
6. The Synagogue in Capernaum was built by a Roman Centurion of whom Jesus healed his servant.

   Luke 7:5: *For he loves our nation, and he is the one* **who built us our synagogue.**
7. The synagogue that existed during Christ's time is made from black basalt stone, and its foundations are under the current synagogue built out of limestone.

Sea of Galilee Sites

8. The current synagogue was built in the 4th century and was quite luxurious and impressive. This happened because Capernaum became a venerated site due to its role as the ministry base and home of Jesus and other apostles.
9. Information about Peter's home.
    - Many substantial archaeological excavations have verified the location of Peter's home.
    - There have been several churches built over Peter's home throughout the centuries.
    - The early Christian believers first built a building over Peter's house in around 50 AD.
    - Peter's home was where Jesus also lived. It contained the central kitchen and living quarters (which are preserved today) and then individual bedrooms connected to it.
    - In the 5th century AD, an octagon-shaped church was built over Peter's house.
    - Recently, in 1990, a church was built over the previous ruins of Peter's house. You can walk inside it and look down at the ruins through a glass floor in the church.

10. At the Greek Orthodox site of Capernaum, the Greek Orthodox Church was built in 1931 and dedicated to the twelve apostles.

Places of Interest

1. Capernaum Franciscan Site
   - Synagogue
   - Peter's Home
   - Village Houses
   - Ancient Artifacts
   - Pillar inscribed with the name of a family (Alphaeus) mentioned in Mark 2:13.
   - Via Maris Roman Road Post Marker
2. Capernaum Greek Orthodox Site
3. Capernaum National Park – Has a peer, which is a great place to walk out onto the Sea of Galilee.

Capernaum in the Bible

1. **Christ left Nazareth to live and set up His ministry base in Capernaum.**

   Matthew 4:13: *And leaving Nazareth he went and lived in **Capernaum** by the sea, in the territory of Zebulun and Naphtali.*

2. **Jesus frequently taught in the Synagogue in Capernaum.**

   Mark 1:21–28: *And they went into **Capernaum**, and immediately on the Sabbath, he entered the synagogue and **was teaching**. 22 And they were astonished at his teaching, for he taught them as one who had authority, and not as the scribes. 23 And immediately there was in their synagogue a man with an unclean spirit. And he cried out, 24 "What have you to do with us, Jesus of Nazareth? Have you come to destroy us? I know who you*

   Capernaum: Greek Orthodox site

   are—the Holy One of God." 25 But Jesus rebuked him, saying, "Be silent, and come out of him!" 26 And the unclean spirit, convulsing him and crying out with a loud voice, came out of him. 27 And they were all amazed, so that they questioned among themselves, saying, "What is this? A new teaching with authority! He commands even the unclean spirits, and they obey him." 28 And at once his fame spread everywhere throughout all the surrounding region of Galilee.

3. **Jesus healed Peter's mother and many others in Capernaum.**

   Mark 1:29–34: *And immediately he left the synagogue and entered the house of Simon and Andrew, with James and John. 30 Now Simon's mother-in-law lay ill with a fever, and immediately they told him about her. 31 And he came and took her by the hand and lifted her up, and the fever left her, and she began to serve them. 32 That evening at sundown they brought to him all who were sick or oppressed by demons. 33 And the whole city was gathered together at the door. 34 And he healed many who were sick with various diseases, and cast out many demons. And he would not permit the demons to speak, because they knew him.*

4. **In Capernaum, Jesus forgave and healed a paralyzed man. This likely happened right at the home where Jesus lived.**

   Mark 2:1–5: *And when he returned to Capernaum after some days, it was reported that he was at home. 2 And many were gathered together, so that there was no more room, not even at the door. And he was preaching the word to them. 3 And they came, bringing to him a paralytic carried by four men. 4 And when they could not get near him because of the crowd, they removed the roof above him, and when they had made an opening, they let down the bed on which the paralytic lay. 5 And when Jesus saw their faith, he said to the paralytic, "Son, your sins are forgiven."*

5. **Christ marveled at the great faith of a centurion in Capernaum.**

   Luke 7:1–10: *After he had finished all his sayings in the hearing of the people, he entered* **Capernaum**. *2 Now a centurion had a servant who was sick and at the point of death, who was highly valued by him. 3 When the centurion heard about Jesus, he*

   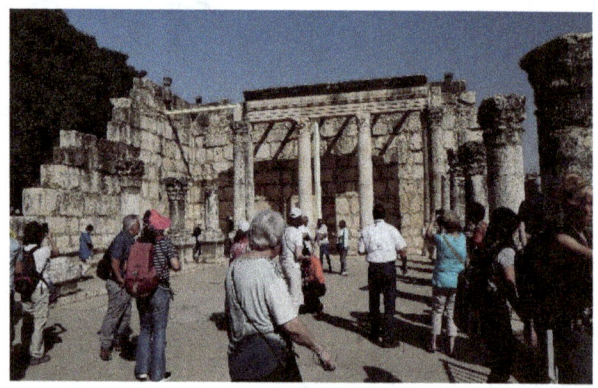
   Synagogue at Franciscan site

   sent to him elders of the Jews, asking him to come and heal his servant. 4 And when they came to Jesus, they pleaded with him earnestly, saying, "He is worthy to have you do this for him, 5 for he loves our nation, and he is the one who built us our synagogue." 6 And Jesus went with them. When he was not far from the house, the centurion sent friends, saying to him, "Lord, do not trouble yourself, for I am not worthy to have you come under my roof. 7 Therefore I did not presume to come to you. But say the word, and let my servant be healed. 8 For I too am a man set under authority, with soldiers under me: and I say to one, 'Go,' and he goes; and to another, 'Come,' and he comes; and to my servant, 'Do this,' and he does it." 9 When Jesus heard these things, he marveled at him, and turning to the crowd that followed him, said, "I tell you, not even in Israel have I found such faith." 10 And when those who had been sent returned to the house, they found the servant well.

6. **The Parables of the Kingdom were preached close to Capernaum.**

    Matthew 13:1-3: *That same day Jesus went out of the house and sat by the lake. 2 Such large crowds gathered around him that he got into a boat and sat in it, while all the people stood on the shore. 3 And He spoke many things to them in parables.*

7. **The miracle of Peter getting money out of the mouth of a fish to pay the temple tax for himself and Jesus happened in Capernaum.**

    Capernaum

    Matthew 17:24-27: *When they came to **Capernaum**, the collectors of the two-drachma tax went up to Peter and said, "Does your teacher not pay the tax?" 25 He said, "Yes." And when he came into the house, Jesus spoke to him first, saying, "What do you think, Simon? From whom do kings of the earth take toll or tax? From their sons or from others?" 26 And when he said, "From others," Jesus said to him, "Then the sons are free. 27 However, not to give offense to them, go to the sea and cast a hook and take the first fish that comes up, and when you open its mouth, you will find a shekel. Take that and give it to them for me and for yourself."*

8. **Jesus called Matthew, the tax collector, close to Capernaum.**

    Matthew 9:9: *As Jesus passed on from there [Capernaum], he saw a man called Matthew sitting at the tax booth, and he said to him, "Follow me." And he rose and followed him.*

9. **Capernaum was one of the 3 towns Christ cursed because of their unbelief in Him.**

    Matthew 11:23-24: *And you, Capernaum, will you be exalted to heaven? You will be brought down to Hades. For if the mighty works done in you had been done in Sodom, it would have remained until this day. 24 But I tell you that it will be more tolerable on the Day of Judgment for the land of Sodom than for you.*

Faith Lesson from Capernaum

1. Christ astonished the large crowds who followed him because He taught with authority. He was completely different from all other teachers because He was God in the flesh. Are we astonished today as we read Christ's teachings in His Word?

2. Christ healed multitudes of people in and around Capernaum. He also showed He was God as He forgave their sins. Forgiving sins is something only God can do. Do we believe Christ was God in the flesh and full deity?

Peter's home – Likely place Jesus lived

3. Christ marveled at the great faith of a Roman Centurion. Do we trust God in such a way that He would marvel at our faith?

4. Unfortunately, Christ cursed the town of Capernaum because of their unbelief in Him. After all they had seen, and after many of them had been healed by Jesus, they were still filled with unbelief. Unbelief is, therefore, a sin. Do we have unbelief in Christ and who He claimed to be? Do we also have unbelief in trusting Him in our daily lives when things don't seem to make sense?

Journal/Notes:

Chorazin

Location

1. Chorazin (Korazim) is located about 2 miles (3 km.) north of the Sea of Galilee.
2. From Chorazin, you can see the Sea of Galilee, Bethsaida, and some of Capernaum.
3. It's located a little off the beaten path.
4. It was built out of black basalt stone, which was common in the Galilee area.

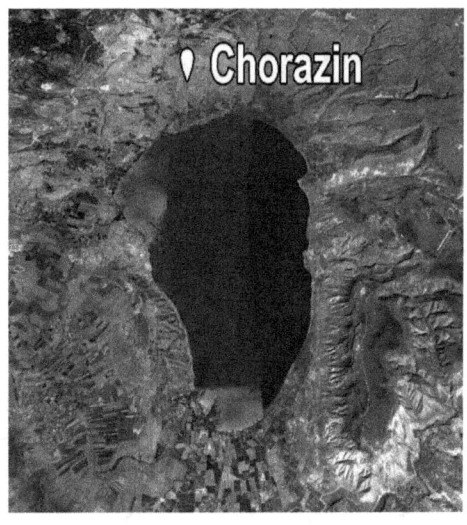

5. The construction of the homes in Chorazin are quite well preserved and show how the home where Jesus lived in Capernaum might have looked.
6. The walls of the homes consisted of stone, and the roofs were of either mud bricks or branches and leaves.
7. This area is very dry, and the water supply was essential for sustaining life in this town. A spring is located on the north-east side of the town, which was the source of the city's water, in addition to the cisterns under the houses.
8. In the time of Jesus, Chorazin was about 15 acres (7 hectares) in size and had an estimated population of around 500–1,000.

Historical Background

1. Chorazin was one of the 3 towns (Chorazin, Bethsaida, and Capernaum), which made up what scholars call "The Evangelical Triangle."
2. Jesus set up His home ministry base in Capernaum, which was nearby to Chorazin.
3. Jesus spent around 50-70% of His ministry time around the northern shore of the Sea of Galilee, so those in Chorazin would

have repeatedly heard and seen all He did.
4. A tree with the kind of thorns that would have been used for the crown of thorns Jesus wore at His crucifixion can be found here.

Places of Interest

1. Synagogue
   - Most of the ruins seen today are from the 3rd century.
   - Jesus would have taught here frequently.
   - It has an ornamental shell which would have been the top part of the cabinet where the Torah and Old Testament Scrolls would have been kept.
2. Chair of Moses
   - An unusual find in the ruins of the synagogue was a Seat of Moses carved out of a single basalt block. From it, the Torah would have been read.
   - The chair seen here is a replica of the original one. The original is in a museum in Jerusalem.

Sea of Galilee Sites

- The "Chair of Moses" was a phrase used by Jesus to signify the place of authority that the scribes and Pharisees had in interpreting the Law and exercising their authority over the Jewish people.

    Matthew 23:1-3: *Then Jesus spoke to the crowds and to His disciples, 2 saying: "The scribes and the Pharisees have seated themselves in the **chair of Moses**; 3 therefore all that they tell you, do and observe, but do not do according to their deeds; for they say things and do not do them."*

3. Mikvah Baths
4. Residential Homes
5. Thorn Trees (the kind used for Jesus' crown of thorns)
6. Public Buildings
7. Sea of Galilee

Chorazin in the Bible

1. **Christ pronounced judgment upon the cities and towns that rejected the gospel.**

    Luke 9:1-6: *And He called the twelve together, and gave them power and authority over all the demons and to heal diseases. 2 And He sent them out to proclaim the kingdom of God and to perform healing. 3 And He said to them, "Take nothing for your journey,*

    Synagogue

    *neither a staff, nor a bag, nor bread, nor money; and do not even have two tunics apiece. 4 Whatever house you enter, stay there until you leave that city. 5 And as for those who do not receive you, as you go out from that city, **shake the dust off your feet as a testimony against them**." 6 Departing, they began going throughout the* *villages, preaching the gospel and healing everywhere.*

2. **Jesus cursed those in Chorazin because they rejected Him, His teachings, and the many miracles He had done in their midst.**

    Matthew 11:21–24: *Woe to you, **Chorazin**! Woe to you, Bethsaida! For if the miracles had occurred in Tyre and Sidon which occurred in you, they would have repented long ago in sackcloth and ashes. 22 Nevertheless, I say to you, it will be more tolerable for Tyre and Sidon in the day of judgment than for you. 23 And you, Capernaum, will not be exalted to heaven, will you? You will descend to Hades; for if the miracles had occurred in Sodom which occurred in you, it would have remained to this day. 24 Nevertheless, I say to you that it will be more tolerable for the land of Sodom in the day of judgment, than for you.*

    Chorazin

3. **To whom much is given, much is required.**

    Luke 12:48: *Everyone to whom much was given, of him much will be required, and from him to whom they entrusted much, they will demand the more.*

4. **Instead of being blessed, Chorazin, Bethsaida, and Capernaum chose to be cursed. Today, each town is a testament to God's curse upon them.**

Faith Lesson from Chorazin

1. Chorazin is a testament to Christ's judgment on a people who rejected His teachings, miracles, healing, and salvation. Are we guilty of rejecting Christ and His teachings in some way?
2. Chorazin stands as a warning to us today not to do the same. Are we walking in close obedience, or living in casual obedience to Christ, or even disobedience?

3. In the same way Chorazin lies in ruins, our lives will lie in ruins if we reject Christ and the life He offers. Are we genuinely living for Christ and putting His Word into practice?
4. It appears there will be different degrees of torment and judgment in hell because Christ said it would be more tolerable in the day of judgment for other cities than for Chorazin. What do you think?
5. Following Christ brings life and blessing; rejecting Him brings death and destruction.

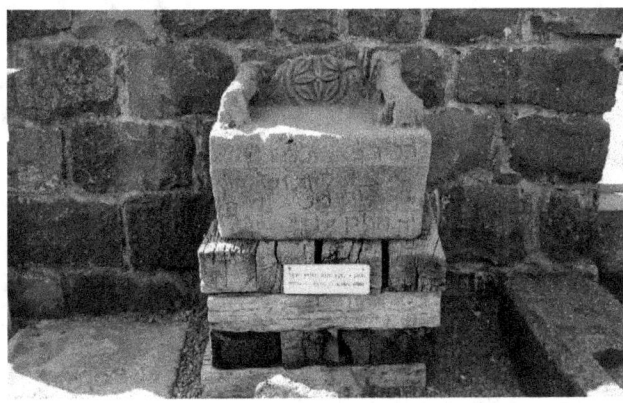

Chair of Moses

Romans 8:6-8: *For the mind set on the flesh is death, but the mind set on the Spirit is life and peace, 7 because the mind set on the flesh is hostile toward God; for it does not subject itself to the law of God, for it is not even able to do so, 8 and those who are in the flesh cannot please God.*

Journal/Notes:

Israel Biblical Sites Travel Guide

Feeding the 5,000

Location

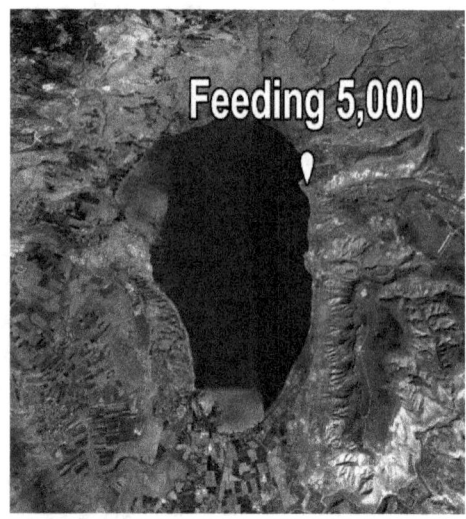

1. The traditional site of this miracle is at Tabgha, located on the northwestern side of the Sea of Galilee.
2. However, we believe this miracle most likely took place on the eastern side of the Sea of Galilee, south of Bethsaida a bit.
3. Scripture says Jesus and His disciples were headed to Bethsaida, a desolate or deserted place (Mark 6:31; Luke 9:10). Tabgha is in a very populated area and on the opposite side of the sea from Bethsaida.
4. The large population area was from Tiberias to Capernaum (the northwestern side). The deserted area was on the northeastern and eastern sides of the sea.
5. Bethsaida was a small fishing village and was about the only town on the northeastern side of the sea.
6. Immediately after feeding the 5,000, Jesus ordered His disciples to cross over to the other side of the sea (Matt. 14:22).
7. While the disciples were crossing over to the other side is when a strong storm arose. Jesus walked on water (Peter attempted to as well), and Jesus calmed the storm.
8. The storm seems to have changed the course of their destination as Scripture says that they ended up arriving in the area of Gennesaret (Matt. 14:34–36).
9. Gennesaret is located on the northwestern side of the sea where all the population is.
10. Gennesaret is less than 2 miles (3 km.) south of Tabgha. If the miracle happened at Tabgha, going from Tabgha to Gennesaret wouldn't be crossing over the other side of the sea as both towns are nearby to each other.

11. After Christ arrived at Gennesaret, many heard he had arrived, and a large multitude gathered for healing. If Christ had just been in the area of Tabgha, it wouldn't make sense that a large crowd would gather again right after Christ had just been there.
12. From the location of the feeding of the 5,000, the disciples headed in the direction toward Bethsaida and Capernaum (Mark 6:45; John 6:16-17). Therefore, they had to be enough south of Bethsaida to head in that direction by boat.

Feeding of the 5,000 in the Bible

13. For these reasons, we believe the best biblical location for the feeding of the multitude is just south of Bethsaida in this open, flat area. It seems to fit the text and the geography of the land best.

Historical Background

1. This miracle happened just after Jesus had sent out the 12 disciples to preach and heal throughout Israel (Luke 9:1-9).
2. You would think after being used so mightily by God that the disciples would have had more faith.
3. It also took place just after the death of John the Baptist (Matt. 14:1-12).
4. Jesus and His disciples were headed to the remote area of Bethsaida to rest after the long ministry period they had just finished (being sent out two by two, preaching and healing).

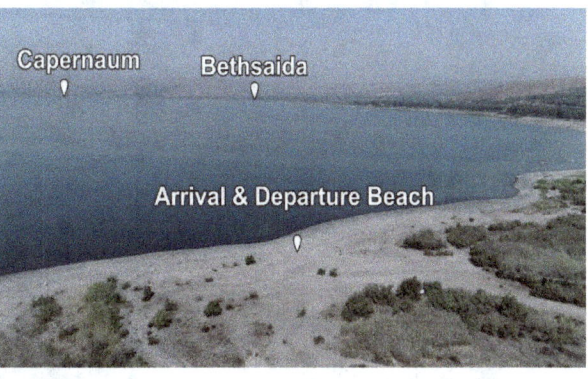

Mark 6:30-32: *The apostles returned to Jesus and told him all that they had done and taught. 31 And he said to them, "Come away by yourselves to a desolate place and rest a while." For many were coming and going, and they had no leisure even to eat. 32 And they went away in the boat to a desolate place by themselves.*

5. However, instead of resting, a huge ministry opportunity awaited

them.

Mark 6:33–34: *Now many saw them going and recognized them, and they ran there on foot from all the towns and got there ahead of them. 34 When he went ashore, he saw a great crowd, and he had compassion on them, because they were like sheep without a shepherd. And he began to teach them many things.*

6. Scripture mentions that there were 5,000 who were fed, not including women and children. This means there could easily have been 15,000 people or more present.

Places of Interest

1. Bethsaida
2. Tabgha
3. Gennesaret
4. Tiberias
5. Feeding of the 5,000 Location
6. Arrival and Departure Beach
7. Desolate side of the Sea of Galilee
8. Populated side of the Sea of Galilee
9. Sea of Galilee

Sea of Galilee Sites

1. **Feeding the multitude.**

    Luke 9:10–11: *On their return, the apostles told him all that they had done. And he took them and withdrew apart to a town called* **Bethsaida**. *11 When the crowds learned it, they followed him, and he welcomed them and spoke to them of the kingdom of God and cured those who had need of healing.*

    Luke 9:12–17: *Now the day began to wear away, and the twelve came and said to him, "Send the crowd away to go into the surrounding villages and countryside to find lodging and get provisions, for we are here in a* **desolate place**.*" 13 But he said to them, "You give them something to eat." They said, "We have no more than five loaves and two fish—unless we are to go and buy food for all these people." 14 For there were about five thousand men. And he said to his disciples, "Have them sit down in groups of about fifty each." 15 And they did so, and had them all sit down. 16 And taking the five loaves and the two fish, he looked up to heaven and said a blessing over them. Then he broke the loaves and gave them to the disciples to set before the crowd. 17 And they all ate and were satisfied. And what was left over was picked up, twelve baskets of broken pieces.*

    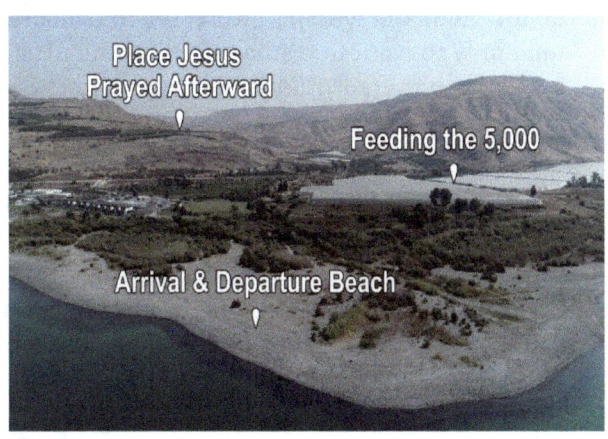

2. **Interestingly, there were twelve baskets. This was no accident as there were 12 tribes of Israel and 12 apostles.**

3. **After feeding the 5,000, the disciples encountered a huge storm. Christ walked on water, calmed the storm, and then they arrived on the northwest side of the sea at Gennesaret (Matt. 14:34–36).**

4. **The crowd Jesus fed later approached Jesus to make Him King; however, Jesus rebuked them.**

    John 6:25–27: *When they found him on the other side of the sea, they said to him, "Rabbi, when did you come here?" 26 Jesus* answered them, *"Truly, truly, I say to you, you are seeking me, not because you saw signs, but because you ate your fill of the loaves. 27 Do not labor for the food that perishes, but for the food that endures to eternal life, which the Son of Man will give to you. For on him God the Father has set his seal."*

Faith Lesson from Feeding the 5,000

1. The disciples should have had more faith after being used mightily by God to preach and heal many people. What about us? Do we lack faith after seeing all God has done for us and others?
2. The crowd later approached Jesus to make Him King. However, Jesus rebuked them because they were just seeking what He could do for them and weren't interested in true discipleship. Do we tend only to want God's blessings but no discipleship, sacrifice, suffering, or persecution?
3. Like the crowd Jesus fed, today, many people come to God for help and want to be fixed up. However, they don't want Christ to be the Lord of their lives. Do we embrace the lordship of Christ, or do we just want our problems solved and then continue living as we please?
4. God also cares for our spiritual needs and likens Himself to spiritual bread. Are you laboring for the bread that endures to eternal life, or are you more focused on temporary things that will soon fade away?
5. Are we feeding our souls daily with God's Word and the Bread of Life?

    John 6:35: *Jesus said to them, "I am the bread of life. The one who comes to me will never become hungry, and the one who believes in me will never become thirsty."*

    Matthew 4:4: *It is written, "Man does not live on bread alone, but on every word that comes from the mouth of God."*

Journal/Notes:

Jesus Walks on the Water, Calms the Storm and Sea

Location

1. This miracle took place in the middle of the widest part of the sea. John 6:19 suggests it was about 3–4 miles (5.5 km.) from the eastern shore. The sea is about 8 miles (13 km.) wide at its widest part, so this would place them in the middle of the sea.

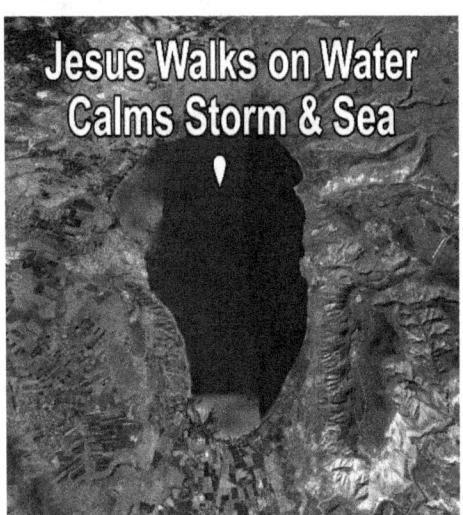

2. They were also a long way from land (Matt. 14:24). This means they were a long way from the northern part of the seashore as well.

Historical Background

1. The disciples had just come off an amazing time of preaching and healing all throughout Israel (Christ had sent them out two by two).
2. Jesus took them to the eastern side of the sea, south of Bethsaida, to rest. However, instead of resting, a large crowd gathered, and Jesus taught them all day and then fed them. There were 5,000 men, not counting women and children present, which means there were probably 15,000–20,000 people or more total.
3. After Christ fed the multitude, they wanted to make Him King by force (John 6:15). However, what they had in mind was an earthly kingdom wherein the Romans would be overthrown, and Jesus would return them to their glory days. This was prophesied in Scripture, but Christ's earthly kingdom would not be realized until His second coming.
4. The disciples were caught up in the frenzy of the crowd's desire to make Jesus King, so He immediately sent them away by boat to the other side of the sea.

5. The disciple's hearts were hard, and Scripture says they didn't learn anything from the feeding of the 5,000 (Matt. 16:5–12).
6. After feeding the 5,000, Jesus went up on a mountain to pray. He likely prayed that His disciples would learn the lesson of faith He was about to teach them. This lesson would involve sending a storm and revealing His deity to them.
7. Jesus purposefully allowed them to get to a state of utter disaster, fear, and desperation, so what He was about to teach them would sink in deeply.
8. The narrative of Scripture would place the disciples sailing from the eastern shore of the Sea of Galilee to the western shore.

Places of Interest

1. Feeding of the 5,000 Location
2. Mountain upon which Jesus prayed.
3. Departure Beach
4. Bethsaida
5. Capernaum

Sea of Galilee Sites

6. Place Jesus walked on water.
7. Gennesaret
8. Sea of Galilee

Jesus Walks on the Water and Calms the Sea in the Bible

1. Immediately after feeding the 5,000, Jesus sent His disciples to the other side of the sea.

Matthew 14:22: *Immediately he made the disciples get into the boat and go before him to the other side, while he dismissed the crowds.*

Mark 6:45: *Immediately he made his disciples get into the boat and go before him to the other side, to **Bethsaida**, while he dismissed the crowd.*

John 6:16–17: *When evening came, his disciples went down to the sea, 17 got into a boat, and started across the sea to **Capernaum**.*

The summary of these verses indicates that they were headed east to the other side of the sea.

2. Jesus went up on a mountain to pray.

Matthew 14:23: *And after he had dismissed the crowds, he went up on the mountain by himself to pray. When evening came, he was there alone.*

3. Jesus sends a strong storm.

Matthew 14:24: *But the boat by this time was a long way from the land, beaten by the waves, for the wind was against them.*

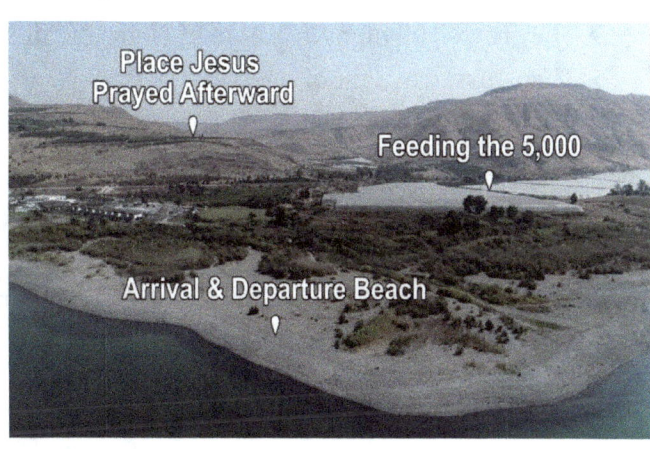

Mark 6:48: *And he saw that they were making headway painfully, for the wind was against them.*

John 6:17–18: *It was now dark, and Jesus had not yet come to them. 18 The sea became rough because a strong wind was blowing.*

Israel Biblical Sites Travel Guide

4. Jesus came to the disciples walking on the sea.

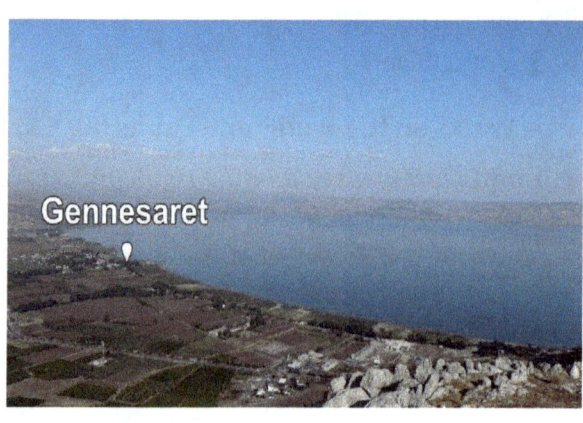

Matthew 14:25: *And in the fourth watch of the night [3:00–6:00 am] he came to them, walking on the sea.*

John 6:19: *When they had rowed about three or four miles, they saw Jesus walking on the sea and coming near the boat.*

5. The disciples became terrified.

Matthew 14:26: *But when the disciples saw him walking on the sea, they were terrified, and said, "It is a ghost!" and they cried out in fear.*

6. The emotional state of the disciples:

- They were already exhausted from their ministry of being sent out two by two.
- They had a long day of ministry.
- They rowed all night in a state of panic and desperation.
- They missed a night of sleep.
- It was still dark, so it was probably around 4:00 am.
- They feared for their lives.
- They were alone.
- It was dark.
- They were terrified when they saw Jesus walking on the sea.

7. Jesus spoke to them.

Matthew 14:27: *But immediately Jesus spoke to them, saying, "Take heart; it is I [I AM, in Greek]. Do not be afraid."*

8. Peter walked on water for a moment.

Matthew 14:28–31: *And Peter answered him, "Lord, if it is you, command me to come to you on the water." 29 He said, "Come." So Peter got out of the boat and walked on the water and came to Jesus. 30 But when he saw the wind, he was afraid, and beginning to sink he cried out, "Lord, save me." 31 Jesus immediately reached out his hand and took hold of him, saying to him, "O you of little faith, why did you doubt?"*

9. **The disciples worshiped Jesus as Lord and Messiah.**

   Matthew 14:32–33: *And when they got into the boat, the wind ceased. 33 And those in the boat **worshiped him**, saying, **"Truly you are the Son of God."***

   Mark 6:52: *And he got into the boat with them, and the wind ceased. And they were **utterly astounded**.*

   This miracle was a major turning point in the lives of the disciples. The deity of Jesus was now deeply embedded in their hearts and lives, and they would never be the same.

10. **Jesus and the disciples miraculously arrived at the other side of the sea at Gennesaret.**

    John 6:21: *Then they were glad to take him into the boat, and **immediately** the boat was at the land to which they were going.*

11. **After already being exhausted and missing a night of sleep, they had more ministry awaiting them.**

    Matthew 14:34–36: *And when they had crossed over, they came to land at **Gennesaret**. 35 And when the men of that place recognized him, they sent around to all that region and brought to him all who were sick 36 and implored him that they might only touch the fringe of his garment. And as many as touched it were made well.*

Gennesaret boat dock

Faith Lesson from Jesus Walking on Water and Calming the Sea

1. Jesus embedded in the lives of His disciples that He was God. Do we believe in the deity of Christ and that He was God in the flesh?
2. Like Peter and the disciples, are we of little faith sometimes?
3. Like the disciples, we, too, are often surrounded by serious problems. Do we realize Jesus cares for us during the storms in

our lives?

4. Like the disciples, we can often feel tired and alone in our trials and problems. Do we understand we are not alone, and God is caring for us?

5. Peter walked on the water a moment and then took his eyes off Jesus and focused on the storm. Therefore, he sank into the water. Do we understand that in order to navigate the storms in our lives, we must keep our eyes on Jesus despite the raging problems around us?

6. Jesus was the one who sent the storm in order to teach His disciples who He was and their need for faith in Him. Do we understand that Jesus also sends storms to teach us the same truths?

7. Jesus and the disciples often had long days of exhausting ministry. Are we willing to do the same?

Journal/Notes:

Kursi

Location

1. Kursi is the place where two demon-possessed men were healed.
2. The demons who lived in these men were cast into a herd of pigs that ran down a steep bank into the sea.
3. It took place on the east side of the Sea of Galilee in the region of the Gerasenes or Gadarenes. This place was also called Kurshi in Hebrew and Kursy in Arabic.

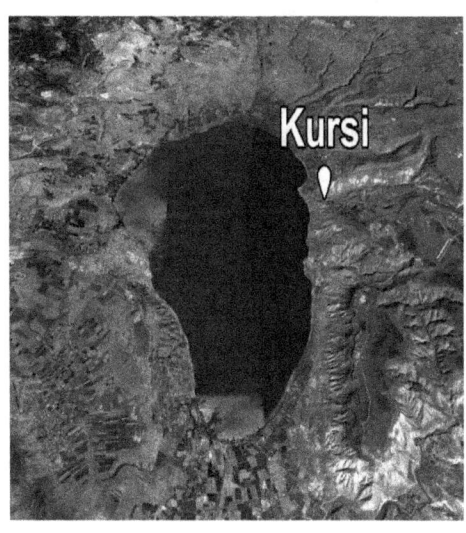

4. It was in the region of the Decapolis.
5. The Decapolis was made up of 10 Roman cities that functioned like city-states. It was a region outside of Jewish authority and inhabited by Jews and Gentiles.
6. It was an immoral area that represented all that sinful humanity had to offer. Therefore, it was considered unclean to the Jews.
7. The caves where the demon-possessed men lived can be seen on the hillside above Kursi.
8. Today, this site contains the ruins of the largest Byzantine monastery complex in Israel. It dates from the middle of the 5th century and was built to commemorate what took place here.

Historical Background

1. Jesus and His disciples were coming from the Capernaum area, where Jesus had just performed many miracles and preached about the Parables of the Kingdom.
2. On the boat ride to this area, Jesus performed an astounding miracle of calming the sea and storm.

   Matthew 8:23–27: *And when he got into the boat, his disciples followed him. 24 And behold, there arose a great storm on the sea, so that the boat was being swamped by the waves; but he was asleep. 25 And they went and woke him, saying, "Save us, Lord; we are perishing." 26 And he said to them, "Why are you afraid, O you of little faith?" Then he rose and rebuked the winds and the sea, and there was a great calm. 27 And the men marveled, saying, "What sort of man is this, that even winds and sea obey him?"*

3. This event is the most detailed account of an exorcism (casting out demons) in the Bible.

Places of Interest

1. Capernaum
2. Calming the Storm and Sea
3. Byzantine Monastery Complex
4. Tombs above Kursi
5. Beach where Jesus and His disciples arrived.
6. Steep hill the pigs ran down into the sea.
7. Decapolis Area

Sea of Galilee Sites

Kursi in the Bible

1. **When Jesus and His disciples arrived at the country of the Gadarenes, they were greeted by two demon-possessed men.**

   Matthew 8:28–29: *And when he came to the other side, to the country of the Gadarenes, two demon-possessed men met him, coming out of the tombs, so fierce that no one could pass that way. 29 And behold, they cried out, "What have you to do with us, O Son of God? Have you come here to torment us before the time?"*

2. **In the account of this story in Mark, it focuses on one of the demon-possessed men.**

   Mark 5:1–2: *They came to the other side of the sea, to the country of the Gerasenes. 2 And when Jesus had stepped out of the boat, immediately there met him out of the tombs a man with an unclean spirit.*

3. **The life of this demon-possessed man was a nightmarish living hell.**

   Mark 5:3–5: *He lived among the tombs. And no one could bind him anymore, not even with a chain, 4 for he had often been bound with shackles and chains, but he wrenched the chains apart, and he broke the shackles in pieces. No one had the strength to subdue him. 5 Night and day among the tombs and on the mountains he was always crying out and cutting himself with stones.*

   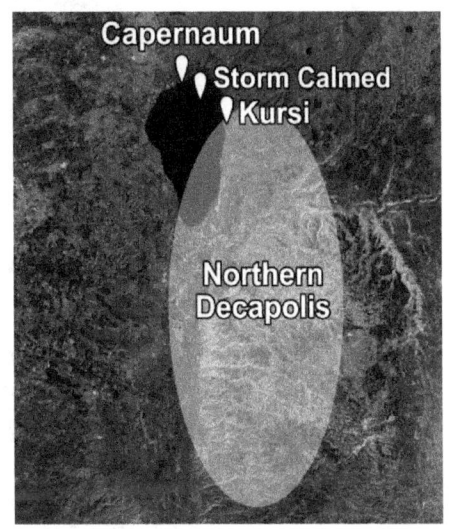

4. **The legion of demons indwelling this man recognized who Jesus was.**

   Mark 5:6–9: *And when he saw Jesus from afar, he ran and fell down before him. 7 And crying out with a loud voice, he said, "What have you to do with me, Jesus, Son of the Most High God? I adjure you by God, do not torment me." 8 For he was saying to him, "Come out of the man, you unclean spirit!" 9 And Jesus asked him, "What is your name?" He replied, "My name is Legion [5,000 demons], for we are many."*

5. **Jesus cast this legion of demons into a herd of pigs who ran into the sea.**

   Mark 5:10–13: *And he begged him earnestly not to send them out of the country. 11 Now a great herd of pigs was feeding there on the hillside, 12 and they begged him, saying, "Send us to the pigs; let us enter them." 13 So he gave them permission. And the unclean spirits came out, and entered the pigs, and the herd, numbering about two thousand, rushed down the steep bank into the sea and were drowned in the sea.*

6. **The demon-possessed man was healed, and news spread rapidly to the whole region.**

   Mark 5:14–17: *The herdsmen fled and told it in the city and in the country. And people came to see what it was that had happened. 15 And they came to Jesus and saw the demon-possessed man, the one who had had the legion, sitting there, clothed and*

   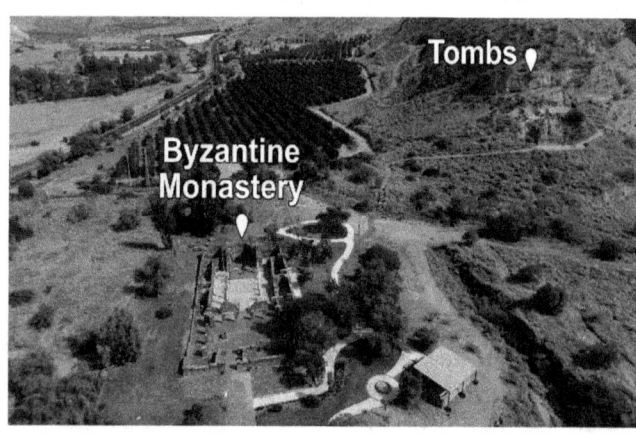

   in his right mind, and they were afraid. 16 And those who had seen it described to them what had happened to the demon-possessed man and to the pigs. 17 And they began to beg Jesus to depart from their region.

7. **Jesus sent the healed man into the Decapolis region to tell them the great things God had done for him.**

   Mark 5:18–20: *As he was getting into the boat, the man who had been possessed with demons begged him that he might be with him. 19 And he did not permit him but said to him, "Go home to your friends and tell them how much the Lord has done for you, and how he has had mercy on you." 20 And he went away and began to proclaim in the Decapolis how much Jesus had done for him, and everyone marveled.*

Sea of Galilee Sites

Faith Lesson from Kursi

1. The demon-possessed man was in deep bondage and torment from the host of demons who lived within him. Do we believe demonic possession and oppression are a reality?
2. Jesus showed His power over the demonic realm by casting the legion of demons into a herd of 2,000 pigs. Do we believe Christ is Lord over Satan and all demonic rulers and principalities in the universe?

Tombs above Kursi

3. Jesus told the demon-possessed man to go and tell others how much the Lord had done for him.
4. History records that as a result of this man's obedience, a large community of believers was established in this area and had great influence on the early church for many centuries.
5. One of our best tools in sharing the gospel is just to tell others what God has done for us. Have we carefully defined our testimony, and are we committed to using it in sharing Christ with others?

Journal/Notes:

Magdala: Mary Magdalene

Location

1. Magdala, also known as Migdal, is located on the northwestern shore of the Sea of Galilee.
2. It was located on the Via Maris (International Highway linking Africa with Asia and Europe).

Historical Background

1. This particular part of Magdala was recently discovered in 2009. It's believed a flash flood covered it sometime in the latter part of the 1st century as there have been no coins or artifacts found dating later than 67 AD.
2. It was a fishing village and had one of the largest fish markets in the northern Galilee area.
3. It has one of the oldest, well-preserved synagogues in Israel.
4. This synagogue was in use during the time of Jesus, and He certainly would have preached here regularly.

    Matthew 4:23: *And he went throughout all Galilee, teaching in their synagogues and proclaiming the gospel of the kingdom and healing every disease and every affliction among the people.*

5. On one occasion, Jesus came to this area after feeding 4,000 people on the eastern side of the Sea of Galilee.

    Matthew 15:38–39: *Those who ate were four thousand men, besides women and children. 39 And after sending away the crowds, he got into the boat and went to the region of Magadan (Magdala).*

6. It had a population of around 1,000–2,000 people during the time of Christ.
7. It had a boat harbor.
8. It has a rare stone replica of the temple in Jerusalem with detailed carvings showing different aspects of the temple.

Sea of Galilee Sites

9. Magdala was the hometown of the famous Jewish historian Josephus.
10. It was the hometown of Mary Magdalene, from whom Christ cast out 7 demons.

Places of Interest

1. Synagogue
2. Beth Midrash (teaching area in the synagogue).
3. Stone with grooves (used for reading the scrolls in the synagogue).
4. A rare stone replica of the temple in Jerusalem in the synagogue.
5. Well preserved mosaics in the synagogue.
6. Scroll storage room in the synagogue.
7. Marketplace
8. Fish Market Area
9. Residential Area
10. Mikvahs
11. Harbor

12. Byzantine Monastery
13. Duc In Altum (Latin for "Put out into the deep") is a spiritual center in Magdala where all can worship. It has a unique Galilean boat as an altar and has a beautiful view behind it of the Sea of Galilee. This center was built in honor of Mary Magdalene. One of its purposes is to honor and support women today.

Magdala (Mary Magdalene) in the Bible

1. **Jesus preached here regularly.**

   Matthew 4:23: *And he went throughout all Galilee, teaching in their synagogues and proclaiming the gospel of the kingdom and healing every disease and every affliction among the people.*

   Matthew 15:38–39: *Those who ate were four thousand men, besides women and children. 39 And after sending away the crowds, he got into the boat and went to the region of **Magadan** (Magdala).*

2. **Jesus cast out 7 demons from Mary Magdalene.**

   Luke 8:1–3: *Soon afterward he went on through cities and villages, proclaiming and bringing the good news of the kingdom of God. And the twelve were with him, 2 and also some women who had been healed of evil spirits and infirmities:* **Mary, called Magdalene**, *from whom seven demons had gone out, 3 and Joanna, the wife of Chuza, Herod's household manager, and Susanna, and many others, who provided for them out of their means.*

   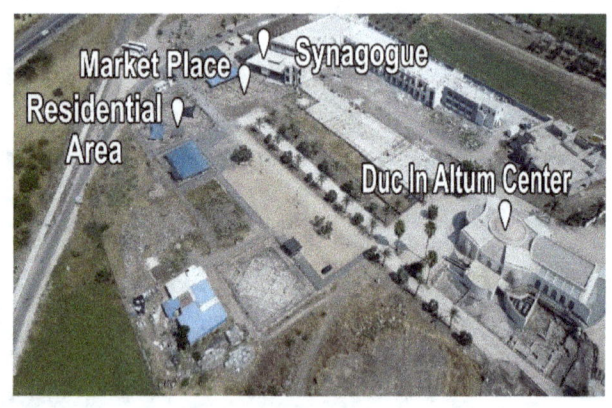

3. **Mary was likely a wealthy widow as she followed Christ everywhere and supported the ministry of Jesus financially.**

4. **A strong case could be made that Mary was one of Christ's most devoted and loyal followers.**

   She followed Jesus everywhere and supported Him financially, she was present at the mock trial of Jesus, she heard Pontius Pilate pronounce the death sentence upon Jesus, she saw Jesus beaten and humiliated by the crowd, she was one of the women who stood near Jesus during the crucifixion to try to comfort Him, and she was the first woman Christ appeared to after rising from the dead.

5. **Mary looked from a distance at Christ's crucifixion and then moved in closer during His last suffering hours on the Cross.**

   Mark 15:40: *There were also women looking on from a distance, among whom were **Mary Magdalene**, and Mary the mother of James the younger and of Joses, and Salome.*

   John 19:25: *But standing by the cross of Jesus were his mother and his mother's sister, Mary the wife of Clopas, and **Mary Magdalene**.*

6. **Mary Magdalene helped buy expensive spices to anoint the body of Jesus after His crucifixion.**

   Mark 16:1: *When the Sabbath was over, **Mary Magdalene**, Mary the mother of James, and Salome bought spices so that they might go to anoint Jesus' body.*

7. **Mary was the earliest witness to the resurrection of Jesus and was sent by Jesus to tell the others.**

   Mark 16:9: *When Jesus rose early on the first day of the week,* ***he appeared first to Mary Magdalene****, out of whom he had driven seven demons.*

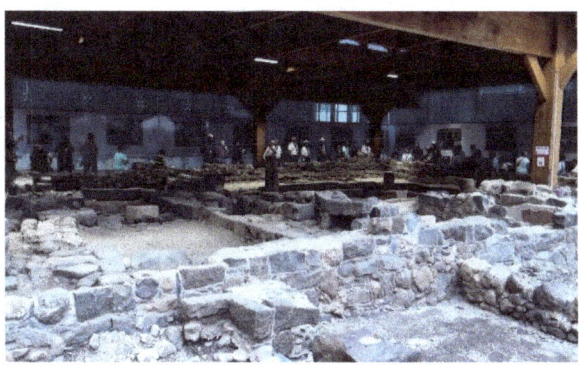

Synagogue

   John 20:11–18: *But **Mary** stood weeping outside the tomb, and as she wept, she stooped to look into the tomb. 12 And she saw two angels in white, sitting where the body of Jesus had lain, one at the head and one at the feet. 13 They said to her, "Woman, why are you weeping?" She said to them, "They have taken away my Lord, and I do not know where they have laid him." 14 Having said this, she turned around and saw Jesus standing, but she did not know that it was Jesus. 15 Jesus said to her, "Woman, why are you weeping? Whom are you seeking?" Supposing him to be the gardener, she said to him, "Sir, if you have carried him away, tell me* *where you have laid him, and I will take him away." 16 Jesus said to her, "Mary." She turned and said to him in Aramaic, "Rabboni!" (which means Teacher). 17 Jesus said to her, "Do not cling to me, for I have not yet ascended to the Father; but go to my brothers and say to them, 'I am ascending to my Father and your Father, to my God and your God.'" 18* **Mary Magdalene** *went and announced to the disciples, "I have seen the Lord"—and that he had said these things to her.*

8. **Even at the very end, Mary never lost her first love for Jesus.**

   Revelation 2:4: *But I have this against you, that you have left your first love.*

9. **There is also no doubt Mary served Christ alongside the apostles the rest of her life.**

Faith Lesson from Magdala and Mary Magdalene

1. Christ cast out 7 demons from Mary. This changed her life forever and filled her with deep gratitude to Jesus. Are we grateful for what God has done for us as well?
2. Mary loved Christ profoundly and was one of His most devoted followers. She is the model of what it means to love the Lord your God with all your heart, soul, mind, and strength. Are we devoted to Christ as Mary was?
3. Mary supported Jesus' ministry financially. Do we support the ministries of Jesus as well?
4. Mary never lost her first love for Christ. Have we lost our first love?

Journal/Notes:

Sea of Galilee Sites

Mount Arbel

Location

1. Mount Arbel is located on the west side of the Sea of Galilee and is the tallest mountain around the sea.
2. It has a spectacular view of the Sea of Galilee.
3. It rises about 1,200 ft. (365 m.) above the Sea of Galilee.
4. It has on its eastern side a cliff that drops right down to the Sea of Galilee basin.
5. This cliff has many natural caves that have been used throughout history for battles and protection purposes.

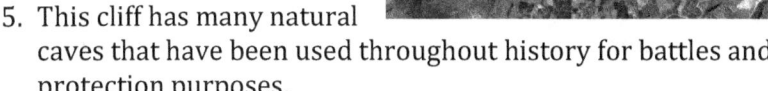

Historical Background

1. History and tradition locate Mount Arbel as the place where Christ gave the Great Commission mandate to go into all the world and preach the gospel.
2. Many theologians believe this is the place because it is the tallest mountain in the area and provides a perfect view of the Sea of Galilee.
3. Because Christ spent around 50–70% of His ministry time around the Sea of Galilee, Mount Arbel would have provided the perfect backdrop when Christ gave the powerful Great Commission mandate to His disciples. From this location, we can easily see:
   - Magdala
   - The area where Christ likely called several of His disciples.
   - Chorazin
   - Tabgha
   - Capernaum
   - Bethsaida

Israel Biblical Sites Travel Guide

- Kursi
- Where Jesus walked on water and calmed the sea.

4. The Great Commission was one of the last contacts Christ had with His disciples, which shows the importance of this commandment.
5. The cliffs of Mount Arbel have natural caves that have been used as shelters for rebels against Herod the Great, revolts against the Romans, and again in later periods. There are ruins of Hellenistic, Roman, and Byzantine villages that lie below the cliffs and on its southwestern side.

Places of Interest

1. Park Entrance
2. Lookout Location
3. Arbel Cliffs
4. Magdala
5. Sea of Galilee
6. Hellenistic, Roman, and Byzantine villages that lie below the cliffs.
7. Ancient Synagogue
8. Fortress
9. Hiking Trail

Mount Arbel in the Bible

1. **Mount Arbel is the believed place where Christ gave the Great Commission.**

   Matthew 28:16–20: *Now the eleven disciples went to **Galilee, to the mountain** to which Jesus had directed them. 17 And when they saw him, they worshiped him, but some doubted. 18 And Jesus came and said to them, "All authority in heaven and on earth has been given to me. 19 Go therefore and make disciples of all nations, baptizing them in the name of the Father and of the Son and of the Holy Spirit, 20 teaching them to observe all that I have commanded you. And behold, I am with you always, to the end of the age."*

2. **What does the phrase "All authority in heaven and on earth has been given to me" mean?**

   Colossians 1:15–17: *He [Christ] is the image of the invisible God, the firstborn of all creation. 16 For by him all things were created, in heaven and on earth, visible and invisible, whether thrones or dominions or rulers or authorities—all things were created through him and for him. 17 And he is before all things, and in him all things hold together.*

   - Christ is the image of the invisible God. He is God in the flesh so we can understand and know Him better.
   - Christ created all things in heaven and on earth.
   - He created all thrones, dominions, rulers, and authorities, and rules over them.
   - He is the head of all things.
   - All creation is held together and sustained by His power.

3. **During Christ's ministry on earth, He performed every class of miracle to show He was Lord of every aspect of creation.**

- Sickness – Christ healed every kind of sickness among countless people.
- Demons and the demonic world – Christ repeatedly cast out demons from many people.
- Weather – Christ calmed the sea and storms.
- Nature – Christ cursed a fig tree, and it died.
- Animals – Christ cast out demons into a herd of swine, He performed the miraculous catches of fish, and He rode into Jerusalem on an untamed donkey.

Caves and fortress on the cliffs of Mt. Arbel

- Food – Christ fed 5,000 and 4,000 people.
- The authority to forgive sins – Only God has this authority, so Christ showed Himself as being fully God.
- Death – Christ raised numerous people from the dead, and He Himself rose from the dead.

4. **Every knee in heaven and earth will bow before the authority of Christ.**

Philippians 2:9–11: *Therefore God has highly exalted him and bestowed on him the name that is above every name, 10 so that at the name of Jesus every knee should bow, in heaven and on earth and under the earth, 11 and every tongue confess that Jesus Christ is Lord, to the glory of God the Father.*

5. **Based upon the authority that Christ possesses, He commands us to go and make disciples.**

Matthew 28:19–20: ***Go therefore*** *and make disciples of all nations, baptizing them in the name of the Father and of the Son and of the Holy Spirit, 20 teaching them to observe all that I have commanded you.*

Sea of Galilee Sites

Faith Lesson from Mount Arbel

1. All authority in heaven and earth has been given to Christ. Do we truly believe this?
2. We are all called to be missionaries.

   Acts 1:8: *But you will receive power when the Holy Spirit has come upon you, and you will be my witnesses in Jerusalem and in all Judea and Samaria, and to the end of the earth.*
3. Missionary means "One Sent."
4. Most missionary work is done on the local level in our own Jerusalem, as most are not called to foreign missions.
5. Just because we are not foreign missionaries does not mean we aren't a missionary at our local level.
6. Making disciples entails evangelizing.
7. To support foreign missions, there are a few ways we can be involved:
   - We can be goers.
   - We can be supporters by helping financially.
   - We can be encouragers to those in the field.
   - We can be helpers when missionaries return from the field and need help back home.
   - We can be prayer supporters.
   - Am I involved in foreign missions in at least one of the above ways?
8. In fulfilling the Great Commission, it's not just enough to be a good person and hope our life will show others we're different. We are commanded to go and speak!

9. While baptism does not save us, we are to emphasize it and baptize in the name of the Father, Son, and Holy Spirit. Have I been baptized, and do I encourage others to be baptized as well?
10. We are to teach others to obey all Christ has commanded. Am I involved in doing this?
11. We have the promise that the one who has all authority in heaven and on earth will be with us as we go to evangelize and make disciples. We should realize that:

    Mt. Arbel and the Sea of Galilee in the background

    - We are not alone in fulfilling the Great Commission but have Christ present and supernaturally helping us.
    - We have all the power and authority necessary in Christ, our helper, so we don't need to fear any demonic or contrary force.
12. Do I realize Christ is with me in every aspect as I strive to fulfill the Great Commission?

Journal/Notes:

Mount of Beatitudes

Location

1. The Mount of Beatitudes is located on a hill overlooking the northern shore of the Sea of Galilee.
2. It has a spectacular view of the sea.
3. It has great acoustics.

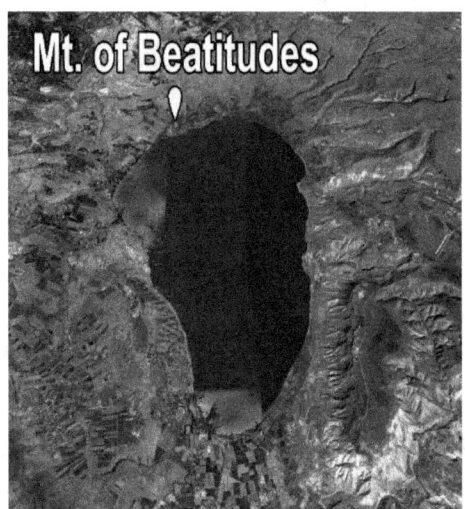

Historical Background

1. This sermon is the most complete and famous teaching Christ preached.
2. It's 3 chapters long and is found in Matthew 5–7.
3. In the same way the Law was given on Mount Sinai, many theologians see the Sermon on the Mount as the summary of the New Covenant.
4. In this sermon, Christ clarifies many Old Testament meanings and misinterpretations by constantly saying, *"You have heard it said, but I say to you."*
5. The view from the Sermon on the Mount is spectacular and provided a perfect backdrop for Christ's hearers to see as they contemplated His powerful message.
6. It was no accident that Christ chose this setting as He used nature and creation to aid in much of His teachings.
7. A Byzantine church was erected here in the 4th century and was used until the 7th century. Its ruins have been discovered just a little downhill from the present church here today.
8. Today, the Church of the Beatitudes is an octagonal building located on this site. It was built in 1938 for a Franciscan order of nuns. The eight sides of the church represent the eight beatitudes shown in Latin in the upper windows.

Places of Interest

1. Entrance
2. Mount of Beatitudes
3. Sea of Galilee
4. Church of the Beatitudes
5. Beatitude Monastery

The Sermon on the Mount in the Bible

1. **In the 8 beatitudes, everything is flipped or reversed from what most would understand as blessings.**

   Matthew 5:1–12: *Seeing the crowds, he went up on the mountain, and when he sat down, his disciples came to him. 2 And he opened his mouth and taught them, saying: 3 "Blessed are the poor in spirit, for theirs is the kingdom of heaven. 4 Blessed are those who mourn, for they shall be comforted. 5 Blessed are the meek, for they shall inherit the earth. 6 Blessed are those who hunger and thirst for righteousness, for they shall be satisfied. 7 Blessed are the merciful, for they shall receive mercy. 8 Blessed are the pure in heart, for they shall see God. 9 Blessed are the peacemakers, for they shall be called sons of God. 10 Blessed are those who are persecuted for righteousness' sake, for theirs is the kingdom of heaven. 11 Blessed* are you when others revile you and persecute you and utter all kinds of evil against you falsely on my account. 12 Rejoice and be glad, for your reward is great in heaven, for so they persecuted the prophets who were before you."

2. **Christ addressed the true essence of anger, adultery, divorce, keeping our word, how to treat our enemies, giving, prayer, and what genuine salvation looks like.**

3. **He taught about storing our riches in heaven and how to handle worry and stress.**

Matthew 6:19–21: *Do not lay up for yourselves treasures on earth, where moth and rust destroy and where thieves break in and steal, 20 but lay up for yourselves treasures in heaven, where neither moth nor rust destroys and where thieves do not break in and steal. 21 For where your treasure is, there your heart will be also.*

Matthew 6:25–34: *Therefore, I tell you, do not be anxious about your life, what you will eat or what you will drink, nor about your body, what you will put on. Is not life more than food, and the body more than clothing? 26 Look at the birds of the air: they neither sow nor reap nor gather into barns, and yet your heavenly Father feeds them. Are you not of more value than they? 27 And which of you by being*

Mount of Beatitudes

anxious can add a single hour to his span of life? 28 And why are you anxious about clothing? Consider the lilies of the field, how they grow: they neither toil nor spin, 29 yet I tell you, even Solomon in all his glory was not arrayed like one of these. 30 But if God so clothes the grass of the field, which today is alive and tomorrow is thrown into the oven, will he not much more clothe you, O you of little faith? 31 Therefore do not be anxious, saying, "What shall we eat?" or "What shall we drink?" or "What shall we wear?" 32 For the Gentiles [nonbelievers] seek after all these things, and your heavenly Father knows that you need them all. 33 **But seek first the kingdom of God and his righteousness, and all these things will be added to you.** 34 Therefore do not be anxious about tomorrow, for tomorrow will be anxious for itself. Sufficient for the day is its own trouble.

4. **Christ ended His message with a sober warning about the importance of obeying and living out His words, not just listening to them.**

   Matthew 7:24–29: *Everyone then who hears these words of mine and does them will be like a wise man who built his house on the rock. 25 And the rain fell, and the floods came, and the winds blew and beat on that house, but it did not fall, because it had been founded on the rock. 26 And everyone who hears these words of mine and does not do them will be like a foolish man who built his house on the sand. 27 And the rain fell, and the floods came, and the winds blew and beat against that house, and it fell, and great was the fall of it. 28 And when Jesus finished these sayings, the crowds were astonished at his teaching, 29 for he was teaching them as one who had authority, and not as their scribes.*

Sea of Galilee from the Mount of Beatitudes

Faith Lesson from the Sermon on the Mount

1. Christ began His sermon by clarifying the principles of true blessings in life. Do we understand each principle, and are we living them out?
2. Christ focused on the heart attitude behind His commands. Do we understand that Christ looks at our hearts and motives for why we obey or don't obey His commands?
3. Christ stressed the importance of storing our riches in heaven and living for eternity. Do we care about our treasures in heaven, or are we mainly just focused on this life and the treasures it has to

offer?

4. Christ defined a wise person as one who lived out what He taught. He defined a foolish person as one who heard but did not put into practice what He taught. Do we tend to know what to do but not actually live it out?

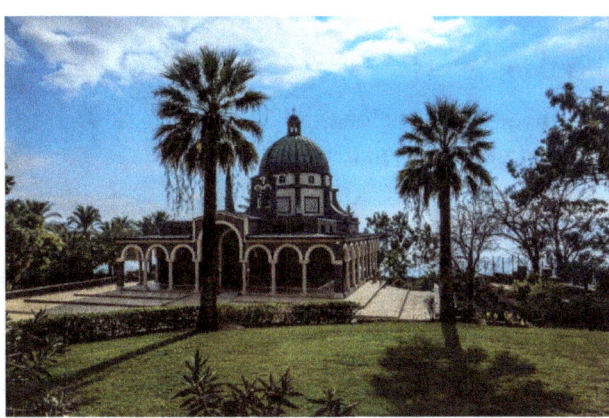
Church of the Beatitudes

5. Are we building our lives on the sand or on the rock?

Journal/Notes:

Sower's Cove: Parables of the Kingdom

Location

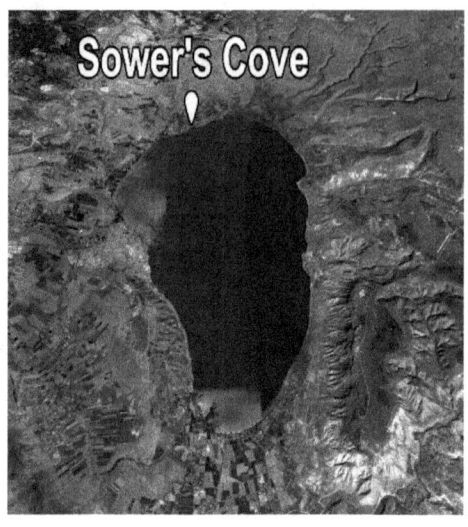

1. Sower's Cove is located between Capernaum and Tabgha on the northern shore of the Sea of Galilee.
2. It's a natural cove with outstanding acoustics.
3. When Christ preached the Parables of the Kingdom, He went out of His house in Capernaum and sat by the sea. Tradition and the natural location of Sower's Cove make it an excellent candidate for the place where Christ preached these parables found in Matthew 13.

Historical Background

1. A parable is a story that illustrates a truth by using an example from nature.
2. The parables tell what the Kingdom of Heaven is like.
3. The term "Kingdom of Heaven" and "Kingdom of God" are the same. Matthew's gospel uses the term "Kingdom of Heaven" as it was directed to more of a Jewish audience. The Jews had such a high reverence for God that they didn't use His name much. They even took out the vowels in Yahweh to show reverence. The other Gospels mainly use the term "Kingdom of God" in their accounts.
4. Part of the reason Christ spoke in parables was to fulfill prophecies regarding judgment on the Israelites because of their dull and hardened hearts (Isaiah 6:9–10).

    Matthew 13:13–17: *This is why I speak to them in parables, because seeing they do not see, and hearing they do not hear, nor do they understand. 14 Indeed, in their case the prophecy of Isaiah is fulfilled that says: "You will indeed hear but never understand, and you will indeed see but never perceive." 15 For this people's heart has grown dull, and with their ears they can barely hear, and their*

Sea of Galilee Sites

eyes they have closed, lest they should see with their eyes and hear with their ears and understand with their heart and turn, and I would heal them. 16 But blessed are your eyes, for they see, and your ears, for they hear. 17 For truly, I say to you, many prophets and righteous people longed to see what you see, and did not see it, and to hear what you hear, and did not hear it.

Places of Interest

1. Sower's Cove
2. Capernaum
3. Northern Shore of the Sea of Galilee
4. Mount of Beatitudes
5. Bethsaida
6. Tabgha
7. Sea of Galilee

Parable of the Sower in the Bible

1. **Jesus went out by the Sea of Galilee and told many parables; one of them was the Parable of the Sower.**

   Matthew 13:1-9: That same day Jesus went out of the house and sat beside the sea. 2 And great crowds gathered about him, so that he got into a boat and sat down. And the whole crowd stood on the beach. 3 And he told them many things in parables, saying: "A sower went out to sow. 4 And as he sowed, some seeds fell along the path, and the birds came and devoured them. 5 Other seeds fell on rocky ground, where they did not have much soil, and immediately they sprang up, since they had no depth of soil, 6 but when the sun rose, they were scorched. And *since they had no root, they withered away. 7 Other seeds fell among thorns, and the thorns grew up and choked them. 8 Other seeds fell on good soil and produced grain, some a hundredfold, some sixty, some thirty. 9 He who has ears, let him hear."*

2. **Jesus used the natural elements of nature found right in this area as illustrations for this parable.**

3. **Christ explains the meaning of the Parable of the Sower.**

   Matthew 13:18-23: Hear then the parable of the sower: 19 When anyone hears the word of the kingdom and does not understand it, the evil one comes and snatches away what has been sown in his heart. This is what was sown along the path. 20 As for what was sown on rocky ground, this is the one who hears the word and immediately receives it with joy, 21 yet he has no root in himself, but endures for a while, and when tribulation or persecution arises on account of the word, immediately he falls away. 22 As for what was sown among thorns, this is the one who hears the word, but the cares of the world and the deceitfulness of riches choke the word, and it proves unfruitful. 23 As for what was sown on good soil, this is the one who hears the word and understands it. He indeed bears fruit and yields, in one case a hundredfold, in another sixty, and in another thirty.

Summary of the Meaning of the Parable of the Sower

1. The seed is the Word of God.
2. The different soils represent the different kinds of hearts people can have.
3. The one who snatches away the seed is the Devil.
4. The hard soil is a hard heart that hears but refuses to let God's Word enter. They are unsaved and under Satan's control.
5. The rocky soil represents those who hear God's Word but don't continue when hard times and persecution come.
6. The weedy soil represents people who allow the worries of life and the pursuit of wealth to choke out God's Word, so they wither up and die.
7. The last soil that produces a harvest represents true believers who persevere in their faith, and in so doing, produce fruit.

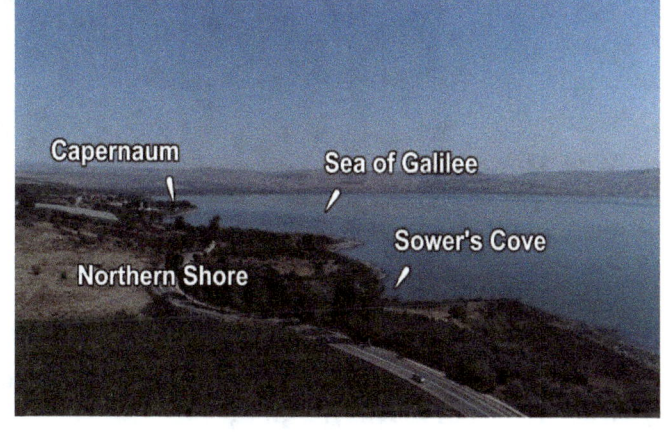

8. It seems clear that the first 3 kinds of soils represent unsaved people.
9. Only the last soil that produced fruit represents the truly saved person, as fruit is the example used throughout Scripture to refer to genuinely saved people.

Other Parables Christ Taught at Sower's Cove

1. Parable of the Weeds (Tares)

2. Parable of the Mustard Seed and the Leaven
3. Parable of the Hidden Treasure
4. Parable of the Pearl of Great Value
5. Parable of the Net

Faith Lesson from Sower's Cove

1. Part of the reason Christ spoke in parables was to fulfill prophecies regarding judgment on the Israelites because of their dull and unbelieving hearts. Are our hearts dull of hearing? What are we doing to protect our hearts from becoming dull of hearing?
2. What kind of soil (heart) do we possess? Is it hard? Is it stony, shallow, and pulls away from God when trials and suffering come? Is it full of the cares and distractions of this world? Or is it producing much fruit for God?
3. The good soil produced different amounts of fruit; some yielded a hundred-fold, some sixty-fold, and some thirty-fold. How much fruit are you producing for God?

Journal/Notes:

Sea of Galilee Sites

Tabgha

Location

1. Tabgha is located on the northwest side of the Sea of Galilee.
2. There are 7 springs found in this area which provided one of the best fishing places around the sea.
3. Some of the springs provided warm sulfuric water that caused the fish to gather here. It was also used for health purposes, and many came from far away to find healing and relief in its waters.

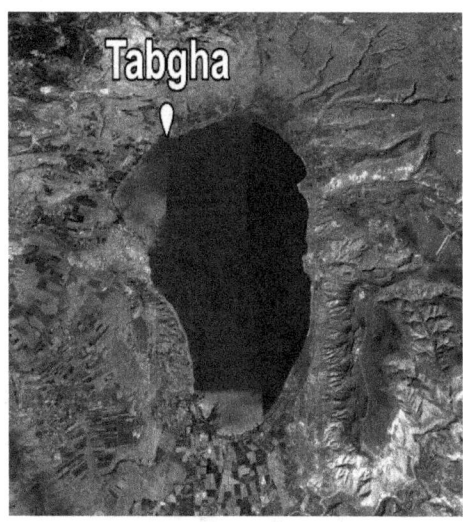

4. Waters from these springs were also taken to nearby fields and villages via canals.
5. This site is the traditional place where it's believed Christ fed the 5,000. The modern Church of the Multiplication stands on the site of a 4th-century church that has undergone several renovations throughout the centuries. In 1982 the church that was here was replaced by the modern Church of the Multiplication.
6. However, we don't believe Tabgha is the biblical place for the feeding of the 5,000 for the following reasons:
   - Scripture says Jesus and His disciples were headed to Bethsaida to a desolate place (Mark 6:31; Luke 9:10). Tabgha is in a very populated area and on the opposite side of the sea from Bethsaida, which was on the eastern side of the sea.
   - The large population area was from Tiberias to Capernaum (the northwestern side). The deserted area was on the northeastern side of the sea in the Bethsaida region.
   - Bethsaida was a fishing village on the northeastern side of the sea.
   - Immediately after feeding the 5,000, Jesus ordered His disciples to cross over to the other side of the sea (Matt. 14:22).

- While the disciples were crossing over to the other side is when a strong storm arose. Jesus walked on water (Peter attempted to as well), and Jesus calmed the storm.
- The storm seems to have changed the course of their destination as Scripture says that they ended up arriving in the area of Gennesaret (Matt. 14:34–36).
- Gennesaret is located on the northwestern side of the sea where all the population is.
- Gennesaret is less than 2 miles (3 km.) south of Tabgha. If the miracle happened at Tabgha, going from Tabgha to Gennesaret wouldn't be crossing over the other side of the sea as both towns are nearby to each other.

Tabgha

- After Christ arrived at Gennesaret, many heard he had arrived, and a large multitude gathered for healing. If Christ had just been in the area of Tabgha, it wouldn't make sense that a large crowd would gather again right after Christ had just been there.
- For these reasons, we believe the best biblical location for the feeding of the 5,000 is just south of Bethsaida in an open flat area. It seems to fit the text and the geography of the land best.

7. Even though Tabgha might not be the location of the feeding of the 5,000, it's a great place to reflect and commemorate this miracle. The important thing is that the miracle really happened, not that we get the place exactly right.

8. It's also the site where it's believed Christ restored Peter after His resurrection. The Church of the Primacy of St. Peter marks the place where this event took place. The church today was built in 1933 and incorporated parts of an earlier 4th-century church. A building made of black basalt was built in 1934 and

Sea of Galilee Sites

commemorates this place.
9. The restoration of Peter will be our focus at this site.

Historical Background

1. The disciples had returned to their hometowns on the northern shore of the Sea of Galilee after the death, burial, and resurrection of Christ in Jerusalem.
2. They undoubtedly felt very depressed, lonely, and as if their whole world had come to an end.
3. Their beloved Master had been crucified, and they were left wondering what would happen now.

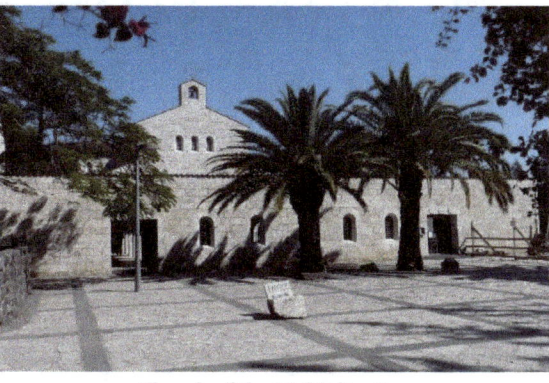
Church of the Multiplication

4. They probably called into question how they had spent their past 3 ½ years following Christ.
5. Peter especially felt depressed and spiritually sick. His last contact with Christ was that of hearing the cock crow in declaration to the fact that he had just denied his Lord and Master 3 times after he had just moments earlier said he would follow Him even to death.

Places of Interest

1. Church of the Multiplication
2. Stone inside the Church of the Multiplication upon which tradition holds that Christ multiplied the fish and bread.
3. Church of the Primacy of St. Peter
4. Stone inside the Church of the Primacy of St. Peter upon which tradition holds that Christ fed the disciples after His resurrection, and where Christ restored Peter.
5. Beach nearby to the Church of the Primacy of St. Peter.
6. Heart-shaped stones by the beach.
7. Rock Monument with a carved cross and verse.
8. Mount of Beatitudes

Restoration of Peter in the Bible

1. **After Christ's crucifixion and resurrection, the disciples went back to fishing like old times.**

   John 21:1–3: *Afterward Jesus appeared again to his disciples, by the Sea of Tiberius. It happened this way: 2 Simon Peter, Thomas (called Didymus), Nathanael from Cana in Galilee, the sons of Zebedee, and two other disciples were together [8 disciples in all]. 3 "I'm going out to fish," Simon Peter told them, and they said, "We'll go with you." So they went out and got into the boat, but that night they caught nothing.*

2. **Jesus appears to the disciples.**

   John 21:4–14: *Early in the morning, Jesus stood on the shore, but the disciples did not realize that it was Jesus. 5 He called out to them, "Friends, haven't you any fish?" "No," they answered. 6 He said, "Throw your net on the right side of the boat, and you will find some." When they did, they were unable to haul the net in because of the large number of fish. 7 Then the disciple whom Jesus loved said to Peter, "It is the Lord!" As soon as Simon Peter heard him say, "It is the Lord," he wrapped his outer garment around him (for he had taken it off) and jumped into the water. 8 The other disciples followed in the boat, towing the net full of fish, for they were not far from shore, about a hundred yards. 9 When they landed, they saw a fire of burning coals there with fish on it, and some bread [in John 18:18 Peter denied Christ by a charcoal fire]. 10 Jesus said to them, "Bring some of the fish you have just caught." 11 Simon Peter climbed aboard and dragged the net ashore. It was full of large fish, 153 [according to Hebrew alphabetics, this number meant "I Am God"], but even with so many, the net was not torn. 12 Jesus said to them, "Come and have breakfast." None of the disciples dared ask him, "Who are you?" They knew it was the Lord. 13 Jesus came, took the bread and gave it to them, and did the same with the fish [same food as the feeding of the 5,000]. 14 This was now the third time Jesus appeared to his disciples after he was raised from the dead.*

3. **Jesus restores Peter.**

   John 21:15–17: *When they had finished eating, Jesus said to Simon Peter, "Simon son of John, do you truly love me more than these?" "Yes, Lord," he said, "you know that I love you." Jesus said, "Feed my lambs." 16 Again Jesus said, "Simon son of John, do you truly love me?"*

   Church of the Primacy of St. Peter

   He answered, "Yes, Lord, you know that I love you." Jesus said, "Take care of my sheep." 17 The third time he said to him, "Simon son of John, do you love me?" Peter was hurt because Jesus asked him the third time, "Do you love me?" He said, "Lord, you know all things; you know that I love you." Jesus said, "Feed my sheep."

4. **This encounter was similar to the first time Christ called Peter to be His disciple.**

   Luke 5:1–11: *On one occasion, while the crowd was pressing in on him to hear the word of God, he was standing by the lake of Gennesaret, 2 and he saw two boats by the lake, but the fishermen had gone out of them and were washing their nets. 3 Getting into one of the boats, which was Simon's, he asked him to put out a little from the land. And he sat down and taught the people from the boat.*

4 And when he had finished speaking, he said to Simon, "Put out into the deep and let down your nets for a catch." 5 And Simon answered, "Master, we toiled all night and took nothing! But at your word, I will let down the nets." 6 And when they had done this, they enclosed a large number of fish, and their nets were breaking. 7 They signaled to their partners in the other boat to come and help them. And they came and filled both the boats, so that they began to sink. 8 But when Simon Peter saw it, he fell down at Jesus' knees, saying, "Depart from me, for I am a sinful man, O Lord." 9 For he and all who were with him were astonished at the catch of fish that they had taken, 10 and so also were James and John, sons of Zebedee, who were partners with Simon. And Jesus said to Simon, "Do not be afraid; from now on you will be catching men." 11 And when they had brought their boats to land, they left everything and followed him.

Faith Lesson from Tabgha

1. Peter's original calling to be a disciple and his restoration follow the same miracle pattern. Christ did this on purpose because He wanted Peter to remember his roots and beginning.
2. Christ was the one who reached out to Peter and took the initiative to restore him.
3. Jesus asked Peter if he loved Him 3 times because Peter denied Him 3 times.
4. God realizes we are human and make mistakes.
5. The main thing God looks for in restoration is a spirit of repentance and a contrite, humble heart.
6. Am I in need of restoration in some way?
7. Do I understand that God is more interested in my restoration with Him than I probably am?

Journal/Notes:

Yardenit Baptismal Site

Location

There are two main baptismal sites on the Jordan River.

Yardenit Baptismal Site

1. Yardenit is just a couple hundred yards (meters) west of Hwy. 90, at the southern tip of the Sea of Galilee.
2. It's a popular spot, and the water is clean and abundant.
3. For those desiring to get baptized here in the Jordan River, the Yardenit gift shop provides white robes and towels for a small fee.
4. Yardenit has a large gift shop for the purchase of souvenirs and other miscellaneous items as well.
5. Yardenit is also a great place to view the Jordan River.
6. Entrance to the site is free.

Jordan River Baptismal Site of Jesus (Qasr al-Yahud)

1. This baptismal site is located about 2 miles (3.2 km.) east of Hwy. 90, across from Jericho.
2. It's also known as Qaser al-Yahud, Kasser al-Yahud, and the Baptismal Site of Jesus.
3. It's the place where it's believed Jesus was baptized and where John the Baptist and the disciples of Jesus baptized many people as well.
4. The water is not as clean as Yardenit, but thousands of pilgrims are baptized there each year because of its spiritual significance.
5. It's also the believed location where the Israelites crossed the Jordan River to enter the Promised Land.

   (For more, please see Jordan River Baptismal Site of Jesus.)

Places of Interest

1. Yardenit Baptismal Site
2. Jordan River
3. Parking Area
4. Hwy. 90
5. Sea of Galilee

Historical Background

1. The concept of baptism is rooted in the Old Testament. As far back as Genesis, eight people were saved from the great flood of God's judgment. The Apostle Peter indicated that the water of the flood "symbolizes baptism that now saves you" (1 Pet. 3:21).
2. Old Testament prophets such as Isaiah, Ezekiel, and King David likewise used water as an external symbol for internal cleansing (Isa. 1:16; Ezek. 36:25; Ps. 51:2).

    Isaiah 1:16: *Wash yourselves; make yourselves clean; remove the evil of your deeds from before my eyes; cease to do evil.*
3. The word baptize, baptized, baptizing, or baptismal is mentioned around 83 times in the New Testament and, therefore, shows the value God places on it.

(For the full Bible teaching on baptism, please see the Jordan River Baptismal Site of Jesus – Qsar al-Yahud Baptismal Site.)

Other Sites Around the Sea of Galilee

Beit Yigal Allon Centre, Ginosar: The Galilee Boat

The main attraction of Kibbutz Ginnosar is the ancient fishing boat, now known as the Sea of Galilee Boat, displayed here in the Beit Yigal Allon Museum. Discovered in 1986, buried near the edge of the lake in

mud, the boat is dated somewhere between 70 BC and 90 AD, meaning that it could have been in use during the time of Jesus. The boat is made from cedar wood and is about 27 ft. (8.27 m.) long and 7.5 ft. (2.3 m.) wide. Although there is no proof that the boat could have been used by Jesus or one of his disciples, many people have nicknamed it the Jesus Boat.

Berko Archaeological Park

The Berko Archaeological Museum provides a unique glimpse into Tiberias of the first century. Tiberias was founded in 18 AD by Herod Antipas, son of Herod the Great and Jewish ruler of the Galilee (4 BC-39 AD). Herod Antipas made the new city his capital, and named the city after the Roman emperor, Tiberius Caesar. The park includes an ancient Roman gate, a theater, bathhouse, and a drainage system that is a thousand years old. It also contains gardens with paths throughout and balconies offering an overall view of the ancient city.

The Theater of Roman Tiberias was constructed in the 1st century AD, then enlarged in the 2nd or 3rd centuries AD, and had a seating capacity of 7,000 people. It continued to be used for gatherings until the end of the Byzantine period and was destroyed by an earthquake that struck the city in 749 AD.

The site is located near the southern entrance of Tiberias, between the ancient cemetery and the hotels of Hammat Tiberias. A parking lot is located near the south gate, north of the Holiday Inn hotel.

Gamla Nature Reserve

High in the Golan Heights of northern Israel stretches the Gamla Nature Reserve, which is home to the ancient city of Gamla, and the Gamla Stream Waterfall (the tallest flowing waterfall in Israel). The park is full of wildlife and breathtaking views.

Gamla (camel in Hebrew) was an ancient fortified city on the Golan Heights located on a high ridge above a crossing of two gorges. During the Great Revolt against the Romans in 66 AD, it became an important stronghold where Jewish rebels fought bravely until their fatal end. The observation terrace provides a view from above the ancient city on its ridge and the remains of the early synagogue. To explore the ruins of Gamla up close, you need to take the hiking trail, aptly named "Ancient Trail," which is about .62 miles (1 km.) each way. However, because it involves some climbing and descending over stones, it can take about 2 hours. There is a viewing place by the park headquarters that grants a beautiful view of the ruins for those who don't care to hike down to them.

Gamla Stream Waterfall lookout point provides a view of the cliffs of the Gamla Stream canyon and a colony of nesting birds of prey. There is an easy 90-minute trail (45 minutes each way) leading to the lookout terrace from which the highest waterfall in Israel, 170 ft. (51 m.), flows year-round. Along the way, you will pass ancient dolmans and a collection of bronze age burial mounds made of huge boulders.

Hamat Tverya National Park

This park is in the ancient village of Hamat and is much older than Tiberias. "Hama" means hot spring. It was one of the fortified cities mentioned in the Bible within the Tribe of Naftali:

> *"And the fortified cities were Tziddim, Tzer, and **Hamat**, and Rakkat, and Chinneret"* (Josh. 19:35).

After the founding of Tiberias, Hamat became Hamat Tverya. The distance between the two cities was one mile (1.6 km.). In the park, the remains of mosaics from 3 different synagogues that were built one on top of the other, can be found. The first synagogue was built about 230 AD, the second existed in the 4th century AD, and the third was rebuilt after being destroyed in an earthquake in the 5th century. The synagogue underwent preservation, restoration, and reconstruction, and is now surrounded by glass walls.

Tiberias Hot Springs – Hamat Tverya National Park – On the Tiberias Hot Springs site, 17 thermo-mineral springs flow at a temperature of about 140 F (60 C). The water flows in a system of underground channels to the Turkish Hamam, a beautifully preserved 18th-century structure. Surplus water that does not flow into the Tiberias hot baths is collected in a pool located on-site. Because of the curative properties attributed to the waters, the Romans erected luxurious baths, attracting

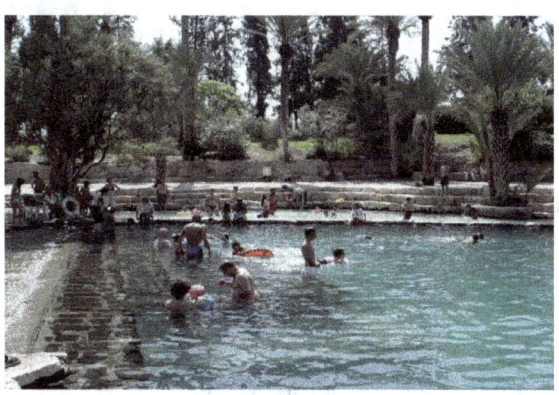

people from all over the empire. The remains of the ancient Roman baths are located at the southern end of the site.

Hippos (Horvat Susita)

The ruins of the ancient city of Hippos (horse in Greek), known today as Horvat Susita, are located 1.2 miles (2 km.) east of the Sea of Galilee on the plateau of a diamond-shaped mountain, 1,148 ft. (350 m.) above the sea. The city was almost entirely isolated from its surroundings, with just a narrow saddle-bridge leading towards the western slopes of the Golan Heights. The entire city was surrounded by an imposing fortification wall.

The ruins of Hippos are of the Hellenistic, Roman, Byzantine, and Umayyad periods, dating back to the time between the 3rd century BC and 7th century AD. During the Roman period, Hippos belonged to the Decapolis, a group of ten cities that were regarded as centers of Greek culture in an area predominantly Jewish. Archaeologists have uncovered a main colonnaded street, Roman fortifications, public baths, and temples from both the Hellenistic and Roman periods. More recently, a Roman basilica and the remains of at least seven different churches built during the Byzantine period

have been uncovered. This confirms that by the 4th century AD, the majority of residents in the city were probably Christian. Hippos continued to exist until the mid-8th century, when the city was destroyed by the catastrophic earthquake of 749 AD and was never again resettled.

Mitzpe Ofir Observation Point

This is a beautiful lookout and rest area in the southern Golan Heights that offers a view of the entire Sea of Galilee. From this viewpoint, not only can you see the whole lake, but you can also see the Lower Galilee mountains, the Upper Galilee, and the Golan Heights. The lookout is also part of a long hiking trail down to old Derech Bnei Yehuda (village settlement). This is a great place to spend a late

afternoon and witness spectacular sunsets. Mitzpe Ofir was established and is maintained by Mr. Shaal of Givat Yoav, who chose this beautiful spot to memorialize his son Ofir, who died of a long illness when he was only 16 years old. A grove of 16 olive trees has been planted there, one for each year of Ofir's life.

Tiberias Promenade

The Yigal Allon Promenade in Tiberias is more commonly known as the Tiberias Promenade. It's located along the Sea of Galilee near the Old City of Tiberias and the small Marina. The Promenade offers a pleasant stroll by the water, allowing visitors to enjoy the beautiful view of the water, boats, and the marina.

You can take a ride on a boat on the Sea of Galilee from here as well. Sunset and the evening are exceptional times to visit the Promenade with its many restaurants and souvenir shops open and busy.

Tiberium Light Show

Israel's world-renowned multimedia design company created a breathtaking water-music-light show for Tiberias. This spectacular show features dancing fountains with artistic laser lights, music, and pyrotechnics screened onto jets of water, reaching over ten meters high to create a dazzling display of water and light. The show takes place at the south end of the Yigal Alon Promenade and is free to the public three times each evening from 7-9 pm, except in rainy weather. (Note: Tiberium depends on the water level of the Sea of Galilee. If the level is too high, the light show will not take place.)

Northern Israel Sites

Northern Israel Sites

Beth-Shean

Location

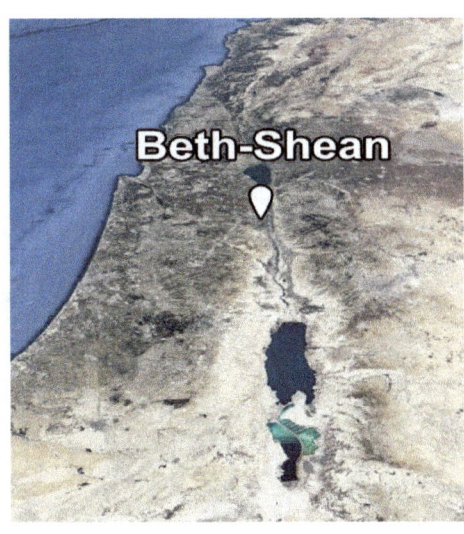

1. Beth-Shean, also known as Beit Shean or Bet She'an, was a major biblical and secular city for thousands of years.
2. It's located in the center of several main crossroads between the Jordan Valley and the Jezreel (Yizreel) Valley.
3. It's about 15 miles (25 km.) south of the southern tip of the Sea of Galilee and about 35 miles (55 km.) east of the Mediterranean Sea.
4. It's located on the Harod Stream, which provides it with much water. This Harod Stream is the same stream that originates at Harod Spring, just west of here about 15 miles, and is where Gideon chose 300 men under God's command to defeat the Midianites and other armies.
5. The main entrance faced the east, as did most other major cities and structures in ancient times. In fact, the word "orientation" comes from the word "orient," which means east. Because creation, the beginning civilizations, and the sun rose from the east, to be oriented was to position yourself focused on the east. Today, maps use the north for orientation, but in ancient days, maps used the east for orientation purposes.

Historical Background

1. Beth-Shean was a key city long before the arrival of the Israelites because of its location. In the late Canaanite period (1600–1400 BC), the Egyptians ruled the area and the entire land of Israel.
2. Later, around 1000 BC, the Philistines also ruled the city for a time as they hung the body of King Saul on its walls after defeating the armies of Israel in the Battle of Gilboa.

3. When King David reigned (1010–970 BC), he conquered Beth-Shean, which became part of Israel's territories.
4. Later, in 732 BC, the Assyrian king, Tiglath-Pileser III, destroyed Beth-Shean after defeating the northern Kingdom of Israel.
5. In the 4th century BC, Hellenistic (Greek) new settlers established a city-state (polis) in Beth-Shean. During the Hellenistic period, the city was named Nisa Scythopolis.
6. In 63 BC, the city was conquered by the Romans and became one of the cities of the Decapolis – a group of cities with a Hellenistic-Roman cultural character, most of them in Transjordan. Beth-Shean was one of the key cities of the Roman Empire in this area south of Galilee.
7. Beth-Shean was not far from Nazareth, so it's very likely when Jesus was young, he worked here with His father as a builder.
8. Undoubtedly Christ ministered here and walked by it regularly.
9. Beth-Shean was destroyed in 749 AD due to an enormous earthquake.
10. The biblical tel of Beth-Shean has around 20 layers of civilizations that have been discovered.

Places of Interest

1. Entrance
2. Old Testament Beth-Shean
3. Egyptian Governor's House
4. Tree marking the place where Saul's body was hanged.
5. Bathhouse – Often, it was a place of prostitution, so Christians avoided places like these.
6. Theater – Often, immoral and indecent acts took place there.

Therefore, early Christians avoided them and were persecuted as a result.

7. Cardo (Palladius Street) – Comes from the word "cardiac," which means the center street of the city.

8. Sigma – A mosaic depicting Tyche, Goddess of the city.
9. Pillars
10. Shopping Stores
11. Nymphaeum – Public Fountain
12. Marketplace (Agora) – Paul would be dragged into places like this (Acts 16:19).
13. Temple – Paul faced the gods of these temples in each Gentile city he ministered in (Acts 14:13).
14. Northern Street
15. Valley Street
16. Silvanus Street
17. Eastern Bathhouse
18. Public Bathrooms
19. Sacred Area
20. City Gate during Greek and Roman times.

Beth-Shean in the Bible

1. **Beth-Shean is mentioned in the division and conquering of the Promised Land.**

   Joshua 17:11: *Also, in Issachar and in Asher, Manasseh had **Beth-Shean** and its villages.*

2. **The Canaanites were a strong and fortified people.**

   Joshua 17:16: *The people of Joseph said, "The hill country is not enough for us. Yet all the Canaanites who dwell in the plain have chariots of iron, both those in **Beth-shean** and its villages and those in the Valley of Jezreel."*

3. **The tribe of Manasseh was not able to conquer the city of Beth-Shean and its villages.**

   Judges 1:27: *Manasseh did not drive out the inhabitants of **Beth-Shean** and its villages.*

4. **The major biblical event of Beth-Shean has to do with the life of King Saul.**

   As a result of Saul's persistent disobedience and presuming upon God's grace, his life was taken by the Lord, and his body, along with his sons, were hanged here on the walls of the biblical Beth-Shean, which is the hill above the lower Beth-Shean.

Theater

Saul's Disobedient Life

1. **Saul had incredible jealousy and tried to kill David for many years.**

   Scripture records many times that Saul tried to kill David: 1 Samuel 18:11, 1 Samuel 18:25, 1 Samuel 19:9–15, 1 Samuel 20:31–33, 1 Samuel 23:9, and 1 Samuel 23:25–26. Saul even gave his daughter, Michal, in marriage to David as a means to ensnare and kill him.

Northern Israel Sites

2. **When Saul felt pressured during a battle, he offered sacrifices that only a priest was allowed to do.**

   1 Samuel 13:5-7: *And the Philistines mustered to fight with Israel, thirty thousand chariots and six thousand horsemen and troops like the sand on the seashore in multitude. They came up and encamped in Michmash, to the east of Beth-aven. 6 When the men of Israel saw that they were in trouble (for the people were hard pressed), the people hid themselves in caves and in holes and in rocks and in tombs and in cisterns, 7 and some Hebrews crossed the fords of the Jordan to the land of Gad and Gilead. Saul was still at Gilgal, and all the people followed him trembling.*

3. **Saul's unlawful sacrifice.**

   1 Samuel 13:8-14: *He waited seven days, the time appointed by Samuel. But Samuel did not come to Gilgal, and the people were scattering from him. 9 So Saul said, "Bring the burnt offering here to me, and the peace offerings." And he offered the burnt offering. 10 As soon as he had finished offering the burnt offering, behold, Samuel came. And Saul went out to meet him and greet him. 11 Samuel said, "What have you done?" And Saul said, "When I saw that the people were scattering from me, and that you did not come within the days appointed, and that the Philistines had mustered at Michmash, 12 I said, 'Now the Philistines will come down against me at Gilgal, and I have not sought the favor of the Lord.' So I forced myself, and offered the burnt offering." 13 And Samuel said to Saul, "You have done foolishly. You have not kept the command of the Lord your God, with which he commanded you. For then the Lord would have established your kingdom over Israel forever. 14 But now your kingdom shall not continue. The Lord has sought out a man after his own heart, and the Lord has commanded him to be prince over his people, because you have not kept what the Lord commanded you."*

Cardo- Palladius Street

4. **Saul failed to obey God by not destroying God's enemies.**

    1 Samuel 15:1-3: *And Samuel said to Saul, "The LORD sent me to anoint you king over his people Israel; now therefore listen to the words of the LORD. 2 Thus says the LORD of hosts, 'I have noted what Amalek did to Israel in opposing them on the way when they came up out of Egypt. 3 Now go and strike Amalek and devote to destruction all that they have. Do not spare them, but kill both man and woman, child and infant, ox and sheep, camel and donkey."*

5. **Samuel confronts Saul's disobedience.**

    1 Samuel 15:22-23: *And Samuel said, "Has the LORD as great delight in burnt offerings and sacrifices, as in obeying the voice of the LORD? Behold, to obey is better than sacrifice, and to listen than the fat of rams. 23 For rebellion is as the sin of divination, and presumption is as iniquity and idolatry. Because you have rejected the word of the LORD, he has also rejected you from being king."*

    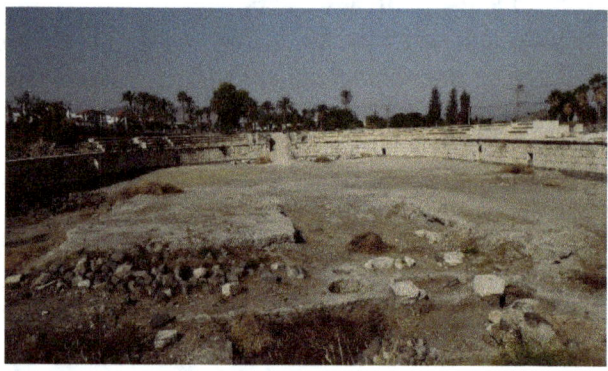
    Amphitheater/Hippodrome

    Interestingly, it would be an Amalekite, whom Saul did not destroy, that would later kill him.

6. **In a heated battle with the Philistines, Saul disobeyed God and visited a witch of Endor.**

    1 Samuel 28:15-19: *Then Samuel said to Saul, "Why have you disturbed me by bringing me up?" Saul answered, "I am in great distress, for the Philistines are warring against me, and God has turned away from me and answers me no more, either by prophets or by dreams. Therefore, I have summoned you to tell me what I shall do." 16 And Samuel said, "Why then do you ask me, since the Lord has turned from you and become your enemy? 17 The Lord has done to you as he spoke by me, for the Lord has torn the kingdom out of your hand and given it to your neighbor, David. 18 Because you did not obey the voice of the Lord and did not carry out his fierce wrath against Amalek, therefore the Lord has done this thing to you*

this day. *19 Moreover, the Lord will give Israel also with you into the hand of the Philistines, and tomorrow you and your sons shall be with me. The Lord will give the army of Israel also into the hand of the Philistines."*

7. **As a result of Saul's repeated disobedience, God took his life.**

1 Samuel 31:1–13: *Now the Philistines fought against Israel, and the men of Israel fled before the Philistines and fell slain on Mount Gilboa. 2 And the Philistines overtook Saul and his sons, and the Philistines struck down Jonathan and Abinadab and Malchi-shua, the sons of Saul. 3 The battle pressed hard against Saul, and the archers found him, and he was badly wounded by the archers. 4 Then Saul said to his armor-bearer, "Draw*

Western Bathhouse & Sigma

your sword, and thrust me through with it, lest these uncircumcised come and thrust me through, and mistreat me." But his armor-bearer would not, for he feared greatly. Therefore, Saul took his own sword and fell upon it. 5 And when his armor-bearer saw that Saul was dead, he also fell upon his sword and died with him. 6 Thus Saul died, and his three sons, and his armor-bearer, and all his men, on the same day together. 7 And when the men of Israel who were on the other side of the valley and those beyond the Jordan saw that the men of Israel had fled and that Saul and his sons were dead, they abandoned their cities and fled. And the Philistines came and lived in them. 8 The next day, when the Philistines came to strip the slain, they found Saul and his three sons fallen on Mount Gilboa. 9 So they cut off his head and stripped off his armor and sent messengers throughout the land of the Philistines, to carry the good news to the house of their idols and to the people. 10 They put his armor in the temple of Ashtaroth, and they fastened his body to the **wall of Beth-shan.** *11 But when the inhabitants of Jabesh-gilead heard what the Philistines had done to Saul, 12 all the valiant men arose and went all night and took the body of Saul and the bodies of his sons from* *the **wall of Beth-shan**, and they came to Jabesh and burned them there. 13 And they took their bones and buried them under the tamarisk tree in Jabesh and fasted seven days.*

Faith Lesson from Beth-Shean

1. Saul cared more about what people thought than what God thought of him.
2. He made big decisions without consulting the Lord.
3. Saul always had an excuse for his sin and disobedience.
4. We need to realize that obedience delights God more than asking forgiveness.
5. Rebellion and arrogance are the same as witchcraft because both attitudes fail to obey God and instead, seeks their own will and pleasure.

Beth-Shean ruins

6. Saul presumed upon God's grace. In other words, he believed he could disobey God, that God would just forgive him, and there would be no consequences. This attitude proved to be dangerous, sinful, and cost him his life and ministry.
7. Are we committed to submitting to God, or do we set ourselves up as our own authority like Saul?

Journal/Notes:

Beth-Shean Amphitheater/Hippodrome

Location

1. Beth-Shean, also known as Beit Shean or Bet She'an, was a major biblical and secular city for thousands of years.

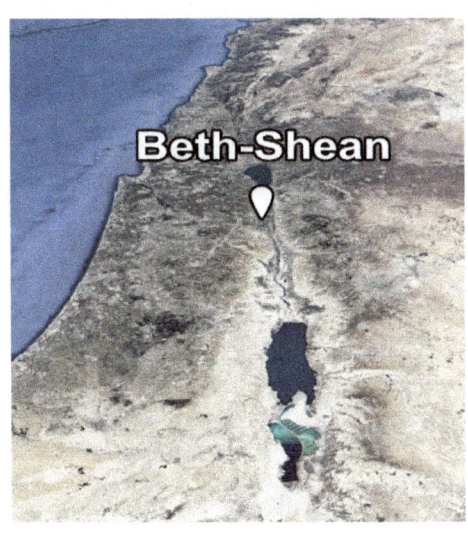

2. It's located in the center of several main crossroads between the Jordan Valley and the Jezreel (Yizreel) Valley.

3. It's about 15 miles (25 km.) south of the southern tip of the Sea of Galilee and about 35 miles (55 km.) east of the Mediterranean Sea.

4. The Romans used the amphitheater/hippodrome in Bet-Shean for pleasure events, games with animals, and gladiator-type activities.

5. This arena seems to have served as both an amphitheater and hippodrome as it has openings into the arena from under the grandstands. It was common in Greek and Roman times that a city would have one stadium that could be used for both purposes because of financial and real estate reasons.

6. An amphitheater is different from a theater. An amphitheater has a full circle of seating, wherein a theater just has a semi-circle of seating.

7. The amphitheater/hippodrome was also used to persecute Christians during the early church period and later.

8. This amphitheater/hippodrome has underground rooms where wild beasts were released to devour people and other animals.

9. On many occasions, they were released in a game-like event where believers who refused to deny Christ were torn to pieces and eaten alive while the crowd roared in a frenzy.

10. It's sobering and gives a person chills to just think about it!

Israel Biblical Sites Travel Guide

Historical Background

1. Beth-Shean was a key city long before the arrival of the Israelites because of its location. In the late Canaanite period (1600–1400 BC), the Egyptians ruled the area and the entire land of Israel.

2. Later, around 1000 BC, the Philistines also ruled the city for a time as they hung the body of King Saul on its walls after defeating the armies of Israel in the Battle of Gilboa.

Amphitheater/Hippodrome

3. When King David reigned (1010–970 BC), he conquered Beth-Shean, and it became part of Israel's territories.

4. Later, in around 732 BC, the Assyrian king, Tiglath-Pileser III, destroyed Beth-Shean and the northern Kingdom of Israel.

5. In the 4th century BC, Hellenistic (Greek) settlers established a city-state (polis) in Beth-Shean. During the Hellenistic period, the city was named Nisa Scythopolis.

6. In 63 BC, the city was conquered by the Romans and became one of the cities of the Decapolis – a group of cities with a Hellenistic-Roman cultural character, most of them in Transjordan. Beth-Shean was one of the key cities of the Roman Empire in this area south of Galilee.

Places of Interest

1. The Arena – Is derived from the word "sand." It's where the activities were carried out and was in the center.
2. Grandstands where the people were seated. The stadium's many seats have crumbled over the years, but it's estimated the seating capacity would have been between 10,000–20,000 people.
3. Entrance openings into the arena from under the grandstands.
4. Rooms under the grandstands where the animals and people

would wait before being released into the arena.

The Amphitheater/Hippodrome in the Bible

1. **Persecution was a common practice**, and the Bible refers to what many believers faced.

   Hebrews 11:35–38: *Some were tortured, refusing to accept release so that they might rise again to a better life. 36 Others suffered mocking and flogging, and even chains and imprisonment. 37 They were stoned, they were sawn in two, they were killed with the sword. They went about in skins of sheep and goats, destitute, afflicted, mistreated 38 of whom the world was not worthy, wandering about in deserts and mountains, and in dens and caves of the earth.*

   Acts 7 records how Stephen was one of the first to suffer early Christian persecution. He was stoned to death outside the gates for the faithful manner in which he preached the gospel. After this, a great persecution arose against all who professed belief in Christ as the Messiah.

   Acts 8:1: *And Saul approved of his [Stephen] execution. And there arose on that day a great persecution against the church in Jerusalem, and they were all scattered throughout the regions of Judea and Samaria, except the apostles.*

2. **History and tradition provide rich data regarding the believed fate of many of the apostles**, along with other believers who suffered persecution for their faith in Christ

during the early church period.

1. James the Great, the elder brother of John the Apostle, was beheaded in 44 AD.
2. Philip, who served in Upper Asia, was scourged in Phrygia, thrown into prison, and later crucified in 54 AD.

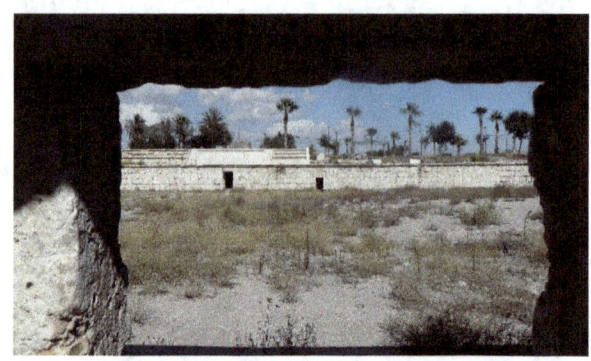

Looking out from an underground room

3. Matthew, the tax collector, served the Lord in Parthia and Ethiopia, where he was slain with a halberd (a shafted weapon with an ax-like cutting blade and a speared end) in the city of Nadabah in 60 AD.
4. James the Less, the brother of the Lord, served the church in Jerusalem and wrote the book of James. He suffered martyrdom at the age of 94 by being beaten and stoned by the Jews.
5. Matthias, the man who was chosen to replace Judas as an apostle, was stoned at Jerusalem and then beheaded.
6. Andrew, the brother of Peter, preached the gospel to many Asiatic nations and was crucified on a cross at Edessa. The ends of his cross were fixed transversely in the ground, thus the derivation of the term, Andrew's Cross.
7. Mark was converted to Christianity by Peter and served as his personal scribe. He was dragged to pieces and died by the people of Alexandria.
8. The Apostle Peter was sought by Nero to be put to death. Jerome wrote that Peter was crucified with his head down and his feet up because he thought himself unworthy to be crucified in the same way as Christ.
9. The Apostle Paul was persecuted all throughout his ministry. He was scourged, stoned, and finally, Nero had him beheaded by a sword.

Northern Israel Sites

10. Jude, the brother of James, commonly called Thaddeus, was crucified at Edessa in 72 AD.
11. Bartholomew preached in several countries and translated the Gospel of Matthew into the language of India. He was cruelly beaten and then crucified by impatient idolaters.

12. Thomas (doubting Thomas) preached the gospel in Parthia and India. His ministry caused the rage of the pagan priests, and he was martyred by being thrust through with a spear.
13. Luke, the author of Luke and Acts, traveled with Paul through various countries and was supposed to have been hanged on an olive tree by the idolatrous priests of Greece.
14. Simon the Zealot preached the gospel in Mauritania, Africa, and even Britain, where he was crucified in 74 AD.
15. John, the apostle whom Jesus loved, was sent from Ephesus to Rome, where he was put into a cauldron of boiling oil. He escaped by a miracle without injury but was then banished to the Isle of Patmos, where he wrote the book of Revelation. Nerva, Domitian's successor, said he was the only apostle who escaped a violent death.

3. **There are ten persecutions mentioned in *Foxe's Book of Martyrs* that are quite gruesome.**
    1. The first mass persecution occurred under Nero in 64 AD. He was the sixth emperor of Rome and is remembered as the one who set Rome aflame and then blamed the Christians for the deaths and destruction caused by the fire. He had some Christians sewn up in skins of wild beasts and thrown to the dogs. Some Christians were dressed in shirts made stiff with wax, fixed to axletrees, and set on fire alongside streets and in Nero's gardens in order to illuminate them. Rather than diminishing the spirit of Christianity, this persecution increased the devotion and commitment of Christians instead.

2. The second persecution happened under Domitian in 81 AD. Anything bad that happened like famine, pestilence, or earthquakes he blamed on the Christians and put them to death.
3. The third persecution occurred under Trajan in 108 AD. Christians were beaten, beheaded, and devoured by wild beasts, causing about ten thousand Christians to be put to death.

Inside an underground room

4. The fourth persecution took place under Marcus Aurelius Antoninus in 162 AD.
5. The fifth persecution is credited to Severus in 192 AD. Christians were burned at the stake, had hot tar poured on their heads, beheaded, placed in boiling water, and ravaged by wild beasts.
6. The sixth persecution took place under Maximus in 235 AD. At this time, numerous Christians were slain without trial and buried indiscriminately in mass graves, sometimes 50 or 60 cast into a pit together.
7. The seventh persecution happened under Decius in 249 AD. The main person martyred was Fabian, the bishop of Rome, who was beheaded on January 20, 250 AD.
8. The eighth persecution occurred under Valerian in 257 AD. Once again, every manner of torture was used to mock those claiming to be Christians. Persecution was also used for the entertainment of the rulers and their guests.
9. The ninth persecution occurred under Aurelian in 274 AD, when Felix, bishop of Rome, was martyred.
10. The tenth persecution took place under Diocletian in 303 AD. This was commonly called the Era of the Martyrs. Persecutions were carried out with racks, scourges, swords, daggers, crosses, poisons, and famine.

11. Today, there are more martyrs for Christ than there have ever been at any time in the history of the church. Many of these take place in the Middle East and go unnoticed by the public eye. According to BBC News, there are around 100,000–250,000 Christians who are martyred every year.

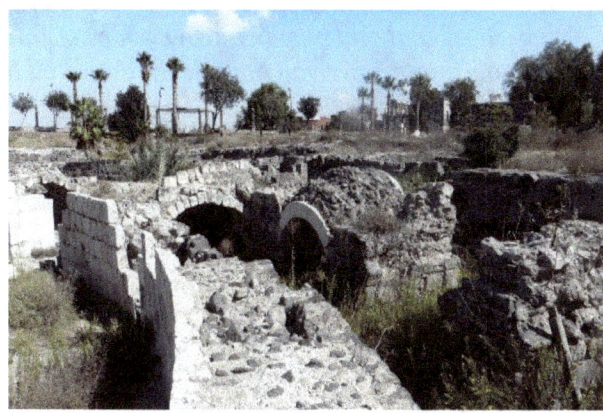
Underground rooms

Faith Lesson from Beth-Shean Amphitheater/Hippodrome

1. God used persecution to give more validity, power, and meaning to the message of the gospel.
2. We show the world the value of our faith by what it cost us to keep and obey it.
3. During the years between 313 and 325 AD, Constantine, the Roman Emperor of that time, became a Christian and later declared Christianity the religion of the Roman Empire.
4. It was the persecution of Christians that God used most to convert the Roman Empire to Christianity.
5. Through persecution, God changed the religion of the most powerful nation on the earth to Christianity.
6. The church has seen its greatest growth and maturity during the periods it was persecuted the most.
7. We are nearing a time when it is going to cost us to follow Christ as well.

   Hebrews 12:1–4: *Therefore, since we are **surrounded by so great a cloud of witnesses**, let us also lay aside every weight, and sin which clings so closely, and let us run with endurance the race that is set before us, 2 looking to Jesus, the founder and perfecter of our faith, who for the joy that was set before him endured the cross,* *despising the shame, and is seated at the right hand of the throne of God. 3 Consider him who endured from sinners such hostility against himself, so that you may not grow weary or fainthearted. 4 In your struggle against sin, you have not yet resisted to the point of shedding your blood.*

8. Are we willing to suffer for our faith?
9. What does it cost us to follow Christ?

10. Do we stand firm on God's Word despite opposition?
11. Do we allow ourselves to be persuaded to compromise our faith because of pressure from our peers?
12. Do we subtly deny Christ in moments when we're around people who don't share our faith?
13. The only thing these Christians who died in this amphitheater here in Beth-Shean would have had to do to save their lives and not be shredded to pieces by the wild beast was to deny Christ.
14. But they didn't, and today they have a special reward in heaven for being a martyr.
15. How about us? Are we willing to do the same?

Journal/Notes:

Caesarea Philippi

Location

1. Few other places in Scripture provide so much meaning by understanding the location.
2. It was here that Peter made the divinely inspired declaration the Jesus was the Christ, the Son of the living God.
3. Caesarea Philippi was an impressive Greco-Roman city near a huge spring that comes out of a cave and is one of the main sources of the Jordan River.

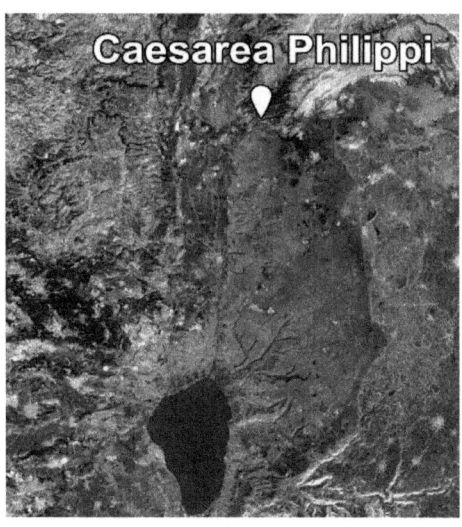

4. It's about 30 miles (48 km.) north of the Sea of Galilee and is at the foothills of Mount Hermon.
5. It was close to a "high place" where Jeroboam set up a golden calf for the northern tribes of Israel to worship, which led to their downfall.
6. In around 1000 AD, an earthquake collapsed part of the cave and changed the water flow. Now the water comes out of the ground below the cave.

Historical Background

1. This place has been associated with intense false god worship and evil for many years.
2. Baal worship took place here during the period of the kings of Israel.
3. King Jeroboam set up a golden calf not far from here and commanded all the Israelites in this area to worship it.
4. Later, under the Greeks, it became the key place of worship to the fertility god, Pan. Pan was a half-human, half-goat-like creature.
5. Then the Romans incorporated it into a place of false god worship

as well.
6. Caesarea Philippi was originally called Panion or Panias, after the Greek god Pan. Later it became known as Banias.
7. Herod the Great's son, Philip, established it as the capital of his territory and named it Caesarea to honor the emperor of Rome. It became a large flourishing Roman city.
8. It was known as Caesarea Philippi to distinguish it from other cities with the same name.
9. During the time of Christ, there were 5 main areas of worship to false gods that took place here.
    - Herod the Great built a temple right at the mouth of this enormous spring to honor Augustus Caesar.
    - A courtyard area to the worship of Pan.
    - A temple dedicated to the false god Zeus.
    - An upper Tomb Temple of the Dancing Goats.
    - A lower Tomb Temple of the Dancing Goats.
10. It was a worldwide gathering place of worship to numerous false gods.
11. It was literally considered the "Gate of the Underworld (Hades)" by the known world at that time.

12. Children would be thrown alive into the entrance to the cave as a sacrifice to the god of Pan, believing this would appease the gods and bring fertility to their crops.
13. Some even believe that men would mate with goats in the courtyard of Pan and on the Tomb Temples in ritualistic fertility acts believing this would help their crops. They would also have goats mating with goats as well in these areas.
14. It was a sick cesspool of evil and represented the worst Satan and sinful humanity could offer.
15. The disciples were very uncomfortable coming to this eerie,

demonic, dark place, and no good Jew would have even considered coming here.

16. However, Jesus purposefully brought His disciples here to embed within their hearts the imperative truth of who He was, what the mission of His church would be, and the astounding power His church would have over evil through Him.

Places of Interest

1. Cave Entrance (place the large spring was located)
2. Temple of Augustus
3. Courtyard of Pan
4. Temple of Zeus
5. Upper Tomb Temple of the Dancing Goats
6. Lower Tomb Temple of the Dancing Goats

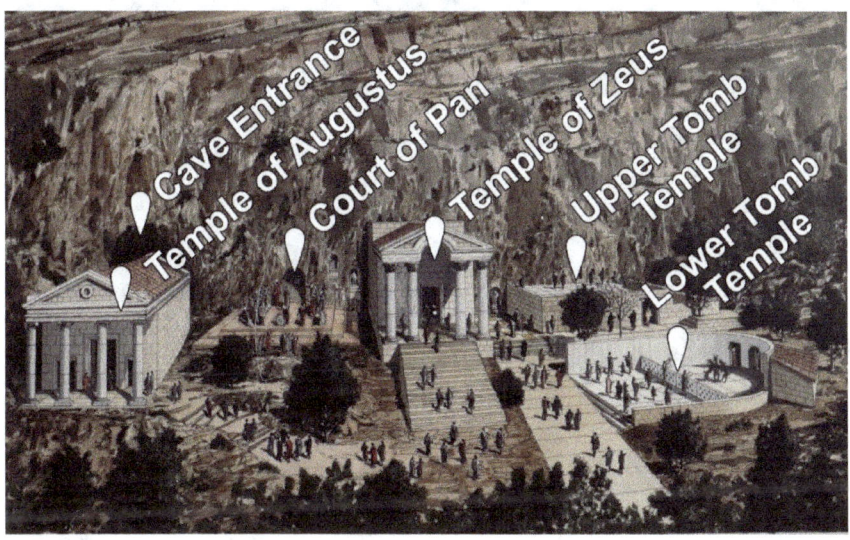

7. Hermon Stream (flows from the cave entrance)
8. Byzantine Church
9. Cardo
10. Moat
11. Church
12. Crusader Church
13. Palace of Agrippa II

14. Flour Mill
15. Roman Bridge

Caesarea Philippi in the Bible

1. **Peter's confession about the identity of Christ.**

   Matthew 16:13–16: *Now when Jesus came into the district of **Caesarea Philippi**, he asked his disciples, "**Who do people say that the Son of Man is?**" 14 And they said, "Some say John the Baptist, others say Elijah, and others Jeremiah or one of the prophets." 15 He said to them, "But who do you say that I am?" 16 Simon Peter replied, "**You are the Christ, the Son of the living God**."*

   - To properly understand the meaning of this passage, we must understand the big question Christ asked and the purpose for which He asked it.
   - The question was about who Christ was, His identity, and His essence.
   - In contrast to all the false gods being worshiped at this site,

Christ established that He was the only true and living God that should be worshiped.

2. Peter's confession was a direct revelation from God.

Matthew 16:17: *And Jesus answered him, "Blessed are you, Simon Bar-Jonah! For flesh and blood has not revealed this to you, but my Father who is in heaven."*

3. Christ will build His Church.

Matthew 16:18: *And I tell you, you are Peter [petros – small pebble], and on this rock [petra – large, massive rock],* **I will build my church**, *and the gates of hell shall not prevail against it.*

This passage has had two main interpretations throughout history. The Roman Catholic Church claims that the rock upon which Christ will build His Church is Peter, upon which they build the papacy. Evangelicals claim that the rock is Christ, based upon Peter's confession.

Evidence that the rock is Christ, not Peter:

- Christ used the word ***petros*** in describing Peter. He used the word ***petra*** in describing upon whom He would build His Church. Christ certainly wouldn't build His Church upon a pebble.

- Christ didn't say He would build His Church upon Peter because He says, *"Upon this rock."* He didn't say to Peter, *"Upon you."*

- Peter had three significant failures in his ministry life: (1) In Matthew 16:23, just shortly after Peter's confession of who Christ was, Christ rebuked Peter and told him, *"Get behind me Satan."* (2) Peter denied Christ shortly before Christ's crucifixion. (3) Paul rebuked Peter in Galatians 2:11 in front of everyone for a serious matter regarding the gospel. Christ certainly wouldn't build His Church upon a frail human.

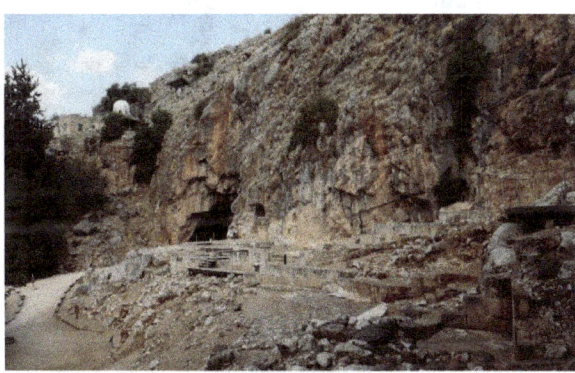

Courtyard to false gods

- Christ is referred to as the Cornerstone and foundation of the Church.
- Peter understood he was not the rock upon which Christ would build His church as he states in 1 Peter 2:4–6:

  As you come to him, a living stone *rejected by men but in the sight of God chosen and precious, 5 you yourselves like living stones are being built up as a spiritual house, to be a holy priesthood, to offer spiritual sacrifices acceptable to God through Jesus Christ. 6 For it stands in Scripture:* "**Behold, I am laying in Zion a stone, a cornerstone** *chosen and precious, and whoever believes in him will not be put to shame."*

  The rock upon which the Church is being built is Christ, the Cornerstone.

4. **The Gates of Hell will not prevail against Christ's Church.**

   Matthew 16:18: *And I tell you, you are Peter, and on this rock, I will build my church, and the **gates of hell shall not prevail against it**.*

   - Christ purposefully took His disciples to this evil Pagan place to show them that His Church would be so powerful that the gates of hell wouldn't be able to prevail or stand against it.
   - Gates were used in the ancient world for defensive purposes. They were used to keep an enemy from entering a certain place.

   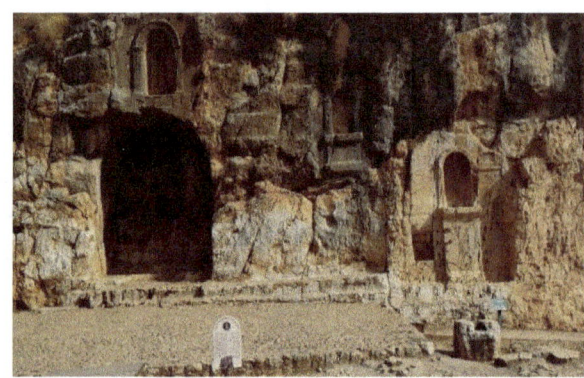

   Court of Pan

   - This means that the church is on the offense, and the gates of hell will not be able to withstand its entry and power.
   - Contrary to what some might believe, the church is not on defense in a stationary mode standing its ground.
   - God has designed His Church to be in the world, but not of it. This means we should be involved in influencing the world for Christ, not retreating and hiding from it.

Northern Israel Sites

- Christ wants His Church involved in society and reaching every hidden corner of it for Him.

5. **From Caesarea Philippi, Jesus began His journey to Jerusalem to be crucified**.

   Matthew 16:21–23: *From that time Jesus began to show his disciples that he must go to Jerusalem and suffer many things from the elders and chief priests and scribes, and be killed, and on the third day be raised. 22 And Peter took him aside and began to rebuke him, saying, "Far be it from you, Lord! This shall never happen to you." 23 But he turned and said to Peter,* **"Get behind me, Satan!** *You are a hindrance to me. For you are not setting your mind on the things of God, but on the things of man."*

6. **Christ teaches about the commitment level He demands from the disciples of His Church.**

   Matthew 16:24–27: *Then Jesus told his disciples, "If anyone would come after me, let him deny himself and take up his cross and follow me. 25 For whoever would save his life will lose it, but whoever loses his life for my sake will find it. 26 For what will it profit a man if he gains the whole world and forfeits his soul? Or what*

   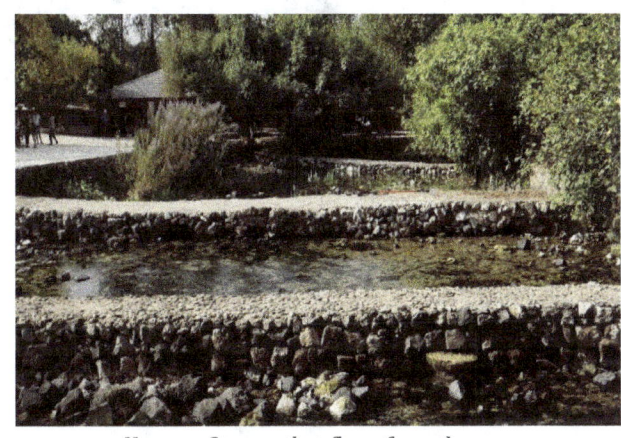
   Hermon Stream that flows from the cave

   shall a man give in return for his soul? 27 For the Son of Man is going to come with his angels in the glory of his Father, and then he will repay each person according to what he has done."

Faith Lesson from Caesarea Philippi

1. Are we on the offense and influencing our world for Christ, or are we retreating and hiding out?
2. Do we truly believe that Christ and His Church are more powerful than Satan and the culture we live in?
3. Do we know God's Word so we can use it effectively in advancing

the truth against the lies of Satan and the world?
4. Do we understand the spiritual battles that are taking place today?
   - The belief that truth is just what each person believes it to be and what works for them personally.
   - The belief that feelings and emotions determine truth and what's right and wrong.
   - The belief that if it feels good, it must be right, or if it makes me happy, it can't be wrong.
   - The belief that there are no absolute standards of right and wrong that apply to everyone.
   - The belief that truth is rigid, intolerant, and judgmental.
   - The belief that if we speak the truth of God's Word to someone, we are judging them and intolerant.

Byzantine Church

5. Are we willing to pay the cost Christ demands to be His disciples?

Journal/Notes:

Caesarea Maritime

Location

Caesarea is located on the beautiful Mediterranean Sea about 35 miles (56 km.) north of Joppa.

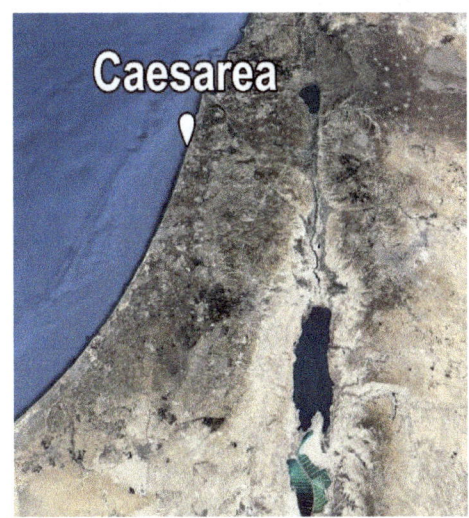

Historical Background

1. Caesarea was built by Herod the Great from about 25 to 13 BC as the port city called "Caesarea Maritime."
2. It was named after the Roman Emperor, Augustus Caesar.
3. King Herod the Great was the one who had all the children 2 years and younger slaughtered in Bethlehem in his attempt to kill Christ. He was a jealous king who feared losing his power and control.
4. King Herod built Caesarea out of nothing and was a master builder. Some of his major building projects included:
    - This seaport of Caesarea
    - An enlarged Temple Mount platform and temple in Jerusalem.
    - Masada
    - The Herodian by Bethlehem.
    - Cave of the Patriarchs in Hebron.
5. He was known for his building ventures, and no one equaled him in this respect.
6. Caesarea was the largest seaport in the Roman Empire during the time of Herod.
7. Caesarea was the capital of Israel during the time of Christ and during the whole Roman occupation of Israel.

Places of Interest

1. Crusader Fortress Entrance

Israel Biblical Sites Travel Guide

2. Crusader Fortress
3. Caesarea Harbor
4. Caesarea Historic Port
5. Governor's Palace
6. Roman Toilet
7. Mosaic Hall
8. Hippodrome
9. Promontory Palace
10. Caesarea Columns
11. Roman Theater
12. Submerged Garden Castle
13. Pontius Pilate Stone
14. Paul Appeals to Caesar Marker

Northern Israel Sites

Caesarea in the Bible

1. **After the Apostle Paul received Christ, he was sent to Tarsus from this seaport.**

   Acts 9:30: *And when the brothers learned this, they brought him down to **Caesarea** and sent him off to Tarsus.*

2. **Cornelius, the first Gentile to receive the Holy Spirit, lived here.**

   Acts 10:1–8: *At **Caesarea** there was a man named Cornelius, a centurion of what was known as the Italian Cohort, 2 a devout man who feared God with all his household, gave alms generously to the people, and prayed continually to God. 3 About the* 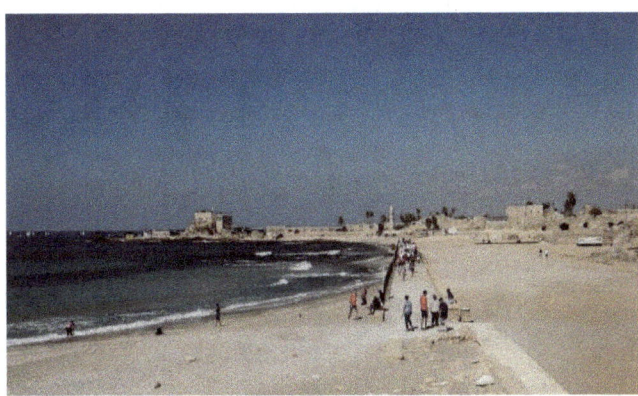 *ninth hour of the day he saw clearly in a vision an angel of God come in and say to him, "Cornelius." 4 And he stared at him in terror and said, "What is it, Lord?" And he said to him, "Your prayers and your alms have ascended as a memorial before God. 5 And now send men to Joppa and bring one Simon who is called Peter. 6 He is lodging with one Simon, a tanner, whose house is by the sea." 7 When the angel who spoke to him had departed, he called two of his servants and a devout soldier from among those who attended him, 8 and having related everything to them, he sent them to Joppa.*

3. **Caesarea was the place where the Holy Spirit was given to the Gentiles.**

   Acts 10:44–48: *While Peter was still saying these things, the Holy Spirit fell on all who heard the word. 45 And the believers from among the circumcised who had come with Peter were amazed, because the gift of the Holy Spirit was poured out even on the Gentiles. 46 For they were hearing them speaking in tongues and extolling God. Then Peter declared, 47 "Can anyone withhold water for baptizing these people, who have received the Holy Spirit just as we have?" 48 And he commanded them to be baptized in the name of*

Jesus Christ. Then they asked him to remain for some days.

4. **King Herod Agrippa the 1st, the son of Herod the Great, met his death in Caesarea.**

   Acts 12:21-24: *On an appointed day Herod put on his royal robes, took his seat upon the throne, and delivered an oration to them. 22 And the people were shouting, "The voice of a god, and not of a man!" 23 Immediately an angel of the Lord struck him down, because he did not give God the glory, and he was eaten by worms and breathed his last. 24 But the word of God increased and multiplied.*

5. **Philip the Evangelist lived in Caesarea.**

   Acts 21:8: *On the next day we departed and came to **Caesarea**, and we entered the house of Philip the evangelist, who was one of the seven, and stayed with him.*

6. **The Apostle Paul sailed to and from Caesarea on his missionary travels.**

   Acts 21:7-8: *When we had finished the voyage from Tyre, we arrived at Ptolemais, and we greeted the brothers and stayed with them for one day. 8 On the next day we departed and came*

   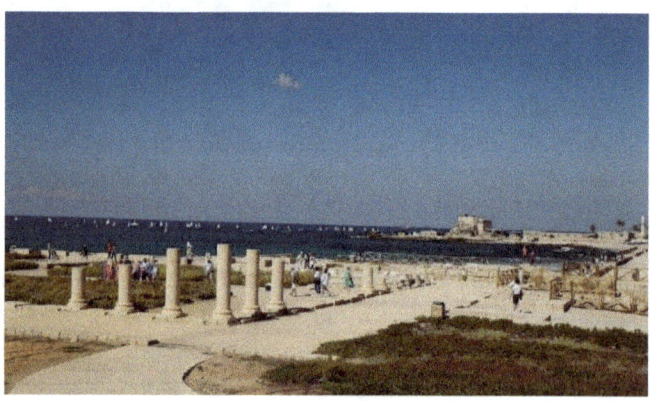

   *to **Caesarea**, and we entered the house of Philip the evangelist, who was one of the seven, and stayed with him.*

7. **The Apostle Paul stood trial here for his faith.**

   Acts 23:33-35: *When they had come to **Caesarea** and delivered the letter to the governor, they presented Paul also before him. 34 On reading the letter, he asked what province he was from. And when he learned that he was from Cilicia, 35 he said, "I will give you a hearing when your accusers arrive." And he commanded him to be guarded in Herod's Praetorium.*

8. **The Apostle Paul was imprisoned here 2 years because of his faith.**

    Acts 24:27: *When two years had elapsed, Felix was succeeded by Porcius Festus. And desiring to do the Jews a favor, Felix left Paul in prison.*

    It's possible that Paul wrote some of the Prison Epistles in Caesarea during the 2 years he spent here in prison.

9. **After spending 2 years of imprisonment in Caesarea, the Apostle Paul sailed from Caesarea to Rome, where he stood trial for his faith.**

    Acts 25:8, 11: *Paul argued in his defense, "Neither against the law of the Jews, nor against the temple, nor against Caesar have I committed any offense."* Paul then declares in verse 11: *"I appeal to Caesar."*

Faith Lesson from Caesarea

1. The Holy Spirit was given to the Gentiles here. This shows that God loves all people from all races and backgrounds and wants them to be saved.

2. Paul spent 2 years in prison here because of his faithfulness to Christ. It's possible he wrote some of the Prison Letters while here. We, too, should be willing to suffer like Paul for the advancement of the gospel.

3. God opposes the proud and caused King Herod Agrippa the 1st, the son of Herod the Great, to meet his death here because of his arrogance. We should be certain we always give God the glory for what He does through us and avoid pride in our lives.

Journal/Notes:

Cana

Location

Cana is in the northern part of Israel in the Galilee area. It's about 11 miles (17 km.) southwest of the Sea of Galilee, about 4 miles (6.4 km.) northeast of Nazareth, and about 22 miles (35 km.) inland from the Mediterranean Sea.

Historical Background

1. Cana's actual location is uncertain, with at least three possible candidates.
2. However, at the Wedding Church, the Franciscans have relied on the testimony of early pilgrims, including Jerome, as being the authentic site. Therefore, they established themselves here in 1641.
3. The Franciscans also believe excavations beneath their present church, dating from the early 1900s, confirm the existence of an early place of worship. They believe it's possible it was a Jewish-Christian synagogue.
4. Beneath the present Franciscan Wedding Church were found remains of dwellings dating back to the 1st century. An ancient basilica with three arch vaults in a cross-like form was also discovered. Additionally, in a crypt, a small stone cistern was found fitted into a flagstone floor.
5. Not far from the Wedding Church is the Greek Orthodox Church of the Marriage Feast. It possesses two large stone jars believed to be two of the original water pots used when Christ turned the water into wine.
6. The town also has a chapel dedicated to Bartholomew, whom some scholars identify with Nathanael of Cana.

Places of Interest

1. Franciscan Wedding Church

Northern Israel Sites

2. Greek Orthodox Church
3. Nathanael Bartholomew Church
4. Cana Baptist Church

Cana in the Bible

1. Jesus changed water into wine.

John 2:1–11: *On the third day there was a wedding at Cana in Galilee, and the mother of Jesus was there. 2 Jesus also was invited to the wedding with his disciples. 3 When the wine ran out, the mother of Jesus said to him, "They have no wine." 4 And Jesus said to her, "Woman, what does this have to do with me? My hour has not yet come." 5 His mother said to the servants, "Do whatever he tells you." 6 Now there were six stone water jars there for the Jewish rites of purification, each holding twenty or thirty gallons. 7 Jesus said to the servants, "Fill the jars with water." And they filled them up to the brim. 8 And he said to them, "Now draw some out and take it to the master of the feast." So they took it. 9 When the master of the feast tasted the water now become wine, and did not know where it came from (though the servants who had drawn the water knew), the* master of the feast called the bridegroom 10 and said to him, "Everyone serves the good wine first, and when people have drunk freely, then the poor wine. But you have kept the good wine until now." 11 **This, the first of his signs, Jesus did at Cana in Galilee**, and manifested his glory. And his disciples believed in him.

2. **Jesus also healed an official's son in Cana.**

    John 4:46–54: *So he came again to Cana in Galilee, where he had made the water wine. And at Capernaum, there was an official whose son was ill. 47 When this man heard that Jesus had come from Judea to Galilee, he went to him and asked him to come down and heal his son, for he was at the point of death. 48 So Jesus said to him, "Unless you see signs and wonders you will not believe." 49 The official said to him, "Sir, come down before my child dies." 50 Jesus said to him, "Go; your son will live." The man believed the word that Jesus spoke to him and went on his way. 51 As he was going down, his servants met him and told him that his son was recovering. 52 So he asked them the hour when he began to get better, and they said to him, "Yesterday at the seventh hour the fever left him." 53 The father knew that was the hour when Jesus had said to him, "Your son will live." And he himself believed, and all his household. 54 This was now the second sign that Jesus did when he had come from Judea to Galilee.*

    Wedding Church

3. **Nathanael, one of the close followers of Christ and close friend (or possibly a brother) of the Apostle Philip, was from Cana.**

    John 21:2: *Simon Peter, Thomas, **Nathanael from Cana** in Galilee, the sons of Zebedee, and two other disciples were together.*

4. **The Apostle Philip led Nathanael, who was from Cana, to Christ.**

    John 1:43–51: *The next day Jesus decided to go to Galilee. He found Philip and said to him, "Follow me." 44 Now Philip was from Bethsaida, the city of Andrew and Peter. 45 Philip found Nathanael and said to him, "We have found him of whom Moses in the Law and also the prophets wrote, Jesus of Nazareth, the son of Joseph." 46 Nathanael said to him, "Can anything good come out of Nazareth?"*

Philip said to him, "Come and see." 47 Jesus saw Nathanael coming toward him and said of him, "Behold, an Israelite indeed, in whom there is no deceit!" 48 Nathanael said to him, "How do you know me?" Jesus answered him, "Before Philip called you, when you were under the fig tree, I saw you." 49 Nathanael answered him, "Rabbi, you are the Son of God! You are the King of Israel!" 50 Jesus answered him, "Because I said to you, 'I saw you under the fig tree,' do you believe? You will see greater things than these." 51 And he said to him, "Truly, truly, I say to you, you will see heaven opened, and the angels of God ascending and descending on the Son of Man."

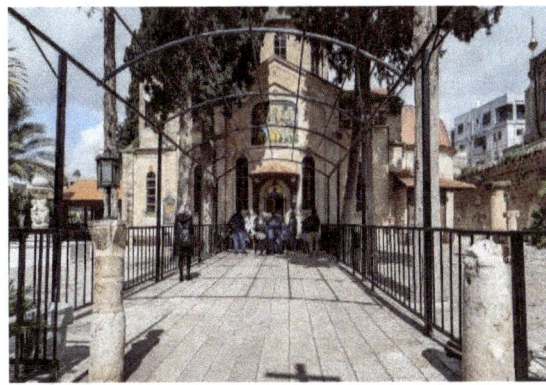
Greek Orthodox Church

Faith Lesson from Cana

1. Christ performed His first public miracle in Cana to authenticate and show that He was the promised Messiah. Do we believe Christ was God in the flesh and the true Messiah?
2. Christ honored the request of His mother in turning the water into wine. Do we honor our parents as Christ did, and as God commands?
3. Jesus also healed an official's son here in Cana. Do we believe Christ can still do miracles today in our own lives?
4. If you could ask Christ for one miracle, what would it be?
5. In the same way Philip led Nathanael to Christ, do we lead others to Christ?
6. Christ turned water into wine to fulfill many Old Testament prophecies that proved He was the Messiah. Do we believe Christ is the Messiah, and have we placed our trust in Him as our Savior?

Journal/Notes:

Dan

Location

1. The city of Dan was in the northernmost part of Israel, about 24 miles (38 km.) north of the Sea of Galilee.
2. It's a well-watered lush area superb for agriculture.

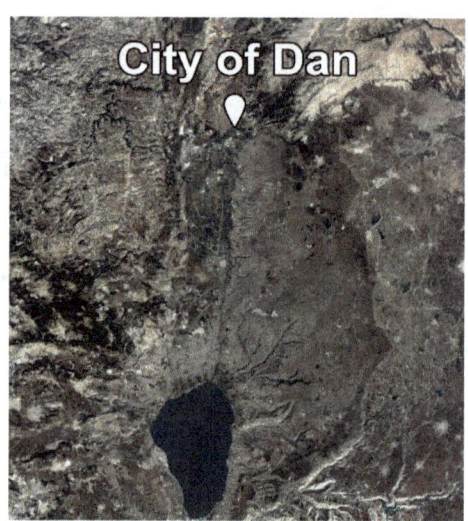

Historical Background

1. The tribe of Dan failed to take the original territory allotted to them, so they captured and moved to this area (Judg. 18).
2. When referring to all Israel, the phrase "From Dan to Beersheba" was commonly used.

   1 Kings 4:25: *Judah and Israel lived safely, every man under his vine and under his fig tree, **from Dan even to Beersheba**, all the days of Solomon.*

3. Just after Solomon's reign, the kingdom of Israel was divided because Solomon turned from the Lord and introduced the worship of false gods into the nation.

   1 Kings 11:1–2: *Now King Solomon loved many foreign women along with the daughter of Pharaoh: Moabite, Ammonite, Edomite, Sidonian, and Hittite women, 2 from the nations concerning which the Lord had said to the sons of Israel, "You shall not associate with them, nor shall they associate with you, for they will surely **turn your heart away** after their gods." Solomon held fast to these in love.*

   1 Kings 11:6–11: *Solomon did what was evil in the sight of the Lord, and did not follow the Lord fully, as David his father had done. 7 Then Solomon built a high place for Chemosh the detestable idol of Moab, on the mountain which is east of Jerusalem, and for Molech the detestable idol of the sons of Ammon. 8 Thus also he did for all*

Northern Israel Sites

his foreign wives, who burned incense and sacrificed to their gods. 9 Now the Lord was angry with Solomon **because his heart was turned away from the Lord**, the God of Israel, who **had appeared to him twice**, 10 and had commanded him concerning this thing, that he should **not go after other gods**; but he did not observe what the Lord had commanded. 11 So the Lord said to Solomon, "Because you have done this, and you have not kept My covenant and My statutes, which I have commanded you, I will surely **tear the kingdom from you**, and will give it to your servant."

4. Rehoboam was given the southern 2 tribes of Israel (called Judah from this time forward), and Jeroboam received the northern 10 tribes of Israel (called Israel from this time forward).

Places of Interest

1. Entrance
2. Dan River
3. Jeroboam's Golden Calf High Place
4. City Ruins
5. Israelite Gate
6. Canaanite Gate
7. Shallow Pool

City of Dan in the Bible

1. **God appeared to Jeroboam and promised to bless him if he would serve Him.**

   1 Kings 11:38: *Then it will be, that if you listen to all that I command you and walk in My ways, and do what is right in My sight by observing My statutes and My commandments, as My servant David did, then I will be with you and build you an enduring house as I built for David, and I will give Israel to you.*

2. **Jeroboam turned away from the Lord and built golden calves in Bethel and Dan.**

   1 Kings 12:25-31: *Then Jeroboam built Shechem in the hill country of Ephraim, and lived there. And he went out from there and built Penuel. 26 Jeroboam said in his heart, "Now the kingdom will return to the house of David. 27 If this people go up to offer sacrifices in the house of the Lord at Jerusalem, then the heart of this people will return to*

   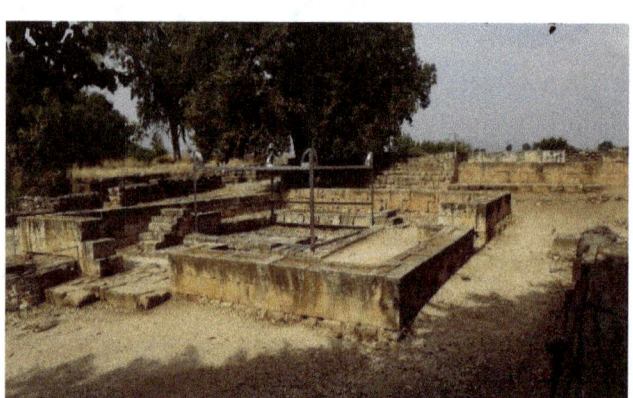
   Golden Calf Altar

   *their lord, even to Rehoboam king of Judah; and they will kill me and return to Rehoboam king of Judah." 28 So the king consulted, and made **two golden calves**, and he said to them, "It is too much for you to go up to Jerusalem; behold your gods, O Israel, that brought you up from the land of Egypt." 29 He set **one in Bethel**, and the other he put in **Dan**. 30 Now this thing became a sin, for the people went to worship before the one as far as **Dan**. 31 And he made **houses on high places**, and made priests from among all the people who were not of the sons of Levi.*

3. **After a severe warning from God, Jeroboam continued in sin. The worship of false gods would eventually seal the doom of the northern 10 tribes of Israel.**

   1 Kings 13:33-34: *Even after this, Jeroboam did not change his evil ways, but once more appointed priests for the high places from all*

*sorts of people. Anyone who wanted to become a priest he consecrated for the high places. 34 This was the sin of the house of Jeroboam that led to its **downfall and to its destruction** from the face of the earth.*

4. **The sin of Jeroboam became a pattern that the rest of the kings of Israel would follow.**

   1 Kings 15:33–34: *In the third year of Asa king of Judah, Baasha son of Ahijah became king of all Israel in Tirzah, and he reigned twenty-four years. 34 He did evil in the eyes of the LORD, **walking in the ways of Jeroboam** and in his sin, which he had caused Israel to commit.*

   1 Kings 16:26: *He [Omri] **walked in all the ways of Jeroboam** son of Nebat and in his sin, which he had caused Israel to commit, so that they provoked the LORD, the God of Israel, to anger by their worthless idols.*

5. **In 722 BC, as judgment from God for their continual disobedience, the 10 northern tribes of Israel were deported by the Assyrian Empire.**

6. **Eighty years later, Josiah became King of Judah and chose to follow God with all his heart. As a result of finding and reading the Scriptures, he led one of the most significant revivals Israel ever experienced.**

   2 Kings 22:1–2: *Josiah was eight years old when he became king, and he reigned in Jerusalem thirty-one years. His mother's name was Jedidah daughter of Adaiah; she was from Bozkath. 2 He did what was right in the eyes of the LORD and walked in all the ways of his father David, not turning aside to the right or to the left.*

   Israelite City Gate

   2 Kings 23:25: *Before him, **there was no king like him who turned to the Lord with all his heart and with all his soul and***

with all his might, *according to all the law of Moses; nor did any like him arise after him.*

7. **As a result of Josiah's obedience, he renewed the covenant of the Lord with Israel and destroyed the golden calves Jeroboam had erected.**

   2 Kings 23:15: *Furthermore, the altar that was at **Bethel** and the **high place** which Jeroboam the son of Nebat, who made Israel sin, had made, even that altar and the high place he broke down. Then he demolished its stones, ground them to dust, and burned the Asherah.*

   2 Kings 23:19: *Josiah also removed all the houses of the **high places** which were in the **cities of Samaria**, which the kings of Israel had made provoking the Lord; and he did to them just as he had done in Bethel.*

Faith Lesson from the city of Dan

1. Despite God supernaturally revealing Himself two times to Solomon, he turned away from the Lord in his latter years. There is a tendency to grow apathetic the longer we are Christians. Are you apathetic and lukewarm in your relationship with God?

2. Despite God supernaturally revealing himself two times to Jeroboam, he turned his back on God and built altars to false gods all throughout the land. God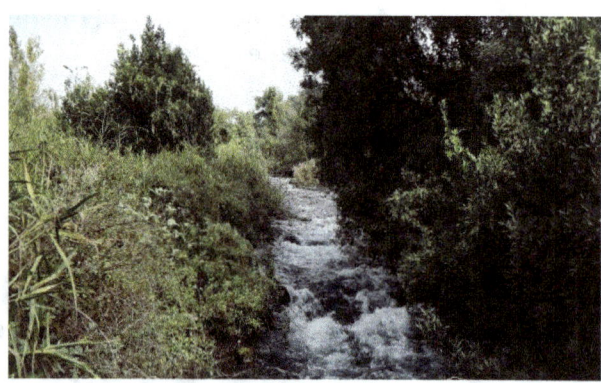

   Dan River

   gives grace to each person to receive and obey Him, but those who reject Him and His grace will be judged accordingly.

3. The sin of Jeroboam became a pattern that the rest of the kings of the northern tribes of Israel followed. What kind of example are we? Are we following the sinful patterns of our parents and those around us?

4. In 722 BC, the 10 northern tribes of Israel were deported because of their refusal to return to God.

Northern Israel Sites

5. The worship of false gods at Bethel and Dan became the downfall of the northern tribes of Israel. False gods and idols can be anything we make more important in our lives than God. Do you have any idols in your life?

6. Josiah chose to follow God with all his heart and tore down the two golden calf altars Jeroboam had set up. Do we follow God with all our heart like Josiah, and work with God to tear down the lies and false philosophies of Satan and the world with God's Word (2 Cor. 10:4–5)?

City ruins

Journal/Notes:

Gideon's Spring

Location

Gideon's Spring, or also known as Harod Spring, is located in the fertile Jezreel Valley about 26 miles (42 km.) from the Mediterranean Sea and about 17 miles (28 km.) south of the Sea of Galilee. Just to the south of Gideon's Spring are the Gilboa Mountains.

Historical Background

1. The period of the Judges saw the nation of Israel experience many cycles of obedience and disobedience.
2. They would walk with God for a bit and then fall away.
3. One verse is repeated several times in the book of Judges that summarizes the mentality of their day: *"In those days there was no king in Israel; everyone did what was right in his own eyes"* (Judg. 17:6, 21:25).
4. In order to bring the nation of Israel back to Himself, God would send them oppressors to make their lives difficult.
5. As a result, the Israelites would look to the Lord, and He would send them a deliverer, or also known as a Judge.
6. Gideon was one of these deliverers that God raised up to deliver the Israelites out of the hand of the Midianites who were oppressing Israel at that time.
7. There were a total of 13 Judges or Deliverers in the book of Judges.
8. Gideon was the 6th Judge.

Places of Interest

1. Hill of Moreh: Hill area where the Midianites camped.
2. Midianite Camp
3. Jezreel Valley

Northern Israel Sites

4. Battle Area
5. Gideon's Spring – Area where Gideon chose 300 men for battle.
6. Gilboa Mountains – Where the Israelites hid out.
7. Hankin House Museum – Located above the spring entrance.

Gideon's Spring in the Bible

1. **God gave the Israelites into the hands of the Midianites because they abandoned and disobeyed Him.**

    Judges 6:1-6: *Then the sons of Israel did what was evil in the sight of the Lord; and the Lord gave them into the hands of Midian seven years. 2 The power of Midian prevailed against Israel. Because of Midian the sons of Israel made for themselves the dens which were in the mountains and the caves and the strongholds. 3 For it was when Israel had sown, that the Midianites would come up with the Amalekites and the sons of the east and go against them. 4 So they would camp against them and destroy the produce of the earth as far as Gaza, and leave no sustenance in Israel as well as no sheep, ox, or donkey. 5 For they would come up with their livestock and their* tents, they would come in like locusts for number, both they and their camels were innumerable; and they came into the land to devastate it. 6 So Israel was brought very low because of Midian, and the sons of Israel cried to the Lord.*

2. **God hears the prayers of the Israelites and decides to deliver them.**

   Judges 6:7–10: *Now it came about when the sons of Israel cried to the Lord on account of Midian, 8 that the Lord sent a prophet to the sons of Israel, and he said to them, "Thus says the Lord, the God of Israel, 'It was I who brought you up from Egypt and brought you out from the house of slavery. 9 I delivered you from the hands of the Egyptians and from the hands of all your oppressors, and dispossessed them before you and gave you their land, 10 and I said to you, I am the Lord your God; you shall not fear the gods of the Amorites in whose land you live. But you have not obeyed Me.'"*

   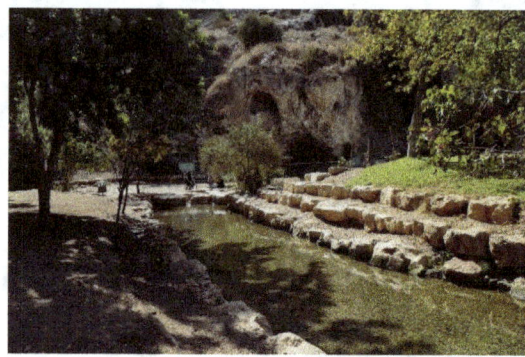

3. **God visits Gideon through an angel and chooses to deliver the Israelites through him.**

   Judges 6:11–12: *Then the angel of the Lord came and sat under the oak that was in Ophrah, which belonged to Joash the Abiezrite as his son **Gideon** was beating out wheat in the winepress in order to save it from the Midianites. 12 The angel of the Lord appeared to him and said to him, "The Lord is with you, O valiant warrior."*

4. **Gideon responds by saying that his family was the least in the tribe of Manasseh and that he was the youngest in his family (Judg. 6:15). This is similar to the response of Moses when God called him.**

5. **God allows the angel to show Gideon a couple of miracles to prove God will help him.**

   Judges 6:21: *Then the angel of the Lord put out the end of the staff that was in his hand and touched the meat and the unleavened bread; and fire sprang up from the rock and consumed the meat and the unleavened bread. Then the angel of the Lord vanished from his sight.*

6. **God commands Gideon to tear down the altars to Baal that his father had erected and to erect an altar to the Lord in their place (Judg. 6:28–32).**

7. **Shortly afterward, many nations gather together to wipe out the Israelites.**

Judges 6:33–35: *Then all the Midianites and the Amalekites and the sons of the east assembled themselves; and they crossed over and camped in the valley of Jezreel [just north of Gideon's Spring]. 34 So the Spirit of the Lord came upon Gideon; and he blew a trumpet, and the Abiezrites were called together to follow him. 35 He sent messengers throughout Manasseh, and they also were called together to follow him; and he sent messengers to Asher, Zebulun, and Naphtali, and they came up to meet them.*

- The Midianites were the descendants of Midian and therefore, children of Abraham. They settled in "the land of the east." When Moses fled the wrath of Pharaoh, he traveled to Midian (Ex. 2:15). There, Moses met and married his wife, Zipporah, and served his father-in-law, Jethro, as a shepherd for 40 years.
- The Amalekites were the first ones to attack the Israelites upon their exodus from Egypt. Genesis 36 refers to the descendants of Amalek, the son of Eliphaz and grandson of Esau, as Amalekites. So, the Amalekites were somehow related to, but distinct from, the Edomites.

8. **As a result of the nations who had gathered together to wipe out the Israelites, Gideon asks for a sign from God that he will be successful. The sign of the wet and dry fleeces is used by Gideon to seek assurance of God's help (Judg. 6:36–40). However, it reveals a lack of faith in what God had said He would do.**

9. **God commands Gideon to choose 300 men for battle so that**

He gets all the glory for the victory.

Judges 7:1–7: *Then Jerubbaal [Gideon] and all the people who were with him rose early and encamped beside the **spring of Harod**. And the camp of Midian was north of them, by the hill of Moreh, in the valley. 2 The LORD said to Gideon,* 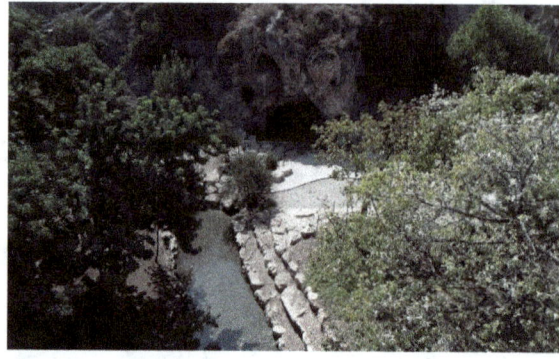 *"The people with you are too many for me to give the Midianites into their hand, lest Israel boast over me, saying, 'My own hand has saved me.' 3 Now therefore proclaim in the ears of the people, saying, 'Whoever is fearful and trembling, let him return home and hurry away from Mount Gilead.'" Then 22,000 of the people returned, and 10,000 remained. 4 And the LORD said to Gideon, "The people are still too many. Take them down to the water, and I will test them for you there, and anyone of whom I say to you, 'This one shall go with you,' shall go with you, and anyone of whom I say to you, 'This one shall not go with you,' shall not go." 5 So he brought the people down to the water. And the LORD said to Gideon, "Everyone who laps the water with his tongue, as a dog laps, you shall set by himself. Likewise, everyone who kneels down to drink." 6 And the number of those who lapped, putting their hands to their mouths, was 300 men, but all the rest of the people knelt down to drink water. 7 And the LORD said to Gideon, "With the 300 men who lapped I will save you and give the Midianites into your hand, and let all the others go every man to his home."*

It's believed God chose those who lapped like dogs because they were less civilized. This would give God even more glory for the victory.

10. The size of the opposing army was enormous.

Judges 7:12: *Now the Midianites and the Amalekites and all the sons of the east were lying in the valley as numerous as locusts; and their camels were without number, as numerous as the sand on the seashore.*

11. God allows Gideon to visit the camp of the opposing army to be assured of victory.

Judges 7:13-14: *When Gideon came, behold, a man was relating a dream to his friend. And he said, "Behold, I had a dream; a loaf of barley bread was tumbling into the camp of Midian, and it came to the tent and struck it so that it fell, and turned it upside down so that the tent lay flat." 14 His friend replied, "This is nothing less than the sword of Gideon the son of Joash, a man of Israel; God has given Midian and all the camp into his hand."*

12. God delivers the Midianites and Amalekites into the hands of the Israelites.

Judges 7:15-25: *As soon as Gideon heard the telling of the dream and its interpretation, he worshiped. And he returned to the camp of Israel and said, "Arise, for the LORD has given the host of Midian into your hand." 16 And he divided the 300 men into three companies and put trumpets into the hands of all of them and empty jars, with torches inside the jars.*

Field by Gideon's Spring

17 And he said to them, "Look at me, and do likewise. When I come to the outskirts of the camp, do as I do. 18 When I blow the trumpet, I and all who are with me, then blow the trumpets also on every side of all the camp and shout, 'For the LORD and for Gideon.'" 9 So Gideon and the hundred men who were with him came to the outskirts of the camp at the beginning of the middle watch, when they had just set the watch. And they blew the trumpets and smashed the jars that were in their hands. 20 Then the three companies blew the trumpets and broke the jars. They held in their left hands the torches, and in their right hands the trumpets to blow. And they cried out, "A sword for the LORD and for Gideon!" 21 Every man stood in his place around the camp, and all the army ran. They cried out and fled. 22 When they blew the 300 trumpets, the LORD set every man's sword against his comrade and against all the army. And the army fled as far as Beth-shittah toward Zererah, as far as the border of Abel-meholah, by Tabbath [cities by the Jordan River directly east]. 23 And the men of Israel were called out from Naphtali and from Asher and from all Manasseh, and they pursued after Midian. 24 Gideon sent messengers throughout all the hill country of Ephraim, saying, "Come down against the Midianites and capture the waters against them, as far as Beth-barah, and also the Jordan." So all the men of Ephraim were called out, and they captured the waters as far as Beth-barah, and also the Jordan. 25 And they captured the two princes of Midian, Oreb and Zeeb. They killed Oreb at the rock of Oreb, and Zeeb they killed at the winepress of Zeeb. Then they pursued Midian, and they brought the heads of Oreb and Zeeb to Gideon across the Jordan.

Faith Lesson from Gideon's Spring

1. God often puts us in difficult situations so He gets all the glory when He helps us with our problems.
2. We, like the Israelites, can worship idols as well. An idol is anything that distracts us from our time and attention on God. What is distracting you away from God at this time in your life?
3. We should look at the size of our God rather than the size of our difficulties.
4. God delights in our faith but is grieved by our lack of it.
5. God chooses the weak things to show His glory.

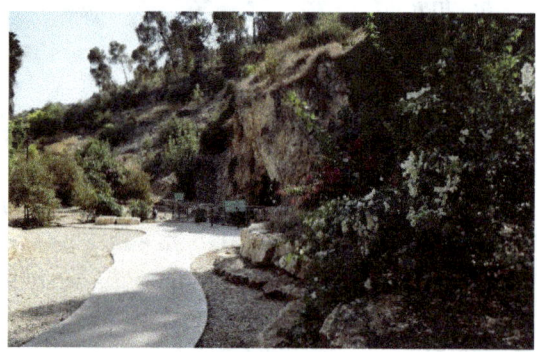

   1 Cor. 1:27–29: But God has chosen the foolish things of the world to shame the wise, and God has chosen the weak things of the world to shame the things which are strong, 28 and the base things of the world and the despised God has chosen, the things that are not, so that He may nullify the things that are, 29 **so that no man may boast before** *God.*
6. Even if you have weaknesses, God can use you if you trust and follow Him.

Journal/Notes:

Hazor

Location

1. Hazor is about 10 miles (16 km.) due north of the Sea of Galilee and just to the east of Hwy. 90.
2. It was on one of the most important travel routes called the "Via Maris," which linked Africa and Egypt with Europe and Asia.
3. It was the largest and most strategic city in northern Galilee due to its size and location.

Historical Background

1. Hazor was one of the most important cities of the Canaanites and was the head of all the northern kingdoms (Josh. 11:10).
2. It was 10 times the size of Jerusalem and totaled 200 acres (81 hectares, 200 football fields) in size.
3. The upper part of the tel is around 30 acres (12 hectares), and the lower part is around 170 acres (69 hectares).
4. What we see today of Hazor is 1/8 the size of what it once was.
5. To the north lies most of the city, which is now a farm field.
6. It's the largest tel in Israel.
7. It's also believed to have been the largest city in ancient Canaan.
8. It was one of three major cities of defense in Israel (Gezer, to the south, Megiddo, in the middle of the country, and Hazor, in the north). All three cities were on the Via Maris.
9. Hazor rivaled Nineveh in size and importance.
10. Hazor is mentioned 19 times in the Bible.

Places of Interest

1. Parking

2. Israelite Walls
3. Lower City
4. Temple Tombs
5. Northern Walls
6. Canaanite Temple/Palace
7. Solomon's Walls and Gate (archaeologists have uncovered a six-chambered gate at Hazor, which is nearly identical in size and design to the gates at Megiddo and Gezer).
8. Ash Layer in the Canaanite Palace.
9. Canaanite Altar
10. Water System (a century after Solomon's time, the Israelites built a massive shaft 131 ft. (40 m.) deep into the tel, reaching the water table below).
11. Citadel
12. Rooms & Buildings
13. Canaanite passage between the upper and lower cities.

Hazor in the Bible

1. **When Jabin, king of Hazor, heard that Joshua and the Israelites had been on a conquering rampage throughout all the southern part of the land, he gathered a host of kings in the northern part of the land to unite and fight against the Israelites.**

   Joshua 11:1–5: *When Jabin, **king of Hazor**, heard of this, he sent to Jobab king of Madon, and to the king of Shimron, and to the king of Achshaph, 2 and to the kings who were in the northern hill country, and in the Arabah south of Chinneroth, and in the lowland, and in Naphoth-dor on the west, 3 to the Canaanites in the east and the west, the Amorites, the Hittites, the Perizzites, and the Jebusites in the hill country, and the Hivites under Hermon in the land of Mizpah. 4 And they came out with all their troops, a great horde, in number like the sand that is on the seashore, with very many horses and chariots. 5 And all these kings joined their forces and came and encamped together at the waters of **Merom** [3.5 miles, 5.5 km. north of Hazor] to fight against Israel.*

2. **All the unified kings and soldiers believed that with their countless armies and gods, Israel would be no match for them.**

3. **God told Joshua and the Israelites not to be afraid because He**

would be with them and deliver all these kings into their hands.

Joshua 11:6–9: *And the Lord said to Joshua, "Do not be afraid of them, for tomorrow at this time I will give over all of them, slain, to Israel. You shall hamstring their horses and burn their chariots with fire." 7 So Joshua and all his warriors came suddenly against them by the waters of **Merom** and fell upon them. 8 And the Lord gave them into the hand of Israel, who struck them and chased them as far as Great Sidon and Misrephoth-maim, and eastward as far as the Valley of Mizpeh. And they struck them until he left none remaining. 9 And Joshua did to them just as the Lord said to him: he hamstrung their horses and burned their chariots with fire.*

4. **After defeating all the armies, Joshua conquered Hazor and burned it with fire.**

Joshua 11:10–13: *Then Joshua turned back at that time, and captured **Hazor** and struck its king with the sword; for **Hazor** formerly was the **head of all these kingdoms**. 11 They struck every person who was in it with the edge of the sword, utterly destroying them; there was no one left who breathed. **And he burned Hazor with fire**.*

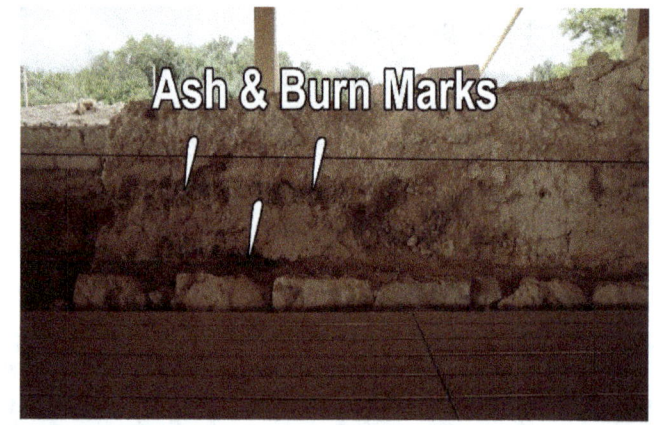

*12 Joshua captured all the cities of these kings, and all their kings, and he struck them with the edge of the sword, and utterly destroyed them; just as Moses the servant of the Lord had commanded. 13 But none of the cities that stood on mounds did Israel burn, **except Hazor alone; that Joshua burned**.*

Evidence of the burn marks and ash layer can be seen in the Canaanite Palace at Hazor.

5. **Hazor was later retaken and rebuilt by the Canaanites. God used the Canaanites to punish Israel for their disobedience to Him.**

Northern Israel Sites

Judges 4:1–3: *And the people of Israel again did what was evil in the sight of the Lord after Ehud died. 2 And the Lord sold them into the hand of Jabin [not the king's actual personal name but his title] king of Canaan, who reigned in **Hazor**. The commander of his army was Sisera, who lived in Harosheth-hagoyim. 3 Then the people of Israel cried out to the Lord for help, for he had 900 chariots of iron and he oppressed the people of Israel cruelly for twenty years.*

6. **God used Deborah and Barak to deliver the Israelites after they repented of their sins and cried out to Him for help.**

   Joshua 4:14–16: *And Deborah said to Barak, "Up! For this is the day in which the Lord has given Sisera into your hand. Does not the Lord go out before you?" So Barak went down from Mount Tabor with 10,000 men following him. 15 And the Lord routed Sisera and all his chariots and all his army before Barak by the edge of the sword. And Sisera got down from his chariot and fled away on foot. 16 And Barak pursued the chariots and the army to Harosheth-hagoyim, and all the army of Sisera fell by the edge of the sword; not a man was left.*

7. **Hazor later came under the control of Israel during the period of King David and Solomon, and Solomon rebuilt and fortified Hazor, along with Megiddo and Gezer.**

   1 Kings 9:15: *Now this is the account of the forced labor which King Solomon levied to build the house of the Lord, his own house, the Millo, the wall of Jerusalem, **Hazor**, Megiddo, and Gezer.*

8. **Jeremiah prophesied against Hazor due to the Israelites disobedience after David and Solomon's time.**

   Jeremiah 49:33: ***Hazor** will become a haunt of jackals, a desolation forever; no one will live there, nor will a son of man reside in it.*

   It's amazing that this once sought-after prime location is now desolate. It shows the power of God and His proclaimed word.

9. **As a result of Israel's disobedience to God, Hazor was destroyed by Assyria in 722 BC, and the northern 10 tribes of Israel were deported.**

   2 Kings 15:29: *In the days of Pekah king of Israel, Tiglath-pileser king of Assyria came and captured Ijon, Abel-beth-maacah, Janoah, Kedesh, **Hazor**, Gilead, and Galilee, all the land of Naphtali, and he carried the people captive to Assyria.*

Faith Lesson from Hazor

1. When the Israelites obeyed God, He blessed them and made them victorious over countless kings and multitudes of soldiers.
2. When they disobeyed God, He caused them to become weak and defeated.
3. The same lesson from the Old Testament applies to us today (Rom. 15:4). When we are obedient and faithful to God, we live victoriously and receive His blessings. However, when we disobey Him, we become weak and defeated.

4. What kind of lives are we living today? Are we victorious or defeated?

Journal/Notes:

Northern Israel Sites

Jordan River Overview

Location

1. The Jordan River begins at Mount Hermon in the northernmost part of Israel, flows into the Sea of Galilee, and then out and down to the Dead Sea.
2. The lower part of the river has the lowest elevation of any river in the world.
3. It's the border between Israel and Jordan for much of its length.
4. Today, because of the high demands of water by both Israel and Jordan, little water makes it to the Dead Sea area.

Historical Background

1. The Jordan River is mentioned over 180 times in the Bible.
2. It is the main River in Israel, supplying much of the country with water.
3. Its total winding length is about 125 miles (200 km.).
4. The meaning of "Jordan" in Hebrew is "descend." This is true of the Jordan River as it literally descends thousands of feet from its inception to its ending, and all but the beginning part is below sea level.
5. However, there's a deeper spiritual meaning to the word. In the same way we must physically descend to access the Jordan River's waters, we must descend and humble ourselves before we can ascend spiritually. This concept is seen in many of the miracles that happened in and around its shores.

Places of Interest

1. Mount Hermon – Rises to around 9,232 ft. (2,813 m.) above sea level and supplies the Jordan River with most of its water.

2. Hermon Stream Nature Reserve – Beginning area of the Jordan River.
3. Jordan River View – Nice viewing place where the river is wide and calm.
4. Sea of Galilee – The Jordan River flows into and out of the Sea of Galilee.
5. Yardenit Baptismal Site – Located just south of the Sea of Galilee. It's a popular place where many pilgrims get baptized in the Jordan River.
6. Adam – Place the waters of the Jordan backed up to when the Israelites crossed the river (20 miles, 32 km. above crossing).
7. Baptismal Site of Jesus – Located across from Jericho, this is the believed place where Jesus was baptized. It's also a popular place where many people get baptized today as well.
8. Crossing of the Jordan River by the Israelites – Located nearby to the Baptismal Site of Jesus.
9. Camp Gilgal
10. Jericho
11. Dead Sea

Northern Israel Sites

Jordan River in the Bible

1. **Abraham entered the Promised Land through the gateway of the Jordan River Valley when he first journeyed from Ur of the Chaldeans (Gen. 12:1–9).**
2. **When Abraham and Lot divided their possessions, Lot chose to settle in the lower part of the Jordan River Valley.**

   Genesis 13:10: *And Lot lifted up his eyes and saw that the **Jordan Valley** was well watered everywhere like the garden of the LORD, like the land of Egypt, in the direction of Zoar. (This was before the LORD destroyed Sodom and Gomorrah.)*
3. **Before entering the Promised Land, the Israelites camped on the east side of the Jordan River, opposite Jericho.**

   Joshua 3:1: *Then Joshua rose early in the morning, and they set out from Shittim. And they came to the **Jordan**, he and all the people of Israel, and lodged there before they passed over.*
4. **The Israelites crossed the Jordan River on dry ground as God miraculously parted the waters.**

   Joshua 3:14–17: *So when the people set out from their tents to pass over the **Jordan** with the priests bearing the ark of the covenant before the people, 15 and as soon as those bearing the ark had come as far as the **Jordan**, and the **feet of the priests** bearing the ark were dipped in the brink*

   Hermon Springs Nature Reserve (Caesarea Philippi)

   *of the water (**now the Jordan overflows all its banks throughout the time of harvest**), 16 the waters coming down from above stood and rose up in a heap very far away, at Adam [20 miles, 32 km. north], the city that is beside Zarethan, and those flowing down toward the Sea of the Arabah, the Salt Sea, were completely cut off. And the people passed over opposite Jericho. 17 Now the priests bearing the ark of the covenant of the Lord stood firmly on dry ground **in the midst of the Jordan**, and all Israel was passing over on dry ground until all the nation finished passing over the **Jordan**.*

5. **Naaman, the Leper, was healed in the Jordan River by the Prophet Elisha.**

   2 Kings 5:10–14: *And Elisha sent a messenger to him, saying, "Go and wash in the **Jordan** seven times, and your flesh shall be restored, and you shall be clean." 11 But Naaman was angry and went away, saying, "Behold, I thought that he would surely come out to me and stand and call upon the name of the LORD his God, and wave his hand over the place and cure the leper. 12 Are not Abana and Pharpar, the rivers of Damascus, better than all the waters of Israel? Could I not wash in them and be clean?" So he turned and went away in a rage. 13 But his servants came near and said to him, "My father, it is a great word the prophet has spoken to you; will you not do it? Has he actually said to you, 'Wash, and be clean?'" 14 So he went down and dipped himself seven times in the **Jordan**, according to the word of the man of God, and his flesh was restored like the flesh of a little child, and he was clean.*

   Jordan River north of the Sea of Galilee

6. **Elijah parted the waters of the Jordan with his cloak.**

   2 Kings 2:6–8: *Then Elijah said to him, "Please stay here, for the Lord has sent me to the Jordan." But he said, "As the Lord lives, and as you yourself live, I will not leave you." So the two of them went on. 7 Fifty men of the sons of the prophets also went and stood at some distance from them, as they both were standing by the **Jordan**. 8 Then Elijah took his cloak and rolled it up and struck the water, and the water was parted to the one side and to the other, till the two of them could go over on dry ground.*

7. **Elisha made the head of an ax float at the Jordan River.**

   2 Kings 6:1–7: *Now the sons of the prophets said to Elisha, "See, the place where we dwell under your charge is too small for us. 2 Let us go to the **Jordan** and each of us get there a log, and let us make a*

place for us to dwell there." And he answered, "Go." 3 Then one of them said, "Be pleased to go with your servants." And he answered, "I will go." 4 So he went with them. And when they came to the **Jordan**, they cut down trees. 5 But as one was felling a log, his axe head fell into the water, and he cried out, "Alas, my master! It was borrowed." 6 Then the man of God said, "Where did it fall?" When he showed him the place, he cut off a stick and threw it in there and made the iron float. 7 And he said, "Take it up." So he reached out his hand and took it.

8. **John the Baptist baptized many people in the Jordan River.**

    Matthew 3:5–6: *Then Jerusalem and all Judea and all the region about the Jordan were going out to him, 6 and they were baptized by him in the **river Jordan**, confessing their sins.*

9. **Jesus was baptized in the Jordan River by John the Baptist.**

    Matthew 3:13–17: *Then Jesus came from Galilee to the **Jordan** to John, to be baptized by him. 14 John would have prevented him, saying, "I need to be baptized by you, and do you come to me?" 15 But Jesus answered him, "Let it be so now, for thus it is fitting for us to fulfill all righteousness." Then he consented. 16 And when Jesus was baptized, immediately he went up from the water, and behold, the heavens were opened to him, and he saw the Spirit of God descending like a dove and coming to rest on him; 17 and behold, a voice from heaven said, "This is my beloved Son, with whom I am well pleased."*

    Yardenit Baptismal Site

10. **The disciples of Jesus baptized many people in the Jordan River.**

    John 4:1–3: *Now when Jesus learned that the Pharisees had heard that Jesus was making and baptizing more disciples than John 2 (although Jesus himself did not baptize, but only his disciples), 3 he left Judea and departed again for Galilee.*

Faith Lesson from the Jordan River

1. The Jordan River represented life and vitality to the Israelites. They were desert people, and water was their life. Therefore, Christ used this concept to teach them that in the same way water was vital for their physical lives, He was vital for their spiritual lives as well. Do we realize the importance of a close relationship with Christ in order to have spiritual life and vitality?

2. The meaning of Jordan means "descend." In a spiritual sense, are we humble before God and submissive to Him in order to grow spiritually?

3. The Israelites crossed the Jordan River on dry ground. In so doing, God reminded them of the miracle of crossing the Red Sea after their exodus from Egypt. Often, God will repeat miracles to show His faithfulness. What things has God done repeatedly to show His faithfulness to us?

Baptismal Site of Jesus

4. Naaman, the leper, had his own idea of how God should operate. Do we often have our own ideas as well as to how we think God should do things?

5. Baptism played a major role in the ministries of John the Baptist, Jesus, and his disciples. It was a baptism of repentance. What is our view of baptism today, and how important is it to us and our ministries?

Journal/Notes:

Megiddo: Valley of Armageddon

Location

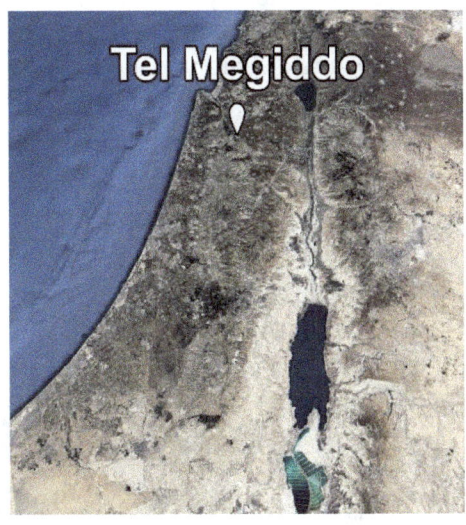

1. Tel Megiddo is about 15 miles (26 km.) east of the Mediterranean Ocean and about 25 miles (40 km.) southwest of the Sea of Galilee.
2. Megiddo lay at the juncture of several key routes (the main route is called the Via Maris) which linked Africa to Asia and Europe. For this reason, any country that rose to world power had to control Megiddo due to its strategic location.
3. More battles have been fought in this location than any other place in the entire world.
4. The name Armageddon is derived from "Har-Megiddo," which is translated, "Armageddon." Har means hill, and Megeddon is the place. When these words are joined together, it is Armageddon.
5. Today, this place is called Megiddo in English. It's located in the most fertile valley in Israel called the Jezreel Valley.
6. It is a "Tel," which is made up of layer upon layer of different civilizations that make up an artificial hill.
7. Tel Megiddo is made up of 25–26 layers of civilizations.
8. Today, you can see a busy highway right beside Tel Megiddo that uses the same ancient travel route that has been used for 6,000 years.
9. One of the Pharaohs, Thutmose the III, said conquering Megiddo was like conquering a thousand cities.

Historical Background

1. 4000 BC: Early Settlements.
2. 2000 BC: Massive city walls were built.

3. 1800 BC: A Canaanite gate was constructed on the north side.
4. 1500 BC: The gate and walls were rebuilt.
5. 1468 BC: The city rebelled against the Egyptians with other Canaanite cities and was conquered by Thutmose III after a great battle and a 7-month siege.
6. 960 BC: New gate and walls were built by the Israelites under Solomon's command.
7. 945 BC: Pharaoh Shishak conquered the city (1 Kings 14:25). A fragment of a tablet with Pharaoh Shishak's name was found here.
8. 850 BC: King Ahab fortified Megiddo and dug a water tunnel to access water within the city walls.
9. 732 BC: The city was captured by the Assyrian King Tiglath-Pileser III. Megiddo became the capital of the Assyrian province of the Galilee.

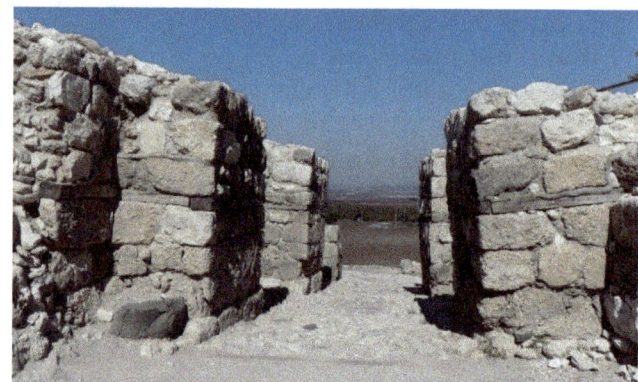

Canaanite Gates

10. 650 BC: Battle between the Egyptian Army and the Kingdom of Judah (King Josiah died in this battle).
11. 609 BC: The Egyptians replaced the Assyrians.
12. 300 BC: The city was abandoned, and the Tel was left in ruins.
13. 1918 AD: Battles between the British and the Turks in WWI. Britain gained control over Israel.
14. 1948 AD: Britain granted independence to Israel.
15. 1949 AD: Kibbutz Megiddo was established on the south side of Tel Megiddo.

Places of Interest

1. Canaanite Gate with 4 Towers
2. Canaanite Palace
3. Israelite Gate with 6 Towers

Northern Israel Sites

4. Northern Horse Stables
5. Northern Palace
6. Large cut through the tel was carried out between 1903 and 1905 by Gottlieb Schumacher for the German Society for Oriental Research.
7. Canaanite Temple and Altar – Place of animal sacrifice, and possibly children, to false gods.
8. Burial Chamber
9. Public Structure
10. Four-room House
11. Grain Silo
12. Southern Palace
13. Southern Horse Stables
14. Assyrian City
15. Water tunnel dug by King Ahab to protect the water source from enemies.
16. View of the Jezreel Valley (Valley of Armageddon).

Tel Megiddo in the Bible

1. **King Solomon fortified Megiddo and used it for a fort of protection.**

   1 Kings 9:15: *Now this is the account of the forced labor which King Solomon levied to build the house of the Lord, his own house, the Millo, the wall of Jerusalem, Hazor,* **Megiddo**, *and Gezer.*

2. **A monumental battle will be fought here and in Jerusalem at the end of the Great Tribulation Period.**

   Revelation 16:1–21: *Then I heard a loud voice from the temple telling the seven angels, "Go and pour out on the earth the **seven bowls of the wrath of God**." 2 So the **first angel** went and poured*

   Jezreel Valley (Armageddon) from Megiddo

   *out his bowl on the earth, and harmful and painful sores came upon the people who bore the mark of the beast and worshiped its image. 3 The **second angel** poured out his bowl into the sea, and it became like the blood of a corpse, and every living thing died that was in the sea. 4 The **third angel** poured out his bowl into the rivers and the springs of water, and they became blood. 5 And I heard the angel in charge of the waters say, "Just are you, O Holy One, who is and who was, for you brought these judgments. 6 For they have shed the blood of saints and prophets, and you have given them blood to drink. It is what they deserve!" 7 And I heard the altar saying, "Yes, Lord God the Almighty, true and just are your judgments!" 8 The **fourth angel** poured out his bowl on the sun, and it was allowed to scorch people with fire. 9 They were scorched by the fierce heat, and they cursed the name of God who had power over these plagues. They did not repent and give him glory. 10 The **fifth angel** poured out his bowl on the throne of the beast, and its kingdom was plunged into darkness. People gnawed their tongues in anguish 11 and cursed the God of heaven for their pain and sores. They did not* *repent of their deeds. 12 The* **sixth angel** *poured out his bowl on the great river Euphrates, and its water was dried up, to prepare the way for the kings from the east. 13 And I saw, coming out of the mouth of the dragon and out of the mouth of the beast and out of the mouth of the false prophet, three unclean spirits like frogs. 14 For they are demonic spirits, performing signs, who go abroad to the kings of the whole world, to assemble them for battle on the great day of God the Almighty. 15 ("Behold, I am coming like a thief! Blessed is the one who stays awake, keeping his garments on, that he may not go about naked and be seen exposed!") 16 And they assembled them at the place that in Hebrew is called* **Armageddon**. *17 The* **seventh angel** *poured out his bowl into the air, and a loud voice came out of the temple, from the throne, saying, "It is done!" 18 And there were flashes of lightning, rumblings, peals of thunder, and a great earthquake such as there had never been since man was on the earth, so great was*

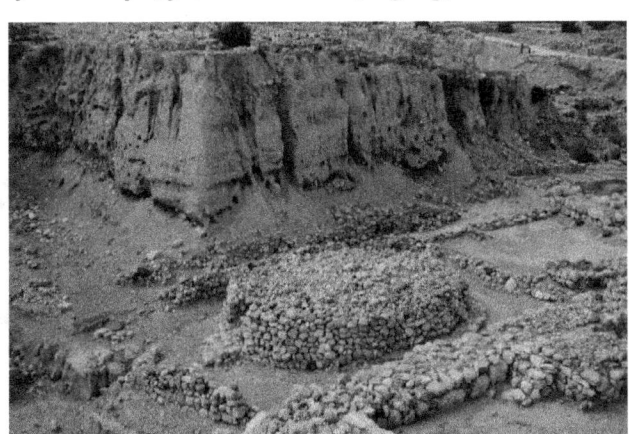

Canaanite Altar

that earthquake. 19 The great city was split into three parts, and the cities of the nations fell, and God remembered Babylon the great, to make her drain the cup of the wine of the fury of his wrath. 20 And every island fled away, and no mountains were to be found. 21 And great hailstones, about one hundred pounds each, fell from heaven on people; and they cursed God for the plague of the hail, because the plague was so severe.

3. **The harvest of the earth in God's winepress of wrath in Jerusalem.**

   Revelation 14:14–20: *Then I looked, and behold, a white cloud, and seated on the cloud one like a son of man, with a golden crown on his head, and a sharp sickle in his hand. 15 And another angel came out of the temple, calling with a loud voice to him who sat on the cloud, "Put in your sickle, and reap, for the hour to reap has come,* for the harvest of the earth is fully ripe." 16 So he who sat on the cloud swung his sickle across the earth, and the earth was reaped. 17 Then another angel came out of the temple in heaven, and he too had a sharp sickle. 18 And another angel came out from the altar, the angel who has authority over the fire, and he called with a loud voice to the one who had the sharp sickle, "Put in your sickle and gather the clusters from the vine of the earth, for its grapes are ripe." 19 So the angel swung his sickle across the earth and gathered the grape harvest of the earth and threw it into the great winepress of the wrath of God. 20 And the winepress was trodden **outside the city** [Jerusalem], and blood flowed from the winepress, as high as a horse's bridle, for 1,600 stadia [180 miles, 300 km.].

Matthew 25:31–34: *When the Son of Man comes in his glory, and all the angels with him, then he will sit on his glorious throne. 32 Before him will be gathered all the nations, and he will separate people one from another as a shepherd separates the sheep from the goats. 33* *And he will place the sheep on his right, but the goats on the left. 34 Then the King will say to those on his right, "Come, you who are blessed by my Father, inherit the kingdom prepared for you from the foundation of the world."*

Matthew 25:46: *And these will go away into eternal punishment, but the righteous into eternal life.*

Faith Lesson from Megiddo

1. Part of the last battle of Armageddon will be fought in Megiddo and the other part in Jerusalem. The war seems to happen simultaneously.
2. This battle will take place at the end of the Great Tribulation

Period.
3. Scripture says that unless these days were shortened, no life would survive.
4. The Tribulation Period will be a time when God pours out His wrath on a world that has rejected Him inspite of all He has done for them.
5. Where will I be at this battle? Will I be fighting with Christ or against Him?
6. Water was the source of life for all cities in ancient days. These cities could be conquered when their enemies cut off their water supply.

7. God's Word is our water source of life. Our enemy, Satan, can defeat us by cutting off our intake of God's Word. When he can do this, he can conquer us. To stand against Satan and his attacks, am I daily drinking abundantly from the water source of God's Word?

Journal/Notes:

Mount Carmel

Location

1. The place marking the great showdown between Elijah and the false prophets is known as Deir Al-Mukhraqa Carmelite Monastery.

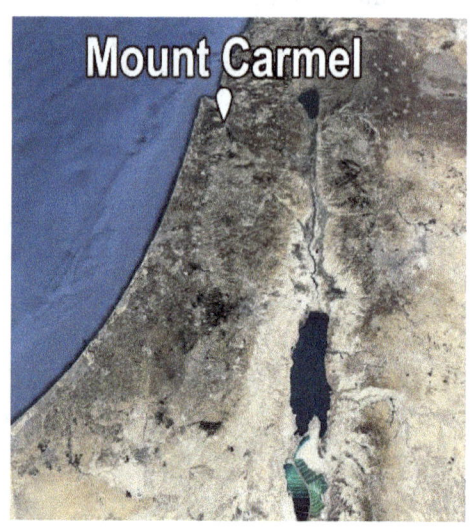

2. Mount Carmel is located about 9 miles (15 km.) east of the Mediterranean Sea in the Carmel Mountain Range, which is in the northern part of Israel. It's also about 28 miles (44 km.) southwest of the Sea of Galilee.
3. Mount Carmel was a High Place of worship to the false god of Baal and Asherah during the period of Judges, 1 & 2 Samuel, and 1 & 2 Kings.
4. It has a spectacular view of the Jezreel Valley, which is also known as the Valley of Armageddon. Armageddon is where part of the last battle on earth takes place at the end of the Great Tribulation Period.
5. From Mount Carmel, Nazareth and Cana can be seen to the northeast.

Historical Background

1. The great showdown between the Prophet Elijah and the 850 prophets of Baal and Asherah began around 100 years earlier when King Solomon sowed the seeds that would destroy Israel morally.
2. Against God's clear commandments to the Israelites, Solomon married many foreign wives.
3. These foreign wives worshiped false gods, and in order to honor them, Solomon built high places of worship all over Israel where these false gods could be worshiped. 1 Kings 11 recounts this

Northern Israel Sites

tragic reality.

4. As a result, the worship of false gods became rampant in the land.
5. Because of the worship of false gods, God pronounced judgment on the nation of Israel, and it was divided into two kingdoms after Solomon's death.
6. Rehoboam, one of Solomon's sons, took the Southern Kingdom of Judah, which consisted of 2 tribes, and Jeroboam, one of Solomon's officials, took the Northern Kingdom, which consisted of 10 tribes.

Mount Carmel

7. Because Jeroboam was afraid many of his people would defect to Rehoboam's kingdom by going to Jerusalem to worship God in the temple there, he introduced false gods into the northern tribes of Israel.
8. Jeroboam erected two golden calf altars at Bethel and Dan for his people to worship at instead of going to the temple in Jerusalem. He told his people that these golden calves were the gods who led them out of Egypt.
9. Several kings later, King Ahab, king of the Northern Kingdom, married a foreign wife named Jezebel, who worshiped the false gods of Baal (a male god) and Asherah (a female god). Jezebel promoted worship to these false gods by employing countless prophets of Baal and Asherah. She even supported them financially and fed them at her royal table.
10. Mt. Carmel was one of the key high places in Israel where the people worshiped Baal and Asherah.
11. Baal and Asherah were the gods of the weather. It was for this reason God sent a drought and then later sent rain. By doing so, He showed He was the true God of the weather and everything else. Baal worship was originally from the Canaanite nations God drove out because of their extreme wickedness.

Places of Interest

1. Mt. Carmel
2. Kishon Stream
3. Jezreel Valley
4. Tel Jezreel
5. Mediterranean Sea

Mount Carmel in the Bible

1. The showdown between Elijah and the false prophets took place during the reign of Ahab, King of Israel.

1 Kings 16:29–33: *In the thirty-eighth year of Asa king of Judah, Ahab the son of Omri began to reign over Israel, and Ahab the son of Omri reigned over Israel in Samaria twenty-two years. 30 And Ahab the son of Omri did evil in the sight of the LORD, more than all who were before him. 31 And as if it had been a light thing for him to walk in the sins of Jeroboam the son of Nebat, he took for his wife Jezebel, the daughter of Ethbaal king of the Sidonians, and went and served Baal and worshiped him. 32 He erected an altar for Baal in*

Northern Israel Sites

the house of Baal, which he built in Samaria. 33 And Ahab made an Asherah. Ahab did more to provoke the LORD, the God of Israel, to anger than all the kings of Israel who were before him.

2. **Because of Ahab's great sin, God sent a severe drought over all the land.**

   1 Kings 17:1: *Now Elijah the Tishbite, of Tishbe in Gilead, said to Ahab, "As the LORD, the God of Israel, lives, before whom I stand, there shall be neither dew nor rain these years, except by my word."*

3. **After these 3 years had ended, Elijah confronts Ahab and promises God will send rain.**

   1 Kings 18:1-2: *After many days the word of the LORD came to Elijah, in the third year, saying, "Go, show yourself to Ahab, and I will send rain upon the earth." 2 So Elijah went to show himself to Ahab. Now the famine was severe in Samaria.*

   Mount Carmel

   1 Kings 18:17-19: *When Ahab saw Elijah, Ahab said to him, "Is it you, you troubler of Israel?" 18 And he answered, "I have not troubled Israel, but you have, and your father's house, because you have abandoned the commandments of the Lord and followed the Baals. 19 Now, therefore, send and gather all Israel to me at Mount Carmel, and the 450 prophets of Baal and the 400 prophets of Asherah, who eat at Jezebel's table."*

4. **The great gathering of all the people.**

   1 Kings 18:20-21: *So Ahab sent to all the people of Israel and gathered the prophets together at Mount Carmel. 21 And Elijah came near to all the people and said, "How long will you go limping between two different opinions? If the Lord is God, follow him; but if Baal, then follow him." And the people did not answer him a word.*

5. The great contest between Elijah and the 850 prophets of Baal and Asherah.

1 Kings 18:22–24: *Then Elijah said to the people, "I, even I only, am left a prophet of the Lord, but Baal's prophets are 450 men. 23 Let two bulls be given to us, and let them choose one bull for themselves and cut it in pieces and lay it on the wood, but put no fire to it. And I will prepare the other bull and lay it on the wood and put no fire to it. 24 And you* 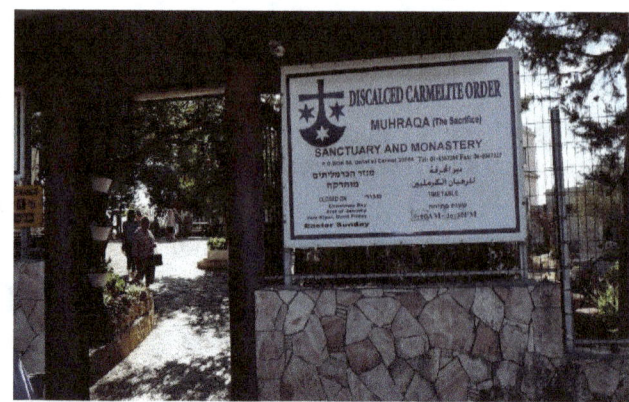 *call upon the name of your god, and I will call upon the name of the Lord, and the God who answers by fire, he is God." And all the people answered, "It is well spoken."*

6. The false prophets of Baal and Asherah go first.

1 Kings 18:25–29: *Then Elijah said to the prophets of Baal, "Choose for yourselves one bull and prepare it first, for you are many, and call upon the name of your god, but put no fire to it." 26 And they took the bull that was given them, and they prepared it and called upon the name of Baal from morning until noon, saying, "O Baal, answer us!" But there was no voice, and no one answered. And they limped around the altar that they had made. 27 And at noon Elijah mocked them, saying, "Cry aloud, for he is a god. Either he is musing, or he is relieving himself, or he is on a journey, or perhaps he is asleep and must be awakened." 28 And they cried aloud and cut themselves after their custom with swords and lances, until the blood gushed out upon them. 29 And as midday passed, they raved on until the time of the offering of the oblation [evening sacrifice], but there was no voice. No one answered; no one paid attention.*

7. Elijah takes his turn.

1 Kings 18:30–35: *Then Elijah said to all the people, "Come near to me." And all the people came near to him. And he repaired the altar of the Lord that had been thrown down. 31 Elijah took twelve stones, according to the number of the tribes of the sons of Jacob, to whom*

the word of the Lord came, saying, "Israel shall be your name," 32 and with the stones he built an altar in the name of the Lord. And he made a trench about the altar, as great as would contain two seahs [about 1 foot deep by 1 foot wide] of seed. 33 And he put the wood in order and cut the bull in pieces and laid it on the wood. And he said, "Fill four jars with water and pour it on the burnt offering and on the wood." 34 And he said, "Do it a second time." And they did it a second time. 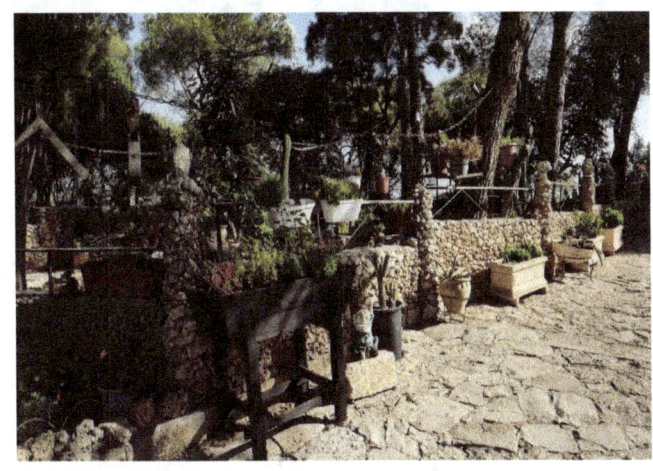 *And he said, "Do it a third time." And they did it a third time. 35 And the water ran around the altar and filled the trench also with water.*

8. God miraculously answers.

1 Kings 18:36–39: *And at the time of the offering of the oblation, Elijah the prophet came near and said, "O Lord, God of Abraham, Isaac, and Israel, let it be known this day that you are God in Israel, and that I am your servant, and that I have done all these things at your word. 37 Answer me, O Lord, answer me, that this people may know that you, O Lord, are God, and that you have turned their hearts back." 38 Then the fire of the Lord fell and consumed the burnt offering and the wood and the stones and the dust, and licked up the water that was in the trench. 39 And when all the people saw it, they fell on their faces and said, "The Lord, he is God; the Lord, he is God."*

9. Elijah then slaughters the false prophets below Mount Carmen at the Kishon Stream.

1 Kings 18:40: *And Elijah said to them, "Seize the prophets of Baal; let not one of them escape." And they seized them. And Elijah brought them down to the brook Kishon and slaughtered them there.*

10. **Afterward, God sent a massive rainstorm which brought a deluge of rain to Israel and ended the drought.**

   1 Kings 18:41–46: *And Elijah said to Ahab, "Go up, eat and drink, for there is a sound of the rushing of rain." 42 So Ahab went up to eat and to drink. And Elijah went up to the top of Mount Carmel. And he bowed himself down on the earth and put his face between his knees. 43 And he said to his servant, "Go up now, look toward the sea." And he went up and looked and said, "There is nothing." And he said, "Go again," seven times. 44 And at the seventh time he said, "Behold, a little cloud like a man's hand is rising from the sea." And he said, "Go up, say to Ahab, 'Prepare your chariot and go down, lest the rain stop you.'" 45 And in a little while, the heavens grew black with clouds and wind, and there was a great rain. And Ahab rode and went to Jezreel. 46 And the hand of the Lord was on Elijah, and he gathered up his garment and ran before Ahab to the entrance of Jezreel.*

   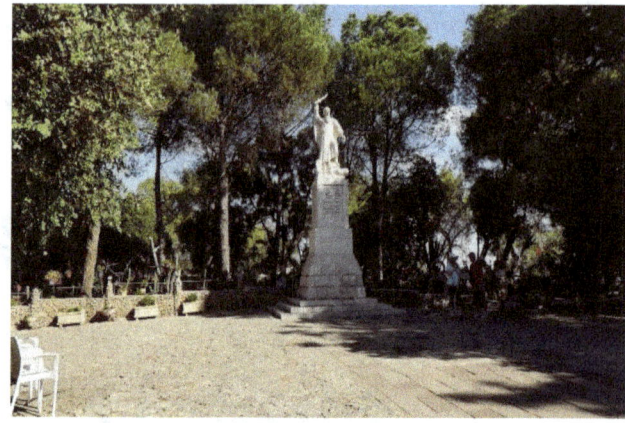
   Statue of Elijah at Mount Carmel

   Jezreel is about 15 miles (24 km.) directly east of Mount Carmel.

11. **Unfortunately, this great miracle and spiritual revival didn't last long. Soon afterward, the country fell back into the worship of false gods and idols.**

Faith Lesson from Mount Carmel

1. Do we fall away easily from the Lord and neglect Him?
2. Does spiritual revival in our lives rapidly fade?
3. Are we undisciplined in our time with God and fail to read His Word and grow in Him?
4. Have we witnessed miracles in our lives where we know that God is real and that He has shown Himself powerful to us?

Northern Israel Sites

5. After seeing miracles and experiencing God's help, do we forget and fall away from God afterward?

6. Are we steadfast in our relationship with God, or are we like the Israelites who were unstable with big ups and downs?

Viewing platform

7. Are we in need of coming back to God today and getting right with Him once again?

Journal/Notes:

Mount Tabor

Location

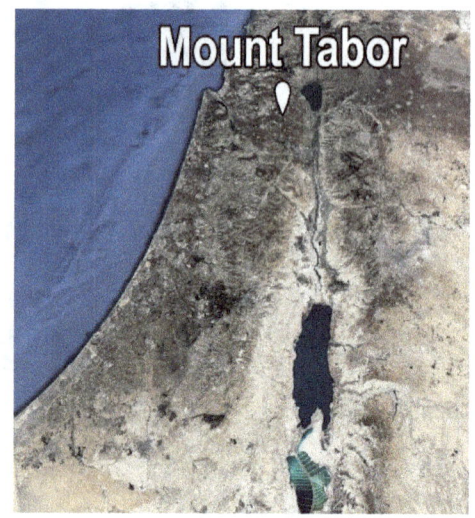

1. Mount Tabor, rising like a dome-like mountain from the Plain of Jezreel, is the place where Christian tradition places the transfiguration of Jesus.
2. It's about 11 miles (15 km.) southwest of the Sea of Galilee and about 5 miles (8 km.) east of Nazareth.
3. Mount Tabor stands some 1,500 ft. (457 m.) above the Jezreel Valley plain in Lower Galilee.
4. It held a strategic position at the junction of several trade routes. For this reason, many battles have been fought around it.
5. It's mentioned as one of the key mountains in Scripture: *The north and the south, you have created them;* **Tabor** *and Hermon joyously praise your name* (Ps. 89:12).

Historical Background

1. In the Old Testament, Mount Tabor is described as a sacred mountain and a place for worship. However, it's not mentioned by name in the New Testament.
2. Throughout its history, it has been a place where mankind has sought contact with the divine.
3. It also served as an important fortress during the Old Testament, Greek, Roman, and Crusader times.
4. It is best known as the believed place where the transfiguration of Christ took place, an event in the Gospels in which Jesus is transfigured upon an unnamed mountain and speaks with Moses and Elijah as described in Matthew 17:1–9; Mark 9:2–8; and Luke 9:28–36.

5. Christian tradition in the early centuries named Mount Tabor as the place of the transfiguration of Christ. This location is cited in early apocryphal writings and was accepted by the Syriac and Byzantine churches.
6. The earliest identification of the Mount of Transfiguration as Mount Tabor is by Origen in the 3rd century.
7. During the Byzantine period, due to the importance of Mount Tabor in Christian tradition, it became a pilgrimage site from the 4th century and onward. According to descriptions of the pilgrims visiting this site during the 6th century, there were three churches that resided on the top of Mount Tabor.

Franciscan Basilica of the Transformation

8. Some biblical scholars today now question this tradition. These scholars see the much higher Mount Hermon as a more likely location as it was closer to Caesarea Philippi, where Peter's confession of Christ took place.
9. However, there is great value in considering the 2,000-year-old traditions of history at this site.
10. Scripture says that the transfiguration of Christ took place 6 days after Peter's confession of Christ in Caesarea Philippi. Mount Tabor is only about 40 miles (65 km.) south of Caesarea Philippi, which could easily have been reached in 6 days.
11. It's really not important where this event happened but that it did happen.
12. Today, there are two main churches and monasteries on top of Mount Tabor, marking the event of the transfiguration of Christ. They include the Franciscan Basilica of the Transfiguration and St. Elias Greek Orthodox Church.

Israel Biblical Sites Travel Guide

Places of Interest

1. Franciscan Basilica of the Transfiguration – Main church that is visited and sits at the highest part of Mount Tabor. This church, which is part of a Franciscan monastery complex, was completed in 1924. It was built on the ruins of an ancient 4th to 6th-century Byzantine church and a 12th-century church of the Crusader Kingdom period.
2. St. Elias Greek Orthodox Church – Located on the northern side of Mount Tabor (named after the Prophet Elijah).
3. Tower & Walls
4. Other ancient structures, chapels, cisterns, and quarries.
5. Descentibus Chapel
6. Melchizedek Chapel
7. Jezreel Valley

Northern Israel Sites

Mount Tabor in the Bible

1. **Mount Tabor is mentioned 12 times in Scripture.**
2. **It's first mentioned in Joshua 19:22 as a border between the 3 tribes of Zebulun, Issachar, and Naphtali. The mountain's prominence is due to its strategic location at the junction of the Galilee's north-south route, along with the east-west highway of the Jezreel Valley.**
3. **According to Judges chapter 4, Hazor was the seat of Jabin, the king of Canaan. His military commander, Sisera, led a Canaanite army against the Israelites. Deborah, the Jewish prophetess, summoned Barak of the tribe of Naphtali and gave him the following command.**

   Judges 4:14–16: *And Deborah said to Barak, "Up! For this is the day in which the Lord has given Sisera into your hand. Does not the Lord go out before you?" So, Barak went down from **Mount Tabor** with 10,000 men following him. 15 And the Lord routed Sisera and all his chariots and all his army before Barak by the edge of the sword.*

   And Sisera got down from his chariot and fled away on foot. 16 And Barak pursued the chariots and the army to Harosheth-hagoyim, and all the army of Sisera fell by the edge of the sword; not a man was left.

4. **Transfiguration of Christ.**

   Matthew 17:1–13: *And after six days Jesus took with him Peter and James, and John, his brother, and led them up a high mountain by themselves. 2 And he was transfigured before them, and his face shone like the sun, and his clothes became white as light. 3 And behold, there appeared to them Moses and Elijah, talking with him. 4 And Peter said to Jesus, "Lord, it is good that we are here. If you wish, I will make three tents here, one for you and one for Moses and one for Elijah." 5 He was still speaking when, behold, a bright cloud overshadowed them, and a voice from the cloud said, "This is my beloved Son, with whom I am well pleased; listen to him." 6 When the disciples heard this, they fell on their faces and were terrified. 7 But Jesus came and touched them, saying, "Rise, and have no fear." 8 And when they lifted up their eyes, they saw no one but Jesus only. 9 And as they were coming down the mountain, Jesus commanded them, "Tell no one the vision, until the Son of Man is raised from the dead." 10 And the disciples asked him, "Then why do the scribes say that first Elijah must come?" 11 He answered, "Elijah does come, and he will restore all things. 12 But I tell you that Elijah has already come, and they did not recognize him, but did to him whatever they pleased. So also, the Son of Man will certainly suffer at their hands." 13 Then the disciples understood that he was speaking to them of John the Baptist.*

5. **After descending Mount Tabor, Christ healed a man and used Mount Tabor as an example of faith.**

   Matthew 17:14–20: *And when they came to the crowd, a man came up to him and, kneeling before him, 15 said, "Lord, have mercy on my son, for he has seizures and he suffers terribly. For often he falls into the fire, and often into the water. 16 And I brought him to your*

   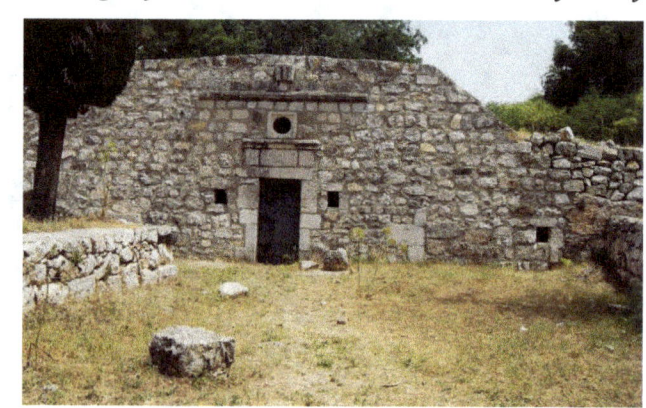
   Melchizedek Chapel

   disciples, and they could not heal him." 17 And Jesus answered, "O faithless and twisted generation, how long am I to be with you? How long am I to bear with you? Bring him here to me." 18 And Jesus rebuked the demon, and it came out of him, and the boy was healed instantly. 19 Then the disciples came to Jesus privately and said, "Why could we not cast it out?" 20 He said to them, "Because of your little faith. For truly, I say to you, if you have faith like a grain of mustard seed, you will say to **this mountain***, 'Move from here to there,' and it will move, and nothing will be impossible for you."*

Northern Israel Sites

Faith Lesson from Mount Tabor

1. The transfiguration of Christ is another proof that He was truly the Son of God and divine.
2. It cemented in the hearts of Peter, James, and John, who would become key leaders in the early church, that Christ was definitely the Messiah and God the Father in the flesh.
3. The Apostle Peter looked back to this landmark event of the transfiguration to speak about how sure and solid our faith in Christ and His Word is.

   1 Peter 1:16–21: *For we did not follow cleverly devised myths when we made known to you the power and coming of our Lord Jesus Christ, but we were eyewitnesses of his majesty. 17 For when he received honor and glory from God the Father, and the voice was borne to him by the Majestic Glory, "This is my beloved Son, with whom I am well pleased," 18 we ourselves heard this very voice borne from heaven, for we were with him on the holy mountain [mount of transfiguration]. 19 And we have the prophetic word more fully confirmed, to which you will do well to pay attention as to a lamp shining in a dark place, until the day dawns and the morning star rises in your hearts, 20 knowing this first of all, that no prophecy of Scripture comes from someone's own interpretation [source or wisdom]. 21 For no prophecy was ever produced by the will of man, but men spoke from God as they were carried along by the Holy Spirit.*
4. Are we anchored in our faith and unmovable?
5. Do we believe Christ was God in the flesh, and are we willing to follow Him and be His disciples?
6. Do we believe we can move spiritual mountains if we have faith in Christ?

Journal/Notes:

Nazareth Overview

Location

1. Nazareth is in the northern part of Israel in the Lower Galilee area.
2. It's about 15 miles (24 km.) southwest of the Sea of Galilee, about 3.5 miles (5.6 km.) southwest of Cana, and about 23 miles (37 km.) inland from the Mediterranean Sea.

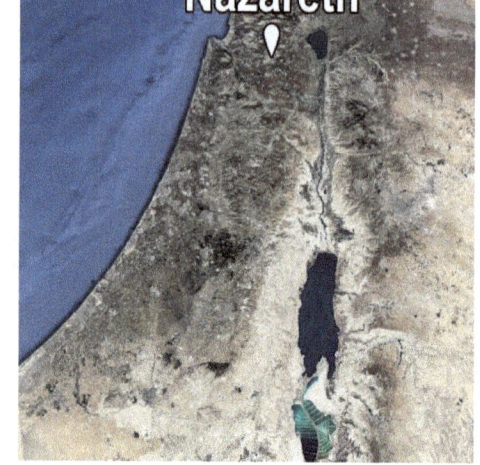

Historical Background

1. Nazareth had an estimated population of around 300 people during the time of Christ.
2. It's a famous town because it's where the Angel Gabriel announced the miraculous virgin birth to Mary.
3. Nazareth is also the place where Jesus grew up.
4. It was a small farming town where everyone knew each other.
5. For some reason, Nazareth had a bad reputation.

   John 1:43–46: *The next day He purposed to go into Galilee, and He found Philip. And Jesus said to him, "Follow Me." 44 Now Philip was from Bethsaida, of the city of Andrew and Peter. 45 Philip found Nathanael and said to him, "We have found Him of whom Moses in the Law and also the Prophets wrote—Jesus of Nazareth, the son of Joseph." 46 Nathanael said to him,* **"Can any good thing come out of Nazareth?"** *Philip said to him, "Come and see."*

Places of Interest

1. Church of the Annunciation (also known as the Basilica of the Annunciation)
2. Mary's Well
3. Greek Catholic Church
4. Synagogue Church

5. Greek Orthodox Church of the Annunciation
6. St. Joseph's Church
7. Mensa Christi Church
8. Greek Catholic Church
9. Mount Precipice

Nazareth in the Bible

1. Nazareth was the home of Joseph and Mary and the place where the angel Gabriel was sent to announce to Mary, a virgin, that she would be the mother of Christ the Messiah.
2. There have been two churches built here to commemorate this announcement. One is called the "Church of the Annunciation," and the other, the "Greek Orthodox Church of the Annunciation." The Church of the Annunciation has the most evidence of being the true site.

Luke 1:26–38: *In the sixth month the angel Gabriel was sent from God to a city of Galilee named Nazareth, 27 to a virgin betrothed to a man whose name was Joseph, of the house of David. And the virgin's name was Mary. 28 And he came to her and said, "Greetings, O favored one, the Lord is with you!" 29 But she was greatly troubled at the saying,*

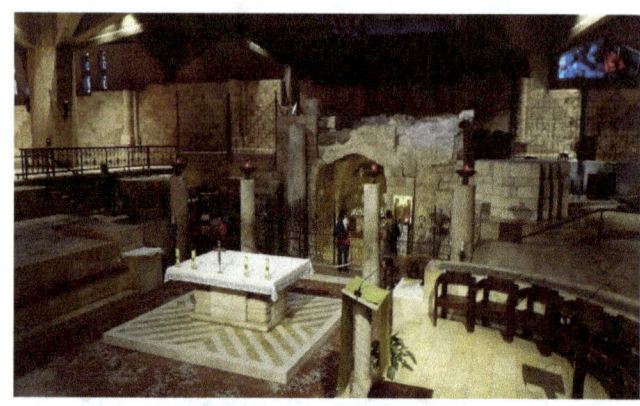

Inside the Church of the Annunciation: Believed Home of Joseph & Mary

and tried to discern what sort of greeting this might be. 30 And the angel said to her, "Do not be afraid, Mary, for you have found favor with God. 31 And behold, you will conceive in your womb and bear a son, and you shall call his name Jesus. 32 He will be great and will be called the Son of the Most High. And the Lord God will give to him the throne of his father David, 33 and he will reign over the house of Jacob forever, and of his kingdom there will be no end." 34 And Mary said to the angel, "How will this be, since I am a virgin?" 35 And the angel answered her, "The Holy Spirit will come upon you, and the power of the Most High will overshadow you; therefore, the child to be born will be called holy—the Son of God. 36 And behold, your relative Elizabeth in her old age has also conceived a son, and this is the sixth month with her who was called barren. 37 For nothing will be impossible with God." 38 And Mary said, "Behold, I am the servant of the Lord; let it be to me according to your word." And the angel departed from her.

3. **After living in Egypt for some time after Christ's birth, His parents returned to Nazareth, where Jesus grew up.**

Matthew 2:19–23: *But when Herod died, behold, an angel of the Lord appeared in a dream to Joseph in Egypt, 20 saying, "Rise, take the child and his mother and go to the land of Israel, for those who sought the child's life are dead." 21 And he rose and took the child and his mother and went to the land of Israel. 22 But when he heard that Archelaus was reigning over Judea in place of his father Herod,*

Northern Israel Sites

he was afraid to go there, and being warned in a dream he withdrew to the district of Galilee. 23 And he went and lived in a city called **Nazareth**, that what was spoken by the prophets might be fulfilled: "He shall be called a Nazarene."

Luke 2:51–52: *And He went down with them and came to **Nazareth**, and He continued in subjection to them; and His mother treasured all these things in her heart. 52 And Jesus kept increasing in wisdom and stature, and in favor with God and men.*

4. **Jesus lived in Nazareth until He started His earthly ministry at the age of 30. From Nazareth, Christ relocated and set up His ministry home base in Capernaum by the Sea of Galilee.**

   Matthew 4:13–17: *And **leaving Nazareth he went and lived in Capernaum** by the sea, in the territory of Zebulun and Naphtali, 14 so that what was spoken by the prophet Isaiah might be fulfilled: 15 "The land of Zebulun*

   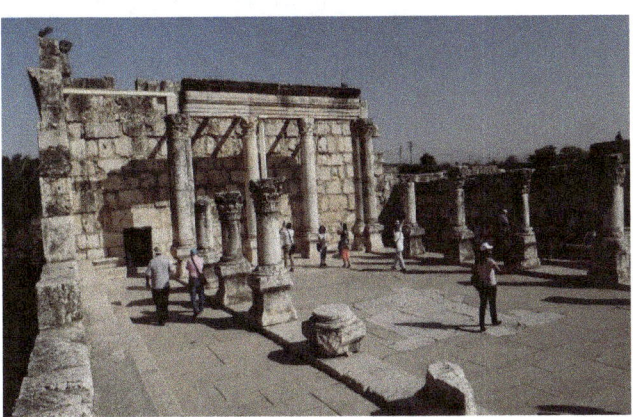
   Synagogue at Capernaum

   and the land of Naphtali, the way of the sea, beyond the Jordan, Galilee of the Gentiles—16 the people dwelling in darkness have seen a great light, and for those dwelling in the region and shadow of death, on them a light has dawned." 17 From that time Jesus began to preach, saying, "Repent, for the kingdom of heaven is at hand."

5. **Jesus was rejected by His own townspeople at Nazareth and was unable to perform many miracles there due to their lack of faith in Him.**

   Luke 4:14–27: *And Jesus returned in the power of the Spirit to Galilee, and a report about him went out through all the surrounding country. 15 And he taught in their synagogues, being glorified by all. 16 **And he came to Nazareth, where he had been brought up**. And as was his custom, he went to the synagogue on* the Sabbath day, and he stood up to read. 17 And the scroll of the prophet Isaiah was given to him. He unrolled the scroll and found the place where it was written, 18 "The Spirit of the Lord is upon me, because he has anointed me to proclaim good news to the poor. He has sent me to proclaim liberty to the captives and recovering of sight to the blind, to set at liberty those who are oppressed, 19 to proclaim the year of the Lord's favor." 20 And he rolled up the scroll and gave it back to the attendant and sat down. And the eyes of all in the synagogue were fixed on him. 21 And he began to say to them, "Today this Scripture has been fulfilled in your hearing." 22 And all spoke well of him and marveled at the gracious words that were coming from his mouth. And they said, "Is not this Joseph's son?" 23 And he said to them, "Doubtless you will quote to me this proverb, 'Physician, heal yourself.' What we have heard you did at Capernaum, do here in your hometown as well." 24 And he said, "Truly, I say to you, no prophet is acceptable in his hometown. 25 But in truth, I tell you, there were many widows in Israel in the days of Elijah, when the heavens were shut up three years and six months, and a great famine came over all the land, 26 and Elijah was sent to none of them but only to Zarephath, in the land of Sidon, to a woman who was a widow. 27 And there were many lepers in Israel in the time of the prophet Elisha, and none of them was cleansed, but only Naaman the Syrian."

Mount Precipice

6. **Those who knew Christ best rejected Him and attempted to throw Him off a cliff close to their town. Today, this place is called Mount Precipice.**

    Luke 4:28–30: *When they heard these things, all in the synagogue were filled with wrath. 29 And they rose up and drove him out of the town and brought him to the brow of the hill on which their town was built, so that they could throw him down the cliff. 30 But passing through their midst, he went away.*

Faith Lesson from Nazareth

1. Nazareth had a bad reputation. God oftentimes places light in the dark so the light can illuminate the darkness. Are we being lights where we live?

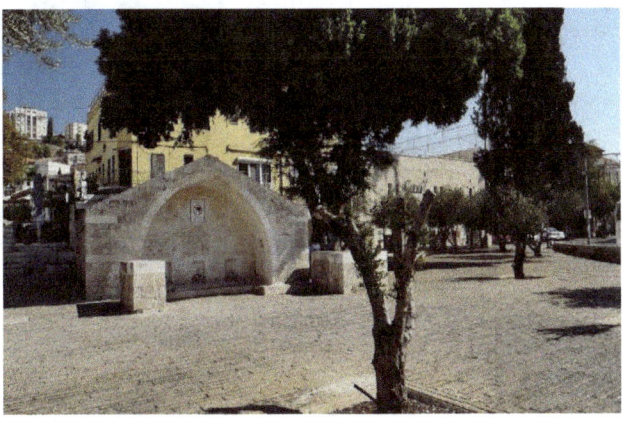
Mary's Well

2. The people of Nazareth largely rejected Christ. It shouldn't surprise us if we, too, are rejected because of our faith in Christ and adherence to His Word.
3. Christ was rejected, so He understands when we are rejected by our close friends and family members because of our faith in Him.
4. Do we reject Christ by refusing His offer of salvation, by refusing to be obedient to Him, or by not sharing our faith with those around us?

Journal/Notes:

Nazareth: Church of the Annunciation

Location

1. Nazareth is about 15 miles (24 km.) southwest of the Sea of Galilee and about 23 miles (37 km.) inland from the Mediterranean Sea.
2. The Church of the Annunciation is in the center of the City of Nazareth, on Casa Nova Street.

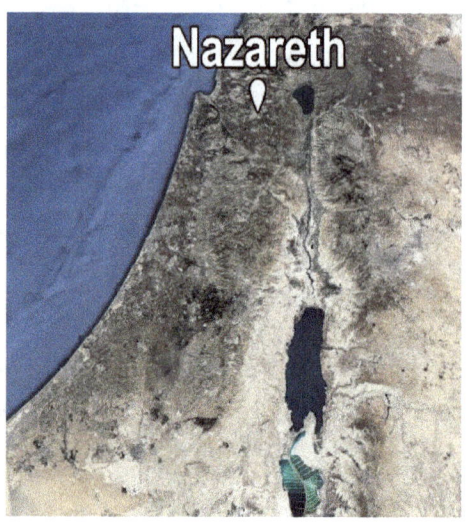

Historical Background

1. Nazareth had an estimated population of around 300 people during the time of Christ.
2. It was a small farming town where everyone knew each other.
3. Nazareth had a bad reputation.

   John 1:46: *Nathanael said to him, "Can **any good thing** come out of Nazareth?" Philip said to him, "Come and see."*
4. Tradition holds that this home is in the cave grotto in the lower level of the Church of the Annunciation.
5. Christians began venerating the home of Mary and Joseph soon after Christ's death and resurrection. Remains of a Judeo-Christian synagogue at this site show proof of this.
6. In the mid-4th century, Helena, the mother of the Roman Emperor Constantine, commissioned the construction of the Church of the Annunciation based upon tradition and evidence she found at the site. The church was built over the remains of the Judeo-Christian synagogue.
7. The church has been destroyed and rebuilt around 5 times. The Muslims destroyed it in the 7th century. In 1100, the Crusaders arrived and rebuilt the church. In 1620, the Franciscans purchased the ruins and rebuilt them. In 1730, the church was rebuilt again, and in 1877, it was enlarged.

Northern Israel Sites

8. From 1955–1969, the church was rebuilt to its current status. It's now a massive two-story church with a modern architectural style. In 1969, when it was completed, it was the largest Christian church in the Middle East.

9. The church has two levels with two separate churches. The upper church level is for Nazareth's Catholic community. The lower level is centered around the grotto, which was the home of Mary and the site of the Annunciation. The remnants of the churches from the second century, Byzantine, and Crusader eras can be seen around the grotto area.

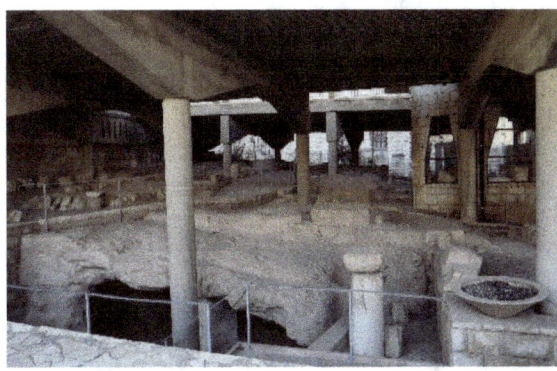

Ruins under the church

10. Another church in Nazareth commemorates the annunciation of the birth of Christ as well. It's the Greek Orthodox Church of the Annunciation, the traditional site held by the Eastern Orthodox churches.

Places of Interest

1. Statue of Mary – Her hands are blackened from touch.
2. Written in Latin across the façade over the triple-doorway entrance is the Bible verse: *"The Word was made flesh and dwelt among us"* (John 1:14).
3. The entryway doors to the church have carvings of significant events that happened in the Old and New Testaments.
4. The current church is a two-story building. The main entrance is on the lower level.
5. On the lower level is the grotto that is believed to be the original home of Mary and the place the angel Gabriel appeared to her.
6. The words written on an altar table at the front of the grotto mean, "Here the Word was made Flesh."
7. On each side of the grotto are the remains of earlier churches.

8. The upper level of the church serves as the local Roman Catholic parish church.
9. Outside the upper level of the church are excavations and buildings during the time of Christ.
10. Outside the church's lower level is a covered area with mosaic panels of many countries from around the world.

Nazareth in the Bible

1. **Nazareth was the home of Joseph and Mary, and the place where the angel Gabriel was sent to announce to Mary, a virgin, that she would be the mother of Christ the Messiah.**

   Luke 1:26–38: *In the sixth month the angel Gabriel was sent from God to a city of Galilee named **Nazareth**, 27 to a virgin betrothed to a man whose name was Joseph, of the house of David. And the virgin's name was Mary. 28 And he came to her and said, "Greetings, O favored one, the Lord is with you!" 29 But she was greatly troubled at the saying, and tried to discern what sort of greeting this might be. 30 And the angel said to her, "Do not be afraid, Mary, for you have found favor with God. 31 And behold, you will conceive in your* *womb and bear a son, and you shall call his name Jesus. 32 He will be great and will be called the Son of the Most High. And the Lord God will give to him the throne of his father David, 33 and he will reign over the house of Jacob forever, and of his kingdom there will be no end." 34 And Mary said to the angel, "How will this be, since I am a virgin?" 35 And the angel answered her, "The Holy Spirit will come upon you, and the power of the Most High will overshadow you; therefore the child to be born will be called holy—the Son of God. 36 And behold, your relative Elizabeth in her old age has also conceived a son, and this is the sixth month with her who was called barren. 37 For nothing will be impossible with God." 38 And Mary said, "Behold, I am the servant of the Lord; let it be to me according to your word." And the angel departed from her.*

Faith Lesson from the Life of Mary

1. Mary was a righteous person whom God saw would honor and obey Him with the great gift of being the mother of Christ. Are we devoted to God in such a way that He would entrust to us abundant blessings?

2. Mary did not remain a virgin after giving birth to Christ, as many believe. She had many other children, as we can see all throughout Scripture (Matt. 15:55–56). Are we students of God's Word so we believe the truth, or do we follow what our church or others teach instead? Who is our highest authority in what we believe: people or God's Word?

Church of the Annunciation

3. Mary is not to be worshiped like some do but is an example to us of a person of deep faith and obedience. Do we revere and honor Mary, or do we worship her?

Journal/Notes:

Israel Biblical Sites Travel Guide

Sepphoris (Tsipori, Zippori)

Location

1. Sepphoris is located about 4 miles (6 km.) northwest of Nazareth, about 14 miles (23 km.) from the Mediterranean Sea, and about 15 miles (25 km.) from the Sea of Galilee.
2. Because of its close proximity to Nazareth, it was easily accessible by Jesus and His earthly father, Joseph.

Historical Background

1. The city started to grow during the 2nd century BC under Greek rule.
2. Later, under Roman rule during the time of Christ, Herod Antipas (the son of Herod the Great) invested in it significantly and made it "the ornament of Galilee." It was a sophisticated Roman city with all the luxuries of modern life at that time. It included a network of colonnaded paved streets, markets, residential houses, public buildings, bathhouses, a theater, and a synagogue.
3. Sepphoris rose to recognized status during the century before Christ because it was located right on one of the main trade routes linking Africa with Europe and Asia called "The Via Maris" (way of the sea). Therefore, it was a wealthy city.
4. It was also a military city guarded well by Roman troops.
5. Sepphoris was the capital of the Galilee area during the time of Christ.
6. In order to rebuild the city, Herod Antipas used a massive workforce.
7. Because Nazareth was so close to Sepphoris, and because Jesus was a Tekton (Greek for a construction worker of various types), Jesus and His father undoubtedly worked here.
8. So, in part, it's also where Jesus grew in wisdom and stature and in

favor with God and man (Luke 2:52).

9. Because it was mainly a Jewish city, it was given its Hebrew name, Zippori, because it sits on a hilltop like a bird (Zippor).

10. Sepphoris is also known as the Mosaic City, as some of the best mosaics in all of Israel are found here. More than 40 mosaic floors reveal the bustling life of a Roman city and the luxury it afforded.

11. After Herod's death in 4 BC, the Roman army rose up and halted a rebellion of Jewish rebels led by a man named Judas. Many of these rebels, numbering several thousand, were killed. However, according to Josephus, 2,000 of them were kept alive to be crucified on its streets and nearby roads in the area. These mass crucifixions were carried out to instill fear in others who might consider rebelling against Roman rule.

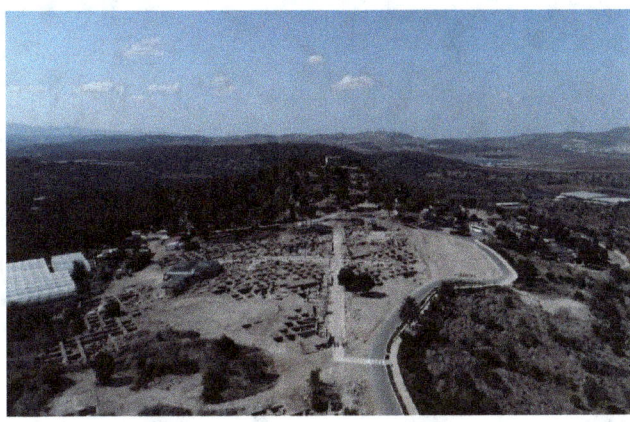

12. Sepphoris did not join the Jewish rebellion in 66-70 AD and was therefore spared destruction.

13. After the destruction of Jerusalem in 70 AD, Sepphoris became a center of Jewish learning and seat of the Sanhedrin supreme court. The Mishnah, the first authoritative collection of Jewish Oral Law, was compiled here.

14. Sepphoris witnessed Byzantine, Crusader, and Ottoman rule in the centuries following.

Places of Interest

1. Park Entrance
2. Water System
3. Decumanus Street
4. Nile House & Mosaics
5. Cardo

6. Public Building
7. Dionysus (god of wine) Building & Mosaics
8. Fortress
9. Residential Area
10. Theater
11. Synagogue

Sepphoris in the Bible

While Sepphoris is not mentioned in the Bible, it is significant for several reasons:

1. **It was nearby to Nazareth and employed many carpenters. Because Jesus was a construction worker, it's very likely Jesus worked here before starting His earthly ministry.**
2. **After the death of Jesus' earthly father, Joseph, Christ became the chief financial provider for His family. Christ was very responsible in caring for His family and expects us to do the same.**

    2 Thessalonians 3:10–11: *For even when we were with you, we*

Northern Israel Sites

would give you this command: If anyone is not willing to work, let him not eat. 11 For we hear that some among you walk in idleness, not busy at work, but busybodies.

John 19:26-27: *When Jesus saw his mother and the disciple whom he loved standing nearby, he said to his mother, "Woman, behold, your son!" 27 Then he said to the disciple, "Behold, your mother!" And from that hour the disciple took her to his own home.*

3. **It appears Jesus used references about this city in His teachings.**

   Matthew 5:14: *You are the light of the world. A city set on a hill cannot be hidden. Nor do people light a lamp and put it under a basket, but on a stand, and it gives light to all in the house.*

   Sepphoris was certainly a city on a hill. In fact, that's what the name of this city means.

   Matthew 6:2-4: *Thus, when you give to the needy, sound no trumpet before you, as the hypocrites do in the synagogues and in the streets, that they may be*

   Fortress

   praised by others. Truly, I say to you; they have received their reward. 3 But when you give to the needy, do not let your left hand know what your right hand is doing, 4 so that your giving may be in secret. And your Father who sees in secret will reward you.

   - The word for actor in Greek is "hypocrite." Because these actors would walk the streets sounding their horns to advertise an upcoming event at the city theater, Jesus used them as an example of what not to do when giving to others and serving God.

4. **Jesus likely used the example of the mass crucifixion carried out by the Romans against the Jewish revolt here to teach about the cost of being His disciple.**

Mark 8:34–38: *And calling the crowd to him with his disciples, he said to them, "If anyone would come after me, let him deny himself and take up his cross and follow me. 35 For whoever would save his life will lose it, but whoever loses his life for my sake and the gospel's will save it. 36 For what does it profit a man to gain the whole world and forfeit his soul? 37 For what can a man give in return for his soul? 38 For whoever is ashamed of me and of my words in this adulterous and sinful generation, of him will the Son of Man also be ashamed when he comes in the glory of his Father with the holy angels."*

- Christ taught about the cost of following him in several places during His ministry. In this account in Mark, He was teaching in the upper Galilee area at Caesarea Philippi, which is not far from Sepphoris.

Cardo showing chariot grooves

- It's very likely Christ's audience would have personally witnessed the crucifixions here in Sepphoris or seen others.
- To the Jewish mind, Christ's teaching would have sent a powerful and sober message of what Christ was asking of His followers. He was calling for total commitment, even commitment to death.
- Christ also used the imagery of crucifixion to teach us how we should daily crucify our personal desires that are contrary to God's desires.
- Sepphoris was certainly an adulterous and sinful city that Christ probably referred to in Mark 8:38.

Faith Lesson from Sepphoris

1. Jesus was a hard worker. Are we hard workers as well?
2. Jesus provided for His family after the death of His father. He also took care of His mother's future needs as He was being crucified. Do we provide and take care of our family members?
3. Jesus was undoubtedly good at what He did as a construction worker. Do we develop our skills to be good at what we do as well?
4. We should emulate Jesus in not only His spiritual side but also in His work ethic, work skills, and family responsibilities.

Crusader Fortress

5. Jesus grew in wisdom and stature and in favor with God and man prior to His earthly ministry. Are we doing the same?
6. Jesus likely used Sepphoris as an example of how we should be lights on a hill. Are we letting our lights shine brightly, or are we dim lights to those who know and see us?
7. Jesus likely used the actors in Sepphoris who blew their loud trumpets as an example of what we should not do when we give and serve God. Do we serve for God's glory alone, or do we serve for the praise and esteem of others?

Journal/Notes:

Other Sites in Northern Israel

Acre (Akko, Acco, Ptolemais)

Located about 9 miles (14 km.) north of Haifa, Acre was one of the best seaports in Israel.

Acre was allotted to the tribe of Asher, but they were never able to conquer it (Josh. 19:24–31; Judg. 1:31).

It was similar to Tyre and Sidon, cities the Israelites failed to conquer. As a result, Acre became a fortress city of unusual strength that stood up against its many attackers.

However, when Assyria arose to power, Acre was conquered and came under its control. When Assyria fell from world power, Acre, along with other Phoenician towns, came under the rule of Babylon, and then later, to Persia.

Modern Acre with seaport

In the Seleucid period (BC 312–65), Acre rose to prominence in the battles between the Seleucids and the Ptolemies. The Ptolemies had control of it during the struggles after the death of Alexander the Great and made it their stronghold on the coast. At this time, the city of Acre was changed to the name Ptolemais. This would be the name it would be known as during the Greek and Roman occupations of Israel. Therefore, the New Testament authors refer to Acre as Ptolemais (Acts 21:7).

In the period of the Crusaders, Acre was the most famous stronghold on the coast.

It declined after the Crusader period and fell into the hands of the Ottomans under Selim I in 1516.

Northern Israel Sites

Belvoir Fortress

This Crusader castle is located on a hill of the Naphtali Plateau, 12 miles (20 km.) south of the Sea of Galilee.

This impressive structure sits about 1,641 ft. (500 m.) above the Jordan Valley, which was a strategic location during the time of the Crusades. Designed to withstand the Muslim invaders, the fortress provided strong combat positioning as well as an amazing view of the surrounding area.

Belvoir Fortress

Built in 1168 by the Hospitallers order, it withstood a year and a half siege by Saladin's forces. The structure itself consists of an outer and an inner square fortress. It is still well-preserved, and visitors can explore the grounds while taking in a stunning view of the Jordan Valley, the Sea of Galilee, and the Golan Heights. It's the most complete and preserved Crusader fortress in Israel.

Tel Jezreel (Yizreel)

Jezreel, located in the fertile Jezreel Valley, is about 24 miles (38 km.) east of the Mediterranean Sea and about 17 miles (28 km.) southwest of the Sea of Galilee.

Jezreel was a major biblical city, and during the 9th century BC,

Tel Jezreel

it was the northern capital of the Israelite Kingdom.

When Saul and Jonathan were killed in battle on Mount Gilboa, news of this event came from Jezreel. Mephibosheth, Jonathan's son, became crippled when his nurse fell while carrying him as she ran in haste after hearing the terrible news of Jonathan's death (2 Sam. 4:4).

After the Kingdom of Israel was divided in around 930 BC, King Ahab made Jezreel one of his royal residences, erecting a palace here (1 Kings 21:1).

At Jezreel lived King Ahab's wife, who instituted the worship to the false gods of Baal and Asherah. This provoked God to send a drought that lasted 3 years. It ended with the great showdown between Elijah and the 850 false prophets of Baal and Asherah. God sent fire from heaven that consumed Elijah's altar to show the nation of Israel He was God. Afterward, Elijah killed all the false prophets (1 Kings 18).

The vineyard of Naboth was by King Ahab's palace in Jezreel. Ahab wanted the vineyard for a vegetable garden, but Naboth refused to sell it. So Ahab's wicked wife, Jezebel, arranged for Naboth to be wrongly accused and executed so Ahab could rob his land (1 Kings 21).

Apparently, it was on the city's eastern wall from which Jehu entered when he ordered Jezebel (King Ahab's wife) to be thrown down according to prophecy. Some of her blood spattered on the wall when she landed, and the dogs ate her body (2 Kings 9:30–37).

Nimrod Fortress National Park

Nimrod Fortress is situated in the northernmost part of Israel, just a few miles north of Caesarea Philippi. It's on a ridge rising some 2,600 ft. (800 m.) above sea level and is the biggest Crusader castle in Israel. The mountain-top stronghold overlooks the deep narrow valley separating Mount

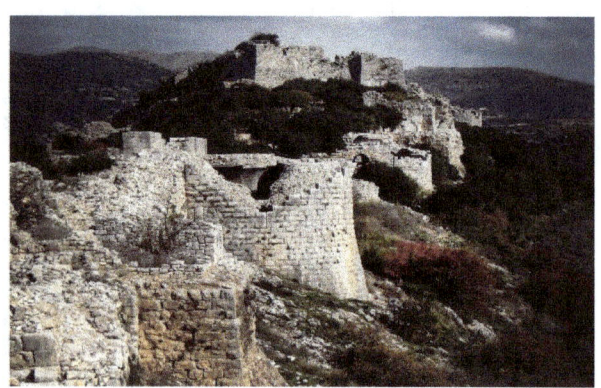

Nimrod Fortress

Hermon from the Golan Heights and the road linking the Galilee with Damascus (present-day Syria).

The Crusaders built it in the Middle Ages to guard this major access route against armies coming from the west. On the eastern edge of the fortress was a large keep (a keep is a fortress within a fortress), protected by large rectangular towers. In the west, it was separated from the main fortress by a moat, accessed by a bridge. The keep served as living quarters for the commander of the fortress. In times of siege, it became an additional defense position. The fortress is named after a biblical hero, the hunter, Nimrod, the great warrior (Gen. 10:8-9) who, according to local tradition, dwelt on this summit.

Central Israel Sites

Central Israel Sites

Tel Ai

Location

1. Ai is in the hill country of the Samaria region about 14 miles (22 km.) west of Jericho and about 10 miles (17 km.) north of Jerusalem.

2. Two locations nearby to one another provide overwhelming evidence as to the location of Tel Ai. The first location, which is the oldest excavation site, is called Et-Tell. The second, and most recent excavation site, is called Khirbet el-Maqatir (Khirbet means ruins in Hebrew). It is the view of HolyLandSite.com that both places are the same biblical Ai. Ai was a large city and had at least 12,000 inhabitants (Josh. 8:25). Because both sites are almost adjacent to one another, it appears that both belong to the same city of Ai and are just different parts of the city.

3. Both places are undeveloped sites, and no fees are charged to visit them. Et-Tell is located to the north of the modern town of Dayr Dibwan, and Khirbet el-Maqatir is located just west of Dayr Dibwan.

Historical Background

1. Ai was the second town Joshua and the Israelites conquered after they entered the Promised Land.

2. It was a small town compared to Jericho, but because of sin among one person, Joshua and the Israelites had a hard time conquering this city and were taught a major lesson about how God feels about sin among His people.

3. Khirbet el-Maqatir is also the believed place of the New Testament town of Ephraim. This is significant because after Christ raised Lazarus from the dead, He and His disciples came here to stay a while.

John 11:54: *Jesus, therefore, no longer walked openly among the Jews, but went from there to the region near the wilderness, to a town called **Ephraim**, and there he stayed with the disciples.*

4. There has been some dispute regarding the location of Ai, with the believed place being Et-Tell for many years. However, in 1995, excavations at Khirbet el-Maqatir were begun by Bryant Wood and sponsored by the Associates of Biblical Research (ABR). They excavated much of the site and made substantial discoveries, all indicating this site as the biblical Ai. ABR deserves the bulk of the credit for the excavations and discoveries at this site. However, as mentioned, we believe both sites of Et-Tell and Khirbet el-Maqatir are part of biblical Ai.

Ai - Khirbet el-Maqatir

5. Byzantine monks built a large monastery on Khirbet el-Maqatir in the 4th century AD. Typically, churches were built at significant holy sites to preserve and commemorate them. This helps confirm this site as Ai.

6. The earliest reports by Edward Robinson in 1838 show that the local people thought Khirbet el-Maqatir was Ai. It's likely that the Byzantine monastery helped preserve the memory of this location.

7. Evidence shows that Khirbet el-Maqatir was occupied and destroyed by fire during the time of Joshua, matching the biblical account. Ash layers have been discovered here supporting destruction by fire.

8. The Bible states that when Joshua arrived at Ai with his army, he stood ***in front of*** Ai on its north side (Joshua 8:11). In 1995, Associates for Biblical Research discovered the remains of a gate on the north side of the city wall. This matches the biblical account for the layout of biblical Ai.

9. At Khirbet el-Maqatir, a Canaanite border fortress was discovered

Central Israel Sites

that shows evidence of being destroyed by military action in around 1406 BC. This matches the exact time of the destruction of Ai in the Bible. The rough outline of the fortress walls have been marked out, and small sections excavated.

10. Many pieces of pottery and artifacts dating to the time of Joshua have been uncovered here. Among these are two Egyptian scarabs (small seals that look like coins).
11. The geography of the land in the area fits the locations of Khirbet el-Maqatir, and Et-Tell perfectly.
12. Both sites are on one of the highest mountains to the east of Bethel.

Places of Interest at Et-Tell

1. Temple
2. Sacred Stones
3. Northern Gate

Places of Interest at Khirbet el-Maqatir

1. City Towers
2. City Gate
3. City Walls
4. Ash remains from the destruction of Ai.
5. Byzantine Church and Monastery
6. Mikvahs
7. Dwellings
8. Silos
9. Cisterns

General Places of Interest around Ai

1. City of Bethel
2. Bethel Site of Abraham and Jacob
3. Bethel High Place of Worship – Currently named Khalom Ya'akov Antiquities Site.
4. Jericho

Places of interest at Khirbet el-Maqatir

Ai in the Bible

1. **Nearby to Ai, Abram (Abraham) built an altar to the Lord.**

   Genesis 12:7–8: *The Lord appeared to Abram and said, "To your descendants I will give this land." So he built an altar there to the Lord who had appeared to him. 8 Then he proceeded from there to the mountain on the east of Bethel, and pitched his tent, with Bethel on the west and Ai on the east; and there he built an altar to the Lord and called upon the name of the Lord.*

2. **Before conquering Jericho, God gave strict orders that the Israelites were not to take any items from it. It was for the Lord as a kind of "First Fruits Offering" because it was the first city the Israelites conquered in the Promised Land.**

   Joshua 6:17–19: *The city shall be under the ban, it and all that is in it belongs to the Lord; only Rahab the harlot and all who are with her in the house shall live, because she hid the messengers whom we sent. 18 But as for you, only keep yourselves from the things under the ban, so that you do not covet them and take some of the things under the ban, and make the camp of Israel accursed and bring trouble on it. 19 But all the silver and gold and articles of bronze and iron are holy to the Lord; they shall go into the treasury of the Lord.*

3. **God gave the Israelites a miraculous victory over Jericho.**

After marching around the city one time each day for six days, and seven times the seventh day, God caused the walls to fall by the shout of His people.

Joshua 6:20: *So the people shouted, and priests blew the trumpets; and when the people heard the sound of the trumpet, the people shouted with a great shout and the wall fell down flat, so that the people went up into the city, every man straight ahead, and they took the city.*

4. **Achan disobeyed God's orders and took forbidden items from Jericho.**

Part of the City Gate

Joshua 7:1: *But the sons of Israel acted unfaithfully in regard to the things under the ban, for Achan, the son of Carmi, the son of Zabdi, the son of Zerah, from the tribe of Judah, took some of the things under the ban, therefore the anger of the Lord burned against the sons of Israel.*

It's interesting that God held all of Israel guilty for the sin of one person. It appears He wanted to show them that they were a family and community, and what affects one person affects everyone.

5. **After seeing a miraculous victory over Jericho, the Israelites then proceeded to Ai, thinking they would take it with ease. However, God was angry over Achan's sin and decided to teach the whole nation of Israel a big life lesson.**

Joshua 7:2–5: *Now Joshua sent men from Jericho to Ai, which is near Beth-aven, east of Bethel, and said to them, "Go up and spy out the land." So the men went up and spied out Ai. 3 They returned to Joshua and said to him, "Do not let all the people go up; only about two or three thousand men need go up to Ai; do not make all the people toil up there, for they are few." 4 So about three thousand men from the people went up there, but they fled from the men of Ai. 5 The men of Ai struck down about thirty-six of their men, and*

Central Israel Sites

pursued them from the gate as far as Shebarim and struck them down on the descent, so the hearts of the people melted and became as water.

6. God spoke to Joshua and revealed the problem.

Joshua 7:10-13: *So the Lord said to Joshua, "Rise up! Why is it that you have fallen on your face? 11 Israel has sinned, and they have also transgressed My covenant which I commanded them. And they have even taken some of the things under the ban and have both stolen and deceived. Moreover, they have also put them among their own things. 12 Therefore, the sons of Israel cannot stand before their enemies; they turn their backs before their enemies, for they have become accursed. I will not be with you anymore unless you destroy the things under the ban from your midst. 13 Rise up! Consecrate the people and say, 'Consecrate yourselves for tomorrow, for thus the Lord, the God of Israel, has said, "There are things under the ban in your midst, O Israel. You cannot stand before your enemies until you have removed the things under the ban from your midst."*

7. Achan's sin is dealt with, and the Israelites are cleansed.

Joshua 7:22-26: *So Joshua sent messengers, and they ran to the tent; and behold, it was concealed in his tent with the silver underneath it. 23 They took them from inside the tent and brought them to Joshua and to all the sons of Israel, and they poured them out before the Lord. 24 Then Joshua and all Israel with him, took Achan the son of Zerah, the silver, the mantle, the bar of gold, his sons,*

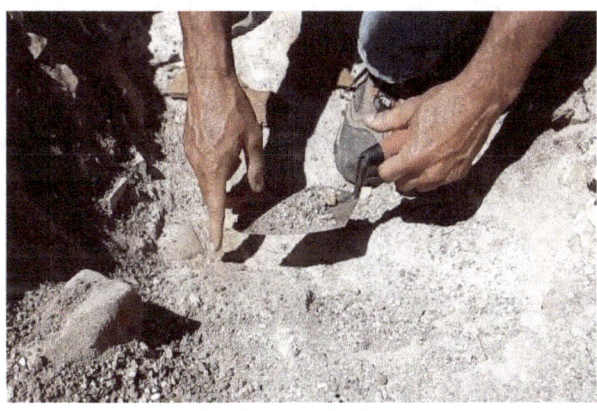

Ash layer from the fire at Ai

his daughters, his oxen, his donkeys, his sheep, his tent and all that belonged to him; and they brought them up to the valley of Achor. 25 Joshua said, "Why have you troubled us? The Lord will trouble you this day." And all Israel stoned them with stones; and they burned them with fire after they had stoned them with stones. 26 They raised over him a great heap of stones that stands to this day, and the Lord turned from the fierceness of His anger.

8. The Israelites easily conquer Ai and burn it with fire.

Joshua 8:11–12: *And all the fighting men who were with him went up and drew near before the city and encamped on the north side of Ai, with a ravine between them and Ai. 12 He took about 5,000 men and set them in ambush between Bethel and Ai, to the west of the city.*

Joshua 8:14–17: *And as soon as the king of Ai saw this, he and all his people, the men of the city, hurried and went out early to the appointed place toward the Arabah to meet Israel in battle. But he did not know that there was an ambush against him behind the city. 15 And Joshua and all Israel pretended to be beaten before them and fled in the direction of the wilderness. 16 So all the people who were in the city were called together to pursue them, and as they pursued Joshua they were drawn away from the city. 17 Not a man was left in Ai or Bethel who did not go out after Israel. They left the city open and pursued Israel.*

Joshua 8:19–21: *And the men in the ambush rose quickly out of their place, and as soon as he had stretched out his hand, they ran and entered the city and captured it. And they hurried to set the city on fire. 20 So when the men of Ai looked back, behold, the* **smoke of the city went up to heaven**, *and they had no power to flee this way or that, for the people who fled to the wilderness turned back against the pursuers. 21 And when Joshua and all Israel saw that the ambush had captured the city, and that the smoke of the city went up, then they turned back and struck down the men of Ai.*

Faith Lesson from Ai

1. Sin is a serious thing in the life of a believer or church.
2. Our sin not only affects us but others around us as well.
3. If there is unconfessed sin in our lives, God will likely allow us to be defeated.
4. If our hearts are right before God, He will give us victory.

Journal/Notes:

Central Israel Sites

Bethel

Location

1. Bethel is in the hill country of the Samaria region about 10 miles (17 km.) north of Jerusalem.

2. Bethel stood at several main crossroads in Israel. It was on the main north-south road that passed through the central hill country from Hebron in the south to Shechem in the north, and it was on the main east-west route leading from Jericho to the Mediterranean Sea.

3. In addition to the main city of Bethel, which today is called, Baytin or Beit El, there are two other key sites close to the main city of Bethel.

    - The first is the original place where Abraham and Jacob pitched their tents and erected altars. This is located just outside Bethel toward the south, a short distance.

    - The second is the high place of worship. It's about 1.5 miles (2.5 km.) north of the main city of Bethel. It's one of the highest places in Israel, sitting at an elevation of 2,900 ft. (886 m.). For this reason, it was a place of worship, both to God and false gods. It's believed the tabernacle resided here for some time during the period of the Judges and was the place Jeroboam set up one of his Golden-Calf altars after the Kingdom of Israel divided. Today, this high place of worship has been recognized by the Israeli government and is called Khalom Ya'akov Antiquities Site. It's fenced and secured.

Historical Background

1. Bethel is mentioned 60 times in the Bible, representing over 30 distinct stories and prophecies, all in the Old Testament. Only is

Jerusalem mentioned more times in the Bible than Bethel.
2. Bethel means "House of God."
3. The site of Bethel, the nearby sites of Abraham and Jacob, and the high place are all holy to Christians, Jews, and Muslims. They have artifacts, buildings, tombs, and ruins pertaining to each religion.

Places of Interest

1. **The site where Abraham and Jacob pitched their tents and built altars.**

   There are ruins at this site which provide strong evidence that this was the place Abraham and Jacob pitched their tents and built altars. Later, a Byzantine church was erected here, marking this spot. Jerome (347-420 AD), an early Christian leader, confirms this. He wrote the following about this site: *"There is also a church built where Jacob slept as he passed to Mesopotamia."*

2. **The original city of Bethel.**

   This site was once excavated and revealed walls, buildings, and remains of ancient Bethel. It has since been abandoned and filled in by those living in the area. However, some remains can still be seen in various places.

3. **The high place of worship.**
   1. Muslim Prayer Shrine
   2. Crusader Chapel
   3. A 1,000-year-old oak tree, and other ancient trees (trees were never cut at holy sites).
   4. Walls & Tower of Protection – These would have been used during times of war between Judah and Israel after the nation divided.
   5. Burial Tombs
   6. Ruins of a foundation measuring the exact size of the tabernacle.
   7. Jeroboam's Golden-Calf Altar

Places of interest at the high place of worship

Bethel in the Bible

1. **It was near Bethel that Abraham built one of the first altars mentioned in the Bible, and there he "invoked the name of the Lord."**

   Genesis 12:8: *From there he moved to the hill country on the east of Bethel and pitched his tent, with Bethel on the west and Ai on the east. And there he built an altar to the LORD and called upon the name of the LORD.*

2. **After Abraham fled to Egypt to escape a famine in the Holy Land, he returned to the same place near Bethel, and once again invoked the name of the Lord.**

   Genesis 13:2–4: *Now Abram was very rich in livestock, in silver, and in gold. 3 And he journeyed on from the Negev as far as **Bethel** to the place where his tent had been at the beginning, between Bethel and Ai, 4 to the place where he had made an altar at the first. And there Abram called upon the name of the LORD.*

3. **When Jacob was fleeing from his brother Esau, he stopped for the night at Bethel, where he had a dream.**

Genesis 28:10–22: *Jacob left Beersheba and went toward Haran. 11 And he came to a certain place and stayed there that night, because the sun had set. Taking one of the stones of the place, he put it under his head and lay down in that place to sleep.*

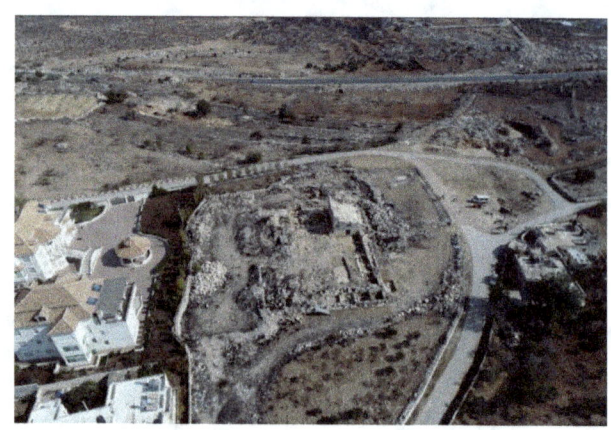

Site where Abraham and Jacob pitched their tents

12 And he dreamed, and behold, there was a ladder set up on the earth, and the top of it reached to heaven. And behold, the angels of God were ascending and descending on it! 13 And behold, the LORD stood above it and said, "I am the LORD, the God of Abraham your father and the God of Isaac. The land on which you lie I will give to you and to your offspring. 14 Your offspring shall be like the dust of the earth, and you shall spread abroad to the west and to the east and to the north and to the south, and in you and your offspring shall all the families of the earth be blessed. 15 Behold, I am with you and will keep you wherever you go, and will bring you back to this land. For I will not leave you until I have done what I have promised you." 16 Then Jacob awoke from his sleep and said, "Surely the LORD is in this place, and I did not know it." 17 And he was afraid and said, "How awesome is this place! This is none other than the house of God, and this is the gate of heaven." 18 So early in the morning Jacob took the stone that he had put under his head and set it up for a pillar and poured oil on the top of it. 19 **He called the name of that place Bethel**, *but the name of the city was Luz at the first. 20 Then Jacob made a vow, saying, "If God will be with me and will keep me in this way that I go, and will give me bread to eat and clothing to wear, 21 so that I come again to my father's house in peace, then the LORD shall be my God, 22 and this stone, which I have set up for a pillar, shall be God's house.*

And of all that you give me I will give a full tenth to you."

4. **When Jacob was in Paddan-aram, God told him to return to the land of Israel.**

   Genesis 31:13: *I am the **God of Bethel**, where you anointed a pillar, where you made a vow to Me; now arise, leave this land, and return to the land of your birth.*

5. **After Jacob returned to the Holy Land, he moved to Bethel to live. God spoke to him and changed his name from Jacob to Israel.**

   Genesis 35:1: *Then God said to Jacob, "Arise, go up to **Bethel and live there**, and make an altar there to God, who appeared to you when you fled from your brother Esau."*

   Genesis 35:9–15: *Then God appeared to Jacob again when he came from Paddan-aram, and He blessed him. 10 God said to him, "Your name is Jacob; You shall no longer be called Jacob, **but Israel shall be your name**." Thus, He called him **Israel**. 11 God also said to him, "I am God Almighty; be fruitful and multiply; a nation and a company of nations shall come from you, and kings shall come forth from you. 12 The land which I gave to Abraham and Isaac, I will give it to you, and I will give the land to your descendants after you." 13 Then God went up from him in the place where He had spoken with him. 14 Jacob set up a pillar in the place where He had spoken with him, a pillar of stone, and he poured out a drink offering on it; he also poured oil on it. 15 So Jacob named the place where God had spoken with him, **Bethel**.*

   Tabernacle location at the high place of worship

6. **Bethel was a place the tabernacle resided for some time.**

   Judges 20:26–27: *Then all the people of Israel, the whole army, went up and **came to Bethel** and wept. They sat there before the LORD and fasted that day until evening, and offered burnt offerings and peace offerings before the LORD. 27 And the people* *of Israel inquired of the* LORD *(for the ark of the covenant of God was there in those days).*

7. **After the Kingdom of Israel was divided, Jeroboam, the king of the northern kingdom, set up golden calves in Bethel and Dan.**

    1 Kings 12:26–29: *And Jeroboam said in his heart, "Now the kingdom will turn back to the house of David. 27 If this people go up to offer sacrifices in the temple of the Lord at Jerusalem, then the heart of this people will turn again to their lord, to Rehoboam king of Judah, and they will kill me and return to Rehoboam king of Judah." 28 So the king took counsel and made* **two calves of gold**. *And he said to the people, "You have gone up to Jerusalem long enough. Behold your gods, O Israel, who brought you up out of the land of Egypt." 29 And he set* **one in Bethel**, *and the other he put in Dan.*

8. **God warned Jeroboam about erecting the golden calves at Bethel. Jeroboam's arm withered and was then restored by a prophet to show Jeroboam that God was serious about his great sin. However, Jeroboam did not heed God's warning (1 Kings 13:1–34).**

9. **The continual disobedience of Jeroboam, and the succeeding kings, sealed the fate of Bethel. By the time of Jesus' birth, Bethel had completely faded away as a place of importance and is not mentioned anywhere in the New Testament.**

10. **Josiah, a righteous king, destroyed the golden-calf altar Jeroboam erected at Bethel.**

    2 Kings 23:15: *Moreover, the* **altar at Bethel**, *the high place erected by Jeroboam the son of Nebat, who made Israel to sin, that altar with the high place he pulled down and burned, reducing it to dust. He also burned the Asherah.*

11. **Just before Elijah ascended to heaven, he and Elisha were in Bethel.**

    2 Kings 2:1–3: *Now when the Lord was about to take Elijah up to heaven by a whirlwind, Elijah and Elisha were on their way from Gilgal. 2 And Elijah said to Elisha, "Please stay here, for the Lord has sent me as far as* **Bethel**." *But Elisha said, "As the Lord lives, and as you yourself live, I will not leave you."* **So they went down to Bethel**. *3 And the sons of the* **prophets who were in Bethel** *came out to Elisha and said to him, "Do you know that today the Lord will take away your master from over you?" And he said, "Yes, I know it; keep*

quiet."

12. After Assyria conquered and exiled the Northern Kingdom of Israel, the king of Assyria sent one of the captured Israelite priests back to Bethel to teach the people from other nations who lived in Israel how to worship Yahweh, the true and living God (2 Kings 17:24–41).

Faith Lesson from Bethel

1. Bethel was a place of two different kinds of responses to God.
    - It was a place where Abraham and Jacob had special encounters with God and worshiped Him, and a place where the Ark of the Covenant dwelt, which represented the presence and glory of God.
    - Unfortunately, it also represents a place of disobedience to God and the worship of false gods and idols.
2. We could learn a great lesson from this biblical site of Bethel.
3. Are we going to be like those who worshiped and obeyed God, or like those who disobeyed and worshiped their own desires and plans?

Journal/Notes:

Bethlehem Overview

Location

1. Bethlehem is located 6 miles (9 km.) south of Jerusalem.
2. In Bible times, Bethlehem was a farming area with grainfields, and sheep and goats grazed the hillsides. Amazingly, little has changed over the past 3,000 years.
3. It's on the edge of the Judean Desert that lies to the southeast.
4. Bethlehem is in the West Bank but is very safe. Thousands visit its Christian sites each month with no issues.

Historical Background

1. Bethlehem was a Canaanite village before the conquest of the Israelites in around 1406 BC.
2. It means "House of Bread." Maybe this is so because many wheat and barley fields were in this area.

Places of Interest

1. Rachel's Tomb
2. Church of the Nativity
3. Shepherds' Fields
4. Herodian Fortress
5. Grainfields
6. Hillsides for livestock to graze on.
7. Deep Ravine – Maybe the valley David had in mind when he wrote Psalm 23.

Bethlehem in the Bible

1. **Jacob's wife, Rachel, died and was buried in Bethlehem.**

   Genesis 35:16–20: *Then they journeyed from Bethel. When they were still some distance from Ephrath **[Bethlehem]**, Rachel went into labor, and she had hard labor. 17 And when her labor was at its hardest, the midwife said to her, "Do not fear, for you have another son." 18 And as her soul was departing (for she was dying), she called his name Ben-oni; but his father called him Benjamin. 19 So Rachel died, and she was buried on the way to Ephrath (that is, Bethlehem), 20 and Jacob set up a pillar over her tomb. It is the pillar of Rachel's tomb, which is there to this day.*

2. **Naomi was from Bethlehem, but because of a famine in Israel, her husband and two sons moved to Moab.**

   Ruth 1:1–2: *In the days when the judges ruled there was a famine in the land, and a man of **Bethlehem** in Judah went to sojourn in the country of Moab, he and his wife and his two sons. 2 The name of the man was Elimelech and the name of his wife, Naomi, and the names of his two sons were Mahlon and Chilion.*

3. **Naomi and Ruth returned from Moab to Bethlehem.**

   Ruth 1:22: *So Naomi returned, and Ruth the Moabite her daughter-*

in-law with her, who returned from the country of Moab. And they came to **Bethlehem** at the beginning of barley harvest.

4. **Ruth gleaned in the grainfields of Boaz in Bethlehem and then married Boaz (Boaz was the Great Grandfather of King David).**

   Ruth 2:1–2: *Now Naomi had a relative of her husband's, a worthy man of the clan of Elimelech, whose name was Boaz. 2 And Ruth the Moabite said to Naomi, "Let me go to the field and glean among the ears of grain after him in whose sight I shall find favor." And she said to her, "Go, my daughter."*

   Ruth 4:13–17: *So Boaz took Ruth, and she became his wife. And he went in to her, and the Lord gave her conception, and she bore a son. 14 Then the women said to Naomi, "Blessed be the Lord, who has not left you this day without a redeemer, and may his name be renowned in Israel! 15 He shall be to you a restorer of life and a nourisher of your old age, for your daughter-in-law who loves you, who is more to you than seven sons, has given birth to him." 16 Then Naomi took the child and laid him on her lap and became his nurse. 17 And the women of the neighborhood gave him a name, saying, "A son has been born to Naomi." They named him Obed. He was the father of Jesse, the father of David.*

   Shepherds' Field

5. **King David was from Bethlehem, so it is also called the "City of David."**

   1 Samuel 17:12: *Now David was the son of an Ephrathite of Bethlehem in Judah, named Jesse, who had eight sons. In the days of Saul, the man was already old and advanced in years.*

6. **David grew up in Bethlehem as a shepherd. Being a shepherd was a lonely, boring job that no one wanted. However, David put his time to good use and learned to play the harp, throw a sling, and grew to love the Lord. Many of the Psalms David wrote have their roots in the area around Bethlehem.**

Central Israel Sites

7. **David was anointed king in Bethlehem.**

   1 Samuel 16:1: *The Lord said to Samuel, "How long will you grieve over Saul, since I have rejected him from being king over Israel? Fill your horn with oil, and go. I will send you to Jesse the Bethlehemite, for I have provided for myself a king among his sons."*

   1 Samuel 16:4: *Samuel did what the Lord commanded and came to* **Bethlehem**.

   1 Samuel 16:6-7: *When they came, he looked on Eliab and thought, "Surely the Lord's anointed is before him." 7 But the Lord said to Samuel, "Do not look on his appearance or on the height of his stature, because I have rejected him. For the Lord sees not as man sees:* **man looks on the outward appearance, but the Lord looks on the heart.**"

   Herodian Fortress

   1 Samuel 16:11-13: *Then Samuel said to Jesse, "Are all your sons here?" And he said, "There remains yet the youngest, but behold, he is keeping the sheep." And Samuel said to Jesse, "Send and get him, for we will not sit down till he comes here." 12 And he sent and brought him in. Now he was ruddy and had beautiful eyes and was handsome. And the Lord said, "Arise, anoint him, for this is he." 13 Then Samuel took the horn of oil and anointed him in the midst of his brothers. And the Spirit of the Lord rushed upon David from that day forward.*

8. **King Herod the Great built a huge fortress called the "Herodian" that was located just outside of Bethlehem. It was built for his protection and glory.**

9. **Bethlehem was the prophesied birthplace of Christ.**

   Micah 5:2: *But you, O Bethlehem Ephrathah, who are too little to be among the clans of Judah, from you shall come forth for me one who is to be ruler in Israel, whose coming forth is from of old, from ancient days.*

   Luke 2:7: *And she gave birth to her firstborn son and wrapped him in swaddling clothes and laid him in a manger, because there was no place for them in the inn.*

10. Angels appeared to shepherds watching their flocks by night in Bethlehem.

Luke 2:8–16: *And there were shepherds living out in the fields nearby, keeping watch over their flocks at night. 9 And an angel of the Lord appeared to them, and the glory of the Lord shone around them, and they were filled with fear. 10 And the angel said to them, "Fear not, for behold, I bring you good news of great joy that will be for all the people. 11 For unto you is born this day in the **city of David**, a Savior, who is Christ the Lord. 12 And this will be a sign for you: you will find a baby wrapped in swaddling clothes and lying in a manger." 13 And suddenly there was with the angel a multitude of the heavenly host praising God*

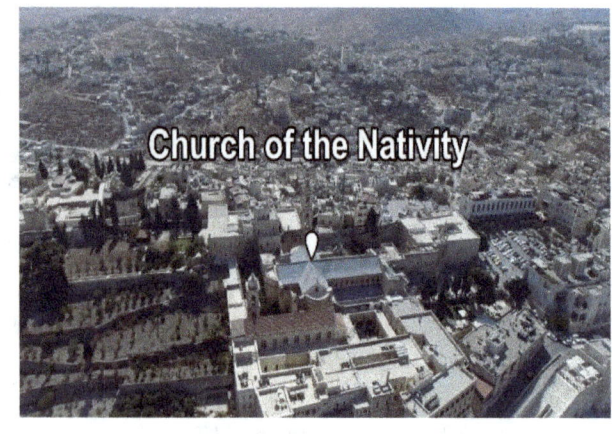

*and saying, 14 "Glory to God in the highest, and on earth peace among those with whom he is pleased!" 15 When the angels went away from them into heaven, the shepherds said to one another, "Let us go over to **Bethlehem** and see this thing that has happened, which the Lord has made known to us." 16 And they went with haste and found Mary and Joseph, and the baby lying in a manger.*

11. Wise men (Magi) from the east visited and worshiped Christ in Bethlehem.

Matthew 2:1: *Now after Jesus was born in **Bethlehem** of Judea in the days of Herod the king, behold, wise men from the east came to Jerusalem saying, "Where is he who has been born king of the Jews? For we saw his star when it rose and have come to worship him."*

12. King Herod had all the male children 2 years and younger murdered in his attempt to kill Christ.

Matthew 2:16–18: *Then Herod, when he saw that he had been tricked by the wise men, became furious, and he sent and killed all the male children in Bethlehem and in all that region who were two years old or under, according to the time that he had ascertained from the wise men. 17 Then was fulfilled what was spoken by the prophet Jeremiah: 18 "A voice was heard in Ramah, weeping and loud lamentation, Rachel weeping for her children; she refused to be comforted, because they are no more."*

Grainfields (center) deep ravine (right)

Faith Lesson from Bethlehem

1. Bethlehem means "House of Bread." Jesus also refers to Himself as the Bread of life.
2. In the same way our bodies need bread to live, so our spirit needs Christ for nourishment and life. Are we feeding daily on God's Word and walking moment by moment in dependence on Him?
3. We have many godly examples of people from Bethlehem who walked with God, i.e., Naomi, Ruth, Boaz, and David.
4. Today, they are in heaven rejoicing in God's presence. Are we following their example and living for our eternal home as well?
5. David used his spare time shepherding wisely and learned many skills that He would eventually use to serve God. Are we developing our abilities to be better servants of Christ?
6. The Lord sees not as man sees: man looks on the outward appearance, but the Lord looks on the heart (1 Sam. 16:7). What kind of heart does God see in us?

Journal/Notes:

Israel Biblical Sites Travel Guide

Bethlehem: Church of the Nativity

Location

1. The Church of the Nativity is in Bethlehem, about 6 miles (9 km.) south of Jerusalem.
2. It's right beside Manger Square and Manger Street.
3. Bethlehem is in the West Bank but is very safe. Thousands of tourists visit its Christian sites each month with no issues whatsoever.

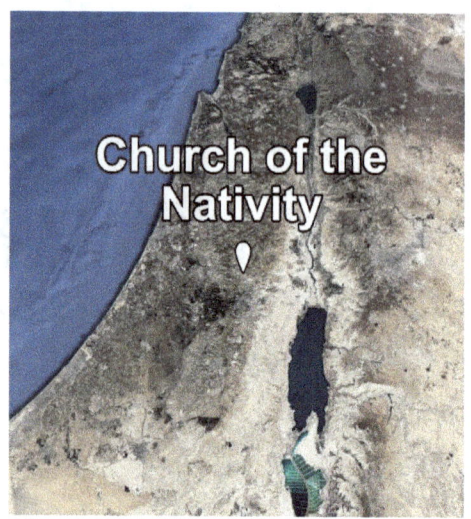

Historical Background

1. Shortly after Christ's ascension back to heaven, worshipers began marking the key places surrounding the life and events of Jesus.
2. Christ's birthplace was marked out, and worshipers began commemorating this site.
3. In 135 AD, Hadrian, a Roman governor, destroyed the Christian sites and built shrines to false gods on top of many of them. He also renamed Jerusalem to Aelia Capitolina and banned Jews from entering the city.
4. On top of Christ's birthplace, he erected a shrine to Adonis, the Greek god of beauty and desire.
5. Evidence that this was the birthplace of Jesus also surfaced in the writings of Justin Martyr in around 160 AD. It was also affirmed later by Origen and Eusebius in the 3rd century.
6. Helena, the mother of the Roman Emperor, Constantine, received Christ as her Savior and came to the Holy Land to build churches on key Christian sites.
7. Constantine and his mother, Helena, commissioned that the Church of the Nativity be built over the cave marking the birthplace of Jesus, and it was dedicated in 339 AD. It consisted of an octagonal floor plan and was placed directly over the cave. In the center of the octagonal part, a viewing area with a railing

Central Israel Sites

provided a view of the cave. Part of the mosaic of the original floor has survived and can still be seen.

8. Jerome, who translated the Hebrew and Greek manuscripts into Latin (the language of the Roman Empire) to form what is called the Latin Vulgate, did much of his translation work in a cave beside the Church of the Nativity from 382–405 AD. He was later buried here, and today it's called Jerome's Grotto. His remains were carried to Rome by the Crusaders in around 1165.

9. The church was burned down during a Samaritan revolt in 529 AD.

10. Justinian, emperor of the Byzantine Empire, rebuilt a larger church in 565 AD that has survived to date. It is the oldest functioning church in the world.

Church of the Nativity

11. The Church of the Nativity was the only church spared by the Persians during their conquest of the Holy Land in 614 AD because they saw paintings on the outside of the church honoring the Magi from the east who were fellow Persians.

12. The Crusaders renovated the church in around 1165 AD and painted murals on the pillars of the main nave.

13. The church has been neglected and renovated several times since the Crusader period to the present.

14. Today, the custody of the church is in the hands of the Roman Catholic, Armenian, and Greek Orthodox churches. The Greek Orthodox Church cares for the Grotto of the Nativity.

Places of Interest

1. Entrance to the Church
   - Door of Humility – To provide a humble entrance and keep horsemen and carts from entering the church to loot it during

the Ottoman Period (1500 AD).
2. Entrance Lobby
3. Main Nave
   - Columns with Crusader murals.
   - Mosaics under the floor.
   - Fragments of 12th-century mosaics on the walls high above the columns.
4. High Altar (front part of the nave)
   - Mosaics of the original church on the left side of the High Altar.

5. Birthplace Grotto
   - Located under the main altar.
   - The entrance is to the right of the altar, and the exit is to the left.
   - Manger where Christ was placed – on the right side of the grotto.
   - A 14-pointed star marking the birthplace of Christ is in the center of the grotto (14 points for the three sets of 14

Central Israel Sites

generations in Matthew 1:17, and for the 14 Stations of the Via Dolorosa).

6. Church of St. Catherine
   - A Roman Catholic Church named after Catherine, a 4th-century martyr from Alexandria.
   - It was built upon the ruins of a 5th-century monastery and a 12th-century Crusader church.
   - Courtyard
   - Statue of Jerome in the courtyard.
   - Burial Caves – Jerome's Grotto
   - The burial caves are accessed by a narrow staircase inside the Church of St. Catherine on the right side.
7. Manger Square – Located across from the Church of the Nativity.

Birth of Christ in the Bible

1. **Bethlehem was the prophesied birthplace of Christ.**

   Micah 5:2: *But you, O **Bethlehem** Ephrathah, who are too little to be among the clans of Judah, from you shall come forth for me one who is to be ruler in Israel, whose coming forth is from of old, from ancient days.*

   Birthplace of Jesus marked by 14-point star

2. **Christ was born in Bethlehem as prophesied.**

   Luke 2:1–7: *In those days Caesar Augustus issued a decree that a census should be taken of the entire Roman world. 2 (This was the first census that took place while Quirinius was governor of Syria.) 3 And everyone went to his own town to register. 4 So Joseph also went up from the town of Nazareth in Galilee to Judea, to **Bethlehem** the town of David, because he belonged to the house and* line of David. 5 He went there to register with Mary, who was pledged to be married to him and was expecting a child. 6 While they were there, the time came for the baby to be born, 7 and she gave birth to her firstborn, a son. She wrapped him in cloths and placed him in a manger, because there was no room for them in the inn.

3. **Many angels appeared to the shepherds near Bethlehem who were watching their flocks.**

   Luke 2:8–16: *And there were shepherds living out in the fields nearby, keeping watch over their flocks at night. 9 An angel of the Lord appeared to them, and the glory of the Lord shone around them, and they were terrified. 10 But the angel said to them, "Do not be afraid. I bring you good news of great joy that will be for all the people. 11 Today in the town of David a Savior has been born to you; he is Christ the Lord. 12 This will be a sign to you: You will find a baby wrapped in cloths and lying in a manger." 13 Suddenly a great company of the heavenly host appeared with the angel, praising God and saying, 14 "Glory to God in the highest, and on earth peace to men on whom his favor rests." 15 When the angels had left them and gone into heaven, the shepherds said to one another, "Let's go to* **Bethlehem** *and see this thing that has happened, which the Lord has told us about." 16 So they hurried off and found Mary and Joseph, and the baby, who was lying in the manger.*

Manger where Jesus was laid

4. **Wise men (Magi) from the east visited and worshiped Christ in Bethlehem.**

   Matthew 2:1–12: *Now after Jesus was born in Bethlehem of Judea in the days of Herod the king, behold, wise men from the east came to Jerusalem, 2 saying, "Where is he who has been born king of the*

Jews? For we saw his star when it rose and have come to worship him." 3 When Herod the king heard this, he was troubled, and all Jerusalem with him; 4 and assembling all the chief priests and scribes of the people, he inquired of them where the Christ was to be born. 5 They told him, "In Bethlehem of Judea, for so it is written by the prophet: 6 "'And you, O Bethlehem, in the land of Judah, are by no means least among the rulers of Judah; for from you shall come a ruler who will shepherd my people Israel.'" 7 Then Herod summoned the wise men secretly and ascertained from them what time the star had appeared. 8 And he sent them to Bethlehem, saying, "Go and search diligently for the child, and when you have found him, bring me word, that I too may come and worship him." 9 After listening to the king, they went on their way. And behold, the star that they had seen when it rose went before them until it came to rest over the place where the child was. 10 When they saw the star, they rejoiced exceedingly with great joy. 11 And going into the house they saw the child with Mary, his mother, and they fell down and worshiped him. Then, opening their treasures, they offered him gifts, gold and frankincense, and myrrh. 12 And being warned in a dream not to return to Herod, they departed to their own country by another way.

Nave of the church with mosaics under the floor

5. **Herod had all the male children 2 years and younger murdered in Bethlehem in his attempt to kill Christ.**

Matthew 2:16–18: *Then Herod, when he saw that he had been tricked by the wise men, became furious, and he sent and killed all the male children in **Bethlehem and in all that region** who were two years old or under, according to the time that he had ascertained from the wise men. 17 Then was fulfilled what was spoken by the prophet Jeremiah: 18 "A voice was heard in Ramah, weeping and loud lamentation, Rachel weeping for her children; she* *refused to be comforted, because they are no more."*

Faith Lesson from the Birth of Christ

1. Bethlehem was the prophesied birthplace of Christ.
2. Christ fulfilled over 300 prophecies regarding his first coming.
3. The birth of Christ was a historical supernatural event witnessed by many.
4. The fulfillment of prophecy proves Christ was the Son of God and that His Word is inspired.
5. Christ's birth, death, and resurrection were all miraculous events, also proving Christ to be the very Son of God.
6. Christ claimed to be God in the flesh and proved it by His supernatural life and miracles.
7. Do we believe Christ is the Son of God, and have we received Him as our Lord and Savior?

Courtyard with statue of Jerome

Journal/Notes:

Central Israel Sites

Bethlehem: Herodian Fortress

Location

1. The Herodian (Herodium) was a fortress and palace of King Herod located about 3 miles (5 km.) south of Bethlehem.
2. It's on the edge of the Judean Wilderness.
3. It was built upon a natural mountain which gave it added protection.
4. It was massive in size and overshadowed everything in the area with its presence and majesty.

Historical Background

1. The Roman Empire appointed King Herod to rule Judea on behalf of Rome from 37 to 4 BC. He was the king in power when Christ was born.
2. He's most known as the one who killed all the babies in Bethlehem 2 years old and younger in his attempt to kill Jesus.

   Matthew 2:16: *Then Herod, when he saw that he had been tricked by the wise men, became furious, and he sent and* **killed all the male children in Bethlehem** *and in all that region who were two years old or under, according to the time that he had ascertained from the wise men.*
3. He was so powerful that with a mere spoken word, he could order a mass execution of children in Bethlehem without approval from anyone.
4. Everything in Israel was dominated by King Herod, and his Herodian Fortress was evidence of his domination and power.
5. He was also a master builder who was known for building things that defied nature and glorified his name.
   - He built Caesarea Maritime, which was a deep-water seaport

larger than any in Rome, Athens, or Greece.
- He built Masada that was a fortress of protection and a winter palace. It had supplies for 1,000 people for 10 years.
- He enlarged the Temple Mount, which was an engineering masterpiece.
- He built a new temple for the Jews that was unparalleled in glory, size, and beauty.
- He built a massive building over the Caves of the Patriarchs in Hebron.
- He built this Herodian Fortress, named after himself, among other accomplishments.

6. War was common in his day, so the Herodian was built to protect himself and his kingship from those who tried to kill or remove him. The Herodian was on the highest mountain in the Judean Desert.
7. He had a great fear of betrayal from others attempting to usurp his throne. He had two of his sons strangled, killed numerous in-laws, and ordered his oldest son to be beheaded just before he died. He even had one of his wives murdered out of fear that she was in a plot to betray him.
8. Construction of the Herodian began in 25 BC using thousands of slaves. Herod reshaped the summit of the hill to create a pleasure palace and fortress that was virtually impregnable.
9. The Herodian was the 3rd largest palace in the known world at the time of Herod, and it was a monument to his power and glory.

The Herodian

10. It could be seen from many miles away and rose in dominance and prestige.
11. It covered 45 acres (18 hectares) and had a small luxurious city at

its base that included swimming pools, spas, a theater, and all the luxuries life could afford. An aqueduct brought water from a spring nearly 4 miles (6 km.) away.

12. On top of the Herodian were four towers that gave it a commanding view of the Judean Desert, the Dead Sea, and the mountains of Moab. By using mirrors to reflect the sun, Herod could send messages from the Herodian to Jerusalem, Masada, and other places.
13. Herod is remembered as a jealous self-serving person who built his own kingdom for his own glory. Because he was so despised and hated, at his death he ordered many prominent Jews to be killed so there would be weeping in Israel. He died at the age of 69 and was buried at the Herodian.
14. Today, all that's left of Herod's kingdom and glory are ancient ruins.
15. The Herodian has been used for defense and religious purposes after the time of Herod to the present.

Places of Interest

1. Lower Section
    - Park Entrance
    - Ballista balls at the park entrance.
    - Water Pool
    - City Ruins
    - Colonnade Pillars
    - Roman Garden
    - Staircase going up the mountain.
2. Upper Section
    - Herodian Palace and Fortress
    - Four Towers of the Palace (north, east, west, and south)
    - Synagogue (used from 66–70 AD)
    - Mikvah
    - Bathhouse
    - Cisterns
    - Bar Kokhba Revolt Tunnels (132–136 AD)
    - Tunnels

- Theater
- Herod's Tomb

Central Israel Sites

A Contrast of Two Kingdoms in the Bible

1. **Christ is the eternal majestic King of His kingdom.**

   Isaiah 9:6–7: *For to us a **child is born**, to us a son is given; and the government shall be upon his shoulder, and his name shall be called **Wonderful Counselor, Mighty God, Everlasting Father, Prince of Peace**. 7 Of the increase of his government and of peace there will be no end, on the throne of David and over his kingdom, to establish it and to uphold it with justice and with righteousness **from this time forth and forevermore**. The zeal of the Lord of hosts will do this.*

   Micah 5:2: *But you, O Bethlehem Ephrathah, who are too little to be among the clans of Judah, from you shall come forth for me one who is to be ruler in Israel, whose coming forth is from of old, from **ancient days**.*

   John 8:58–59: *Jesus said to them, "Truly, truly, I say to you, before Abraham was, **I AM**." 59 So they picked up stones to throw at him, but Jesus hid himself and went out of the temple.*

   John 10:31–33: *The Jews picked up stones again to stone him. 32 Jesus answered them, "I have shown you many good works from the Father; for which of them are you going to stone me?" 33 The Jews answered him, "It is not for a good work that we are going to stone you but for blasphemy, because you, being a man, **make yourself God**."*

   Pool & Roman Garden at the base of the Herodian

   Revelation 22:12–13: *Behold, I am coming soon, bringing my recompense with me, to repay each one for what he has done. 13 I am the **Alpha and the Omega**, the first and the last, the beginning and the end.*

2. **Unlike Herod, who only cared about building his own kingdom, Christ came as a lowly servant to serve others.**

   - Christ was born in a humble manger in the small frontier town

of Bethlehem.
- He owned no home and had nowhere to lay His head.
- He held no public office.
- He rode into Jerusalem on the colt of a donkey, which was a lowly symbol of peace.
- He washed His disciples' feet.
- He died a criminal's death between two thieves.

3. **Unlike Herod, who glorified himself, Christ set aside His glory to become an obedient servant, even unto death on a cross.**

    Philippians 2:5–11: *Have this attitude in yourselves which was also in Christ Jesus, 6 who, although He existed in the form of God, did not regard **equality with God a thing to be grasped**, 7 **but emptied Himself**, taking the form of a bondservant, and being made in the likeness of men. 8 Being found in appearance as a man, **He humbled Himself** by becoming obedient to the point of death, even death on a cross. 9 For this reason also, God highly exalted Him, and bestowed on Him the name which is above every name, 10 so that at the name of Jesus every knee will bow, of those who are in heaven and on earth and under the earth, 11 and that every tongue will confess that Jesus Christ is Lord, to the glory of God the Father.*

    Herodian Palace on top of the Herodian

4. **Unlike Herod, whose kingdom came to ruins, Christ changed people and the course of history like no other person.**

Faith Lesson from the Herodian Fortress

1. Herod mainly cared about his own glory and kingdom. What about us? Are we more like King Herod or King Jesus?
2. We all have an element of King Herod living within us. Are we

going to follow those tendencies and desires?

1 John 2:15-17: *Do not love the world or the things in the world. If anyone loves the world, the love of the Father is not in him. 16 For all that is in the world—***the desires of the flesh, and the desires of the eyes, and pride of life**—*is not from the Father but is from the world. 17 And the world is passing away along with its desires, but whoever does the will of God abides forever.*

View of the pool and city ruins from the top of the Herodian

3. Do we have a prideful attitude like Herod or a humble spirit like Christ?
4. Are we mainly building our own kingdom or God's?
5. What will be our legacy, and what will we leave behind?

   Matthew 6:19-21: *Do not lay up for yourselves treasures on earth, where moth and rust destroy and where thieves break in and steal, 20 but lay up for yourselves treasures in heaven, where neither moth nor rust destroys and where thieves do not break in and steal. 21* ***For where your treasure is, there your heart will be also****.*

Journal/Notes:

Israel Biblical Sites Travel Guide

Bethlehem: Shepherds' Field

Location

1. There are two main sites that have their own Shepherds' Field, where the angels appeared to the shepherds announcing Christ's birth. Less than a half-mile (1 km.) separates them from one another.

    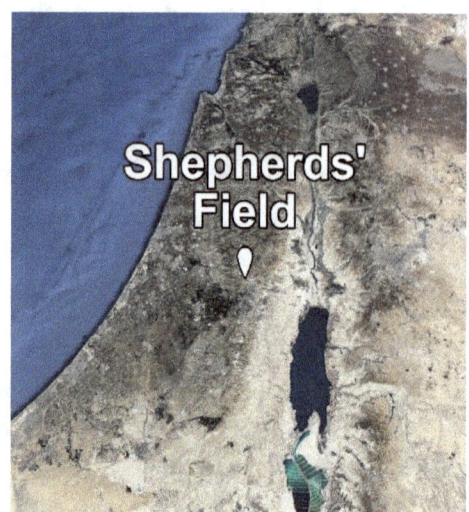

    - Franciscan Shepherds' Field (the most visited as it's more easily accessed and is set up for tourists).
    - The Greek Orthodox Shepherds' Field.

2. Both sites have substantial archaeological evidence and tradition supporting them. However, the Greek Orthodox site has more ruins and longer continuous usage.
3. Both places are located about a mile (2 km.) east of Bethlehem in the Beit Sahour village. The Church of the Nativity can be seen from each site.
4. Because the sites are so close to one another, it's very possible that the angels' appearance was seen from both places as there could have easily been numerous shepherds in close proximity. There are also various other ruins, churches, and monasteries in the area, which testify to the fact that this event happened here.

Historical Background

General Evidence

1. At the end of the 4th century, Jerome, who was translating the Hebrew and Greek Bible manuscripts into Latin at the Church of the Nativity, mentioned that the church in Jerusalem celebrated a feast-day at the Church of the Shepherds in this area on Christmas Eve.
2. In 384 AD, the pilgrim Egeria was shown the church called "At the

Shepherds" in a valley near Bethlehem. She reported, *"A big garden is there now, protected by a neat wall all around, and also there is a very splendid cave with an altar."*

3. In the 7th century, Bishop Archulph spoke of a burial place of three shepherds in the church at the Shepherds' Field.
4. In the 12th century, Peter the Deacon, a Benedictine monk, quoted an anonymous pilgrim who said, *"Not far from there, there is a church called of the Shepherds, where a large garden is fully enclosed by a wall, and there, there is a very luminous grotto which has an altar where an angel, appearing to the shepherds in a vigil, announced the birth of Christ."*

Franciscan Shepherds' Field

1. It has a cave with a soot-blackened roof that has been partly enclosed to make a modern chapel.
2. A church built in the 4th century was erected by the cave.
3. The church was destroyed by the time the Crusaders arrived, but pilgrims continued to visit and commemorate this site.

Franciscan Shepherds' Church

4. It has ruins of a monastery dating from the 4th century to the 7th century.
5. A large complex of caves containing Mikvahs, tunnels, and rooms can be found here.
6. Today, above the cave is a modern church shaped like a tent and decorated with a bronze angel that was built near the ruins of an ancient monastery in 1953.

Greek Orthodox Shepherds' Field

1. The original church was in a cave located on the site.
2. Helena, the mother of Constantine, modified the cave into a church in 326 AD. It is the only original church Helena built that has survived to this day.

3. In the 5th century, a barrel-vaulted roof was built on the cave-church, and a monastery was built on the site later.
4. Above the 5th-century cave-church, a Byzantine chapel was built that was replaced by a larger church, which was destroyed in 614 AD. The Byzantine church and monastery were rebuilt in the 7th century and survived until the 10th century.
5. In 1972, in order to build a new church above the cave-church, excavations verified the remains of three different churches dating to the 5th, 6th, and 7th centuries.

Greek Orthodox Shepherds' Church

6. The cave-church Helena built served the Orthodox community from the 4th century to 1955.
7. Today, a new large church has been built, the 4th-century cave-church has been restored, and the remains of the upper church and monastery have been preserved.
8. According to tradition dating from the 4th century, this site was associated with the place where Jacob pastured his flock and built Mignal Eder (Tower of the Flocks), referred to in Genesis 35:16. The remains of the base of this tower are still visible today.
9. If Mignal Eder is the site where Jacob erected a tower in Rachel's memory, this would also be the biblical location of Rachel's Tomb, and Jacob would have lived in this area for some time.

Places of Interest

1. Rachel's Tomb.
2. Church of the Nativity
3. Franciscan Shepherds' Field
4. Greek Orthodox Shepherds' Field
    - Mignal Eder Tower

Central Israel Sites

5. Fields of Boaz

Shepherds' Fields in the Bible

1. **The Greek Orthodox Church site is associated with Mignal Eder, the place Jacob erected a tower of memorial to Rachel after her death.**

   Genesis 35:16–21: *Then they journeyed from Bethel. When they were still some distance from Ephrath [Bethlehem], Rachel went into labor, and she had hard labor. 17 And when her labor was at its hardest, the midwife said to her, "Do not fear, for you have another son." 18 And as her soul was departing (for she was dying), she called his name Ben-oni; but his father called him Benjamin. 19 So Rachel died, and she was buried on the way to Ephrath (that is, Bethlehem), 20 and Jacob set up a pillar over her tomb. It is the pillar of Rachel's tomb, which is there to this day. 21 Israel journeyed on and pitched his tent beyond the tower of Eder.*

2. **Ruth gleaned in the grainfields of Boaz and then married him (Boaz was the Great Grandfather of King David).**

   Ruth 2:1–2: *Now Naomi had a relative of her husband's, a worthy man of the clan of Elimelech, whose name was Boaz. 2 And Ruth the Moabite said to Naomi, "Let me go to the field and glean among the ears of grain after him in whose sight I shall find favor." And she said* to her, "Go, my daughter."

3. **Angels appeared to the shepherds out in the field, watching their flocks by night.**

   Luke 2:8–14: *And in the same region there were shepherds out in the field, keeping watch over their flock by night. 9 And an angel of the Lord appeared to them, and the glory of the Lord shone around them, and they were filled with great fear. 10 And the angel said to them, "Fear not, for behold, I bring you good news of great joy that will be for all the people. 11 For unto you is born this day in the city of David a Savior, who is Christ the Lord. 12 And this will be a sign for you: you will find a baby wrapped in swaddling cloths and lying in a manger." 13 And suddenly there was with the angel a multitude of the heavenly host praising God and saying, 14 "Glory to God in the highest, and on earth peace among those with whom he is pleased!"*

   Fields by Bethlehem

4. **The shepherds went in haste to see Jesus.**

   Luke 2:15–16: *When the angels went away from them into heaven, the shepherds said to one another, "Let us go over to Bethlehem and see this thing that has happened, which the Lord has made known to us." 16 And they went with haste and found Mary and Joseph, and the baby lying in a manger.*

5. **The shepherds spread the good news of Jesus' birth and returned, glorifying and praising God.**

   Luke 2:17–20: *And when they saw it, they made known the saying that had been told them concerning this child. 18 And all who heard it wondered at what the shepherds told them. 19 But Mary treasured up all these things, pondering them in her heart. 20 And the shepherds returned, glorifying and praising God for all they had heard and seen, as it had been told them.*

Faith Lesson from the Shepherds' Fields

1. The shepherds were the first to hear the announcement of Jesus' birth.
2. Shepherds were considered among the lowliest people. To be a shepherd was to be a nobody. It was a boring, lonely, despised job no one wanted.
3. Because Christ came to save all people and show his humility, the angels appeared to the shepherds as a sign that the "Good News" was available for all, from the lowliest shepherds to the noblest kings (the Magi).

Ruins of Mignal Eder Tower

4. Do we believe salvation is for everyone?
5. Are we humble like the shepherds were?
6. The shepherds went in haste to see Jesus. Do we show zeal and fervor in our desire to be with Jesus?
7. The shepherds spread the good news about Jesus. Do we share the good news (gospel) with others as well?

Journal/Notes:

Beth-Shemesh

Location

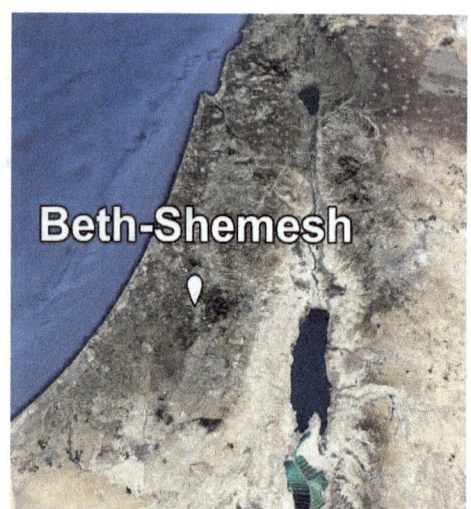

1. Beth-Shemesh lies 13 miles (21 km.) west of Jerusalem and 20 miles (32 km.) east of the Mediterranean Sea. It's on Hwy. 38, about 5.5 miles (8 km.) south of Hwy. 1.
2. Beth-Shemesh was the most important city in the Sorek Valley as it was a guard-city to both east-west and north-south traffic through the region.
3. It was a border city between Judah and Dan that was given to the Levites.
4. Just across the valley (north) is the town of Zorah, where Samson lived. Some ruins and his tomb can be seen today.
5. Down the Sorek Valley (west) a short distance was the town of Timnah, the hometown of Samson's first wife, and the area where his girlfriend Delilah lived.
6. Beth-Shemesh means "House of the Sun" and probably got its name from sun worship by the Canaanites.
7. Beth-Shemesh is most known as the place where the Ark of the Covenant arrived when the Philistines returned it as found in 1 Samuel 6.

Historical Background

1. Beth-Shemesh was a large thriving city belonging to the Canaanites when the Israelites arrived in about 1406 BC.
2. The Philistines were part of the Canaanite people group who lived in the land (Gen. 21:34). They possessed iron and were the high-tech people of the day.
3. At the time of Judges and 1 Samuel (1050 AD), the Philistines had a stronghold in the coastal plain area.

Central Israel Sites

4. As the Philistines gained territory, they moved inland. Beth-Shemesh and the cities in the Sorek Valley were affected and became border towns between the Philistines and the Israelites.
5. Samson, who lived across from Beth-Shemesh in Zorah, engaged in battle with the Philistines to liberate the area from their grasp and return it to the Israelites.
6. The Philistines worshiped the false god, Dagon, who was supposedly the father of Baalsabul, or Baal. He was a fish god of fertility and was represented as a half-man, half-fish creature.

Places of Interest

1. Tel Beth-Shemesh
   - 5th-Century AD Byzantine Monastery
   - Underground Water Reservoir
   - Northern Double Chambered Gate
   - Southern Gate
   - Mosque Ruins
   - Tombs

- Large rock where the Israelites likely sacrificed the oxen who pulled the cart after receiving the Ark of the Covenant from the Philistines.
2. Sorek Valley
3. Nahal Sorek Stream
4. Zorah
   - Samson's Tomb
5. Tel Timnah
6. Modern Beth-Shemesh

Beth-Shemesh in the Bible

1. **God gave the Israelites over to the Philistines because they had done evil in His sight.**

   Judges 13:1: *And the people of Israel again did what was evil in the sight of the LORD, so the LORD gave them into the hand of the Philistines for forty years.*

2. **God raised up Samson to begin the deliverance of the area from the hand of the Philistines (Judg. 13–16).**

3. **Not long after the death of Samson, the Ark of the Covenant was captured in a battle against the Philistines. This was due**

Central Israel Sites

   to judgment against the priest Eli and his two sons, Hophni and Phinehas, who all died in battle because of their wickedness (1 Sam. 4).

4. **The Philistines believed they were victorious in battle because their god, Dagon, was stronger than the true God of the Israelites. As a result, the Philistines took the Ark to the temple of their god, Dagon, to honor him for the victory.**

5. **However, God made the false god, Dagon, fall down in worship before the Ark.**

   1 Samuel 5:1–4: *When the Philistines captured the ark of God, they brought it from Ebenezer to Ashdod. 2 Then the Philistines took the ark of God and brought it into the house of Dagon and set it up beside Dagon. 3 And when the people of Ashdod rose early the next day, behold, Dagon had fallen face downward on the ground before the ark of the LORD. So they took Dagon and put him back in his place. 4 But when they rose early on the next morning, behold, Dagon had fallen face downward on the ground before the ark of the LORD, and the head of Dagon and both his hands were lying cut off on the threshold. Only the trunk of Dagon was left to him.*

   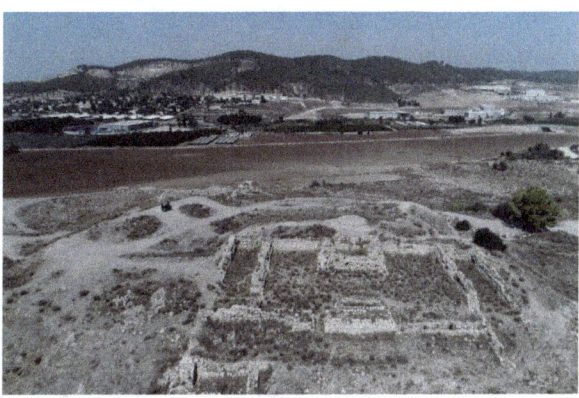
   Tel Beth-Shemesh

6. **God sent the Philistines many sicknesses as a result of possessing the Ark. So they moved it from town to town, thinking their diseases were just coincidental.**

7. **Finally, they realized that it was God who was behind their diseases and decided to send the Ark of the Covenant back to the Israelites.**

8. **The Philistines prepare to return the Ark to the Israelites in Beth-Shemesh.**

   1 Samuel 6:1–9: *The ark of the LORD was in the country of the Philistines seven months. 2 And the Philistines called for the priests and the diviners and said, "What shall we do with the ark of the*

LORD? Tell us with what we shall send it to its place." 3 They said, "If you send away the ark of the God of Israel, do not send it empty, but by all means return him a guilt offering. Then you will be healed, and it will be known to you why his hand does not turn away from you." 4 And they said, "What is the guilt offering that we shall return to him?" They answered, "Five golden tumors and five golden mice, according to the number of the lords of the Philistines, for the same plague was on all of you and on your lords. 5 So you must make images of your tumors and images of your mice that ravage the land, and give glory to the God of Israel. Perhaps he will lighten his hand from off you and your gods and your land. 6 Why should you harden your hearts as the Egyptians and Pharaoh hardened their hearts? After he had dealt severely with them, did they not send the people away,

Tel Beth-Shemesh & Sorek Valley

and they departed? 7 Now then, take and prepare a new cart and two milk cows on which there has never come a yoke, and yoke the cows to the cart, but take their calves home, away from them. 8 And take the ark of the LORD and place it on the cart and put in a box at its side the figures of gold, which you are returning to him as a guilt offering. Then send it off and let it go its way 9 and watch. If it goes up on the way to its own land, to **Beth-Shemesh**, then it is he who has done us this great harm, but if not, then we shall know that it is not his hand that struck us; it happened to us by coincidence."

9. **The Ark miraculously arrives at Beth-Shemesh.**

1 Samuel 6:10–13: *The men did so and took two milk cows and yoked them to the cart and shut up their calves at home. 11 And they put the ark of the LORD on the cart and the box with the golden mice and the images of their tumors. 12 And the cows went straight in the direction of* **Beth-Shemesh** *along one highway, lowing as they went. They turned neither to the right nor to the left, and the lords of the*

Central Israel Sites

*Philistines went after them as far as the border of **Beth-Shemesh**. 13 Now the people of **Beth-Shemesh** were reaping their wheat harvest in the valley. And when they lifted up their eyes and saw the ark, they rejoiced to see it.*

10. The Israelites offer a burnt offering to the Lord in gratitude for receiving the Ark.

1 Samuel 6:14–16: *The cart came into the field of Joshua of **Beth-Shemesh** and stopped there. A great stone was there. And they split up the wood of the cart and offered the cows as a burnt offering to the LORD. 15 And the Levites took down the ark of the LORD and the box that was beside it, in which were the golden figures, and set them upon the great stone. And the men of **Beth-Shemesh** offered burnt offerings and sacrificed sacrifices on that day to the LORD. 16 And when the five lords of the Philistines saw it, they returned that day to Ekron.*

11. The Beth-Shemesh area is where Philip the Evangelist witnessed to the Ethiopian Eunuch.

Acts 8:26–31: *Now an angel of the Lord said to Philip, "Rise and go toward the south to the **road that goes down from Jerusalem to Gaza**." This is a desert place. 27 And he rose and went. And there was an Ethiopian, a eunuch, a court official of Candace, queen of the Ethiopians, who was in charge of all her treasure. He had come to Jerusalem to worship 28 and was returning,*

Road from Jerusalem to Gaza in the Sorek Valley

seated in his chariot, and he was reading the prophet Isaiah. 29 And the Spirit said to Philip, "Go over and join this chariot." 30 So Philip ran to him and heard him reading Isaiah the prophet and asked, "Do you understand what you are reading?" 31 And he said, "How can I, unless someone guides me?" And he invited Philip to come up and sit with him.

Faith Lesson from Beth-Shemesh

1. The Israelites adopted the sinful culture of those around them and did evil in the sight of the Lord. Am I careful not to adopt the sinful lifestyles and beliefs of the culture in which I live?

2. Even though the Israelites sinned and failed to be a faithful witness to the surrounding nations, God protected His glory and showed Himself to them as the true and living God. Am I a faithful witness to my culture in living out God's truth and reflecting His glory?

Northern City Gate of Beth-Shemesh

3. Do I use the miracles God has done in my life as a tool to witness and teach others who God is?

4. Like Philip, am I obedient in listening to God's voice and sharing the gospel when He prompts me?

Journal/Notes:

Central Israel Sites

Emmaus Nicopolis

Location

1. Emmaus is about 10 miles (14 km.) west of the outskirts of Jerusalem on Hwy. 1.
2. Emmaus is also known as Emmaus Nicopolis and is in Ayalon Canada Park.
3. It's believed to be the site of the village of Emmaus, which is referred to in Luke 24, where Jesus met two of His followers on the road to Emmaus after his resurrection.
4. The ruins of the old city are scattered over a vast area inside the park and on its west side.

Historical Background

1. Emmaus was a large city that existed from the Hellenistic period through the Byzantine period.
2. It's strategically located on the main road that links Joppa and the coastal cities to Jerusalem.
3. It has served as an administrative, military, and economic center.
4. Eusebius (260–340 AD) mentioned Nicopolis as biblical Emmaus in his writings.
5. Jerome (347–420 AD) spoke of a church in Nicopolis, built in the house of Cleopas, where Jesus broke bread with His disciples.
6. From the 4th century on, the site has been widely identified as the biblical Emmaus.
7. A Byzantine church was built here in the 5th century.
8. Another Byzantine church was built beside the 5th-century church in around the 7th century.
9. Later, the Crusaders built a basilica over the Byzantine church in the 12th century.

Places of Interest

1. 5th-Century Church
2. 7th-Century Church
3. 12th-Century Church
4. Byzantine Inscription
5. Byzantine Baptistry Chapel
6. 5th-Century Bishop's House
7. Ancient Tombs
8. Roman Bathhouse – Located north of the church several hundred yards (meters).

Emmaus in the Bible

1. After Christ's resurrection, two of His followers were walking to Emmaus.

Luke 24:13–14: *And behold, two of them were going that very day to a village named* **Emmaus**, *which was about seven miles [60 stadia, Greek and Roman measurement that varied somewhat in length] from Jerusalem. 14 And they were talking with each other about all these things which had taken place.*

2. **Jesus talked to the disciples and enlightened them, but He didn't let them know who He was.**

   Luke 24:15-27: *While they were talking and discussing, Jesus Himself approached and began traveling with them. 16* ***But their eyes were prevented from recognizing Him****. 17 And He said to them, "What are these words that you are exchanging with one another as you are walking?" And they stood still, looking sad. 18 One of them, named Cleopas, answered and said to Him, "Are You the only one visiting Jerusalem and unaware of the things which have happened here in these days?" 19 And He said to them, "What things?" And they said to Him, "The things about Jesus the Nazarene, who was a prophet mighty in deed and word in the sight of God and all the people, 20 and how the chief priests and our rulers delivered Him to the sentence of death and crucified Him. 21 But we were hoping that it was He who was going to redeem Israel. Indeed, besides all this, it is the third day since these things happened. 22 But also some women among us amazed us. When they were at the tomb early in the morning, 23 and did not find His body, they came, saying that they had also seen a vision of angels who said that He was alive. 24 Some of those who were with us went to the tomb and found it just exactly as the women also had said; but Him they did not see." 25 And He said to them, "O foolish men and slow of heart to believe in all that the prophets have spoken! 26 Was it not necessary for the Christ to suffer these things and to enter into His glory?" 27 Then* ***beginning with Moses and with all the prophets, He explained to them the things concerning Himself in all the Scriptures.***

   Churches at Emmaus

3. **Jesus made Himself known to the disciples.**

   Luke 24:28-32: *And they approached the village where they were going, and He acted as though He were going farther. 29 But they urged Him, saying, "Stay with us, for it is getting toward evening,* and the day is now nearly over." So He went in to stay with them. 30 When He had reclined at the table with them, He took the bread and blessed it, and breaking it, He began giving it to them. 31 Then **their eyes were opened, and they recognized Him**; and He vanished from their sight. 32 They said to one another, "Were not our hearts burning within us while He was speaking to us on the road, while He was explaining the Scriptures to us?"

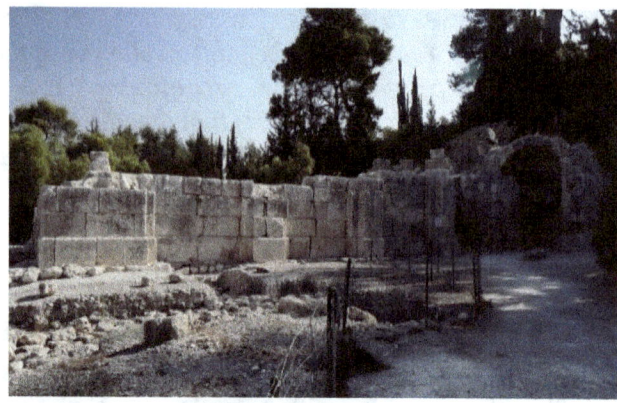
Church at Emmaus

4. **The two men returned to Jerusalem and told the rest of the disciples that they had seen the risen Christ.**

    Luke 24:33–35: *And they got up that very hour and **returned to Jerusalem**, and found gathered together the eleven and those who were with them, 34 saying, "The Lord has really risen and has appeared to Simon." 35 They began to **relate their experiences** on the road and how He was recognized by them in the breaking of the bread.*

Faith Lesson from Emmaus

1. There are hundreds of prophecies in the Old Testament that verify Christ as the Messiah. Do we believe Jesus is the Messiah and the Son of God, and have we received Him as our Lord and Savior?
2. The New Testament is built upon the Old Testament as the Old Testament is quoted 855 times in the New Testament. Do we read and teach out of the Old Testament, or do we neglect it?
3. Being God, Christ knew every detail of the Bible and handled it with precision and clarity. Do we know God's Word in detail, and do we handle it with precision (2 Tim. 2:15)?
4. Christ taught the Scriptures in such a way that they reached the very depths of a person's heart. Are we master teachers or mediocre teachers?

5. Christ appeared to many after His resurrection, and to over 500 at one time. Do we believe the resurrection of Christ was a real historical event?

1 Corinthians 15:3–8: *For I delivered to you as of first importance what I also received, that Christ died for our sins according to the Scriptures, 4 and that He was buried, and that He was raised on the third day according to the Scriptures, 5 and that He appeared to Cephas [Peter], then to the twelve. 6 After that He appeared to more than* **five hundred brethren at one time**, *most of whom remain until now, but some have fallen asleep; 7 then He appeared to James, then to all the apostles; 8 and last of all, as to one untimely born, He appeared to me also.*

5th-century church

Journal/Notes:

Gezer

Location

1. Gezer is in the eastern foothills of the coastal plain (Shaphelah) of western Israel. It's about 14 miles (22.5 km.) east of the Mediterranean Sea and about 19 miles (30.5 km.) west of Jerusalem. Tel Aviv sits about 17 miles (27 km.) to the northwest of Gezer.

2. Gezer was on the international north-south travel route called the Via Maris. It was also on a major east-west route that linked the coastal plain to Jerusalem and beyond.

   - The Via Maris connected three continents: Africa, Asia, and Europe.
   - This location is significant because Israel forms a narrow land bridge to connect these three continents.
   - To the east is a desert and to the west is the Mediterranean Sea. This forced trade and travelers to use the Via Maris.
   - Whatever happened in Israel was taken to the known world at that time.

3. Whoever controlled Gezer controlled the trade and influence of the ancient world in biblical times.
4. God, in His sovereignty, placed Israel on the crossroads of the known world so they could be a light to the world and communicate His message to them.
5. Gezer was in the territory of Ephraim.

Historical Background

1. Gezer is one of the largest tels in Israel.
2. Whoever controlled Gezer had significant control over the ancient

Central Israel Sites

world.
3. Gezer began to be inhabited some 5,000 years ago.
4. It has around 21 layers of civilizations.
5. A tel is a mound of earth that develops as one civilization builds upon another.
6. The Canaanites first lived here from around 3000 BC to around 2000 BC.
7. Sadly, there has been found on this site many sacrificed babies.
8. When the Israelites arrived in 1406 BC, they failed to drive out the Philistines and occupy Gezer.
9. As a result, the Philistines lived here from around 2000 BC until King David subdued them in around 1000 BC.
10. Gezer existed during the time of Christ.

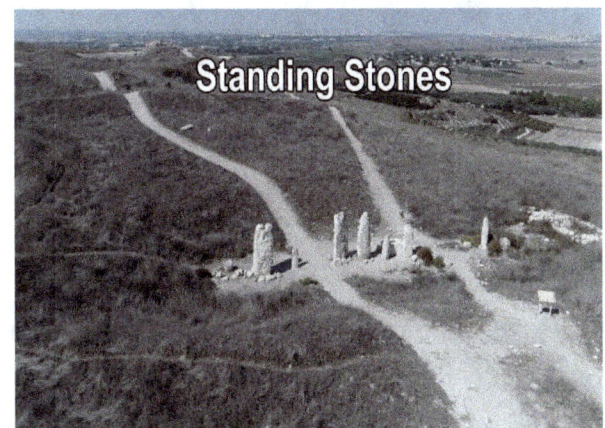

11. Gezer is mentioned 14 times in the Bible.
12. During the Hasmonean revolt (167 BC), the Jews lived close to Gezer and used it for battle purposes.
13. The Ottomans (15th and 16th centuries) lived here as well.

Places of Interest

1. Parking
2. Canaanite Tower
3. Canaanite Gate
4. Water System
5. Sheikh's Tomb
6. Israelite City
7. Solomon's Gate
8. Standing Stones
9. Lookout Point

Gezer in the Bible

1. **In the conquest of the Promised Land, God gave the Israelites victory over Gezer.**

    Joshua 10:33: *Then Horam king of **Gezer** came up to help Lachish. And Joshua struck him and his people, until he left none remaining.*

2. **The tribe of Ephraim was allotted Gezer, but they didn't fully drive out its inhabitants and conquer them.**

    Joshua 16:10: *However, they did not drive out the Canaanites who lived in **Gezer**, so the Canaanites have lived in the midst of Ephraim to this day but have been made to do forced labor.*

3. **Gezer was one of the cities given to the Kohathite clans of the Levites. It was also a city of refuge.**

    Joshua 21:20–22: *As to the rest of the Kohathites belonging to the Kohathite clans of the Levites, the cities allotted to them were out of the tribe of Ephraim. 21 To them were given Shechem, the city of refuge for the manslayer, with its pasturelands in the hill country of Ephraim, **Gezer** with its pasturelands, 22 Kibzaim with its pasturelands, Beth-horon with its pasturelands—four cities.*

4. **King David, some 200 years later, conquered the Philistines who lived in Gezer.**

    2 Samuel 5:25: *Then David did so, just as the Lord had commanded*

Central Israel Sites

*him, and struck down the Philistines from Geba as far as **Gezer**.*

5. **After King David, it appears Egypt also conquered Gezer and gave it to Solomon, who rebuilt and fortified it.**

1 Kings 9:15–17: *And this is the account of the forced labor that King Solomon drafted to build the house of the Lord and his own house and the Millo and the wall of Jerusalem and Hazor and Megiddo and **Gezer** 16 (Pharaoh king of Egypt had gone up and captured **Gezer** and burned it with fire, and had killed the Canaanites who lived in the city, and had given it as dowry to his daughter, Solomon's wife; 17 so Solomon rebuilt **Gezer**) and Lower Beth-horon.*

Faith Lesson from Gezer

1. In the same way Gezer is on a hill found on the crossroads of the world, we too have been placed by God in the world to influence those around us.

2. Unlike the Ephraimites who failed to conquer Gezer and attain what God had promised them, we should subdue what God wants us to become and accomplish for Him.

3. Like the standing stones at Gezer, we should be firm in our faith and persevere under persecution and pressure. We should not allow the world to mold us, but instead, we should impact the world for Christ.

Journal/Notes:

Gibeon

Location

1. Gibeon is about 6 miles (10 km.) northwest of Jerusalem on Hwy. 436.
2. Today, it's known as Nabi Samuel or Nebi Samwil, which means "The Prophet Samuel" because it's believed Samuel's tomb is located here.
3. Just below this high place and to the north is the ancient city of Gibeon with its ruins, known today as Al Jib.

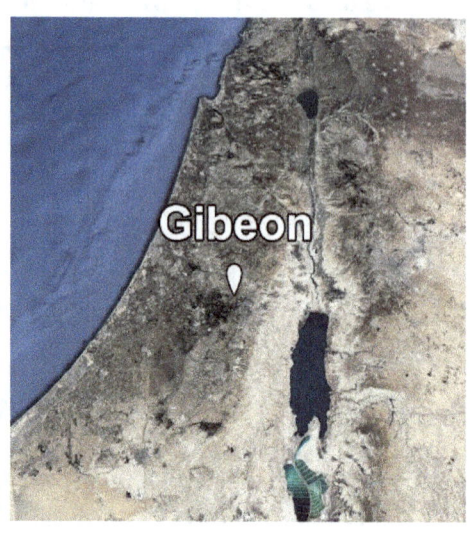

4. Gibeon is on top of a high mountain with a spectacular view of Jerusalem and the surrounding area. In fact, you can see Jerusalem quite easily from this site. It becomes clear that this spot was a significant high place and fits the biblical descriptions of many events found in Scripture and history.
5. This high place is about 3,000 feet or 908 meters above sea level.
6. It's located on an ancient route that led from the coastal plain passing through Beit Horon, this high place of Gibeon, and on to Jerusalem. Today highways 436 and 443 mark this route.

Historical Background

1. Before the conquest of the Israelites, Gibeon was a Canaanite city.
2. Gibeon was a popular place in the Bible and is mentioned 43 times.
3. Its name means "Hill City," and it's located in the heart of the Tribe of Benjamin.
4. It was a high place of worship throughout much of Israel's history, and the tabernacle was here during the times of King David and King Solomon.
5. The tomb of the Prophet Samuel is believed to be located inside the synagogue part of the mosque/synagogue building.

6. Excavations, which are still ongoing, have uncovered the remains of settlements from both the First Temple (7th century BC) and the Second Temple (Hasmonean Period 167 BC–63 BC) can be found here.
7. During the Byzantine period (5th–7th century AD), a church and monastery were built at Gibeon.

8. The Crusaders then built a church and fortress over the monastery in the 12 century AD. The main structure that can be seen today is a magnificent Crusader-era church, and it's one of only four that survived after the Muslim conquests of the Crusaders. It survived because the Muslims turned this church into a mosque, which they still use today.
9. After Saladin conquered much of Israel in 1187, the church and monastery were damaged.
10. In 1267 the Mamluks captured the area and controlled the Holy Land until 1517. In the 14th century, the Mamelukes converted the church to a mosque. Remains from this period include two ceramic ovens near the stables.
11. Because it's believed Samuel was buried here, along with the biblical history of the site, it was used as a synagogue during the 15th and 16th centuries.
12. It appears that later on, the mosque was renovated by the Ottomans in 1730.
13. The building that we see today was rebuilt by the British after

World War 1. Both the mosque and synagogue share the same building.

Places of Interest

1. Tabernacle Location

The original tabernacle is believed to be directly under the synagogue and mosque of this site. This would make sense as we have a long history of one thing built on top of another, which is a strong sign of authenticity in archaeology. As mentioned, this synagogue and mosque were built upon the ruins of a Crusader church, built on the ruins of a Byzantine church, built upon where the tabernacle was located during the reigns of King David and King Solomon. It also has other ruins dating back to the first temple period of the 7th century BC.

2. Hannah's Spring

Just down the hill below the ruins is a place called Hannah's Spring. It's named after Samuel's mother, Hannah, who is believed to have traversed this area and lived nearby. Today, women come here to pray for God's blessing for conception and childbirth. An ancient road passing through an orchard of strawberry, olive, and fig trees leads to a small spring flowing from a cave. Picnic tables have been set up in a pleasant and tranquil corner in the shade of the fig trees. Above Hannah's Spring, entrances to First Temple period burial caves can be seen.

3. Hasmonean Ruins

During extensive archaeological excavations, archaeologists found remains dating to the Hasmonean period, which was from around 164 to 63 BC. We can see a number of well-preserved two-story houses and streets in this section.

4. Byzantine Church and Monastery

During the Byzantine period in around 400 AD, a large monastery was constructed at this site.

Original tabernacle location

There are few remains from that period since the Crusaders built their church and fortress over the monastery. The monastery served as a hostel for the Christian pilgrims who came to visit Jerusalem. It existed until around 900 AD.

5. Crusader Ruins

The crusade to liberate the Holy Land and free Jerusalem started in 1096. On June 7, 1099, three years after the military expedition started in Europe, the Crusaders finally approached the gates of Jerusalem. They first arrived at this site of Nebi Samuel, where they could see Jerusalem in the distance. They were so joyful on viewing the Holy City for the first time that they later named this site the "Mountain of Joy."

In 1140 the Crusaders upgraded the site as a military fortress as well as a holy shrine. They cut into the bedrock on the west, north, and east sides, creating a defensive moat. However, only part of the moat was finished. The hewn rocks were used for the building material of the church of St. Samuel on the top of the hill. The church was completed in 1157. The fortress was a rectangular structure with the church at its center, built over the traditional tomb of the prophet.

On the north and north-east sides, the Crusaders cut away the bedrock to around 15 ft. or 5 m. below the surface. The stones were used to build their structures and fortress. This large flat area was then used as a campsite for armies and a hostel for Christian pilgrims headed to Jerusalem.

On the north side, within the quarried area, are a number of hewn structures. We can see a large stable with rock-cut troughs. There are also pools, cisterns, rock-hewn tombs, and agriculture installations here.

6. **Synagogue**

   An earlier synagogue was preserved at a lower level where the actual tomb of Samuel is located. The entrance to the Synagogue is on the north side and houses the believed tomb of the prophet Samuel. There is a women's section and a men's section. The men's section is accessed by going down some stairs and is where the tomb of Samuel can be found. It's located below because its level was the original level of the Byzantine Church and monastery.

7. **Rooftop Viewing Area**

   On the roof above the mosque and synagogue is a large area that provides a spectacular view of the area. Jerusalem, the Mt. of Olives, and many other sites can be seen from this high place.

8. **Quarry**
9. **Stables**

Gibeon in the Bible

1. **This ancient city is named after the Gibeonites, who tricked Joshua into making a treaty with them.**

   Joshua 9:3–6: *When the **inhabitants of Gibeon** heard what Joshua had done to Jericho and to Ai, 4 they also acted craftily and set out as envoys, and took worn-out sacks on their donkeys, and wineskins worn-out and torn and mended, 5 and worn-out and patched sandals on their feet, and worn-out clothes on themselves; and all the bread of their provision was dry and had become crumbled. 6 They went to Joshua to the **camp at Gilgal** and said to him and to the men of Israel, "We have come from a far country; now therefore, make a covenant with us."*

   Gilgal is only 29 miles (32 km.) from Gibeon.

   Joshua 9:14–15: *So the men of Israel took some of their provisions, and **did not ask for the counsel of the Lord**. 15 Joshua made peace with them and made a covenant with them, to let them live; and the leaders of the congregation swore an oath to them.*

2. **The amazing miracle of the sun and moon standing still happened at Gibeon.**

   Joshua 10:1–14: *Now it came about when Adoni-zedek king of Jerusalem heard that Joshua had captured Ai, and had utterly destroyed it (just as he had done to Jericho and its king, so he had done to Ai and its king), and that the inhabitants of Gibeon had made peace with Israel and were within their land, 2 that he feared greatly, because **Gibeon was a great city**, like one of the royal cities, and because it was greater than Ai, and all its men were mighty. 3 Therefore Adoni-zedek king of Jerusalem sent word to Hoham king of Hebron and to Piram king of*

High Place at Gibeon

Jarmuth and to Japhia king of Lachish and to Debir king of Eglon, saying, 4 "Come up to me and help me, and let us attack Gibeon, for it has made peace with Joshua and with the sons of Israel." 5 So the five kings of the Amorites, the king of Jerusalem, the king of Hebron, the king of Jarmuth, the king of Lachish, and the king of Eglon, gathered together and went up, they with all their armies, and camped by Gibeon and fought against it. 6 Then the men of Gibeon sent word to Joshua to the camp at Gilgal, saying, "Do not abandon your servants; come up to us quickly and save us and help us, for all the kings of the Amorites that live in the hill country have assembled against us." 7 So Joshua went up from Gilgal, he and all the people of war with him and all the valiant warriors. 8 The Lord said to Joshua, "Do not fear them, for I have given them into your hands; not one of

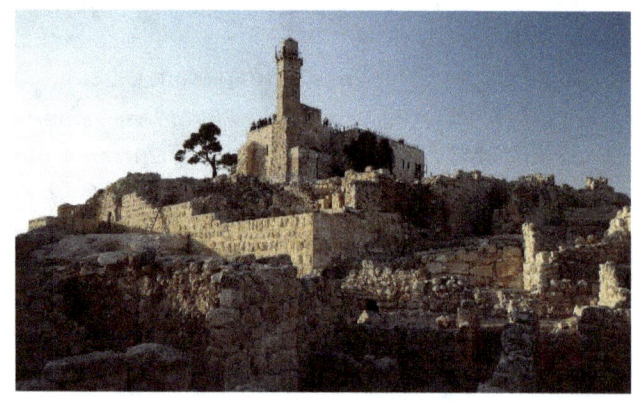

them shall stand before you." 9 So Joshua came upon them suddenly by marching all night from Gilgal. 10 And the Lord confounded them before Israel, and He slew them with a great slaughter at **Gibeon**, and pursued them by the way of the ascent of Beth-horon and struck them as far as Azekah and Makkedah. 11 As they fled from before Israel, while they were at the descent of Beth-horon, the Lord threw large stones from heaven on them as far as Azekah, and they died; there were more who died from the hailstones than those whom the sons of Israel killed with the sword. 12 Then Joshua spoke to the Lord in the day when the Lord delivered up the Amorites before the sons of Israel, and he said in the sight of Israel, "**O sun, stand still at Gibeon, and O moon in the valley of Aijalon.**" 13 So the **sun stood still, and the moon stopped**, until the nation avenged themselves of their enemies. Is it not written in the book of Jashar? And the sun stopped in the middle of the sky and did not hasten to go down for **about a whole day**. 14 There was no day like that before it or after it, when the Lord listened to the voice of a man; for the Lord fought for Israel.

Central Israel Sites

3. **Gibeon (Gibeah) was the hometown of King Saul.**

   1 Samuel 10:26: *Saul also went to his house at Gibeah.*

4. **The tabernacle resided at the high place of Gibeon during the reigns of David and Solomon.**

   1 Chronicles 21:28–29: *At that time, when David saw that the Lord had answered him on the threshing floor of Ornan the Jebusite, he offered sacrifice there. 29 For the tabernacle of the Lord, which Moses had made in the wilderness, and the altar of burnt offering were in the **high place at Gibeon** at that time.*

   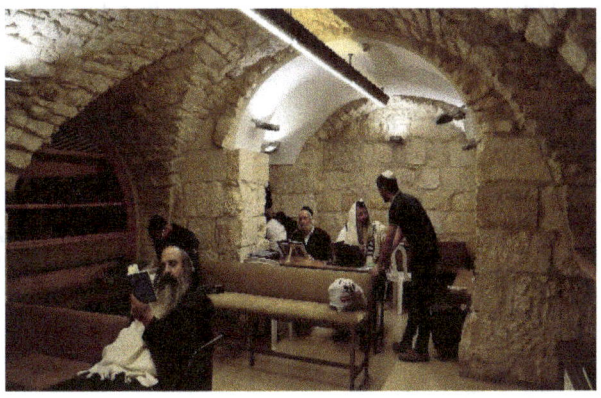
   Synagogue at Gibeon

   2 Chronicles 1:2–3: *Solomon spoke to all Israel, to the commanders of thousands and of hundreds and to the judges and to every leader in all Israel, the heads of the fathers' households. 3 Then Solomon and all the assembly with him went to the **high place, which was at Gibeon**, for **God's tent of meeting was there**, which Moses the servant of the Lord had made in the wilderness.*

5. **God caused a famine in Israel because King Saul broke the covenant Joshua made with the Gibeonites.**

   2 Samuel 21:1: *Now there was a famine in the days of David for three years, year after year; and David sought the presence of the Lord. And the Lord said, "It is for Saul and his bloody house, because he put the Gibeonites to death."*

6. **Soon after Solomon became king, he went to Gibeon. Here he received supernatural wisdom, wealth, and power to use for ruling God's people.**

   1 Kings 3:3–5: *Now Solomon loved the Lord, walking in the statutes of his father David, except he sacrificed and burned incense on the high places. 4 The **king went to Gibeon** to sacrifice there, for that was **the great high place**; Solomon offered a thousand burnt offerings on that altar. 5 In Gibeon, the Lord appeared to Solomon in*

a dream at night; and God said, "Ask what you wish Me to give you."

In response, God not only gave him supernatural wisdom, but wealth and power as well.

Faith Lesson from Gibeon

1. The Gibeonites tricked Joshua because he failed to seek the Lord in prayer. Do we make poor decisions as well because we fail to seek the Lord?

    Proverbs 3:5–6: *Trust in the Lord with all your heart and do not lean on your own understanding. In all your ways acknowledge Him, and He will make your paths straight.*

2. God heard Joshua's prayer, and the sun and moon stood still for a day. There is nothing we can ask in prayer that is too big for God to answer.

    James 5:16–18: *The effective prayer of a righteous man can accomplish much. Elijah was a man with a nature like ours, and he prayed earnestly that it would not rain, and it did not rain on the earth for three years and six months. Then he prayed again, and the sky poured rain and the earth produced its fruit.*

    Do we believe God truly hears our prayers?

3. God punished the Israelites because they broke their word with the Gibeonites.

    Psalm 15:4: *But he honors those who fear the Lord; he who swears to his own hurt and does not change.*

    What about us? Do we keep our word with others?

4. God gave Solomon supernatural wisdom, wealth, and power to serve others and glorify God. How do we use our wisdom, wealth, and power? Do we mainly use it for the Lord, or primarily for our own good and benefit?

Journal/Notes:

Central Israel Sites

Gilgal

Location

There are two locations for Gilgal.

1. **Tel Gilgal** is situated in the Jordan Valley plain at the place of the modern city of Gilgal, which is located about 8 miles (12 km.) north of Jericho on Hwy. 90.
2. **Camp Gilgal** is located on the eastern edge of Jericho on Hwy. 90.

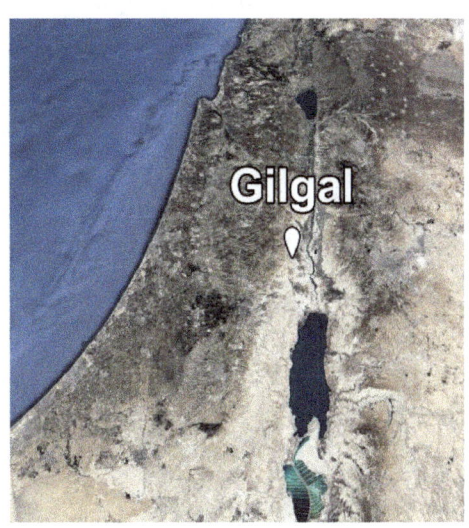

Historical Background

1. The late professor, Adam Zertal (University of Haifa), did much research on the biblical location of Gilgal and discovered that it's possible it wasn't necessarily a specific location but a common name for a camp or religious site in its early period.
2. In Zertal's research, he discovered 6 sites where the Israelites likely camped after crossing the Jordan into the Promised Land. Each place is uniquely shaped like a human right footprint. This is likely attributed to the promise given to them in Deuteronomy 11:24: *Every place on which the **sole of your foot treads** shall be yours; your border will be from the wilderness to Lebanon, and from the river, the river Euphrates, as far as the western sea.*
3. Joshua 4:19 places Gilgal on the eastern edge of Jericho: *Now the people came up from the Jordan on the tenth of the first month and camped at Gilgal on the **eastern edge of Jericho**.* The place of Tel Gilgal (modern-day Gilgal) doesn't seem to fit the qualifications found in Joshua 4:19.
4. If Zertal's claims are true, then it's possible Tel Gilgal (located at modern Gilgal) was the more permanent Gilgal that is referred to 35 times in Scripture and the place on the eastern edge of Jericho was a temporary place where the Israelites camped. This seems reasonable as there are no remains of a permanent city on the

eastern edge of Jericho.
5. Tel Gilgal became a central meeting place throughout the rest of the Old Testament and appears to have been a small city.

Places of Interest
1. Tel Gilgal
2. Tower
3. Heel part of the footprint shape of Tel Gilgal.
4. Center part of the footprint shape of Tel Gilgal.
5. Tabernacle
6. 12 Stone Monument (it appears it was moved from Camp Gilgal to Tel Gilgal as a permanent monument at a later date).
7. Altar
8. Toe part of the footprint shape of Tel Gilgal.

9. Modern Gilgal
10. Jericho
11. Jordan River
12. Camp Gilgal on the eastern edge of Jericho.

Central Israel Sites

Gilgal in the Bible

1. **Camp Gilgal is the first place the Israelites camped after crossing the Jordan River and entering the Promised Land.**

   Joshua 4:19: *Now the people came up from the Jordan on the tenth of the first month and **camped at Gilgal** on the **eastern edge of Jericho**.*

2. **At Camp Gilgal, Joshua erected 12 stones taken from the Jordan River as a monument of remembrance.**

   Joshua 4:18-24: *It came about when the priests who carried the ark of the covenant of the Lord had come up from the middle of the Jordan, and the soles of the priests' feet were lifted up to the dry ground, that the waters of the Jordan returned to their place, and went over all its banks as before. 19 Now the people came up from the Jordan on the tenth of the first month and **camped at Gilgal on the eastern edge of Jericho**. 20 Those twelve stones which they had taken from the Jordan, Joshua set up at **Gilgal**. 21 He said to the sons of Israel, "When your children ask their fathers in time to come, saying, 'What are these stones?' 22 then you shall inform your* children, saying, 'Israel crossed this Jordan on dry ground.' 23 For the Lord your God dried up the waters of the Jordan before you until you had crossed, just as the Lord your God had done to the Red Sea, which He dried up before us until we had crossed; 24 that all the peoples of the earth may know that the hand of the Lord is mighty, so that you may fear the Lord your God forever."

3. **Camp Gilgal was the first place the Israelites celebrated the Passover after entering the Promised Land.**

   Joshua 5:10: *While the sons of Israel camped at **Gilgal**, they observed the Passover on the evening of the fourteenth day of the month on the **desert plains of Jericho**.*

4. **At Gilgal, the Gibeonites tricked the Israelites into making a covenant with them so they wouldn't be destroyed.**

   Joshua 9:3–6: *When the inhabitants of Gibeon heard what Joshua had done to Jericho and to Ai, 4 they also acted craftily and set out as envoys, and took worn-out sacks on their donkeys,*

   Aerial view of Tel Gilgal – Outline of footprint

   *and wineskins worn-out and torn and mended, 5 and worn-out and patched sandals on their feet, and worn-out clothes on themselves; and all the bread of their provision was dry and had become crumbled. 6 They went to Joshua to the **camp at Gilgal** and said to him and to the men of Israel, "We have come from a far country; now, therefore, make a covenant with us."*

5. **Gilgal was where Caleb, one of the two faithful spies Moses sent to spy out the Promised Land, asked Joshua for his portion of the land.**

   Joshua 14:6–9: *Then the sons of Judah drew near to Joshua in **Gilgal**, and Caleb the son of Jephunneh the Kenizzite said to him, "You know the word which the Lord spoke to Moses the man of God concerning you and me in Kadesh-barnea. 7 I was forty years old* *when Moses the servant of the Lord sent me from Kadesh-barnea to spy out the land, and I brought word back to him as it was in my heart. 8 Nevertheless my brethren who went up with me made the heart of the people melt with fear; but I followed the Lord my God fully." 9 So Moses swore on that day, saying, "Surely the land on which your foot has trodden will be an inheritance to you and to your children forever, because you have followed the Lord my God fully."*

View looking north

Joshua 14:13: *So Joshua blessed him and gave Hebron to Caleb the son of Jephunneh for an inheritance.*

6. The Prophet Samuel visited and taught the Word of God regularly at Tel Gilgal.

1 Samuel 7:15–16: *Now Samuel judged Israel all the days of his life. 16 He used to go annually on circuit to Bethel and **Gilgal** and Mizpah, and he judged Israel in all these places.*

7. Saul, the first king of Israel, was made king at Tel Gilgal.

1 Samuel 11:14–15: *Then Samuel said to the people, "Come and let us go to **Gilgal** and renew the kingdom there." 15 So all the people went to **Gilgal**, and there they made Saul king before the Lord in **Gilgal**. There they also offered sacrifices of peace offerings before the Lord; and there Saul and all the men of Israel rejoiced greatly.*

8. Tel Gilgal was a central gathering place for the Israelites.

1 Samuel 13:4: *All Israel heard the news that Saul had smitten the garrison of the Philistines, and also that Israel had become odious to the Philistines. The people were then summoned to Saul at **Gilgal**.*

9. King Saul's reign over Israel came to an end at Tel Gilgal because of his disobedience.

1 Samuel 13:8–14: *Now he waited seven days, according to the appointed time set by Samuel, but Samuel did not come to* **Gilgal**; *and the people were scattering from him. 9 So Saul said, "Bring to me the burnt offering and the peace offerings." And he offered the burnt offering. 10 As soon as he finished offering the burnt offering, behold, Samuel came; and Saul went out to meet him and to greet him. 11 But Samuel said, "What have you done?" And Saul said, "Because I saw that the people were scattering from me, and that you did not come within the appointed days, and that the Philistines were assembling at Michmash,*

Tower at Tel Gilgal

12 therefore I said, 'Now the Philistines will come down against me at **Gilgal**, *and I have not asked the favor of the Lord.' So I forced myself and offered the burnt offering." 13 Samuel said to Saul, "You have acted foolishly; you have not kept the commandment of the Lord your God, which He commanded you, for now the Lord would have established your kingdom over Israel forever. 14 But now your kingdom shall not endure. The Lord has sought out for Himself a man after His own heart, and the Lord has appointed him as ruler over His people, because you have not kept what the Lord commanded you."*

10. **God pronounced judgment upon Israel at Tel Gilgal because of their disobedience to Him.**

Hosea 9:15: *All their evil is at* **Gilgal**; *Indeed, I came to hate them there! Because of the wickedness of their deeds I will drive them out of My house! I will love them no more; all their princes are rebels.*

Amos 5:4–5: *For thus says the Lord to the house of Israel, "Seek Me that you may live. 5 But do not resort to Bethel and do not come to* **Gilgal**, *nor cross over to Beersheba; for* **Gilgal** *will certainly go into captivity and Bethel will come to trouble."*

Faith Lesson from Gilgal

1. Like the Israelites who took 12 stones out of the Jordan River to mark the fulfillment of God's miracle in bringing them into the Promised Land, we too should set up remembrances to help us remember what God has done in our lives.
2. Like Caleb, who was faithful in trusting God, we should emulate his faith and strength.
3. Unlike Joshua, who failed to pray and seek the Lord regarding the trickery of the Gibeonites, we should bring our cares and decisions to the Lord.
4. We should heed the warnings from the life of King Saul, who presumed upon God's grace and disobeyed the Lord regularly.

Drone flight at Tel Gilgal

5. Lastly, we should not be like the Israelites, who slowly turned away from the Lord and were disciplined by God.

Journal/Notes:

Inn of the Good Samaritan

Location

1. The Inn of the Good Samaritan is located about 8.5 miles (13.5 km.) east of Jerusalem on Hwy. 1 and about 6.5 (10.5 km.) west of Jericho.

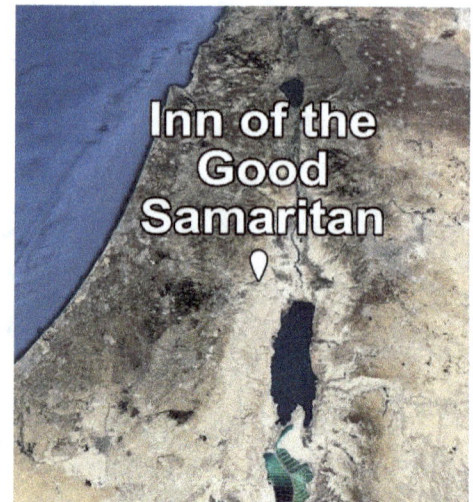

2. The Inn is about halfway between Jerusalem and Jericho on an ancient road that linked traffic from the Jordan Valley to Jerusalem and the coastal towns of the Mediterranean Ocean.
3. The famous story of the Good Samaritan took place on this road.

Historical Background

1. Interestingly, Jesus used real places and people in the story of the Good Samaritan, i.e., road, Jerusalem, Jericho, robbers, Samaritans, priests, Levites, and the Inn. Therefore, the possibility exists that the story was actually a real event that had happened.
2. The ancient road connecting the Jordan Valley to Jerusalem and beyond had an elevation difference of 3,400 ft. (1,036 m.). Jericho is at 800 ft. (244 m.) below sea level, and Jerusalem is at 2,600 ft. (792 m.) above sea level.
3. It was a dangerous road that was desolate in places, steep, curvy, with crooks, crannies, and caves where bandits and robbers could hide out and get away easily in the desert. It also lacked police protection in many places.
4. It was about 15 miles (24 km.) between Jerusalem and Jericho.
5. Around 12,000 priests and Levites lived in Jericho who used this road whenever they were summoned to serve in the temple in Jerusalem.
6. The rocky desert terrain around the Inn of the Good Samaritan was notorious for robbers. The local name for the area is Ma'ale

Adummim, which means red rocks. It's believed the name was derived from the limestone stained red by iron oxide, but it's also believed its name is due to the amount of blood that was spilled here by bandits and robbers.
7. Jesus and His disciples would have used this road repeatedly as they traveled between Jerusalem and Jericho.
8. The Inn of the Good Samaritan.
    - Although it's not certain that the inn Jesus mentioned in the story of the Good Samaritan was a real place, a site was proposed in the early Christian centuries as a place to commemorate this event. Today, it's called the Inn of the Good Samaritan.
    - The site was inhabited in the Hellenistic and Roman periods, and remains from the 1st century BC to the 1st century AD were discovered during the excavations of the Inn.

    Inn of the Good Samaritan

    - In the 6th century, a Byzantine church and monastery with pilgrim accommodations were erected on the site of what was probably some sort of travelers' hostel before the time of Jesus.
    - Later, the Crusaders built a fortress on a nearby hill to protect pilgrims against robbers.
    - The remains of the monastery later became an Ottoman Inn.
    - In the 1800s, the Ottomans built a rectangular structure over the ruins of the southern wall of the Crusader Fortress.
    - The current museum at this site was opened in 2009.

Places of Interest

1. Byzantine Church
2. Museum (has many mosaics and artifacts from around Israel)
3. Caves 1 and 2
4. Crusader Fortress

Israel Biblical Sites Travel Guide

Central Israel Sites

5. Hwy. 1
6. Jericho
7. Jerusalem
8. Ancient Road from Jericho to Jerusalem.
9. Wadi Qelt

The Story of the Good Samaritan in the Bible

1. **A lawyer (student of Scripture) tested Jesus regarding what a person had to do to receive eternal life.**

   Luke 10:25–28: *And a lawyer stood up and put Him to the test, saying, "Teacher, **what shall I do to inherit eternal life**?" 26 And He said to him, "What is written in the Law? How does it read to you?" 27 And he answered, "You shall love the Lord your God with all your heart, and with all your soul, and with all your strength, and with all your mind [Deut. 6:5]; and your neighbor as yourself [Lev. 19:18]." 28 And He said to him, "You have answered correctly; do this and you will live."*

2. **Attempting to justify himself, the lawyer asked a follow-up question about what the term "neighbor" meant.**

   Luke 10:29: *And He said to him, "You have answered correctly; do this and you will live." But wishing to justify himself, he said to Jesus, "And who is my **neighbor**?"*

3. **To illustrate who our neighbor is, Jesus told the story of the Good Samaritan.**

   Luke 10:30–34: *Jesus replied and said, "A man was **going down** from Jerusalem to Jericho, and fell among robbers, and they stripped him and beat him, and went away leaving him half dead. 31 And by chance a priest was going down*

   Inn of the Good Samaritan

   on that road, and when he saw him, he passed by on the other side. 32 Likewise, a Levite also, when he came to the place and saw him, passed by on the other side. 33 But a Samaritan who was on a journey, came upon him; and when he saw him, he felt compassion, 34 and came to him and bandaged up his wounds, pouring oil and wine on them; and he put him on his own beast, and brought him to an inn and took care of him."

- The priests were the spiritual leaders and oversaw the temple.
- The Levites were servants in the temple.
- Samaritans were unfaithful Jews who intermarried with foreign unbelievers and established their own religion.
- The Samaritans were despised and rejected by the Jews and considered unclean.
- The Samaritans, likewise, despised the Jews and had few dealings with them.
- Under the Hasmonean Reign (167-63 BC), the Jews destroyed the temple and city of the Samaritans in Shechem.
- Any traveler from Samaria would have been regarded as an alien in Judea.

Luke 10:35–37: On the next day, he took out two denarii and gave them to the innkeeper and said, "Take care of him; and whatever more you spend, when I return, I will repay you." 36 Which of these three do you think proved to be a neighbor to the man who fell into the robbers' hands? 37 And he said, "The one who showed mercy toward him." Then Jesus said to him, **"Go and do the same."**

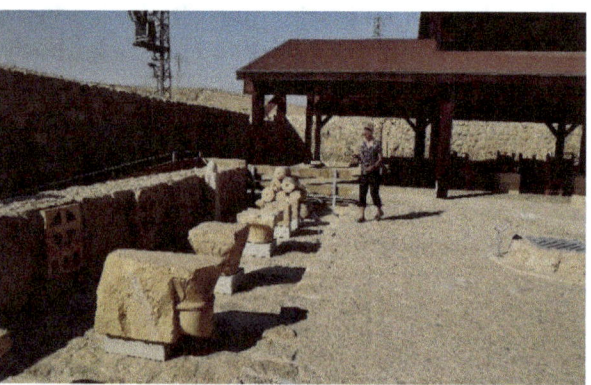

Inn of the Good Samaritan

- A denarius was about a day's wage. Today, it would be around $200 dollars for an average worker. The Samaritan gave the innkeeper two denarii for a total of $400 dollars.
- The Good Samaritan was willing to spend even more money on the hurt man, meaning that what he had already given was just a start.

Faith Lesson from the Good Samaritan

1. Our neighbor is anyone with a genuine need whom we find in our path.
2. The wounded man the Samaritan helped was not a family member, a friend, or an acquaintance; he was a total stranger.
3. The Samaritan spent a large sum of money to help heal the wounded man with no expectation or guarantee of being repaid.
4. It's not what we see but what we do that makes us a neighbor.
5. Jesus emphasized that it's not just what we believe that matters, but what we do that shows we are truly saved.
6. While we should help the wounded with physical needs, we should also help the wounded with their spiritual needs as well. The greatest need everyone has is salvation. Do we share our faith and give the greatest gift possible to those in need spiritually?

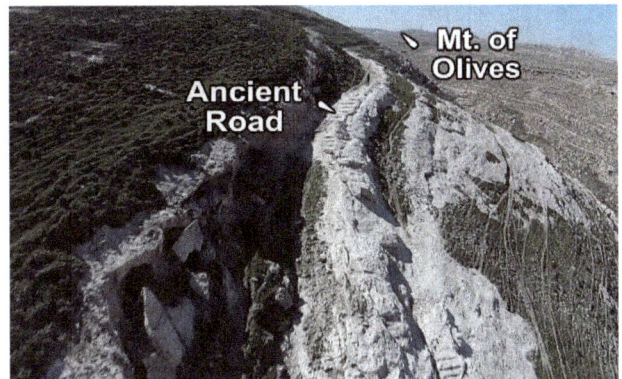

7. We should keep in mind that not every want or need others might have are legitimate.
8. God doesn't want us to reward wrong motives and laziness.

    2 Thessalonians 3:10–11: *For even when we were with you, we used to give you this order:* ***if anyone is not willing to work, then he is not to eat****, either. 11 For we hear that some among you are leading an **undisciplined life, doing no work at all**, but acting like busybodies.*

Journal/Notes:

Jericho

Location

1. Jericho is in the Jordan Valley about 8 miles (13 km.) north of the Dead Sea and about 15 miles (24 km.) east of Jerusalem.
2. It's situated at 800 ft. (244 m.) below sea level, making it the lowest city in the world.
3. Jericho claims to be the oldest city in the world that has been continuously inhabited.
4. Its name means "City of Palms."
5. It was located at the crossroads of two main travel routes. It had a north-south route that ran through the Jordan Valley, and an east-west route that connected the east side of the Jordan River with Jerusalem, the Samaritan cities, and the coastal plain cities of the Mediterranean Sea.
6. It has a year-round climate with lots of sun.
7. Tel Jericho is also known today as Tell Es-Sultan.

Historical Background

1. Jericho was a well-fortified Canaanite city before the arrival of the Israelites.
2. It's an ancient city with about 6 thousand years of history.
3. Archaeologists have uncovered 23 levels of civilizations at Tel Jericho.
4. The city was fortified with double walls.
    - The walls were constructed of large stones at the base and mud bricks continuing upwards.
    - The exterior wall's stone base was about 10–12 ft. high (3 m.), and the mud-brick wall on top of it was another 20–25 ft. tall (7

m.), for a total of around 35 ft. (11 m.).
- The inner wall was constructed the same way; only it rose even higher than the exterior wall for a total height of around 50 ft. (15 m.).
- The width of the walls were around 8 ft. (2.5 m.) wide each, and people lived between them (Josh. 2:15).
- These double walls were enormous and overwhelming in size and strength.
5. Jericho was given by Marc Antony (Roman general under Julius Caesar) to Cleopatra (Pharaoh of Egypt) as a wedding gift in 36 BC.
6. King Herod built a winter palace in Jericho around 20 BC and would later die there as well.
7. During the Byzantine period, homes and churches were built in the area.
8. During the Crusader period, the town was moved about a mile (1.6 km.) southeast of Tel Jericho.

Places of Interest in General

1. Tel Jericho
2. Mount of Temptation Monastery
3. Jericho Cable Cars – Access to Mount of Temptation Monastery.
4. Hisham's Palace – 8th century Muslim Palace.
5. Modern Jericho
6. Shittim – Place the Israelites camped on the east side of the Jordan River before entering the Promised Land.
7. Camp Gilgal – Place the Israelites camped after entering the Promised Land.
8. Zacchaeus Tree
9. Herod's Palace
10. St. George's Monastery – Hanging monastery with Cave of Elijah.
11. Baptismal Site of Jesus
12. Jordan River
13. Dead Sea

Israel Biblical Sites Travel Guide

Places of Interest at Tel Jericho

1. Elisha's Spring – Tourist viewing place.
2. Tower
3. Walls
4. Ancient Homes
5. Burn & Ash Layers
6. Palace
7. Building
8. Neolithic Tower
9. Byzantine Homes
10. Walls
11. Preserved Wall and Homes – This area is likely where Rahab lived as it was spared in the destruction by the Lord.
12. Elisha's Spring – Main source of water for Jericho.

Central Israel Sites

Archaeological Evidence at Tel Jericho that Proves the Bible is True

1. Retaining Walls
2. Fallen Mudbrick Walls
3. Preserved section of the wall where Rahab likely lived.
4. Burn Layer
5. Burnt full jars of barley.
6. The battle was short, as shown in the archaeology.
7. The battle took place in the Spring during the barley harvest.
8. Discovered abandonment layer due to Joshua's curse on Jericho.
9. Jericho was rebuilt by the Israelites during the time of King Ahab, according to Joshua's prophecy.
10. Israelite occupation layer.

Jericho in the Bible

1. **Rahab the prostitute, who hid the Israelite Spies, was from Jericho.**

   Joshua 2:1: *And Joshua the son of Nun sent two men secretly from Shittim as spies, saying, "Go, view the land, especially **Jericho**." And they went and came into the house of a prostitute whose name was **Rahab** and lodged there.*

   Joshua 2:8–15: *Before the men lay down, she came up to them on the roof, 9 and said to the men, "I know that the Lord has given you the land, and that the fear of you has fallen upon us, and that all the inhabitants of the*

   Walls where Rahab might have lived

   *land melt away before you. 10 For we have heard how the Lord dried up the water of the Red Sea before you when you came out of Egypt, and what you did to the two kings of the Amorites who were beyond the Jordan, to Sihon and Og, whom you devoted to destruction. 11 And as soon as we heard it, our hearts melted, and there was no spirit left in any man because of you, for the Lord your God, he is God in the heavens above and on the earth beneath. 12 Now then, please swear to me by the Lord that, as I have dealt kindly with you, you also will deal kindly with my father's house, and give me a sure sign 13 that you will save alive my father and mother, my brothers and sisters, and all who belong to them, and deliver our lives from death." 14 And the men said to her, "Our life for yours even to death! If you do not tell this business of ours, then when the Lord gives us the land we will deal kindly and faithfully with you." 15 Then she let them down by a rope through the window, for her house was built into the city wall, so that **she lived in the wall**.*

2. **The Children of Israel crossed the Jordan River near Jericho.**

   Joshua 3:14–16: *So when the people set out from their tents to pass over the Jordan with the priests bearing the ark of the covenant before the people, 15 and as soon as those bearing the ark had come as far as the Jordan, and the feet of the priests bearing the ark were* dipped in the brink of the water (now the Jordan overflows all its banks throughout the time of harvest), 16 the waters coming down from above stood and rose up in a heap very far away, at Adam, the city that is beside Zarethan, and those flowing down toward the Sea of the Arabah, the Salt Sea, were completely cut off. And the people passed over opposite **Jericho**.

3. **The Israelites camped at Camp Gilgal after entering the Promised Land.**

   Joshua 4:19: *The people came up out of the Jordan on the tenth day of the first month, and they encamped at **Gilgal on the east border of Jericho**.*

4. **The Israelites celebrated the Passover after crossing the Jordan River.**

   Joshua 5:10: *While the sons of Israel camped at Gilgal they celebrated the Passover on the evening of the fourteenth day of the month on the desert plains of Jericho.*

5. **Jericho was the first city captured by the Israelites when they entered the Promised Land.**

   Joshua 6:1–5: *Now **Jericho** was shut up inside and outside because of the people of Israel. None went out, and none came in. 2 And the Lord said to Joshua, "See, I have given **Jericho** into your hand, with its king and mighty men of valor. 3 You shall march around the city, all the men of war going around the city once. Thus shall you do for six days. 4 Seven priests shall bear seven trumpets of rams' horns before the ark. On the seventh day you shall march around the city seven times, and the priests shall blow the trumpets. 5 And when they make a long blast with the ram's horn, when you hear the sound of the trumpet, then all the people shall shout with a great shout, and the wall of the city will fall down flat, and the people **shall go up**, everyone straight before him."*

   Jericho had double-walled fortification

   Joshua 6:15–16: *On the seventh day they rose early, at the dawn of* day, and marched around the city in the same manner seven times. It was only on that day that they marched around the city seven times. 16 And at the seventh time, when the priests had blown the trumpets, Joshua said to the people, "Shout, for the Lord has given you the city."

Walls of Jericho

6. The mud-brick walls of Jericho fell flat (beneath themselves) and formed a ramp.

Joshua 6:20–22: *So the people shouted, and the trumpets were blown. As soon as the people heard the sound of the trumpet, the people shouted a great shout, and the wall fell down flat, so that the people went up into the city, every man straight before him, and they captured the city. 21 Then they devoted all in the city to destruction, both men and women, young and old, oxen, sheep, and donkeys, with the edge of the sword. 22 But to the two men who had spied out the land, Joshua said, "Go into the prostitute's house and bring out from there the woman and all who belong to her, as you swore to her."*

7. Joshua burned the city of Jericho with fire. Burn layer found throughout the tel.

Walls of Jericho fell flat towards the outside of the city

Joshua 6:24: *And they burned the city with fire, and everything in it.*

8. Joshua cursed Jericho, and it laid abandoned for many centuries.

This formed an abandonment layer that can be seen today.

Joshua 6:26: *Then Joshua made them take an oath at that time, saying, "Cursed before the Lord is the man who rises up and builds this city Jericho; with the loss of his firstborn he will lay its foundation, and with the loss of his youngest son he will set up its gates."*

9. **Jericho was rebuilt during the time of King Ahab around 875 BC.**

   1 Kings 16:34: *In his days Hiel the Bethelite rebuilt Jericho; he laid its foundations with the loss of Abiram his firstborn, and set up its gates with the loss of his youngest son Segub, in accordance with the word of the Lord, which He spoke by Joshua the son of Nun.*

10. **The prophets, Elijah and Elisha, traversed in Jericho often.**

    2 Kings 2:4: *Elijah said to him, "Elisha, please stay here, for the LORD has sent me to **Jericho**." But he said, "As the LORD lives, and as you yourself live, I will not leave you." So they came to **Jericho**.*

11. **Elisha healed the water source of Jericho.**

    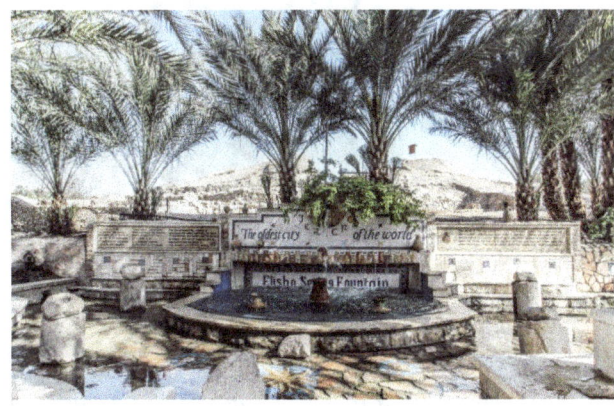

    Elisha's Spring

    2 Kings 2:19–22: *Now the men of the city said to Elisha, "Behold, the situation of this city is pleasant, as my lord sees, but the water is bad, and the land is unfruitful." 20 He said, "Bring me a new bowl, and put salt in it." So they brought it to him. 21 Then he went to the spring of water and threw salt in it and said, "Thus says the LORD, I have healed this water; from now*

on neither death nor miscarriage shall come from it." 22 So the water has been healed to this day, according to the word that Elisha spoke.

12. The miracle of a blind man healed by Jesus occurred in Jericho.

Luke 18:35–43: *As he [Jesus] drew near to **Jericho**, a blind man was sitting by the roadside begging. 36 And hearing a crowd going by, he inquired what this meant. 37 They told him, "Jesus of Nazareth is passing by." 38 And he cried out, "Jesus, Son of David, have mercy on me!" 39 And those who were in front rebuked him, telling him to be silent. But he cried out all the more, "Son of David, have mercy on me!" 40 And Jesus stopped and commanded him to be brought to him. And when he came near, he asked him, 41 "What do you want me to do for you?" He said, "Lord, let me recover my sight." 42 And Jesus said to him, "Recover your sight; your faith has made you well." 43 And immediately he recovered his sight and followed him, glorifying God. And all the people, when they saw it, gave praise to God.*

13. Zacchaeus, the Tax Collector, was from Jericho.

Luke 19:1–10: *He [Jesus] entered **Jericho** and was passing through. 2 And there was a man named Zacchaeus. He was a chief tax collector and was rich. 3 And he was seeking to see who Jesus was, but on*

Tel Jericho

account of the crowd he could not, because he was small of stature. 4 So he ran on ahead and climbed up into a sycamore tree to see him, for he was about to pass that way. 5 And when Jesus came to the place, he looked up and said to him, "Zacchaeus, hurry and come down, for I must stay at your house today." 6 So he hurried and came down and received him joyfully. 7 And when they saw it, they all grumbled, "He has gone in to be the guest of a man who is a sinner." 8 And Zacchaeus stood and said to the Lord, "Behold, Lord, the half of my goods I give to the poor. And if I have defrauded anyone of anything, I restore it fourfold." 9 And Jesus said to him, "Today salvation has come to this house, since he also is a son of Abraham. 10 For the Son of Man came to seek and to save the lost."

14. **The famous story of the Good Samaritan happened on the route from Jericho to Jerusalem (Luke 10:25-37).**

Faith Lesson from Jericho

1. The crumbling of the walls of Jericho by the shout of the Israelites proves to be one of the greatest miracles in the Bible. Do we believe God can crumble the obstacles in our lives today as well?
2. Rahab was a sinner who chose to fear the Lord and turn to Him. She was welcomed into the Jewish faith and became part of the lineage of Christ, along with Ruth the Moabitess.

    Matthew 1:5-6: *And Salmon the father of Boaz by **Rahab**, and Boaz the father of Obed by **Ruth**, and Obed the father of Jesse, 6 and Jesse the father of David the king.*

    Amazingly, in the genealogy of Christ, two generations in a row include foreign women who were saved by grace through faith and welcomed into the Jewish faith.
3. The lives of Rahab and Ruth illustrate that salvation has always been and always will be open to anyone willing to listen to God's call of salvation.
4. Jesus healed a blind man in Jericho because of his persevering faith. What about us? What kind of faith do we have in Christ? Do we give up easily, or do we persevere?
5. Zacchaeus, the Tax Collector, was another outsider who was willing to embrace Christ's love and offer of salvation. Jericho resounds with examples of outsiders who were rejected by others but sought out by God. Do we believe God loves outsiders today, and do we welcome them into our lives and churches?

Journal/Notes:

Joppa (Jaffa, Yafo)

Location

1. Joppa (Jaffa, Yafo) is one of the oldest port cities in the land of Israel and the Mediterranean area.
2. It's located on a hill and has a strategic location on the crossroads of Israel and the main travel route linking Africa with Asia and Europe. This travel route was called the "Via Maris."
3. Joppa is about 45 miles (72 km.) west of Jerusalem.

Historical Background

1. Legend holds that the founder of Joppa (also called Jaffa) was Japheth, one of Noah's sons.
2. Joppa was inhabited by the Canaanites, the Egyptians, the Israelites, the Greeks, Romans, and others.
3. Joppa was the main seaport and entry gate to Israel for thousands of years until just before the time of Christ when Herod the Great built another seaport at Caesarea, about 35 miles (56 km.) north of Joppa.

Places of Interest

1. House of Simon the Tanner
2. St. Peter's Church
3. Ramses II Fortress, built in about 1250 BC.
4. Old Port of Joppa
5. Suspended Orange Tree
6. Abrasha Park
7. Alma Beach

8. Llana Goor Museum
9. Tel Joppa
10. Old City Joppa
11. Jaffa Museum

Joppa in the Bible

1. **The seaport of Joppa is where the trees of Lebanon arrived that Solomon used to build the Temple in Jerusalem around 950 BC.**

   2 Chronicles 2:16: Hiram king of Tyre replied by letter to Solomon: *"And we will cut whatever timber you need from Lebanon and bring it to you in rafts by sea to **Joppa**, so that you may take it up to Jerusalem."*

2. **Joppa was also the seaport from which King Solomon's ships came and went on their journeys around the known world.**

3. **Joppa was the seaport from which Jonah sailed when he attempted to disobey the Lord's calling and flee to Tarshish rather than preach a message of repentance to the Ninevites.**

Jonah 1:3: *But Jonah rose to flee to Tarshish from the presence of the LORD. He went down to **Joppa** and found a ship going to Tarshish. So, he paid the fare and went on board, to go with them to Tarshish, away from the presence of the LORD.*

4. **Joppa was the seaport where logs arrived for rebuilding the second temple after the return of the Israelites from their deportations in about 535 BC.**

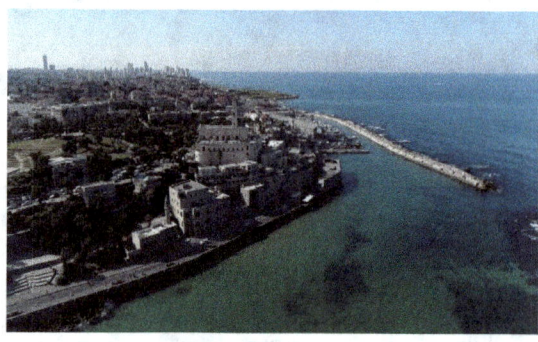

Ezra 3:7: *So they gave money to the masons and the carpenters, and food, drink, and oil to the Sidonians and the Tyrians to bring cedar trees from Lebanon to the sea, to **Joppa**, according to the grant that they had from Cyrus king of Persia.*

5. **After preaching to the Ethiopian Eunuch, Philip the Evangelist passed through Joppa preaching the gospel on his way to Caesarea.**

Acts 8:39–40: *When they came up out of the water, the Spirit of the Lord snatched Philip away; and the eunuch no longer saw him, but went on his way rejoicing. 40 But Philip found himself at Azotus (modern-day Ashdod), and as he passed through, he kept preaching the gospel to all the cities until he came to Caesarea.*

6. **Joppa was the place a famous woman, Dorcas, lived and was raised from the dead.**

Acts 9:36–43: *Now there was in **Joppa** a disciple named Tabitha, which, translated, means Dorcas. She was full of good works and acts of charity. 37 In those days she became ill and died, and when they had washed her, they laid her in an upper room. 38 Since Lydda was near **Joppa**, the disciples, hearing that Peter was there, sent two men to him, urging him, "Please come to us without delay." 39 So, Peter rose and went with them. And when he arrived, they took him to the upper room. All the widows stood beside him weeping and showing tunics and other garments that Dorcas made while she was with them. 40 But Peter put them all outside, and knelt down and prayed; and turning to the body he said, "Tabitha, arise." And she opened her eyes, and when she saw Peter she sat up. 41 And he gave* *her his hand and raised her up. Then calling the saints and widows, he presented her alive. 42 And it became known throughout all **Joppa**, and many believed in the Lord. 43 And he stayed in **Joppa** for many days with one Simon, a tanner.*

7. **Simon the Tanner lived in Joppa, and it was the place the Apostle Peter was staying when he received the vision to take the Gospel to the Gentiles.**

Acts 10:9–15: *The next day, as they were on their journey and approaching the city, Peter went up on the housetop about the sixth hour to pray. 10 And he became hungry and wanted something to eat, but while they were preparing it, he fell into a trance 11 and saw the heavens opened and something like a great sheet descending, being let down by its four corners upon the earth. 12 In it were all kinds of animals and reptiles and birds of the air. 13 And there came a voice to him: "Rise, Peter; kill and eat." 14 But Peter said, "By no means, Lord; for I have never eaten anything that is common or unclean." 15 And the voice came to him again a second time, "What God has made clean, do not call common."*

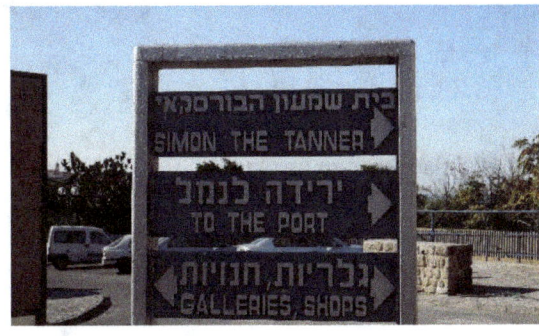

Faith Lesson from Joppa

1. Jonah disobeyed the Lord here and ran from the presence of the Lord. Are we running away from something God wants us to do?
2. Peter obeyed the Lord here, trusted in God, and took the gospel to the Gentiles in Caesarea. Are we taking the gospel to those around us?
3. When we obey, we find life, and when we disobey, we find destruction and problems. What kind of problems are we facing because of some area of disobedience in our lives?

Journal/Notes:

Jordan River: Baptismal Site of Jesus

Location

There are two main baptismal sites on the Jordan River.

Qasr al-Yahud Baptismal Site

1. It's located about 2 miles (3.2 km.) east of Hwy. 90, across from Jericho.
2. It's also known as Qaser al-Yahud, Kasser al-Yahud, and the Baptismal Site of Jesus.
3. It's the believed place where Jesus was baptized, and where John the Baptist and the disciples of Jesus baptized many people as well.
4. The water is not quite as clean as Yardenit, but thousands of pilgrims are baptized here each year because of its spiritual significance.
5. It's also the believed location where the Israelites crossed the Jordan River to enter the Promised Land.
6. For those desiring to get baptized here in the Jordan River, the Qsar al-Yahud gift shop provides white robes and towels for a small fee.
7. Qsar al-Yahud also has a gift shop for the purchase of souvenirs and other miscellaneous items.

Yardenit Baptismal Site

1. Yardenit is just a couple hundred yards (meters) west of Hwy. 90, at the southern tip of the Sea of Galilee.
2. It's a popular spot, and the water is clean and abundant.
3. For those desiring to get baptized in the Jordan River at Yardenit, their gift shop provides white robes and towels for a small fee.
4. Yardenit has a large gift shop for the purchase of souvenirs and other miscellaneous items as well.

   (For more, please see Yardenit Baptismal Site.)

Central Israel Sites

Historical Background

1. The concept of baptism is rooted in the Old Testament. As far back as Genesis, eight people were saved from the great flood of God's judgment. The Apostle Peter indicated that the water of the flood "symbolizes baptism that now saves you" (1 Pet. 3:21).

Qasr al-Yahud Baptismal Site – Jordanian sites in background

2. Old Testament prophets such as Isaiah, Ezekiel, and David likewise used water as an external symbol for internal cleansing (Isa. 1:16; Ezek. 36:25; Ps. 51:2).

    Isaiah 1:16: *Wash yourselves; make yourselves clean; remove the evil of your deeds from before my eyes; cease to do evil.*

3. The word baptize, baptized, or baptismal is mentioned around 72 times in the New Testament and, therefore, shows the value God places upon it.

Places of Interest

1. Qasr al-Yahud Baptismal Site
2. Hwy. 90
3. Jew's Palace (Castle of the Jews)
4. Jordanian Baptismal Site of Jesus
5. St. John the Baptist Romanian Church: On the Jordanian Site of the river.
6. Original Church of John the Baptist. There have been at least 5 churches built at this location dating back to the first and second centuries AD.
7. Cave of John the Baptist
8. Greek Orthodox Church of St John the Baptist

9. The believed location where the Israelites crossed the Jordan River to enter the Promised Land.
10. This area is also associated with the ascension of the Prophet Elijah into heaven, which is commemorated at a hill called Tell Mar Elias or Jabal Mar-Elias (Elijah's Hill).

Baptism in the Bible

1. Baptism in the Old Testament.

Baptism in the Old Testament had a different name and purpose than believers' baptism in the New Testament.

- It served as a purification ritual that happened regularly.
- Before entering the temple, a synagogue, or any religious building, the Jews would purify themselves (ritual cleansing) in Mikvahs (purification pools).
- They also purified themselves before the Sabbath, feast days, and so forth. Purification for a Jew was a regular part of life.
- Purification involved confession of sin, entering a pool of water, immersing oneself completely, and putting on a new change of clothes. Mikvahs were found everywhere, and some of the wealthier population had their own private mikvahs.

2. **The Baptism of John the Baptist.**

   John's baptism picked up on this Jewish concept and took it a step further. His baptism was primarily a baptism of repentance in preparation for the coming Messiah.

   Matthew 3:1–6: *In those days John the Baptist came preaching in the wilderness of Judea, 2 "Repent, for the kingdom of heaven is at hand." 3 For this is he who was spoken of by the prophet Isaiah when he said, "The voice of one crying in the wilderness: 'Prepare the way of the Lord; make his paths straight.'" 4 Now John wore a garment of camel's hair and a leather belt around his waist, and his food was locusts and wild honey. 5 Then Jerusalem and all Judea and all the region about the Jordan were going out to him, 6 and they were **baptized** by him in the river Jordan, **confessing their sins**.*

3. **Jesus was baptized by John.**

   Matthew 3:13–17: *Then Jesus came from Galilee to the Jordan to John, to be **baptized** by him. 14 John would have prevented him, saying, "I need to be **baptized** by you, and do you come to me?" 15 But Jesus answered him, "Let it be so now, for thus it is fitting for us to fulfill all righteousness." Then he consented. 16 And when **Jesus was baptized**, immediately he went up from the water, and behold, the heavens were opened to him, and he saw the Spirit of God descending like a dove and coming to rest on him; 17 and behold, a voice from heaven said, "This is my beloved Son, with whom I am well pleased."*

   Qasr al-Yahud Baptismal Site

4. **Why did Jesus get baptized if He was God in the flesh and perfect? After all, the purpose of Baptism in Jesus' day was a baptism of repentance.**

   - Jesus permitted John the Baptist to baptize Him in order to fulfill all righteousness.

- He was setting an example for all to follow.
- Jesus didn't repent of anything because He was perfect.
- It also allowed God to speak audibly and show His pleasure and affirmation of Christ as the Son of God.

5. **Jesus' baptism of others.**

   The message and baptism of Jesus dealt with repentance from sin and acceptance of Himself as the Messiah.

   - Matthew 4:17: *From that time Jesus began to preach, saying, "Repent, for the kingdom of heaven is at hand."*
   - John 4:1–3: *Now when Jesus learned that the Pharisees had heard that Jesus was making and **baptizing** more disciples than John 2 (although Jesus himself did not baptize, but only his disciples), 3 he left Judea and departed again for Galilee.*

6. **Baptism in the rest of the New Testament.**

   Baptism always followed salvation and was an outward proclamation of an inner conversion.

   - On the day of Pentecost, 3,000 people were saved and were baptized. They would have used the existing Jewish mikvahs as baptismal pools.

     Acts 2:41: *So those who received his word were **baptized**, and there were added that day about three thousand souls.*

   - Baptism was an act of obedience symbolizing the believer's faith in a crucified, buried, and risen Savior.

   Romans 6:1–4: *What shall we say then? Are we to continue in sin that grace may abound? 2 By no means! How can we who died to sin still live in it? 3 Do you not know that all of us who have been **baptized** into Christ Jesus were **baptized** into his death? 4 We were buried therefore with him by **baptism** into death, in order*

that, just as Christ was raised from the dead by the glory of the Father, we too might walk in newness of life.

- In the same way Jesus died, was buried, and rose again to new life, baptism follows this same pattern. The believer's placement under the water symbolizes burial and death to sin, and rising up out of the water symbolizes new life in Christ.
- Baptism does not save us in and of itself; it follows salvation and expresses what has already taken place in the heart of a believer.
- Baptism is a declaration to others that we are identifying ourselves with Christ and are now one of His disciples.
- Baptism is commanded in many passages of the Bible, and unless we are unable to do so for some unique reason, we should get baptized.

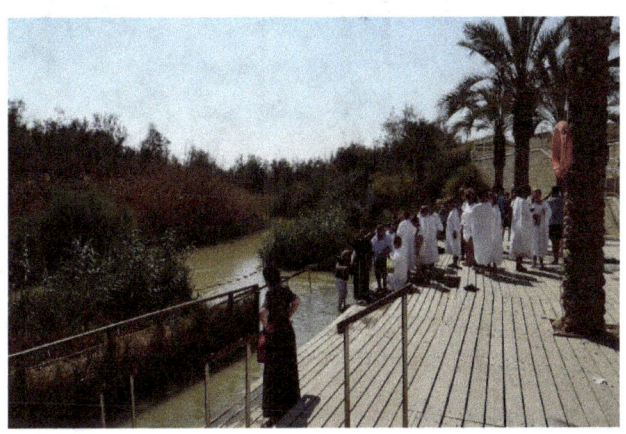

Matthew 28:18-20: *And Jesus came and said to them, "All authority in heaven and on earth has been given to me. 19 Go therefore and make disciples of all nations,* **baptizing them** *in the name of the Father and of the Son and of the Holy Spirit, 20 teaching them to observe all that I have commanded you. And behold, I am with you always, to the end of the age."*

Acts 2:37-38: *Now when they heard this they were cut to the heart, and said to Peter and the rest of the apostles, "Brothers, what shall we do?" 38 And Peter said to them, "Repent and be* **baptized** *every one of you in the name of Jesus Christ for the forgiveness of your sins, and you will receive the gift of the Holy Spirit."*

Faith Lesson on Baptism

1. Jesus didn't need to be baptized but did so in order to be an example for us to follow.
2. If we are genuine believers in Christ and have not been baptized, we should do so in order to obey Christ.
3. Baptism does not save us in and of itself, but when connected with our faith in Christ, it cleanses us of sin, identifies us with the death, burial, and resurrection of Christ, and declares to others that we are followers of Christ.
4. Baptism symbolizes our newness of life in Christ and that we are now dead to being controlled and defeated by sin.

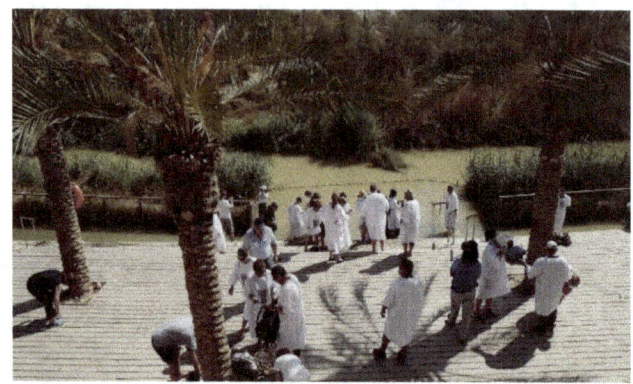

Romans 6:4: *We were buried therefore with him by* **baptism** *into death, in order that, just as Christ was raised from the dead by the glory of the Father,* ***we too might walk in newness of life***.

Journal/Notes:

Central Israel Sites

Jordan River: Crossing into the Promised Land

Location

1. The crossing place where the Israelites entered the Promised Land is just opposite Jericho.
2. It's amazing that it's in the same area where John the Baptist baptized many and where John baptized Jesus.
3. Today, it's known as Qasr el Yahud (Kasser Al Yahud, Qaser), the Baptismal Site of Jesus.
4. It's about 2 miles (3.2 km.) east of Hwy. 90, opposite Jericho.

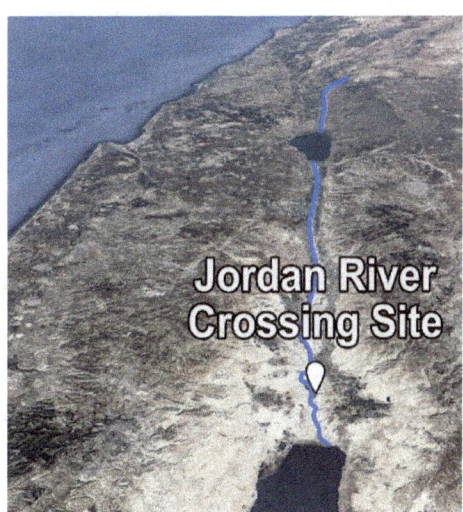

Historical Background

1. The nation of Israel spent 430 years in Egypt. Four hundred of these years, they were slaves (Gen. 15:13), and for 30 years, they enjoyed peace during the time Joseph was alive.
2. God supernaturally delivered the Israelites out of the hands of the Egyptians through Moses.
3. After the Exodus, they crossed the Red Sea on dry ground.
4. They spent a year at Mount Sinai receiving the Law and then headed to Kadesh Barnea to enter the Promised Land.
5. After the 12 spies returned from scouting out the land, 10 spies convinced the people that the inhabitants of the land were too strong for them to conquer, and they should return to Egypt (Num. 13:25–33).
6. Because of their unbelief and disobedience, they were banned from entering the Promised Land and ordered to wander in the desert 40 years until every person 20 years old, and older died (Num. 14:20–25).
7. During the 40 years of wandering in the desert, entering the

Promised Land became a deep yearning within the souls of the new generation. Day after day, they dreamt about a new life in the Promised Land, which would bring an end to their seemingly vain wandering in the desert eating Manna day after day.

8. After 40 long years, they were poised to enter the Promised Land, and their hearts were overflowing with enthusiasm and expectation as the time had finally arrived.

Jordan River crossing location

9. The word "Hebrew" means to cross over. Abraham crossed over from false gods to the one and only true God. He crossed over physically by leaving his homeland and coming to the Promised Land. The Israelites were delivered by God from the Egyptians as they crossed through the Red Sea, and then crossed through the Jordan River into the Promised Land. All these acts are pictures of deliverance and salvation. We also cross over from death to life through Christ.

Places of Interest

1. Crossing Site of the Israelites into the Promised Land.
2. Baptismal Site of Jesus – Believed place where Jesus was baptized and where many are baptized today.
3. Adam – The place where the waters of the Jordan backed up to when the Israelites crossed the river (20 miles, 32 km., above the crossing site).
4. Shittim
5. Camp Gilgal
6. Jericho

Crossing the Jordan River in the Bible

1. **Before entering the Promised Land, the Israelites camped on the east side of the Jordan River, opposite Jericho.**

   Joshua 3:1: *Then Joshua rose early in the morning, and they set out from **Shittim**. And they came to the **Jordan**, he and all the people of Israel, and lodged there before they passed over.*

2. **The Israelites crossed the Jordan River on dry ground as God miraculously parted the waters.**

   Joshua 3:14–17: *So when the people set out from their tents to pass over the **Jordan** with the priests bearing the ark of the covenant before the people, 15 and as soon as those bearing the ark had come as far as the **Jordan**, and the **feet of the priests** bearing the ark were dipped in the brink of the water (**now the Jordan overflows all its banks throughout the time of harvest**), 16 the waters coming down from above stood and rose up in a heap very far away, at **Adam** [20 miles, 32 km. north], the city that is beside Zarethan, and those flowing down toward the Sea of the Arabah, the Salt Sea [Dead Sea], were completely cut off. And the people passed over opposite Jericho. 17 Now the priests bearing the ark of the covenant of the Lord stood firmly on dry ground **in the midst of the Jordan**,* *and all Israel was passing over on dry ground until all the nation finished passing over the **Jordan**.*

Using the geographical layout of the land from Adam to the crossing of the Jordan site, the body of water that would have accumulated would have been 20 miles (32 km.) long, 2 miles (3.2 km.) wide, and around 120 ft. (37 m.) high.

3. God ordered that 12 stones be taken out of the Jordan River for a monument.

*Joshua 4:1-7: When all the nation had finished passing over the **Jordan**, the Lord said to Joshua, 2 "Take twelve men from the people, from each tribe a man, 3 and command them, saying, 'Take twelve stones from here out of the midst of the Jordan, from the very place where the priests' feet stood firmly, and bring them over with you and lay them down in the place where you lodge tonight [Gilgal].'" 4 Then Joshua called the twelve men from the people of Israel, whom he had appointed, a man from each tribe. 5 And Joshua said to them, "Pass on before the ark of the Lord your God into the midst of the **Jordan**, and take up each of you a stone upon his shoulder,* *according to the number of the tribes of the people of Israel, 6 that this may be a sign among you. When your children ask in time to come, 'What do those stones mean to you?' 7 then you shall tell them that the waters of the Jordan were cut off before the ark of the covenant of the Lord. When it passed over the **Jordan**, the waters of the **Jordan** were cut off. So these stones shall be to the people of Israel a memorial forever."*

It appears that the 12-Stone Monument was later moved to the permanent Gilgal located about 7 miles north of Camp Gilgal. For more, please see Gilgal.

4. **Joshua also erected a monument in the middle of the Jordan River.**

Jordan River crossing location

Joshua 4:9–10: *And Joshua set up twelve stones in the **midst of the Jordan**, in the place where the feet of the priests bearing the ark of the covenant had stood; and they are there to this day. 10 For the priests bearing the ark stood in the midst of the Jordan until everything was finished that the Lord commanded Joshua to tell the people, according to all that Moses had commanded Joshua.*

5. **After crossing the river, the water flowed again, and the Israelites arrived at Camp Gilgal.**

Joshua 4:15–19: *And the Lord said to Joshua, 16 "Command the priests bearing the ark of the testimony to come up out of the Jordan." 17 So Joshua commanded the priests, "Come up out of the Jordan." 18 And when the priests bearing the ark of the covenant of the Lord came up from the **midst of the Jordan**, and the soles of the priests' feet were lifted up on dry ground, the waters of the Jordan returned to their place and **overflowed all its banks, as before**. 19 The people came up out of the **Jordan** on the tenth day of the first month, and they encamped at **Gilgal** on the east border of Jericho.*

6. Joshua set up 12 stones as a monument of remembrance.

Joshua 4:20–24: *And those twelve stones, which they took out of the **Jordan**, Joshua set up at Gilgal. 21 And he said to the people of Israel, "When your children ask their fathers in times to come, 'What do these stones mean?' 22 then you shall let your children know, 'Israel passed over this Jordan on dry ground.' 23 For the Lord your God dried up the waters of the Jordan for you until you passed over, as the Lord your God **did to the Red Sea**, which he dried up for us until we passed over, 24 so that all the peoples of the earth may know that the hand of the Lord is mighty, that you may fear the Lord your God forever."*

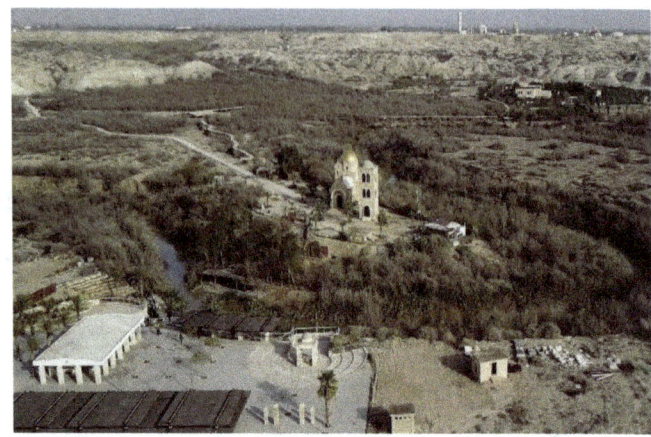
Jordan River crossing location

Faith Lesson from Crossing the Jordan River

1. Entering the Promised Land was a long-awaited dream for the new generation of Israelites after wandering in the desert for 40 years. It was also the fulfillment of the Abrahamic Covenant of promise, one of the foundational covenants in the Bible. Is there some hope and dream you have that seems like it will never happen? Do you also really believe that God will fulfill His promise of heaven and that one day you'll actually be there? And are you living in such a way that shows this?

2. Crossing into the Promised Land is also a picture of living in victory. Unfortunately, many Christians today choose to live in the wilderness in defeat and disobedience. Are you living in obedience and victory or living in the wilderness?

3. The crossing of the Jordan was a much bigger miracle than we think as the river was at flood stage, overflowing its banks. As mentioned, the body of water that would have accumulated would

Central Israel Sites

have been 20 miles (32 km.) long, 2 miles (3.2 km.) wide, and around 120 ft. (37 m.) high. This was a massive body and wall of water the 3 million or more Israelites would have witnessed as they walked alongside it for about 2 miles (3.2 km.).

4. The miracle was similar to the crossing of the Red Sea after the Israelite's Exodus from Egypt. God repeated this miracle to reveal His glory and faithfulness.

5. The waters of the Jordan stopped flowing the moment the priests' stepped into the water. God required the priests to take a step of faith, and then He acted.

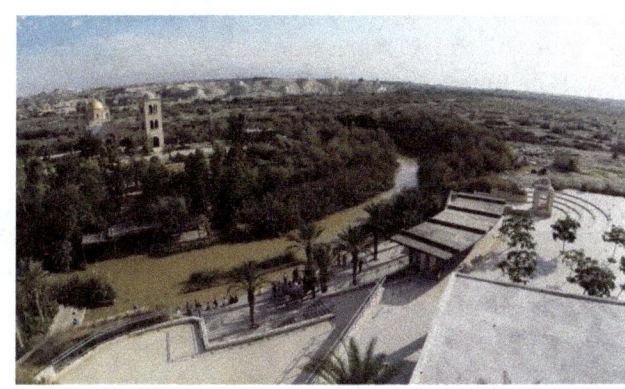
Jordan River crossing location

In the same way, God often asks us to take a step of faith before He moves. What step of faith do we need to take in our lives today?

6. God ordered Joshua to set up a memorial after crossing the Jordan. Do we have memorials in our minds as reminders of the miracles God has done for us, and do we pass these memorials on to our offspring?

Journal/Notes:

Judean Wilderness

Location

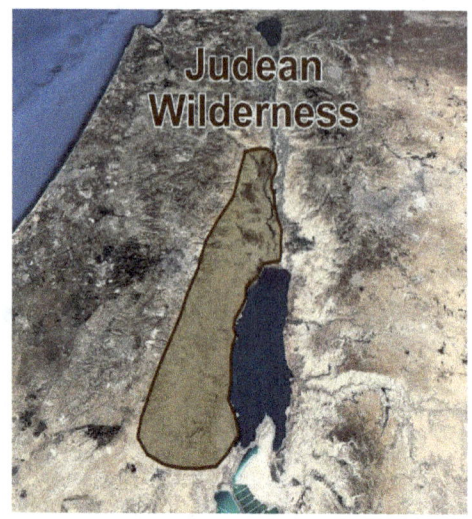

1. The Judean Wilderness runs from north of Jericho to the southern end of the Dead Sea.
2. It lies on the western side of the lower Jordan Valley and the Dead Sea area.
3. It's about 60 miles (95 km.) long and about 13 miles (21 km.) wide.
4. It receives less than 2 inches (50 mm.) of rain per year.
5. Average high temperatures in the winter run in the 70s (21 C.), and highs in the summer run over 100 (40 C.).
6. Water is scarce and hard to find, and very little vegetation grows in the wilderness due to its lack of water and poor soil composition.

Historical Background

1. Even though the Judean Desert is dry and barren, it was settled long before recorded history began. Jericho, which dates to 5000 BC, is the oldest city in the Judean Desert and the oldest continually inhabited city in the world.
2. En Gedi is another notable place that dates to about the same time as Jericho. It's a large oasis that had cities built around it for over 5,000 years.
3. Sodom, Gomorrah, and the other three cities around the Dead Sea date back to ancient times as well.
4. It appears God changed the climate of the Judean Wilderness after He destroyed Sodom and Gomorrah and the surrounding cities. Scripture says that this area used to be like a watered garden of the Lord.

    Genesis 13:10: *And Lot lifted up his eyes and saw that the Jordan*

*Valley was **well watered everywhere like the garden of the Lord**, like the land of Egypt, in the direction of Zoar. (This was before the **Lord destroyed Sodom and Gomorrah**.)*

5. God will cause the Judean Wilderness to flourish again during the Millennial Reign of Christ on this earth.

   Ezekiel 47:6–10: *Then he led me back to the bank of the river. 7 As I went back, I saw on the bank of the river very many trees on the one side and on the other. 8 And he said to me, "This water flows toward the eastern region and goes down into the Arabah, and enters the sea; when the water flows into the sea, the water will become fresh. 9 And wherever the river goes, every living creature that swarms will live, and there will be very many fish. For this water goes there, that the waters of the sea may become fresh; so everything will live where the river goes. 10 Fishermen will stand beside the sea. From **En Gedi to Eneglaim** it will be a place for the spreading of nets."*

Places of Interest

1. Judean Wilderness
2. Jordan River

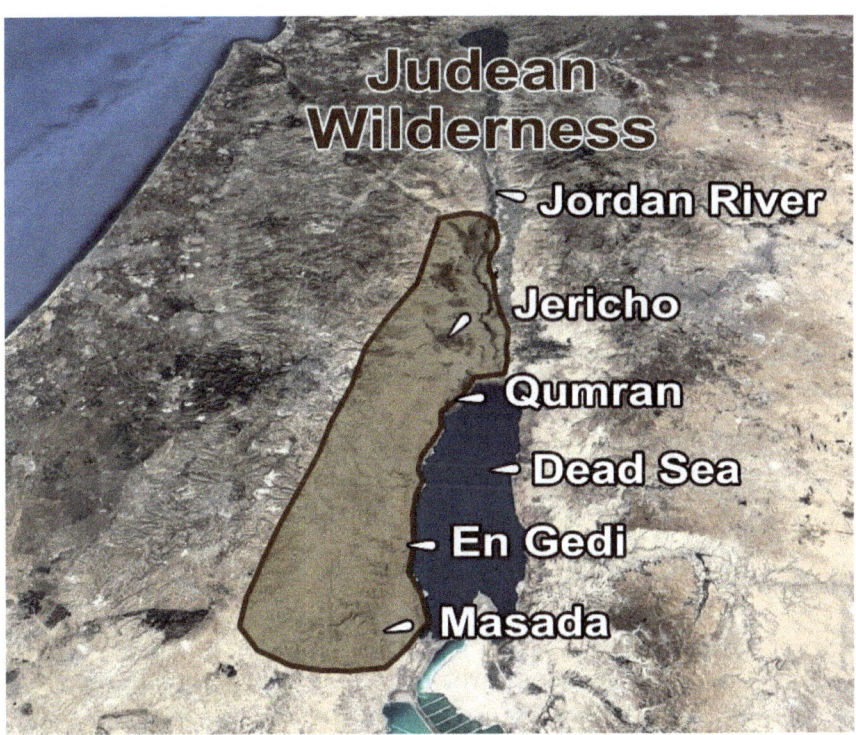

3. Jericho
4. Qumran
5. Dead Sea
6. En Gedi
7. Masada

Judean Wilderness in the Bible

En Gedi and King David

1. **En Gedi was one of David's main hideouts when Saul was pursuing his life.**

   1 Samuel 23:28-29: *So Saul returned from pursuing after David and went against the Philistines. Therefore, that place was called the Rock of Escape. 29 And David went up from there and lived in the* **strongholds of En Gedi**.

Qumran and the Essenes

1. The Essenes lived in the Judean Wilderness from about 200 BC to around 68 AD. They were a spiritually devoted group who left Jerusalem due to their belief that the priesthood had become corrupt. They devoted themselves to the study and strict obedience of Scripture.

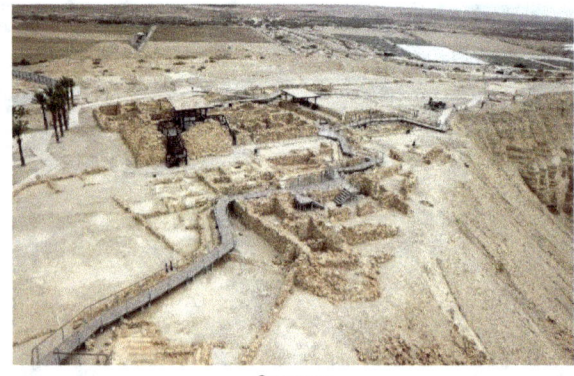
Qumran

2. They also devoted themselves to copying and translating the Bible. When they saw the nation of Israel falling to the Romans in 68 AD, they hid their translations in caves by the Dead Sea.

3. These translated manuscripts are called the Dead Sea Scrolls and were discovered in eleven caves along the northwest shore of the Dead Sea between the years 1947 and 1956.

John the Baptist

1. **He was the prophesied forerunner of Christ, whose purpose was to prepare the way of the Lord (Isa. 40:3).**

2. His main message was a message of repentance.

Matthew 3:1-12: *In those days John the Baptist came preaching in the **wilderness of Judea**, 2 "Repent, for the kingdom of heaven is at hand." 3 For this is he who was spoken of by the prophet Isaiah when he said, "The voice of one **crying in the wilderness**: 'Prepare the way of the Lord; make his paths straight.'" 4 Now John wore a garment of camel's hair and a leather belt around his waist [similar to Elijah], and his food was locusts and wild honey. 5 Then Jerusalem and all Judea and all the region about the Jordan were going out to him, 6 and they were baptized by him in the river Jordan, confessing their sins. 7 But when he saw many of the Pharisees and Sadducees coming to his baptism, he said to them, "You brood of vipers! Who warned you to flee from the wrath to come? 8 Bear fruit in keeping with repentance. 9 And do not presume to say to yourselves, 'We have Abraham as our father,' for I tell you, God is able from these stones to raise up children for Abraham. 10 Even*

Judean Wilderness

now the axe is laid to the root of the trees. Every tree, therefore, that does not bear good fruit is cut down and thrown into the fire. 11 I baptize you with water for repentance, but he who is coming after me is mightier than I, whose sandals I am not worthy to carry. He will baptize you with the Holy Spirit and fire. 12 His winnowing fork is in his hand, and he will clear his threshing floor and gather his wheat into the barn, but the chaff he will burn with unquenchable fire."

3. He had the privilege of baptizing Jesus.

Matthew 3:13-17: *Then Jesus came from Galilee to the Jordan to John, to be **baptized by him**. 14 John would have prevented him, saying, "I need to be baptized by you, and do you come to me?" 15 But Jesus answered him, "Let it be so now, for thus it is fitting for us to fulfill all righteousness." Then he consented. 16 And when Jesus was baptized, immediately he went up from the water, 17 and behold, the heavens were opened to him, and he saw the Spirit of God descending like a dove and coming to rest on him; and behold, a* voice from heaven said, "This is my beloved Son, with whom I am well pleased."

4. He was beheaded for taking a stand against sin.

Herod Antipas became the ruler (tetrarch) of Galilee and Perea from 4 BC to 39 AD. He ruled from his capital at Tiberias on the western shore of the Sea of Galilee. He divorced his first wife in order to marry Herodias, the wife of his half-brother Herod Philip. He imprisoned and beheaded John the Baptist for criticizing his marriage (Matt. 14:1–12).

Testing of Jesus

1. After Jesus was baptized, He was immediately led into the wilderness to be tested.

Matthew 4:1–11: *Then Jesus was led up by the Spirit* **into the wilderness** *to be tempted [tested] by the devil. 2 And after fasting forty days and forty nights, he was hungry. 3 And the tempter came and said to him, "If you are the Son of God, command these stones to become loaves of bread." 4 But he answered, "It is written,*

Judean Wilderness

"'Man shall not live by bread alone, but by every word that comes from the mouth of God.'" 5 Then the devil took him to the holy city and set him on the pinnacle of the temple 6 and said to him, "If you are the Son of God, throw yourself down, for it is written, "'He will command his angels concerning you,' and "'On their hands they will bear you up, lest you strike your foot against a stone.'" 7 Jesus said to him, "Again it is written, 'You shall not put the Lord your God to the test.'" 8 Again, the devil took him to a very high mountain and showed him all the kingdoms of the world and their glory. 9 And he said to him, "All these I will give you, if you will fall down and worship me." 10 Then Jesus said to him, "Be gone, Satan! For it is written, "'You shall worship the Lord your God and him only shall you serve.'" 11 Then the devil left him, and behold, angels came and were ministering to him.

Faith Lesson from the Judean Wilderness

1. John the Baptist was a strong and serious witness for Jesus. John's life is an example to us of the seriousness with which we are to approach the Christian life and our call to ministry.

Judean Wilderness, Dead Sea

2. John shows us how to stand firm in our faith no matter what the circumstances. Paul reminds us that "everyone who wants to live a godly life in Christ Jesus will be persecuted" (2 Tim. 3:12).
3. Christ was tested and overcame each test of Satan with Scripture.
4. God tested many of His servants before He called them to ministry, i.e., Moses, David, and the prophets.
5. We are often tested by God as well.
6. Scripture says that leaders are to be tested before being placed into ministry (1 Tim. 3:10).
7. Has God tested me in various ways in my lifetime?
8. How have I responded to the tests He sends my way?
9. Do I know God's Word so I can overcome the temptations of Satan?

Journal/Notes:

Qumran and the Dead Sea Scrolls

Location

1. Qumran is located on the northwest side of the Dead Sea on Hwy. 90 about 13 miles (21 km.) east of Jerusalem.
2. It's in the Judean Wilderness, where it's barren and hot.
3. It's located 1200 ft. (366 m.) below sea level.
4. Its water source comes from the Judean Mountains to the west of the community via an aqueduct.

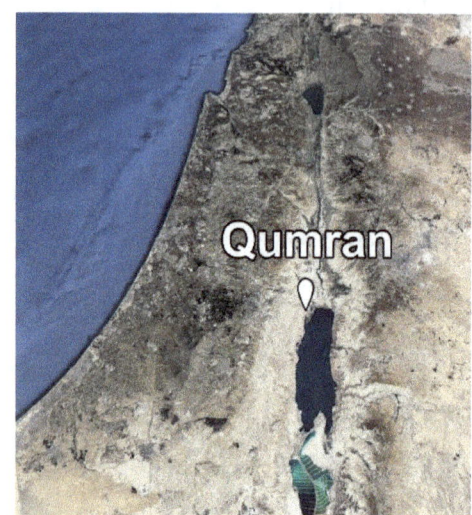

5. There are many caves in the area.
6. At Qumran, one of the most important discoveries in the history of biblical archaeology took place in around 1947.

Historical Background

1. It's believed the ancient settlement of Qumran was established by a Jewish group called the Essenes.
2. They lived here from about 200 BC to around 68 AD.
3. There were around 200 people who inhabited Qumran.
4. The ruins were excavated in the 1950s by a French archaeological team.
5. The Essenes were a spiritually devoted group of folks who left Jerusalem due to their belief that the priesthood had become corrupted beyond repair and separated themselves to study the Bible, copy it, and seek the Lord in the desert.
6. They were a strict Torah observant, Messianic, apocalyptic, new covenant Jewish sect. They were led by a priest they called the "Teacher of Righteousness." They were highly educated and very familiar with writing and study.
7. The future monastery lifestyle followed similar patterns of the

Essene community.

8. Josephus wrote that the men of Qumran rejected marriage, and instead, cared for the needy and neglected children of others. However, later discoveries have found skeletons of women, so it's believed some men possibly were married and that women were part of the community as well.
9. The Essenes most likely wrote the Dead Sea Scrolls from about 200 BC to 68 AD. Josephus and other secular sources mention the Essenes. However, they are not mentioned in the New Testament.
10. When the Essenes saw the nation of Israel falling to the Romans in around 68 AD, they hid their manuscripts in caves around Qumran. These manuscripts are what we refer to as the Dead Sea Scrolls.

Historical Background of the Dead Sea Scrolls

1. In around 1947, Bedouin shepherds were tending their goats and sheep near the ancient settlement of Qumran. One of the shepherds threw a rock into a cave and heard an echo sound. He and his friends later climbed into the cave and found a collection of large clay jars, seven of which contained leather and papyrus scrolls. An antiquities dealer from Bethlehem bought the scrolls, which later wound up in the possession of numerous scholars who estimated that the manuscripts were around 2,000 years old. After news of the discovery was made public, Bedouin treasure hunters and archaeologists discovered tens of thousands of additional scroll fragments from 10 nearby caves.

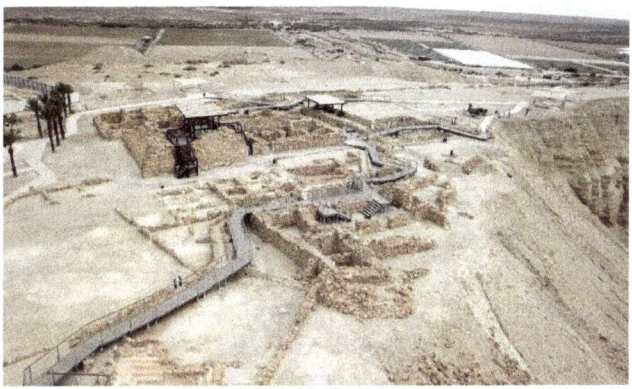

Qumran

2. The scrolls were discovered in eleven caves between the years of 1947 and 1956. The manuscripts are numbered according to the caves in which they were found.

3. There are around 972 manuscripts (15,000 fragments) that have been found to date. The longest is 26 ft. (8 m.) long.
4. They include fragments from every book of the Old Testament except for the Book of Esther (Esther might have been lost or decomposed due to time or may have been damaged by the Bedouin shepherds).
5. The writings consist of biblical manuscripts and other religious writings that circulated during the Second Temple era (516 BC to 70 AD). About 230 of the manuscripts are referred to as biblical scrolls. However, many of the manuscripts were fragmented and had to be assembled.

Qumran Caves

6. Cave 4, which is right beside ancient Qumran, had around 75% of all the material from the Qumran caves.
7. The Isaiah Scroll, found relatively intact, is 1,000 years older than any previously known copy of Isaiah, and the other scrolls are the oldest group of Old Testament manuscripts ever found.
8. The major intact manuscripts from Caves 1 and 11 were published by the late fifties and are now housed in the Shrine of the Book Museum in Jerusalem.
9. Recently, an additional cave (Cave 12) has been discovered, but no manuscripts have been found there yet.
10. Amazingly, the biblical manuscripts are virtually identical to the manuscripts we have today of the Old Testament part of the Bible. This proves God's ability to preserve His word through the ages.
11. Interestingly, the inhabitants of Qumran were either killed or fled, as no one ever came back to retrieve the scrolls.

Central Israel Sites

Places of Interest

1. Aqueduct Entrance
2. Reservoirs
3. Cisterns
4. Tower
5. Kitchen
6. Scriptorium
7. Pottery Shop
8. Kiln
9. Mikvah (ritual bath)
10. Assembly Hall
11. Pantry
12. Animal Pen
13. Aqueduct

14. Cave viewing area (caves 4–10)
15. Caves 1, 2, 3, and 11 are located 1 mile (1.62 km.) north of Qumran.

16. Dead Sea

Qumran and the Bible

1. The Dead Sea Scrolls would have been the same Hebrew Bible that Christ and the apostles used.

2. The Hebrew Bible was divided into 3 sections: the Law (Torah), the Writings (Historical Books), and the Prophets (Major and Minor Prophets).

3. Christ gave full validity to the authority and accuracy of Scripture and used every section of it in His teachings. He repeatedly said, *"So that it might be fulfilled," "It is written," "Have you not read?"* and so forth.

4. Christ used the Old Testament to explain His purpose on earth.
   Luke 24:27: *And beginning with Moses and all the Prophets, he explained to them what was said in all the Scriptures concerning himself.*

5. In the New Testament, there are 850 quotes or references to the Old Testament.

6. The New Testament is built upon the Old Testament and cannot be fully understood without it.

The Uniqueness of the Bible

1. The Bible was written by 40 different authors on 3 different continents and written over a period of 1,600 years. Yet all the books of the Bible harmonize and keep the same themes like a puzzle pieced together in perfect harmony.
2. This harmony is a miracle in and of itself. For example, if an accident happened on a street corner and 10 witnesses were asked what they saw, there would be many different accounts or versions of the incident. However, this is not so with the Bible. It has one guiding theme despite having many authors writing over a long period of time on different continents.

The Bible Was Written and Preserved Supernaturally by God

1. 2 Timothy 3:16–17: *All Scripture is breathed out by God and profitable for teaching, for reproof, for correction, and for training in righteousness, 17 that the man of God may be competent, equipped for every good work.*
2. 2 Peter 1:19–21: *And we have something more sure, the prophetic word, to which you will do well to pay attention as to a lamp shining in a dark place, until the day dawns and the morning star rises in your hearts, 20 knowing this first of all, that no prophecy of Scripture comes from someone's own interpretation. 21 For no prophecy was ever produced by the will of man, but men spoke from God as they were carried along by the Holy Spirit.*

Qumran

3. Hebrews 4:12–13: *For the word of God is living and active, sharper than any two-edged sword, piercing to the division of soul and of spirit, of joints and of marrow, and discerning the thoughts and intentions of the heart. 13 And no creature is hidden from his sight, but all are naked and exposed to the eyes of him to whom we must*

give account.

4. Matthew 4:4: *But he answered, "It is written, 'Man shall not live by bread alone, but by every word that comes from the mouth of God.'"*
5. Matthew 5:18: *For truly, I say to you, until heaven and earth pass away,* **not an iota, not a dot***, will pass from the Law until all is accomplished.*
6. Luke 21:33: *Heaven and earth will pass away, but* **my words** *will not pass away.*

Faith Lesson from Qumran

1. The Dead Sea Scrolls were one of the most important discoveries in the history of mankind. God supernaturally allowed this in order to prove the reliability of His Word. Do we believe in the Bible and that it's God's divine revelation to us?
2. Christ referred to every section of the Hebrew Bible (Old Testament) and repeatedly said, *"So that it might be fulfilled," "It is written," "Have you not read?"* and so forth. If Christ claimed the Hebrew Bible of His day was accurate, do we trust in the accuracy of the Bible we have today as well?
3. The New Testament contains around 850 references from the Old Testament. This shows how the New Testament is built upon the Old Testament. Do we read the Old Testament in order to understand the New Testament better?
4. If Christ was so passionate about the truthfulness of Scripture and claimed it was the very Word of God, then we too, like Christ, can certainly trust God's ability to preserve Scripture. Like Christ, are we passionate about the Bible, and do we read it regularly?
5. If God supernaturally preserved the accuracy of the Old Testament, do we believe He could do the same for the New Testament?

Journal/Notes:

Central Israel Sites

Samaria

Location

1. The biblical city of Samaria, also known as Sabastia, is located at Samaria National Park (Shomron National Park).
2. Samaria is about 33 miles (54 km.) north of Jerusalem and about 20 miles (32 km.) east of the Mediterranean Sea.
3. The city of Samaria was in the Samaria region of Israel in the territory of Ephraim and Manasseh during Bible times.
4. It was on a main east-west route that linked the coastal plain of Israel with the Jordan Valley.

Historical Background

1. Samaria was a central focus point in Israel and is mentioned around 117 times in the Bible.
2. The word "Samaria" is used 3 different ways in the Bible and can mean:
    - The capital city of Samaria.
    - The geographical region in the hill country north of Jerusalem.
    - The entire Northern Kingdom of Israel.
3. After the nation of Israel was divided in around 936 BC (after Solomon's reign), the capital of the Northern Kingdom was first established in Shechem and then moved to Tirzah. Both capitals were founded by Jeroboam (931–910 BC).
4. King Omri began his reign in 882 BC and moved the capital of the Northern Kingdom from Tirzah, and established it in the city of Samaria.
5. The city of Samaria was to the Northern Kingdom what Jerusalem

was to the Southern Kingdom. As a result, it became the second most important city in Israel after Jerusalem.
6. The city sits on a flat-topped, oblong hill with steep slopes on all sides. It was a huge city fortified with walls.
7. King Omri named the city "Shomron" (Samaria).
8. King Ahab built a palace at Samaria and overlaid it with ivory (1 Kings 22:39). This palace has been discovered with ivory in it, as mentioned in Scripture.

9. Samaria fell to the Assyrians in 722 BC, after 3 years of battle.
10. Samaria was given to Herod the Great by the emperor Augustus. Herod rebuilt Samaria and called it Sebaste (Greek form of Augustus) in honor of the emperor.
11. In order to honor John the Baptist, a Byzantine church was built on the southern side of the Acropolis in the 5th century. It was believed John's body was buried here, but this seems quite unlikely, according to the evidence.
12. During the Crusader Period (12th century), a church was built on the ruins of the eastern gate.

Places of Interest

1. Visitor Center
2. Western Gate

Central Israel Sites

3. Colonnade Street
4. Ahab's Palace
5. Temple
6. Theater
7. Acropolis
8. Hippodrome
9. Modern-day Sabastia (Sabaste)

Samaria in the Bible

1. **Samaria was established as the capital of the Northern Kingdom under King Omri's reign.**

    1 Kings 16:24: *He bought the hill of **Samaria** from Shemer for two talents of silver, and he fortified the hill and called the name of the city that he built **Samaria**, after the name of Shemer, the owner of the hill.*

2. **King Ahab erected an altar to the false god Baal in Samaria.**

    1 Kings 16:29–33: *In the thirty-eighth year of Asa king of Judah, Ahab the son of Omri began to reign over Israel, and Ahab the son of Omri reigned over Israel in **Samaria** twenty-two years. 30 And Ahab the son of Omri did evil in the sight of the Lord, more than all who*

were before him. 31 And as if it had been a light thing for him to walk in the sins of Jeroboam the son of Nebat, he took for his wife Jezebel the daughter of Ethbaal king of the Sidonians, and went and served Baal and worshiped him. 32 **He erected an altar for Baal in the house of Baal, which he built in Samaria***. 33 And Ahab made an Asherah. Ahab did more to provoke the Lord, the God of Israel, to anger than all the kings of Israel who were before him.*

3. **Because of Ahab's great sin, God sent a famine upon Samaria, and the great prophet Elijah paid a visit here.**

   1 Kings 18:1–2: *After many days the word of the Lord came to Elijah, in the third year, saying, "Go, show yourself to Ahab, and I will send rain upon the earth." 2 So Elijah went to show himself to Ahab. Now the famine was severe in* **Samaria***.*

4. **Later, the great showdown between the 850 false prophets of Baal and Asherah and Elijah took place on Mount Carmel, just 28 miles (48 km.) north of Samaria.**

   1 Kings 18:20–21: *So Ahab sent to all the people of Israel and gathered the prophets together at Mount Carmel. 21 And Elijah came near to all the people and said, "How long will you go limping between two different opinions? If the Lord is God, follow him; but if Baal, then follow him." And the people did not answer him a word.*

   Acropolis

5. **Ben-hadad, the king of Syria, came up against Samaria and attempted to defeat it. However, because Ben-hadad mocked God, God gave King Ahab victory over him.**

   1 Kings 20:26–28: *In the spring, Ben-hadad mustered the Syrians and went up to Aphek to fight against Israel. 27 And the people of Israel were mustered and were provisioned and went against them. The people of Israel encamped before them like two little flocks of*

goats, but the Syrians filled the country. 28 And a man of God came near and said to the king of Israel, "Thus says the Lord, '**Because the Syrians have said, "The Lord is a god of the hills but he is not a god of the valleys**," therefore I will give all this great multitude into your hand, and you shall know that I am the Lord.'"

6. **King Ahab killed Naboth to acquire his vineyard here.**

   1 Kings 21:1–3: *Now Naboth the Jezreelite had a vineyard in Jezreel, beside the* **palace of Ahab king of Samaria**. *2 And after this Ahab said to Naboth, "Give me your vineyard, that I may have it for a vegetable garden, because it is near my house, and I will give you a better vineyard for it; or, if it seems good to you, I will give you its value in money." 3 But Naboth said to Ahab, "The Lord forbid that I should give you the inheritance of my fathers."*

   Temple

7. **God killed King Ahab because of his great wickedness.**

   1 Kings 22:37–38: *So the king died, and was brought to* **Samaria**. *And they buried the king in Samaria. 38 And they washed the chariot by the pool of Samaria, and the dogs licked up his blood, and the prostitutes washed themselves in it, according to the word of the Lord that he had spoken.*

8. **God sent the prophets Elijah and Elisha to minister and perform many miracles to persuade the Northern Kingdom of Israel (Samaria) to turn from their false gods and serve Him.**

9. **Despite Israel's great sins, God had mercy on them and delivered them from warring armies.**

   2 Kings 6:24–25: *Afterward Ben-hadad king of Syria mustered his entire army and went up and besieged* **Samaria**. *25 And there was a great famine in Samaria, as they besieged it, until a donkey's head was sold for eighty shekels of silver, and the fourth part of a kab [8 oz., .23 ltr.] of dove's dung for five shekels of silver.*

2 Kings 7:1: *But Elisha said, "Hear the word of the Lord: thus says the Lord, 'Tomorrow about this time a seah [2.75 gal., 10.5 ltr.] of fine flour shall be sold for a shekel, and two seahs [5.5 gal., 21 ltr.] of barley for a shekel, at the **gate of Samaria**.'"*

2 Kings 7:3–7: *Now there were four men who were lepers at the **entrance to the gate**. And they said to one another, "Why are we sitting here until we die? 4 If we say, 'Let us enter the city,' the famine is in the city, and we shall die there. And if we sit here, we die also. So now come, let us go over to the camp of the Syrians. If they spare our lives we shall live, and if they kill us we shall but die." 5 So they arose at twilight to go to the camp of the Syrians. But when they came to the edge of the camp of the Syrians, behold, there was no one there. 6 For the Lord had made the army of the Syrians hear the sound of chariots and of horses, the sound of a great army, so that they said to one another, "Behold, the king of Israel has hired against us the kings of the Hittites and the kings of Egypt to come against us." 7 So they fled away in the twilight and abandoned their tents, their horses, and their donkeys, leaving the camp as it was, and fled for their lives.*

Visitor Center

2 Kings 7:16: *Then the people went out and plundered the camp of the Syrians. So a seah of fine flour was sold for a shekel, and two seahs of barley for a shekel, according to the word of the Lord.*

10. The Northern Kingdom continued to reject God, so He allowed Assyria to conquer and lead them into captivity.

2 Kings 17:5–8: *Then the king of Assyria invaded all the land and came to Samaria, and for three years he besieged it. 6 In the ninth year of Hoshea, the king of Assyria captured Samaria, and he carried the Israelites away to Assyria and placed them in Halah, and on the Habor, the river of Gozan, and in the cities of the Medes. 7 And this*

occurred because the people of Israel had sinned against the Lord their God, who had brought them up out of the land of Egypt from under the hand of Pharaoh king of Egypt, and had feared other gods 8 and walked in the customs of the nations whom the Lord drove out before the people of Israel, and in the customs that the kings of Israel had practiced.

11. **As a common Assyrian conquest practice, the Israelite exiles were replaced by people from Mesopotamia and other areas. However, some of the Israelites were left in the land by the Assyrians.**

Theater

2 Kings 17:24: *And the king of Assyria brought people from Babylon, Cuthah, Avva, Hamath, and Sepharvaim, and placed them in the* **cities of Samaria** *instead of the people of Israel. And they took possession of* **Samaria** *and lived in its cities.*

12. **The beginning of the Samaritan people.**

Assyria led into captivity most of the inhabitants of the Northern Kingdom of Israel. However, some were left in the land. Those who were left intermarried with foreign unbelievers that were placed there by the Assyrians and were thereafter called Samaritans. When Ezra and Nehemiah returned with many Jews to rebuild Jerusalem and the temple, these Samaritans and others would attempt to stop them.

The Samaritans established their own religion at Mount Gerizim and built their own temple. They were despised and rejected by the Jews and considered unclean because they weren't pure bloodline Jews. The Samaritans, likewise, despised the Jews and had few dealings with them. The Samaritan people still exist today and only believe in the Torah (first 5 books of the Old Testament).

13. **Part of Samaria was repopulated by Jews from Judah (Southern Kingdom of Israel), and worship of God was restored.**

    2 Kings 23:19: *And Josiah [King of Judah] removed all the shrines also of the high places that were in the **cities of Samaria**, which kings of Israel had made, provoking the Lord to anger. He did to them according to all that he had done at Bethel.*

14. **Jesus ministered in the area of Samaria.**

    John 4:1–5: *Now when Jesus learned that the Pharisees had heard that Jesus was making and baptizing more disciples than John 2 (although Jesus himself did not baptize, but only his disciples), 3 he left Judea and departed again for Galilee. 4 And he had to pass through **Samaria**. 5 So he came to a town of **Samaria** called **Sychar [Shechem]**, near the field that **Jacob had given to his son Joseph**.*

    Ahab's Palace

15. **In the New Testament, believers from Jerusalem spread to the Samaria region due to persecution.**

    Acts 8:1: *And Saul approved of his execution. And there arose on that day a great persecution against the church in Jerusalem, and they were all scattered throughout the regions of Judea and **Samaria**, except the apostles.*

16. **Philip preached Christ in the city of Samaria.**

    Acts 8:4–8: *Now those who were scattered went about preaching the word. 5 Philip went down to the **city of Samaria** and proclaimed to them the Christ. 6 And the crowds with one accord paid attention to what was being said by Philip, when they heard him and saw the signs that he did. 7 For unclean spirits, crying out with a loud voice, came out of many who had them, and many who were paralyzed or lame were healed. 8 So there was much joy in that city.*

Central Israel Sites

Faith Lesson from Samaria

1. Unfortunately, the division of the Nation of Israel into two parts was born out of disobedience to God.
2. Nonetheless, God sent prophet after prophet to warn them to leave their false Gods and return to Him.
3. God extended mercy and patience upon them despite their continual rejection of Him.
4. Because of their hardhearted rejection, God had no choice but to discipline the Northern Kingdom and deport most of them to Assyria.

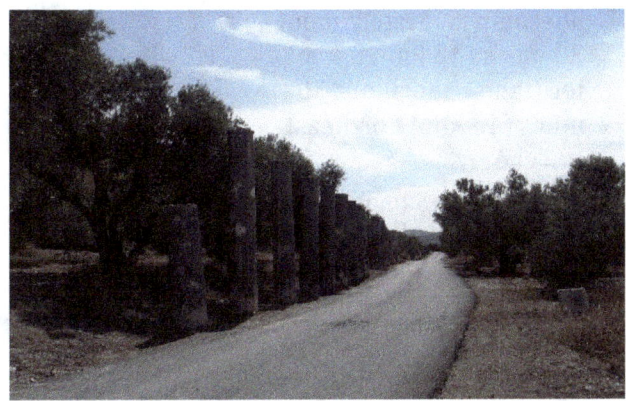

Colonnade Street

5. Do we really believe that disobedience to God causes pain and suffering (Rom. 8:6)?
6. Do we understand that God is merciful and patient but disciplines those He loves (Heb. 12:7–11)?
7. The Samaritan people gladly received the gospel under Philip's preaching. Do we realize that those living in darkness are the most receptive to the light?

Journal/Notes:

Shechem

Location

1. Biblical Shechem is also known as Sychar in the New Testament and as Tel Balata and Nablus today.
2. Shechem is located about 30 miles (48 km.) north of Jerusalem and about 30 miles (48 km.) northeast of Tel Aviv.
3. It was in the Samaria region of Israel in the territories of Ephraim and Manasseh during Bible times.

4. It was on a main north-south travel route that linked the northern and southern parts of Israel.
5. It was also on a main east-west route that linked the coastal plain of Israel with the Jordan Valley.
6. Shechem lies between the two famous mountains of Gerizim and Ebal.

Historical Background

1. Shechem had a significant role in the Bible and is mentioned 58 times.
2. God first appeared to Abraham in Shechem and gave him the promise that he would inherit the land.
3. Abraham and Jacob lived here.
4. Jacob lived here and built a well.
5. Joseph's bones are buried here.
6. The blessings and curses that were given on Mount Gerizim and Mount Ebal took place here.
7. Joshua rallied all Israel and made a covenant with them in Shechem.
8. Abimelech, son of Gideon, reigned wickedly over Shechem for

Central Israel Sites

three years. It was he who burned down the fortress temple here called "El-Berith," and killed 1,000 people who had taken refuge in it. Later, he was killed by a woman who threw a millstone down on his head.

9. The nation of Israel became divided in Shechem.
10. Shechem became the capital of the northern tribes of Israel under King Jeroboam's rule.
11. The Samaritans worshiped on top of Mount Gerizim, and there are substantial ruins there today.
    - The Samaritans first built a temple here for worship in the 5th century. Later, in the 2nd century, they built walls around the temple to protect it.
    - In the latter part of the 2nd century, the Hasmoneans (Jewish rule from 167–63 BC) destroyed the Samaritan's temple on Mount Gerizim and the city at the base of the mountain (ancient Shechem).
    - During the Roman occupation of Israel, the Samaritans were given permission by the Romans to rebuild their temple and city.

Mt. Gerizim ruins

    - In 475 AD, under Byzantine rule, the Samaritan temple was destroyed, and a Byzantine church was erected. Later, a monastery was built as well.
12. Jesus met with a Samaritan woman (John 4) at Jacob's Well in Shechem. Today, this well is located in a Greek Orthodox church called "The Church of Jacob's Well."
13. The Samaritans were a small group of unfaithful Israelites who remained in the land of Israel and intermarried with foreign unbelievers after the deportation of Israel by the Assyrians in 722

BC. They established their own religion at Mount Gerizim and built their own temple. They were despised and rejected by the Jews and considered unclean. The Samaritans, likewise, despised the Jews and had few dealings with them. The Samaritans only believe in the Torah (the first 5 books of the Old Testament).

Places of Interest

1. Tel Balata
   - Visitor Center
   - Northwest Gate
   - City Wall
   - Fortress Temple

   - Joshua's Stone (Erected after Joshua made a covenant with the Israelites).
   - Sacred Courtyard
   - Houses
   - Eastern Gate
2. Mount Gerizim

Central Israel Sites

- 2nd-Century Buildings
- Fortified Enclosure
- Citadel
- Courtyards
- 2nd-Century Mansion
- 12-Stone Altar
- Byzantine Church
- Byzantine Gate
- 2nd-Century Gate
- Byzantine Monastery
- Eastern Gate

3. Mount Ebal
   - Joshua's Rectangular Altar
   - Circular Altar below Rectangular Altar (possibly that of Abraham or Jacob)
4. Jacob's Well (120 ft., 40 m. deep)

5. Joseph's Tomb
6. Modern Shechem (Nablus)

Shechem in the Bible

1. **Shechem is the place where God first appeared to Abraham after he entered the Promised Land.**

   Genesis 12:4–7: *So Abram went, as the Lord had told him, and Lot went with him. Abram was seventy-five years old when he departed from Haran. 5 And Abram took Sarai his wife, and Lot his brother's son, and all their possessions that they had gathered, and the people that they had acquired in Haran, and they set out to go to the land of Canaan. When they came to the land of Canaan, 6 Abram passed through the land to the place at **Shechem**, to the oak of Moreh. At that time the Canaanites were in the land. 7 Then the Lord appeared to Abram and said, "To your **offspring I will give this land**." So he **built there an altar to the Lord**, who had appeared to him.*

2. **It was at Shechem where Jacob settled after reuniting with his estranged brother, Esau, upon his return from Paddan-aram.**

   Genesis 33:18–20: *And Jacob came safely to the city of **Shechem**, which is in the land of Canaan, on his way from Paddan-aram, and he camped before the city. 19 And from the sons of Hamor,*

*Shechem's father, he bought for a hundred pieces of money the piece of land on which he had pitched his tent. 20 There he **erected an altar** and called it El-Elohe-Israel (God; the God of Israel).*

3. **The defilement of Dinah, Jacob's daughter, took place at Shechem.**

   Genesis 34:1–4: *Now Dinah, the daughter of Leah, whom she had borne to Jacob, went out to see the women of the land. 2 And when Shechem the son of Hamor the Hivite, the prince of the land, saw her, he seized her and lay with her and humiliated her. 3 And his soul was drawn to Dinah, the daughter of Jacob. He loved the young woman and spoke tenderly to her. 4 So Shechem spoke to his father Hamor, saying, "Get me this girl for my wife."*

   Tel Balata – Ancient Shechem

   Genesis 34:25–27: *On the third day, when they were sore [from being circumcised], two of the sons of Jacob, Simeon and Levi, Dinah's brothers, took their swords and came against the city while it felt secure and killed all the males. 26 They killed Hamor and his son Shechem with the sword and took Dinah out of Shechem's house and went away. 27 The sons of Jacob came upon the slain and plundered the city, because they had defiled their sister.*

4. **In Shechem, Jacob buried his foreign gods and committed himself fully to the true and living God of his forefathers.**

   Genesis 35:4: *So they gave to Jacob all the foreign gods that they had, and the rings that were in their ears. Jacob hid them under the terebinth tree that was near **Shechem**.*

5. **To the rich pastureland near Shechem, Joseph came to seek his brethren and was sold into slavery and taken to Egypt.**

   Genesis 37:12–14: *Now his brothers went to pasture their father's* flock near **Shechem**. 13 And Israel said to Joseph, "Are not your brothers pasturing the flock at **Shechem**? Come, I will send you to them." And he said to him, "Here I am." 14 So he said to him, "Go now, see if it is well with your brothers and with the flock, and bring me word." So he sent him from the Valley of Hebron, and he came to **Shechem**.

6. **The bones of Joseph were buried in Shechem.**

    Joshua 24:32: *Now they **buried the bones of Joseph**, which the sons of Israel brought up from Egypt, at **Shechem**, in the piece of ground which Jacob had bought from the sons of Hamor the father of Shechem for one hundred pieces of money; and they became the inheritance of Joseph's sons.*

    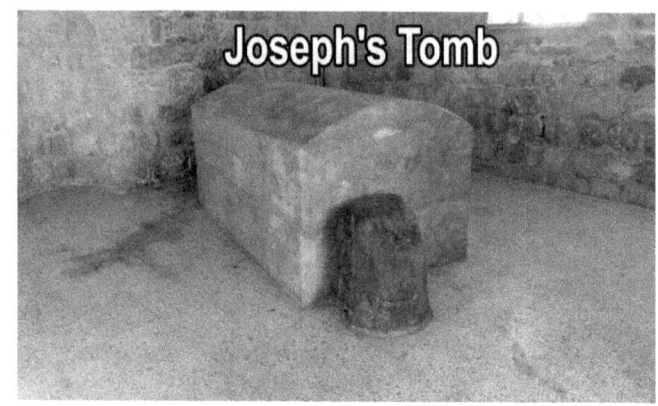

7. **On the mountains of Gerizim and Ebal, Moses commanded the Israelites to pronounce blessings and curses for their obedience or disobedience to Him.**

    Deuteronomy 27:11–13: *That day Moses charged the people, saying, 12 "When you have crossed over the Jordan, these shall stand on **Mount Gerizim** to **bless** the people: Simeon, Levi, Judah, Issachar, Joseph, and Benjamin. 13 And these shall stand on **Mount Ebal** for the **curse**: Reuben, Gad, Asher, Zebulun, Dan, and Naphtali."*

    The blessings and curses pronounced on Gerizim and Ebal would become the foundational reference point to which God would refer in punishing Israel and Judah by sending them wars, famines, and pestilences. Eventually, their disobedience would lead to their deportations. Because they had broken the covenant on Gerizim and Ebal repeatedly, they deserved the discipline God gave them.

8. **As commanded by Moses, Joshua erected an altar on Mount Ebal with uncut stones.**

    Deuteronomy 27:1–8: *Now Moses and the elders of Israel commanded the people, saying, "Keep the whole commandment that*

I command you today. 2 And on the day you cross over the Jordan to the land that the Lord your God is giving you, you shall set up large stones and plaster them with plaster. 3 And you shall write on them all the words of this law, when you cross over to enter the land that the Lord your God is giving you, a land flowing with milk and honey, as the Lord, the God of your fathers, has promised you. 4 And when you have crossed over the Jordan, you shall set up these stones, concerning

Joshua's Altar on Mount Ebal

which I command you today, on Mount Ebal, and you shall plaster them with plaster. 5 And there you shall **build an altar** *to the Lord your God, an altar of stones. You shall wield no iron tool on them; 6 you shall* **build an altar** *to the Lord your God of* **uncut stones***. And you shall offer burnt offerings on it to the Lord your God, 7 and you shall sacrifice peace offerings and shall eat there, and you shall rejoice before the Lord your God. 8 And you shall write on the stones all the words of this law very plainly."*

9. **When his end was approaching, Joshua gathered the tribes of Israel at Shechem and gave them his final words of counsel and exhortation. Afterward, he erected a large stone as a monument to mark the covenant with the people and God. This stone can be seen today at Tel Balata.**

Joshua 24:1: *Joshua gathered all the tribes of Israel to* **Shechem** *and summoned the elders, the heads, the judges, and the officers of Israel. And they presented themselves before God.*

Joshua 24:14–15: *Now, therefore, fear the Lord and serve him in sincerity and in faithfulness. Put away the gods that your fathers served beyond the River and in Egypt, and serve the Lord. 15 And if it is evil in your eyes to serve the Lord, choose this day whom you will serve, whether the gods your fathers served in the region beyond the River, or the gods of the Amorites in whose land you dwell.* **But as** *for me and my house, we will serve the Lord.*

Joshua 24:25–27: *So Joshua **made a covenant** with the people that day, and put in place statutes and rules for them at **Shechem**. 26 And Joshua wrote these words in the Book of the Law of God. And he took a **large stone** and set it up there under the terebinth that was by the **sanctuary of the Lord**. 27 And Joshua said to all the people, "Behold, this **stone shall be a witness against** us, for it has heard all the words of the Lord that he spoke to us. Therefore, it shall be a witness against you, lest you deal falsely with your God."*

10. **Abimelech, son of Gideon, reigned wickedly over Shechem for three years. He burned down the fortress temple here called "El-Berith," and killed 1,000 people who had taken refuge in it. Later, he was killed by a woman who threw a millstone down on his head.**

Mt. Gerizim (left) Mt. Ebal (right)

Judges 9:46, 49: *When all the leaders of the tower of Shechem heard about it, they entered the inner chamber of the temple of El-berith. 49 So all the people also cut down, each one, his branch and followed Abimelech, and put them on top of the inner chamber and set the inner chamber on fire over those inside, so that all the people of the tower of Shechem also died, about a thousand men and women.*

Judges 9:52-54: *So Abimelech came to the tower and fought against it, and approached the entrance of the tower to burn it down with fire. 53 But a woman threw an upper millstone on Abimelech's head, crushing his skull. 54 Then he called quickly to the young man, his armor bearer, and said to him, "Draw your sword and kill me, so that it will not be said of me, 'A woman killed him.'"*

11. **At Shechem, the nation of Israel became divided, and Jeroboam reigned over the northern part (Israel) and**

Rehoboam over the southern part (Judah).

1 Kings 12:1-2: *Rehoboam went to **Shechem**, for all Israel had come to **Shechem** to make him king. 2 And as soon as Jeroboam the son of Nebat heard of it (for he was still in Egypt, where he had fled from King Solomon), then Jeroboam returned from Egypt.*

1 Kings 12:16-17: *And when all Israel saw that the king (Rehoboam) did not listen to them, the people answered the king, "What portion do we have in David? We have no inheritance in the son of Jesse. To your tents, O Israel! Look now to your own house, David." So Israel went to their tents. 17 But Rehoboam reigned over the people of Israel who lived in the cities of Judah.*

12. **King Jeroboam fortified Shechem and ordered that two golden calves be erected in Bethel and Dan.**

    1 Kings 12:25-29: *Then Jeroboam built **Shechem** in the hill country of Ephraim and **lived there**. And he went out from there and built Penuel. 26 And Jeroboam said in his heart, "Now the kingdom will turn back to the house of David. 27 If this people go up to offer sacrifices in the temple of the Lord at Jerusalem, then the heart of this people will turn again to their lord, to Rehoboam king of Judah, and they will kill me and return to Rehoboam king of Judah." 28 So the king took counsel and made two calves of gold. And he said to the people, "You have gone up to Jerusalem long enough. Behold your gods, O Israel, who brought you up out of the land of Egypt." 29 And he set one in Bethel, and the other he put in Dan.*

    Jacob's Well

13. **Later, Shechem became the central city of the Samaritans, who built their own temple on Mt. Gerizim.**

14. **Shechem, called Sychar, is the place Jesus met a woman at Jacob's well and conversed with her.**

John 4:1–26: *Now when Jesus learned that the Pharisees had heard that Jesus was making and baptizing more disciples than John 2 (although Jesus himself did not baptize, but only his disciples), 3 he left Judea and departed again for Galilee. 4 And he had to pass through Samaria. 5 So he came to a town of Samaria called* **Sychar**, *near the field that* **Jacob had given to his son Joseph**. *6 Jacob's well was there; so Jesus, wearied as he was from his journey, was sitting beside the well. It was about the sixth hour [12:00 pm]. 7 A woman from Samaria came to draw water. Jesus said to her, "Give me a drink." 8 (For his disciples had gone away into the city to buy food.) 9 The Samaritan woman said to him, "How is it that you, a Jew, ask for a drink from me, a woman of Samaria?" (For Jews have no dealings with Samaritans.) 10 Jesus answered her, "If you knew the gift of God, and who it is that is saying to you, 'Give me a drink,' you would have asked him, and he would have given you living water."*

Church over Jacob's Well

11 The woman said to him, "Sir, you have nothing to draw water with, and the well is deep [120 ft., 40 m.]. Where do you get that living water? 12 Are you greater than our father Jacob? He gave us the well and drank from it himself, as did his sons and his livestock." 13 Jesus said to her, "Everyone who drinks of this water will be thirsty again, 14 but whoever drinks of the water that I will give him will never be thirsty again. The water that I will give him will become in him a spring of water welling up to eternal life." 15 The woman said to him, "Sir, give me this water, so that I will not be thirsty or have to come here to draw water." 16 Jesus said to her, "Go, call your husband, and come here." 17 The woman answered him, "I have no husband." Jesus said to her, "You are right in saying, 'I have no husband'; 18 for you have had five husbands, and the one you now have is not your husband. What you have said is true." 19 The woman said to him, "Sir, I perceive that you are a prophet. 20

*Our fathers worshiped on **this mountain [Gerizim]**, but you say that in Jerusalem is the place where people ought to worship." 21 Jesus said to her, "Woman, believe me, the hour is coming when neither on this mountain nor in Jerusalem will you worship the Father. 22 You worship what you do not know; we worship what we know, for salvation is from the Jews. 23 But the hour is coming, and is now here, when the true worshipers will worship the Father in spirit and truth, for the Father is seeking such people to worship him. 24 God is spirit, and those who worship him must worship in spirit and truth." 25 The woman said to him, "I know that Messiah is coming (he who is called Christ). When he comes, he will tell us all things." 26 Jesus said to her, "I who speak to you am he."*

John 4:39–42: *Many Samaritans from that town believed in him because of the woman's testimony, "He told me all that I ever did." 40 So when the Samaritans came to him, they asked him to stay with them, and he stayed there two days. 41 And many more believed because of his word. 42 They said to the woman, "It is no longer because of what you said that we believe, for we have heard for ourselves, and we know that this is indeed the Savior of the world."*

Faith Lesson from Shechem

1. Of all the events that happened at Shechem, Jesus summed up God's desire for us when He told the woman at the well: *"The hour is coming, and is now here, when the true worshipers will worship the Father in spirit and truth, for the Father is seeking such people to worship him. God is spirit, and those who worship him must worship in spirit and truth"* (John 2:23–24).
2. Do we worship God in spirit?
3. Do we walk in the Spirit and stay in close fellowship with God (Gal. 5:16–26)?
4. Do we worship God in truth?
5. Do we know God's Word well and the truth it contains (2 Tim. 2:15)?
6. We will only know God to the degree we know His Word. How well do you know God?

Journal/Notes:

Shiloh

Location

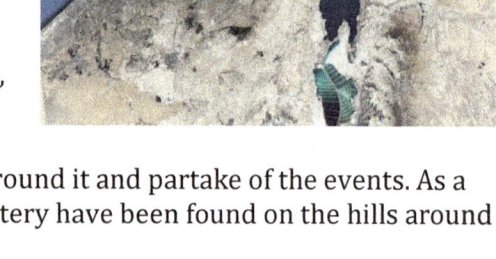

1. Shiloh is about 20 miles (32 km.) north of Jerusalem on Hwy. 60.
2. It was on a major north-south travel route that linked Beersheba in the south to Shechem and the northern cities of Israel.
3. Shiloh was located on a hilltop which made it defensible.
4. It had hills surrounding it, so when the nation gathered at Shiloh for feasts, they could camp around it and partake of the events. As a result, many pieces of pottery have been found on the hills around Shiloh.
5. Tel Shiloh is at an archaeological park called "Ancient Shiloh," located at the entrance to modern-day Shiloh.
6. Shiloh was in the hill country of Samaria within the tribal allotment of Ephraim.
7. It was likely chosen as the capital and military base of Israel due to its central location within the country.

Historical Background

1. Shiloh was the religious and military capital of Israel during the times of the Judges, and the tabernacle resided here for 369 years.
2. It was the first place where the tabernacle became a permanent structure.
3. Two million Jews would gather at Shiloh on the main festivals and would camp on the surrounding hills.
4. The Ark of the Covenant resided here within the tabernacle. The ark contained the following 3 items:
    - Tablets of the 10 Commandments.

Central Israel Sites

- Aaron's staff, or rod that budded.
- Jar of Manna

5. During the Byzantine Period, a church and structures were built at Shiloh. A Mosque was built on the west side of the ruins of the Byzantine church and named Jamia el Arbain.
6. North of the Byzantine church, archaeologists have discovered two more Byzantine churches under a Mosque that is partially standing today. One of the churches was built in the 6th century, and the lower one in the 4th century. The lower level may have been built over the ruins of an ancient synagogue.

Places of Interest

1. Byzantine Church (A Danish team in the 1930s added the building over the Byzantine church base seen today).
2. Mosque (Byzantine churches underneath).
3. Byzantine Ruins
4. Oil Press
5. Storerooms
6. Canaanite Wall
7. Visitor Tower
8. Tabernacle Location

Shiloh in the Bible

1. **During the conquest of the Promised Land (7-year period), the tabernacle resided principally at Gilgal (Josh. 4:19–24).**

2. **After the conquest of the land was basically complete, the tabernacle was set up in Shiloh, where it would reside for 369 years.**

   Joshua 18:1: *Then the whole congregation of the people of Israel assembled at **Shiloh and set up the tent of meeting there**. The land lay subdued before them.*

3. **At Shiloh, lots were cast to divide the land among the 7 tribes who had not yet received their inheritance on the west side of the Jordan River. Ruben, Gad, and the half-tribe of Manasseh had already received their portion on the east side of the Jordan, and Judah and Joseph had already received theirs on the west side.**

   Joshua 18:2–3: *There remained among the people of Israel **seven tribes** whose inheritance had not yet been apportioned. 3 So Joshua said to the people of Israel, "How long will you put off going in to take possession of the land, which the Lord, the God of your fathers, has given you?"*

   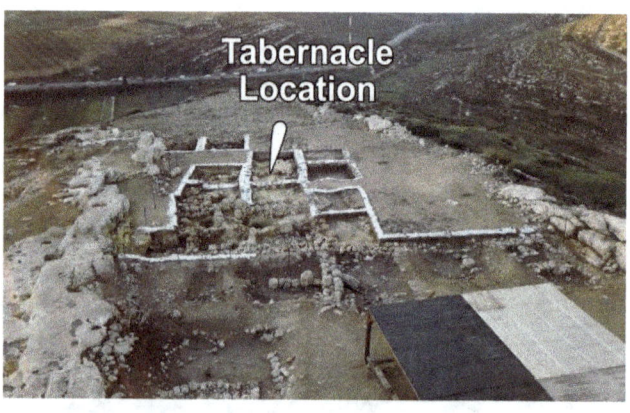

   Joshua 18:8–10: *So the men arose and went, and Joshua charged those who went to write the description of the land, saying, "Go up and down in the land and write a description and return to me. And I will cast lots for you here before the Lord in **Shiloh**." 9 So the men went and passed up and down in the land and wrote in a book a description of it by towns in seven divisions. Then they came to Joshua to the camp at **Shiloh**, 10 and Joshua cast lots for them in **Shiloh** before the Lord. And there Joshua apportioned the land to the people of Israel, to each his portion.*

4. **From Shiloh, Reuben, Gad, and the half-tribe of Manasseh departed for their homes east of the Jordan River.**

   Joshua 22:9: *So the people of Reuben and the people of Gad and the half-tribe of Manasseh returned home, parting from the people of Israel at **Shiloh**, which is in the land of Canaan, to go to the land of Gilead, their own land of which they had possessed themselves by command of the LORD through Moses.*

5. **After departing from Shiloh to return home, the tribes of Reuben, Gad, and the half-tribe of Manasseh built an altar at the Jordan River. The rest of the tribes misunderstood their purpose for the altar and met at Shiloh to go and fight against them.**

   Joshua 22:12: *And when the people of Israel heard of it, the whole assembly of the people of Israel gathered at **Shiloh** to make war against them.*

   Visitor Tower

   The intent of the 2 ½ tribes was to erect an altar as a witness to future generations that they were part of the 9 ½ tribes on the west side of the Jordan River. When the 9 ½ tribes understood their purpose, they returned home in peace.

6. **During a dark time in the book of Judges, the Benjamite tribe was almost wiped out by the other tribes of Israel because of their severe disobedience to God. In order to revive the population of Benjamin, wives were provided for them at Shiloh.**

   Judges 21:19–21: *So they said, "Behold, there is the yearly feast of the Lord at **Shiloh**, which is north of Bethel, on the east of the highway that goes up from Bethel to Shechem, and south of Lebonah." 20 And they commanded the people of Benjamin, saying, "Go and lie in ambush in the vineyards 21 and watch. If the **daughters of Shiloh** come out to dance in the dances, then come out of the vineyards and snatch each man his wife from the* *daughters of **Shiloh**, and go to the land of Benjamin."*

7. At Shiloh, Hannah prayed for a son. God heard her prayers and blessed her with Samuel.

1 Samuel 1:3–5: *Now this man used to go up year by year from his city to worship and to sacrifice to the Lord of hosts at **Shiloh**, where the two sons of Eli, Hophni and Phinehas, were priests of the Lord. 4 On the day when Elkanah sacrificed, he would give portions to Peninnah his wife and to all her sons and daughters. 5 But to **Hannah**, he gave a double portion, because he loved her, though the Lord had closed her womb.*

1 Samuel 1:9–11: *After they had eaten and drunk in **Shiloh**, Hannah rose. Now Eli the priest was sitting on the seat beside the doorpost of the temple of the Lord. 10 She was deeply distressed and prayed to the Lord and wept bitterly. 11 And she vowed a vow and said, "O Lord of hosts, if you will indeed look on the affliction of your servant and remember me and not forget your servant, but will give to your servant a son, then I will give him to the Lord all the days of his life, and no razor shall touch his head."*

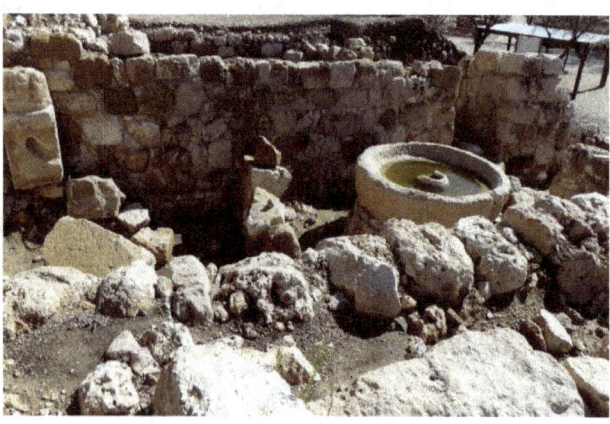
Oil Press

8. To Shiloh, Hannah brought Samuel and consecrated him to the Lord's service.

1 Samuel 1:24–28: *And when she had weaned him, she took him up with her, along with a three-year-old bull, an ephah of flour, and a skin of wine, and she brought him to the house of the Lord at **Shiloh**. And the child was young. 25 Then they slaughtered the bull, and they brought the child to Eli. 26 And she said, "Oh, my lord! As you live, my lord, I am the woman who was standing here in your presence, praying to the Lord. 27 For this child, I prayed, and the Lord has granted me my petition that I made to him. 28 Therefore I have lent him to the Lord. As long as he lives, he is lent to the Lord." And he*

worshiped the Lord there.

9. **The sanctuary in Shiloh was called a "temple," as noted in 1 Samuel 1:9, 3:3. It had doorposts and doors, as seen in 1 Samuel 1:9, 3:15. It was, therefore, a more durable structure than the Tent of Meeting (tabernacle).**

10. **The tabernacle at Shiloh was presided over by Eli and his wicked sons. Then, through the prophet Samuel, the doom of their house was announced.**

    1 Samuel 3:11–13: *Then the Lord said to Samuel, "Behold, I am about to do a thing in Israel at which the two ears of everyone who hears it will tingle. 12 On that day I will fulfill against Eli all that I have spoken concerning his house, from beginning to end. 13 And I declare to him that I am about to punish his house forever, for the iniquity that he knew,*

    Byzantine Buildings

    because his sons were blaspheming God, and he did not restrain them."

11. **In a battle with the Philistines, the ark was captured. As a result, the fall of Hophni and Phinehas, and the death of Eli happened near Shiloh.**

    1 Samuel 4:16–18: *And the man said to Eli, "I am he who has come from the battle; I fled from the battle today." And he said, "How did it go, my son?" 17 He who brought the news answered and said, "Israel has fled before the Philistines, and there has also been a great defeat among the people. Your two sons also, Hophni and Phinehas, are dead, and the ark of God has been captured." 18 As soon as he mentioned the ark of God, Eli fell over backward from his seat by the side of the gate, and his neck was broken and he died, for the man was old and heavy. He had judged Israel forty years.*

12. **The Ark of the Covenant was returned to Beth-Shemesh by the Philistines and wound up staying at the house of Abinadab for**

20 years (1 Sam. 7:1).

13. Eventually, King David would take the ark to the City of David (1 Chron. 13-15), and then it would be moved to the temple Solomon built (2 Chron. 5:2). The tabernacle was taken to Gibeon (1 Chron. 21:29) but didn't have the ark in it. After the temple was built in Jerusalem, the tabernacle at Gibeon went by the wayside.

14. After the Kingdom of Israel was divided, Jeroboam, king of the Northern Tribes, erected golden calf altars in Bethel and Dan for the worship of false gods. Over time, Shiloh fell into ruins and came under judgment from God.

Psalm 78:59-61: *When God heard, he was full of wrath, and he utterly rejected Israel. 60 He forsook his dwelling at **Shiloh**, the tent where he dwelt among mankind, 61 and delivered his power to captivity, his glory to the hand of the foe.*

Jeremiah 7:12: *Go now to my place that was in **Shiloh**, where I made my name dwell at first, and see what I did to it because of the evil of my people Israel.*

Faith Lesson from Shiloh

1. Shiloh was a place of rich blessing and rejoicing when the Israelites obeyed God. Do we understand that obeying and serving God brings life and fulfills our souls?
2. Because of the sins of Eli and his sons, God judged Shiloh. What kind of leaders are we, and do we realize how our leadership affects our families and ministries?
3. Hannah prayed for a child at Shiloh, and God heard her. Like Hannah, do we pray for our needs, and do we pray with the right motives?
4. Shiloh was also a place of grave disaster with a bitter ending. Its end was judgment because of the continual sin of God's people. Do we realize the danger of allowing sin in our lives and the consequences it can bring?

Journal/Notes:

Central Israel Sites

St. George's Monastery

Location

1. St. George's Monastery is located about 2.5 miles (4 km.) west of Jericho in a deep and breathtaking gorge called "Wadi Qelt."
2. It's located on the ancient road connecting the Jordan Valley to Jerusalem and beyond. Jesus would have used this well-traveled road regularly.
3. The story of the Good Samaritan took place on this road. (For more on this story and event, please see the Inn of the Good Samaritan.)

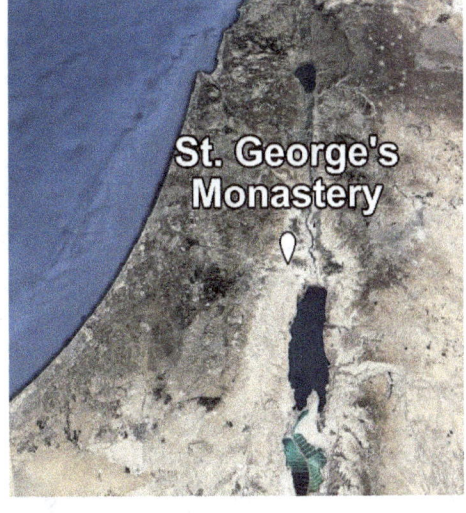

Historical Background

1. St. George's Monastery is a Greek Orthodox cliff-hanging complex carved into a sheer rock wall in the Judaean Desert and is one of the most breathtaking sights in the Holy Land.
2. Starting in the 4th century, monks began to live in the many caves of Wadi Qelt.
3. The monastery of St. George was founded in the 5th century by John of Thebes, an Egyptian. He gathered a small band of five Syrian hermits who had settled around the cave where they believed the prophet Elijah was fed by ravens (1 Kings 17:1–7).
4. Tradition also holds that Elijah visited the cave by the monastery while traveling to the Sinai Peninsula as he fled the threats of Jezebel after he had killed the false prophets of Baal and Asherah (1 Kings 19:1–3).
5. However, it was named after its most famous monk, St George of Koziba, who came as a teenager from Cyprus in the 6th century to follow the ascetic life in the Holy Land after his parents died.
6. The monastery was destroyed in 614 AD by the Persians and was more or less abandoned after the Persians swept through the

valley and massacred the fourteen monks who dwelt there. The bones and skulls of the martyred monks can still be seen today in the monastery chapel.

7. The Crusaders made some attempts at restoration of the monastery in 1179 AD. However, it was abandoned after Muslims regained control of the Holy Land and drove out the Crusaders.

St. George's Monastery from lookout point

8. In 1878, a Greek monk, Kalinikos, settled here and restored the monastery, finishing it in 1901.

History of Christian Monasticism

1. Today, in Israel, there are 33 functioning monasteries. During the 4th century, there were hundreds of monasteries built as almost every holy site had a monastery on it.
2. Because Christianity was prohibited in the Roman Empire before Constantine embraced Christianity, no monasteries or churches were permitted until 313 AD. After this point, monasteries sprung up everywhere throughout the empire.
3. The idea of a monastic lifestyle was taken from both the Old and New Testaments.
    - The Nazarite Vow
    - The prophets (Elijah being fed by ravens in the desert).
    - John the Baptist living in the desert.
    - Christ fasting for 40 days in the desert.
4. There were also the Essenes who lived in the desert by the Dead Sea at Qumran during the time of John the Baptist and Jesus.
5. Monasticism took on different forms and meanings throughout its history.

Central Israel Sites

- Some lived like hermits all alone.
- Later, many lived in monasteries in communal groups.
- They withdrew from society to live a separated life fully devoted to seeking the Lord and becoming godly.
- Over the years, monasticism changed so that many monasteries prepared men and women for a life of service to God. They would live in the monastery for a few years then go out to serve the Lord.
- Monasteries were not always Catholic. There were many monasteries before Catholicism became what it is today, and there were different kinds of monasteries from different religious orientations, i.e., Greek Orthodox, Russian Orthodox, Armenian, etc.

6. In general, monasticism is a religious way of life wherein a person denounces worldly pursuits and fully devotes themselves to seeking the Lord through religious vows and disciplines.
7. The word monk, or monastery, originates from Greek (monos) and means to "dwell alone."
8. In different periods of monasticism, some chose lives of celibacy as well.

Places of Interest

1. St. George's Monastery – It is quite a hike down into the gorge to see the monastery, so only those in good physical shape should attempt it. It can also be extremely hot during the summer.
2. Lookout – Just to the west of the parking area is a trail that leads to a beautiful lookout area over the monastery for those just wanting to see the site without hiking down to it.
3. Monastery Upper Level – Elijah's Cave

4. Monastery Middle Level – Main Church
5. Monastery Lower Level – Storehouses and vault where the remains of the early monks are kept.
6. Stairs from the inner court of the monastery lead to the cave-church of St. Elijah. From this cave, a narrow tunnel provides an escape route to the top of the mountain.
7. Wadi Qelt – Fertile ravine where small-scale farming and irrigation takes place.
8. Caves where monks lived.
9. Small Chapel

St. George's Monastery in the Bible

1. **It seems very unlikely that St. George's Monastery is the location where God supernaturally fed Elijah by ravens. The Bible says the place was east of the Jordan River, and St. George's Monastery is west of the Jordan River.**

   1 Kings 17:1–7: Now Elijah the Tishbite, of Tishbe in Gilead, said to Ahab, "As the Lord, the God of Israel, lives, before whom I stand, *there shall be neither dew nor rain these years, except by my word." 2 And the word of the Lord came to him: 3 "Depart from here and turn eastward and hide yourself by the brook Cherith, **which is east of the Jordan**. 4 You shall drink from the brook, and I have commanded the ravens to feed you there." 5 So he went and did according to the word of the Lord. He went and lived by the brook Cherith that is **east of the Jordan**. 6 And the ravens brought him bread and meat in the morning, and bread and meat in the evening, and he drank from the brook. 7 And after a while the brook dried up, because there was no rain in the land.*

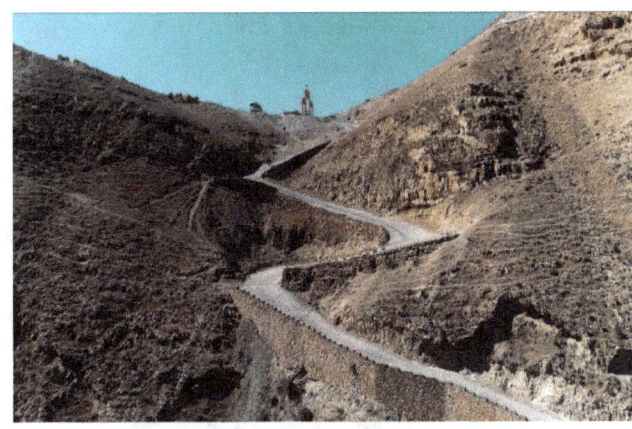

Walkway down to St. George's Monastery

2. **It is possible Elijah stayed in the cave at St. George's Monastery when he fled after being threatened by Jezebel, but it's not certain.**

   1 Kings 19:3: *Then he was afraid, and he arose and ran for his life and came to Beersheba, which belongs to Judah, and left his servant there.*

Faith Lesson from St. George's Monastery

1. We can certainly admire those who took God so seriously that they often sold their possessions and chose a life of solitude and strict discipline to seek the Lord. Do we love the Lord to such a degree we are willing to give up whatever God might ask us so we can be more devoted followers of Him?

2. Do we set time aside to remove the distractions of life and just seek God?

3. While it's good to set time apart for solitude and seeking the Lord, we are also called to be in the world but not of it. Are we doing a good job of being in the world but not a part of its values and

philosophies?
4. Are we disciplined in our Christian lives?
5. While monasticism has many admirable qualities, it does have some unbiblical concepts. For some, it was a withdrawal and escape from society. Like Christ, we are called to influence society and be lights to the world. Are we influencing those around us with the light of God's Word and His love? And are we fulfilling the Great Commission in one way or another?

Wadi Qelt and St. George's Monastery

6. Are we part of a Bible-believing church community where we can grow and serve others?

Journal/Notes:

Central Israel Sites

Valley of Elah

Location

1. The Valley of Elah is about 15 miles (23 km.) west of Bethlehem and about 20 miles (32 km.) east of the Mediterranean Sea.
2. It's located on the western edge of the Judean lower hills and was an important travel route from the coastal cities up to the center of the land of Judah and its main cities of Bethlehem, Jerusalem, and Hebron.

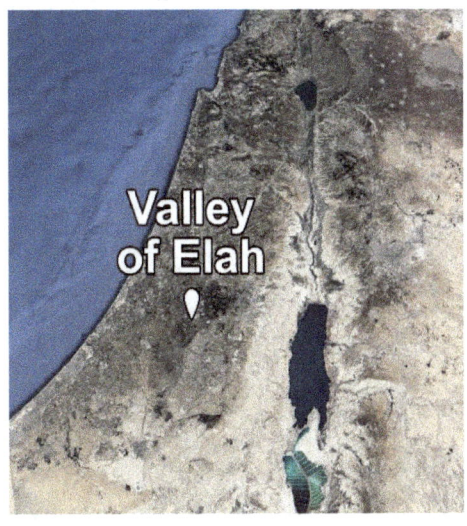

3. It's an undeveloped site that can be seen in its natural state. It has parking alongside Hwy. 38.
4. The Valley of Elah is best known for the epic battle between young David and the giant, Goliath, a skilled veteran warrior.

Historical Background

1. The Philistines were a Canaanite people who inhabited Israel before the Israelites arrived.
2. The Israelites were unable to conquer them, and there were battles between the two nations for much of Israel's history.
3. The Philistine's stronghold was on the coastal plain in the Gaza area.
4. They were powerful, cultured, and possessed iron. They were the high-tech people of the day and did all they could to prohibit Israel from gaining iron and access to their technology (1 Sam. 13:19).
5. They worshiped many false gods.
6. At this time in Israel's history, the Philistines were attempting to push up through the Valley of Elah towards the heart of Judah. King Saul and his army engaged with the Philistines to stop them.
7. The battle was one of the most pivotal between the two nations,

with the loser agreeing to serve the winner. It was a "winner takes all" kind of battle.
8. Later, King Saul would be killed by the Philistines in the Gilboa area.
9. David would eventually subdue the Philistines, and during the time of Solomon, there was peace between the two nations.
10. David was probably around 16–18 years old when he fought Goliath. We'll see why this is so as the story unfolds.

Places of Interest

1. Israelite Camp
2. Philistine Camp at Ephes-dammin
3. Valley of Elah
4. Azekah
5. Socoh
6. HaEla Stream – Place where David selected 5 smooth stones.
7. Battle Location
8. King David's Palace – Built by David when he became King as a memorial to his victory.

Valley of Elah in the Bible

1. **The battlefield setting.**

    1 Samuel 17:1–3: *Now the Philistines gathered their armies for battle. And they were gathered at* **Socoh**, *which belongs to Judah, and encamped between* **Socoh** *and* **Azekah**, *in* **Ephes-dammim**. *2 And Saul and the men of Israel were gathered, and encamped in the* **Valley of Elah**, *and drew up in line of battle against the Philistines. 3 And the Philistines stood on the mountain on the one side, and Israel stood on the mountain on the other side,* **with a valley between them**.

2. **The battle terms defined.**

    1 Samuel 17:4–10: *And there came out from the camp of the Philistines a champion named Goliath of Gath, whose height was six cubits and a span [more than 9 ft., 2.74 m. tall]. 5 He had a helmet of bronze on his head, and he was armed with a coat of mail [bronze scale armor], and the weight of the coat was five thousand* *shekels of bronze [about 125 lbs., 57 kg.]. 6 And he had bronze armor on his legs, and a javelin of bronze slung between his shoulders. 7 The shaft of his spear was like a weaver's beam, and his spear's head weighed six hundred shekels of iron [15 lbs., 7 kg.]. And his shield-bearer went before him. 8 He stood and shouted to the ranks of Israel, "Why have you come out to draw up for battle? Am I not a Philistine, and are you not servants of Saul? Choose a man for yourselves and let him come down to me. 9* **If he is able to fight with me and kill me, then we will be your servants. But if I prevail against him and kill him, then you shall be our servants and serve us**.*" 10 And the Philistine said, "I defy the ranks of Israel this day. Give me a man, that we may fight together."*

3. **The hearts of the Israelites were jolted to their core, and they**

became terrified.

1 Samuel 17:11: *When Saul and all Israel heard these words of the Philistine, they were **dismayed and greatly afraid**.*

4. **David arrived at the Valley of Elah and accepted the challenge to fight Goliath.**

   1 Samuel 17:20-27: *And David rose early in the morning and left the sheep with a keeper and took the provisions and went, as Jesse had commanded him. And he came to the encampment as the host was going out to the battle line, shouting the war cry. 21 And Israel and the Philistines drew up for battle, army against army. 22 And David left the things in charge of the keeper of the baggage and ran to the ranks and went and greeted his brothers. 23 As he talked with them, behold, the champion, the Philistine of Gath, Goliath by name, came up out of the ranks of the Philistines and spoke the same words as before. And David heard him.*

Stream where David picked up 5 smooth stones

   *24 All the men of Israel, when they saw the man, **fled from him and were much afraid**. 25 And the men of Israel said, "Have you seen this man who has come up? Surely he has come up to defy Israel. And the king will enrich the man who kills him with great riches and will give him his daughter and make his father's house free in Israel." 26 And David said to the men who stood by him, "What shall be done for the man who kills this Philistine and takes away the reproach from Israel? For who is this uncircumcised Philistine, that he should defy the armies of the living God?" 27 And the people answered him in the same way, "So shall it be done to the man who kills him."*

5. **King Saul reluctantly agreed to allow David to fight Goliath.**

   1 Samuel 17:31-37: *When the words that David spoke were heard, they repeated them before Saul, and he sent for him. 32 And David said to Saul, "Let no man's heart fail because of him. Your servant*

will go and fight with this Philistine." 33 And Saul said to David, "You are not able to go against this Philistine to fight with him, for **you are but a youth**, *and he has been a* **man of war from his youth**.*" 34 But David said to Saul, "Your servant used to keep sheep for his father. And when there came a lion, or a bear, and took a lamb from the flock, 35 I went after him and struck him and delivered it out of his mouth. And if he arose against me, I caught him by his beard and struck him and killed him. 36 Your servant has struck down both lions and bears, and this uncircumcised Philistine shall be like one of them, for he has defied the armies of the living God." 37 And David said, "The LORD who delivered me from the paw of the lion and from the paw of the bear will deliver me from the hand of this Philistine." And Saul said to David, "Go, and the LORD be with you!"*

View of Elah Valley from the Israelite camp

6. David chose not to use King Saul's armor in the battle with Goliath.

1 Samuel 17:38–39: *Then Saul clothed David with his armor. He put a helmet of bronze on his head and clothed him with a coat of mail, 39 and David strapped his sword over his armor. And he tried in vain to go, for he had not tested them. Then David said to Saul,* **"I cannot go with these, for I have not tested them**.*" So David put them off.*

7. David, with just 5 smooth stones and a sling, went into battle against a heavily armed, experienced fighting machine, who was a giant of a man and had his armor-bearer with him.

1 Samuel 17:40–47: *Then he took his staff in his hand and* **chose five smooth stones from the brook** *and put them in his shepherd's pouch. His* **sling was in his hand**, *and he approached the Philistine. 41 And the Philistine moved forward and came near to David,* **with his shield-bearer in front of him**. *42 And when the Philistine looked and saw David, he disdained him, for he was but a youth, ruddy and handsome in appearance. 43 And the Philistine said to*

David, "Am I a dog, that you come to me with sticks?" And the Philistine cursed David by his gods. 44 The Philistine said to David, "Come to me, and I will give your flesh to the birds of the air and to the beasts of the field." 45 Then David said to the Philistine, "You come to me with a sword and with a spear and with a javelin, but I come to you in the name of the LORD of hosts, the God of the armies of Israel, whom you have defied. 46 This day the LORD will deliver you into my hand, and I will strike you down and cut off your head. And I will give the dead bodies of the host of the Philistines this day to the birds of the air and to the wild beasts of the earth, **that all the earth may know that there is a God in Israel**, 47 and that all this assembly may know that the LORD saves not with sword and spear. For the **battle is the LORD's**, and he will give you into our hand."

View of Elah Valley from the Philistine camp

8. **The outcome of the epic battle showdown.**

    1 Samuel 17:48-51: *When the Philistine arose and came and drew near to meet David, David ran quickly toward the battle line to meet the Philistine. 49 And David put his hand in his bag and took out a stone and slung it and struck the Philistine on his forehead. The stone sank into his forehead, and he fell on his face to the ground. 50 So David prevailed over the Philistine* **with a sling and with a stone**, *and struck the Philistine and killed him. There was no sword in the hand of David. 51 Then David ran and stood over the Philistine and took his sword and drew it out of its sheath and killed him and cut off his head with it.*

9. **David's defeat of Goliath led to a great victory over the Philistines.**

    1 Samuel 17:51-52: *When the Philistines saw that their champion was dead, they fled. 52 And the men of Israel and Judah rose with a shout and pursued the Philistines as far as Gath and the gates of Ekron, so that the wounded Philistines fell on the way from Shaaraim as far as Gath and Ekron.*

Faith Lesson from the Valley of Elah

1. The outcome of the battle was far more significant than we might realize. If the Israelites lost, they would become the servants of the Philistines. It was a "winner takes all" battle.

2. David's motivation in the battle was the glory of God and the protection of His name: *"So that all the earth may know that there is a God in Israel"* (1 Sam. 17:46).

3. During David's youth as a shepherd, he developed many skills. He learned music, how to write, use a sling, how to fight to protect his sheep, and how to love the Lord and obey Him.

4. God used David's skill of using a sling, along with his love for the Lord, to defeat Goliath.

5. The skills David developed as a youth he used throughout his life. He faithfully led the nation Israel, instilled a love for the Lord in his kingdom, and wrote many psalms that were used in his time and throughout history to this day.

6. David knew that it's not the size of our weapons but the size of our faith in God that matters. So he went into the battle full of faith, and confident God would give him the victory.

7. Do I understand that it's my responsibility to develop my abilities and God's responsibility to direct me in how I use them?

8. Do I realize that the most important skill I possess is my love for the Lord and my heart to obey Him?

9. What miracles might God want to do in my life that would show the whole earth that there is a God in the land?

Journal/Notes:

Other Sites in Central Israel

Ashdod (Azotos)

Ashdod is a coastal city on the Mediterranean Sea about 18 miles (29 km.) south of Jaffa and Tel Aviv.

It was one of the 5 main stronghold cities of the Philistines and was well-fortified.

Ancient Ashdod

During the conquest of the Promised Land under Joshua and the Israelites, giants known as Anakim were found here (Josh. 11:22). Ashdod was allotted to Judah, but they failed to conquer it (Josh. 13:3, 15:46–47).

During the time of Samuel, Ashdod, and the other main cities of the Philistines were still independent

When the Israelites were defeated in battle under the priesthood of Eli and his wicked sons (Hophni and Phinehas), the ark was taken to the house of Dagon in Ashdod (1 Sam. 5:1–2). Later, it would be returned to the Israelites at Beth-Shemesh.

Ashdod was conquered and came under the authority of Assyria in around 711 BC. Later, Babylon conquered it as well in around 605 BC.

Ashdod was the recipient of many prophecies proclaiming its doom and destruction, i.e., Isaiah 20:11, Amos 1:8, Jeremiah 25:20, and Zechariah 2:4, 9:6. However, Ashdod continued to be inhabited as the Jews intermarried with its inhabitants after returning from Babylon (Neh. 13:23–24).

In the New Testament, Ashdod is called Azotus.

Acts 8:40: *But Philip found himself at **Azotus**, and as he passed through, he preached the gospel to all the towns until he came to Caesarea.*

Bethany Beyond the Jordan

Tradition and archaeology hold that this site is the believed location of Bethany Beyond the Jordan. It's located on a tributary that connects to the Jordan River known as Wadi Kharrar. Just before the place this wadi joins the Jordan River is called Bethany Beyond the Jordan.

It's also just across from Qasr al-Yahud Baptismal Site on Israel's side of the river. (For more on Qasr al-Yahud Baptismal Site, please see Jordan River Baptismal Site of Jesus.)

Ancient baptismal site at Bethany Beyond the Jordan

This area is where Jesus is believed to have been baptized by John the Baptist (John 1:28), where John baptized many people, and where John lived for periods of time. It's on the Jordanian side of the Jordan River and consists of two distinct areas: Tell Al-Kharrar, also known as Jabal Mar-Elias (Elijah's Hill), and the area of the churches of John the Baptist. There are Roman and Byzantine ruins of churches, chapels, a monastery, caves that hermits have used, and pools in which baptisms were held.

Excavations at this site began in 1996, following Jordan's peace treaty with Israel in 1994, and have uncovered more than 20 churches, caves, and baptismal pools, all dating from the Roman and Byzantine periods.

This area is also associated with the ascension of the Prophet Elijah into heaven, which is commemorated at a hill called Tell Mar Elias or Jabal Mar-Elias (Elijah's Hill).

Ekron (Tel Makna Akron)

Ekron is located about 20 miles (32 km.) east of Ashdod and the

Mediterranean Sea.

Ekron is the northernmost of the 5 main cities of the Philistines, all located in the coastal plain along the Mediterranean Sea.

Joshua and the Israelites failed to conquer Ekron in the conquest of the Promised Land (Josh. 13:3). It was allotted to Judah in the division of the land and then to the tribe of Dan (Josh. 15:11, 45–46, 19:43). However, Dan moved to the northern part of Israel, and Judah wound up conquering Ekron and inhabiting it (Judg. 1:18).

Tel Ekron

When the Philistines captured the Ark of the Covenant, it was the people of Ekron who proposed to have it sent back to Israel (1 Sam. 5:10, 6:16–17). The Ark went up the valley to Beth-Shemesh, where the Israelites received it with joy (1 Sam. 6:9–18).

After David killed Goliath in the Valley of Elah, the Israelites pursued and defeated the Philistines all the way to Ekron.

Ekron seems to have been the center of worship to the false god Baalzebub. This is seen in the account of the sickness and death of King Ahaziah (2 Kings 1:2–3, 6:16).

Ekron is included, among other cities, in pronouncements of judgment by the prophets Amos 1:8, Jeremiah 25:20, Zephaniah 2:4, and Zechariah 9:5–7.

Gath (Tell es Safi)

Biblical Gath (known today as Tell es-Safi, is 14 miles (23 km.) east of Ashdod and Ashkelon, which are close to the Mediterranean Sea.

Gath was one of the five main cities of the Philistines (Josh. 13:3; 1 Sam. 6:17).

It was a well-fortified walled city (2 Chron. 26:6).

Joshua and the Israelites were unable to conquer Gath despite the numerous conflicts between the Israelites and the inhabitants of Gath.

It wasn't until King David that the city was conquered and became part of the Israelite Kingdom (1 Chron. 18:1).

Tel Gath

Its name is most remembered as the home of the giant, Goliath, whom David slew (1 Sam. 17:4).

The people of Ashdod took the Ark of the Covenant to Gath when they were smitten with tumors from God. Later, the people of Gath were smitten as well with tumors and took the ark to Ekron (1 Sam. 5:8–10).

David sought refuge in Gath on two occasions when King Saul was seeking his life (1 Sam. 21:10, 27:2–4).

Gath appears to have been destroyed after being taken by David because Rehoboam restored it under his reign (2 Chron. 11:8).

Later, the Philistines regained control of Gath, for we see that King Uzziah conquered it and destroyed its walls (2 Chron. 26:6).

Once again, it must have been restored and rebuilt because Hazael, of Damascus, captured it once more (2 Kings 12:17).

During the time of the prophet Amos, Gath seems to have been destroyed (Amos 6:2), and is only mentioned in Micah 1:10, as a proverb, *"Tell it not in Gath."*

Since the time Gath was destroyed, most likely in the middle of the 8th century BC, it has laid desolate.

Mizpah

Mizpah was located centrally in the country within the territory of Benjamin, about 8 miles north of Jerusalem. Its importance as an administrative center is demonstrated not only by its use during the days of the Judges and Samuel but also by its utilization by conquering nations years later when the Empires of Assyria and Babylon would take over Judah. Mizpah means watchtower or lookout and was a central meeting place where Israel gathered for much of its history.

At Mizpah, Jacob and Laban made a covenant wherein Jacob promised Laban that he would take care of his daughters and grandchildren (Gen. 31:48-49).

Ruins of wall at Mizpah

The city of Mizpah was established as an important site early in the history of Israel in the time of the Judges and was used as a national rallying point for a man of the Levites who asked for national justice at the end of the time period of the Judges when his concubine was raped and killed by several members of the Benjamite tribe.

Samuel judged the nation from Mizpah and held national gatherings at the city, and Israel's first king, Saul, was presented to the nation at Mizpah.

Southern Israel Sites

Tel Arad

Location

1. Tel Arad is in the Negev about 16 miles (26 km.) east of Tel Beersheba, and 33 miles (54 km.) south of Jerusalem.
2. Tel Arad covers an area of about 100 acres (40 hectares) and is on the west side of Hwy. 80.
3. Although this part of the Negev receives little rain, Arad is strategically situated on ancient trade routes.

Historical Background

1. Tel Arad has two major settlement periods, a Canaanite and an Israelite period. The lower part of the tel is from the Canaanite period, and the upper fortress part is from the Israelite period.
2. The Canaanites were the original settlers of Arad and established a large city here around 3500 BC. It had an estimated population of approximately 2,500 residents.
3. Israel captured Arad in the conquest under Joshua. Later, in around 940 BC, an Israelite settlement was established here.
4. Because Tel Arad is so strategically located and important, it was destroyed and rebuilt 6 times from the 9th to the 6th centuries. It was most likely destroyed in 701 BC by the Assyrians and again by the Babylonians in 586 BC.
5. Over 100 pottery shards (ostraca) were discovered at Tel Arad dating to the 7th and 6th centuries BC. Two of these are of great value as they mention two people from priestly families in the Bible, "Pashhur" from Ezra 2:38, and "Meremoth" from Ezra 8:33.
6. Two other pottery shards found at Tel Arad have written on them the name Arad, which confirms the city's identity.

Southern Israel Sites

Places of Interest

1. Canaanite City
   - City Walls
   - City Gate
   - Temple
   - Palace
   - City Well
   - Homes
2. Entrance to Tel Arad
3. Upper Parking – Easy access to the Fortress Mound.

4. Israelite Fortress at Tel Arad
   - Although there was a small settlement during the time of Solomon, it was during the divided kingdom period that a fortress was set up at Tel Arad. The fortress served to protect Judah's southern border against its enemies.
   - The southern area of Judah was dangerous, and the fortress at Arad was destroyed 6 times during the divided kingdom period.
   - One of the destructions of the fortress likely occurred during Hezekiah's reign when he rebelled against the Assyrian King,

Sennacherib, in 701 BC. Scripture recounts how all the fortified cities of Judah were destroyed at this time (2 Kings 18:13).

- The fortress was rebuilt but destroyed again as a result of Nebuchadnezzar's conquest of Judah in 586 BC.
- During the Hellenistic period of the 3rd to 2nd centuries BC, a tower was built in the center of the fortress compound. During the Persian, Hellenistic, and Roman periods, the tower was repaired and used as a military post. During the early Arab period, the structure served as an inn for caravans.
- The fortress was finally abandoned in the 10th century AD.
- Entrance Towers
- Outer Court

5. Israelite Temple at Tel Arad

Arad had a functioning temple during the time of the divided kingdom that was somewhat similar to the temple in Jerusalem.

The temple at Arad was forbidden by God because the Israelites were to worship at no other place but Jerusalem at that time (Deut. 12:5–6).

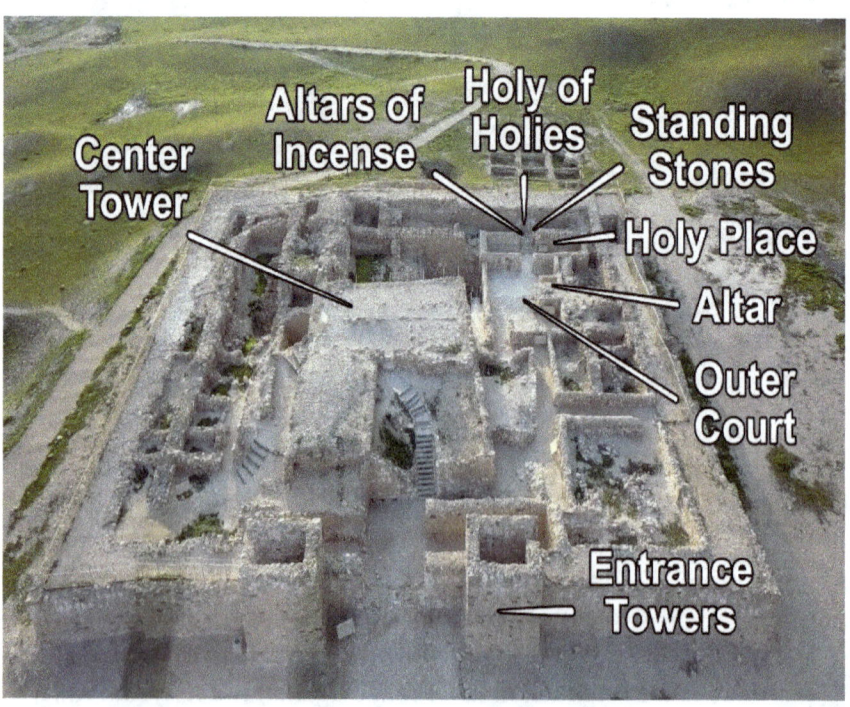

Southern Israel Sites

- Outer Courtyard
- Altar
- Holy Place – In Scripture, the holy place was a long rectangular room. At Arad, it's a wide and rectangular room.
- Altars of Incense
- Holy of Holies
- Dimensions of the Holy of Holies – In the tabernacle God ordered Moses to erect, the required dimensions of the Holy of Holies were to be 10 cubits by 10 cubits (15 ft., 9 m.) (Ex. 26:31–33). In Solomon's temple, the Holy of Holies measured 20 cubits by 20 cubits (30 ft., 9 m.) (1 Kings 6:16). When the second temple was rebuilt under Ezra, the measurements of the Holy of Holies of Solomon's temple were kept.

Holy of Holies at the temple in Tel Arad

- The Holy of Holies at Arad measures about 7 ft. by 7 ft. (2.13 m.), much smaller than the tabernacle of Moses and the First and Second Temples in Jerusalem.
- Standing Stones – There are two standing stones in the Holy of Holies. One represents Yahweh and the other, Asherah, a false female god. This shows the worship of false gods mixed with the worship of God. Clearly, this was strictly forbidden.
- According to archeological data, the temple in Arad was destroyed during King Josiah's reign in about 630 BC (2 Kings 23:4–20). It's possible, though, that King Hezekiah could have removed the temple under his reforms (2 Kings 18:22).
- Even though the worshipers at Arad were commanded to tear down the temple there, they refused to do so and covered it over with dirt instead.

Arad in the Bible

1. **The King of Arad attacked Israel while they were making their way toward the Promised Land.**

   Numbers 21:1–3: *When the Canaanite, the king of **Arad**, who lived in the Negeb, heard that Israel was coming by the way of Atharim, he fought against Israel, and took some of them captive. 2 And Israel vowed a vow to the Lord and said, "If you will indeed give this people into my hand, then I will devote their cities to destruction." 3 And the Lord heeded the voice of Israel and gave over the Canaanites, and they devoted them and their cities to destruction. So the name of the place was called Hormah.*

   Tel Arad

2. **After the confrontation with the king of Arad, the Israelites turned around and headed south toward the Red Sea instead of entering the Promised Land from the Negev region (Num. 21:4).**

3. **The area of Arad was given to the tribe of Simeon during the conquest of the land (Josh. 19:1–8).**

4. **The relatives of Moses' father-in-law (Kenites) also settled in the area around Arad.**

   Judges 1:16–17: *And the descendants of the Kenite, Moses' father-in-law, went up with the people of Judah from the city of palms into the wilderness of Judah, which lies in the Negeb near **Arad**, and they went and settled with the people. 17 And Judah went with Simeon his brother, and they defeated the Canaanites who inhabited Zephath and devoted it to destruction. So the name of the city was called Hormah.*

Southern Israel Sites

Josiah's Reforms and destruction of the temple in Arad.

1. **Josiah became king and did what was right in the eyes of the Lord.**

   2 Kings 22:1–2: *Josiah was eight years old when he began to reign, and he reigned thirty-one years in Jerusalem. His mother's name was Jedidah the daughter of Adaiah of Bozkath. 2 **And he did what was right in the eyes of the Lord** and walked in all the way of David his father, and he did not turn aside to the right or to the left.*

2. **Josiah's grandfather, Manasseh, was very wicked until God humbled him, and he repented. His father, Amon, was so wicked that his servants killed him (2 Kings 21).**

   Josiah's heritage was wicked and could have given him an excuse to live the same way. However, even at an extremely young age of 8, he loved the Lord and did what was right. Interestingly, the Book of the Law wasn't found until Josiah was 26 years old (2 Kings 22:3). This meant Josiah did what was right from a young age, even without Scripture to guide him.

3. **The Book of the Law (Bible) was found and read to Josiah.**

   2 Kings 22:8–11: *And Hilkiah the high priest said to Shaphan the secretary, "I have found the **Book of the Law** in the house of the Lord." And Hilkiah gave the book to Shaphan, and he read it. 9 And Shaphan the secretary came to the king, and reported to the king, "Your servants have*

   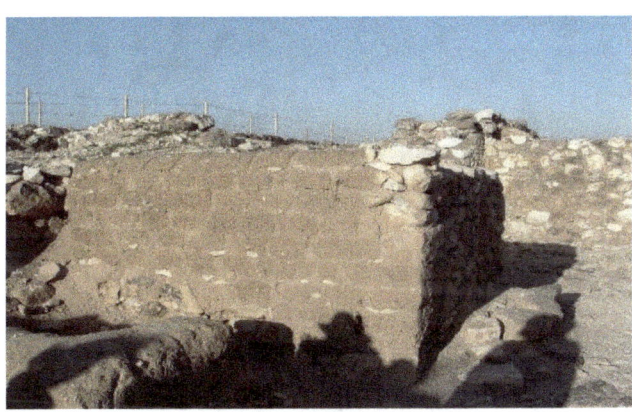
   Altar at the Israelite temple at Tel Arad

   *emptied out the money that was found in the house and have delivered it into the hand of the workmen who have the oversight of the house of the Lord." 10 Then Shaphan the secretary told the king, "Hilkiah the priest has given me a book." And Shaphan read it before the king. 11 When the king heard the words of the **Book of the Law**, he tore his clothes.*

4. **Josiah read the Bible to his whole kingdom and made a covenant with them to follow the Lord.**

    2 Kings 23:1–3: *Then the king sent, and all the elders of Judah and Jerusalem were gathered to him. 2 And the king went up to the house of the Lord, and with him all the men of Judah and all the inhabitants of Jerusalem and the priests and the prophets, all the people, both small and great. And he read in their hearing all the words of the* **Book of the Covenant** *that had been found in the house of the Lord. 3 And the king stood by the pillar and made a covenant before the Lord, to walk after the Lord and to keep his commandments and his testimonies and his statutes with all his heart and all his soul, to perform the words of this covenant that were written in this book. And* ***all the people joined in the covenant***.

5. **Josiah cleansed the temple and ordered that all the altars and shrines to the false gods be destroyed throughout the land (2 Kings 23:4–20). It was most likely Josiah who ordered the temple removed at Tel Arad.**

6. **Josiah reinstitutes and celebrates the Passover.**

    2 Chronicles 35:18: *No Passover like it had been kept in Israel since the days of Samuel the prophet. None of the kings of Israel had kept such a Passover as was kept by Josiah, and the priests and the Levites, and all Judah and Israel who were present, and the inhabitants of Jerusalem.*

    Israelite temple at Arad

    2 Chronicles 35:7: *Then* ***Josiah contributed*** *to the lay people, as Passover offerings for all who were present, lambs and young goats from the flock to the number of 30,000, and 3,000 bulls; these were* ***from the king's possessions***.

Southern Israel Sites

7. **There was no king like Josiah, who turned to the Lord with all his heart.**

   2 Kings 23:25: *Before him there was no king like him, who turned to the Lord with all his heart and with all his soul and with all his might, according to all the Law of Moses, nor did any like him arise after him.*

8. **Unfortunately, Josiah's two sons who reigned after him did not follow the Lord but acted wickedly (2 Kings 23:31-37).**

Faith Lesson from Arad

1. The Israelites in Arad set up their own temple and worshiped God their own way, which was forbidden to do. Do we realize that worshiping the right God in the wrong way is still wrong?
2. Josiah's heritage was rooted in sin, yet he chose to follow the Lord at a very young age. Do we realize that God can still use us mightily regardless of our past if we turn to Him with all our hearts as Josiah did?

Israelite Fortress at Tel Arad

3. Even though Josiah followed God with all his heart, his children chose evil. Each person has a free will to do as they please regardless of the kind of parents they have.

Journal/Notes:

Israel Biblical Sites Travel Guide

Tel Beersheba

Location

1. Beersheba is located in the Negev, which is a semi-desert.
2. The tel of Beersheba lies a little east of the modern city, which is the region's largest city and administrative capital.
3. It's about 45 miles (70 km.) south of Jerusalem and about 30 miles (45 km.) from the Mediterranean Ocean.
4. It's located between the Beersheba and Hebron Streams (which are dry much of the time).
5. It was located on a significant travel route linking Africa and Egypt with Asia and Europe. The Nabateans, who were centralized in Petra, passed through here on caravans with trade goods.

Historical Background

1. Beersheba is the beginning place of God's master plan for the Nation of Israel.
2. In essence, each person has the same tendencies as the Nation of Israel. Therefore, when God wanted to speak to all mankind, He used Israel as the example (1 Cor. 10:11).
3. The name Negev means "dry land" in Hebrew, but the Bible often uses the term to refer to the southern part of Israel.
4. Because Beersheba is in the Negev, which receives an annual rainfall of 6–8 inches (18 cm.), there was not much population in the area, and most of the people living here were nomadic shepherds.
5. Beersheba was in the territory of the Philistines (Gen. 21:33–34).
6. After a conflict over Abraham's well, which he had dug in Beersheba, a covenant was made between Abimelech and

Abraham to settle the dispute (Gen. 21:25–34). To ratify the covenant, Abraham gave Abimelech seven ewe lambs. Therefore, Beersheba means "well of the oath" or "well of the seven lambs."

7. When the writers of Scripture wanted to speak of all Israel, they would often use the expression "from Dan (the northern-most city) to Beersheba" (the southern-most city).

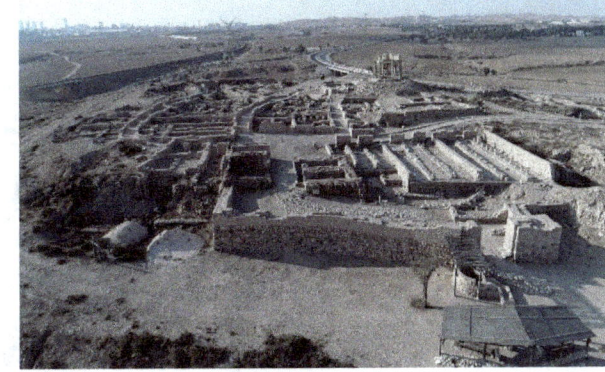
Tel Beersheba

Places of Interest

1. Four-Horned Altar

    This altar belonged to cult worship or was misused by the Israelites as it doesn't comply with Scripture. Altars were to be made of "stones on which you have not used an iron tool" (Deut. 27:5). This altar used hand-shaped stones. The altar was likely one of those torn down during the religious reforms of King Josiah (2 Kings 23:8).

2. Abraham's Well – 230 ft. deep (70 m.)
3. Outer Gate
4. Inner Gate
5. City Square
6. Governor's Palace
7. Roman Bath Pools
8. Basement House
9. Four-room House
10. Casement Wall
11. Roman Fortress
12. Observation Tower
13. Storerooms

14. Street with Shops
15. Beersheba Stream
16. Hebron Stream
17. Water Cistern

Beersheba in the Bible

1. **About 2,000 years before Christ, God called Abraham from Mesopotamia to leave his family and possessions and journey to a new land with the promise that his descendants would become a great nation.**

    Genesis 12:1–3: *Now the Lord said to Abram, "Go from your country and your kindred and your father's house to the land that I will show you. 2 And I will make of you **a great nation**, and I will bless you and make your name great, so that you will be a blessing. 3 I will bless those who bless you, and him who dishonors you I will curse, and in you all the families of the earth shall be blessed."*

2. **After Abraham passed through the Land of Israel, he settled in the Negev area (Gen. 12:9).**

3. **When a severe famine came upon the land, Abraham left the Negev for a bit and went to Egypt (Gen. 12:10).**

4. **After the famine, Abraham returned to the Negev (close to Hebron), and God confirmed His covenant with him.**

   Genesis 13:14–17: *The Lord said to Abram, after Lot had separated from him, "Lift up your eyes and look from the place where you are, northward and southward and eastward and westward, 15 **for all the land that you see I will give to you and to your offspring forever. 16 I will make your offspring as the dust of the earth**, so that if one can count the dust of the earth, your offspring also can be counted. 17 Arise, walk through the length and the breadth of the land, for I will give it to you."*

   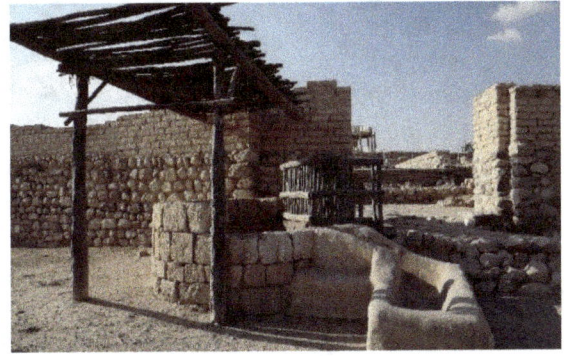
   Abraham's Well

   The Abrahamic Covenant includes two promises: (1) a land, and (2) a nation of people. From this covenant comes the Nation of Israel and their land.

5. **After the destruction of Sodom and Gomorrah, Abraham settled in Beersheba and "Lived there many days" (Gen. 21:34), probably meaning the rest of his life.**

6. **Nearby to Beersheba, Hagar, the mother of Ismael, was sent away by Abraham. However, an angel of the Lord ministered to her, saying that her offspring would be blessed (Gen. 21:14–18).**

7. **Isaac, the son and heir Abraham and Sarah had waited all their lives to have, was born in Beersheba.**

8. **It was from Beersheba that Abraham journeyed with his son Isaac to Mount Moriah at Jerusalem, where God tested him to see if he would be willing to sacrifice his son Isaac as a burnt offering. Mount Moriah is the exact place that Solomon would later build the temple in Jerusalem where countless sacrifices would be made, the most significant being the sacrifice of Christ on the Cross.**

   Genesis 22:1–5: *After these things, God tested Abraham and said to him, "Abraham!" And he said, "Here am I." 2 He said, "Take your son,* your only son Isaac, whom you love, and go to the land of **Moriah**, and offer him there as a burnt offering on one of the mountains of which I shall tell you." 3 So Abraham rose early in the morning, saddled his donkey, and took two of his young men with him, and his son Isaac. And he cut the wood for the burnt offering and arose and went to the place of which God had told him. 4 On the third day, Abraham lifted up his eyes and saw the place from afar. 5 Then Abraham said to his young men, "Stay here with the donkey; I and the boy will go over there and worship and come again to you."

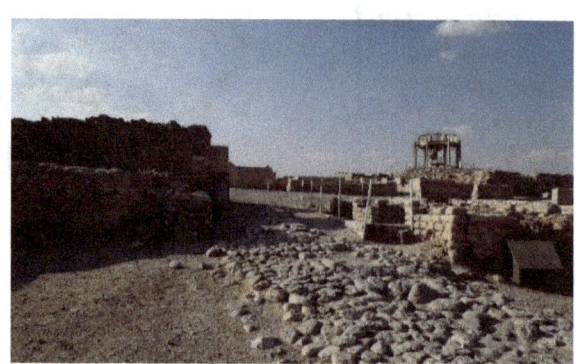

Entering Tel Beersheba

Genesis 22:10–19: Then Abraham reached out his hand and took the knife to slaughter his son. 11 But the angel of the LORD called to him from heaven and said, "Abraham, Abraham!" And he said, "Here am I." 12 He said, "Do not lay your hand on the boy or do anything to him, **for now I know that you fear God, seeing you have not withheld your son, your only son, from me**." 13 And Abraham lifted up his eyes and looked, and behold, behind him was a ram, caught in a thicket by his horns. And Abraham went and took the ram and offered it up as a burnt offering instead of his son. 14 So Abraham called the name of that place, "The LORD will provide"; as it is said to this day, "**On the mount of the LORD it shall be provided**." 15 And the angel of the LORD called to Abraham a second time from heaven 16 and said, "By myself I have sworn, declares the LORD, **because you have done this and have not withheld your son, your only son**, 17 I will surely bless you, and I will surely multiply your offspring as the stars of heaven and as the sand that is on the seashore. And your offspring shall possess the gate of his enemies, 18 and in your offspring shall all the nations of the earth be blessed, because you have obeyed my voice." 19 So Abraham returned to his young men, and they arose and went together to Beersheba. And Abraham lived at Beersheba.

9. **It was at Beersheba that Isaac and Rebecca met, falling in love at first sight (Gen. 24:62–67).**

Southern Israel Sites

10. Isaac's son, Jacob, stole the birthright from his brother Esau while the family lived in Beersheba (Gen. 27).
11. Jacob lived in Beersheba when he and all his family moved to Egypt to live with Joseph (Gen. 46:45–47).
12. The Prophet Elijah came to Beersheba when he fled from Jezebel after the great showdown on Mount Carmel between God and the 450 prophets of Baal and the 400 prophets of Asherah. Elijah had the prophets killed, whom Jezebel supported, so he was running for his life.

Four-Horned Altar

Faith Lesson from Beersheba

1. Beersheba is the beginning place of God's sovereign master plan for the Nation of Israel, and through them, all mankind.
2. Beersheba played a key role in the lives of all the patriarchs.
3. Abraham left his family and country in Mesopotamia in obedience to God and settled in Beersheba.
4. God tested Abraham at Beersheba, and he proved he loved God more than any earthly treasure, even his own son.
5. Do we understand that God often tests us as well?
6. Do we understand that God's greatest question for us is, "What do you love more than me?"
7. Do I have anything in my life that stands between God and me?
8. Do I know what my "Isaac" is, and would I be willing to give it up to God if He asked me to?
9. Abraham is called "Our father of faith" because of his obedience and devotion to God. Do we have faith like Abraham?

Journal/Notes:

En Gedi

Location

1. En Gedi is on the west side of the lower Dead Sea area about 11 miles (17 km.) north of Masada on Hwy. 90.
2. It's a beautiful oasis fed by a large spring in a barren, dry place.

Historical Background

1. The Canaanites inhabited en Gedi during the time of Abraham and Lot.
2. The Dead Sea basin was once like a Garden of the Lord.

    Genesis 13:10–12: *Lot lifted up his eyes and saw all the valley of the Jordan, that it was **well watered everywhere**—this was **before the Lord destroyed Sodom and Gomorrah**—**like the garden of the Lord**, like the land of Egypt as you go to Zoar. 11 So Lot chose for himself all the valley of the Jordan, and Lot journeyed eastward. Thus, they separated from each other. 12 Abram settled in the land of Canaan, while Lot settled in the cities of the valley, and moved his tents as far as **Sodom**.*
3. Due to the abundant water supply, the village by En Gedi Park has had a long history of habitation from ancient days to the present.
4. Today, this area is extremely dry, and En Gedi is an oasis of living water in the desert.

Places of Interest

1. Park Entrance
2. Hiking Trail
3. Nahal David Stream
4. Lower Pools
5. Upper Pools
6. Upper Waterfall

Southern Israel Sites

7. Synagogue at Tel Goren (Jorn)
8. Ancient and Modern En Gedi Town
9. Dead Sea

En Gedi in the Bible

1. **En Gedi was used in a love poem in the book of Song of Solomon.**

   Song of Solomon 1:14: *My beloved is to me a cluster of henna blossoms in the vineyards of **En Gedi**.*

2. **In the Millennial Reign of Christ on earth, God speaks of how He will change the Dead Sea region again to be like a garden due to a supernatural river flowing from Jerusalem.**

   Ezekiel 47:9–10: *And wherever the river goes, every living creature that swarms will live, and there will be very many fish. For this water goes there, that the waters of the sea may become fresh; so everything will live where the river goes. 10 Fishermen will stand beside the sea. **From En Gedi to Eneglaim** it will be a place for the spreading of nets. Its fish will be of very many kinds, like the fish of the Great Sea.*

3. **En Gedi was one of David's main hideouts when Saul was pursuing his life.**

   1 Samuel 23:28-29: *So Saul returned from pursuing after David and went against the Philistines. Therefore, that place was called the Rock of Escape. 29 And David went up from there and lived in the strongholds of* **En Gedi**.

4. **En Gedi is a perfect example of living water in the desert.**
   - The Israelites were a desert people whose whole history was related to the desert. Abraham, Isaac, Jacob, Joseph, along with the Israelite's time in Egypt, and their wandering in the desert for 40 years, all took place in a desert. Also, much of Israel is a desert as well.
   - The Israelites fully knew that living water meant life and survival.

5. **God used the desert and living water as examples of judgment upon Israel.**

   Jeremiah 2:12-13: *Be appalled, O heavens, at this; be shocked, be utterly desolate, declares the LORD, 13 for my people have committed two evils: they have forsaken me,* **the fountain of living waters**, *and* **hewed out cisterns for themselves**, *broken cisterns that can hold no water.*

   En Gedi ravine

6. **God used desert imagery to show how those who abandon Him are like a parched desert without water.**

   Jeremiah 17:5-8: *Thus says the LORD:* "**Cursed is the man who trusts in man** *and makes flesh his strength, whose heart turns away from the LORD. 6 He is like a* **shrub in the desert**, *and shall not see any good come. He shall dwell in the* **parched places of the wilderness**, *in an uninhabited salt land. 7* **Blessed is the man who trusts in the LORD**, *whose trust is the LORD. 8 He is like a tree planted by water, that sends out its roots by the stream, and does not fear when heat comes, for its leaves remain green, and is not* *anxious in the year of drought, for it does not cease to bear fruit."*

7. Christ referred to Himself as the source of living water.

John 7:37–38: *On the last day of the feast, the great day, Jesus stood up and cried out, "If anyone thirsts, let him **come to me and drink**. 38 Whoever believes in me, as the Scripture has said, 'Out of his heart will **flow rivers of living water**."*

Upper waterfall

Faith Lesson from En Gedi

1. Living Water in the Bible refers to spiritual life and vitality found only in being right with God.
2. Stagnant water is full of sickness and diseases and refers to the person who lives life without being right with God.
3. Have we received Christ, the source of living water?
4. Do we fellowship regularly with God in order to receive living water for our souls?
5. Do we read God's Word, which gives living water to our spirits and nourishes our hearts?
6. Are we seeking to find life and joy in our own pursuits and neglecting our relationship with God?

   *Be appalled, O heavens, at this; be shocked, be utterly desolate, declares the LORD, 13 for my people have committed two evils: they have forsaken me, the **fountain of living waters**, and **hewed out cisterns for themselves**, broken cisterns that can hold no water* (Jer. 2:12–13).

Journal/Notes:

Israel Biblical Sites Travel Guide

Exodus, Red Sea, and Mount Sinai

Location

1. For many years it was believed that the Israelites crossed the Suez finger of the Red Sea just southeast of what is now Cairo, Egypt. However, there are no deep bodies of water in these areas but just shallow marshes and lakes. For this reason, the biblical account of this astounding miracle has been attempted to be discredited or erased altogether by liberal scholars.

2. Many recent archeologists and scholars now believe the Israelites crossed the Red Sea at the Aqaba finger of the Red Sea and that Mount Sinai is in Midian, which is part of modern-day Saudi Arabia.

Historical Background

1. God called Abraham and promised him He would make a great nation out of his offspring. Abraham obeyed and left everything to follow God.
2. Abraham birthed Isaac, who birthed Jacob, who birthed 12 sons. God changed Jacob's name to Israel.
3. Jacob and his 12 sons moved to Egypt according to God's sovereign plan (about 70–75 total people).
4. The Israelites spent 430 years in Egypt (30 years as free people under Joseph and 400 years as slaves). During this time, they grew into a nation of around 2.5 to 3 million people.
5. God performed a miraculous deliverance of the Israelites from Egypt by performing 10 amazing miracles.
6. The last miracle, known as the Passover, happened when God killed the firstborn of all the Egyptians who did not put the blood

Southern Israel Sites

of a lamb over the doorposts of their homes.

Places of Interest

1. Egypt
2. Goshen
3. Suez Finger of the Red Sea
4. Traditional Red Sea Crossing Place
5. Sinai Peninsula
6. Aqaba Finger of Red Sea
7. Nuweiba Beach
8. Saudi Arabia Beach
9. Red Sea Crossing
10. Elim
11. Caves of Jethro
12. Rephidim
13. Mount Sinai

Israel Biblical Sites Travel Guide

The Exodus, Red Sea Crossing, and Mount Sinai in the Bible

1. **How many Israelites left Egypt and crossed the Red Sea?**

   Exodus 12:37: *Now the sons of Israel journeyed from Rameses to Succoth, about **six hundred thousand men** on foot, aside from children.*

   Using the number of 600,000 men only, we can estimate that there were probably 2.5 to 3 million Israelites.

2. **How many Egyptian soldiers were chasing the Israelites?**

   Exodus 14:6–7: *So he made his chariot ready and took his people with him; 7 and he took six hundred select chariots, and all the other chariots of Egypt with officers over all of them.*

   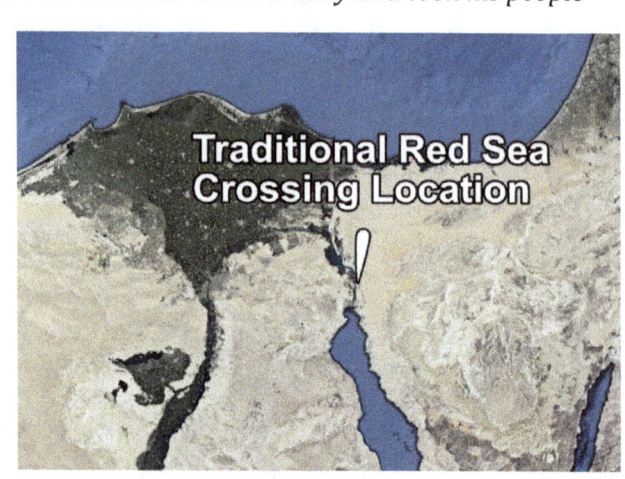

   According to Josephus, a historian writer, there were 50,000 horsemen and 200,000 footmen, all armed.

3. **Did the Israelites cross the Red Sea by Egypt?**

   For many years, it has been generally believed that the Israelites crossed the Suez finger of the Red Sea just east of Cairo, Egypt. However, the sea is not very deep there, so many have discredited the biblical miracle by claiming the Israelites crossed in shallow marshes of water.

   It should be noted that over the years, no archaeological evidence has supported this Red Sea crossing location. It also would have been virtually impossible for such a large army to drown in the shallow lakes and marshes in this area.

4. **Over the past several decades, substantial archeological investigation shows convincing evidence for a different location for the Red Sea crossing.**

   The new location places the crossing at Nuweiba Beach on the Aqaba finger of the Red Sea about 40 miles (64 km.) south of Eilat,

Israel.

5. **God said he brought the Israelites out of Egypt on the very same day they left.**

   Exodus 12:51: *And on that same day the Lord brought the sons of Israel **out of the land of Egypt** by their hosts.*

   The Red Sea crossing happened after they had left Egypt. The border of Egypt at that time was the Suez finger of the Red Sea. Any place the Israelites would have crossed the sea in this area they would still have been in Egypt and not outside of it.

6. **The Suez finger of the Red Sea is about 72 miles (116 km.) south of Goshen (place where the Israelites lived and departed Egypt). However, the land directly east of Goshen is dry and easily crossable.**

   The Israelites had exited Egypt on the same day they left. The route directly east of Goshen would have allowed them to leave Egypt on dry ground. Afterward, they would have been in the wilderness of Sinai, which fits well with the biblical narrative, as we will see in the next point.

7. **Scripture strongly indicates that the Israelites traveled a long time through a wilderness before crossing the Red Sea.**

   Exodus 13:18–22: *Hence, God led the people around by the **way of the wilderness to the Red Sea**; and the sons of Israel went up in martial array from the land of Egypt. 19 Moses took the bones of Joseph with him, for he had made the sons of Israel solemnly swear, saying, "God will surely take care of you, and you shall carry my bones from here with you." 20 Then they set out from Succoth and camped in Etham on the edge of the wilderness. 21 The Lord was going before them in a pillar of cloud by day to lead them on the way, and in a pillar of fire by night to give them light, that they* might **travel by day and by night**. *22 He did not take away the pillar of cloud by day, nor the pillar of fire by night, from before the people.*

These verses clearly reveal that the Israelites walked a long way traveling both day and night through a wilderness before crossing the Red Sea. Because the Red Sea crossing miracle happened several days after the Exodus, it couldn't have happened at the Suez finger of the Red Sea because Goshen is just 20 miles (32 km.) from the sea, a distance of just a few hours walk. Moreover, between Goshen and the believed traditional crossing place of the Red Sea is not a wilderness.

The Sinai Peninsula is a wilderness that would fit the biblical narrative of the Israelites traveling by day and by night before crossing the sea.

Research shows that a person could cross the Sinai Peninsula in 3 days traveling day and night at a normal walking pace of just 3 or so miles an hour.

Scripture also says that there were no feeble ones among them, and that God carried them supernaturally on eagle's wings during their exodus. These factors provide more evidence that the Israelites could have easily crossed the Sinai Peninsula and arrived at the Aqaba finger of the Red Sea at Nuweiba Beach.

Coral growth in the Red Sea by Nuweiba Beach

8. **There has been found in the Aqaba finger of the Red Sea at Nuweiba Beach amazing evidence of coral growth on objects that look like old chariot wheels, axles, etc. These same objects have also been found on the shore across from Nuweiba Beach on the Saudi Arabian side of the Red Sea.**

Coral doesn't grow in sandy areas and must have some object to grow on. The Red Sea is very sandy from Nuweiba Beach to the

Saudi Arabian shore, so there's no reason coral would grow in this area unless there were foreign objects for it to grow on.

9. **Nuweiba Beach is very large and could have easily accommodated the 3 million or so Israelites.**

   The beach at Nuweiba is large, flat, and sandy, a perfect place for the 2.5 to 3 million Israelites to camp.

10. **The ocean floor of the Red Sea by Nuweiba Beach gradually goes down and then gradually goes up to the shore of Saudi Arabia.**

    Just north or south of this area, there are deep impassible ravines on the ocean floor. The Nuweiba Beach location is the only place on the Aqaba finger of the Red Sea that would have allowed the Israelites to cross. It seems reasonable to suggest that God, in His

sovereignty, divinely created this sandy, gradual crossing place for the Israelites to use for this magnanimous miracle.

The maximum depth of the ocean floor at this crossing place is about 2,500 ft. deep (762 m.). This fits the biblical narrative that God divided the "mighty waters" of the sea.

Exodus 14:29: *But the sons of Israel walked on dry land through the **midst of the sea**, and the waters were **like a wall** to them on their right hand and on their left.*

Exodus 15:10: *You blew with Your wind, the sea covered them; They sank like lead in the **mighty waters**.*

Isaiah 51:10: *Was it not You who dried up the sea, the **waters of the great deep**; who made the **depths of the sea** a pathway for the redeemed to cross over?*

The shallow lakebeds and marshes by Egypt were certainly not waters of the **great deep**.

11. **Solomon referred to the Aqaba finger of the Red Sea, and archaeological discoveries have found two pillars he erected on each side of the Red Sea crossing.**

    1 Kings 9:26: *King Solomon also built a fleet of ships in Ezion-geber, which is near Eloth [modern-day Eilat] on the shore of the **Red Sea**, in the land of Edom.*

    At Nuweiba Beach, and on the beach of Saudi Arabia across from Nuweiba Beach, are pillars Solomon erected marking the crossing of the Red Sea by the Israelites.

    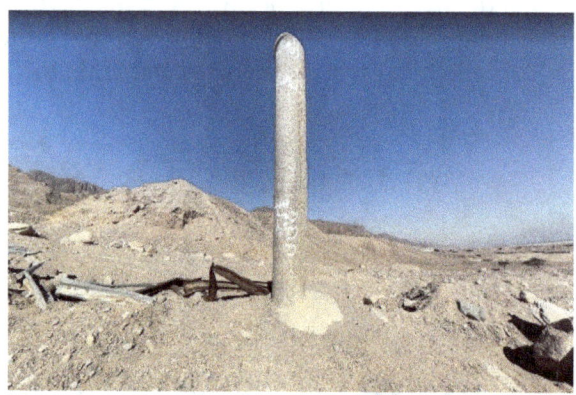
    Solomon Pillar at Nuweiba Beach

12. **When the Israelites arrived at the location of Nuweiba Beach, they were certainly hemmed in, as Scripture says.**

    Exodus 14:1–3: *Then the Lord said to Moses, 2 "Tell the people of Israel to turn back and encamp in front of Pi-hahiroth, between Migdol **and the sea**, in front of Baal-zephon; you shall encamp facing it, **by the sea**. 3 For Pharaoh will say of the people of Israel, 'They are wandering in the land; the wilderness has **shut them in**.'"*

    The landscape at Nuweiba Beach is unique and mountainous and would fit the biblical narrative.

13. **As a result of being hemmed in and threatened by the Egyptian army, the Israelites cried out to Moses in anger and desperation.**

    Exodus 14:13–14: *But Moses said to the people, "Do not fear! Stand by and see the salvation of the Lord which He will accomplish for you today; for the Egyptians whom you have seen today, you will never see them again forever. 14 The Lord will fight for you while you keep silent."*

14. Then the hand of God performed one of the greatest miracles ever recorded in Scripture.

Exodus 14:15–31: *Then the Lord said to Moses, "Why are you crying out to Me? Tell the sons of Israel to go forward. 16 As for you, lift up your staff and stretch out your hand over the sea and divide it, and the sons of Israel shall go through the* **midst of the sea** *on dry land. 17 As for Me, behold, I will harden the hearts of the Egyptians so that they will go in after*

them; and I will be honored through Pharaoh and all his army, through his chariots and his horsemen. 18 Then the Egyptians will know that I am the Lord, when I am honored through Pharaoh, through his chariots and his horsemen."

19 The angel of God, who had been going before the camp of Israel, moved and went behind them; and the pillar of cloud moved from before them and stood behind them. 20 So it came between the camp of Egypt and the camp of Israel; and there was the cloud along with the darkness, yet it gave light at night. Thus, the one did not come near the other all night.

21 Then Moses stretched out his hand over the sea; and the Lord swept the sea back by a strong east wind all night and turned the sea into dry land, so the waters were divided. 22 The sons of Israel went through the midst of the sea on the dry land, and the waters were **like a wall to them** *on their right hand and on their left. 23 Then the Egyptians took up the pursuit, and all Pharaoh's horses, his chariots and his horsemen went in after them into the midst of the sea. 24 At the morning watch, the Lord looked down on the army of the Egyptians through the pillar of fire and cloud and brought the army of the Egyptians into confusion. 25 He caused their chariot wheels to swerve, and He made them drive with difficulty; so the*

Egyptians said, "Let us flee from Israel, for the Lord is fighting for them against the Egyptians."

26 Then the Lord said to Moses, "Stretch out your hand over the sea so that the waters may come back over the Egyptians, over their chariots and their horsemen." 27 So Moses stretched out his hand over the sea, and the sea returned to its normal state at daybreak, while the Egyptians were fleeing right into it; then the Lord overthrew the Egyptians in **the midst of the sea**. *28 The waters returned and covered the chariots and the horsemen, even Pharaoh's entire army that had gone into the sea after them; not even one of them remained. 29 But the sons of Israel walked on dry land through* **the midst of the sea**, *and the* **waters were like a wall** *to them on their right hand and on their left.*

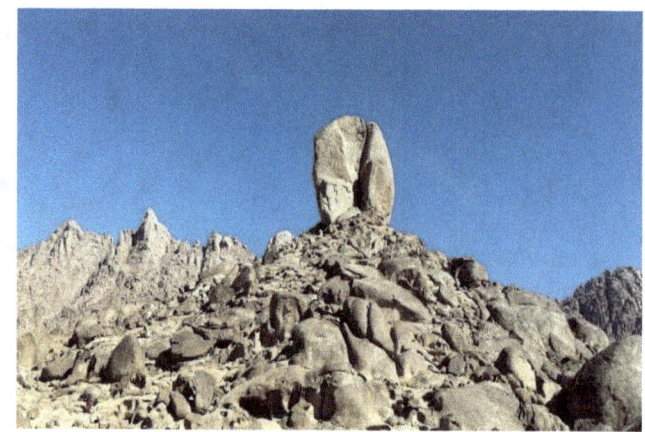
Split Rock at Rephidim

30 Thus the Lord saved Israel that day from the hand of the Egyptians, and Israel saw the Egyptians dead on the seashore. 31 When Israel saw the great power which the Lord had used against the Egyptians, the people feared the Lord, and they believed in the Lord and in His servant Moses.

The entire Egyptian army drowned in the sea, and if the army was around 250,000, this couldn't have happened in the shallow marshes east of Egypt. So it had to occur in a wide and deep body of water.

15. After crossing the Red Sea, the Bible says the Israelites then traveled to Mount Sinai. Does the location of Mount Sinai in Saudi Arabia (biblical Midian) fit the biblical narrative?

When Moses fled to Egypt to save his life, Scripture says he went to Midian.

Exodus 2:15: *When Pharaoh heard of this matter, he tried to kill*

*Moses. But Moses fled from the presence of Pharaoh and settled in the **land of Midian**, and he sat down by a well.*

Midian is in Saudi Arabia, not in the Sinai Peninsula.

Galatians 4:25: *Now this Hagar is **Mount Sinai in Arabia** and corresponds to the present Jerusalem, for she is in slavery with her children.*

When God appeared to Moses in a burning bush at Mount Sinai, God said that Moses would bring the people out of Egypt and worship at the same Mount Sinai (also known as Mount Horeb). Moses was in Midian when this event occurred, so it seems very convincing that Mount Sinai is in Midian.

Exodus 3:1–2: *Now Moses was pasturing the flock of Jethro his father-in-law, the priest of **Midian**; and he led the flock to the west side of the wilderness and came to **Horeb, the mountain of God**. 2 The angel of the Lord appeared to him in a blazing fire from the midst of a bush; and he looked, and behold, the bush was burning with fire, yet the bush was not consumed.*

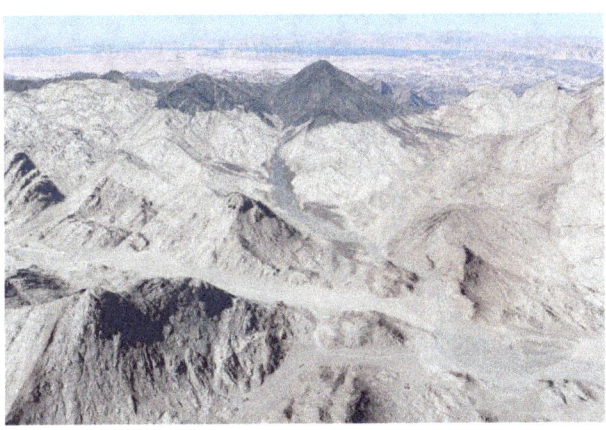
Mount Sinai with dark top

Exodus 3:12: *And He said, "Certainly I will be with you, and this shall be the sign to you that it is I who have sent you: when you have brought the people out of Egypt, you shall worship God **at this mountain**."*

16. **Evidence from the places the Israelites camped on their way from the Red Sea crossing to Mount Sinai supports Mount Sinai's location in Midian.**

    Location of Elim

    Exodus 15:27: *Then they came to **Elim** where there were twelve springs of water and seventy date palms, and they camped there beside the waters.*

The location of Elim has been identified in Saudi Arabia, about 26 miles (42 km.) south of the Red Sea crossing.

Caves of Jethro

There are caves named after Jethro the Midianite (Moses' father-in-law) that have been found by the route the Israelites took from the Red Sea crossing to Mount Sinai. This shows that Jethro lived in this area and that it was the land of Midian at that time.

Split Rock at Rephidim

Exodus 17:1: *Then all the congregation of the sons of Israel journeyed by stages from the wilderness of Sin, according to the command of the Lord, and camped at* **Rephidim**, *and there was no water for the people to drink.*

Exodus 17:6: *Behold, I will stand before you there on the rock at Horeb; and you shall strike the rock, and* **water will come out of it**, *that the people may drink."*

This rock at Rephidim is believed to have been found. It is a large rock that is split from top to bottom and shows water grooves where massive amounts of water ran down from it.

17. **Evidence for the location of Mount Sinai in Midian.**

Mount Sinai in Midian (Saudi Arabia) has a blackened and burnt top, which fits the biblical narrative.

Exodus 19:18: *Now Mount Sinai was all in smoke because the Lord descended upon it in fire; and its smoke ascended like the smoke of a furnace, and the whole mountain quaked violently.*

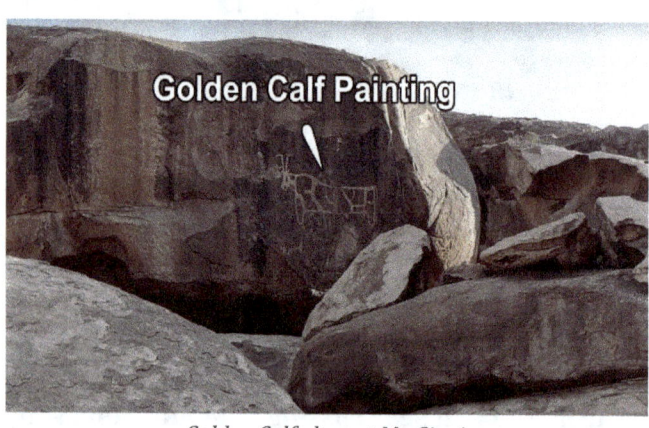

Golden Calf altar at Mt. Sinai

At the base of Mount Sinai in Midian is an altar Moses erected, 12 stones Moses erected by the altar, an altar to a Golden Calf with paintings of calves and animals, a rock painting of a menorah, a cave where Elijah could have stayed, and archaeological findings. Today, sections of the area and the mountain are fenced off by the Saudi Arabian government and designated as archeological sites. However, there are no excavations permitted on them at this time.

18. **Other Evidence from ancient historians.**

    Several Jewish documents dating 600 years before Christ locate Mount Sinai in Midian, and Philo and Josephus (Jewish historians) also located Mount Sinai in Midian of Arabia.

Faith Lesson from the Exodus, Red Sea Crossing, and Mount Sinai

1. The deliverance of the Israelites from Egypt was done to show several deep theological truths:
   - To show God's power and glory (He is above all gods and is the only true God).
   - To be a foreshadow of salvation and deliverance (God can save and deliver us as He did the Israelites).
   - To teach His chosen people how to follow and obey Him.
   - To show his power and glory to the other nations.
2. The important thing to realize is that the location of the events of the Exodus, Red Sea crossing, and Mount Sinai are not the determining factor for whether the Bible is true. However, this evidence does strengthen our faith to know the events spoken of in Scripture are true and historical.
3. The miracles surrounding the Exodus, Red Sea crossing, and Mount Sinai are some of the greatest miracles found in Scripture.
4. All of this should inspire us to trust and obey God more fully.

Journal/Notes:

Hebron

Location

1. The city of Hebron is set in the Judean Mountains about 20 miles (32 km.) south of Jerusalem.
2. Hebron stands 3,000 ft. (914 m.) above sea level, making it the highest city in Israel.
3. While there have been tensions in the past between Israelis and Arabs, the Cave of the Patriarchs and Tel Hebron (Tel Rumeida) is protected by Israeli forces, and around 250,000 tourists visit Hebron annually.

Historical Background

1. Hebron is one of the most popular places in the Bible, being mentioned 72 times.
2. It was inhabited by the Canaanites before Abraham and the Israelites arrived.
3. Hebron is the beginning place and roots of the nation of Israel. The promises and covenants God made with Abraham and his descendants happened here or nearby. These promises would also have wide-reaching implications and include all the nations of the earth.
4. All the patriarchs and their wives, except Rachel, one of Jacob's wives, are buried in Hebron.
5. Located in Hebron is Machpelah, the Cave of the Patriarchs.
    - Abraham purchased the cave and the adjoining field at full market price as a burial place for his family some 3,700 years ago.
    - The Cave of the Patriarchs building is the second holiest site in

Southern Israel Sites

Judaism (after the Western Wall in Jerusalem) and is also sacred to Christians and Muslims.

- In the cave are the tombs of Abraham and Sarah, Isaac and Rebekah, and Jacob and Leah.
- King Herod built a massive wall around the cave around 20 BC to preserve it and establish a memorial place for the Jews. He used the same style of stones as he did for the Temple Mount walls in Jerusalem.
- This is the only building in Israel that has remained intact and undamaged since it was built.
- It was used over the centuries as a church by the Byzantine and Crusaders, then as a mosque by the Muslims.

Machpelah: Cave of the Patriarchs

- The Byzantines erected a small basilica with a roof over part of the interior, and the Crusaders built the roof that exists today that covers the entire building.
- Today, the Cave of the Patriarch building is shared by the Jews and Muslims. On one side of the building is a synagogue and on the other side is a mosque.
- The tombs of the patriarchs are under the foundation of the building, but their memorial monuments are visible in the building on the first floor.

Places of Interest

1. Cave of the Patriarchs (Machpelah)
    - Jewish Synagogue
    - Mosque
    - Tombs of the Patriarchs and Matriarchs
2. Tel Hebron (Tel Rumeida)
    - Abraham's Well

- Ancient Stairs
- Tomb of Jesse and Ruth (King David's father and great grandmother)
- Old Olive Trees
- Ancient City Walls
- Mikvahs
- Ancient Synagogue
- New Excavations
3. Oaks of Mamre

Hebron in the Bible

1. **After God affirmed His covenant with Abraham in Hebron, he built an altar to the Lord and lived there.**

   Genesis 13:17–18: *Arise, walk about the land through its length and breadth; for I will give it to you. 18 Then Abram moved his tent and came and dwelt by the oaks of Mamre, which are in **Hebron**, and there he built an altar to the Lord.*

2. **At Hebron, Abraham learned in a dream that his descendants would spend 400 years as slaves in Egypt.**

Genesis 15:12–14: *Now when the sun was going down, a deep sleep fell upon Abram; and behold, terror and great darkness fell upon him. 13 God said to Abram, "Know for certain that your descendants will be strangers in a land that is not theirs, where they will be enslaved and oppressed four hundred years. 14 But I will also judge the nation whom they will serve, and afterward, they will come out with many possessions."*

3. **At Hebron, Ismael was born to Abraham and Sarah's handmaid, Hagar (Gen. 16:4).**

4. **Near Hebron, God made a covenant with Abraham that he would be "the ancestor of a multitude of nations."**

Genesis 17:1–8: *When Abram was ninety-nine years old the LORD appeared to Abram and said to him, "I am God Almighty; walk before me, and be blameless, 2 that I may make my covenant between me and you, and may multiply you greatly." 3 Then Abram fell on his face. And God said to him, 4 "Behold, my covenant is with you, and you shall be the father of a multitude of nations. 5 No longer shall your name be called Abram, but your*

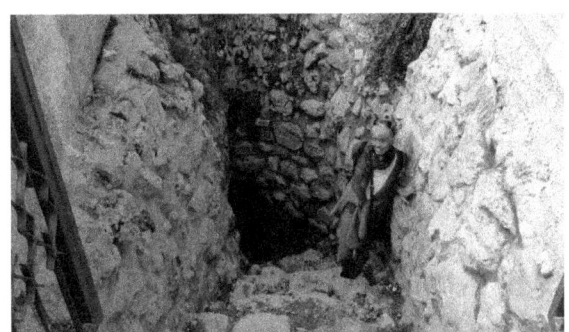

Abraham's Well

name shall be Abraham, for I have made you the father of a multitude of nations. 6 I will make you exceedingly fruitful, and I will make you into nations, and kings shall come from you. 7 And I will establish my covenant between me and you and your offspring after you throughout their generations for an everlasting covenant, to be God to you and to your offspring after you. 8 And I will give to you and to your offspring after you the land of your sojournings, all the land of Canaan, for an everlasting possession, and I will be their God."

5. **At Hebron, Abraham offered hospitality to three servant angels of God and received the promise of a son.**

Genesis 18:10–14: *They said to him, "Where is Sarah your wife?" And he said, "She is in the tent." 10 The LORD said, "I will surely return to you about this time next year, and Sarah your wife shall* have a son." And Sarah was listening at the tent door behind him. 11 Now Abraham and Sarah were old, advanced in years. The way of women had ceased to be with Sarah. 12 So Sarah laughed to herself, saying, "After I am worn out, and my lord is old, shall I have pleasure?" 13 The LORD said to Abraham, "Why did Sarah laugh and say, 'Shall I indeed bear a child, now that I am old?' 14 Is anything too hard for the LORD? At the appointed time I will return to you, about this time next year, and Sarah shall have a son."

Ancient synagogue at Hebron

6. **At Hebron, Abraham bought the Cave of Machpelah as a burial place for his wife, Sarah, and his family.**

    Genesis 23:19: *After this, Abraham buried Sarah his wife in the cave of the field at Machpelah facing Mamre (that is, **Hebron**) in the land of Canaan.*

7. **Later, Abraham, Isaac, Rebecca, Jacob, and Leah would be buried in the Cave of Machpelah as well.**

8. **Jacob returned to Hebron after he had sojourned in Paddan-aram.**

    Genesis 35:27: *Jacob came to his father Isaac at Mamre of Kiriath-arba (that is, **Hebron**), where Abraham and Isaac had sojourned.*

9. **Joseph was sent from Hebron to Shechem, where he would be sold into slavery and taken to Egypt.**

    Genesis 37:14: *Then he said to him, "Go now and see about the welfare of your brothers and the welfare of the flock, and bring word back to me." So he sent him from the valley of **Hebron**, and he came to Shechem.*

10. **Nearby to Hebron, two of the spies who researched the Promised Land returned with a large cluster of grapes.**

    Numbers 13:21–23: *So the men explored the land from the Desert of Zin to the border of Hamath. 22 They went through the Negev and came to **Hebron**, where Ahiman, Sheshai, and Talmai lived. They are* descendants of Anak. (Hebron was built seven years before Zoan in Egypt.) 23 When they came to the Eshcol Valley, they cut off a branch with **only one bunch of grapes** on it. They carried it on a pole between two of them.

11. **Hebron was given to Caleb as an inheritance for his faithfulness to the Lord.**

Joshua 14:13-14: *So Joshua blessed him and gave **Hebron** to Caleb the son of Jephunneh for an inheritance. 14 Therefore, Hebron became the inheritance of Caleb, the son of Jephunneh the Kenizzite until this day, because he followed the Lord God of Israel fully.*

Tombs of Jesse and Ruth

12. **Samson carried the gates of Gaza 35 miles (55 km.) up to Hebron (Judg. 16:1-3).**
13. **David was anointed king in Hebron and reigned here for 7 ½ years (2 Sam. 2:1-4, 11).**

Faith Lesson from Hebron

1. God confirmed His promises and covenants with Abraham at Hebron and fulfilled them all. Do we believe and embrace the promises of God?
2. Caleb was one of the faithful spies who received Hebron as a reward. Are we faithful like Caleb, and do we have our hope placed in our eternal home in heaven as our reward?
3. David was anointed king in Hebron because he was a person after God's own heart. Do we love the Lord like David, and are we desiring to serve Him in significant ways as David did?

Journal/Notes:

Kadesh Barnea

Location

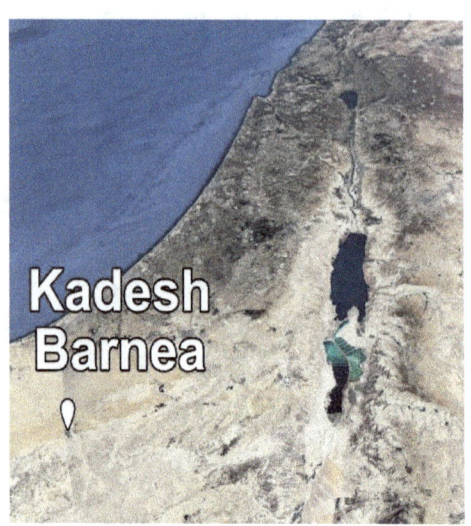

1. Kadesh Barnea is on the southern border area between Israel and Egypt.
2. It's about 31 miles (51 km.) east of the Mediterranean Ocean and about 33 miles (53 km.) southwest of Beer Sheba.
3. Kadesh Barnea was the original place where God intended the Israelites to enter the Promised Land.
4. Today, a community lives at Kadesh Barnea, and the town retains its same name.

Historical Background

1. At Kadesh Barnea, one of the most tragic events in Israel's history happened.
2. It's here they rebelled against God's plan for them to enter the Promised Land. As a result, they were severely judged for their lack of faith and condemned to wander in the wilderness 40 years until those 20 years old, and older died.
3. The Israelites had seen many spectacular miracles.
   - They saw 10 supernatural plagues God sent upon the Egyptians.
   - They witnessed the first Passover wherein God spared the Israelites as they put blood from a lamb around the doors of their dwellings.
   - They saw God open the hearts of the Egyptians so that they gave them many possessions.
   - They experienced supernatural help to cross the Sinai Peninsula on eagle's wings to reach the Aqaba finger of the Red Sea.

Southern Israel Sites

- They beheld a pillar of cloud by day and a pillar of fire by night to guide and protect them.
- They experienced the miraculous crossing of the Red Sea (10.5 miles wide, 17 km.) in which they were approximately 2,500 ft. (762 m.) under sea level in the midst of the depths and mighty waters of the sea (Isa. 51:10).
- They saw God supernaturally provide water out of a rock at Rephidim.
- God helped the Israelites supernaturally defeat the Amalekites as Aaron and Hur held up the arms of Moses.
- They stood in fear and trembling as God sent fire and smoke upon Mt. Sinai when he gave them the Ten Commandments written on stone by His own finger.

Modern-day Kadesh Barnea

- They received supernatural provisions of Manna and quail in the desert.

4. The Israelites had been bathed in miracles for well over a year from when they left Egypt until they reached Kadesh Barnea.
5. They had seen enough miracles to be able to trust God for anything.
6. However, despite all the miracles they had witnessed, they viewed God as too weak to help them enter the Promised Land and rebelled against Him.

Places of Interest

1. Kadesh Barnea
2. Egypt
3. Sinai Peninsula
4. Aqaba Finger of the Red Sea Crossing
5. Rephidim

6. Mt. Sinai
7. Israel

Kadesh Barnea in the Bible

1. **Twelve spies were sent into the Promised Land from Kadesh Barnea to give a report.**

   Numbers 13:1–3: *Then the Lord spoke to Moses saying, 2 "Send out for yourself men so that they may spy out the **land of Canaan**, which I am going to **give to the sons of Israel**; you shall send a man from each of their fathers' tribes, every one a leader among them." 3 So Moses sent them from the wilderness of Paran at the command of the Lord, all of them men who were heads of the sons of Israel.*

2. **Ten Spies give a bad report of the difficulty in possessing the land.**

   Numbers 13:25–29: *When they returned from **spying out the land**, at the end of forty days, 26 they proceeded to come to Moses and Aaron and to all the congregation of the sons of Israel in the wilderness of Paran, at **Kadesh**; and they brought back word to them and to all the congregation and showed them the fruit of the* land. 27 Thus, they told him, and said, "We went in to the land where you sent us; and it certainly does flow with milk and honey, and this is its fruit. 28 Nevertheless, the people who live in the land are strong, and the cities are fortified and very large; and moreover, we saw the descendants of Anak there. 29 Amalek is living in the land of the Negev and the Hittites and the Jebusites and the Amorites are living in the hill country, and the Canaanites are living by the sea and by the side of the Jordan."*

3. **Two spies (Joshua and Caleb) give a good report of faith. Caleb is the spokesman.**

    Numbers 13:30: *Then Caleb quieted the people before Moses and said, "We should by all means go up and take possession of it, for we will surely overcome it."*

4. **The 10 spies convince the people that they are unable to possess the land.**

    Numbers 13:31–33: *But the men who had gone up with him said, "We are **not able to go up against the people**, for they are **too strong for us**."*
    32 So they gave out to the sons of Israel a bad report of the land which they had spied out, saying, "The land through which we have gone, in spying it out, is a land that devours its inhabitants; and all the people whom we saw in it are men of great size. 33 There also we saw the Nephilim (the sons of Anak are part of the Nephilim); and we became like grasshoppers in our own sight, and so we were in their sight."

    Modern-day Kadesh Barnea

5. **The Israelites rebel against God and decide to return to Egypt as slaves again.**

    Numbers 14:1–4: *Then all the congregation lifted up their voices and cried, and the people wept that night. 2 All the sons of Israel grumbled against Moses and Aaron; and the whole congregation said to them, "Would that we had died in the land of Egypt! Or would that we had died in this wilderness! 3 Why is the Lord bringing us* into this land, to fall by the sword? Our wives and our little ones will become plunder; would it not be better for us to return to Egypt?" 4 So they said to one another, "**Let us appoint a leader and return to Egypt**."

6. **Moses, Aaron, Joshua, and Caleb plead with the people not to rebel against God's will for them.**

   Numbers 14:5–10: *Then Moses and Aaron fell on their faces in the presence of all the assembly of the congregation of the sons of Israel. 6 Joshua the son of Nun and Caleb the son of Jephunneh, of those who had spied out the land, tore their clothes; 7 and they spoke to all the congregation of the sons of Israel, saying, "The land which we passed through to spy out is an exceedingly good land. 8 If the Lord is pleased with us, then He will bring us into this land and give it to us— a land which flows with milk and honey. 9 Only do not rebel against the Lord; and do not fear the people of the land, for they will be our prey. Their protection has been removed from them, and the Lord is with us; do not fear them." 10 But all the congregation said to stone them with stones. Then the glory of the Lord appeared in the tent of meeting to all the sons of Israel.*

   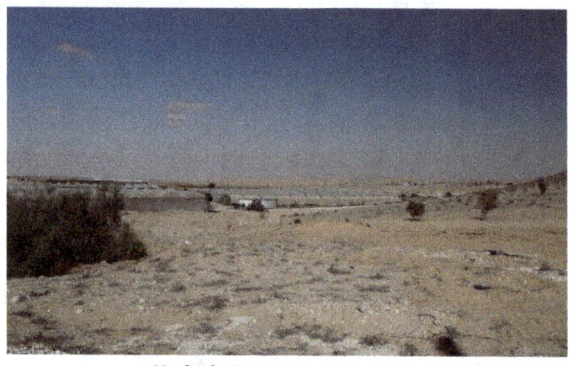
   Kadesh Barnea countryside

7. **God threatens to destroy the Israelites and make a great nation out of Moses' offspring.**

   Numbers 14:11–12: *The Lord said to Moses, "How long will this people spurn Me? And how long will they not believe in Me, despite all the signs which I have performed in their midst? 12 I will smite them with pestilence and dispossess them, and I will make you into a nation greater and mightier than they."*

8. **Moses prays on behalf of the people (Num. 14:13–19).**
9. **God forgives the Israelites but still judges them.**

   Numbers 14:20–38: *So the Lord said, "**I have pardoned them according to your word**; 21 but indeed, as I live, all the earth will be filled with the glory of the Lord. 22 Surely all the men who have* *seen My glory and My signs which I performed in Egypt and in the wilderness, yet have put Me to the test these ten times and have not listened to My voice, 23* **shall by no means see the land which I swore to their fathers**, *nor shall any of those who spurned Me see it. 24 But My servant Caleb, because he has had a different spirit and has followed Me fully, I will bring into the land which he entered, and his descendants shall take possession of it. 25 Now the Amalekites and the Canaanites live in the valleys; turn tomorrow and set out to the wilderness by the way of the Red Sea."*

26 The Lord spoke to Moses and Aaron, saying, 27 "How long shall I bear with this evil congregation who are grumbling against Me? I have heard the complaints of the sons of Israel, which they are making against Me. 28 Say to them, 'As I live,' says the Lord, 'just as you have spoken in My hearing, so I will surely do to you; 29 your corpses will fall in this wilderness, even all your numbered men,

Kadesh Barnea countryside

according to your complete number from twenty years old and upward, who have grumbled against Me. 30 Surely you shall not come into the land in which I swore to settle you, except Caleb the son of Jephunneh and Joshua the son of Nun. 31 Your children, however, whom you said would become a prey—I will bring them in, and they will know the land which you have rejected. 32 But as for you, your corpses will fall in this wilderness. 33 Your sons shall be shepherds for forty years in the wilderness, and they will suffer for your unfaithfulness, until your corpses lie in the wilderness. 34 According to the number of days which you spied out the land, forty days, for every day you shall bear your guilt a year, even forty years, and you will know My opposition. 35 I, the Lord, have spoken, surely this I will do to all this evil congregation who are gathered together against Me. In this wilderness they shall be destroyed, and there they will die.'" 36 As for the men whom Moses sent to spy out the land and who returned and made all the congregation grumble against him by bringing out a bad report concerning the land, 37 even those men who brought out the very bad report of the land died by a plague before the Lord. 38 But Joshua the son of Nun and Caleb the son of Jephunneh remained alive out of those men who went to spy out the land.

Faith Lesson from Kadesh Barnea

1. The reality of the judgment of God is sobering. God forgave the Israelites, but He did not remove the consequences of their disobedience. We frequently find this in Scripture, i.e., Moses striking the rock and David and his sin with Bathsheba.
2. There were approximately 1.2 million Israelites 20 years old and above who died in the desert over a 40-year period. This means there were 30,000 funerals per year, 82 funerals a day, and 7 funerals an hour.
3. God has written these examples in the Bible for our instruction today.

   Romans 15:4: *For whatever **was written in earlier times was written for our instruction**, so that through perseverance and the encouragement of the Scriptures we might have hope.*

   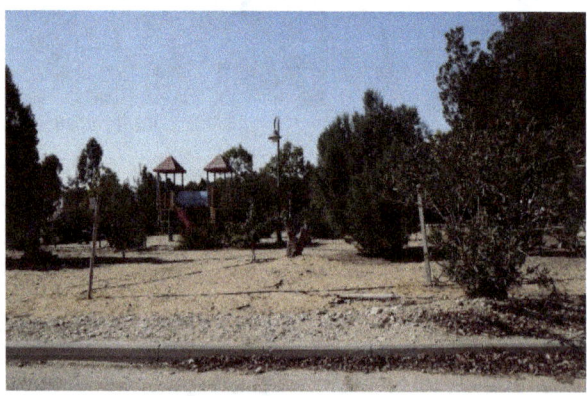
   Modern-day Kadesh Barnea

   1 Corinthians 10:1–13: *For I do not want you to be unaware, brethren, that our fathers were all under the cloud and all passed through the sea; 2 and all were baptized into Moses in the cloud and in the sea; 3 and all ate the same spiritual food; 4 and all drank the same spiritual drink, for they were drinking from a spiritual rock which followed them; and the rock was Christ. 5 Nevertheless, with most of them God was not well-pleased; for they were laid low in the wilderness. 6 Now these things happened as examples for us, so that we would not crave evil things as they also craved. 7 Do not be idolaters, as some of them were; as it is written, "The people sat*

down to eat and drink, and stood up to play." 8 Nor let us act immorally, as some of them did, and twenty-three thousand fell in one day. 9 Nor let us try the Lord, as some of them did, and were destroyed by the serpents. 10 Nor grumble, as some of them did, and were destroyed by the destroyer. 11 **Now these things happened to them as an example, and they were written for our instruction**, *upon whom the ends of the ages have come. 12 Therefore, let him who thinks he stands take heed that he does not fall. 13 No temptation has overtaken you but such as is common to man; and God is faithful, who will not allow you to be tempted beyond what you are able, but with the temptation will provide the way of escape also, so that you will be able to endure it.*

Wilderness of Paran by Kadesh Barnea

4. Do I grumble and complain about God's provisions, trials, or difficulties He has sent my way?
5. Do I have faith that God can help me in whatever He has called me to do and be?

Journal/Notes:

Lachish

Location

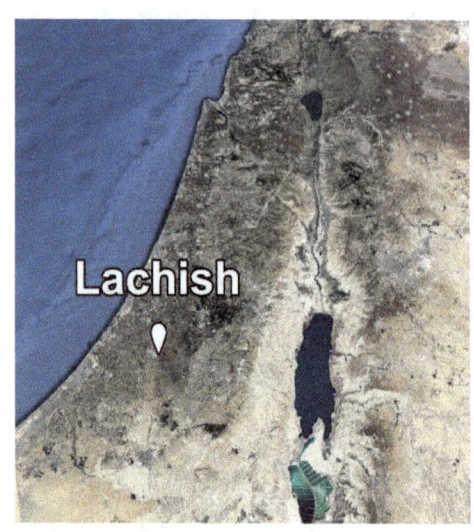

1. Tel Lachish is in the foothills (Shaphelah) of the Judean Mountains, about 18 miles (30 km.) from the Mediterranean Sea and about 25 miles (41 km.) southwest of Jerusalem.
2. Lachish is regarded as the second most important city after Jerusalem in the Southern Kingdom of Judah and was strategically located on the Via Maris travel route.
3. It was a well-fortified military city with double walls and provided protection to Israel's southern region.

Historical Background

1. Lachish has two major settlement periods, a Canaanite and an Israelite settlement period.
2. Lachish was first settled and inhabited by the Canaanites around 3000 BC.
3. It was then conquered by the Israelites under Joshua during the conquest of the Promised Land.
4. After the Kingdom of Israel was divided, Lachish became a thriving Israelite city during king Rehoboam's reign (920 BC), and around 10,000 people lived in the city at that time.
5. It was destroyed by the Assyrians in 701 BC and by the Babylonians in 587 BC.
6. Numerous pottery shards (ostraca) were found at Lachish. One spoke of the fall of the nearby city of Azekah (above the Valley of Elah) by the Assyrians. This realization must have sent fear into the hearts of those in Lachish. Another pottery shard spoke of a prophet, most likely Jeremiah.

Southern Israel Sites

7. Writings and relief pictures at Nineveh (modern-day Mosul) reveal the destruction of Lachish.
8. Interestingly, ostraca pieces and other findings in Israel reveal the evidence of around 100 biblical names of people in the Bible.
9. There are 2 caves filled with skulls nearby to Lachish, giving evidence of its destruction.
10. In 539 BC, the Persians defeated the Babylonians and allowed the exiles to return to Israel from 538–445 BC. Jerusalem and Lachish were reconstructed at this time (Nehemiah 11:1, 30).
11. Lachish was finally abandoned after the Hellenistic rule in Israel (332–167 BC).

Places of Interest

1. Entrance
2. Large Building
3. Siege Ramp
4. City Gate
5. Palace
6. Palace Courtyard

7. Quarry/Reservoir
8. Israelite Temple – Similar layout as the temple in Tel Arad. This temple was also prohibited (Deut. 12:5-7).
9. City Well
10. City Walls

Lachish in the Bible

1. **The King of Lachish joined 4 other kings to fight against the Gibeonites because they had made peace with Israel during the conquest of the Promised Land.**

    Joshua 10:1-5: *As soon as Adoni-zedek, king of Jerusalem, heard how Joshua had captured Ai and had devoted it to destruction, doing to Ai and its king as he had done to Jericho and its king, and how the inhabitants of Gibeon had made peace with Israel and were among them, 2 he feared greatly, because Gibeon was a great city,*

    Lachish replica

    *like one of the royal cities, and because it was greater than Ai, and all its men were warriors. 3 So Adoni-zedek king of Jerusalem sent to Hoham king of Hebron, to Piram king of Jarmuth, to **Japhia king of Lachish**, and to Debir king of Eglon, saying, 4 "Come up to me and help me, and let us strike Gibeon. For it has made peace with Joshua and with the people of Israel." 5 Then the five kings of the Amorites, the king of Jerusalem, the king of Hebron, the king of Jarmuth, the **king of Lachish**, and the king of Eglon, gathered their forces and went up with all their armies and encamped against Gibeon and made war against it.*

2. **Joshua prayed that the sun would stand still so the Israelites could defeat the 5 kings who had gathered to make war against the Gibeonites and the Israelites.**

    Joshua 10:10-14: *And the Lord threw them into a panic before*

*Israel, who struck them with a great blow at Gibeon and chased them by the way of the ascent of Beth-horon and struck them as far as Azekah and Makkedah. 11 And as they fled before Israel, while they were going down the ascent of Beth-horon, the Lord threw down **large stones** from heaven on them as far as Azekah, and they died. There were more who died because of the hailstones than the sons of Israel killed with the sword. 12 At that time Joshua spoke to the Lord in the day when the Lord gave the Amorites over to the sons of Israel, and he said in the sight of Israel, "**Sun, stand still** at Gibeon, and moon, in the Valley of Aijalon." 13 And the **sun stood still, and the moon stopped**, until the nation took vengeance on their enemies. Is this not written in the Book of Jashar? The sun stopped in the midst of heaven and did not hurry to set for about a whole day. 14 There has been no day like it before or since, when the Lord heeded the voice of a man, for the Lord fought for Israel.*

City Gate

3. **Joshua and the Israelites conquer Lachish.**

   Joshua 10:31–32: *Then Joshua and all Israel with him passed on from Libnah to **Lachish** and laid siege to it and fought against it. 32 And the Lord gave **Lachish** into the hand of Israel, and he captured it on the second day and struck it with the edge of the sword, and every person in it, as he had done to Libnah.*

4. **King Rehoboam, Solomon's son, fortified Lachish in about 920 BC after the kingdom of Israel was divided.**

   2 Chronicles 11:5–12: *Rehoboam lived in Jerusalem, and he built cities for defense in Judah. 6 He built Bethlehem, Etam, Tekoa, 7 Beth-zur, Soco, Adullam, 8 Gath, Mareshah, Ziph, 9 Adoraim, **Lachish**, Azekah, 10 Zorah, Aijalon, and Hebron, fortified cities that are in Judah and in Benjamin. 11 He made the **fortresses strong**, and put commanders in them, and stores of food, oil, and wine. 12*

And he put shields and spears in all the cities and made them very strong. So he held Judah and Benjamin.

5. **King Amaziah fled to Lachish after his defeat to the Northern Kingdom of Israel and was killed by his own countrymen in 767 BC.**

   2 Chronicles 25:14–15: *After Amaziah came from striking down the Edomites, he brought the gods of the men of Seir and set them up as his gods and worshiped them, making offerings to them. 15 Therefore the Lord was angry with Amaziah and sent to him a prophet, who said to him, "Why have you sought the gods of a people who did not deliver their own people from your hand?"*

   Siege Ramp at Lachish

   2 Chronicles 25:27: *From the time when he [Amaziah] turned away from the Lord, they made a conspiracy against him in Jerusalem, and he fled to **Lachish**. But they sent after him to **Lachish** and put him to death there.*

6. **God destroyed Lachish because of their continual rejection of Him and sinful choices.**

   Micah 1:13: *Harness the steeds to the chariots, inhabitants of **Lachish**; it was the beginning of sin to the daughter of Zion, for in you were found the transgressions of Israel.*

7. **Lachish was attacked and destroyed by the Assyrians in 701 BC.**

   After Assyria conquered the Northern Kingdom of Israel and led them into captivity to Assyria in 722 BC, King Sennacherib set his sights on Egypt and Judah in 701 BC.

   2 Kings 18:13: *In the fourteenth year of King Hezekiah, Sennacherib king of Assyria came up against **all the fortified cities of Judah** and took them.*

   2 Chronicles 32:9–10: *After this, Sennacherib king of Assyria, who*

*was besieging **Lachish** with all his forces, sent his servants to Jerusalem to Hezekiah king of Judah and to all the people of Judah who were in Jerusalem, saying, 10 "Thus says Sennacherib king of Assyria, 'On what are you trusting, that you endure the siege in Jerusalem?'"*

In the destruction of Lachish, as many as 50,000 people were tortured and killed when Sennacherib took it. Based on archaeological discoveries and writings in Nineveh, the Assyrians beheaded, burned, flayed, and impaled those they conquered. Those who escaped death were deported to Assyria, led by rings pierced through their lips.

In the writings of Sennacherib, he mentions how his army penetrated fortifications using ramps, battering rams, mines, breeches, and siege engines. The evidence of these tactics can be seen in the siege ramp at Lachish.

Palace and Courtyard

8. God supernaturally protected Jerusalem from the Assyrian conquest.

After King Sennacherib conquered Lachish and the southern cities of Judah, he set his sights on Jerusalem. The deliverance of Jerusalem in 701 BC, under King Hezekiah's godly leadership, is one of the most pivotal and monumental miracles in Israel's history. Assyria rose to world domination and had conquered all the Northern Kingdom of Israel and all the southern cities of Judah. Jerusalem was the only city left in the whole region that had not fallen. Assyria was hungry and ready to devour Jerusalem by its merciless iron-toothed war machine.

2 Kings 19:8–10: *The Rabshakeh returned, and found the king of Assyria fighting against Libnah, for he heard that the king had left **Lachish**. 9 Now the king heard concerning Tirhakah king of Cush, "Behold, he has set out to fight against you." So he sent messengers*

again to Hezekiah, saying, 10 "Thus shall you speak to Hezekiah king of Judah: 'Do not let your God in whom you trust deceive you by promising that Jerusalem will not be given into the hand of the king of Assyria.'"

2 Kings 19:20: *Then Isaiah the son of Amoz sent to Hezekiah, saying, "Thus says the Lord, the God of Israel:* **Your prayer** *to me about Sennacherib king of Assyria I have heard."*

2 Kings 19:35-37: *And that night the angel of the Lord went out and* **struck down 185,000** *in the camp of the Assyrians. And when people arose early in the morning, behold, these were all dead bodies. 36 Then Sennacherib king of Assyria departed and went home and lived at Nineveh. 37 And as he was worshiping in the house of Nisroch his god, Adrammelech and Sharezer, his sons, struck him down with the sword and escaped into the land of Ararat. And Esarhaddon his son reigned in his place.*

Tel Lachish aerial view

The defeat over Sennacherib at Jerusalem was a devastating blow to the Assyrian Empire, which caused it to spiral downward thereafter. Later, the Babylonian Empire would arise and become the new world power.

9. Lachish was again destroyed by the Babylonians in around 587 BC.

Jeremiah 34:6-7: *Then Jeremiah the prophet spoke all these words to Zedekiah king of Judah, in Jerusalem, 7 when the army of the king of Babylon was fighting against Jerusalem and against all the cities of Judah that were left,* **Lachish** *and Azekah, for these were the only fortified cities of Judah that remained.*

10. The destruction and deportations of the Israelites into Assyria and Babylon were because of their continual disobedience to God.

Ezra 5:12: *But because our fathers had provoked the God of heaven*

Southern Israel Sites

to wrath, He gave them into the hand of Nebuchadnezzar king of Babylon, the Chaldean, who destroyed this temple and deported the people to Babylon.

Ezra 9:7: *Since the days of our fathers to this day we have been in great guilt, and on account of our iniquities we, our kings and our priests have been given into the hand of the kings of the lands, to the sword, to captivity and to plunder and to open shame, as it is this day.*

Faith Lesson from Lachish

1. God gave the Israelites a great victory over the king of Lachish by causing the sun to stand still and sending great hailstones. Joshua demonstrated great faith in asking God to cause the sun to stand still. Do we realize God is able to do great miracles in our lives if we have faith like Joshua?

2. God supernaturally protected Jerusalem because of King Hezekiah's devotion and faith and defeated the Assyrians by ordering one angel to kill 185,000 soldiers. If our hearts are right before God, there is nothing we should fear.

Tel Lachish entry

3. However, around 115 years later, God allowed the Israelites to be conquered by the Babylonians because of their continual sinful choices. When we are not right with God, we find ourselves in the hand of a disciplining God who will deal with us according to His wisdom.

Journal/Notes:

Masada

Location

1. Masada is at the southern end of the Dead Sea, about 40 miles (64 km.) southeast of Jerusalem.
2. It's a natural flat mountain that rises up from the valley floor some 1,000 ft. (305 m.). It's like a huge column with sheer cliffs on every side that makes it virtually unreachable.
3. Ancient Gomorrah lies at the base of Masada, and ancient Sodom is south of Masada, about 14 miles (23 km.).
4. The base of Masada is in a desert region about 1,000 ft. (305 m.) below sea level.
5. The word Masada means fortress.

Historical Background Leading up to the Fall of Masada

1. Masada was one of 3 fortified fortresses King Herod built for pleasure purposes and from which to protect his territories. He built Masada in about 24 BC.
2. Masada was fortified with elaborate water cisterns that were fed by diverting water from the nearby mountains. It even had swimming pools and most of the luxuries life afforded at that time.
3. In addition to ample water storage, Masada had 15 storehouses of food, enough for 10,000 people for 10 years.
4. In 66 AD, events began to unfold in Israel that caused the Jews to rebel against Roman rule. This revolt began in Caesarea Maritime.
5. In 66–70 AD, when the nation was in revolt, Jewish Zealots who had fled from Jerusalem and the surrounding areas took the fortress of Masada from Roman occupation. They were national Freedom Fighters who opposed Roman rule. In their conquest, they gained possession of all the stored food and water at Masada.

Southern Israel Sites

6. Between 66–70 AD, Rome conquered all the northern cities of Israel.
7. In 70 AD, under the command of Titus, the Romans totally destroyed Jerusalem in a bloody battle that lasted well over 4 months. Josephus (Jewish Historian) claims that 1.1 million Jews lost their lives in this battle, and another 97,000 were captured and enslaved. The temple was leveled in the siege at this time as well.
8. In 73 AD, there had amassed a total of 967 Jews, counting their families, at Masada. They were under the command of Eleazar Ben-Yair, a Jewish Zealot Freedom Fighter.
9. After conquering Jerusalem and most of Israel, the Romans headed south to conquer the southern strongholds around the Dead Sea region and Masada.
10. Masada was the last stronghold of the Israelites that existed, and the Romans amassed their troops there in the fall of 73 AD.

Masada view from the north

Places of Interest

1. Cistern
2. Living Quarters
3. Ritual Baths
4. Small Palace 1
5. Southern Fort
6. Pool
7. Small Palace 2
8. Small Palace 3
9. Western Palace
10. Byzantine Church

11. Cable Car Access

12. Eastern Gate
13. Storerooms
14. Baths
15. Northern Palace
16. Officers' Quarters
17. Administrative Building
18. Western Gate
19. Synagogue
20. Siege Ramp
21. En Gedi
22. Dead Sea
23. Ancient Gomorrah
24. Ancient Sodom

Masada in the Bible

1. **After a confrontation between King Saul and David close to En Gedi, David likely hid out on top of Masada afterward.**

   1 Samuel 24:22: *And David swore this to Saul. Then Saul went home, but David and his men went up to the **stronghold [fortress]**.*

2. **Because of Israel's rejection of Christ as their Messiah, Christ foretold the destruction of Jerusalem and the nation of Israel. This destruction occurred between 66–74 AD.**

   Luke 19:41–44: *And when he drew near and saw the city, he wept over it, 42 saying, "Would that you, even you, had known on this day the things that make for peace! But now they are hidden from your eyes. 43 For the days will come upon you, when your enemies will set up a barricade around you and surround you and hem you in on every side 44 and tear you down to the ground, you and your children within you. And they will not leave one stone upon another in you, because you did not know the time of your visitation."*

3. **Zechariah prophesied about Jerusalem's destruction as well.**

   Zechariah 14:1–2: *Behold, a day is coming for the Lord, when the spoil taken from you will be divided in your midst. 2 For I will gather all the nations against Jerusalem to battle, and the city shall be taken and the houses plundered and the women raped. Half of the city shall go out into exile, but the rest of the people shall not be cut off from the city.*

The Fall of Masada

1. In 73 AD, the 10th Roman Army Legion, totaling around 10,000 soldiers and 6,000 Jewish slaves under a commander by the name of Silva, arrived at the base of Masada.
2. This Roman legion first built a wall around the base of Masada, much of it by using Jewish slave labor.
3. Next, they built 8 camps around the base of the mountain. The remains of most of these camps can still be seen today. Silva set up his headquarters at the northwest camp.
4. After several months of unsuccessful engagement with the Jewish Zealots atop Masada, the Romans decided to build a massive siege ramp out of dirt on the west side of Masada using Israelite slave labor to help in the process.
5. As the siege ramp grew closer to the top of Masada, the Romans primarily used Jewish slave labor so that their fellow Jews on Masada wouldn't shoot arrows and throw spears at their own countrymen.

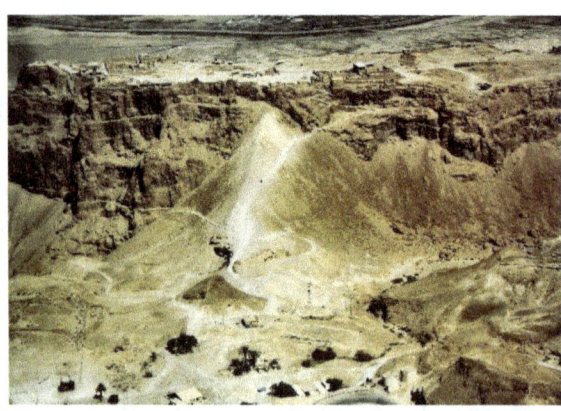
Siege Ramp

6. After several months of building the siege ramp, the Romans finally reached the top of Masada and severely damaged the exterior wall.
7. When the Jewish Zealots realized they were in grave danger of being conquered, they built another interior wall just inside the exterior wall using wood beams from many of their buildings.

Southern Israel Sites

They layered the beams with earth in between in order to fortify the new wall.

8. The Romans set this inner wall on fire and were now poised to enter. However, this all happened late at night, so the Romans decided to wait until the next morning to make their attack.

9. Eleazar Ben-Yair, the commander of the Zealots, gave an impassioned speech about how God had not created them to be slaves and about what would happen to them if they surrendered to the Romans. This is what he proposed:

   - The Romans are angry after the long battle and will kill most of us by torture. Those who are not killed will be mistreated and forced to be slaves. Our women will be raped before our eyes and violated, and our children will be tortured and forced to be slaves as well.
   - The only option we have as free people is to take our own lives.
   - So the men gathered in a special meeting and drew lots picking out 10 courageous men who knew about killing and understood how to die.
   - Then every father went home and killed their wives and children.
   - Then all the men gathered again together, and 10 of these men in the group killed the remaining men. Then one man killed the other 9, and then the last man killed himself.

Northern Palace

10. On May 3, 74 AD, after 7 months or so of long battled weariness, the Romans entered the top of Masada and stood in awe-stricken silence as they beheld the mass suicide of the Jews before them. The Zealots chose to die by suicide rather than be conquered by the Romans to be abused or killed.

Faith Lesson from Masada

1. While we don't endorse and believe the Jewish Zealots should

have committed suicide as it's only God's place to take a person's life, we do understand these Zealots' decision.

2. While some of the Zealots may have believed in Christ and were devoted servants to God, the Jewish nation as a whole, and their leaders, had largely rejected Christ as their Messiah. As a result, Christ spoke judgment upon the nation in Luke 19:41–44.
3. Almost every instance in which a country falls, it's due mainly to the decisions of its leaders.
4. The sad reality is that the righteous always suffer at the hands of the wicked.
5. Today, it's the same; while there may be many righteous people in a country, God will still judge it because of the sinful and immoral decisions its leaders and the majority of the people make.
6. Israel didn't return to be a nation again until 1948, and this was due to God's sovereign plan for them. God prophesied that He would bring them back again to be a nation, and it's a miracle that after almost 2,000 years, this has been fulfilled. This is unheard of in the history of any civilization.
7. However, the price Israel paid for their rejection of Christ cost them dearly and should be a sober warning to us today as well.

Cable cars headed up to Masada

Journal/Notes:

Sodom and Gomorrah

Location

1. Sodom and Gomorrah are located on the eastern side of the Dead Sea.
2. Gomorrah is situated at the base of Masada, and Sodom is about 13 miles (20 km.) south of Gomorrah.
3. Though the actual locations of the cities are somewhat disputed, growing evidence reveals that the locations are quite certain.

Historical Background

1. Josephus, a historian writer during the time of Christ, said the ruins could still be clearly seen in his day.
2. Archeologists have discovered around 1.5 million bodies in graves in these areas around Sodom and Gomorrah.
3. There are a lot of brimstone (old name for sulfur) balls in these cities.
4. This sulfur is unique and different from all other sulfur found in the world.
   - It's around 90-95% pure.
   - It's white, unlike any other place in the world.
   - It's so pure you can light it on fire, and it burns a hot blue flame.
   - These sulfur balls are not found between the cities.
5. There is a lot of ash in these areas that fits the biblical narrative.

   2 Peter 2:6: *And if He condemned the cities of **Sodom and Gomorrah** to destruction by **reducing them to ashes**, having made them an example to those who would live ungodly lives thereafter.*
6. The material of these city formations is calcium sulfate, which is what limestone and sulfur become when heated.

7. The preferred building material in Israel is limestone, so these cities fit the scientific evidence as well.
8. There is a lot of charcoal layers found in the strata of these cities.
9. The amount of ash, charcoal, and calcium sulfate reveal overwhelming evidence of extreme heat in these cities.
10. There is also no geothermal activity in these areas to explain the ash, charcoal, and calcium sulfate.
11. In addition, there are many unexplained shapes in these areas that look like buildings, Sphinxes, pyramids, and palaces.
12. These cities existed around 4,000 years ago, so their remains would be difficult to distinguish. Plus, God destroyed and reduced them to ashes as well.

Sphinx at Gomorrah

13. These cities fit the location as described in the Bible.

    Genesis 13:10: *Lot lifted up his eyes and saw all the valley of the Jordan, that it was well watered everywhere—this was before the Lord destroyed Sodom and Gomorrah—like the garden of the Lord,* **like the land of Egypt as you go to Zoar** *[Zoar has been identified as being south of Sodom and Gomorrah].*

14. Because the Dead Sea basin used to be like the Garden of Eden, it was an extremely desirable climate that was great for agriculture and life in general. It was, therefore, a very populated area.
15. The thought of God raining down fire and brimstone upon the cities and people in this area is staggering and gives me chills up and down my spine. This fire and brimstone were so hot and intense they destroyed everything in its wake.
16. God also used Sodom and Gomorrah to refer to all of the cities of the Dead Sea basin.

Southern Israel Sites

Places of Interest
1. Sodom
2. Gomorrah
3. Zoar
4. Admah
5. Zeboiim
6. Masada
7. Sphinx
8. Pyramid

Sodom and Gomorrah in the Bible

1. **God told Abraham through two angels about His plan to destroy Sodom and Gomorrah.**

    Genesis 18:20–21: *And the Lord said, "The outcry of **Sodom and Gomorrah** is indeed great, and their sin is exceedingly grave. 21 I will go down now and see if they have done entirely according to its outcry, which has come to Me; and if not, I will know."*

2. **During a dialogue between Abraham and God, Abraham pleaded with God to spare the cities on account of the righteous ones living in them (Gen. 18:22–31).**

3. **God told Abraham that He would spare the cities if only 10 righteous people could be found in them.**

    Genesis 18:32–33: *And He said, "I will not destroy it on account of the ten." 33 As soon as He had finished speaking to Abraham the Lord departed, and Abraham returned to his place.*

4. **In the cities of Sodom and Gomorrah lived hundreds of thousands of people. The fact that there were not even 10 righteous people speaks of the extreme wickedness of these cities.**

    Genesis 13:13: *Now the men of **Sodom were wicked exceedingly** and sinners against the Lord.*

5. **The wickedness of Sodom revealed.**

    Genesis 19:1–11: *Now the two angels came to **Sodom** in the evening as Lot was sitting in the gate of **Sodom**. When Lot saw them, he rose to meet them and bowed down with his face to the ground. 2 And he said, "Now behold, my lords, please turn aside into your servant's house, and spend the night, and wash your feet; then you may rise early and go on your way." They said however, "No, but we shall spend the night in the square." 3 Yet he urged them strongly, so they turned aside to him and entered his*

Gomorrah

*house; and he prepared a feast for them, and baked unleavened bread, and they ate. 4 Before they lay down, the men of the city, the men of **Sodom**, surrounded the house, both young and old, all the people from every quarter; 5 and they called to Lot and said to him, "Where are the men who came to you tonight? Bring them out to us that we **may have relations with them**." 6 But Lot went out to them at the doorway, and shut the door behind him, 7 and said, "Please, my brothers, do not act wickedly. 8 Now behold, I have two daughters who have not had relations with man; please let me bring them out to you, and do to them whatever you like; only do nothing to these men, inasmuch as they have come under the shelter of my roof." 9 But they said, "Stand aside." Furthermore, they said, "This one came in as an alien, and already he is acting like a judge; now we will treat you worse than them." So they pressed hard against Lot and came near to break the door. 10 But the men [two angels] reached out their hands and brought Lot into the house with them, and shut the door. 11 They struck the men who were at the doorway of the house with blindness, both small and great, so that they wearied themselves trying to find the doorway.*

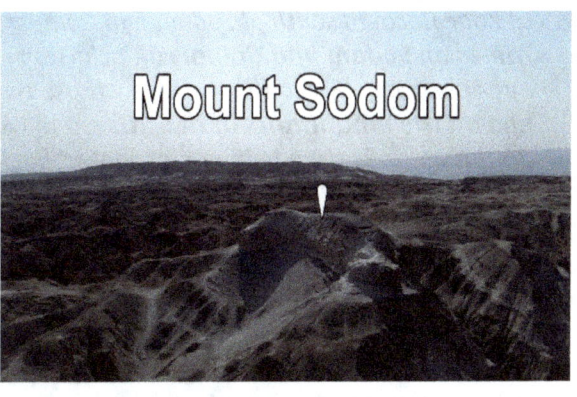

6. God warns Lot and his family to flee for their lives.

Genesis 19:12–17: Then the two men said to Lot, "Whom else have you here? A son-in-law, and your sons, and your daughters, and whomever you have in the city, bring them out of the place; 13 for we are about to destroy this place, because their outcry has become so great before the Lord that the Lord has sent us to destroy it." 14 Lot went out and spoke to his sons-in-law, who were to marry his daughters, and said, "Up, get out of this place, for the Lord will destroy the city." But he appeared to his sons-in-law to be jesting. 15 When morning dawned, the angels urged Lot, saying, "Up, take your wife and your two daughters who are here, or you will be swept away in the punishment of the city." 16 But he hesitated. So the men seized his hand and the hand of his wife and the hands of his two daughters, for the compassion of the Lord was upon him; and they brought him out, and put him outside the city. 17 When they had brought them outside, one [angel] said, "Escape for your life! Do not look behind you, and do not stay anywhere in the valley; escape to the mountains, or you will be swept away."

7. **God destroys Sodom and Gomorrah.**

   Genesis 19:23–29: *The sun had risen over the earth when Lot came to Zoar [located south of Sodom and Gomorrah]. 24 Then the Lord rained on* **Sodom and Gomorrah** *brimstone and fire from the Lord out of heaven, 25 and He overthrew those cities, and all the valley, and* **all the inhabitants of the cities***, and what grew on the ground. 26 But his wife, from behind him, looked back, and she became a pillar of salt. 27 Now Abraham arose early in the morning and went to the place where he had stood before the Lord; 28 and he looked down toward* **Sodom and Gomorrah***, and toward all the land of the valley, and he saw, and*

   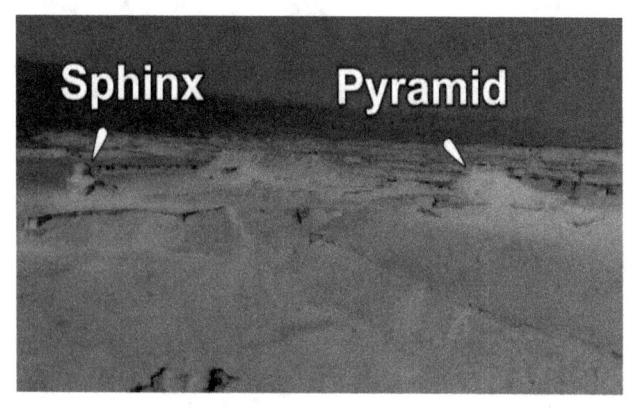

   behold, the smoke of the land ascended like the smoke of a furnace. 29 Thus, it came about, when God destroyed the **cities of the valley***, that God remembered Abraham, and sent Lot out of the midst of the overthrow, when He overthrew the cities in which Lot lived.*

God uses Sodom and Gomorrah as examples of judgment upon the ungodly throughout the Bible.

1. **Moses used Sodom and Gomorrah as warnings for the future generations of the Israelites.**

   Deuteronomy 29:23: *All its land is brimstone and salt, a burning waste, unsown and unproductive, and no grass grows in it, like the overthrow of* **Sodom** *and* **Gomorrah***,* **Admah** *and* **Zeboiim***, which the Lord overthrew in His anger and in His wrath.*

   God specifically states that He destroyed two other cities besides

Sodom and Gomorrah (Admah and Zeboiim). However, it appears He also destroyed Zoar because after Lot left Zoar, his two daughters said there was no one in the land for them to marry.

2. **The prophets continually used Sodom and Gomorrah as examples of God's wrath on the ungodly.**

    Jeremiah 49:18: "*Like the overthrow of **Sodom and Gomorrah with its neighbors**,*" says the Lord, "*no one will live there, nor will a son of man reside in it.*"

    Lamentations 4:6: *For the iniquity of the daughter of my people Is greater than the sin of **Sodom**, which was overthrown as in a moment, and no hands were turned toward her.*

3. **Jesus used Sodom and Gomorrah as examples of God's judgment on the ungodly.**

    Luke 17:28–30: *It was the same as happened in the days of Lot: they were eating, they were drinking, they were buying, they were selling, they were planting, 29 they were building; but on the day that Lot went out from **Sodom** it rained fire and brimstone from heaven and destroyed them all. 30 It will be just the same on the day that the Son of Man is revealed.*

    Gomorrah

4. **The Apostles used Sodom and Gomorrah as examples of God's coming judgment on the ungodly.**

    2 Peter 2:4–10: *For if God did not spare angels when they sinned, but cast them into hell and committed them to pits of darkness, reserved for judgment; 5 and did not spare the ancient world, but preserved Noah, a preacher of righteousness, with seven others, when He brought a flood upon the world of the ungodly; 6 and if He condemned the cities of **Sodom and Gomorrah** to destruction by reducing them to ashes, having made them **an example** to those who would live ungodly lives thereafter; 7 and if He rescued*

righteous Lot, oppressed by the sensual conduct of unprincipled men 8 (for by what he saw and heard that righteous man, while living among them, felt his righteous soul tormented day after day by their lawless deeds), 9 then the Lord knows how to rescue the godly from temptation, and to keep the unrighteous under punishment for the day of judgment, 10 and especially those who indulge the flesh in its corrupt desires and despise authority.

Jude 1:5-7: *Now I want to remind you, although you once fully knew it, that Jesus, who saved a people out of the land of Egypt, afterward destroyed those who did not believe. 6 And the angels who did not stay within their own position of authority, but left their proper dwelling, he has kept in eternal chains under gloomy darkness until the judgment of the great day— 7 just as* **Sodom and Gomorrah and the surrounding cities**, *which likewise indulged in* **sexual immorality and pursued unnatural desire**, *serve as an example by undergoing a punishment of eternal fire.*

Sulfur balls at Sodom and Gomorrah

Repeatedly, throughout the accounts of the destruction of Sodom and Gomorrah, the sin of homosexuality is highlighted as the main wickedness for which God destroyed them.

Some, who defend homosexuality, claim that God destroyed them because of their lack of hospitality.

5. **God uses the same imagery of fire and brimstone in the destruction of Sodom and Gomorrah as for what hell will be like.**

   Revelation 20:10: *And the devil who deceived them was thrown into the lake of* **fire and brimstone**, *where the beast and the false prophet are also; and they will be tormented day and night forever and ever.*

Faith Lesson from Sodom and Gomorrah

1. The lesson from Sodom and Gomorrah is a serious, sobering message we should allow to sink in deeply.
2. The primary sin for which God destroyed Sodom and Gomorrah was homosexuality. However, they sinned in many other ways as well.
3. Sodom and Gomorrah are a foreshadow of what hell will be like.
4. Jesus talked about how His second coming would be like that of Sodom and Gomorrah. Jesus also spoke more about hell than heaven.
5. If God, the prophets, Christ, and the apostles used Sodom and Gomorrah as an example of the eternal judgment in hell that awaits the ungodly, then we should do the same today as well.

Burning sulfur ball – Copyright Discovered Media

6. God is a God of love and has done everything He can to save us, but for those who reject His offer of salvation, eternal suffering in the Lake of Fire awaits them (Rev. 20:10).

Journal/Notes:

Timna Park: Tabernacle Replica

Location

1. Timna Park is 17 miles (27 km.) north of Eilat and the Red Sea, on Hwy. 90.
2. Located within Timna Park is another park that has an exact replica of the tabernacle God ordered Moses to build while he was on Mount Sinai.
3. This tabernacle contains every piece of furniture, Brazen Altar, Table of Shewbread, Ark of the Covenant, and everything the original tabernacle had. It's the only life-size model of its kind in Israel that is exactly like the original one. It has been researched extensively and built according to the specifications given to Moses.
4. Timna Park is in the arid desert of Arava and is on the route the Israelites would have taken in their travels. It's not for certain, but it's possible the Israelites could have camped in the same area.
5. The landscape around Timna Park is very similar to that of biblical times when the children of Israel wandered in the desert for 40 years. The arid country, lack of water, and heat all paint a picture of what it would have been like to live in the desert at that time.

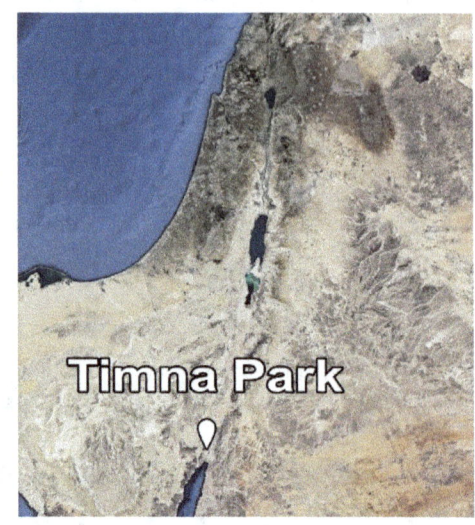

Historical Background

1. The tabernacle was portable, and its specifications are found in Exodus chapters 25–40.
2. Most Christians skim over or don't read the sections and books of the Bible that deal with the details of the Law and the tabernacle.
3. Some might wonder why God spent 40 days instructing Moses about the tabernacle but only spent 6 days creating the entire universe?
4. And if God only needed a little over one chapter to describe the

structure of the world, why did He need 15 chapters to describe the design and details of the tabernacle?

5. For most Christians, reading from Genesis to Exodus chapter 20 is great. Then, they get bogged down in the rest of Exodus, Leviticus, and part of Numbers.

6. The fact that God spends so much time on the details of how mankind can be right with Him reveals that He is more concerned about having a relationship with us than the importance of His creation.

Places of Interest

1. Tabernacle Courtyard Fence
   - It measures 75 ft. wide (23 m.) by 150 ft. long (46 m.).
   - The Courtyard has 60 posts with linen curtains all around it.
   - The Courtyard posts were 7.5 ft. high (2.29 m.).
   - Each post had a bronze base with silver hooks and rings on top.
   - Acacia wood was used for the tabernacle. These trees can be seen close to the tabernacle in Timna Park today.
   - The Eastern Gate, which was the entrance, had 4 posts and a colored curtain.

2. Courtyard
   - The Bronze (copper) Altar measured 7.5 ft. wide square (2.29 m.) by 4.5 ft. high (1.37 m.) and had 4 horns on each corner (also called the horns of the altar).
   - The Bronze Laver or washbasin made from brass.
   - Sacrifices and cleansing took place in the courtyard outside the Holy Place. Judgment and cleansing had to take place first before the priests could enter the tabernacle or temple.
3. The Tabernacle (also known as the tent of meeting)
   - It measured 45 ft. long (13.72 m.) by 15 ft. wide by 15 ft. high (4.57 m.).
   - It was made with 10 curtains of fine linen of blue, purple, and scarlet yarn.
   - Each curtain was made with an embroidered cherub.
4. The Holy Place
   - Only the priests and High Priest could enter the Holy Place.
   - It measured 15 ft. wide (4.57 m.) by 30 ft. long (9.14 m.).
   - It contained the Menorah made from a single piece of gold.
   - The Table of Showbread (representing the unleavened bread of the first Passover) measured 36 inches wide (91.44 cm.) by 18 inches deep (45.72 cm.) by 27 inches tall (68.58 cm.). On it

were 12 loaves of bread which represented the 12 tribes of Israel.
- The Altar of Incense measured 18 inches square (45.72 cm.) by 36 inches tall (91.44 cm.). Only a special kind of incense was to be burned upon it.
- The priests wore white linen robes with a colorful sash.
- The High Priest wore special garments (a turban, ephod, breastplate, and robe). The breastplate contained 12 stones, each representing the 12 tribes of Israel. There were bells and pomegranates at the bottom of the robe.

5. The Veil Curtain separated the Holy Place from the Holy of Holies. It was made of blue, purple, and scarlet thread.
6. The Holy of Holies.
   - It measured 15 ft. by 15 ft. (4.6 m. by 4.6 m.).
   - Only the High Priest could enter the Holy of Holies once a year on the day of Yom Kippur, and he wore a holy linen coat (Lev. 16:4).
   - He had to be purified from all sin before entering.
   - Tradition holds that a rope was tied to the waist of the High Priest in case God smote him for being impure in His sight. By doing so, he could be drug out with the rope because they were forbidden to enter the Holy of Holies. This tradition might very well be true, but it's not mentioned in the Bible.

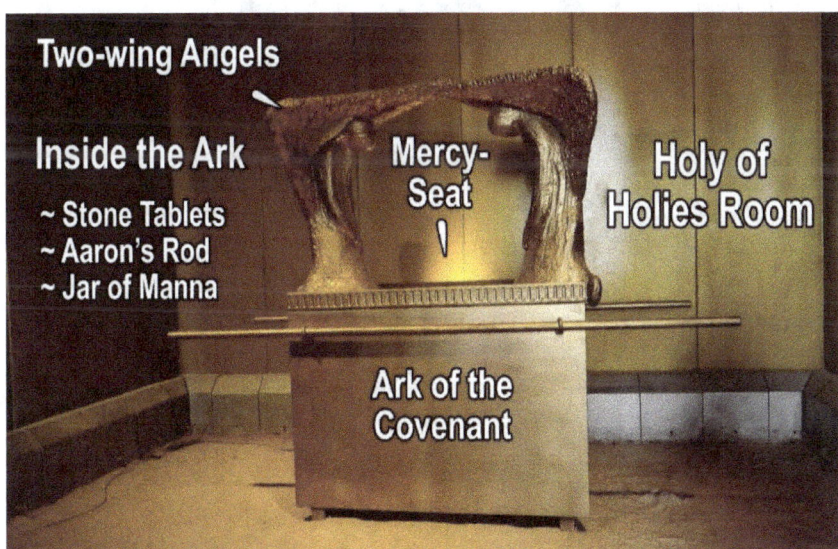

- Inside the Holy of Holies was the Ark of the Covenant, which measured 45 inches wide (114 cm.) by 27 inches deep by 27 inches tall (68.58 cm.).
- On top of the Ark of the Covenant was the Mercy Seat, which measured 27 inches high (68.58 cm.). Molded to it were 2-winged cherubim angel figures made from one piece of gold.
- Inside the Ark of the Covenant were the Ten Commandments written on Stone Tablets by the finger of God, Aaron's Rod that budded, and a Jar of Manna.

Tabernacle in the Bible

1. **God gave the instructions of how to build the tabernacle to Moses while he was on Mount Sinai.**

   Exodus 24:15–18: *Then Moses went up on the mountain, and the cloud covered the mountain. 16 The glory of the Lord dwelt on Mount Sinai, and the cloud covered it six days. And on the seventh day he called to Moses out of the midst of the cloud. 17 Now the appearance of the glory of the Lord was like a devouring fire on the top of the mountain in the sight of the people of Israel. 18 Moses entered the cloud and went up on the mountain. And Moses was on the mountain forty days and forty nights.*

   Mount Sinai with blackened top

   Hebrews 8:5: *They serve a copy and shadow of the heavenly things. For when Moses was about to erect the tent, he was instructed by God, saying, "See that you make everything according to the pattern that was shown you on the mountain."*

2. **The tabernacle was to be God's special dwelling place among His people.**

Southern Israel Sites

Exodus 25:1-9: *The Lord said to Moses, 2 "Speak to the people of Israel, that they take for me a contribution. From every man whose heart moves him you shall receive the contribution for me. 3 And this is the contribution that you shall receive from them: gold, silver, and bronze, 4 blue and purple and scarlet yarns and fine twined linen, goats' hair, 5 tanned rams' skins, goatskins, acacia wood, 6 oil for the lamps, spices for the anointing oil and for the fragrant incense, 7 onyx stones, and stones for setting, for the ephod and for the breastpiece. 8 And let them* **make me a sanctuary, that I may dwell in their midst**. *9 Exactly as I show you concerning the pattern of the tabernacle, and of all its furniture, so you shall make it."*

3. **The presence of God was over the tabernacle in the form of a cloud by day and fire by night.**

   Numbers 9:15-17: *On the day that the tabernacle was set up, the* **cloud covered the tabernacle**, *the tent of the testimony. And at evening it was over the tabernacle like the appearance of fire until morning. 16 So it was always: the* **cloud covered it by day and the appearance of fire by night**. *17 And whenever the cloud lifted from over the tent, after that the*

Tabernacle replica at Timna Park

   people of Israel set out, and in the place where the cloud settled down, there the people of Israel camped.

4. **Part of the reason the Levites were chosen to be the priests and servants of the temple was because of the zeal for the Lord they displayed regarding the Golden Calf at Mount Sinai.**

   Exodus 32:25-29: *And when Moses saw that the people had broken loose (for Aaron had let them break loose, to the derision of their enemies), 26 then Moses stood in the gate of the camp and said, "Who is on the Lord's side? Come to me." And all the* **sons of Levi gathered around him**. *27 And he said to them, "Thus says the Lord*

*God of Israel, 'Put your sword on your side each of you, and go to and fro from gate to gate throughout the camp, and each of you kill his brother and his companion and his neighbor.'" 28 And the sons of Levi did according to the word of Moses. And that day about three thousand men of the people fell. 29 And Moses said, "**Today you have been ordained for the service of the Lord**, each one at the cost of his son and of his brother, so that he might bestow a blessing upon you this day."*

Faith Lesson from the Tabernacle

1. God focused on the details of the tabernacle because He wanted to embed some essential concepts in our minds.
2. The details of the tabernacle reveal how sinful people must approach a holy God.
3. The tabernacle was God's special dwelling place among mankind.
4. The tabernacle and sacrificial system details reveal that God is more concerned about having a relationship with us than His creation.
5. It reveals the honor and respect we should have toward God.
6. The tabernacle and sacrificial system show the consequences of sin and the value of Christ's sacrifice on the Cross. When a person sinned in the Old Testament, it cost them financially as they had to offer a sacrifice from their flocks or purchase one.

Tabernacle courtyard with altar and laver basin

7. The tabernacle was a pattern of heavenly things.

   Hebrews 8:5-6: *They serve a copy and shadow of the heavenly things. For when Moses was about to erect the tent, he was instructed by God, saying, "See that you make everything according to the pattern that was shown you on the mountain." 6 But as it is, Christ has obtained a ministry that is as much more excellent than the old as the covenant he mediates is better, since it is enacted on better promises.*

8. The tabernacle gives insight and understanding regarding the privilege believers have today of being the temple of the living God.

   1 Corinthians 3:16–17: *Do you not know that you are a **temple of God** and that the Spirit of God dwells in you? 17 If any man destroys the temple of God, God will destroy him, for the **temple of God is holy, and that is what you are.***

9. The concepts of the tabernacle provide understanding for believers today about how we are a living temple made with living stones.

   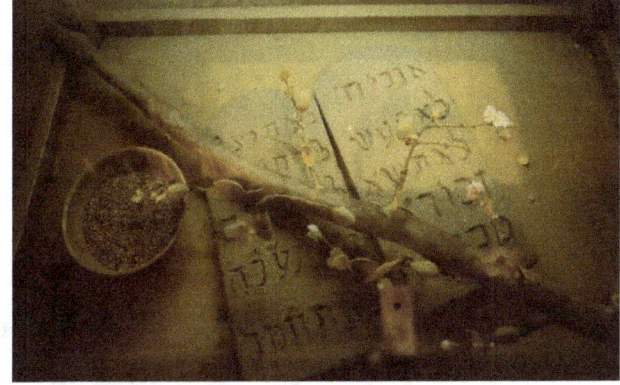
   Inside the Ark of the Covenant

   1 Peter 2:4–5: *And coming to Him as to a living stone which has been rejected by men, but is choice and precious in the sight of God, 5 you also, as living stones, are being built up as a **spiritual house** for a **holy priesthood**, to offer up **spiritual sacrifices** acceptable to God through **Jesus Christ**.*

10. Those who skim over or neglect to read the details in Exodus, Leviticus, and Numbers will miss the foundational truths of who Christ is and what He did in redeeming us through His work on the Cross.

11. The New Testament is built upon the foundation of the Old Testament. Therefore, if our understanding of the Old Testament is weak, so will be our understanding of the New Testament.

Journal/Notes:

Other Sites in Southern Israel

Ashkelon

Ashkelon is a coastal city on the Mediterranean Sea about 27 miles (43 km.) south of Jaffa and Tel Aviv. It's also just a bit north of modern-day Gaza.

Ashkelon was one of the 5 main coastal cities of the Philistines.

Joshua and the Israelites conquered Ashkelon in the conquest of the Promised Land (Josh. 13:3), and it was allotted to Judah, who then occupied it (Judg. 1:18).

One of the golden tumors (emerods) that was returned with the Ark of the Covenant by the Philistines was from Ashkelon (1 Sam. 6:17).

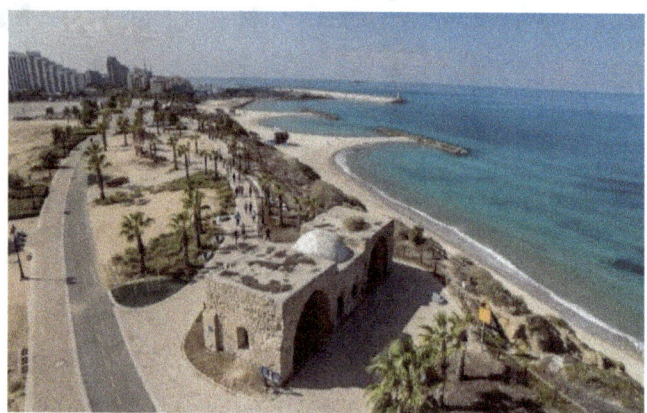
Ruins at Ashkelon

Both Ashkelon and Gath are mentioned in David's lament over Saul and Jonathan, revealing their importance (2 Sam. 1:20).

Ashkelon is also mentioned with Gaza, Ashdod, and Ekron, in the prophet Amos' denunciations of their sin and coming judgment (Amos 1:7–8).

Ashkelon was also denounced by Jeremiah (Jer. 25:20, 47:5–7), Zephaniah (2:4–7), and Zechariah (9:5).

Dead Sea

What would a trip to Israel be without taking a dip in the famous Dead Sea? Following is some helpful info for helping you decide which beach is best for you.

Northern Beaches

The northern beaches are privately owned and charge a fee to enter, even if your stay is for a quick dip in the sea. They have more of the mud for skincare, the water is a little cooler, they have higher waves and a little less salt content. However, there is still plenty of salt, so you can float quite easily.

For health reasons, a strong warning is given regarding swallowing the saltwater in the Dead Sea. It has 7 times more salt than any other body of water in the world, and it's easy to get salt poisoning if even a small amount of water is ingested.

All the beaches have changing rooms, restrooms, showers, and bathrooms. All have great places to eat at and shop. The northern beaches have gift shops, while the southern beaches have access to gift shops, but they're not always right at the resorts.

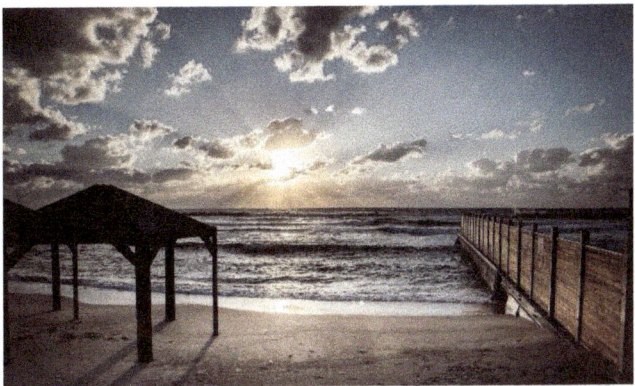

Dead Sea Beach

1. Kalia Beach – Less waves, cheaper entrance fee.
2. Biankini Beach
3. Neve Midbar
4. Ein Gedi Hot Springs – More expensive entrance fees, natural hot mineral springs.

Southern Beaches

The southern beaches have a higher concentration of salt, are more turquoise in color, have more transparent water, are more gradual with fewer waves, are smoother, and are free as they are public beaches.

1. Ein Bokek Public Beach
2. Zohar Public Beach

3. Segregated Public Beach – This beach separates the men from the women for Jewish reasons.

Gaza

Gaza is one of the 5 main cities of the Philistines and seems to be the oldest of them all.

It's a coastal city on the Mediterranean Sea about 40 miles (64 km.) south of Joppa (Jaffa). Gaza was also located on the Via Maris.

Gaza was on a hill rising about 200 ft. (61 m.) above the valley floor. There were sand dunes between it and the sea, which was about 2 miles away.

In the conquest of the Promised Land, Joshua and the Israelites failed to conquer Gaza, along with several other main cities of the Philistines (Josh. 10:41, 11:22).

Gaza ruins 1898 (American Colony or Matson photo service, Library of Congress)

Later, the tribe of Judah captured Gaza but couldn't control it for long, and it fell back into the hands of the Philistines (Judg. 1:18).

During the time of Samson, it was the heavy gates of Gaza that Samson carried all the way up to Hebron (Judg. 16:1–3).

After the Philistines defeated the Israelites in battle and captured the Ark of the Covenant during the priesthood of Eli and his two wicked sons, Gaza, along with the other main cities of the Philistines, sent a trespass offering to God when the ark was returned to the Israelites at Beth-Shemesh (1 Sam. 6:17–18).

When Hezekiah reigned, he defeated and pursued the Philistines to Gaza but did not seem to have captured the city. However, the Assyrians later captured it in 720 BC.

In the New Testament, Philip was sent to Gaza to evangelize the Ethiopian eunuch (Acts 8:26).

Today, because ancient Gaza lies in the Gaza Strip, where land is scarce and Israeli interests are not valued, the remains of ancient Gaza are practically nonexistent.

Ziklag

While the exact location of biblical Ziklag is debated, most archaeologists now place it at Tel Ser'a (Tel esh-Shariah), which is in the southernmost area of Judea about 14 miles (23 km.) northwest of Tel Beer Sheba and about 15 miles (24 km.) east of Gaza.

Ziklag is first mentioned in the Bible as part of the inheritance of the tribe of Judah (Josh. 15:31). It was allotted to the tribe of Simeon (within the tribe of Judah), but the Israelites apparently failed to conquer it because Ziklag was still under Philistine control when Saul reigned as king (Josh. 19:5).

Because for many years King Saul sought to harm David, David fled to Ziklag seeking refuge after the death of Samuel. As a result, he lived in Ziklag with six hundred men and their households in Philistine territory.

While living in Ziklag, David petitioned Achish, the Philistine king of Gath, to give him the city of Ziklag (1 Sam. 27:5–6). Achish consented and gave Ziklag to David.

During David's rule over Ziklag, which lasted 16 months, he made it his military home base. From Ziklag, David raided many of the cities of the Amalekites. Because many soldiers from Israel were disappointed with Saul's leadership, they joined forces with David's private army during this time (1 Chron. 12:1–22). When war broke out between the Philistines and Israel during the reign of King Saul, David and his small army attempted to join the Philistine army to fight against Saul. However, the Philistine leaders rejected David and sent him away from the battle. While David and the Philistines were away, the Amalekites attacked Ziklag. They burned the city and took captive all the women, children, and the elderly.

When David and his men returned to Ziklag, they found it had been destroyed by fire, and their families had been taken captive (1 Sam. 30:1–3). In response, David and his army pursued the Amalekites and recovered their families and possessions. (1 Sam. 30:16–31).

While David was living in Ziklag, he received the news of the defeat of Israel by the Philistines and Saul and Jonathan's deaths (2 Samuel 4:10).

Ziklag remained in control of Israel from this point on and is last mentioned in the Bible as one of the cities the Jews inhabited after returning from exile in Babylon (Neh. 11:28).

Timeline of Israel

Israel Biblical Sites Travel Guide

Why it's so important to understand a brief overview of the historical periods of Israel.

The Holy Land is an old place, about the oldest in the world! While in the Holy Land, you'll be seeing things as old as 6,000 years. That's old! Different periods of history will be referred to when describing Israel's holy sites and places. Please realize that there will likely be several key events at a particular site that have taken place there. Each event will have happened during a specific period in Israel's history. If you can understand the different periods a little, you'll get much more out of your experience.

Chronology of Time Used by Archaeologist and Historians
- Early Bronze Age   4000–2000 BC
- Middle Bronze Age   2000–1500 BC
- Late Bronze Age   1500–1200 BC
- Iron 1 Age   1200–1000 BC
- Iron 2 Age   1000–586 BC

Canaanite Period   4000–1875 BC
- 4000 BC – Canaanites inhabit the land of Israel.
- 2500 BC – Noah and the Great Flood.
- 2100 BC – Tower of Babel
- 2095 BC – Abraham moves to the land of Canaan from Ur of the Chaldeans.
- 1880 BC – Jacob and his family move to Egypt to live with Joseph.

Israelite Period   1450–965 BC
- 1450 BC – Exodus of the Israelites from Egypt.
- 1406 BC – Jews enter the Promised Land.
- 1012 BC – Saul unifies the 12 Hebrew tribes into the United Kingdom of Israel.
- 1010–970 BC – David's reign.

First Temple Period   970–586 BC
- 970–925 BC – Solomon's reign; glory years of the Kingdom of Israel.
- 950 BC – Solomon builds the magnificent temple on Mount

Moriah in Jerusalem (same place Abraham intended to sacrifice Isaac).

- 926 BC – Kingdom of Israel divides because of Solomon's sins. Jeroboam reigns over the northern Kingdom of Israel from Samaria. Rehoboam reigns over the southern Kingdom of Israel from Jerusalem.
- 722 BC – Assyrians conquer and deport most of the northern Kingdom of Israel to Assyria.
- 586 BC – Babylonians conquer Jerusalem and Judah under Nebuchadnezzar and deport most of the southern Kingdom of Judah to Babylon.

Second Temple Period   535–444 BC

- 535 BC – Many Jews return from Babylonia; Second Temple began to be rebuilt.
- 458 BC – Ezra returns to Jerusalem with second wave of Jews to continue rebuilding the Second Temple.
- 444 BC – Nehemiah returns to Jerusalem to rebuild the city walls.

Hellenistic Period (Greek Rule)   333–167 BC

- 333 BC – Alexander the Great defeats the Persian Empire and sets out to conquer the world. After his sudden death in 323 BC, the Greek Empire is divided. During this period the Bible is translated into Greek (the Septuagint).

Hasmonean Period (Maccabean Rule)   167–63 BC

- 167 BC – When the Jews were prohibited from practicing Judaism, and their temple was desecrated as part of an effort to impose Greek-oriented culture and customs on the entire population, the Jews revolted. First led by Mattathias of the priestly Hasmonean family and then by his son Judah the Maccabee, the Jews subsequently entered Jerusalem and purified the temple. This purification of the temple is remembered by the Jewish Holiday, Hanukkah (164 BC).

Roman Period (Roman Rule)   63 BC–330 AD

- 63 BC – Jerusalem is captured by Roman general Pompey.
- 37 BC–4 BC – Herod, Roman vassal king, rules the Land of Israel. He enlarges the Temple Mount and rebuilds the temple. He also

builds other monumental projects, including Caesarea, Herodian, Cave of the Patriarchs, and Masada.

- 4 BC – Jesus is born in Bethlehem.
- 27–30 AD – Ministry of Jesus.
- 30 AD – Jesus crucified.
- 66 AD – Jewish revolt against the Romans.
- 70 AD – Destruction of Jerusalem and Second Temple.
- 74 AD – Fall of Masada.
- 132 AD – Bar Kokhba Revolt. Roman Emperor Hadrian destroys Jerusalem and builds Aelia Capitolina, a pagan city in its place. Many holy sites are preserved, but with pagan shrines on them.

Byzantine Period (Eastern Roman Empire Rule)   330–614 AD

- 313 – Emperor Constantine recognizes Christianity, later becoming a Christian himself.
- 326 – Constantine's mother, Helena, goes to the Holy Land and builds many churches and basilicas on holy sites.

Persian Period   614–628 AD

- 614 – Persian conquest of the Holy Land. Many churches and monasteries destroyed.

Byzantine Period Reestablished   628–638 AD

- 628 – Holy Land recaptured by the Byzantines.

Muslim/Arab Period   638–1099 AD

- 638 – Muslim/Arab conquest of the Holy Land completed. Rule is by Caliphs from Damascus, then from Baghdad, and then Egypt.
- 691 – On top of the First and Second Temples in Jerusalem, the Dome of the Rock is built by Caliph Abd el-Malik.

Crusader Period   1099–1291 AD

- 1099 – Crusaders (Catholic armies from Rome) conquer Jerusalem and many parts of Israel.
- 1147 – Second Crusade arrives in the Holy Land.
- 1187 – Destruction of the Crusader army by Muslim leader Saladin. Collapse of Crusader Kingdom begins.

Timeline of Israel

- 1265 – Mamelukes, led by Sultan Beybars, conquer the Holy Land.
- 1270 – Final Crusade arrives, and all its participants massacred.
- 1291 – Last Crusader stronghold of Acco taken, ending Crusader rule.

Mamluk (Muslim) Period   1291–1517 AD

- 1291 – Mamluk rule begins.
- 1333 – Franciscan Order established in Jerusalem. Its members care for holy places and pilgrims.
- By the end of the Middle Ages, the country's urban centers were virtually in ruins, most of Jerusalem was abandoned, and the small Jewish community was poverty-stricken. The period of Mamluk decline was darkened by political and economic upheavals, plagues, locust invasions, and devastating earthquakes.

Ottoman (Muslim) Period   1517–1917 AD

- 1517 – Following the Ottoman conquest in 1517, the land was divided into four districts and attached administratively to the province of Damascus and ruled from Istanbul.
- 1520 – Suleiman the Magnificent rebuilds the city walls of Jerusalem.
- 1799 – Napoleon Bonaparte invades Israel but fails to capture it and is forced to leave.
- 1860 – The first neighborhood, Mishkenot Sha'ananim, is built outside of Jerusalem's city walls.
- 1882 – First large-scale immigration to Israel, mainly from Russia.
- 1904 – Second large-scale immigration from Russia and Poland.

British Period   1917–1948 AD

- 1917 – British Foreign Minister Lord Balfour issued on November 2, 1917, the so-called Balfour Declaration, which gave official support for the "establishment in Israel of a national home for the Jewish people" with the commitment not to be prejudiced against the rights of the non-Jewish communities.
- 1947 – The United Nations approved the partition of Israel into separate Jewish and Arab states on November 29, 1947.

State of Israel Period   1948 to Present

- 1948 – On the day when the British Mandate in Palestine expired, the State of Israel was instituted on May 14, 1948, by the Jewish National Council under the presidency of David Ben Gurion.
- 1948–1949 – The Arab-Israeli War; the Arabs refused to accept the newly established State of Israel. Egypt, Syria, Transjordan, Lebanon, and Iraq attack Israel, but within a year, Israel defeated its attackers.
- 1950 – Western Jerusalem was proclaimed the capital city of Israel on January 23, 1950.
- 1956 – The Suez Crisis: Israelis invade Egyptian territory in October of 1956.
- 1956 – After Egyptian President Gamal Abdel Nasser nationalized the company which administered the Suez Canal, a joint attack by the French and British was launched. Egypt suffered military disaster on November 2, 1956. Israel captured the Sinai Peninsula, but after international condemnation, Israel was forced to withdraw.
- 1967 – Six-Day War: after Egypt closed the Straits of Tiran on May 22, 1967, Israel launched an attack on Egyptian, Jordanian, Syrian, and Iraqi airports on June 5, 1967. After six days, Israel conquered Jerusalem, the Golan Heights, Sinai, and the West Bank.
- 1973 – Yom Kippur War: on October 6, 1973, on the Jewish holiday of Yom Kippur, Syria and Egypt launched a surprise attack against Israel. After initial success of the attackers, Israel managed to cross the Suez into Egypt and endangered Cairo. After the intervention of the USA and USSR, military operations ended on October 25, 1973.
- 1978 – The Camp David Accord was signed by Israeli Prime Minister Menahen Begin, and Egyptian President Anvar as Sadat in September 1978, in Camp David, USA. Israel agreed to withdraw from the occupied Sinai Peninsula.
- 1979 – The Israel-Egypt Peace Treaty was signed on March 26, 1979, in Washington.

Maps of Israel

Israel Biblical Sites Travel Guide

Twelve Tribes of Israel

Divided Kingdom

Regions of Israel

Maps of Israel

Israel Today

Travel Orientation

Travel Orientation

Understanding the Holy Sites in Israel

The Need to Understand What You're Going to See

It would be wonderful if the Holy Land was exactly the same as it was 2,000 years ago when Christ walked its paths, or 4,000 years ago when Abraham traversed its hillsides and valleys. However, 4,000 years is a long time, and there have been many changes that have taken place during this time span. It's hard for us to understand, but 4,000 or even 2,000 years is a long time! Because of its strategic location in the world, no other country has had as many kingdoms occupy it or as many battles fought on its soil as Israel. This, along with time, has led to much change to Israel and its holy sites.

The good news is that many of the biblical sites are in their natural state and appear much the same as they did when the events that happened there occurred. Other sites have had monuments, churches, or basilicas built near, or on them, and are not exactly as they appeared when the events that occurred there happened. Also, many sites have had many events happen in one spot over thousands of years, so it would be impossible to have each event preserved just the way it happened.

Understanding What Some of The Holy Sites Will Be Like

Many of these monuments, churches, or basilicas will have a Catholic, Arabic, or Mid-Eastern look. They're very different from what we're accustomed to seeing, and at first glance, you might find this unattractive. You also might disagree with the religious backgrounds of some of these sites and feel somewhat uncomfortable as well. In addition, you most likely will find other people visiting the Holy Land from other countries who are actually worshiping and kissing some of the adornments on these sites. On a previous trip to Israel, some in our group found all this a little repulsive and chose not to enter some of these holy sites. Because of these possible negative reactions, we would like to provide you with a little background and history about how these holy sites have been preserved so your sightseeing experience can be the best as possible during your time in the Holy Land.

Israel Biblical Sites Travel Guide

A Little History

Even before the time of Christ and afterward, many of the holy sites were marked out and preserved. Then, about 300 years after the time of Christ, the Roman Empire (world power at that time) embraced Christianity. At that time, the mother of Emperor Constantine (Helena) was one of the first of the royal family to convert to Christianity. Later, Emperor Constantine did as well. Helena came to the Holy Land and wanted to preserve some of the holy sites, so she had churches, monuments, and basilicas built over some of the key holy places. These included the Church of the Holy Sepulture, Church of the Nativity, Basilica in the Garden of Gethsemane, Church of the Annunciation, and others. Helena, and others throughout history, felt such emotion and awe at these holy sites that they wanted to honor and preserve them for future generations. The Early Church during this period was the first to be in charge of these sites, and then because the Early Church slowly evolved into what we know as the Catholic Church, many of these holy sites came under the care of the Catholic Church. The monuments, churches, and basilicas were not always Catholic in nature, so we shouldn't assume that they shared the same religious views at their inception.

There were others as well that came to the Holy Land to build churches, monuments, and basilicas on these holy sites (Eastern Orthodox Church, Armenians, Russians, Greeks, etc.). Their hearts felt the same awe and emotion as others who came, so they too built on or by these holy sites to honor and preserve them.

Some of these holy sites are ancient (from as old as 5,000 years), and the churches have a Mid-Eastern style look.

Gratefulness to Those Who Preserved the Biblical Sites

If it hadn't been for those who built monuments or churches on or by the holy sites, they would have had other buildings, roads, and infrastructure built over them and lost to the world forever. These early pilgrims felt the same awe and emotion you will feel, and we certainly can't fault them for this.

Because of all the adornments and construction over the centuries, it's hard to imagine how some of these sites would have looked in their original setting. However, the years of activity and tradition at these holy sites give greater weight to their authenticity. And while we might disagree with the decorations, atmosphere of these places, and religious backgrounds, we can certainly appreciate and admire all the devotion and sacrifice made to preserve them.

Some Might Find These Churches, Monuments, and Basilicas Repulsive

Part of the reason some might find the places they see in Israel as repulsive will have to do with a difference in religious faith. Another reason is due to a misunderstanding of style. These holy sites have a very different style than what we're accustomed to in modern churches. Most of the oldest churches we see today in our own countries are just a few hundred years old and have somewhat the same architecture and style from our modern era. As a result, we're just not used to seeing churches close to 1,500 years old, and older.

Closing Thoughts

1. Entering these churches, monuments, and basilicas to see these holy sites doesn't mean we're in any way embracing and accepting their religious beliefs.

2. While the style, religious background, and adornments might not be to our taste, the motives of those who preserved these sites seem to be noble and honorable. As you see these sites, you will understand why these early pilgrims wanted to preserve them.

3. It's important to note that we, from a modern mindset, have a different view and taste regarding building styles. Because to us, something 200-400 years old seems really ancient, we need to realize that seeing something 1,500 years old has an entirely different architectural look and sense to it than what we're accustomed to seeing.

Hopefully, this info will help you. As mentioned, on a previous trip to Israel, some didn't really understand these things beforehand, and it took them a bit to get themselves wrapped around some of these concepts. It was kind of a self-discovery process. For this reason, this orientation and background are provided so you can get the most out of your Holy Land Experience and not get bogged down in this area.

Israel Biblical Sites Travel Guide

How to Get the Most Out of Your Holy Land Trip

How to See What Many Don't See in the Holy Land

Understand that half of what there is to see in the Holy Land is hidden from most that walk her paths. They are unseen spiritual truths, only revealed to the sensitive and spiritual of heart. Try to get as close to God as you can prior, and during your time in the Holy Land, so you can see and hear things that many don't see during their visit there. The Holy Land is not just places and historical artifacts; it's an experience — an experience that is spiritual in nature and eye-opening for those who can see in this realm.

You Won't Be Able to See Everything

It would be great to see every detail at every holy site, but that would take months, if not years, to do. It's important to understand that there is a lot to see and, therefore, just the highlights can be seen. You'll be eating the frosting off the cake and won't be able to eat the whole thing. As a result, please don't be discouraged if you can't spend as much time in each place as you'd wish. You'll have to move along to see just the highlights, and if you stay too long at one place, that means you'll be saying "No" to another.

Your Trip Won't be Perfect

It would be wonderful if you could be guaranteed a perfect trip with a perfect experience, but that's just not reality. Going to the Holy Land is undoubtedly the closest you'll get to the "Trip of a Lifetime," but please don't get your hopes up so high that you're let down and feel discouraged if it doesn't turn out as you dreamed. Your trip won't be perfect. Your leader and the rest in your group will probably not live up to your expectations either. The only perfect person on the trip will be you (well, maybe not exactly perfect, but pretty close to it, lol). So just prepare yourself to understand that things just aren't going to be flawless.

Trust God for Your Experience

It's also easy to have preconceived ideas of what to expect; the emotions you're going to feel, the dreams you might have of the Holy Land, and the experience you want to have. Please try to set some of these aside and trust God to give you the experience He has for you. Don't get everything built up so high that it would be impossible to fulfill them. Trust God to bless you and teach you what He has for you. He's the One who's worked everything out for you to go, and I'm certain He has special things to teach you. Trust in Him and be looking for what He has for you. And after everything is said and done, be content with what He gives you.

Understanding Group Travel Dynamics

Traveling with Others

Part of the joy and richness of your Holy Land Experience will come from sharing it with others. Going somewhere alone is never as much fun as doing it with someone else. The impact and fullness of the experience will come alive as it's experienced as a group rather than as an individual or couple. For this reason, you'll want to consider a few things to make your Holy Land Experience the best as possible.

Try to Think as a Group and Not as an Individual

Traveling as a group is very different from traveling as an individual or couple. There will be other team members in your group, and each person needs to realize they're part of a larger event than just themselves. The whole team will be depending on others to be punctual, courteous, thoughtful, and pleasant. Try to take into consideration that what you do affects everyone else on the team.

Try to Keep Up with the Group

It will be important that you keep up with the group and not linger too long seeing things during your travels. Each day it is wise to appoint a "Follow-up Person" who'll bring up the group's rear and make sure everyone stays together. Because you'll be seeing some really interesting things, it will be easy to get lost in these and forget that there are other things to see as well.

Try to Be Punctual

Everything from wake-up times, mealtimes, arrival times, departure times, and the site-seeing schedule for each day needs to be considered. Because you are spending a lot of money and taking precious time out of your busy life to experience the Holy Land, you'll want to be as punctual as possible so you and your team can see everything as planned. Your group can only be as fast as the slowest person, so try to be punctual and thoughtful of others. If you tend to be a late person, consider getting a head start on things by starting earlier than normal so you can be on time.

Travel Orientation

Try to Be Patient and Courteous

Be aware that sometime during the trip, you'll likely feel tired, a bit irritated with others, or upset at something that's happened. Do your best to overlook the faults of others and try to keep yourself in check. Also, realize that we have an enemy who will do his best to take away from our experience by using others or problems. Be alert and prayerful! Keep yourself close to God and do your best to love others and take everything in stride.

Try to Be Rested Up Before Your Holy Land Trip

Because you're going to be expending a lot of energy during the trip, try to get as rested as possible before departure. To illustrate this point, we'll use the term "gauges" to help us out. We all know that most of our vehicles have gauges: gas gauge, temperature gauge, oil gauge, etc. Using this analogy for our bodies, we all have bodily gauges as well. We have physical, emotional, mental, and spiritual gauges. Before your trip, try to get your bodily gauges as full as possible. By doing so, you'll get more out of your trip and be more joyful and patient with others.

Tips for filling up your bodily gauges before trip departure:

- Try and scale down on your activities and output before the trip. For example, cut back on meetings, outings, get-togethers, and social events.
- Get plenty of sleep.
- Get plenty of exercise (you'll be doing quite a bit of walking, so try to get in walking shape before the trip).
- Get as much of your responsibilities and commitments done ahead of time, and don't wait until the last minute to take care of things. There will be plenty of last-minute things to do, so don't add to them by procrastinating.
- Try to get packed and ready at your earliest convenience. If you need to shop for trip items, try to do so plenty of time in advance.

By taking into consideration these tips, you'll start your trip with your bodily gauges full and not empty. And when you think about it, who would start a long journey with their car having an empty gas tank and little or no oil in the engine?

Israel Biblical Sites Travel Guide

Travel Tips for Israel

1. Get in shape physically before you go to Israel. You will be doing a lot of walking, so the better shape you're in, the easier and more pleasant your time will be. At least a month before your trip, start walking at least 15-30 minutes a day.
2. Activate your credit/debit cards before departure to Israel.
3. Make sure your Passport is up to date and valid. It must have at least 6 months before expiration from your last day in Israel to be valid.
4. Don't shave your body before taking a dip in the Dead Sea. The salt and minerals will irritate your skin.
5. Don't show public affection with the opposite sex, especially on the Temple Mount and Muslim sites.
6. Don't be afraid to bargain for purchases at marketplaces. It's expected, so take part in it.
7. Establish meeting places at each site so that if for some reason you get lost or separated, you can find each other.
8. Carry a water bottle and stay hydrated.
9. Pack layered types of clothing instead of heavy clothes.
10. Carry your personal items in a safe place on your person.
11. Take a good camera or video camera.
12. Get used to people smoking as it's very common in Israel and the Middle East.
13. Many Israelis are not religious but secular. This might seem strange, but it's true.
14. Carry a copy of your Passport.
15. Women should dress very modestly, especially when visiting holy sites.
16. Men should wear hats when visiting Jewish holy sites.
17. Men should not wear hats when visiting Christian holy sites.

Travel Orientation

Packing List

Clothes

Dressing in layers is best when considering your clothes. For the most part, the weather will be warm and sunny during the summer and cooler in the winter. Following are some suggested items that might be helpful:

- Casual pants for hiking and sightseeing (casual can be worn the whole trip).
- Nicer shorts are okay at many places. However, at some sites like the Temple Mount, Western Wall, etc., pants are recommended. Also, for women, being very modest is recommended at these sites as well.
- Casual long sleeve shirts
- Short sleeve shirts
- Bathing suit (for the Dead Sea if you want to take a dip)
- 2 Plastic bags for wet clothes.
- Undergarments
- Socks
- Light jacket
- Sturdy walking shoes with traction for many stone paths and roads you'll traverse. FYI- many of the streets are paved with stone, and it's challenging to wear shoes with awkward heels/soles on uneven pavement.
- Sleepwear
- Hat for sun protection purposes.
- Men will need to wear a hat or equivalent on their heads when entering Jewish sites and synagogues.
- Ladies will need a shawl or equivalent when entering Muslim areas.

General Items

- Slimline travel Bible
- Small notebook and pen for taking notes
- Travel alarm
- Flashlight (mini) or cell phone with flashlight

- Camera/video camera
- Film or storage disks for your camera (bring plenty, because they're much more expensive in Israel)
- Daypack/backpack (can be used as an airplane carry-on and for travel in Israel).
- Ziplock bags for lunches and for putting the relics in you might gather along the way in Israel.
- Umbrella – small contractible type
- Sunglasses
- Plug adapter for plugging devices into the outlets in Israel.
  Note: The outlets in Israel are different than the states. You'll need this adapter for plugging things in to be charged, etc.
- Charger converter needed for Israel (needed for charging cameras, etc.) Note: Electricity in Israel is 220 volts. In America, and many other countries, it's 110 volts. Many electronic devices today can adapt to both voltages. However, if you plan to take an item that cannot use 220 volts, you will need a converter.

Personal Items

- Toothbrush
- Toothpaste
- Deodorant
- Lip balm
- Razor
- After-shave
- Band-Aids
- Feminine items
- Sunscreen
- Tylenol/Ibuprofen
- Eyeglasses/contact lenses
- Prescription medicines

Travel Orientation

Documents & Items to Carry with You at all Times

There are several options for carrying your money and important documents with you on your trip. For example, you can use a money belt (waist style or necklace style) or pockets on your pants or shirt that can be buttoned and are secure.

- Passport – Must have 6 months left before expiring from the dates of your trip.
- Copy of your Passport
- Driver's License
- Cash
- Credit/Debit Card (make sure to activate your cards for Israel or international travel).

    Note: It's handy to use your debit card for drawing out Shekels for spending money in Israel. You'll also get the best exchange rate by using it as well.

- Travel Visa received in Israel at customs.

    Special Note: When arriving in Israel, you'll go through customs to receive your visa for your stay in Israel. It will be a small piece of paper. ***Please don't lose it!*** You will need it on several occasions while in the country. You can tuck it away in your Passport if you'd like.

About the Author

Todd M. Fink is the founder and director of Go Missions to Mexico and Holy Land Site Ministries. He holds the following degrees: Bachelor of Theology from Freelandia Bible College, Master of Divinity studies at Western Seminary, Master of Theology from Freedom Bible College and Seminary, Master of Divinity from Trinity Theological Seminary, and a Ph.D. in theology from Trinity Theological Seminary.

He served as youth/associate pastor for 11 years at an Evangelical church in Oregon (1987–1998).

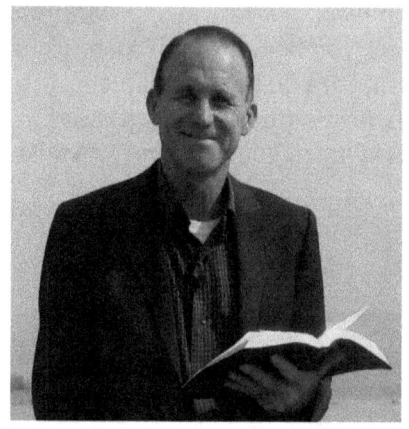

Todd is currently serving as pastor and missionary with Go Missions to Mexico Ministries in Mexico (1998–present).

He also is serving with Holy Land Site ministries and has a passion for the Holy Land. He has developed a large website and YouTube channel with videos and teachings about almost every site in Israel. In addition, he leads tour trips to Israel and has written books about the Holy Land.

Todd is an author, speaker, and teacher. He has a deep passion for God's Word and enjoys helping people understand its eternal truths.

He is married to his lovely wife, Letsy, and has four grown children.

Books by Todd M. Fink

Israel Biblical Sites Travel Guide

Israel Biblical Sites Bible Companion

Jerusalem & Central Israel Biblical Sites Guide

Sea of Galilee & Northern Israel Biblical Sites Guide

Negev & Southern Israel Biblical Sites Guide

Biblical Discipleship: Essential Components for Reaching Spiritual Maturity

Biblical Discipleship: Essential Components for Reaching Spiritual Maturity 16 Week Study Guide

What is the Gospel and How to Share It

Discovering the True Riches of Life

A Biblical Analysis of Corrective Church Discipline

Discipulado Bíblico

Discipulado Bíblico Guía de Estudio

Please visit: ToddMichaelFink.com to see or purchase books.

Connect with Todd

Email: holylandsite.com@gmail.com

Facebook: Todd Mike Fink

Facebook Ministry Page: Holy Land Site

YouTube Channel: Holy Land Site

Websites:

HolyLandSite.com

ToddMichaelFink.com

SelahBookPress.com

GoMissionsToMexico.com

MinisteriosCasaDeLuz.com

www.ingramcontent.com/pod-product-compliance
Lightning Source LLC
Chambersburg PA
CBHW050146130526
44591CB00033B/697